HONOLULU
WAIKIKI
HANDBOOK

THE ISLAND OF OAHU

HONOLULU
WAIKIKI
HANDBOOK

SECOND EDITION

J.D. BISIGNANI

MOON
PUBLICATIONS INC.

HONOLULU-WAIKIKI HANDBOOK: THE ISLAND OF OAHU
SECOND EDITION

Published by
Moon Publications, Inc.
P.O. Box 3040
Chico, California 95927-3040, USA

Printed by
Colorcraft Ltd., Hong Kong

ISBN: 1-56691-058-7
ISSN: 1077-288X

Editor: Pauli Galin
Copy Editor: Deana Corbitt
Production & Design: Karen McKinley, David Hurst,
Carey Wilson, Chris Parmenter
Cartographers: Bob Race, Brian Bardwell
Index: Nicole Revere

Cover Art: Allure of the Tropics by Roy Tabora

Distributed in the continental United States by Publishers Group West
Distributed in Hawaii by Island Heritage Publishing
Printed in Hong Kong

Please send all comments,
corrections, additions,
amendments, and critiques to:

**J.D. BISIGNANI
MOON PUBLICATIONS, INC.
P.O. BOX 3040
CHICO, CA 95927-3040, USA**

Printing History
1st edition—July 1990
2nd edition—January 1995

Although the author and publisher have made every effort to ensure that the information was correct at the time of going to press, the author and publisher do not assume and hereby disclaim any liability to any party for any loss or damage caused by errors, omissions, or any potential travel disruption due to labor or financial difficulty, whether such errors or omissions result from negligence, accident, or any other cause.

WARNING: Nothing in this book is intended to be used for navigation. Mariners are advised to consult official sailing directions and nautical charts.

IS THIS BOOK OUT OF DATE?

In today's world, things change so rapidly that it's impossible for one person to keep up with everything happening in any one place. This is particularly true in Hawaii, where situations are always in flux. Travel books are like automobiles: they require fine tuning and frequent overhauls to keep in shape. Help us keep this book in shape! We require input from our readers so that we can continue to provide the best, most current information available. Please write to let us know about any inaccuracies, new information, or misleading suggestions. Although we try to make our maps as accurate as possible, errors do occur. If you have any suggestions for improvement or places that should be included, please let us know about them.

We especially appreciate letters from female travelers, visiting expatriates, local residents, and hikers and outdoor enthusiasts. We also like hearing from experts in the field as well as from local hotel owners and individuals wishing to accommodate visitors from abroad.

As you travel through the islands, keep notes in the margins of this book. Notes written on the spot are always more accurate than those put down on paper later. If you take a photograph during your trip that you think should be included in future editions, please send it to us. Send only good slide duplicates or glossy black-and-white prints. Drawings and other artwork are also appreciated. If we use your photo or drawing, you'll be mentioned in the credits and receive a free copy of the book. Keep in mind, however, that the publisher cannot return any materials unless you include a self-addressed, stamped envelope. Moon Publications will own the rights on all material submitted. Address your letter to:

J.D. Bisignani
Moon Publications
P.O. Box 3040
Chico, CA 95927-3040
USA

ACKNOWLEDGMENTS

Writing the acknowledgments for a book is supercharged with energy. It's a time when you look forward, hopefully, to a bright future for your work, and a time when you reflect on all that has gone into producing it. Mostly it's a time to say thank you. Thank you for the grace necessary to carry out the task, and thank you to all the wonderful people whose efforts have helped so much along the way. To the following people, I offer my most sincere thank you.

Firstly, to the Moon staff, professionals every one. As time has passed, and one book has followed another, they've become amazingly adept at their work, to the point where their mastery is a marvel to watch.

I would also like to thank the following people for their special help and consideration: Dr. Greg Leo, an adventurer and environmentalist who has done remarkable field research and provided me with invaluable information about the unique flora and fauna of Hawaii; Roger Rose of the Bishop Museum; Lee Wild, Hawaiian Mission Houses Museum; Marilyn Nicholson, State Foundation on Culture and the Arts; the Hawaii Visitors Bureau; Donna Jung, Donna Jung and Associates, who has shown confidence in me since day one; Haunani Vieira, Dollar Rent A Car; Keoni Wagner, Hawaiian Airlines; Jim and John Costello; Dr. Terry and Nancy Carolan; Elizabeth Demotte, Ritz-Carlton Mauna Lani; Barbara Schonley, Destination Molokai; Elisa Josephsohn, Public Relations; Faith Ogawa, for helping me keep the faith; Carol Zahorsky, Four Seasons Resort; Joyce Matsumoto, Halekulani Hotel; Jeanne Datz, Hilton Hotels; Nancy Daniels, Kahala Hilton; Dianne Doer, Kona Hilton; Rudy Bosma, Lanai City Service; Donn Takahashi and Carol Dawson, Maui Prince Hotel; Dennis Costa, Maui Hill; Kim Marshall, Grand Wailea Resort; Sheila Donnelly, Diana Reutter, Julie Char, Sweetie Aiwohi Nelson, Deborah Sharkey of Sheila Donnelly and Associates; Sandi Kato-Klutke, Aston Kauai Beach Villa; Barbara Sheehan, Sheraton Moana Surfrider; Sally Proctor, Aston Hotels; Norm Manzione, Suntrips; Renee Cochran and Will Titus, Colony Resorts; Linda Darling-Mann, Coco Palms Resort. To all of you, my deepest aloha.

CONTENTS

MAPS

MAP SYMBOLS

───────	FREEWAY	●	STATE OR COUNTY PARK	⬭	STATE HIGHWAY
───────	MAIN ROAD	■ ○	POINT OF INTEREST		WATER
───────	SECONDARY ROAD	○	TOWN/VILLAGE	⚠	CAMPGROUND
─ ─ ─ ─	UNPAVED ROAD	▨	LARGE TOWN/CITY		HEIAU
─·─·─·─	TRAIL	▲	MOUNTAIN	✈	AIRPORT
	INTERSTATE HIGHWAY	●	HOTEL/ACCOMMODATION		

CHARTS AND SPECIAL TOPICS

BOB RACE

INTRODUCTION

It is the destiny of certain places on earth to be imbued with an inexplicable magnetism, a power that draws people whose visions and desires combine at just the right moment to create a dynamism so strong that it becomes history. The result for these "certain places" is greatness . . . and Oahu is one of these.

It is difficult to separate Oahu from its vibrant metropolis, Honolulu, whose massive political, economic, and social muscle dominates the entire state, let alone its home island. But to look at Honolulu *as* Oahu is to look only upon the face of a great sculpture, ignoring the beauty and subtleness of the whole. Just the words "Honolulu, Waikiki, Pearl Harbor" conjure up visions common to people the world over. Immediately imaginations flush with palm trees swaying, a healthy tan, bombs dropping with infamy, and a golden moon rising romantically over coiled lovers on a white-sand beach.

Oahu is called the "Gathering Place," and to itself it has indeed gathered the noble memories of old Hawaii, the vibrancy of a bright-eyed fledgling state, and the brawny power so necessary for the future. On this amazing piece of land adrift in the great ocean, 835,000 people live;

five times that number visit yearly, and as time passes Oahu remains strong as one of those "certain places."

OVERVIEW

Oahu is partly a tropical garden, bathed by soft showers and sunshine, and swaying with a gentle but firm rhythm. You can experience this feeling all over the island, even in pockets of downtown Honolulu and Waikiki. However, its other side is brash—dominated by the confidence of a major American city perched upon the Pacific Basin whose music is a pounding staccato jackhammer, a droning bulldozer, and the mechanical screech of the ever present building-crane. The vast majority of first-time and return visitors land at Honolulu International and spend at least a few days on Oahu, usually in Waikiki.

People are amazed at the diversity of experiences the island has to offer. Besides the obvious (and endless) beach activities are museums, botanical gardens, a fantastic zoo and aquarium, nightclubs, extravagant shows, free

OAHU
(OVERVIEW)

© MOON PUBLICATIONS, INC.

ONLY MAIN TOWNS AND ROADS SHOWN

5 mi

5 km

Waikiki

entertainment, cultural classes, theaters, sporting events, a major university, historical sights galore, an exotic cosmopolitan atmosphere, backcountry trekking, and an abundance of camping—all easily accessible via terrific public transportation. Finally, to sweeten the pot, Oahu can easily be the least expensive of the Hawaiian Islands to visit.

Waikiki

Loosely, this world-famous beach is a hunk of land bordered by the **Ala Wai Canal** and running eastward to **Diamond Head.** Early last century these two golden miles were little more than a string of dirty beaches backed by a mosquito-infested swamp. Until 1901, when the Moana Hotel was built, only Hawaii's few remaining *ali'i* and a handful of wealthy *kamaaina* families had homes here. Now, over 125 hotels and condos provide more than 30,000 rooms, and if you placed a $20 bill on the ground, it would barely cover the land that it could buy!

This hyperactive area will delight and disgust you, excite and overwhelm you, but never bore you. Waikiki gives you the feeling that you've arrived *someplace.* Besides lolling on the beach and walking the gauntlet of restaurants, hotels, malls, and street merchants, you can visit the **Waikiki Aquarium** or **Honolulu Zoo.** Then, ever present Diamond Head, that monolith of frozen lava so symbolic of Hawaii, is easily reached by a few minutes' drive and a leisurely stroll to its summit. Head eastward around the bulge passing exclusive residential areas and you quickly find a string of secluded beaches. Around this tip you pass **Koko Head Crater,** a trekker's haven; **Hanauma Bay,** an underwater conservation park renowned for magnificent family-class snorkeling; **Sea Life Park,** an extravaganza of the deep; and the sleepy village of **Waimanalo Beach.** Nearby at **Bellow's Field Beach Park** is camping, where it's hard to believe the city's just 10 miles back.

Downtown Honolulu

Head for downtown and give yourself a full day to catch all the sights. It's as if a huge grappling hook, attached to the heart of a Mainland city, hauled it down to the sea. But don't get the idea that Honolulu is not unique, because it is! You'll find a delightful mixture of quaintly historic and future-shock new, exotic, and ordinary. The center is **Iolani Palace,** the only royal palace in America, heralded by the gilded statue of Kamehameha I. In an easy walking radius is the **State Capitol** and attendant government buildings. Chrome and glass skyscrapers holding the offices of Hawaii's economically mighty shade small stone and wooden structures from last century: **Mission Houses Museum, Kawaiahao Church,** and **St. Andrew's Cathedral.**

Down at the harbor **Aloha Tower** greets the few passenger ships that still make port; nearby is the floating museum ship, *Falls of Clyde,* a nostalgic reminder of simpler times. Hotel Street takes you to old but not always venerable **Chinatown,** filled with alleyways housing tiny temples, herbalists, aromatic markets, inexpensive eateries, rough night spots, dives, and the strong, distinctive flavor of transplanted Asia.

If the hustle and bustle gets to be too much, head for **Foster Botanical Gardens.** Or hop a special London bus for the serenity of the **Bishop Museum and Planetarium,** undoubtedly *the* best Polynesian cultural and anthropological museum in the world.

Pearl Harbor

Hawaii's major interstate, H-1, runs west of the city center to Pearl Harbor. You can't help noticing the huge military presence throughout the area, and it becomes clear why Hawaii is considered the most militarized state in the country. The attraction here, which shouldn't be missed, is the **USS *Arizona* Memorial.** The museum, visitor center, and tours, operated jointly by the U.S. Navy and the National Park Service, are both excellent and free.

Heading For The Hills

Behind the city is the **Koolau Range.** As you head for these beckoning hills, you can take a sidetrip over to the **University of Hawaii** and the **East-West Center** while passing through Manoa Valley, epitome of the "good life" in Hawaii. Route 61 takes you up and over Nuuanu Pali to Oahu's windward side. En route you'll pass **Punchbowl,** an old crater holding some of the dead from WW II and the Korean and Vietnam wars in the **National Cemetery of the Pacific.**

As you climb, the road passes the **Royal Mausoleum,** final resting place for some of Hawaii's last kings, queens, and nobility. Then comes **Queen Emma's Summer Palace,** a Victorian home of gentility and lace. Next is **Nuuanu Pali,** where Kamehameha drove 16,000 Oahu warriors over the cliff, sealing his dominance of the island kingdom with their blood. The view is hauntingly beautiful, as the mountains drop suddenly to the coast of windward Oahu.

Windward Oahu

On the windward side, **Kailua** and **Kaneohe** have become suburban bedroom communities for Honolulu; this entire coast has few tourist accommodations, so it remains relatively uncrowded. The beaches are excellent, with beach parks and camping spots one after another, and the winds make this side off the island perfect for windsurfing. North of Kaneohe is **Valley of the Temples,** where a Christian cross sits high on a hill, and Buddha rests calmly in **Byodo-In Temple.**

Just up Route 83, the coastal highway, comes **Waiahole,** Oahu's outback, where tiny farms and taro patches dot the valleys and local folks move with the slow beat of bygone days. Then a quick succession of beaches follows, many rarely visited by more than a passing fisherman. **Punaluu** comes next, offering some of the only accommodations along this coast and a lovely walk to **Kaliuwaa,** the Sacred Falls. In **Laie** is the **Polynesian Cultural Center,** operated by the Mormon Church. **Brigham Young University** is here too, along with a solid Mormon temple that's open to visitors.

North Shore

The North Shore is famous for magnificent surf. From **Sunset Beach** to **Haleiwa,** world-class surfers come to be challenged by the liquid thunder of the **Banzai Pipeline** and **Waimea Bay.** Art shops, boutiques, tiny restaurants, and secluded hideaways line these sun-drenched miles. At the far western end is **Dillingham Airfield** where you can take a glider or air tour of the island. The road ends with a very rugged jeep trail leading to **Kaena Point,** renowned for the most monstrous surf on the North Shore.

Northwest

The northwestern end of the island is the **Waianae coast.** The towns of **Maili, Waianae,** and **Makaha** are considered the last domain of the locals of Oahu. This coastal area has escaped development so far, and it's one of the few places on the island where ordinary people can afford to live near the beach. Sometimes an attitude of resentment spills over against tourists; mostly though, lovely people with good hearts live here, who will treat you as nicely as you're willing to treat them.

World-class surfing beaches along this coast are preferred by many of the best-known surfers from Hawaii. Many work as lifeguards in the beach parks, and they all congregate for the annual surfing championships held in Makaha. Here is a perfect chance to mingle with the people and soak up some of the last real *aloha* left on Oahu.

THE LAND

When Papa, the Hawaiian earth mother, returned from vacationing in Tahiti, she was less than pleased. She had learned through a gossiping messenger that her husband, Wakea, had been playing around. Besides simple philandering, he'd been foolish enough to impregnate Hina, a lovely young goddess who bore him island children. Papa, scorned and furious, showed Wakea that two could play the same game by taking a handsome young lover, Lua. Their brief interlude yielded the man-child Oahu, sixth of the great island children. Geologically, Oahu is the second oldest main island after Kauai. It emerged from beneath the waves as hissing lava a few million years after Kauai, and cooled a little quicker than Papa's temper to form Hawaii's third largest island.

The modern geological theory concerning the formation of the Hawaiian Islands is no less fanciful than the Polynesian legends sung about their origins. Science maintains that 30 million years ago, while the great continents were being geologically tortured into their rudimentary shapes, the Hawaiian Islands were a mere ooze of bubbling magma 20,000 feet below the surface of the primordial sea. For millions of years this molten rock flowed up from fissures in the sea floor. Slowly, layer upon layer of lava was deposited until an island rose above the surface of the sea. The great weight then sealed the fissure, whose own colossal forces progressively crept in a southwestern direction, to burst out again and again building the chain of what

we now call the Hawaiian Islands. At the same time the entire Pacific plate was afloat on the giant sea of molten magma, and it slowly glided to the northwest, carrying the newly formed islands with it.

In the beginning the spewing crack formed Kure and Midway islands in the extreme northwestern sector of the Hawaiian chain. This process continued for eons, and today more than 130 islands, islets, and shoals make up the Hawaiian Islands, stretching 1,600 miles across an expanse of the North Pacific. Some geologists maintain that the "hot spot" now primarily under the Big Island remains relatively stationary, and that the 1,600-mile spread of the Hawaiian archipelago is due to a northwest drifting effect of about three to five inches per year. Still, with the center of activity under the Big Island, Mauna Loa and Kilauea volcanoes regularly add more land to the only state in the country that is literally still growing. About 30 miles southeast of the Big Island is Loihi Sea Mount, waiting 3,000 feet below the waves. Frequent eruptions bring it closer and closer to the surface until one day it will emerge and become the newest Hawaiian island.

Land Facts

Oahu has a total land area of 608 square miles, and measured from its farthest points it is 44 miles long by 30 miles wide. The 112-mile coastline holds the two largest harbors in the state, **Honolulu** and **Pearl**. The **Koolau Range** runs north-south for almost the entire length of the island, dramatically creating windward and leeward Oahu. The **Waianae Range** is smaller, confined to the northwestern section of the island. It too runs north-south, dividing the **Waianae coast** from the massive **Leilehua Plateau** of the interior. **Mount Ka'ala,** at 4,020 feet, in the northern portion of the Waianae Range, is Oahu's highest peak. The huge Leilehua Plateau is still covered in pineapple and sugarcane, and lies between the two mountain ranges running all the way from Waialua on the north shore to Ewa, just west of Pearl Harbor. At its widest point, around Schofield Barracks, it's more than six miles across.

Oahu's most impressive natural features were formed after the heavy volcanic activity ceased and erosion began to sculpt the island. The most obvious are the wall-like cliffs of the *pali*—mountain heads eroded by winds from the east, valleys cut by streams from the west. Perfect examples of these eroded valleys are **Nuuanu** and **Kalihi.** Other impressive examples are **Diamond Head, Koko Head,** and **Punchbowl,** three "tuff-cone" volcanoes created after the heavy volcanic activity of early Oahu. A tuff cone is volcanic ash cemented together to form solid rock. Diamond Head is the most dramatic, formed after a minor eruption about 100,000 years ago and rising 760 feet from its base.

Oahu has the state's longest stream, **Kaukonahua,** which begins atop Puu Kaaumakua at 2,681 feet in the central Koolaus and runs westward for over 30 miles through the Leilehua Plateau. En route it bypasses the **Wahiawa Reservoir** which, at 302 acres, forms the second largest body of fresh water in Hawaii. Oahu's tallest waterfalls are 80-feet **Kaliuwaa** (Sacred Falls), just west of Punaluu, and **Waihee Falls,** in the famous Waimea Park on the North Shore, which have a sheer drop of over 40 feet. Oahu's main water concern is that usage is outstripping supply, and major municipal water shortages are expected by the year 2000 unless conservation measures and new technology are employed.

Island Builders

The Hawaiians worshipped Madame Pele, the fire goddess. Her name translates equally as "volcano," "fire pit," or "eruption of lava." When she was angry, she complained by spitting fire, which cooled and formed land. Volcanologists say that the islands are huge mounds of cooled basaltic lava surrounded by billions of polyp skeletons that have formed coral reefs. The Hawaiian Islands are shield volcanos that erupt gently and form an elongated dome much like a turtle shell. Oahu, like the rest, is a perfect example of this. Once above the surface of the sea, the tremendous weight of lava seals the fissure below. Eventually the giant tube that carried lava to the surface sinks in on itself and forms a caldera, as evidenced at Hanauma Bay, the famous snorkeling spot on Oahu's southeast coast. More eruptions occur periodically, and they cover the already existing island like frosting on a titanic cake. Wind and water next take over and relentlessly sculpt the raw lava into deep crevices and cuts that become valleys. The once smooth *pali* of windward Oahu are now undulating green monoliths due to this process.

Lava

Lava flows in two distinct types, for which the Hawaiian names have become universal geological terms: *a'a* and *pa'hoehoe.* They're easily distinguished in appearance, but chemically they're the same. *A'a* is extremely rough and spiny, and will quickly tear up your shoes if you do much hiking over it. Also, if you have the misfortune to fall down, you'll immediately know why they call it *a'a.* Pa'hoehoe is billowy, ropey lava that looks like burned pancake batter and can mold itself into fantastic shapes. Examples of both are encountered on various hikes throughout Oahu. Other lava oddities that you may spot on Oahu are peridots, green gemlike stones called "Maui Diamonds"; clear feldspar; and gray lichens covering the older flows known as "Hawaiian snow."

Rivers And Lakes

Oahu has no navigable rivers, but there are hundreds of streams. The two largest are Kaukonahua Stream, which runs through central Oahu, and Waikele Stream, which drains the area around Schofield Barracks. A few reservoirs dot the island; Wahiawa Reservoir and Nuuanu Pali Reservoir are both excellent freshwater fishing spots (see "Sports and Recreation —Gone Fishing" in the Out and About chapter), but there are no natural bodies of water on Oahu. Hikers should be aware that the uncountable streams and rivulets can quickly turn from trickles to torrents, causing flash floods in valleys that were the height of hospitality only minutes before.

Tsunamis

Tsunami is the Japanese word for tidal wave. It ranks up there with the worst in causing horror in human beings. But if you were to count up all the people in Hawaii who have been swept away by tidal waves in the last 50 years, the toll wouldn't come close to those killed on bicycles in only a few Mainland cities in just five years.

A Hawaiian tsunami is actually a seismic sea wave generated by an earthquake that could easily have had its origins thousands of miles away in South America or Alaska. Some waves have been clocked at speeds up to 500 miles per hour. The safest place, besides high ground well away from beach areas, is out on the open ocean where even an enormous wave is perceived only as a large swell—a tidal wave is only dangerous when it is opposed by land. The worst tsunami to strike the islands in modern times occurred on April 1, 1946. The Hana Coast of windward east Maui bore the brunt with a tragic loss of many lives as entire villages were swept away.

Earthquakes

These rumblings can be a concern in Hawaii, offering a double threat because they can cause tsunamis. If you ever feel a tremor and are close to a beach, get as far away as fast as possible. A few tremors are felt on Oahu, but the Big Island, because of its active volcanoes, experiences hundreds of technical earthquakes, although 99% can only be felt on very delicate equipment. The last major quake occurred on the Big Island in late November 1975, reaching 7.2 on the Richter scale and causing many millions of dollars worth of damage in the island's southern regions. The only loss of life occurred when a beach collapsed and two people from a large camping party were drowned. Oahu, like the rest of the state, has an elaborate warning system against natural disasters. You will notice loudspeakers high atop poles along many beaches and coastal areas; these warn of tsunamis, hurricanes, and earthquakes. They are tested at 11 a.m. on the first working day of each month. All island telephone books contain a civil defense warning and procedures section with which you should acquaint yourself. Note the maps in the telephone books, which show the areas traditionally inundated by tsunamis and what procedures to follow in case an emergency occurs.

THE CLIMATE

Oahu, like all the Hawaiian Islands, has equitable weather year-round with the average daily temperature about 80 degrees F. The mountainous interior experiences about the same temperatures as the coastal areas because of the small difference in elevation. However, the *pali* are known for strong, chilly winds that rise up the mountainside from the coast. Precipitation is the biggest differentiating factor in the climate of Oahu. Generally, the entire leeward coast, from Makaha to Koko Head, is dry. Rain falls much more frequently and heavily in the Koolau Mountains and along the windward coast. Although rain can occur at any time of year, it is more plentiful in winter. Huge surf also pummels the North Shore during this period, closing off many beaches to the neophyte, but making them absolutely perfect for expert surfers. The maxim throughout the islands is "don't let rain spoil your day." If it's raining, simply move on to the next beach, or around to the other side of the island where it'll probably be dry. You can most often depend on the beaches of Waikiki and Waianae to be sunny and bright.

"So Good" Weather

The ancient Hawaiians had words to describe climatic specifics such as rain, wind, fog, and even snow, but they didn't have a general word for *weather*. The reason is that the weather is just about the same throughout the year and depends more on where you are on any given island than what season it is. The Hawaiians did distinguish between *kau* (summer, May-Oct.) and *hoo'ilo* (winter, Nov.-April), but this distinction included social, religious, and even navigational factors, far beyond a mere distinction of weather variations.

The average daytime temperature throughout Hawaii is about 80° F (26° C), with the average January day registering 78 degrees, and the average August day raising the thermometer only seven degrees to 85 degrees. Nighttime temperatures drop less than 10 degrees. Elevation, however, does drop temperatures about three degrees for every 1,000 feet you climb. The lowest temperatures ever recorded in Hawaii were atop Haleakala in January 1961, when the mercury dropped well below freezing to a mere 11 degrees; the hottest day occurred in 1931 in the Puna District of the Big Island with a scorching (for Hawaii) 100 degrees.

The Trade Winds

One factor that keeps the Hawaiian temperatures both constant and moderate is the trade winds. These breezes are so reliable that the northeast sides of the islands are always referred to as "windward," regardless of where the wind happens to be blowing on any given day. You can count on the trades to be blowing on an average of 300 days per year: hardly missing a day during summer, and half the time in winter. They blow throughout the day but are strongest during the heat of the afternoon and weakest at night. Just when you need a cooling breeze, there they are, and when the temperature drops at night, it's as if someone turned down the giant fan.

The trade winds are also a factor in keeping down the humidity. They will suddenly disappear, however, usually in winter, and might not resume for a few weeks. The Tropic of Cancer runs through the center of Hawaii, yet its famed oppressively hot and muggy weather is joyfully absent. Honolulu, on the same latitude as sweaty Hong Kong and Havana, has only a 50-60% daily humidity factor.

Kona Winds

Kona means "leeward" in Hawaiian, and when the northeasterly trades stop blowing these southerly winds often take over, bringing in hot sticky air. To anyone from Hawaii, kona wind is euphemistic for bad weather. Luckily, they are most common during the cooler months, from October to April, when they appear roughly half the time. The temperatures drop slightly during the winter so these hot winds are tolerable, and even useful for moderating the thermometer. In the summer they are awful, but luckily—again—they hardly ever blow during this season.

A "kona storm" is another matter. These subtropical low-pressure storms develop west of the Hawaiian Islands, and as they move east they draw winds up from the south. Usual only in winter, they can cause considerable damage to crops and real estate. There is no real pattern to kona storms—some years they come every few weeks while in other years they don't appear at all.

Rain

Hardly a day goes by that it isn't raining somewhere on *all* the main islands. The islands have a windward (northeast, wet) and leeward (southwest, dry) side. It rains much more on the windward side, and much more often during winter than summer. (However, kona storms—because they come from the south—hit the islands' leeward sides most often.) Another important rain

WIND AND WAVES

SHORE   BREAKERS   SWELLS   CHOPS   RIPPLES   WIND

TEMPERATURE AND RAINFALL

TOWN		JAN.	MARCH	MAY	JUNE	SEPT.	NOV.
Honolulu	High	80°	82°	84°	85°	82°	81°
	Low	60°	62°	68°	70°	71°	68°
	Rain	4"	2"	0"	0"	0"	4"
Kaneohe	High	80°	80°	80°	82°	82°	80°
	Low	67°	62°	68°	70°	70°	68°
	Rain	5"	5"	2"	0"	2"	5"
Waialua	High	79°	79°	81°	82°	82°	80°
	Low	60°	60°	61°	63°	62°	61°
	Rain	2"	1"	0"	0"	1"	3"

Note: Rainfall in inches; temperature in degrees Fahrenheit

factor is the mountains, which act like water magnets. Moist winds gather around them and eventually build rain clouds. The ancient Hawaiians used these clouds and the reflected green light on their underbellies to spot land from great distances.

Precipitation mostly occurs at and below the 3,000-foot level; thus the upper slopes of taller mountains are quite dry. The average annual rainfall on the seas surrounding Hawaii is only 25 inches, while a few miles inland around the windward slopes of mountains it can be 250 inches! Conversely, the best beach weather is on the leeward sides: Kaanapali, Waikiki, Kailua-Kona, Poipu. They all sit in the "rain shadows" of interior mountains, and if it happens to be raining at one leeward beach, just move down the road to the next.

One more thing about Hawaiian rains—they aren't very nasty. Much of the time just a light drizzle, they hardly ever last all day. Mostly localized to a relatively small area, you can oftentimes spot them by looking for the rainbows. Rain should never spoil your outings in Hawaii. Just "hang loose, brah," and follow the sunshine.

Bad Weather

With all this talk of ideal weather it might seem like there isn't any bad. Read on. When a storm does hit an island it can be bleak and miserable. The worst storms occur in the winter and often have the warped sense of humor to drop their heaviest rainfalls on areas that are normally quite dry. It's not unusual for a storm to dump more than three inches of rain an hour; this can go as high as 10, making Hawaiian rainfalls some of the heaviest on earth.

Hawaii has also been hit with some walloping hurricanes in the last few decades. There haven't been many but they've been destructive. The vast majority of hurricanes originate far to the southeast off the coast of Mexico and Latin America. They mostly pass harmlessly south of Hawaii, but some, swept along by kona winds, strike the islands. The most recent and destructive was Hurricane Iniki, which battered the islands in 1992. It had its greatest effect on Niihau, the Poipu Beach area of Kauai, and the leeward coast of Oahu.

DIANA LASICH HARPER

FLORA AND FAUNA

Anyone who loves a mystery will be intrigued by the speculation about how plants and animals first came to Hawaii. Most people's idea of an island paradise includes swaying palms, dense mysterious jungles ablaze with wild-flowers, and luscious fruits just waiting to be plucked. In fact, for millions of years these were raw and barren islands where no plants grew and no birds sang. Why? Because they are geological orphans that spontaneously popped up in the middle of the Pacific Ocean. The islands, more than 2,000 miles from any continental landfall, were therefore exempted from the normal ecological spread of plants and animals. Even the most tenacious travelers of the fauna and flora kingdoms would be sorely tried in crossing the mighty Pacific. Those that made it by pure chance found a totally foreign ecosystem. Luckily, the soil of Hawaii was virgin and rich, the competition from other plants or animals was nonexistent, and the climate was sufficiently varied, perfect for most growing things.

The evolution of plants and animals on the isolated islands was astonishingly rapid. A tremendous change in environment, coupled with a limited gene pool, accelerated natural selection. For example, many plants lost their protective thorns and spines because there were no grazing animals or birds to destroy them. Many plants and birds became so specialized that they were not only limited to specific islands in the chain but to habitats that frequently encompassed only a single isolated valley. It was as if after traveling so far and finding a niche they never budged again.

Pre-human Hawaii had no fruits, vegetables, palms, edible land animals, conifers, mangroves, or banyans. Flowers were relatively few. In a land where thousands of orchids now brighten every corner, there were only four native varieties, the least in any of the 50 states. Today, the original plants and animals of Hawaii have the highest rate of extinction anywhere on earth. By the beginning of this century, native plants below 1,500 feet were almost completely extinct or totally replaced by introduced species.

The land and its living things have been greatly transformed by man and his agriculture. This inexorable process began when Hawaii was the domain of its original Polynesian settlers, then greatly accelerated when the land was inundated by Western man.

FLORA

Hawaii's indigenous and endemic plants, flowers, and trees are both fascinating and beautiful, but unfortunately, like everything else that was native, they are quickly disappearing. The majority of flora found exotic by visitors was either introduced by the original Polynesians or later by white settlers. The Polynesians who colonized Hawaii brought foodstuffs, including coconut, banana, taro, breadfruit, sweet potato, yam, and sugarcane. They also carried along gourds to use as containers, *awa* plant to make a basic intoxicant, and the ti plant to use for offerings or to string into hula skirts. Non-Hawaiian settlers over the years have brought mangoes, papayas, passion fruit, pineapples, and all the other tropical fruits and vegetables associated with the islands. Also, most of the flowers, including protea, plumeria, anthuriums, orchids, heliconia, ginger, and most hibiscus have come from every continent on earth. Tropical America, Asia, Java, India, and China have all contributed their most beautiful and delicate blooms. Hawaii is blessed with state parks, gardens, undisturbed rainforests, private reserves, and commercial nurseries that offer an exhaustive botanical survey. The following is just a sampling of common, native, and introduced flora that add the dazzling colors and exotic tastes to the landscape.

ohia lehua

KAREN McKINLEY

Native Trees

Koa and ohia are two native trees still commonly seen on the main islands. Both have been greatly reduced by the foraging of introduced cattle and goats, and through logging and forest fires. The koa, a form of acacia, is Hawaii's finest native tree. It can grow to over 70 feet high and has a strong straight trunk, which can measure more than 10 feet in circumference. The foliage is sickle shaped and produces an inconspicuous pale yellow flower. The koa does best in well-drained soil in deep forest areas, but scruffy specimens will grow in poorer soil. The Hawaiians used koa as the main log for their dugout canoes, and elaborate ceremonies were performed when a log was cut and dragged to a canoe shed. Koa wood was also preferred for paddles, spears, even surfboards. Today it is still considered an excellent furniture wood.

The ohia is a survivor and therefore the most abundant of all the native Hawaiian trees. Coming in a variety of shapes and sizes, it grows as miniature trees in wet bogs or as 100-foot giants on the cool dark slopes of higher elevations. This tree is often the first life in new lava flows. The *ohia* produces a tuftlike flower that re-

KAREN McKINLEY

koa

sembles a natural pompon. Considered sacred to Pele, it was said that she would cause a rainstorm if you picked them without the proper prayers. The flowers were fashioned into a lei that resembled a feather boa. The strong hard wood was also used in canoe building, for poi bowls, and especially for temple images.

Tropical Rainforests

When it comes to possessing a pure and diverse natural beauty, the U.S. is one of the finest pieces of real estate on earth. As if purple mountains' majesty and fruited plains weren't enough, it even received a tiny living emerald of tropical rainforest. A tropical rainforest is where the earth itself takes a breath and exhales pure sweet oxygen through its vibrant living green canopy. Located in the territories of Puerto Rico and the Virgin Islands, and in the state of Hawaii, these forests comprise only one-half of one percent of the world's total, and they must be preserved. The U.S. Congress passed two bills in 1986 designed to protect the unique biological diversity of its tropical areas, but their destruction has continued unabated.

The lowland rainforests of Hawaii, comprised mostly of native ohia, are being razed. Landowners slash, burn, and bulldoze them to create more land for cattle, agriculture, and—most distressingly—for wood chips to generate electricity! Introduced wild boar gouge the forest floor, exposing sensitive roots and leaving tiny, fetid ponds where mosquito larvae thrive. Feral goats that roam the forests are hoofed locusts that strip all vegetation within reach. Maui's Nature Conservancy Preserve in Waikamoi has managed to fence in a speck of this forest, keeping it safe from these animals for the time being.

Almost half of the birds classified in the U.S. as endangered are from Hawaii, and almost all of these make their home in the rainforests. For example, Maui's rainforests have yielded the *poouli*, a new species of bird discovered only in 1974. Another forest survey in 1981 rediscovered the **Bishop's o'o**, a bird thought to be extinct at the turn of the century. We can only lament the passing of the rainforests that have already fallen to ignorance, but if this ill-fated destruction continues on the global level, we will soon be lamenting our own passing. We must nurture the rainforests that remain with the simple enlightenment to let them be.

National Wildlife Refuges And Others

Two areas at opposite ends of the island have been set aside as national wildlife refuges (NWR): **James Campbell NWR**, above the town of Kahuku on the extreme northern tip, and **Pearl Harbor NWR,** at the harbor entrance. Both were established in the mid-'70s and are managed by the U.S. Fish and Wildlife Service. They serve mainly as wetland habitats for the endangered Hawaiian gallinule (*alae'ula*), stilt (*aeo*), and coot (*alae ke'oke'o*). Clinging to existence, these birds should have a future as long as their nesting grounds remain undisturbed. These refuges also attract a wide variety of other birds, mostly introduced species such as **cattle egrets, herons,** a few species of **doves, munia, cardinals,** and the **common finch.**

Much of the area within the refuges is natural marshland, but ponds, complete with water-regulating pumps and dikes, have been built. The general public is not admitted to these areas without permission from the refuge managers. For more information, and to arrange a visit, contact Refuge Manager, Hawaiian and Pacific Islands NWR, U.S. Fish and Wildlife Service, Federal Bldg., Room 5302, P.O. Box 50167, Honolulu, HI 96850.

The Nature Conservancy of Hawaii (see "Environmental Resource Groups" following) maintains two nature preserves: **Honouliuli,** located on the southeast slope of the Waianae Mountains above Makakilo, is home to more than 45 native plants found nowhere else on earth—guided hikes are offered monthly; **Ihi'ihilauakea** is in a shallow crater on the dry southeast coastline above Hanauma Bay where there is a totally unique vernal pool and a very rare fern, *marsilea villosa.* Because of the nature of this extremely fragile ecosystem, visitation is limited.

FAUNA

You would think that with Oahu's dense human population, little room would be left for animals. In fact, they are environmentally stressed, but they do survive. The interior mountain slopes are home to **wild pigs,** and a small population of

feral goats survive in the Waianae Range. Migrating **whales** pass by, especially along the leeward coast where they can be observed from lookouts ranging from Waikiki to Koko Head. Half a dozen introduced game birds are found around the island, but Oahu's real animal wealth is its indigenous birdlife.

Birds

One of the great tragedies of natural history is the continuing demise of Hawaiian birdlife. Perhaps only 15 original species of birds remain of the more than 70 native families that thrived before the coming of humans. Since the arrival of Captain Cook in 1778, 23 species have become extinct, with 31 more in danger. And what's not known is how many species were wiped out before the coming of white explorers. Experts believe that the Hawaiians annihilated about 40 species, including seven other species of geese besides the *nene*, a rare one-legged owl, ibis, lovebirds, sea eagles, and hunting creepers—all gone before Captain Cook arrived. Hawaii's endangered birds account for more than 50% of the birds listed in the U.S. Sport Fisheries and Wildlife's *Red Book* (which cites rare and endangered animals). In the last 200 years, more than four times as many birds have become extinct In Hawaii as in all of North America. These figures unfortunately suggest that a full 40% of Hawaii's endemic birds no longer exist. Almost all of Oahu's native birds are gone and few indigenous Hawaiian birds can be found on any island below the 3,000-foot level.

Native birds have been reduced in number because of multiple factors. The original Polynesians helped wipe out many species. They altered large areas for farming and used fire to destroy patches of pristine forests. Also, bird feathers were highly prized for the making of lei, for featherwork in capes and helmets, and for the large *kahili* fans that indicated rank among the *ali'i*. Introduced exotic birds and the new diseases they carried are another major reason for reduction of native bird numbers, along with predation by the mongoose and rat—especially upon ground-nesting birds. Bird malaria and bird pox are also devastating to the native species. Mosquitoes, unknown in Hawaii until a ship named the *Wellington*

introduced them at Lahaina in 1826 through larvae carried in its water barrels, infect most native birds, causing a rapid reduction in birdlife. Feral pigs rooting deep in the rainforests knock over ferns and small trees, creating fetid pools in which mosquito larvae thrive. However, the most damaging factor by far is the assault upon native forests by agriculture and land developers. The vast majority of Hawaiian birds evolved into specialists. They lived in only one small area and ate a very limited number of plants or insects, which once removed or altered resulted in the birds' deaths.

The shores around Oahu, including those off Koko Head and Sand Island, but especially on the tiny islets of Moku Manu and Manana on the windward side, are home to thriving colonies of marine birds. On these diminutive islands it's quite easy to spot a number of birds from the *tern* family, including the white, gray, and sooty tern. All have distinctive screeching voices, and approximate wingspans of 30 inches. Part of

Hawaiian stilt

their problem is that they have little fear of humans. Along with the terns are **shearwaters.** These birds have normal wingspans of about 36 inches and make a series of moans and wails, oftentimes while in flight. For some reason shearwaters are drawn to the bright lights of the city, where they fall prey to house cats and automobiles. Sometimes Moku Manu even attracts an enormous **Laysan albatross** with its seven-foot wingspan. **Tropicbirds** with their lovely streamerlike tails, are often seen along the windward coast.

To catch a glimpse of exotic birds on Oahu you don't have to head for the sea or the hills. The city streets and beach parks are constantly aflutter with wings. Black **myna birds** with their sassy yellow eyes are common mimics around town. **Sparrows,** introduced to Hawaii through Oahu in the 1870s, are everywhere, while **munia,** first introduced as cage birds from Southeast Asia, have escaped and are generally found anywhere around the island. Another escaped cage bird from Asia is the **bulbul,** a natural clown that perches on any likely city roost and draws attention to itself with loud calls and generally ridiculous behavior.

If you're lucky, you can also catch a glimpse of the *pueo* (Hawaiian owl) in the mountainous areas of Waianae and the Koolaus. Also, along trails and deep in the forest from Tantalus to the Waianae Range you can sometimes see elusive native birds like the *elepaio, amakihi,* and the fiery red *i'iwi.*

pueo *(owl)*

KAREN McKINLEY

The *amakihi* and *i'iwi* are endemic birds not endangered at the moment. The *amakihi* is one of the most common native birds; yellowish green, it frequents the high branches of the ohia, koa, and sandalwood trees looking for insects, nectar, or fruit. It is less specialized than most other Hawaiian birds, the main reason for its continued existence. The *i'iwi,* a bright red bird with a salmon-colored, hooked bill, is found in the forests above 2,000 feet. It too feeds on a variety of insects and flowers. The *i'iwi* is known for a harsh voice that sounds like a squeaking hinge, but it's also capable of a melodious song. The *elepaio,* with its long tail (often held upright), is a five-inch brown bird (appearance can vary considerably) that can be coaxed to come within touching distance of the observer. Sometimes it will sit on lower branches above your head and scold you. This bird was the special *amakua* (personal spirit) of canoe builders in ancient lore. Fairly common, it is basically a species of flycatcher.

Oahu also is home to a number of game birds mostly found in the dry upland forests. These include two varieties of **dove,** the **Japanese quail,** both the **green** and **ring-necked pheasant,** and **Erkel's francolin.** Hunting of these birds occurs year-round and information can be had by contacting the Oahu branch of the Division of Forestry and Wildlife.

Note: Also see "The Northwestern Islands" chapter for more wildlife, including the Hawaiian monk seal, green sea turtle, and various marine birds.

ENVIRONMENTAL RESOURCE GROUPS

Anyone interested in Hawaii's environmental issues can contact the following for more information: **The Nature Conservancy of Hawaii,** 1116 Smith St., Honolulu, HI 96817, tel. 537-4508; **Hawaii Green Movement,** P.O. Box 61508, Honolulu, HI 96839; **Sierra Club Legal Defense Fund,** 212 Merchant St., Suite 202, Honolulu, HI 96813, tel. 599-2436; **Pele Defense Fund,** P.O. Box 404, Volcano, HI 96875, tel. 935-1663; **Rainforest Action Network,** 301 Broadway, Suite A, San Francisco, CA 94133, tel. (415) 398-4404.

Environment Hawaii (733 Bishop St., Honolulu, HI 96813, tel. 934-0115, individual subscription rate $35 per year) is a savvy monthly newsletter that focuses on environmental and political issues facing Hawaii today. The well-researched and concisely written newsletter attempts to be fair to all parties concerned, explaining both sides to most controversies. Short on preaching and long on common sense, *Environment Hawaii* is an excellent resource for anyone interested in sociopolitical and environmental issues.

Note: For **environmental tours** *to* Hawaii see (in the Out and About chapter) "Getting There"; for environmental tours *in* Hawaii see "Getting Around"; also see "Camping and Hiking."

HISTORY

THE ROAD FROM TAHITI

Until the 1820s, when New England missionaries began a phonetic rendering of the Hawaiian language, the past was kept vividly alive only by the sonorous voices of special *kahuna* who chanted the sacred *mele*. The chants were beautiful flowing word pictures that captured the essence of every aspect of life. These *mele* praised the land (*mele aina*), royalty (*mele ali'i*), and life's tender aspects (*mele aloha*). Chants were dedicated to friendship, hardship, and to favorite children. Entire villages sometimes joined together to compose a *mele*—every word was chosen carefully, and the wise old *kapuna* would decide if the words were lucky or unlucky. Some *mele* were bawdy or funny on the surface, but contained secret meanings, often with biting sarcasm, that ridiculed an inept or cruel leader. But the most important chants took the listeners back into the dim past, even before people lived in Hawaii. From these genealogies (*ko'ihonua*) the *ali'i* derived the right to rule, since these chants went back to the gods Wakea and Papa from whom the *ali'i* were directly descended.

The Kumulipo

The great genealogies, finally compiled in the late 1800s by order of King Kalakaua, were collectively known as *The Kumulipo, A Hawaiian Creation Chant,* basically a Polynesian account of Genesis. Other chants related to the beginning of this world, but *The Kumulipo* sums it all up and is generally considered the best. The chant relates that after the beginning of time, there is a period of darkness. The darkness, however, mysteriously brims with spontaneous life; during this period plants and animals are born, as well as Kumulipo, the man, and Po'ele, the woman. In the eighth chant darkness gives way to light and the gods descend to earth. Wakea is "the sky father" and Papa is "the earth mother," whose union gives birth to the islands of Hawaii. First born is Hawaii, followed by Maui, then Kahoolawe. Apparently, Papa becomes bushed after three consecutive births and decides to vacation in Tahiti. While Papa is away recovering from post-partum depression and working on her tan, Wakea gets lonely, and takes Kaula as his second wife, who bears him the island-child of Lanai. Not fully cheered up, but getting the hang of it, Wakea takes a third wife, Hina, who promptly bears the island of Molokai. Meanwhile, Papa gets wind of these shenanigans, returns from Polynesia, and retaliates by taking up with Lua, a young and virile god, and soon gives birth to the island of Oahu. Papa and Wakea finally decide that they really are meant for each other and reconcile to conceive Kauai, Niihau, Kaula, and Nihoa. These two progenitors are the source from which all the *ali'i* ultimately traced their lineage, and from which they derived their god-ordained power to rule.

Basically, there are two major genealogical families: the **Nana'ulu,** who became the royal *ali'i* of Oahu and Kauai; and the **Ulu,** who provided the royalty of Maui and Hawaii. The best sources of information on Hawaiian myth and legend are Martha Beckwith's *Hawaiian Mythology* and the monumental three-volume opus *An Account of the Polynesian Race* compiled by Abraham Fornander from 1878 to 1885. Fornander, after settling in Hawaii, married an *ali'i* from Molokai and had an illustrious career as a newspaper man, Maui circuit judge, and finally

Supreme Court justice. For years Fornander sent scribes to every corner of the kingdom to listen to the elder *kupuna*. They returned with the first-hand accounts and he dutifully recorded them.

Polynesians

Since prehistory, Polynesians have been seafaring people whose origins cannot be completely traced. They seem to have come from Southeast Asia mostly through the gateway of Indonesia, and their racial strain pulls features from all three dominant races: caucasian, negro, and asian. They learned to navigate on tame narrow waterways along Indonesia and New Guinea, then fanned out eastward into the great Pacific. They sailed northeast to the low islands of Micronesia and southwest to Fiji, the New Hebrides (now called Vanuatu), and New Caledonia. Fiji is regarded as the "cradle of Polynesian culture"; carbon dating places humans there as early as 3500 B.C. Many races blended on Fiji, until finally the negroid became dominant and the Polynesians moved on. Wandering, they discovered and settled Samoa and Tonga, then ranged far east to populate Tahiti, Easter Island, and the Marquesas. Ultimately, they became the masters of the "Polynesian Triangle," which measures more than 5,000 miles on each leg, stretching across both the North and South Pacific studded with islands. The great Maori

POLYNESIAN TRIANGLE

"How shall we account for this nation spreading itself so far over this vast ocean? We find them from New Zealand to the south, to these islands to the north and from Easter Island to the Hebrides; . . . how much farther is not known. . . ."

Captain James Cook

HAWAII

PALMYRA

BAKER   CHRISTMAS

PHOENIX   EQUATOR

TOKELAU   MARQUESAS

SOCIETY   TUAMOTU

SAMOA   NIUE   TAHITI

TONGA   COOK   MANGAREVA

AUSTRAL   PITCAIRN

RAPA

KERMADEC   EASTER

-N-

NEW ZEALAND

CHATHAM

0   1000 mi

0   1000 km

© MOON PUBLICATIONS, INC.

The Polynesians, attuned to every nuance in their environment, noticed that a migratory land bird called the golden plover arrived from the north every year. They reasoned that since the plover is not a seabird, there must be land to the north.

LOUISE FOOTE

kingdom of New Zealand is the southern apex of the triangle, with Easter Island marking the point farthest east; Hawaii, farthest north, was the last to be settled.

Migrations And Explorations

Ancient legends common throughout the South Pacific speak of a great Polynesian culture that existed on the island of Raiatea about 150 miles north of Tahiti. Here a powerful priesthood held sway in an enormous *heiau* called Toputapuatea in the Opoa district. Kings from throughout Polynesia came here to worship. Human sacrifice was common, as it was believed that the essence of the spirit could be utilized and controlled in this life; therefore the mana of Toputapuatea was great. Defeated warriors and commoners were used as living rollers to drag canoes up onto the beach, while corpses were dismembered and hung in trees. The power of the priests of Opoa lasted for many generations, evoking trembling fear in even the bravest warrior just by the mention of their names. Finally, their power waned and Polynesians lost their centralized culture, but the constant coming and going from Raiatea for centuries sharpened the Polynesians' already excellent sailing skills and convinced them that the world was vast, and unlimited opportunities existed to better their lot.

Now explorers, many left to look for the "heavenly homeland to the north." Samoans called it "Savai'i"; Tongans "Hawai"; Rarotongans "Avaiki"; and Society Islanders "Havai'i." Others abandoned the small islands throughout Polynesia where population pressures exceeded the limits of natural resources, prompting famine. Furthermore, Polynesians were also very warlike among themselves; power struggles between members of a ruling family were common, as were marauders from other islands. So, driven by hunger or warfare, countless refugee Polynesians headed north. Joining them were a few who undoubtedly went for the purely human reason of wanderlust.

The Great Navigators

No one knows exactly when the first Polynesians arrived in Hawaii, but the great "deliberate migrations" from the southern islands seems to have taken place between A.D. 500 and 800, though anthropologists keep pushing the date backward in time as new evidence becomes available. Even before that, however, it's reasonable to assume that the first people to set foot on Hawaii were probably fishermen, or perhaps defeated warriors whose canoes were blown hopelessly northward into unfamiliar waters; they arrived by a combination of extraordinary good luck and an uncanny ability to sail and navigate by the seat of their pants. With no instruments they could navigate, using the sun by day and the moon and rising stars by night. They could feel the water and determine direc-

The canoe hull was a log shaped by masterly stone adze work. The sides were planks that were drilled and sewn together with fiber cord.

LOUISE FOOTE

tion by swells, tides, and currents. The movements of fish and cloud formations were also utilized to give direction. Since their arrival was probably an accident, they were unprepared to settle on the fertile but barren lands, having no stock animals, plant cuttings, or women. Forced to return southward, undoubtedly many lost their lives at sea, but a few wild-eyed stragglers must have made it home where they told tales of a paradise to the north where land was plentiful and the sea bounteous. This is affirmed by ancient navigational chants from Tahiti, Moorea, and Bora Bora, which passing from father to son revealed how to follow the stars to the "heavenly homeland in the north." Possibly a few migrations followed, but it's known that for centuries there was no real reason for a mass exodus, so the chants alone remained and eventually became shadowy legend.

From Where They Came

It's generally agreed that the first planned migrations were from the violent cannibal islands that Spanish explorers called the Marquesas, 11 islands in extreme eastern Polynesia. The islands themselves are harsh and inhospitable, breeding a toughness into these people which enabled them to withstand the hardships of long unsure ocean voyages and years of resettlement. Marquesans were a fiercely independent people whose chiefs could rise from the ranks because of bravery or intelligence. They must have also been a fierce-looking lot. Both men and women tattooed themselves in complex blue patterns from head to foot. The warriors carried massive, intricately designed ironwood war clubs and wore carved whale teeth in slits in their earlobes, which became stretched to the shoulders. They shaved the sides of their heads with sharks' teeth, tied their hair in two topknots that looked like horns, and rubbed their heavily muscled and tattooed bodies with scented coconut oils. Their religion worshipped mummified ancestors; the bodies of warriors of defeated neighboring tribes were consumed. They were masters at building great double-hulled canoes launched from huge canoe sheds. Two hulls were fastened together to form a catamaran, and a hut in the center provided shelter in bad weather. The average voyaging canoe was 60-80 feet long and could comfortably hold an extended family of about 30 people. These small family bands carried all the staples they would need in the new lands.

The New Lands

For five centuries the Marquesans settled and lived peacefully on the new land, as if Hawaii's *aloha* spirit overcame most of their fierceness. The tribes coexisted in relative harmony, especially since there was no competition for land. Cannibalism died out. There was much coming and going between Hawaii and Polynesia and new people came to settle for hundreds of years. Then, it appears that in the 12th century a deliberate exodus of warlike Tahitians arrived and subjugated the settled islanders. They came to conquer. This incursion had a terrific significance on the Hawaiian religious and social system. Oral tradition relates that a Tahitian priest, Paao, found the mana of the Hawaiian chiefs to be low, signifying that their gods were weak. Paao built a *heiau* at Wahaula on the Big Island, then introduced the warlike god Ku and the rigid *kapu* (taboo) system through which the new rulers became dominant. Voyages between Tahiti and Hawaii continued for about 100 years and Tahitian customs, legends, and language became the Hawaiian way of life. Then suddenly, for no recorded or apparent reason, the voyages discontinued and Hawaii returned to total isolation. It remained forgotten for almost 500 years until the indomitable English seaman, Capt. James Cook, sighted Oahu on January 18, 1778. At that time Hawaii's isolation was so complete that even the Polynesians had forgotten about it. On an earlier voyage, Tupaia, a high priest from Raiatea, had accompanied Capt. Cook as he sailed throughout Polynesia. Tupaia's knowledge of existing archipelagos throughout the South Pacific was vast, which he demonstrated by naming over 130 islands and drawing a map that included the Tonga group, the Cook Islands, the Marquesas, and even tiny Pitcairn, a rock in far eastern Polynesia; where the mutinous crew of the *Bounty* found solace. In mentioning the Marquesas Tupaia said, *"he ma'a te ka'ata,"* which equals "food is man" or simply "cannibals!" But remarkably absent from Tupaia's vast knowledge was the existence of Easter Island, New Zealand, and Hawaii. The next waves of people to Hawaii would be white men, and the Hawaiian world would be changed quickly and forever.

THE WORLD DISCOVERS HAWAII

The late 18th century was an extraordinary time in Hawaiian history. Monumental changes seemed to happen all at once. First, Capt. James Cook, a Yorkshire farm boy, fulfilling his destiny as the all-time greatest Pacific explorer, found Hawaii for the rest of the world. For better or worse, it could no longer be an isolated Polynesian homeland. For the first time in Hawaiian history, a charismatic leader named Kamehameha emerged, and after a long civil war united all the islands into one centralized kingdom. The death of Captain Cook in Hawaii marked the beginning of a long series of tragic misunderstandings between white man and native. When Kamehameha died, the old religious system of *kapu* came to an end, leaving the Hawaiians in a spiritual vortex. Many takers arrived to fill the void: missionaries after souls, whalers after their prey and a good time, traders and planters after profits and a home. The islands were opened and devoured like ripe fruit, as powerful nations, including Russia, Great Britain, France, and the United States, yearned to bring this strategic Pacific jewel under their own influence. The 19th century brought the demise of the Hawaiian people as a dominant political force in their own land and with it the end of Hawaii as a sovereign monarchy. An almost bloodless yet bitter military coup followed by a brief period of a Hawaiian Republic ended in annexation by the United States. As the U.S. became completely entrenched politically and militarily, a new social and economic order was founded on the plantation system. Amazingly rapid population growth occurred with the importation of plantation workers from Asia and Europe, which yielded a unique cosmopolitan blend of races like nowhere else on earth. By the dawning of the 20th century, the face of old Hawaii had been altered forever; the "sacred homeland in the north" was hurled into the modern age. The attack on Pearl Harbor saw a tremendous loss of life and brought Hawaii closer to the U.S. by a baptism of blood. Finally, on August 21, 1959, after 59 years as a "terri-

Captain James Cook

HAWAII STATE ARCHIVES

tory," Hawaii officially became the 50th state of the United States of America.

Captain Cook Sights Hawaii
In 1776, Capt. James Cook set sail for the Pacific from Plymouth, England, on his third and final expedition into this still vastly unexplored region of the world. On a fruitless quest for the fabled Northwest Passage across the North American continent, he sailed down the coast of Africa, rounded the Cape of Good Hope, crossed the Indian Ocean, traveled past New Zealand, Tasmania, and the Friendly Islands (where an unsuccessful plot was hatched by the *friendly* natives to murder him), and finally spotted Hawaii. On January 18, 1778, Captain Cook's 100-foot flagship HMS *Resolution* and its 90-foot companion HMS *Discovery* sighted Oahu. Two days later, they sighted Kauai and went ashore at the village of Waimea on January 20, 1778. Though anxious to get on with his mission, Cook decided to make a quick sortie to investigate this new land and reprovision his ships. He did take time to remark in his diary about the close resemblance of these newfound people to others he had encountered as far south as New Zealand, and marveled at their widespread habitation across the Pacific.

The first trade was some brass medals for a mackerel. Cook also stated that he had never before met natives so astonished by a ship, and that they had an amazing fascination for iron, which they called *toe,* the Hawaiian word for "adze." There is even some conjecture that a Spanish ship under one Captain Gaetano had landed in Hawaii as early as the 16th century, trading a few scraps of iron that the Hawaiians valued even more than the Europeans valued gold. It was also noted that the Hawaiian women gave themselves freely to the sailors with the apparent good wishes of the island men. This was actually a ploy by the *kahuna* to test if the newcomers were gods or men—gods didn't need women. These sailors proved immediately mortal. Cook, who was also a physician, tried valiantly to keep the 66 men (out of 112) who had measurable cases of VD away from the women. The task proved impossible as women literally swarmed the ships; when Cook returned less than a year later, it was logged that signs of VD were already apparent on some natives' faces.

Cook was impressed with their swimming and with their well-bred manners. They had happy dispositions and sticky fingers, stealing any object made of metal, especially nails. The first item stolen was a butcher's cleaver. An unidentified native grabbed it, plunged overboard, swam to shore, and waved his booty in triumph. The Hawaiians didn't seem to care for beads and were not at all impressed with a mirror. Cook provisioned his ships by trading chisels for hogs, while common sailors gleefully traded nails for sex. Landing parties were sent inland to fill casks with fresh water. On one such excursion a Mr. Williamson, who was eventually drummed out of the Royal Navy for cowardice, unnecessarily shot and killed a native. After a brief stop on Niihau, the ships sailed away, but both groups were indelibly impressed with the memory of each other.

Cook Returns

Almost a year later, when winter weather forced Cook to return from the coast of Alaska, his discovery began to take on far-reaching significance. Cook had named Hawaii the "Sandwich Islands" in honor of one of his patrons, John Montague, the Earl of Sandwich. On this return voyage he spotted Maui on November 26, 1778. After eight weeks of seeking a suitable harbor it was bypassed, but not before the coastline was duly drawn by Lt. William Bligh, one of Cook's finest and most trusted officers. (Bligh would find his own drama almost 10 years later as commander of the infamous HMS *Bounty.*) The *Discovery* and *Resolution* finally found a safe anchorage at Kealakekua on the Kona coast of the Big Island. It is very lucky for history that on board was Mr. Anderson, ship's chronicler, who left a handwritten record of the strange and tragic events that followed. Even more important were the drawings of John Webber, ship's artist, who rendered invaluable impressions in superb drawings and etchings. Other noteworthy men aboard were George Vancouver, who would himself lead the first British return to Hawaii after Cook's death and introduce many fruits, vegetables, cattle, sheep, and goats, and James Burney, who would become a longstanding leading authority on the Pacific.

The Great God Lono Returns

By all accounts Cook was a humane and just captain, greatly admired by his men. Unlike many other supremacists of that time, he was known to have a respectful attitude to any people he discovered, treating them as equals and recognizing the significance of their cultures. Not known as a violent man, he would use his superior weapons against natives only in an absolute case of self-defense. His hardened crew had been at sea facing untold hardship for almost three years; returning to Hawaii was truly like reentering paradise.

A strange series of coincidences sailed with Cook into Kealakekua Bay on January 16, 1779. It was *makahiki* time, a period of rejoicing and festivity dedicated to the fertility god of the earth, Lono. Normal *kapu* days were suspended, and willing partners freely enjoyed each other sexually, along with dancing, feasting, and the islands' version of Olympic games. It was long held in Hawaiian legend that the great god Lono would return to earth. Lono's image was a small wooden figure perched on a tall mastlike crossbeam; hanging from the crossbeam were long white sheets of *tapa.* Who else could Cook be but Lono, and what else could his ships with their masts and white sails be but his sacred floating *heiau*? This explained the Hawaiians' previous fascination with his ships, but to add to the remarkable coincidence, Kealakekua Bay happened to be considered Lono's private sacred harbor. Natives from throughout the land prostrated themselves and paid homage to the returning god. Cook was taken ashore and brought to Lono's sacred temple where he was afforded the highest respect. The ships badly needed fresh supplies and the Hawaiians readily gave all they had, stretching their own provisions to the limit. To the sailors' delight this included full measures of the *aloha* spirit.

The Fatal Misunderstandings

After an uproarious welcome and generous hospitality for over a month, it became obvious that the newcomers were beginning to overstay their welcome. During the interim a seaman named William Watman died, convincing the Hawaiians that the *haole* were indeed mortals, not gods. Watman was buried at Hikiau Heiau where a plaque commemorates the event to this day. Incidents of petty theft began to increase dramatically. The lesser chiefs indicated it was time to leave by "rubbing the Englishmen's bellies." Inadvertently many *kapu* were broken by the Englishmen, and once friendly relations became strained. Finally, the ships sailed away on February 4, 1779. After plying terrible seas for only a week, the foremast on the *Resolution* was badly damaged, and Cook sailed back into Kealakekua Bay, dragging the mast ashore on February 13. The natives, now totally hostile, hurled rocks at the marines. Orders were given to load muskets with ball; firearms had previously only been loaded with shot and a light charge. Confrontations increased when some Hawaiians stole a small boat and marines set after them, capturing the fleeing canoe, which held an *ali'i* named Palea. The Englishmen treated him roughly; to the Hawaiians horror, they even smacked him on the head with a paddle. The Hawaiians then furiously attacked the marines who abandoned the small boat.

Cook Goes Down

Next the Hawaiians stole a small cutter from the *Discovery* that had been moored to a buoy and partially sunk to protect it from the sun. For the first time Capt. Cook became furious. He ordered Captain Clerk of the *Discovery* to sail to the southeast end of the bay, and to stop any canoe trying to leave Kealakekua. Cook then made a fatal error in judgment. He decided to take nine armed marines ashore in an attempt to convince the venerable King Kalaniopuu to accompany him back aboard ship where he would hold him for ransom in exchange for the cutter. The old king agreed, but his wife prevailed upon him not to trust the *haole*. Kalaniopuu sat down on the beach to think while the tension steadily grew. Meanwhile, a group of marines fired upon a canoe trying to leave the bay and a lesser chief, Nookemai, was killed. The crowd around Cook and his men reached an estimated 20,000, and warriors outraged by the killing of the chief armed themselves with clubs and protective straw-mat armor. One bold warrior advanced on Cook and struck him with his *pahoa*. In retaliation Cook drew a tiny pistol lightly loaded with shot and fired at the warrior. His bullets spent themselves on the straw armor and harmlessly fell to the ground. The Hawaiians went wild. Lieutenant Molesworth Phillips, in charge of the nine marines, began a withering fire; Cook himself slew two natives. Overpowered by sheer numbers, the marines headed for boats standing offshore, while Lt. Phillips lay wounded. It is believed that Captain Cook, the greatest seaman ever to enter the Pacific, stood helplessly in knee-deep water instead of making for the boats because he could not swim! Hopelessly surrounded, he was knocked on the head, then countless warriors passed a knife around and hacked and mutilated his lifeless body. A sad Lt. King lamented in his diary, "Thus fell our great and excellent commander."

The Final Chapter

Captain Clerk, now in charge, settled his men and prevailed upon the Hawaiians to return Cook's body. On the morning of February 16 a grisly piece of charred meat was brought aboard: the Hawaiians, according to their custom, had afforded Cook the highest honor by baking his body in an underground oven to remove the flesh from the bones. On the 17th a group of Hawaiians in a canoe taunted the marines by brandishing Cook's hat. The Englishmen, strained to the limit and thinking that Cook was

"The Death of Captain Cook," by John Webber, ship's artist on Cook's third Pacific exploration, circa 1779.

HAWAII STATE ARCHIVES

being desecrated, finally broke. Foaming with blood-lust, they leveled their cannon and muskets on shore and shot anything that moved. It is believed that Kamehameha the Great was wounded in this flurry, along with four *ali'i* and 25 *maka'ainana* (commoners). Finally, on February 21, 1779, the bones of Capt. James Cook's hands, skull, arms, and legs were returned and tearfully buried at sea. A common seaman, one Mr. Zimmerman, summed up the feelings of all who sailed under Cook when he wrote, ". . . he was our leading star." The English sailed next morning after dropping off their Hawaiian girlfriends who were still aboard.

Captain Clerk, in bad health, carried on with the fruitless search for the Northwest Passage. He died and was buried at the Siberian village of Petropavlovisk. England was at war with upstart colonists in America, so the return of the expedition warranted little fanfare. The *Resolution* was converted into an army transport to fight the pesky Americans; the once proud *Discovery* was reduced to a convict ship ferrying inmates to Botany Bay, Australia. Mrs. Cook, the great captain's steadfast and chaste wife, lived to the age of 93, surviving all her children. She was given a stipend of 200 pounds per year and finished her days surrounded by Cook's mementos, observing the anniversary of his death to the very end by fasting and reading from the Bible.

THE UNIFICATION OF OLD HAWAII

Hawaii was already in a state of political turmoil and civil war when Cook arrived. In the 1780s the islands were roughly divided into three kingdoms: venerable Kalaniopuu ruled Hawaii and the Hana district of Maui; wily and ruthless warrior-king Kahekili ruled Maui, Kahoolawe, Lanai, and later Oahu; and Kaeo, Kahekili's brother, ruled Kauai. War ravaged the land until a remarkable chief, Kamehameha, rose and subjugated all the islands under one rule. Kamehameha initiated a dynasty that would last for about 100 years, until the independent monarchy of Hawaii forever ceased to be. To add a zing to this brewing political stew, Westerners and their technology were beginning to come in ever increasing numbers. In 1786, Captain LaPerouse and his French exploration party landed in what's now LaPerouse Bay, near Lahaina, foreshadowing European attention. In 1786 two American captains, Portlock and Dixon, made landfall in Hawaii. Also, it was known that a fortune could be made on the fur trade between the great Northwest and Canton, China; stopping in Hawaii could make it all feasible. After this was reported, the fate of Hawaii was sealed.

Hawaii under Kamehameha was ready to enter its "golden age." The social order was medieval, with the *ali'i* as knights, owing their military allegiance to the king, and the serflike *maka'ainana* paying tribute and working the lands. The priesthood of *kahuna* filled the posts of advisors, sorcerers, navigators, doctors, and historians. This was Polynesian Hawaii at its apex. But like the uniquely Hawaiian silversword, the old culture blossomed, and as soon as it did, it began to wither. Ever since, all that was purely Hawaiian has been supplanted by the relentless foreign influences that began bearing down upon it.

Young Kamehameha

Kamehameha was a man noticed by everyone; there was no doubt he was a force to be reckoned with. He had met Captain Cook when the *Discovery* unsuccessfully tried to land at Hana on Maui. While aboard, he made a lasting impression, distinguishing himself from the multitude of natives swarming the ships by his royal bearing. Lt. James King, in a diary entry, remarked that Kamehameha was a fierce-looking man, almost ugly, but that he was obviously intelligent, observant, and very good-natured. Kamehameha received his early military training from his uncle Kalaniopuu, the great king of Hawaii and Hana, who fought fierce battles against Alapai, the usurper who stole his hereditary lands. After regaining Hawaii, Kalaniopuu returned to his Hana district and turned his attention to conquering all of Maui. During this period young Kamehameha distinguished himself as a ferocious warrior and earned himself the nickname of "the hard-shelled crab," even though old Kahekili, Maui's king, almost annihilated Kalaniopuu's army at the sand hills of Wailuku.

When the old king neared death he passed on the kingdom to his son Kiwalao. He also, however, empowered Kamehameha as the keeper of the family war god, Kukailimoku: Ku of the Bloody Red Mouth, Ku the Destroyer. Oddly enough, Kamehameha had been born not 500 yards from Ku's great *heiau* at Kohala, and had heard the chanting and observed the ceremonies dedicated to this fierce god from his first breath. Soon after Kalaniopuu died, Kamehameha found himself in a bitter war that he did not seek against his two cousins, Kiwalao and his brother Keoua, with the island of Hawaii at stake. The skirmishing lasted nine years until Kamehameha's armies met the two brothers at Mokuohai in an indecisive battle in which Kiwalao was killed. The result was a shaky truce with Keoua, a much embittered enemy. During this fighting, Kahekili of Maui conquered Oahu, where he built a house of the skulls and bones of his adversaries as a reminder of his omnipotence. He also extended his will to Kauai by marrying his half brother to a high-ranking chieftess of that island. A new factor would be needed to resolve this stalemate of power—the coming of the *haole*.

The Olowalu Massacre

In 1790 the American merchant ship *Ella Nora*, commanded by Yankee captain Simon Metcalfe, was looking for a harbor after its long voyage from the Pacific Northwest. Following a day behind was the *Fair American*, a tiny ship manned by Metcalfe's son Thomas and a crew of five. Metcalfe, perhaps by necessity, was a stern and humorless man who would broach no interference. While anchored at Olowalu, a beach area about five miles east of Lahaina, some natives slipped close in their canoes and stole a small boat, killing a seaman in the process. Metcalfe decided to trick the Hawaiians by first negotiating a truce and then unleashing full fury upon them. Signaling he was willing to trade, he invited canoes of innocent natives to visit his ship. In the meantime, he ordered that all cannon and muskets be readied with scatter shot. When the canoes were within hailing distance, he ordered his crew to fire at will. Over 100 people were slain; the Hawaiians remembered this killing as "the day of spilled brains." Metcalfe then sailed away to Kealakekua Bay and in an unrelated incident succeeded in insulting Kameiamoku, a ruling chief, who vowed to annihilate the next *haole* ship that he saw.

Fate sent him the *Fair American* and young Thomas Metcalfe. The little ship was entirely overrun by superior forces. In the insuing battle, the mate, Isaac Davis, so distinguished himself by open acts of bravery that his life alone was spared. While harbored at Kealakekua, Simon Metcalfe sent John Young to reconnoiter. Kamehameha, learning of the capture of the *Fair American,* detained Young so he could not report, and Metcalfe, losing patience, marooned his own man and sailed off to Canton. (Metcalfe never learned of the fate of his son Thomas, and was later killed with another son while trading with the Indians along the Pacific coast.) Kamehameha quickly realized the significance of his two captives and the *Fair American* with its brace of small cannon. He appropriated the ship and made Davis and Young trusted advisors, eventually raising them to the rank of chief. They would all play a significant role in the unification of Hawaii.

Kamehameha The Great

Later in 1790, supported by the savvy of Davis and Young and the cannon from the *Fair American,* which he mounted on carts, Kamehameha invaded Maui using Hana as his power base. The island defenders under Kalaniekupule, son of Kahekili who was lingering on Oahu, were totally demoralized, then driven back into the deathtrap of Iao Valley. There, Kamehameha's forces annihilated them. No mercy was expected and none given, although mostly commoners were slain with no significant *ali'i* falling to the vic-

Kamehameha I as drawn by Louis Choris, ship's artist for the Von Kotzebue expedition, circa 1816, supposedly the only time that Kamehameha sat to have his portrait rendered.

HAWAII STATE ARCHIVES

tors. So many were killed in this sheer-walled, inescapable valley that the battle was called *"ka pani wai"* which means "the damming of the waters" . . . literally with dead bodies. While Kamehameha was fighting on Maui, his old nemesis Keoua was busy running amok back on Hawaii, again pillaging Kamehameha's lands. The great warrior returned home flushed with victory, but in two battles could not subdue Keoua. Finally, Kamehameha had a prophetic dream in which he was told that Ku would lead him to victory over all the lands of Hawaii if he would build a *heiau* to the war god at Kawaihae. Even before the temple was finished, old Kahekili attempted to invade Waipio, Kamehameha's stronghold. But Kamehameha summoned Davis and Young, and with the *Fair American* and an enormous fleet of war canoes defeated Kahekili at Waimanu. Kahekili had no choice but to accept the indomitable Kamehameha as the king of Maui, although he himself remained the administrative head until his death in 1794.

Now only Keoua remained in the way and he would be defeated not by war, but by the great mana of Ku. While Keoua's armies were crossing the desert on the southern slopes of Kilauea, the fire goddess Pele trumpeted her disapproval and sent a huge cloud of poisonous gas and mud-ash into the air. It descended upon and instantly killed the middle legions of Keoua's armies and their families. The footprints of this ill-fated army remain to this day outlined in the mud-ash as clearly as if they were deliberately encased in wet cement. Keoua's intuition told him that the victorious mana of the gods had swung to Kamehameha and that his own fate was sealed. Kamehameha sent word that he wanted Keoua to meet with him at Ku's newly dedicated temple in Kawaihae. Both knew that Keoua must die. The old nemesis came riding proudly in his canoe, gloriously outfitted in the red and gold feathered cape and helmet signifying his exalted rank. When he stepped ashore he was felled by Kamehameha's warriors and his body was ceremoniously laid upon the altar along with 11 others who were slaughtered and dedicated to Ku, of the Maggot-Dripping Mouth.

Increasing Contact

By the time Kamehameha had won the Big Island, Hawaii was becoming a regular stopover for numerous ships seeking the lucrative sandalwood trade with China. In February 1791, Capt. George Vancouver, still seeking the Northwest Passage, returned to Kealakekua where he was greeted by a throng of 30,000. The captain at once recognized Kamehameha, who was wearing a Chinese dressing gown that he had received in tribute from another chief who in turn had received it directly from the hands of Cook himself. The diary of a crewmember, Thomas Manby, relates that Kamehameha, missing his front teeth, was more fierce-looking than ever as he approached the ship in an elegant double-hulled canoe sporting 46 rowers. The king invited all to a great feast prepared for them on the beach. Kamehameha's appetite matched his tremendous size. It was noted that he ate two sizable fish, a king-size bowl of poi, a small pig, and an entire baked dog. Kamehameha personally entertained the Englishmen by putting on a mock battle in which he deftly avoided spears by rolling, tumbling, and catching them in midair, all the while hurling his own a great distance. The English reciprocated by firing cannon bursts into the air, creating an impromptu fireworks display. Kamehameha requested from Vancouver a full table setting, with which he was provided, but his request for firearms was prudently denied. The captain did, however, leave beef cattle, fowl, and breeding stock of sheep and goats. The ship's naturalist, Archibald Menzies, was the first *haole* to climb Mauna Kea; he also introduced a large assortment of fruits and vegetables. The Hawaiians were cheerful, outgoing, and showed remorse when they indicated that the remainder of Cook's bones had been buried at a temple close to Kealakekua. John Young, by this time firmly entrenched into Hawaiian society, made no request to sail away with Vancouver. During the next two decades of Kamehameha's rule, the French, Russians, English, and Americans discovered the great whaling waters off Hawaii, and their increasing visits shook and finally tumbled the ancient religion and social order of *kapu*.

Finishing Touches

After Keoua was laid to rest it was only a matter of time till Kamehameha consolidated his power over all of Hawaii. In 1794 the old warrior Ka-

hekili of Maui died and gave Oahu to his son Kalanikupule, while Kauai and Niihau went to his brother Kaeo. Warring between themselves, Kalanikupule was victorious, though he did not possess the grit of his father nor the great mana of Kamehameha. He had previously murdered a Captain Brown who had anchored in Honolulu. Kalanikupule seized Brown's ship, the *Jackall*. With the aid of this ship, Kalanikupule now determined to attack Kamehameha. However, while en route the sailors regained control of their ship and cruised to the Big Island to inform and join with Kamehameha. An army of 16,000 was raised and sailed for Maui, where they met only token resistance, destroyed Lahaina, pillaged the countryside, and vanquished Molokai in one bloody battle. The war canoes next sailed for Oahu and the final showdown. The great army landed at Waikiki, and though defenders fought bravely, giving up Oahu by the inch, they were steadily driven into the surrounding mountains. The beleaguered army made its last stand at Nuuanu Pali, a great precipice in the mountains behind present-day Honolulu. Kamehameha's warriors mercilessly drove the enemy into the great abyss. Kalanikupule, who hid in the mountains, was captured after a few months and sacrificed to Ku, The Snatcher of Lands, thereby ending the struggle for power. Kamehameha put down a revolt on Hawaii in 1796 and the king of Kauai, Kaumuali, accepting the inevitable, recognized Kamehameha as supreme ruler without suffering the hopeless ravages of a needless war. Kamehameha, for the first time in Hawaiian history, was the undisputed ruler of all the islands of "the heavenly homeland in the north."

Kamehameha's Rule

Kamehameha was as gentle in victory as he was ferocious in battle. His rule lasted until his death on May 8, 1819, under which Hawaii enjoyed a peace unlike any the warring islands had ever known before. The king moved his royal court to Lahaina, where in 1803 he built the "Brick Palace," the first permanent building of Hawaii. The benevolent tyrant also enacted the "Law of the Splintered Paddle." This law, which protected the weak from the exploitation of the strong, had its origins when, many years before, a brave defender of a small overwhelmed the great Queen Kaahumanu, by ship's artist Louis Choris from the Otto Von Kotzebue expedition, circa 1816

HAWAII STATE ARCHIVES

village broke a paddle over Kamehameha's head and taught the chief—literally in one stroke—about the nobility of the common man.

However, just as Old Hawaii reached its "golden age," its demise was at hand. The relentless waves of *haole* both innocently and determinedly battered the old ways into the ground. With the foreign ships came prosperity and fanciful new goods after which the *ali'i* lusted. The *maka'ainana* were worked mercilessly to provide sandalwood for the China trade. This was the first "boom" economy to hit the islands, but it set the standard of exploitation that would follow. Kamehameha built an observation tower in Lahaina to watch for ships, many of which were his own, returning laden with riches from the world at large. In the last years of his life Kamehameha returned to his beloved Kona coast where he enjoyed the excellent fishing renowned to this day. He had taken Hawaii from the darkness of warfare into the light of peace. He died true to the religious and moral *kapu* of his youth, the only ones he had ever known, and with him died a unique way of life. Two loyal retainers buried his bones after the baked flesh had been ceremoniously stripped away. A secret burial cave was chosen so that no one could desecrate the remains of the great chief, thereby absorbing his mana. The tomb's whereabouts remains unknown, and disturbing the dead remains one of the strictest *kapu* to this day. "The

Lonely One's" kingdom would pass to his son, Liholiho, but true power would be in the hands of his beloved but feisty wife Kaahumanu. As Kamehameha's spirit drifted from this earth, two forces sailing around Cape Horn would forever change Hawaii: the whalers and the missionaries.

MISSIONARIES AND WHALERS

The year 1819 is of the utmost significance in Hawaiian history. It marked the death of Kamehameha, the overthrow of the ancient *kapu* system, the arrival of the first "whaler" in Lahaina, and the departure of Calvinist missionaries from New England determined to convert the heathen islands. Great changes began to rattle the old order to its foundations. With the *kapu* system and all of the ancient gods abandoned (except for the fire goddess Pele of Kilauea), a great void permeated the souls of the Hawaiians. In the coming decades Hawaii, also coveted by Russia, France, and England, was finally consumed by America. The islands had the first American school, printing press, and newspaper west of the Mississippi. Lahaina, in its heyday, became the world's greatest whaling port, accommodating over 500 ships of all types during its peak years.

The Royal Family

Maui's Hana District provided Hawaii with one of its greatest queens, Kaahumanu, born in 1768 in a cave within walking distance of Hana Harbor. At the age of 17 she became the third of Kamehameha's 21 wives and eventually the love of his life. At first she proved to be totally independent and unmanageable, and was known to openly defy her king by taking numerous lovers. Kamehameha placed a *kapu* on her body and even had her attended by horribly deformed hunchbacks to curb her carnal appetites, but she continued to flaunt his authority. Young Kaahumanu had no love for her great, lumbering, unattractive husband, but (even Captain Vancouver was pressed into service as a marriage counselor) in time she learned to love him dearly. She in turn became his favorite wife, although she remained childless throughout her life. Kamehameha's first wife was the supremely royal Keopuolani, who so outranked even him that the king himself had to approach her naked and crawling on his belly. Keopuolani produced the royal children Liholiho and Kauikeaouli, who became King Kamehameha II and III, respectively. When Kamehameha I died in 1819 he appointed Liholiho his successor, but he also had the wisdom to make Kaahumanu the *kuhina nui* or queen regent. Initially, Liholiho was weak and became a drunkard. Later he became a good ruler, but he was always supported by his royal mother Keopuolani and by the ever-formidable Kaahumanu.

Kapu Is *Pau*

Kaahumanu was greatly loved and respected by the people. On public occasions, she donned Kamehameha's royal cloak and spear: so attired and infused with the king's mana, she demonstrated that she was the real leader of Hawaii. For six months after Kamehameha's death, Kaahumanu counseled Liholiho on what he must do. The wise *kuhina nui* knew that the old ways were *pau* (finished) and Hawaii could not hope to function in a rapidly changing world under the *kapu* system. In November 1819, Kaahumanu and Keopuolani prevailed upon Liholiho to break two of the oldest and most sacred *kapu:* to eat together with women and to allow women to eat previously forbidden foods, such as bananas and certain fish. Kaahumanu

sat with Liholilho, heavily fortified with strong drink, and attended by other high-ranking chiefs and a handful of foreigners, they ate in public. This feast became known as Ai Noa ("Free Eating"), and as the first morsels passed her lips the ancient gods of Hawaii tumbled. Throughout the land revered *heiau* were burned and abandoned and the idols knocked to the ground. Now the people had nothing but their own weakened inner selves to rely on. Nothing and no one could answer their prayers; their spiritual lives were empty and in shambles.

Missionaries

In October 1819 the brig *Thaddeus* left Boston carrying 14 missionaries bound for Hawaii. On April 4, 1820, they landed at Kailua, on the Big Island, where Liholiho had moved the royal court. The Reverends Bingham and Thurston went ashore and were granted a one-year, trial missionary period by King Liholiho. They established themselves on Hawaii and Oahu and from there began the transformation of Hawaii. The missionaries were men of God, but also practical-minded Yankees. They brought education, enterprise, and most importantly, unlike the transient seafarers, a commitment to stay and build. In 1823, Reverend Richards established the first mission in Lahaina, a village of about 2,300 inhabitants.

Rapid Conversions

The year 1823 also marked the death of Keopuolani, who was given a Christian burial. Setting the standard by accepting Christianity, a number of the *ali'i* followed the queen's lead. Liholiho had sailed off to England, where he and his wife contracted measles and died. Their bodies were returned by the British in 1825, on the HMS *Blonde* captained by Lord Byron, cousin of *the* Lord Byron. During these years, Kaahumanu allied herself with Reverend Richards and together they wrote Hawaii's first code of laws based upon the Ten Commandments. Foremost was the condemnation of murder, theft, brawling, and the desecration of the Sabbath by work or play. The early missionaries had the best of intentions, but, like all zealots, were blinded by the singlemindedness that was also their greatest ally. They were not surgically selective in their destruction of the native beliefs.

Anything native was felt to be inferior, and they set about to wipe out all traces of the old ways. In their rampage they reduced the Hawaiian culture to ashes, plucking self-will and determination from the hearts of a once proud people. More so than the whalers, they terminated the Hawaiian way of life.

The Early Seamen
A good portion of the common seamen of the early 19th century were the dregs of the Western world. Many a whoremongering drunkard had awoken from a stupor and found himself on the pitching deck of a ship, discovering to his dismay that he had been "pressed into naval service." For the most part these sailors were a filthy, uneducated, lawless rabble. Their present situation was dim, their future hopeless, and they would live to be 30 if they were lucky and didn't die from scurvy or a thousand other miserable fates. They snatched brief pleasure in every port, and jumped ship at every opportunity, especially in an easy berth like Lahaina. They displayed the worst elements of Western culture— which the Hawaiians naively mimicked. In exchange for *aloha* they gave drunkeness, sloth, and insidious death by disease. By the 1850s, the population of native Hawaiians tumbled from the estimated 300,000 reported by Captain Cook in 1778 to barely sixty thousand. Common conditions such as colds, flu, venereal disease, and sometimes small pox and cholera decimated the Hawaiians, who had no natural immunities to these foreign ailments. By the time the missionaries arrived, *hapa haole* children were common in Lahaina streets. The earliest lawless opportunists had come seeking sandalwood after first filling their holds with furs from the Pacific Northwest. Aided by *ali'i* hungry for manufactured goods and Western finery, they raped Hawaiian forests of this fragrant wood so coveted in China. Next, droves of sailors came in search of the whales. The whalers, decent men at home, left their morals back in the Atlantic and lived by the slogan "no conscience east of the Cape." The delights of Hawaii were just too tempting for most.

Two Worlds Tragically Collide
The 1820s were a time of confusion and soul-searching for the Hawaiians. When Kame-

Kamehameha III

hameha II died the kingdom passed to Kaui-keaouli (Kamehameha III), who made his life-long residence in Lahaina. The young king was only nine years old when the title passed to him, but his power was secure because Kaahumanu was still a vibrant *kuhina nui*. The young prince, more so than any other, was raised in the cultural confusion of the times. His childhood was spent during the very cusp of the change from old ways to new, and he was often pulled in two directions by vastly differing beliefs. Since he was royal born, according to age-old Hawaiian tradition he must mate and produce an heir with the highest ranking *ali'i* in the kingdom. This natural mate happened to be his younger sister, the Princess Nahienaena. To the old Hawaiian advisors, this arrangement was perfectly acceptable and encouraged. To the increasingly influential missionaries, incest was an unimaginable abomination in the eyes of God. The problem was compounded by the fact that Kamehameha III and Nahienaena were drawn to each other and were deeply in love. The young king could not stand the mental pressure imposed by

HAWAII STATE ARCHIVES

conflicting worlds. He became a teenage alcoholic too royal to be restrained by anyone in the kingdom, and his bouts of drunkenness and womanizing were both legendary and scandalous. Meanwhile, Nahienaena was even more pressured because she was a favorite of the missionaries, baptized into the church at age 12. She too vacillated between the old and the new; at times a pious Christian, at others she drank all night and took numerous lovers. As the prince and princess grew into their late teens, they became even more attached to each other and hardly made an attempt to keep their relationship from the missionaries. Whenever possible, they lived together in a grass house built for the princess by her father.

In 1832, the great Kaahumanu died, leaving the king on his own. In 1833, at the age of 18, Kamehameha III announced that the "regency" was over and that all the lands in Hawaii were his, personally, and that he alone was the ultimate law. Almost immediately, however, he decreed that his half sister Kinau would be "premier," signifying that he would leave the actual running of the kingdom in her hands. Kamehameha III fell into total drunken confusion, until one night he attempted suicide. After this episode he seemed to straighten up a bit and mostly kept a low profile. In 1836, Princess Nahienaena was convinced by the missionaries to take a husband. She married Leleiohoku, a chief from the Big Island, but continued to sleep with her brother. It is uncertain who fathered the child, but Nahienaena gave birth to a baby boy in September 1836. The young prince survived for only a few hours, and Nahienaena never recovered from her convalescence. She died in December 1836 and was laid to rest in the mausoleum next to her mother, Keopuolani, on the royal island in Mokuhina Pond, still in existence in modern-day Lahaina. After the death of his sister, Kamehameha III became a sober and righteous ruler. Oftentimes seen paying his respects at the royal mausoleum, he ruled longer than any other king until his death in 1854.

The Missionaries Prevail

In 1823, the first mission was established in Lahaina under the pastorage of Reverend Richards and his wife. Within a few years, many of the notable *ali'i* had been, at least in appearance, converted to Christianity. By 1828 the cornerstones for Wainee Church, the first stone church on the island, were laid just behind the palace of Kamehameha III. The struggle between missionaries and whalers centered around public drunkenness and the servicing of sailors by local native girls. The normally god-fearing whalers had signed on for perilous duty that lasted up to three years, and when they anchored in Lahaina they sought their pleasure. The missionaries were instrumental in placing a curfew on sailors and prohibiting native girls from boarding ships, which had become customary. These measures certainly did not stop the liaisons between sailor and *wahine,* but it did impose a modicum of social sanction and tolled the end of the wide-open days. The sailors were outraged; in 1825 the crew from the *Daniel* attacked the home of the meddler, Reverend Richards. A year later a similar incident occurred. In 1827, confined and lonely sailors from the whaler *John Palmer* fired their cannon at Reverend Richards' newly built home.

Slowly the tensions eased, and by 1836 many sailors were regulars at the Seamen's Chapel, adjacent to the Baldwin Home. Unfortunately, even the missionaries couldn't stop the pesky mosquito from entering the islands through the port of Lahaina. The mosquitoes arrived in 1826, from Mexico, aboard the merchant *Wellington.* They were inadvertently carried as larvae in the water barrels and democratically pestered everyone in the islands from that day forward regardless of race, religion, or creed.

Lahaina Becomes A Cultural Center

By 1831, Lahaina was firmly established as a seat of Western influence in Hawaii. That year marked the founding of Lahainaluna School, the first *real* American school west of the Rockies. Virtually a copy of a New England normal school, it attracted the best students, both native and white, from throughout the kingdom. By 1834, Lahainaluna had an operating printing press publishing the islands' first newspaper, *The Torch of Hawaii,* starting a lucrative printing industry centered in Lahaina that dominated not only the islands but also California for many years.

An early native student was David Malo. He was brilliant and well-educated, but more importantly, he remembered the "old ways." One of the first Hawaiians to realize his native land was being swallowed up by the newcomers, Malo compiled the first history of precontact Hawaii and the resulting book, *Hawaiian Antiquities,* became a reference masterpiece which has yet to be eclipsed. David Malo insisted that the printing be done in Hawaiian, not English. Malo is buried in the mountains above Lahainaluna where, by his own request, he is "high above the tide of foreign invasion." By the 1840s, Lahaina was firmly established as the "whaling capital of the world"; the peak year of 1846 saw 395 whaling ships anchored here. A census in 1846 reported that Lahaina was home to 3,445 natives, 112 permanent *haole,* 600 sailors, and over 500 dogs. The populace was housed in 882 grass houses, 155 adobe houses, and 59 relatively permanent stone and wooden-framed structures. Lahaina would probably have remained the islands' capital, had Kamehameha III not moved the royal capital to the burgeoning port of Honolulu on the island of Oahu.

Foreign Influence

By the 1840s Honolulu was becoming the center of commerce in the islands; when Kamehameha III moved the royal court there from Lahaina the ascendant fate of the new capital was guaranteed. In 1843, Lord Paulet, commander of the warship *Carysfort,* forced Kamehameha III to sign a treaty ceding Hawaii to the British. London, however, repudiated this act and Hawaii's independence was restored within a few months when Queen Victoria sent Admiral Thomas as her personal agent of good intentions. The king memorialized the turn of events by a speech in which he uttered the phrase, *"Ua mau ke ea o ka aina i ka pono,"* ("The life of the land is preserved in righteousness"), now Hawaii's motto. The French used similar bullying tactics to force an unfavorable treaty on the Hawaiians in 1839; as part of these heavyhanded negotiations they exacted a payment of $20,000, as well as the right for Catholics to enjoy religious freedom in the islands. In 1842 the U.S. recognized and guaranteed Hawaii's independence without a formal treaty, and by 1860 over 80% of the islands' trade was with the United States.

The Great *Mahele*

In 1840, Kamehameha III ended his autocratic rule and instituted a constitutional monarchy. This brought about the Hawaiian Bill of Rights, but the most far-reaching change was the transition to private ownership of land. Formerly, all land belonged to the ruling chief, who gave wedge-shaped parcels called *ahupua'a* to lesser chiefs to be worked for him. The commoners did all the real labor, their produce heavily taxed by the *ali'i.* The fortunes of war, the death of a chief, or the mere whim of a superior could force a commoner off his land. The Hawaiians, however, could not think in terms of "owning" land. No one could *possess* land, one could only *use* land, and its *ownership* was a strange foreign concept. (As a result, naive Hawaiians gave up their lands for a song to unscrupulous traders, which remains an integral, unrectified problem to this day.) In 1847 Kamehameha III and his advisers separated the lands of Hawaii into three groupings: crown land (belonging to the king), government land (belonging to the chiefs), and the people's land (the largest parcels). In 1848, 245 *ali'i* entered their land claims in the *Mahele Book,* assuring them ownership. In 1850, the commoners were given title in fee simple to the lands they cultivated and lived on as tenants, not including house lots in towns. Commoners without land could buy small *kuleana* (farms) from the government at 50 cents per acre. In 1850, foreigners were also allowed to purchase land in fee simple, and the ownership of Hawaii from that day forward slipped steadily from the hands of its indigenous people.

KING SUGAR

The sugar industry began at Hana, Maui, in 1849. A whaler named George Wilfong hauled four blubber pots ashore and set them up on a rocky hill in the middle of 60 acres he had planted in sugar. A team of oxen turned "crushing rollers" and the cane juice flowed down an open trough into the pots, under which an attending native kept a roaring fire burning. Wilfong's methods of refining were crude, but the resultant high-quality sugar turned a neat profit in Lahaina. The main problem was labor. The Hawaiians, who had participated willingly as whalers,

Women of many ethnic backgrounds worked the plantations at the turn of the century.

were basically indentured workers. They became extremely disillusioned with their contracts, which could last up to 10 years. Most of their wages were eaten up by manufactured commodities sold at the company store, and it didn't take long for them to realize that they were little more than slaves. At every opportunity they either left the area or just refused to work.

Imported Labor
The **Masters and Servants Act of 1850,** which allowed importation of laborers under the contract system, ostensibly guaranteed an endless supply of cheap labor for the plantations. Chinese laborers were imported, but were too enterprising to remain in the fields for a meager $3 per month. They left as soon as opportunity permitted and went into business as small merchants and retailers. In the meantime, Wilfong had sold out, releasing most of the Hawaiians previously held under contract, and his plantation fell into disuse. In 1860, two Danish brothers, August and Oscar Unna, bought land at Hana to raise sugar. They solved the labor problem by importing Japanese laborers who were extremely hardworking and didn't balk at the long hours. The workday lasted 10 hours, six days a week, for a salary of $20 per month with housing and medical care thrown in. Plantation life was very structured with stringent rules governing

even bedtimes and lights out. A worker could be fined for being late or for smoking on the job. Even the Japanese couldn't function under these circumstances, and improvements in benefits and housing were slowly gained.

Sugar Grows
The demand for "Sandwich Island Sugar" grew as California was populated during the gold rush, and increased dramatically when the American Civil War demanded a constant supply. The only sugar plantations on the Mainland were small plots confined to the Confederate states, whose products could hardly be bought by the Union and whose fields, later in the war, were destroyed. By the 1870s it was clear to the planters, still mainly New Englanders, that the U.S. was their market; they tried often to gain closer ties and favorable tariffs. The Americans also planted rumors that the British were interested in annexing Hawaii; this put pressure on the U.S. Congress to pass the long-desired **Reciprocity Act,** which would exempt sugar from import duty. It finally passed in 1875, in exchange for U.S. long-range rights to the strategic naval port of Pearl Harbor, among other concessions. These agreements gave increased political power to a small group of American planters, whose outlooks were similar to the post-Civil War South where a few powerful

whites were the virtual masters of a multitude of dark-skinned laborers. Sugar was now big business and the Hana District alone exported almost 3,000 tons per year. All of Hawaii would have to reckon with the "sugar barons."

Changing Society

The sugar plantation system changed life in Hawaii physically, spiritually, politically, and economically. Now boatloads of workers came not only from Japan, but from Portugal, Germany, and even Russia. The white-skinned workers were most often the field foremen (*luna*). With the immigrants came new religions, new animals and plants, unique cuisines, and a plantation language known as pidgin or da kine. Many Asians, but also portions of all the other immigrant groups including the white plantation owners, intermarried with Hawaiian women. A new class of people properly termed "cosmopolitan" but more familiarly and aptly known as "locals" was emerging. These were the people of multiple race backgrounds who couldn't exactly say *what* they were, but it was clear to all just *who* they were. The plantation owners became the new "chiefs" of Hawaii who would carve up the land and dispense favors. The Hawaiian monarchy was soon eliminated.

A KINGDOM PASSES

The fate of Lahaina's Wainee Church through the years has been a symbol of the political and economic climate of the times. Its construction heralded the beginning of missionary dominance in 1828. It was destroyed by a tornado or "ghost wind" in 1858, just when whaling began to falter. The previously dominant missionaries began losing their control to the merchants and planters. In 1894, Wainee Church was burned to the ground by Royalists supporting the besieged Queen Liliuokalani. It was then rebuilt with a grant from H.P. Baldwin in 1897, while Hawaii was a republic ruled by the sugar planters. It wasn't until 1947 that the Wainee was finally completed and remodeled.

The Beginning Of The End

Like the Hawaiian people themselves, the Kamehameha dynasty in the mid-1800s was dying from within. King Kamehameha IV (Alexander Liholiho) ruled from 1854 to 1863; his only child died in 1862. He was succeeded by his older brother Kamehameha V (Lot Kamehameha), who ruled until 1872. With his passing the Kamehameha line ended. William Lunalilo, elected king in 1873 by popular vote, was of royal, but not Kamehameha, lineage. He died after only a year in office, and being a bachelor left no heirs. He was succeeded by David Kalakaua, known far and wide as "The Merry Monarch." He made a world tour and was well received wherever he went. He built Iolani Palace in Honolulu and was personally in favor of closer ties with the U.S., helping push through the Reciprocity Act. Kalakaua died in 1891 and was replaced by his sister Lydia Liliuokalani, last of the Hawaiian monarchs.

The Revolution

When Liliuokalani took office in 1891 the native population was at a low of 40,000 and she felt the U.S. had too much influence over her homeland. She was known to personally favor the English over the Americans. She attempted to replace the liberal constitution of 1887 (adopted by her pro-American brother) with an autocratic mandate in which she would have much more political and economic control of the islands. When the McKinley Tariff of 1890 brought a decline in sugar profits, she made no attempt to improve the situation. Thus, the planters saw her as a political obstacle to their economic growth; most of Hawaii's American planters and merchants were in favor of a rebellion. She would have to go! A central spokesman and firebrand was Lorrin Thurston, a Honolulu publisher who, with a central core of about 30 men, challenged the Hawaiian monarchy. Although Liliuokalani rallied some support and had a small military potential in her personal guard, the coup was ridiculously easy—it took only one casualty. Captain John Good shot a Hawaiian policeman in the arm and that did it. Naturally, the conspirators could not have succeeded without some solid assurances from a secret contingent in the U.S. Congress as well as outgoing President Benjamin Harrison, who favored Hawaii's annexation. Marines from the *Boston* went ashore to "protect American lives," and on January 17, 1893, the Hawaiian monarchy came to an end.

Queen Liliuokalani

The provisional government was headed by Sanford B. Dole, who became president of the Hawaiian Republic. Liliuokalani actually surrendered not to the conspirators, but to U.S. Ambassador John Stevens. She believed that the U.S. government, which had assured Hawaiian independence, would be outraged by the overthrow and would come to her aid. Actually, incoming President Grover Cleveland *was* outraged and Hawaii wasn't immediately annexed as expected. When queried about what she would do with the conspirators if she were reinstated, Liliuokalani said that they would be hung as traitors. The racist press of the times, which portrayed the Hawaiians as half-civilized, bloodthirsty heathens, publicized this widely. Since the conspirators were the leading citizens of the land, the queen's words proved untimely. In January 1895, a small, ill-fated counterrevolution headed by Liliuokalani failed, and she was placed under house arrest in Iolani Palace. Forced to abdicate her throne, officials of the Republic insisted that she use her married name (Mrs. John Dominis) to sign the documents.

She was also forced to swear allegiance to the new Republic. Liliuokalani went on to write *Hawaii's Story* and also the lyric ballad *Aloha O'e*. She never forgave the conspirators and remained to the Hawaiians "queen" until her death in 1917.

Annexation

The overwhelming majority of Hawaiians opposed annexation and desired to restore the monarchy. But they were prevented from voting by the new Republic because they couldn't meet the imposed property and income qualifications—a transparent ruse by the planters to control the majority. Most *haoles* were racist and believed that the "common people" could not be entrusted with the vote because they were childish and incapable of ruling themselves. The fact that the Hawaiians had existed quite well for 1,000 years before the white man even reached Hawaii was never considered. The Philippine theater of the Spanish-American War also prompted annexation. One of the strongest proponents was Alfred Mahon, a brilliant naval strategist who, with support from Theodore Roosevelt, argued that the U.S. military must have Hawaii to be a viable force in the Pacific. In addition, Japan, flushed with victory in its recent war with China, protested the American intention to annex, and in so doing prompted even moderates to support annexation in fear that the Japanese themselves coveted the prize. On July 7, 1898, President McKinley signed the annexation agreement, and this "tropical fruit" was finally put into the U.S.'s basket.

MODERN TIMES

Hawaii entered the 20th century totally transformed from what it had been. The old Hawaiian language, religion, culture, and leadership were all gone. Western dress, values, education, and recreation were the norm. Native Hawaiians were now unseen citizens who lived in dwindling numbers in remote areas. The plantations, new centers of social order, had a strong Asian flavor; more than 75% of their work force was Asian. There was a small caucasian middle class, an all-powerful caucasian elite, and a single political party ruled by that elite. Education, however, was always highly prized, and by the turn of the century all racial groups were encouraged to attend school. By 1900, almost 90% of Hawaiians were literate (far above the national norm) and schooling was mandatory for all children between ages six and 15. Intermarriage was accepted, and there was a mixing of the races like nowhere else on earth. The military became increasingly important to Hawaii. It brought in money and jobs, dominating the island economy. The Japanese attack on Pearl Harbor, which began U.S. involvement in World War II, bound Hawaii to America forever. Once the islands had been baptized by blood, the average Mainlander felt that Hawaii was American soil. A movement among Hawaiians to become part of the United States began to grow. They wanted a real voice in Washington, not merely a voteless delegate as provided under their territory status. Hawaii became the 50th state in 1959 and the jumbo jet revolution of the 1960s made it easily accessible to growing numbers of tourists from all over the world.

Military History

A few military strategists realized the importance of Hawaii early in the 19th century, but most didn't recognize the advantages until the Spanish-American War. It was clearly an unsinkable ship in the middle of the Pacific from which the U.S. could launch military operations. Troops were stationed at Camp McKinley, at the foot of Diamond Head, the main military compound until it became obsolete in 1907. Pearl Harbor was first surveyed in 1872 by General Schofield. Later a military base named in his honor, Schofield Barracks, became a main military post in central Oahu. It first housed the U.S. 5th Cavalry in 1909 and was heavily bombed by the Japanese at the outset of WW II. Pearl Harbor, first dredged in 1908, was officially opened on December 11, 1911. The first warship to enter was the cruiser *California*. Ever since, the military has been a mainstay of island economy. Unfortunately, there has been long-standing bad blood between locals and military personnel. Each group has tended to look down upon the other.

Pearl Harbor Attack

On the morning of December 7, 1941, the Japanese carrier *Akagi*, flying the battle flag of the famed Admiral Togo of the Russo-Japanese War, received and broadcast over its PA system island music from Honolulu station KGMB. Deep in the bowels of the ship a radio man listened for a much different message, coming thousands of miles from the Japanese mainland. When the ironic poetic message "east wind rain" was received, the attack was launched. At the end of

Honolulu Star-Bulletin 1st EXTRA

8 PAGES—HONOLULU, TERRITORY OF HAWAII, U. S. A., SUNDAY, DECEMBER 7, 1941—8 PAGES

★ PRICE FIVE CENTS

WAR!

(Associated Press by Transpacific Telephone)

SAN FRANCISCO, Dec. 7.— President Roosevelt announced this morning that Japanese planes had attacked Manila and Pearl Harbor.

OAHU BOMBED BY JAPANESE PLANES

SIX KNOWN DEAD. 21 INJURED, AT EMERGENCY HOSPITAL

The Honolulu Star Bulletin banner headline announces the beginning of U.S. involvement in WW II on Sunday, December 7, 1941.

HONOLULU STAR BULLETIN

the day, 2,325 U.S. servicemen and 57 civilians were dead; 188 planes were destroyed; 18 major warships were sunk or heavily damaged; and the U.S. was in the war. Japanese casualties were ludicrously light and the ignited conflict would rage for four years until Japan, through the atomic bombs dropped on Nagasaki and Hiroshima, was vaporized into total submission. By the end of hostilities, Hawaii would never again be considered separate from America (see "Central Oahu—Aiea, Pearl City, and Vicinity" for more details).

Statehood

A number of economic and political reasons explain why the ruling elite of Hawaii desired statehood, but simply, the vast majority of people who lived there, especially after WW II, considered themselves Americans. The first serious mention of making "The Sandwich Islands" a state was in the 1850s under President Franklin Pierce, but it wasn't taken seriously until the monarchy was overthrown in the 1890s. For the next 50 years statehood proposals were made repeatedly to Congress, but there was stiff opposition, especially from the southern states. With Hawaii a territory, an import quota system beneficial to Mainland producers could be enacted on produce, especially sugar. Also, there was prejudice against creating a state in a

place where the majority of the populace was not caucasian. This situation was illuminated by the infamous Massie Rape case of 1931 (see "People—The Massie Rape Case"), which went down as one of the greatest miscarriages of justice in American history. During WW II, Hawaii was placed under martial law, but no serious attempt to intern the Japanese population was made, as in California. There were simply too many Japanese, who went on to gain the respect of the American people by their outstanding fighting record during the war. Hawaii's own 100th Battalion became the famous 442nd Regimental Combat Team, which gained notoriety by saving the Lost Texas Battalion during the Battle of the Bulge, and went on to be *the* most decorated battalion in all of WW II. When these GIs returned home, *no one* was going to tell them that they were not loyal Americans. Many of these AJAs (Americans of Japanese Ancestry) took advantage of the GI Bill and received higher education. They were from the common people, not the elite, and they rallied grassroots support for statehood. When the vote finally occurred, approximately 132,900 voted in favor of statehood with only 7,800 votes against. Congress passed the Hawaii State Bill on March 12, 1959, and on August 21, 1959, President Eisenhower announced that Hawaii was officially the 50th state.

DIANA LASICH HARPER

GOVERNMENT

The only difference between the government of the state of Hawaii and other states is that it's "streamlined," and in theory more efficient. There are only two levels of government: the state and the county. With no town or city governments to deal with, considerable bureaucracy is eliminated.

Hawaii, in anticipation of becoming a state, drafted a constitution in 1950 and was ready to go when statehood came. Politics and government are taken seriously in the "Aloha State," which consistently turns in the best national voting record per capita. For example, in the first state elections 173,000 of 180,000 registered voters voted—a whopping 94% of the electorate. In the election to ratify statehood, hardly a ballot went uncast, with 95% of the voters opting for statehood. The bill carried every island of Hawaii except for Niihau, where, coincidentally, the majority of people (total population 250 or so) are of relatively pure Hawaiian blood. The present governor is John Waihee III, first Hawaiian gov-

ernor in the United States. Mr. Waihee has held this office since 1986.

Oahu has been the center of government for about 150 years, since King Kamehameha III permanently established the royal court there in the 1840s. In 1873-74, King David Kalakaua built Iolani Palace as the central showpiece of the island kingdom. Liliuokalani, the last Hawaiian monarch, lived after her dethronement in the nearby residence Washington Place. While Hawaii was a territory, and for a few years after it became a state, the palace was used as the capitol building, the governor residing in Washington Place. Modern Oahu, besides being the center of state government, governs itself as the **City and County of Honolulu.** The county not only covers the entire island of Oahu, but all the far-flung Northwestern Islands, except for Midway, which is under federal jurisdiction.

State Representation
Oahu has four times as many people as the

other islands combined. Nowhere is this more evident than in the representation of Oahu in the state House and Senate. Oahu claims 19 of the 25 state senators and 39.7 of the 51 state representatives. (The 0.7 state representative covers the split district of the north Waianae area of Oahu, and the north shore of Kauai chips in with the remainder 0.3 of the representative.) These lopsided figures make it obvious that Oahu has plenty of clout, especially Honolulu urban districts, which elect more than 50% of Oahu's representatives.

Frequent political battles ensue, since what's good for the city and county of Honolulu isn't always good for the rest of the state. More often than not, the political moguls of Oahu, backed by huge business interests, prevail. The Oahu state senators are overwhelmingly Democratic, except for three Republicans, all from the Honolulu urban districts. State representation is similar: only nine are Republicans, all from urban Honolulu or the suburban communities around Kailua.

OFFICE OF HAWAIIAN AFFAIRS

In 1979, constitutional mandate created the Office of Hawaiian Affairs (OHA). This remarkable piece of legislature recognized, for the first time since the fall of the monarchy in 1893, the special plight of native Hawaiians. For 75 years, no one in government was eager to face the "native question," but since 1979, OHA has opened a Pandora's box of litigation and accusation. For example, in 1983, a presidential commission investigated U.S. involvement in the overthrow of Hawaii's last queen, Liliuokalani, to decide if the federal government owed reparations to her Hawaiian people. After listening to testimony from thousands attesting to personal family loss of land and freedom, complete with old deeds documenting their claims, the commission concluded that the U.S. was guiltless and that native Hawaiians have nothing coming from Uncle Sam. Jaws dropped, and even those opposed to native Hawaiian rights couldn't believed this whitewash. Then-governor George Ariyoshi said in a newspaper interview, "A recent congressional study did not accurately portray what went on here at the turn of the century. . . . To say that the monarchy was not overthrown . . . is something that I cannot accept. It is not historically true."

Trouble In Paradise

The OHA, as the vanguard of native political activism, has focused on gaining monies guaranteed in the state constitution as recently as 1959 for "ceded lands." They have also been instrumental in regaining disputed Hawaiian lands and have helped in the fight to save the sacred island of Kahoolawe, which is now uninhabited and has been used as a bombing target since WW II. To simply state a complex issue, native Hawaiians have been eligible for benefits from revenues accrued from ceded lands and haven't been receiving them. These lands (1.8 million acres) were crown and government lands belonging to the Hawaiian monarchy and, therefore, to its subjects. When the kingdom was overthrown, the lands passed on to the short-lived Republic, followed by the U.S. Protectorate, and then finally to the state in 1959. No one disputed that these lands belonged to *the people*, who were entitled to money collected from rents and leases. For the last 26 years, however, these tens of millions of dollars have gone into a "general fund" used by various state agencies such as the Department of Transportation and the Department of Land and Natural Resources; the state is extremely reluctant to turn these funds over to what they derisively call an "unconstitutional special interest group." A Constitutional Convention scheduled in 1988 supposedly addressed this issue, but many problems still exist.

Native Hawaiian Rights

The question has always been, "Just what is a native Hawaiian?" The answer has always been ambiguous. The government has used the "blood quantum" as a measuring stick. This is simply the percentage of Hawaiian blood in a person's ancestry—customarily 50% qualifies a person as Hawaiian. The issue is compounded by the fact that no other group of people has been so racially intermarried for so many years. Even though many people have direct ancestry to pre-Republic Hawaiians, they don't have enough "Hawaiianness" to qualify. An overwhelming number of these people fall into the

HOUSE DISTRICTS

KAUAI
49

OAHU

42

43

49
41
40
38
39
35
10-34, 44-48
37
36
HONOLULU

HONOLULU CITY & COUNTY: 10-49

SENATORIAL DISTRICTS

22

OAHU

21

19
20

18
6-17, 23, 24

HONOLULU CITY
& COUNTY: 6-24
N.B. ALSO INCLUDES
NORTHWESTERN ISLANDS

© MOON PUBLICATIONS, INC.

category of "locals": they "feel" Hawaiian, but blood-wise they're not. They suffer all of the negativity of second-class citizens and reap none of the benefits accorded Hawaiians. Those who do qualify according to blood quantum don't have the numbers or the political clout necessary to get results. In fact, many people involved with OHA would not qualify themselves, at least not according to the blood quantum! Strong factionalism within the native Hawaiian movement itself threatens its credibility. Many people who do qualify by the blood quantum

view the others as impinging on their rightful claims. The most vocal activists point out that only a coalition of people who have Hawaiian blood, combined with those who "identify" with the movement, will get results. Walter Ritte, a political firebrand and OHA trustee from Molokai, says that "anti-Hawaiian rights" lobbyists such as the tourist industry, airlines, large corporations, etc., are now stronger than the Hawaiians. Ritte advises that the only way the Hawaiian rights movement can win is to become active "political warriors" and vote for legislators who will support their cause. The rhetoric of OHA is reminiscent of the equal rights movement of the 1960s.

Obviously compromise is necessary. Perhaps certain social entitlements (such as tuition grants) could be equal for all, whereas money and land entitlements could be granted by percentages equal to the claiming person's actual "blood quantum." OHA members appeal directly to the Hawaiian people and can build political constituencies at a grassroots level. Since they are elected by the people and not appointed by the government (the case with the Hawaiian Home Lands Department and the trustees of the Bishop Estate, two other *supposedly* Hawaiian institutions), the status quo political parties of Hawaii are wary of them. Their candidates may be opposed and defeated in the future. What makes the issue even more ludicrous is that some of the state's most powerful corporate families opposed to Hawaiian rights have direct lineage to not only pre-Republic Hawaiian ancestors, but to Hawaiian royalty! They themselves would receive "entitlements" from the ceded land according to blood quantum, but socioeconomically they are the natural enemies of OHA. The problem is difficult and it is improbable that all concerned will get satisfaction. OHA maintains offices at 567 S. King Street, Honolulu 96813. They publish a newspaper entitled *Ka Wai Ola O OHA* ("The Living Waters of OHA"), which is available upon request.

ECONOMY

Hawaii's mid-Pacific location makes it perfect for two primary sources of income: tourism and the military. Tourists come in anticipation of endless golden days on soothing beaches, while the military is provided with the strategic position of an unsinkable battleship. Each economic sector nets Hawaii about $4 billion annually, which should keep flowing smoothly and increasingly into the foreseeable future. These revenues mostly remain aloof from the normal ups and downs of the Mainland U.S. economy. Together they make up 60% of the islands' income, and both attract either gung-ho enthusiasts or rabidly negative detractors. The remaining 40% comes in descending proportions from manufacturing, construction, and agriculture (mainly sugar and pineapples). As long as the sun shines and the balance of global power requires a military presence, the economic stability of Hawaii is guaranteed.

Economically, Oahu dwarfs the rest of the islands combined. It generates income from government spending, tourism, and agriculture. A huge military presence, an international airport that receives the lion's share of visitors, and unbelievably, half of the state's best arable lands keep Oahu in the economic catbird seat. The famous "Big Five" all maintain their corporate offices in downtown Honolulu, from which they oversee vast holdings throughout Hawaii and the Mainland. Located in about the same spots as when their founders helped to overthrow the monarchy, things are about the same as then, except that they're going strong, while the old royalty of Hawaii has vanished.

TOURISM

"The earthly paradise! Don't you want to go to it? Why, of course!" This was the opening line of *The Hawaiian Guide Book* by Henry Whitney, which appeared in 1875. In print for 25 years, it sold for 60 cents during a time when a roundtrip sea voyage between San Francisco and Honolulu cost $125. The technique is a bit dated, but the human desires remain the same: some of us

seek paradise, all seek escape, some are drawn to play out a drama in a beautiful setting. Tourists have been coming to Hawaii ever since steamship service began in the 1860s. Until WW II, luxury liners carried the financial elite on exclusive voyages to the islands. By the 1920s 10,000 visitors a year were spending almost $5 million dollars—cementing the bond between Hawaii and tourism.

A $25,000 prize offered by James Dole of pineapple fame sparked a trans-Pacific air race in 1927. The success of the aerial daredevils who answered the challenge proved that commercial air travel to Hawaii was feasible. Two years later, **Hawaiian Air** was offering regularly scheduled flights between all of the major islands. By 1950 airplanes had captured over 50% of the transportation market, and ocean voyages were relegated to "specialty travel," catering to the elite. By 1960 the large airbuses made their debut; 300,000 tourists arrived on eight designated airlines. The Boeing 747 began operating in 1969. These enormous planes could carry hundreds of passengers at reasonable rates, so travel to Hawaii became possible for the average-income person. In 1970, two million arrived, and by 1980 close to four million passengers arrived on 22 international air carriers. The first hotel in Honolulu was the **Hawaiian,** built in 1872. It was predated by **Volcano House,** which overlooked Kilauea Crater on the Big Island and was built in 1866. The coral-pink **Royal Hawaiian,** built in 1927, is Waikiki's graciously aging grand dame, a symbol of days gone by. As late as the 1950s it had Waikiki Beach almost to itself. Only 10,000 hotel units were available in the islands in 1960; today there are over 60,000, and thousands of condos as well.

The flow of visitors to Oahu has remained unabated ever since tourism outstripped sugar and pineapples in the early 1960s, becoming Hawaii's top moneymaker. Of the nearly five million people who visit the state yearly, two-thirds stay on Oahu; almost all the rest, en route to the Neighbor Islands, at least pass through. Hotels directly employ over 15,000 workers, half the state's total, not including all the shop assistants, waiters and waitresses, taxi drivers, and everyone else needed to ensure a carefree vacation. Of Hawaii's 60,000 hotel rooms, Oahu claims 34,000. The visitor industry generates over $2 billion of yearly revenue, and this is only the amount that can be directly related to the hotel and restaurant trades. With the flow of visitors seemingly endless, Oahu has a bright economic future.

Tourists: Who, When, And Where

Tourism-based income outstripped pineapples and sugar by the mid-'60s and the boom was on. Long-time residents could even feel a physical change in air temperature: many trees were removed from Honolulu to build parking lots, and reflected sunlight made Honolulu much hotter and at times unbearable. Even the trade winds, known to moderate temperatures, were not up to that task. So many people from the outlying farming communities were attracted to work in

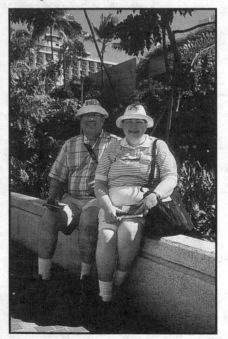

Mainland visitors

the hotels that there was a poi famine in 1967. But for the most part, islanders knew that their economic future was tied to this "nonpolluting industry."

Most visitors (75%) are American, and the largest numbers come from the West Coast. Sun-seeking refugees from frigid Alaska, however, make up the greatest proportional number, according to population figures. The remaining arrivals are in descending order from Japan, Canada, Australia, and England. Europe, as a whole, sends proportionately fewer visitors than North America or Asia, while the least amount come from South America. The Japanese market is constantly growing and by the year 1990 over a million Japanese had visited Hawaii. This is particularly beneficial to the tourist market because the average Western tourist spends about $90 per day, while his Japanese counterpart spends just over $200 per day. However, they stay only about five days, shorter than the typical visit. Up until very recently the Japanese traveled only in groups and primarily stayed on Oahu. Now the trend is to travel independently, or come with a group and then peel off, with a hefty percentage heading for the Neighbor Islands.

The typical visitor is slightly affluent, about 35, with 20% more women than men. The average age is a touch higher than most vacation areas because it reflects an inflated proportion of retirees heading for Hawaii, especially Honolulu, to fulfill a lifelong "dream" vacation. A typical stay lasts about 12 days, down from a month in the 1950s; a full 50% are repeat visitors. On any given day there are about 70,000 travelers on Oahu, 15,000 on Maui, and about 7,000 each on Kauai and Hawaii. Molokai and Lanai get so few that the figures are hardly counted. In 1964 only 10% of the islands' hotel rooms were on the Neighbor Islands, but by 1966 the figure jumped to 25%, with more than 70% of tourists opting to visit the Neighbor Islands. Today four out of 10 hotel rooms are on the Neighbor Islands and that figure should reach 50% shortly.

The overwhelming number of tourists are on package tours, and the largest number of people congregate in Waikiki, which has a 74% average hotel occupancy rate and attracts 2.5 times as many visitors as the Neighbor Islands together.

Waikiki growing rice, circa 1920

HAWAII STATE ARCHIVES

Obviously, Waikiki is still most people's idea of paradise. Those seeking a more intimate experience can have it with a 20-minute flight from Oahu or a direct flight to Hilo (Hawaii) and now Maui and Kauai.

Joaquin Miller, the 19th-century poet of the Sierra, said, "I tell you my boy, the man who has not seen the Sandwich Islands, in this one great ocean's warm heart, has not seen the world." The times have certainly changed, but the sentiments of most visitors to Hawaii remain consistently the same.

Tourism-related Problems

Tourism is both boon and blight to Hawaii. It is the root cause of two problems: one environmental, the other socioeconomic. The environmental impact is obvious and best described in the lament of songstress Joni Mitchell's "They paved paradise and put up a parking lot." Simply, tourism can draw too many people to an area and overburden it. In the process, it stresses the very land and destroys the natural beauty that attracted people in the first place. Tourists come to Hawaii for what has been called its "ambient resource": a balanced collage of indulgent climate, invigorating waters, intoxicating scenery, and exotic people all wrapped up neatly in one area which can both soothe and excite at the same time. It is in the best interest of Hawaii to preserve this "resource."

Changing Lifestyle

Like the land, humans are stressed by tourism. Local people, who once took the "Hawaiian lifestyle" for granted, become displaced and estranged in their own land. Some areas, predominantly along gorgeous beaches that were average-to-low-income communities, are now overdeveloped with prices going through the roof. The locals are not only forced to move out, but often must come back as service personnel in the tourist industry and cater to the very people who displaced them. At one time the psychological blow was softened because, after all, the newcomers were merely benign tourists who would stay a short time, spend a wad of money, and leave.

Today, condos are being built and a different sort of visitor is arriving. Many condo owners are in the above-average income bracket: well-educated businesspeople and professionals. The average condo owner is a Mainlander who purchases one as a second or retirement home. These people are not islanders and have a tough time relating to the locals, who naturally feel resentment. Moreover, since they don't *leave* like normal tourists, they use all community facilities, find those special nooks and crannies for shopping or sunbathing that were once exclusively the domain of locals, and have a say as voters in community governments. The islanders become more and more disenfranchised. Many believe that the new order instigated by tourism is similar to what has always existed in Hawaii: a few from the privileged class being catered to by many from the working class. In a way it's an extension of the plantation system, but instead of carrying pineapples, most islanders find themselves carrying luggage, cocktails, or broiled fish. One argument, however, remains undeniable: whether it's people or pineapples, one has to make a living. The days of a little grass shack on a sunny beach aren't gone; it's just that you need a wallet full of credit cards to afford one.

THE MILITARY

Hawaii is the most militarized state in the country: all five services are represented. Camp H.M. Smith, overlooking Pearl Harbor, is the headquarters of CINCPAC (Commander in Chief Pacific), which is responsible for 70% of the earth's surface, from California to the east coast of Africa and to both poles. The U.S. military presence dates back to 1887, when Pearl Harbor was given to the Navy as part of the "Sugar Reciprocity Treaty." The sugar planters were given favorable "duty-free" treatment for their sugar, while the U.S. Navy was allowed exclusive rights to one of the best harbors in the Pacific. In 1894, when the monarchy was being overthrown by the sugar planters, the USS *Boston* sent a contingency of Marines ashore to "keep order," which really amounted to a show of force, backing the revolution. The Spanish-American War saw U.S. troops billeted at Camp McKinley at the foot of Diamond Head, and Schofield Barracks opened to receive the 5th Cavalry in 1909. Pearl Harbor's flames ignited WW II, and there has been no looking back since then.

About 60,000 military personnel are stationed in Hawaii, with a slightly higher number of dependents. The Navy and Marines combined have the most personnel with about 36,000, followed by the Army's 17,000, 6,000 in the Air Force, and 1,000 or so Coast Guard members. Besides this, 20,000 civilian support personnel account for 65% of all federal jobs in Hawaii. The combined services are one of the largest landholders with over 242,000 acres, accounting for six percent of Hawaiian land. The two major holdings are the 100,000-acre Pohahuloa Training Area on Hawaii and 100,000 acres on Oahu, which is a full 26% of the entire island. The Army controls 71% of the military lands, followed by the Navy at 25%, and the remainder goes to the Air Force and a few small installations to the Coast Guard.

The Military Has No *Aloha*

Not everyone is thrilled about the strong military presence in Hawaii. Two factions, native Hawaiians and antinuclear groups, are downright angry. Radical contingencies of native

Pearl Harbor Yards, Joseph Strauss missile destroyer

Hawaiian-rights groups actually consider Hawaii to be an independent country, besieged and "occupied" by the U.S. government. They date their loss of independence to Liliuokalani's overthrow in 1894. The vast majority of ethnic Hawaiians, though they consider themselves Americans, are concerned with loss of their rightful homelands, with no financial reparation, and a continuing destruction and disregard for their traditional religious and historical sites. A long list of grievances is cited by native Hawaiian action groups, but the best and clearest example is the controversy over the sacred island, Kahoolawe, which is used as a bombing target by the Navy.

The second controversy raised by the military presence focuses on Hawaii as a nuclear target. The ultimate goal of the antinuclear protestors is to see the Pacific, and the entire world, free from nuclear arms. They see Hawaii as a big target that the international power merchants on the Mainland use as both pawn and watchdog. There is no doubt that Hawaii is a nuclear time bomb/powderkeg and the antinuke groups say that if war breaks out the Hawaiian Islands will be reduced to cinders. The military naturally counters that a strong Hawaii is a deterrent to nuclear war and that Hawaii is not only a powerful offensive weapon, but one of the best-defended regions of the world. Unfortunately, when you are on an island there is no place to go: like a boxer in a ring, you can run, but you can't hide.

AGRICULTURE

You'd think that with all the people living on Oahu, coupled with the constant land development, there'd hardly be any room left for things to grow. But that's not the case. The land is productive, though definitely stressed. It is startling that in downtown Honolulu and Waikiki, so many trees have been removed to build parking lots that the asphalt becomes overheated from the lack of shade, allowing temperatures, once moderated by the trade winds, to rise demonstrably.

Changing times and attitudes led to a "poi famine" that hit Oahu in 1967 because very few people were interested in the hard work of farm-

LEAF JOINT (COLLARS)

STALK

LEAF

INTERNODE

NODE

ROOTS — SEED PIECE

YOUNG SUGARCANE

LOUISE FOOTE

ing this staple. However, with half the state's best arable land, Oahu manages to produce a considerable amount of sugarcane, pineapples, and the many products of diversified agriculture. Sugar lands account for 33,000 acres, most owned by the James Campbell Estate, located around Ewa, north and west of Pearl Harbor, with some acreage around Waimea and Waialua on the north shore. Pineapples cover 11,500 acres, with the biggest holdings in the Leilehua Plateau belonging to Dole, a subsidiary of Castle and Cooke. In the hills, entrepreneurs raise *pakalolo,* which has become the state's most productive cash crop. Oahu is also a huge agricultural consumer, demanding more than four times as much vegetables, fruits, meats, and poultry to feed its citizens and visitors than the remainder of the state combined.

THE "BIG FIVE"

Until statehood, Hawaii was ruled economically by a consortium of corporations known as "the Big Five": **C. Brewer and Co.,** sugar, ranching, and chemicals, founded 1826; **Theo. H. Davies & Co.,** sugar, investments, insurance, and transportation, founded 1845; **Amfac Inc.** (originally H. Hackfield Inc.—a German firm that changed its name and ownership during the anti-German sentiment of WW I to American Factors), sugar, insurance, and land development, founded 1849; **Castle and Cooke Inc.** (Dole), pineapple, food packing, and land development, founded 1851; and **Alexander and Baldwin Inc.,** shipping, sugar, and pineapple, founded 1895. This economic oligarchy ruled Hawaii with a velvet glove and a steel grip.

With members on all important corporate boards, they controlled all major commerce, including banking, shipping, insurance, hotel development, agriculture, utilities, and wholesale and retail merchandising. Anyone trying to buck the system was ground to dust, finding it suddenly impossible to do business in the islands. The Big Five were made up of the islands' oldest and most well-established *haole* families; all included bloodlines from Hawaii's own *ali'i.* They looked only among themselves for suitable husbands and wives, so breaking in from the outside

even through marriage was hardly possible. The only time they were successfully challenged prior to statehood was when Sears, Roebuck and Co. opened a store on Oahu. Closing ranks, the Big Five decreed that their steamships would not carry Sears freight. When Sears threatened to buy its own steamship line, the Big Five relented. The original Sears, managed by W.G. McDermid, in downtown Honolulu along Beretania Street is now a temporary police station, but it was renowned as the very first building in Hawaii to be air-conditioned (the entire roof was flooded with water to achieve the result). The Honolulu Sears was also the very first store to sell coordinated aloha wear for the entire family, the very succesful brainchild of Sears manager, Morley Theaker, who in 1956 wanted to incorporate the idea of "this is Hawaii" into his store.

Actually, statehood, and more to the point, tourism, broke their oligarchy. After 1960 too much money was at stake for Mainland-based corporations to ignore. Eventually the grip of the Big Five was loosened, but they are still enormously powerful and richer than ever, though unlike before, they don't control every-

LAND OWNERSHIP

OAHU
380,800 ACRES

- ▦ STATE
- ▥ FEDERAL
- ▧ HAWAIIAN HOMES
- ■ SMALL PRIVATE
- ☐ LARGE PRIVATE

© MOON PUBLICATIONS, INC.

thing. Now their power is land. With only five other major landholders, they control 65% of all the privately held land in Hawaii.

LAND OWNERSHIP

Landwise, Hawaii is a small pie, and its slices are not at all well divided. Of 6,425 square miles of land, the six main inhabited islands make up 98%. (This figure does not include Niihau, which is privately owned by the Robinson family and inhabited by the last remaining pure-blooded Hawaiians, nor does it include Kahoolawe, the uninhabited Navy bombing target just off Maui's south shore.) Of the 4,045,511 acres that make up the inhabited islands, 36% is owned by the state, 10% by the federal government, and the remaining 54% is in private hands. But only 40 owners with 5,000 or more acres own 75% of all private lands. Moreover, only 10 private concerns own two-thirds of these lands. To be more specific, Castle and Cooke Inc. owns 99% of Lanai, while 40-60% of Maui, Oahu, Molokai, Kauai, and Hawaii are owned by less than a dozen private parties. The largest private landowner is the Kamehameha Schools/Bishop Estate, which recently lost a Supreme Court battle that allows the state of Hawaii to acquire privately owned land for "the public good."

More than in any other state, Hawaii's landowners tend to lease land instead of selling it, and many private homes are on rented ground. Many feel that with land prices going up all the time, only the very rich land developers will be able to purchase, and the "people" of Hawaii will become even more land-poor.

The land and industries of Hawaii are owned by old families and large corporations, and Hawaii is only so large.

—JACK LONDON

HAWAII STATE ARCHIVES

PEOPLE

Nowhere else on earth can you find such a kaleidoscopic mixture of people. Every major race is accounted for, and over 50 ethnic groups are represented throughout the islands, making Hawaii the most racially integrated state in the country. Its population of 1.1 million includes 120,000 permanently stationed military personnel and their dependents, and it's the only state where caucasians are not the majority. About 60% of the people living in Hawaii were born there, 25% were born on the Mainland U.S., and 15% of the people are foreign-born.

The population of Hawaii has been growing steadily in recent times, but it fluctuated wildly in times past. In 1876 it reached its lowest ebb, with only 55,000 permanent residents in the islands. This was the era of large sugar plantations, and their constant demand for labor was the primary cause for the importation of various peoples from around the world, which is what led to Hawaii's very racially integrated society. World War II saw Hawaii's population swell from 400,000 just prior to the war to 900,000 during the war. Naturally, 500,000 were military personnel who left at war's end, but many returned to settle after getting a taste of island living.

Of the 1.1 million people in the islands today, 835,000 live on Oahu, with over half of these living in the Honolulu Metropolitan Area. The rest of the population is distributed as follows: 120,000 on Hawaii, with 38,000 living in Hilo;

91,000 on Maui, with the largest concentration, 28,000, in Wailuku/Kahului; 51,000 on Kauai, including 230 pure-blood Hawaiians on Niihau; Molokai with 6,500; and Lanai with 2,500. The population density, statewide, is 173 people per square mile, slightly less than California's 191 people per square mile. The population is not at all evenly distributed, with Oahu claiming about 1,400 people per square mile, and Maui the second-most densely populated island with only 125 people per square mile. City dwellers outnumber those living in the country by four to one.

For most visitors, regardless of where they've come from, Oahu (especially Honolulu) will be the first place they've ever encountered such an integrated multiracial society. Various countries may be cosmopolitan, but nowhere will you meet so many individuals from such a diversity of ethnic groups, and mixes of these groups. You could be driven to your hotel by a Chinese-Portuguese cab driver, checked in by a Japanese-Hawaiian clerk, served lunch by a Korean waiter, serenaded by a Hawaiian-Italian-German musician, while an Irish-English-Filipino-French chambermaid tidies your room. This racial symphony is evident throughout Hawaii, but it's more apparent on Oahu, where the large population creates more opportunity for a racial hodgepodge. The warm feeling you get almost immediately upon arrival is that everyone belongs.

Population Figures

Oahu's 835,000 residents account for 75% of the state's population. All these people are on an island comprising only 10% of the state's land total. Sections of Waikiki can have a combined population of permanent residents and visitors as high as 90,000 per square mile, making cities like Tokyo, Hong Kong, and New York seem quite roomy by comparison. The good news is that Oahu *expects* all these people and knows how to accommodate them comfortably.

Over 400,000 people live in greater Honolulu, generally considered the built-up area from Ewa to Koko Head. The next most populous urban centers after Honolulu are the Kailua/Kaneohe area with about 100,000 residents, followed by Pearl City and Waipahu with a combined total of about 75,000 or so. With all of these people, and such a finite land resource, real estate on the island is sky-high. A typical one-family home sells for $180,000, while a condo averages about $110,000. And for plenty of prime real estate, these figures would barely cover the down payment!

So where is everybody? Of the major ethnic groups you'll find the Hawaiians clustered around Waianae and on the windward coast near Waiahole; the caucasians tend to be in Wahiawa, around Koko Head, in Waikiki, and in Kailua/Kaneohe; those of Japanese ancestry prefer the valleys heading toward the *pali,* including Kalihi, Nuuanu, and Tantalus; Filipinos live just east of the airport, in downtown Honolulu, around Barbers Point, and in Wahiawa; the Chinese are in Chinatown and around the Diamond Head area. Of the minor ethnic groups the highest concentration of blacks is in the Army towns around Schofield Barracks; Samoans live along with the Hawaiians in Waianae and the windward coastal towns, though they are most concentrated in downtown Honolulu not far from Aloha Tower; Koreans and Vietnamese are scattered here and there, but mostly in Honolulu.

THE HAWAIIANS

The study of the native Hawaiians is ultimately a study in tragedy because it ends in their demise as a viable people: when Captain Cook first

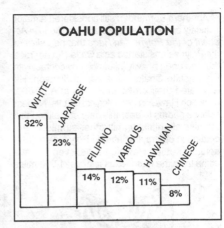

OAHU POPULATION

WHITE 32%
JAPANESE 23%
FILIPINO 14%
VARIOUS 12%
HAWAIIAN 11%
CHINESE 8%

sighted Hawaii in 1778, there were an estimated 300,000 natives living in perfect harmony with their ecological surroundings; within 100 years a scant 50,000 demoralized and dejected Hawaiians existed almost as wards of the state. Today, although 115,000 people claim varying degrees of Hawaiian blood, experts say that less than 1,000 are pure Hawaiian, and this is stretching the point.

It's easy to see why people of Hawaiian lineage could be bitter over what they have lost, being strangers in their own land now, much like the American Indians. The overwhelming majority of "Hawaiians" are of mixed heritage, and the wisest take the best from all worlds. From the Hawaiian side comes simplicity, love of the land, and acceptance of people. It is the Hawaiian legacy of *aloha* that remains immortal and adds that special elusive quality that *is* Hawaii.

Polynesian Roots

The Polynesians' original stock is muddled and remains an anthropological mystery, but it's believed that they were nomadic wanderers who migrated from both the Indian subcontinent and Southeast Asia through Indonesia, where they learned to sail and navigate on protected waterways. As they migrated they honed their sailing skills until they could take on the Pacific, and as they moved, they absorbed people from other cultures and races until they had coalesced into what we now know as Polynesians.

Abraham Fornander, still considered a major authority on the subject, wrote in his 1885 *An Account of the Polynesian Race* that he believed the Polynesians started as a white (Aryan) race that had been heavily influenced by contact with the Cushite Chaldeo-Arabian civilization. He estimated their arrival in Hawaii at A.D. 600, based on Hawaiian genealogical chants. Modern science seems to bear this date out, although it remains skeptical on his other surmises. According to others, the intrepid Polynesians who actually settled Hawaii are believed to have come from the Marquesas Islands, 1,000 miles southeast of Hawaii. The Marquesans were cannibals known for their tenacity and strength, attributes that would serve them well.

The Caste System

Hawaiian society was divided into rankings by a strict caste system determined by birth, and from which there was no chance of escaping. The highest rank was the *ali'i*, the chiefs and royalty. The impeccable genealogies of the *ali'i* were traced back to the gods themselves, and the chants (*mo'o ali'i*) were memorized and sung by professionals (called *ku'auhau*) who were themselves *ali'i*. Ranking passed from both father and mother and custom dictated that the first mating of an *ali'i* be with a person of equal status.

A *kahuna* was a highly skilled person whose advice was sought before any major project was undertaken, such as building a house, hollowing a canoe log, or even offering a prayer. The *mo'o kahuna* were the priests of Ku and Lono, and they were in charge of praying and following rituals. They were very powerful *ali'i* and kept strict secrets and laws concerning their various functions.

Besides this priesthood of *kahuna*, there were other *kahuna* who were not *ali'i* but commoners. The two most important were the healers (*kahuna lapa'au*) and the black magicians (*kahuna ana'ana*); the latter could pray a person to death. The *kahuna lapa'au* had a marvelous pharmacopeia of herbs and spices that could cure over 250 diseases common to the Hawaiians. The *kahuna ana'ana* could be hired to cast a love spell over a person or cause his untimely death. They seldom had to send out a reminder of payment!

A special group called *kauwa* was a landless, untouchable caste confined to living on reservations. Their origins were obviously Polynesian, but they appeared to be descendants of castaways who had survived and become perhaps the aboriginals of Hawaii before the main migrations. It was *kapu* for anyone to go onto *kauwa* lands, and doing so meant instant death. If a human sacrifice was needed, the *kahuna* would simply summon a *kauwa*, who had no recourse but to mutely comply. To this day, to call someone *kauwa*, which now supposedly only means servant, is still considered a fight-provoking insult.

LOUISE FOOTE

The ali'i wore magnificent feathered capes that signified their rank. The noblest colors were red and yellow, provided by specialized hunters who snared and plucked just the right birds.

Kapu And Day-to-day Life

There were occasional horrible wars, but mostly the people lived a quiet and ordered life based on a strict caste society and the *kapu* (taboo) system. Famine was known but only on a regional level, and the population was kept in check by birth control, crude abortions, and the distasteful practice of infanticide, especially of baby girls. The Hawaiians were absolutely loving and nurturing parents under most circumstances, and would even take in an adopted *hanai* (child or oldster), a lovely practice that lingers to this day.

A strict division of labor existed among men and women. Men were the only ones permitted to have anything to do with taro: this foodstuff was so sacred that it had a greater *kapu* than man himself. Men pounded poi and served it to the women. Men also were the fishermen and the builders of houses, canoes, irrigation ditches, and walls. Women tended to other gardens and shoreline fishing, and were responsible for making tapa cloth. The entire family lived in the common house called the *hale noa*.

Certain things were *kapu* between the sexes. Primarily, women could not enter the *mua* (man's house), nor could they eat with men. Certain foods such as pork and bananas were forbidden to women, and it was *kapu* for a man to have intercourse before going fishing, engaging in battle, or attending a religious ceremony. Young boys lived with the women until they underwent a circumcision rite called *pule ipu*. After this was performed, they were required to keep the *kapu* of men.

Ali'i could also declare a *kapu,* and often did so. Certain lands or fishing areas were temporarily made *kapu* so that they could revitalize. Even today, it is *kapu* for anyone to remove all the *opihi* (a type of limpet) from a rock. The great King Kamehameha I even placed a *kapu* on the body of his notoriously unfaithful child bride, Kaahumanu. It didn't work! The greatest *kapu (kapu moe)* was afforded to the highest ranking *ali'i*: anyone coming into their presence had to prostrate themselves. Lesser ranking *ali'i* were afforded the *kapu noho:* lessers had to sit or kneel in their presence. Commoners could not let their shadows fall upon an *ali'i* or enter their houses except through a special door. Breaking a *kapu* meant immediate death.

Fatal Flaws

Less than 100 years after Captain Cook's arrival, King Kalakaua found himself with only 48,000 Hawaiian subjects, down more than 80%. Wherever the king went, he would beseech his people, *"Hooulu lahui,"* "Increase the race," but it was already too late. It was as if nature herself had turned her back on these

Ship's artist Jacques Arago depicts the harsh verdict delivered to a kapu breaker, circa 1819.

once proud people. Many of their marriages were barren and in 1874, when only 1,400 children were born, a full 75% died in infancy. The Hawaiians sat around and could do nothing as their race faded from existence.

The Causes Of Decline

The ecological system of Hawaii has always been exceptionally fragile and this included its people. When the white man came he found a great people who were large, strong, and virile, but when it came to fighting off the most minor diseases they proved as delicate as hothouse flowers. To exacerbate the situation, the Hawaiians were totally uninhibited toward sexual intercourse between willing partners, and they engaged in it openly and with abandon. Unfortunately, the sailors who arrived were full of syphilis and gonorrhea. The Hawaiian women brought these diseases home and, given the nature of Hawaiian society at the time, they spread like wildfire. By the time the missionaries came in 1820 and helped to halt the unbridled fornication, they estimated the native population at only 140,000, less than half of what it had been only 40 years since initial contact! In the next 50 years measles, mumps, influenza, and tuberculosis further ravaged the people. Hawaiian men were excellent sailors and it's estimated that during the whaling years at least 25% of all able-bodied Hawaiian men sailed away, never to return.

But the coup de grace that really ended the Hawaiian race, as such, was that all racial newcomers to the islands were attracted to the Hawaiians and the Hawaiians were in turn attracted to them. With so many interracial marriages, the Hawaiians literally bred themselves out of existence. By 1910, there were still twice as many full-blooded Hawaiians as mixed-bloods, but by 1940 mixed-blooded Hawaiians were the fastest-growing group, and full-blooded the fastest declining.

Hawaiians Today

Many of the Hawaiians who moved to the cities became more and more disenfranchised. Their folk society stressed openness and a giving nature, but downplayed the individual and the ownership of private property. These cultural traits made them easy targets for the users and

Aloha *still shows.*

schemers until they finally became either apathetic or angry. Most surveys reveal that although Hawaiians number only 12% of the population (11% on Oahu), they account for almost 50% of the financially destitute families, and similarly, about half of arrests and illegitimate births. Niihau, a privately owned island, is home to about 230 pure-blood Hawaiians, representing the largest concentration of them, per capita, in the islands. The Robinson family, which owns the island, restricts visitors to invited guests only.

The second largest concentration is on Molokai, where 3,300 Hawaiians, living mostly on 40-acre *kuleana* of Hawaiian Homes Lands, make up 50% of that island's population. The majority of mixed-blood Hawaiians, 80,000 or so, live on Oahu, where they are particularly strong in the hotel and entertainment fields. People of Hawaiian extraction are still a delight to meet, and anyone so lucky as to be befriended by one long regards this friendship as the highlight of his travels. The Hawaiians have always given their *aloha* freely to all the people of the world, and it is we who must acknowledge this precious gift.

THE CHINESE

Next to Yankees from New England, the Chinese are the oldest migrant group in Hawaii, and their influence has far outshined their meager numbers. They brought to Hawaii, along with their individuality, Confucianism, Taoism, and Buddhism, although many have long since become Christian. The Chinese population at 69,000 makes up only six percent of the state's total, and the majority (63,000, eight percent of Oahu's total) reside on Oahu. As an ethnic group they account for the least amount of crime, the highest per capita income, and a disproportionate number of professionals.

The First Chinese
No one knows his name, but an unknown Chinese man is credited with being the first person in Hawaii to refine sugar. This Asian wanderer tried his hand at crude refining on Lanai in 1802. Fifty years later the sugar plantations desperately needed workers, and the first Chinese brought to Hawaii under the newly passed Masters and Servants Act were 195 coolies from Amoy who arrived in 1852. These conscripts were contracted for three to five years and given $3 per month plus room and board. This was for 12 hours a day, six days a week, and even in 1852 these wages were the pits. The Chinese

almost always left the plantations the minute their contracts expired. They went into business for themselves and promptly monopolized the restaurant and small shop trades.

The Chinese Niche
Although almost all people in Hawaii considered all Chinese the same, they were actually quite different. The majority came from Guangdong Province in southern China. They were two distinct ethnic groups: the Punti made up 75% of the immigrants, and the Hakka made up the remainder. In China, they remained separate from each other, never mixing; in Hawaii, they mixed out of necessity. For one, hardly any Chinese women came over at first, and the ones who followed were at a premium and gladly accepted as wives, regardless of ethnic background. The Chinese were also one of the first groups who willingly intermarried with the Hawaiians, from whom they gained a reputation for being exceptionally caring husbands.

The Chinese accepted the social order and kept a low profile. For example, during the turbulent labor movements of the 1930s and '40s in

HAWAII STATE ARCHIVES

Many believed that the devastating Chinatown fire of 1900 was deliberately allowed to burn in order to displace the Chinese population of Honolulu.

Hawaii, the Chinese community produced not one labor leader, radical intellectual, or left-wing politician. However, when Hawaii became a state, one of the two senators elected was Hiram Fong, a racially mixed Chinese. Since statehood, the Chinese community has carried on business as usual as they continue to rise both economically and socially.

THE JAPANESE

Most scholars believe that (inevitably) a few Japanese castaways floated to Hawaii long before Captain Cook arrived and might have introduced iron, which the islanders seemed to be familiar with before the white men arrived. The first official arrivals were ambassadors sent by the Japanese shogun to negotiate in Washington; they stopped en route at Honolulu in March 1860. But it was as plantation workers that the Japanese were brought to the islands. A small group arrived in 1868, and mass migration started in 1885.

In 1886, because of famine, the Japanese government allowed farmers, mainly from southern Honshu, Kyushu, and Okinawa, to emigrate. Among these were members of Japan's little-talked-about untouchable caste, called *eta* or *burakumin* in Japan and *chorinbo* in Hawaii. They gratefully seized this opportunity to better their lot, an impossibility in Japan. The first Japanese migrants were almost all men. Between 1897 and 1908 migration was steady,

with about 70% men and 30% women arriving. Afterwards, migration slowed because of a "Gentlemen's Agreement," a euphemism for racism against the "yellow peril." By 1900 there were over 60,000 Japanese in the islands, constituting the largest ethnic group.

AJAs, Americans Of Japanese Ancestry

Parents of most Japanese children born before WW II were *issei* (first generation), who considered themselves apart from other Americans and clung to the notion of "We Japanese." Their children, the *nisei* or second generation, were a different matter altogether. In one generation they had become Americans, and they put into practice the high Japanese virtues of obligation, duty, and loyalty to the homeland, and that homeland was now unquestionably America. After Pearl Harbor was bombed, the FBI kept close tabs on the Japanese community, and the menace of the "enemy within" prompted the decision to place Hawaii under martial law for the duration of the war. It has since been noted that not a single charge of espionage or sabotage was ever reported against the Japanese community in Hawaii during the war.

AJAs As GIs

Although Japanese had formed a battalion during WW I, they were insulted by being considered unacceptable as American soldiers in WW II. Some Japanese-Americans volunteered to serve in labor battalions, and because of their

indentured Japanese plantation workers and mounted overseer

HAWAII STATE ARCHIVES

flawless work and loyalty, it was decided to put out a call for a few hundred volunteers to form a combat unit. Over 10,000 signed up! AJAs formed two distinguished units in WW II: the 100th Infantry Battalion, and later the 442nd Regimental Combat Team. They landed in Italy at Salerno and even fought from Guadalcanal to Okinawa. They distinguished themselves by becoming *the* most decorated unit in American military history.

The AJAs Return

Many returning AJAs took advantage of the G.I. Bill and received college educations. The

The Japanese-American GIs returned as "our boys."

"Big Five" Corporations (see "Economy—The Big Five") for the first time accepted former AJA officers as executives and the old order was changed. Many Japanese became involved with Hawaiian politics and the first elected to Congress was Daniel Inouye, who had lost an arm fighting in WW II. Hawaii's past governor, George Ariyoshi, elected in 1974, was the country's first Japanese-American ever to reach such a high office. Most Japanese, even as they climb the economic ladder, tend to remain Democrats.

Today, one out of every two political offices in Hawaii is held by a Japanese-American. In one of those weird quirks of fate, it is now the Hawaiian-Japanese who are accused by other ethnic groups of engaging in unfair political practices— nepotism and reverse discrimination. Many of these accusations against AJAs are undoubtedly motivated by jealousy, but the AJAs' record with social fairness issues is not without blemish; true to their custom of family loyalty, they do stick together.

There are now 247,000 people in Hawaii of Japanese ancestry, one-quarter of the state's population. On Oahu, 195,000 make up 23% of the population. They are the least likely of any ethnic person in Hawaii to marry outside of their group—especially the men—and they enjoy a higher-than-average standard of living.

CAUCASIANS

White people have a distinction from all other ethnic groups in Hawaii: they are all lumped together as one. You can be anything from a Protestant Norwegian dockworker to a Greek Orthodox shipping tycoon, but if your skin is white, in Hawaii, you're a *haole*. What's more, you could have arrived at Waikiki from Missoula, Montana, in the last 24 hours, or your *kamaaina* family can go back five generations, but again, if you're white, you're a *haole*.

The word *haole* has a floating connotation that depends upon the spirit in which it's used. It can mean everything from a derisive "honky" or "cracker" to nothing more than "white person." The exact Hawaiian meaning is clouded, but some say it meant "a man of no background," because white men couldn't chant a genealogical *kanaenae* telling the Hawaiians who they were. *Haole* then became euphemised into "foreign white man" and today, simply "white person."

White History

Next to Hawaiians themselves, white people have the oldest stake in Hawaii. They've been there as settlers in earnest since the missionaries of the 1820s, and were established long before any other migrant group. From last century until statehood, old *haole* families owned and controlled everything, and although they were generally benevolent, philanthropic, and paternalistic, they were also racist. They were established *kamaaina* families, many of whom made up the boards of the Big Five Corporations or owned huge plantations and formed an inner social circle that was closed to the outside. Many managed to find mates from among close family acquaintances.

Their paternalism, which they accepted with grave responsibility, at first only extended to the Hawaiians, who saw them as replacing their own *ali'i*. Asians were considered "primarily as instruments of production." These supremacist attitudes tended to drag on in Hawaii until quite recent times. They are today responsible for the sometimes sour relations between white and nonwhite people in the islands. Today, all individual white people are resented to a certain degree because of these past acts, even though they personally were in no way involved.

White Plantation Workers

In the 1880s the white landowners looked around and felt surrounded and outnumbered by Asians, so they tried to import white people for plantation work. None of their schemes seemed to work out. Europeans were accustomed to a much higher wage scale and better living conditions than were provided on the plantations. Although only workers and not considered the equals of the ruling elite, they still were expected to act like a special class. They were treated preferentially, which meant higher wages for the same job performed by an Asian. Some of the imported workers included: 600 Scandinavians in 1881; 1,400 Germans 1881-85; 400 Poles 1897-98; and 2,400 Russians, 1909-12. Many proved troublesome, like the Poles and Russians who staged strikes after only months on the job. Many quickly moved to the Mainland. A contingency of Scots, who first came as mule skinners, did become successful plantation managers and supervisors. The Germans and Scandinavians were well received and climbed the social ladder rapidly, becoming professionals and skilled workers.

The Depression years, not as economically bad in Hawaii as in the continental U.S., brought many Mainland whites seeking opportunity, mostly from the South and the West. These new people were even more racist toward people of color than the *kamaaina haoles,* and they made matters worse. They also competed more intensely for jobs. The racial tension generated during this period came to a head in 1932 with the infamous "Massie Rape Case."

The Massie Rape Case

Thomas Massie, a naval officer, and his young wife Thalia attended a party at the Officers Club. After drinking and dancing all evening, they got into a row and Thalia rushed out in a huff. A few hours later, Thalia was at home, confused and hysterical, claiming to have been raped by some local men. On the most circumstantial evidence, Joseph Kahahawai and four friends of mixed ethnic background were accused. In a highly controversial trial rife with racial tensions, the verdict ended in a hung jury.

While a new trial was being set, Kahahawai and his friends were out on bail. Seeking revenge, Thomas Massie and Grace Fortescue, Thalia's mother, kidnapped Joseph Kahahawai with a plan of extracting a confession from him. They were aided by two enlisted men assigned to guard Thalia. While questioning Joseph, they killed him and attempted to dump his body in the sea but were apprehended. Another controversial trial—this time for Mrs. Fortescue, Massie, and the accomplices—followed. Clarence Darrow, the famous lawyer, sailed to Hawaii to defend them. For killing Kahahawai, these people served *one hour* of imprisonment in the judge's private chambers. The other four, acquitted with Joseph Kahahawai, maintain innocence of the rape to this day. Later, the Massies divorced, and Thalia went on to become a depressed alcoholic who eventually took her own life.

The Portuguese

The last time anyone looked, Portugal was still attached to the European continent, but for some anomalous reason the Portuguese weren't considered *haoles* in Hawaii for the longest time. About 12,000 arrived from 1878 to 1887 and another 6,000 came between 1906 and 1913. Accompanied during this period by 8,000 Spanish, they were considered one and the same. Most of the Portuguese were illiterate peasants from Madeira and the Azores, and the Spanish hailed from Andalusia. They were very well received, and because they were white but not *haole* they made a perfect "buffer" ethnic group. Committed to staying in Hawaii, they rose to be skilled workers—the *luna* class on the plantations. They, however, de-emphasized education and became very racist toward Asians, regarding them as a threat to their job security.

By 1920 the 27,000 Portuguese made up 11% of the population. After that they tended to blend with the other ethnic groups and weren't counted separately. Portuguese men tended to marry within their ethnic group, but a good portion of Portuguese women married other white men and became closer to the *haole* group, while another large portion chose Hawaiian mates and grew further away. Although they didn't originate pidgin English (see "Language"), the unique melodious quality of their native tongue did give pidgin that certain lilt it has today. Also, the ukulele ("jumping flea") was closely patterned after the *cavaquinho,* a Portuguese stringed folk instrument.

The White Population

Today all white people together make up the largest racial, if not ethnic, group in the islands at 33% (about 370,000) of the population. There are heavy white concentrations throughout Oahu especially in Waikiki, Kailua/Kaneohe, and around Pearl City. The white population is the fastest growing in the islands, because most people resettling in Hawaii are white Americans predominantly from the West Coast.

FILIPINOS AND OTHERS

The Filipinos who came to Hawaii brought high hopes of making a fortune and returning home as rich heroes: for most it was a dream that never came true. Filipinos had been American nationals ever since the Spanish-American War of 1898, and as such weren't subject to immigration laws that curtailed the importation of Asian workers at the turn of this century. The first to arrive were 15 families in 1906, but a large number came in 1924 as strikebreakers. The majority were illiterate peasants called Ilocanos from the northern Philippines, with about 10% Visayans from the central cities. From the first, Filipinos were looked down upon by all the other immigrant groups, and were considered particularly uncouth by the Japanese. They put the least amount of value on education of any group, and even by 1930 only about half could speak rudimentary English, the majority remaining illiterate. They were billeted in the worst housing, performed the most menial jobs, and were the last hired and first fired.

One big difference with Filipinos was that they had no women to marry, so they clung to the idea of returning home. In 1930 there were 30,000 men and only 360 women. This hopeless situation led to a great deal of prostitution and homosexuality; many of these terribly lonely bachelors would feast and drink on weekends and engage in their gruesome but exciting pastime of cockfighting on Sundays. When some did manage to find wives, their mates were inevitably part Hawaiian. Today, there are still plenty of old Filipino bachelors who never managed to get home, and the Sunday cockfights remain a way of life.

The Filipinos constitute 14% of Hawaii's population (147,000), with almost 70% living on Oahu. Many visitors to Hawaii mistake Filipinos for Hawaiians because of their dark skin, and this is a minor irritant to both groups. Some streetwise Filipinos even claim to be Hawaiians, because being Hawaiian is "in" and goes over well with the tourists, especially the young women tourists. For the most part, these people are hardworking, dependable laborers who do tough work for little recognition. They still remain the low man on the social totem pole and have not yet organized politically to stand up for their rights.

Other Groups

About 10% of Hawaii's population is made up of a conglomerate of small ethnic groups. Of these, the largest is Korean with 14,000 people. About

8,000 Koreans came to Hawaii from 1903 until 1905, when their own government halted emigration. During the same period about 6,000 Puerto Ricans arrived, but they have become so assimilated that only 4,000 people in Hawaii today consider themselves Puerto Rican. There were also two attempts made last century to import other Polynesians to strengthen the dying Hawaiian race, but they were failures. In 1869 only 126 central Polynesian natives could be lured to Hawaii, and from 1878 to 1885 2,500 Gilbert Islanders arrived. Both groups became immediately disenchanted with Hawaii. They pined away for their own islands and departed for home as soon as possible.

Today, however, 12,000 Samoans have settled in Hawaii, and with more on the way they are the fastest growing minority in the state. For unexplainable reasons, Samoans and native Hawaiians get along extremely poorly and have the worst racial tensions and animosity between any of the groups. The Samoans ostensibly should represent the archetypal Polynesians that the Hawaiians are seeking, but it doesn't work that way. Samoans are criticized by Hawaiians for their hot tempers, lingering feuds, and petty jealousies. They're clannish and often are the butt of "dumb" jokes. This racism seems especially ridiculous, but that's the way it is.

Just to add a bit more exotic spice to the stew, there are about 27,000 blacks, a few thousand American Indians, and a smattering of Vietnamese refugees.

LANGUAGE

Hawaii is the U.S. and people speak English there, but that's not the whole story. If you turn on the TV to catch the evening news, you'll hear "Walter Cronkite" English, unless of course you happen to tune in a Japanese-language broadcast designed for tourists from that country. You can easily pick up a Chinese-language newspaper, or groove to the music on a Filipino radio station, but let's not confuse the issue. All your needs and requests at airports, car rental agencies, restaurants, hotels, or wherever you happen to travel will be completely understood, as well as answered, in English. However, when you happen to overhear "islanders" speaking, what they're saying will sound somewhat familiar, but you won't be able to pick up all the words, and the beat and melody of the language will be noticeably different.

Hawaii, like New England, the deep South, and the Midwest, has its own unmistakable linguistic regionalism. The many ethnic people who make up Hawaii have enriched the English spoken there with words, expressions, and subtle shades of meaning that are commonly used and understood throughout the islands. The greatest influence on English has come from the Hawaiian language itself, and words such as aloha, hula, and muumuu are familiarly used and understood by most Americans.

Other migrant people, especially the Chinese, Japanese, and Portuguese, influenced the local dialect to such an extent that the simplified plantation lingo that they spoke has become known as "pidgin." A fun and enriching part of the "island experience" is picking up a few words of Hawaiian and pidgin. English is the official language of the state, business, education, and perhaps even the mind; but pidgin is the language of the people, the emotions, and life, while Hawaiian remains the language of the heart and the soul.

Note: Many Hawaiian words are commonly used in English, appear in English dictionaries, and therefore would ordinarily be subject to the rules of English grammar. The Hawaiian language, however, does not pluralize nouns by adding an "s"; the singular and plural are differentiated in context. For purposes of this book, and to highlight rather than denigrate the Hawaiian culture, the Hawaiian style of pluralization will be followed for common Hawaiian words. The following are some examples of plural Hawaiian nouns treated this way in this book: *haole* (not haoles), hula (not hulas, etc.) *kahuna,* lei, *nene.*

PIDGIN

The dictionary definition of pidgin is: a simplified language with a rudimentary grammar used as a means of communication between people speaking different languages. Hawaiian pidgin is a little more complicated than that. It had its roots during the plantation days of last century when white owners and *luna* had to communicate with recently arrived Chinese, Japanese, and Portuguese laborers. It was designed as a simple language of the here and now, and was primarily concerned with the necessary functions of working, eating, and sleeping. It has an economical noun-verb-object structure (not necessarily in that order).

CAPSULE PIDGIN

The following are a few commonly used words and expressions that should give you an idea of pidgin. It really can't be written properly, merely approximated, but for now, *"Brah, study da' kine an' bimbye you be hele on, brah! OK? Lesgo."*

an' den—and then? big deal; so what's next; how Fboring

bimbye—after a while; bye and bye. "Bimbye, you learn pidgin."

blalah—brother, but actually only refers to a large, heavy-set, good-natured Hawaiian man

brah—all the bros in Hawaii are brahs; brother; pal. Used to call someone's attention. One of the most common words used even among people who are not acquainted. After a fill-up at a gas station, a person would say "Tanks, brah."

cockaroach—steal; rip off. If you really want to find out what *cockaroach* means, just leave your camera on your beach blanket when you take a little dip.

da' kine—a catchall word of many meanings that epitomizes the essence of pidgin. *Da' kine* is easily used as a euphemism for pidgin and is substituted whenever the speaker is at a loss for a word or just wants to generalize. It can mean: you know? watchamacallit; of that type.

geev um—give it to them; give them hell; go for it. Can be used as an encouragement. If a surfer is riding a great wave, the people on the beach might yell, "Geev um, brah!"

hana ho—again. Especially after a concert the audience shouts "hana ho" (one more!).

hele on—right on! hip; with it; groovy

howzit?—as in "howzit brah?" what's happening? how is it going? The most common greeting, used in place of the more formal "How do you do?"

hu hu—angry! "You put the make on the wrong da' kine wahine brah, and you in da' kine trouble, if you get one big Hawaiian blalah plenty hu hu."

kapu—a Hawaiian word meaning forbidden. If *kapu* is written on a gate or posted on a tree it means "No trespassing." *Kapu*-breakers are still very unpopular in the islands.

lesgo—Let's go! Do it!

li'dis an' li'dat—like this or that; a catch-all grouping especially if you want to avoid details; like, ya' know?

lolo buggah—stupid or crazy guy (person). Words to a tropical island song go, "I want to find the lolo who stole my pakalolo."

mo' bettah—real good! great idea. An island sentiment used to be, "mo' bettah you *come* Hawaii." Now it has subtly changed to, "mo' bettah you *visit* Hawaii."

ono—number one! delicious; great; groovy. "Hawaii is ono, brah!"

pakalolo—literally "crazy smoke"; marijuana; grass; reefer. "Hey, brah! Maui-wowie da' kine ono pakalolo."

pakiki head—stubborn; bull-headed

pau—a Hawaiian word meaning finished; done; over and done with. *Pau hana* means end of work or quitting time. Once used by plantation workers, now used by everyone.

stink face—basically frowning at someone; using facial expression to show displeasure. Hard looks. What you'll get if you give local people a hard time.

swell head—burned up; angry

talk story—spinning yarns; shooting the breeze; throwing the bull; a rap session. If you're lucky enough to be around to hear *kapuna* (elders) "talk story," you can hear some fantastic tales in the tradition of old Hawaii.

tita—sister, but only used to describe a fun-loving, down-to-earth country girl

waddascoops—what's the scoop? what's up? what's happening?

Hawaiian words make up most of pidgin's non-English vocabulary. There is a good smattering of Chinese, Japanese, and Samoan, and the distinctive rising inflection is provided by the melodious Mediterranean lilt of the Portuguese. Pidgin is not a stagnant language. It's kept alive by hip new words introduced by people who are "so radical," or especially by slang words introduced by teenagers. It's a colorful English, like "jive" or "ghettoese" spoken by American blacks, and is as regionally unique as the speech of Cajuns from Louisiana's bayous. *Maka'ainana* of all socioethnic backgrounds can at least understand pidgin. Most islanders are proud of it, while some consider it a low-class jargon. The Hawaiian House of Representatives has given pidgin an official sanction, and most people feel that it adds a real local style and should be preserved.

Pidgin Lives

Pidgin is first learned at school, where all students, regardless of background, are exposed to it. The pidgin spoken by young people today is "fo' real" different from that of their parents. It's no longer only plantation talk, but has moved to the streets and picked up some sophistication. At one time there was an academic movement to exterminate it, but that idea died away with the same thinking that insisted on making left-handed people write with their right hand. It is strange, however, that pidgin has become the unofficial language of Hawaii's grassroots movement, when it actually began as a white owners' language used to supplant Hawaiian and all other languages brought to the islands.

Although hip young *haole* use it all the time, it has gained some of the connotation of being the language of the nonwhite locals, and is part of the "us against them" way of thinking. All local people, *haole* or not, do consider pidgin their own island language, and don't really like it when it's used by *malihini* (newcomers). If you're in the islands long enough, you don't have to bother learning pidgin; it'll learn you. There's a book sold all over the islands called *Pidgin to da Max*, written by (you guessed it) a *haole* from Nebraska named Doug Simonson. You might not be able to understand what's being said by locals speaking pidgin (that's usually the idea), but you should be able to *feel* what's being meant.

HAWAIIAN

The Hawaiian language sways like a palm tree in a gentle wind. Its words are as melodious as a love song. Linguists say that you can learn a lot about people through their language: when you hear Hawaiian you think of gentleness and love, and it's hard to imagine the ferocious side so evident in Hawaii's past. With many Polynesian root words that are easily traced to Indonesian and Malayan, it's evident that Hawaiian is from this same stock. The Hawaiian spoken today is very different from old Hawaiian. Its greatest metamorphosis occurred when the missionaries began to write it down in the 1820s. There is a movement to reestablish the Hawaiian language, and courses in it are offered at

THE ALPHABET.

VOWELS.

	Names.	SOUND. Ex. in Eng.	Ex. in Hawan.
A a	â	as in *father,*	la—sun.
E e	a	— *tete,*	hemo—cast off.
I i	e	— *marine,*	marie—quiet.
O o	o	— *over,*	ono—sweet.
U u	oo	—*rule,*	nui—large.

CONSONANTS.	Names.	CONSONANTS.	Names.
B b	be	N n	nu
D d	de	P p	pi
H h	he	R r	ro
K k	ke	T t	ti
L l	la	V v	vi
M m	mu	W w	we

The following are used in spelling foreign words:

F f	fe	S s	se
G g	ge	Y y	yi

Cover page of the first Hawaiian primer, showing the phonetic rendering of the ancient Hawaiian language before five of the consonants were dropped.

the University of Hawaii. Many scholars have put forth translations of Hawaiian, but there are endless, volatile disagreements in the academic sector about the real meanings of Hawaiian words. Hawaiian is no longer spoken as a language except on Niihau, and the closest tourists will come to it is in place names, street names, and in words that have become part of common usage, such as aloha and *mahalo*. A few old Hawaiians still speak it at home and there are sermons in Hawaiian at some local churches. Kawaiahao Church in downtown Honolulu is the most famous of these. (See the Glossary for lists of commonly used Hawaiian words.)

Wiki Wiki Hawaiian
Although the missionaries were instrumental in destroying the widespread use of Hawaiian, they did create a written alphabet that rendered it phonetically using only 12 letters. They are the five vowels, a-e-i-o-u, sounded as they are in Italian, and seven consonants, h-k-l-m-n-p-w, sounded exactly as they are in English. Sometimes "w" is pronounced as "v," but this only occurs in the middle of a word and always follows a vowel. A consonant is always followed by a vowel, forming two-letter syllables, but vowels are often found in pairs or even triplets. A slight oddity about Hawaiian is the "glottal stop." This is merely an abrupt break in sound in the middle of a word such as "oh-oh" in English, and is denoted with an apostrophe ('). A good example is *ali'i*, or even better, the Oahu town of **Ha'iku,** which actually means "abrupt break."

Pronunciation Key
For those unfamiliar with the sounds of Italian or other Romance languages, the vowels are sounded as follows:

A—in stressed syllables, long *a* as in "Ah" (that feels good!). For example, Haleakala (Hah lay ah kah lah.) Unstressed syllables get a short "a" as in "again" or "above." For example, Kamehameha (**Ka me ha me ha**).

E—short e as in pen or dent (Ha**le**). Long e sounded as "ay" as in s**way** or d**ay.** For example, the Hawaiian goose (**ne ne**) is a "nay nay," not a "knee knee."

I—a long i as in s**ee** or w**e** (Hawa*ii* or pal**i**).

O—round **o** as in n**o** or **oh** (k**o**a, or **ono**).

U—round **u** like "d**o**" or "st**ew**."(ka**pu**, or p**u**na).

Diphthongs
There are also eight vowel pairs known as "diphthongs" (ae-ai-ao-au-ei-eu-oi-ou). These are the sounds made by gliding from one vowel to another within a syllable. The stress is placed on the first vowel. In English, examples would be s**oi**l and **eu**phoria. Common examples in Hawaiian are lei (lay) and *heiau.*

Stress
The best way to learn which syllables are stressed in Hawaiian is just by listening closely. It becomes obvious after a while. There are also some vowel sounds that are held longer than others and these can occur at the beginning of a word such as the first "a" in *aina* or in the middle of a word like the first "a" in *lanai*. Again, it's a matter of tuning your ear and paying attention. No one is going to give you a hard time if you mispronounce a word. It's good, however, to pay close attention to the pronunciation of street and place names because many Hawaiian words sound alike and a misplaced vowel here or there could be the difference in getting to where you want to go and getting lost.

CAPSULE HAWAIIAN

The list on the following pages is merely designed to give you a "taste" of Hawaiian and to provide a basic vocabulary of words in common usage which you are likely to hear. Becoming familiar with them is not a strict necessity, but they will definitely enhance your experience and make it more congenial when talking with local people. You'll soon notice that many islanders spice their speech with certain words, especially when they're speaking "pidgin," and you too can use them just as soon as you feel comfortable. You might even discover some Hawaiian words that are so perfectly expressive that they'll become a regular part of your vocabulary. Many Hawaiian words have actually made it into the English dictionary. Place names, historical names, and descriptive terms used throughout the text may not appear in the lists below, but will be cited in the glossary at the back of the book. Also see "Capsule Pidgin," "Food," and "Getting Around" for applicable Hawaiian words and phrases in these categories. The definitions given are not exhaustive, but are generally considered the most common.

BASIC VOCABULARY

a'a—rough clinker lava. *A'a* has become the correct geological term to describe this type of lava found anywhere in the world.

ae—yes

akamai—smart; clever; wise

ali'i—a Hawaiian chief or nobleman

aloha—the most common greeting in the islands. Can mean both hello and goodbye, welcome or farewell. It also can mean romantic love, affection or best wishes.

aole—no

hale—house or building; often combined with other words to name a specific place such as Haleakala ("House of the Sun"), or Hale Pai at Lahainaluna, meaning "Printing House"

hana—work; combined with *pau* means end of work or quitting time

haole—a word that at one time meant foreigner, but now means a white person or caucasian. Many etymological definitions have been put forth, but none satisfy everyone. Some feel that it signified a person without a background, because the first white men could not chant their genealogies as was common to Hawaiians.

hapai—pregnant. Used by all ethnic groups when a *keiki* is on the way.

hapa—half, as in a mixed-blooded person being refered to as *hapa haole*

heiau—a traditional Hawaiian temple. A platform made of skillfully fitted rocks, upon which structures were built and offerings made to the gods.

holomuu—an ankle-length dress that is much more fitted than a muumuu, and which is often worn on formal occasions

hoolaulea—any happy event, but especially a family outing or picnic

hoomalimali—sweet talk; flattery

hu hu—angry; irritated; mad

huli huli—barbecue, as in *huli huli* chicken

hula—a native Hawaiian dance where the rhythm of the islands is captured in swaying hips and the stories told by lyrically moving hands

hui—a group; meeting; society. Often used to refer to Chinese businessmen or family members who pool their money to get businesses started.

imu—an underground oven filled with hot rocks and used for baking. The main cooking feature at a luau, used to steam-bake the pork and other succulent dishes. Traditionally the tending of the *imu* was for men only.

ipo—sweetheart; lover; girl or boyfriend

kahuna—priest; sorcerer; doctor; skillful person. *Kahuna* had tremendous power in old Hawaii, which they used for both good and evil. The *kahuna ana'ana* was a feared individual because he practiced "black magic" and could pray a person to death, while a *kahuna lapa'au* was medical practitioner bringing aid and comfort to the people.

kalua—means roasted underground in an *imu*. A favorite island food is *kalua* pork.

kamaaina—a child of the land; an old-timer; a longtime island resident of any ethnic background; a resident of Hawaii or native son. Oftentimes, hotels and airlines offer discounts called "*kamaaina* rates" to anyone who can prove island residency.

kane—means man, but is actually used to signify a husband or boyfriend. Written on a door, it means "Men's Room."

kapu—forbidden; taboo; keep out; do not touch

kapuna—a grandparent or old-timer; usually means someone who has gained wisdom. The statewide school system now invites *kapuna* to talk to the children about the old ways and methods.

kaukau—slang word meaning food or chow; grub. Some of the best eating in Hawaii is from *"kaukau* wagons," which are trucks from which plate lunches and other morsels are sold.

keiki—child or children; used by all ethnic groups. "Have you hugged your *keiki* today?"

kokua—help. As in "Your *kokua* is needed to keep Hawaii free from litter."

kona wind—a muggy subtropical wind that blows from the south and hits the leeward side of the islands. It usually brings sticky hot weather, and is one of the few times when air-conditioning will be appreciated.

lanai—veranda or porch. You'll pay more for a hotel room if it has a lanai with an ocean view.

lei—a traditional garland of flowers or vines. One of Hawaii's most beautiful customs. Given at any auspicious occasion, but especially when arriving or leaving Hawaii.

limu—varieties of edible seaweed gathered from the shoreline. It makes an excellent salad, and is used to garnish many island dishes—a favorite at luau.

lomi lomi—traditional Hawaiian massage; also, a vinegared salad made up of raw salmon, chopped onions, and spices

lua—the toilet; the head; the bathroom

luau—a Hawaiian feast featuring poi, *imu* baked pork and other traditional foods. A good luau provides some of the best gastronomical delights in the world.

mahalo—thanks; thank you. *Mahalo nui* means big thanks or thank you very much.

mahu—a homosexual; often used derisively like "fag" or "queer"

makai—toward the sea; used by most islanders when giving directions

malihini—what you are if you have just arrived: a newcomer; a tenderfoot; a recent arrival

manauahi—free; gratis; extra

manini—stingy; tight. A Hawaiianized word taken from the name of Don Francisco Marin, who was instrumental in bringing many fruits and plants to Hawaii. He was known for never sharing any of the bounty from his substantial gardens on Vineyard Street in Honolulu; therefore his name came to mean stingy.

mauka—toward the mountains; used by most islanders when giving directions

mauna—mountain. Often combined with other words to be more descriptive, as in Mauna Kea ("White Mountain").

moana—the ocean; the sea. Many businesses and hotels as well as place-names have *moana* as part of their name.

muumuu—the garment introduced by the missionaries to cover the nakedness of the Hawaiians. A "Mother Hubbard," a long dress with a high neckline that has become fashionable attire for almost any occasion in Hawaii.

ohana—a family; the fundamental social division; extended family. Now used to denote a social organization with "grassroots," as in the "Save Kahoolawe Ohana."

okolehau—literally "iron bottom"; a traditional booze made from ti root; *okole* means your "rear end" and *hau* means iron, which was descriptive of the huge blubber pots that it was made in. Also, if you drink too much it'll surely knock you on your *okole.*

ono—delicious; delightful; the best. *Ono ono* means "extra or absolutely" delicious.

opu—belly; stomach

pa'hoehoe—smooth ropey lava that looks like burnt pancake batter. *Pa'hoehoe* is now the correct geological term used to describe this type of lava found anywhere in the world.

pakalolo—"crazy smoke"; marijuana; grass; smoke; dope

pali—a cliff; precipice. Hawaii's geology makes them quite common. The most famous are the *pali* of Oahu, where a major battle was fought.

paniolo—a Hawaiian cowboy. Derived from the Spanish *espaniola.* The first cowboys brought in during the early 19th century were Mexicans from California.

pau—finished; done; completed. Often combined into *pau hana,* which means end of work or quitting time.

pilau—stink; smells bad; stench

pilikia—trouble of any kind, big or small; bad times

pono—righteous or excellent

poi—a glutinous paste made from the pounded corn of taro which, slightly fermented, has a light sour taste. Purplish in color, it is a staple at luau, where it is called one-, two-, or three-finger poi, depending upon its thickness.

puka—a hole of any size. *Puka* is used by all island residents and can be employed when talking about a tiny *puka* in a rubber boat or a *puka* (tunnel) through a mountain.

punee—bed; narrow couch. Used by all ethnic groups. To recline on a *punee* on a breezy lanai is a true island treat.

pupule—crazy; nuts; out of your mind

pu pu—an appetizer; a snack; hors d'oeuvres; can be anything from cheese and crackers to sushi. Oftentimes, bars or nightclubs offer them free.

tapa—a traditional paper cloth made from beaten bark. Intricate designs were stamped in using beaters, and color was added with natural dyes. The tradition was lost in Hawaii, but it is now making a comeback and provides some of the most beautiful folk art in the islands.

tutu—grandmother; granny; older woman. Used by all as a term of respect and endearment.

ukulele—*uku* means "flea" and *lele* means "jumping," thus ukelele means "jumping flea," which was the way the Hawaiians perceived the quick finger movements on the banjo-type Portuguese folk instrument called a *cavaquinho*. The ukulele quickly became synonymous with the islands.

wahine—young woman; female; girl; wife. Used by all ethnic groups. When written on a door means "Women's Room."

wai—fresh water; drinking water

wela—hot. *Wela kahao* is a "hot time" or "making whoopee."

wiki—quickly; fast; in a hurry. Often seen as *wiki wiki* (very fast), as in "Wiki Wiki Messenger Service."

USEFUL PHRASES

Aloha ahiahi—Good evening
Aloha au ia oe—I love you!
Aloha kakahiaka—Good morning
aloha nui loa—much love; fondest regards
Hauoli la hanau—Happy Birthday

Hauoli makahiki hau—Happy New Year
komo mai—please come in; enter; welcome
Mele Kalikimaka—Merry Christmas
okole maluna—bottoms up; salute; cheers; kampai

RELIGION

The Lord saw fit to keep His island paradise secret from humanity for a few million years, but once we finally arrived we were awfully thankful. Hawaii sometimes appears like a floating tabernacle; everywhere you look there's a church, temple, shrine, or *heiau*. The islands are either a very holy place, or there's a powerful lot of sinning going on that would require so many houses of prayer. Actually, it's just America's "right to worship" concept fully employed . . . in microcosm. Each of the different people who came to Hawaii brought their own form of devotion. The Polynesian Hawaiians praised the primordial creators, Wakea and Papa, from whom their pantheon of animistically inspired gods sprang. Obviously, to a modern world, these old gods would never do. Unfortunately for the old gods, there were simply too many of them, and belief in them was looked upon as mere superstition, the folly of semicivilized pagans. So the famous missionaries of the 1820s brought Congregational Christianity and the "true path" to heaven.

Inconveniently, the Catholics, Mormons, Reformed Mormons, Adventists, Episcopalians, Unitarians, Christian Scientists, Lutherans, Baptists, Jehovah's Witnesses, Salvation Army, and every other major and minor denomination of Christianity that followed in their wake brought their own brand of enlightenment and never quite agreed with each other. The Chinese and Japanese migrants came and established all the major sects of Buddhism, Confucianism, Taoism, and Shintoism. Allah is praised, the Torah is chanted in Jewish synagogues, and nirvana is available at a variety of Hindu temples. If the spirit moves you, a Hare Krishna devotee will be glad to point you in the right direction and give you a free flower for only a dollar or two. If the world is still too much with you, you might find peace at a Church of Scientology, or meditate at a Kundalini Yoga institute, or perhaps find relief at a local assembly of Baha'i. Anyway, rejoice, because in Hawaii you'll not only find paradise, but you might even find salvation.

HAWAIIAN BELIEFS

The Polynesian Hawaiians worshipped nature. They saw its forces manifested in a multiplicity of forms to which they ascribed godlike powers, and daily life was based on this animistic philosophy. Handpicked and specially trained storytellers chanted the exploits of the gods. These ancient tales, kept alive in a special oral tradition called *moolelo,* were recited only by day. Entranced listeners encircled the chanter; in respect for the gods and in fear of their wrath, they were forbidden to move once the tale was begun. This was serious business where a life could be at stake. It was not like the telling of *kaao,* which were simple fictions, tall tales, and yarns of ancient heroes, merely related for amusement and to pass the long nights. Any object, animate or inanimate, could be a god. All could be infused with mana, especially a dead body, or a respected ancestor.

Ohana had personal family gods called *amakua* whom they called on in times of danger or strife. There were children of gods called *kupua* who were thought to live among men and were distinguished either for their beauty and strength or for their ugliness and terror. It was told that processions of dead *ali'i,* called "Marchers of the Night," wandered through the land of the living and unless you were properly protected it could mean death if they looked upon you. There were simple ghosts known as *akua lapu* who merely frightened people. Forests, waterfalls, trees, springs, and a thousand forms of nature were the manifestations of *akua li'i* (little spirits), who could be invoked at any time for help or protection. It made no difference who or what you were in old Hawaii, the gods were ever-present and they took a direct and active role in your life.

Behind all of these beliefs was an innate sense of natural balance and order. It could be interpreted as positive-negative, yin-yang, plus-minus, life-death, light-dark, whatever, but the main idea was that everything had its opposite. The time of darkness when only the gods lived was *po.* When the great gods descended to the earth and created light, this was *ao* and man was born. All of these *moolelo* are part of the *Kumulipo,* the great chant that records the Hawaiian version of creation. From the time the gods descended and touched earth at Ku Moku on Lanai, where the genealogies were kept. Unlike the Bible, these included the noble families of female *ali'i* as well as males. **Note:** For more information regarding life in precontact Hawaii please see the "History" section.

Kukailimoku, Kamehameha's war god, was 30 inches tall. Fashioned from feathers, it presented a horrible sight with its gaping mouth of dog's teeth and was reputed to utter loud cries while battle was being waged.

THE STRIFES OF MAUI

Of all the heroes and mythological figures of Polynesia, Maui is the best known. His "strifes" are like the great Greek epics, and they make excellent tales of daring that elders loved to relate to youngsters around the evening campfire. Maui was abandoned by his mother, Hina of Fire, when he was an infant. She wrapped him in her hair and cast him upon the sea where she expected him to die; he lived and returned home to become her favorite. She knew then that he was a born hero and had strength far beyond that of ordinary mortals. His first exploit was to lift the sky. In those days the sky hung so low that men had to crawl around on all fours. Then a seductive young woman approached Maui and asked him to use his great strength to lift the sky. In fine heroic fashion, the big boy agreed, if the beautiful woman would euphemistically "give him a drink from her gourd." He then obliged her by lifting the sky, and he might even have made the earth move for her once or twice.

More Land

The territory of man was small at that time. Maui decided that more land was needed, so he conspired to "fish up islands." He descended into the land of the dead and petitioned an ancestress to fashion him a hook out of her jawbone. She obliged, and created the mythical hook *Manai ikalani*. Maui then secured a sacred *alae* bird that he intended to use for bait and bid his brothers to paddle him far out to sea. When he arrived at the deepest spot, he lowered *Manai ikalani* baited with the sacred bird, and his sister, Hina of the Sea, placed it into the mouth of "Old One Tooth," who held the land fast to the bottom of the waters. Maui then exhorted his brothers to row, but warned them not to look back. They strained at the oars with all their might and slowly a great landmass arose. One brother, overcome by curiosity, looked back, and when he did so, the land shattered into all of the islands of Polynesia.

Further Exploits

Maui still desired to serve mankind. People were without fire, the secret of which was held by the sacred *alae* birds, who learned it from Maui's far distant mother. Hina of Fire gave Maui her burning fingernails, but he oafishly kept dropping them into streams until all had fizzled out and he had totally irritated his generous progenitor. She pursued him, trying to burn him to a cinder; Maui chanted for rain to put out her scorching fires. When she saw that they were all being quenched she hid her fire in the barks of special trees and informed the mud hens where they could be found, but first made them promise never to tell men. Maui knew of this and captured a mud hen, threatening to wring its scrawny, traitorous neck unless it gave up the secret. The bird tried trickery and told Maui first to rub together the stems of sugarcane, then banana and even taro. None worked, and Maui's determined rubbing is why these plants have hollow roots today.

Finally, with Maui's hands tightening around the mud hen's gizzard, the bird confessed that fire could be found in the *hau* tree and also the sandalwood, which Maui named *ili aha* (fire bark) in its honor. He then rubbed all the feathers off the mud hen's head for being so deceitful, which is why their crowns are featherless today.

The Sun Is Snared

Maui's greatest deed, however, was in snaring the sun and exacting a promise that it would go slower across the heavens. The people complained that there were not enough daylight hours to fish or farm. Maui's mother could not dry her tapa cloth because the sun rose and set so quickly. She asked her son to help. Maui went to his blind grandmother, who lived on the slopes of Haleakala and was responsible for cooking the sun's bananas, which he ate every day in passing. She told him to personally weave 16 strong ropes with nooses out of his sister's hair. Some say these came from her head, but other versions insist that it was no doubt Hina's pubic hair that had the power to hold the sun-god. Maui positioned himself with the rope, and as each of the 16 rays of the sun came across Haleakala, he snared them until the sun was defenseless and had to bargain for his life. Maui agreed to free him if he promised to go more slowly. From that time forward the sun agreed to move slowly and Haleakala ("The House of the Sun") became his home.

HEIAU AND IDOLS

A *heiau* is a Hawaiian temple. The basic *heiau* was a masterly built and fitted rectangular stone wall that varied in size from as large as a basketball court to the size of a football field. Once the restraining outer walls were built, the interior was backfilled with smaller stones and the top dressing was expertly laid and then rolled, perhaps with a log, to form a pavementlike surface. All that remains of Hawaii's many *heiau* are the stone platforms. The buildings upon them, made from perishable wood, leaves, and grass, have long since disappeared.

Some *heiau* were dreaded temples where human sacrifices were made. Tradition says that this barbaric custom began at Wahaula Heiau on the Big Island in the 12th century and was introduced by a ferocious Tahitian priest named Paao. Other *heiau,* such as Puuhonua o Honaunau, also on the Big Island, were temples of refuge where the weak, widowed, orphaned, and vanquished could find safety and sanctuary.

Idols

All the people worshipped gods who took the form of idols fashioned from wood, feathers, or stone. The eyes were made from shells and until these were inlaid, the idol was dormant. The hair used was often human hair, and the arms and legs were usually flexed. The mouth was either gaping or formed a wide figure-eight lying on its side, and more likely than not, it was lined with glistening dog teeth. There were small figures made of woven basketry that were expertly covered with feathers. Red and yellow were favorite colors that were taken from specific birds by men whose only work was to roam the forests in search of them.

Ghosts

The Hawaiians had countless superstitions and ghost legends, but two of the more interesting involve astral travel of the soul, and the "death Marchers of the Night." The soul, *uhane,* was considered by Hawaiians to be totally free and independent of its body, *kino.* The soul could separate, leaving the body asleep or very drowsy. This disincorporated soul (*hihi'o*) could visit people, and it was considered quite different from a *lapu,* an ordinary spirit of a dead person. A *kahuna* could immediately recognize if a person's *uhane* had left his body, and a special wreath was placed upon his head to protect him and to facilitate reentry. If a person was confronted by an apparition, he could test to see if it was indeed dead or still alive by placing leaves of an *ape* plant upon the ground. If the leaves tore when they were walked upon, the spirit was merely human, but if they remained intact it was a ghost. Also, you could sneak up and startle the vision and if it disappeared it was a ghost, or if no reflection of the face appeared when it drank water from an offered calabash, it was also a ghost. Unfortunately, there were no instructions to follow once you had determined that you indeed had a ghost on your hands. Maybe it was better not to know! Some people would sprinkle salt and water around their houses, but this only kept away evil spirits, not ghosts.

There are also many stories of *kahuna* restoring a soul to a dead body. First they had to catch it and keep it in a gourd. They then placed beautiful tapa and fragrant flowers and herbs about the body to make it more enticing. Slowly, they would coax the soul out of the gourd. Finally, the soul reentered the body through the big toe.

Death Marchers

One inexplicable phenomenon that many people attest to is *ka huakai o ka po,* "Marchers of the Night." This march of the dead is fatal if you gaze upon it, unless one of the marchers happens to be a friendly ancestor who will protect you. The peak time for "the march" is from 7:30 p.m. till 2 a.m. The marchers can be dead *ali'i* and warriors, the gods themselves, or the lesser *amakua.* When the *amakua* march there is usually chanting and music. *Ali'i* marches are more somber. The entire procession, lit by torches, oftentimes stops at the house of a relative and might even carry them away. When the gods themselves march, there is often thunder, lightning, and heavy seas. The sky is lit with torches, and they walk six abreast, three gods and three goddesses. If you get in the way of a march, remove your clothing and prostrate yourself. If the marching gods or *amakua* happen to be ones to which you prayed, you might be spared. If it's a march of the *ali'i* you might make it if you lie face upward and feign death. If you *do* see a death march, the last thing that you'll worry about is lying naked on the ground and looking ridiculous.

MISSIONARIES ONE AND ALL

In Hawaii, when you say "missionaries," it's taken for granted you're referring to the small

HAWAII STATE ARCHIVES

William Alexander preaching on Kauai. Drawing by A. Agate, circa 1840.

and determined band of Congregationalists who arrived aboard the brig *Thaddeus* in 1820, and the follow-up groups called "companies" or "packets" that reinforced them. They were sent from Boston by the American Board of Commissioners for Foreign Missions (ABCFM), which learned of the supposed sad and godless plight of the Hawaiian people through returning sailors and especially through the few Hawaiians who had come to America to study.

The person most instrumental in bringing the missionaries to Hawaii was a young man named Opukahaia. He was an orphan befriended by a ship's captain and taken to New England, where he studied theology. Obsessed with the desire to return home and save his people from certain damnation, his accounts of life in Hawaii were published and widely read. These accounts were directly responsible for the formation of the Pioneer Company to the Sandwich Islands Missions in 1819. Unfortunately, Opukahaia died in New England from typhus the year before they left.

"Civilizing" Hawaii

The first missionaries had the straightforward task of bringing the Hawaiians out of paganism and into Christianity and civilization. They met with terrible hostility—not from the natives, but from the sea captains and traders who were very happy with the open debauchery and wanton whoremongering that was status quo in the Hawaii of 1820. Many direct con-

frontations between these two factions even included the cannonading of missionaries' homes by American sea captains, who were denied the customary visits of island women, thanks to meddlesome "do-gooders." The most memorable of these incidents involved "Mad Jack" Percival, the captain of the USS *Dolphin,* who bombed a church in Lahaina to show his rancour. In actuality, the truth of the situation was much closer to the sentiments of James Jarves, who wrote, "The missionary was a far more useful and agreeable man than his Catholicism would indicate; and the trader was not so bad a man as the missionary would make him out to be." The missionaries' primary aim might have been conversion, but the most fortuitous by-product was education, which raised the consciousness of every Hawaiian, regardless of his religious affiliation. In 40 short years Hawaii was considered a civilized nation well on its way into the modern world, and the American Board of Missions officially ended its support in 1863.

Non-Christians

By the turn of the century, both Shintoism and Buddhism, brought by the Japanese and Chinese, were firmly established in Hawaii. The first official Buddhist temple was Hongpa Hongwanji, established on Oahu in 1889. All the denominations of Buddhism account for 17% (170,000 parishioners) of the island's religious total, and there are about 50,000 Shintoists.

The Hindu religion has perhaps 2,000 adherents, and about the same number of Jewish people live throughout Hawaii, with only one synagogue, Temple Emanuel, on Oahu. The largest number of people in Hawaii (300,000) remain unaffiliated, and about 10,000 people are in new religious movements and lesser-known faiths such as Baha'i and Unitarianism.

Ti plants are always found around heiau, *where their leaves are still used to wrap stones as simple offerings to the gods.*

DIANA LASICH HARPER

OUT AND ABOUT
CAMPING AND HIKING

CAMPING

Few people equate visiting Oahu with camping. The two seem mutually exclusive, especially when you focus on the mystique of Waikiki, and the dominance of a major city like Honolulu. But between state, county, and private campgrounds, and even a military reserve or two, you have about 20 spots to choose from all over the island. Camping on Oahu, however, is a little different from camping on the Neighbor Islands, which are simply more amenable to camping. In an island state, they're considered "the woods, the sticks, the backcountry," and camping seems more acceptable there.

Although totally legal to camp, and done by both visitors and residents, Oahu's camping problems are widely divergent, with social and financial implications. When the politically powerful tourist industry thinks of visitors, it imagines people sitting by a hotel pool, drinking mai tais,

and dutifully spending money! Campers just won't cooperate in parting with their quota of dollars, so there's not much impetus to cater to their wants and needs. Moreover, Honolulu is an international city that attracts both the best and worst kinds of people. The tourist industry, supported by the civil authorities, has a mortal dread that low-lifers, loafers, and bums will ensconce themselves on Oahu's beaches. This would be disastrous for Oahu's image! Mainland cities, not so dependent upon tourism, can obviously be more tolerant of their citizens who have fallen through the social net. So in Oahu they keep a close eye on the campgrounds, enforcing the rules, controlling the situation. The campgrounds are patrolled, adding a measure of strictness along with a measure of security. Even decent people can't bend the rules and slide by a little, where they normally might on the Neighbor Islands.

An odd, inherent social situation adds to the problem. Not too long ago, the local people ei-

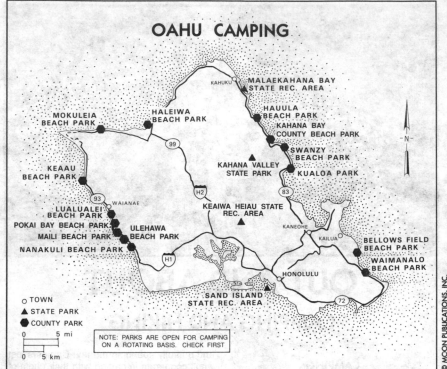

OAHU CAMPING

KAHUKU

MALAEKAHANA BAY
STATE REC. AREA

MOKULEIA
BEACH PARK

HALEIWA
BEACH PARK

HAUULA
BEACH PARK

KAHANA BAY
COUNTY BEACH PARK

KEAAU
BEACH PARK

KAHANA VALLEY
STATE PARK

SWANZY
BEACH PARK

KUALOA PARK

WAIANAE

KEAIWA HEIAU STATE
REC. AREA

LUALUALEI
BEACH PARK

POKAI BAY BEACH PARK

MAILI BEACH PARK

NANAKULI BEACH PARK

ULEHAWA
BEACH PARK

KANEOHE

KAILUA

BELLOWS FIELD
BEACH PARK

WAIMANALO
BEACH PARK

HONOLULU

SAND ISLAND
STATE REC. AREA

○ TOWN
▲ STATE PARK
⬣ COUNTY PARK

0   5 mi

0   5 km

NOTE: PARKS ARE OPEN FOR CAMPING
ON A ROTATING BASIS. CHECK FIRST

© MOON PUBLICATIONS, INC.

ther lived on the beach or used them extensively, oftentimes for their livelihoods. Many, especially fishermen and their families, would set up semipermanent camps for a good part of the year. You can see the remnants of this practice at some of the more remote and ethnically claimed campgrounds. As Oahu, much more than the Neighbor Islands, felt the pressures of growing tourism, beachfront property became astronomically expensive. Local people had to relinquish what they thought of as their beaches. The state and county, in an effort to keep some beaches public and therefore undeveloped, created beach parks. This ensured that all could use the beaches forever, but it also meant that their access would be governed and regulated.

Local people, just like visitors, must follow the rules and apply for camping permits limited by the number of days that you can spend in

any one spot. Out went the semipermanent camp and with it, for the local people, the idea of *our* beach. Now, you have the same rights to camp in a spot that may have been used, or even owned, in past generations, by the family of dark-skinned people next to you. They feel dispossessed, infringed upon, and bitter. And you, especially if you have white skin, can be the focus of this bitterness. This situation, although psychologically understandable, can be a monumental drag. Of course, not all island people have this attitude, and chances are very good that nothing negative will happen. But you must be aware of underlying motivations so that you can read the vibes of the people around your camp spot.

If all of these "problems" haven't made you want to pull up your tent stakes and head into a more congenial sunset, you can have a great and inexpensive time camping on Oahu. All of this is just the social climate that you *may* have to face, but most likely, nothing unpleasant will happen, and you'll come home tanned, relaxed, and singing the praises of the great outdoors on Hawaii's capital island.

State Parks

Oahu boasts 23 state parks and recreation areas. The majority offer a beach for day use, walks, picnicking, toilets, showers, and pavilions. A few of these, including some very important *heiau,* along with **Washington Place,** the state capitol, **Iolani Palace,** the **Royal Mausoleum,** and **Diamond Head** are designated as state monuments.

Oahu state parks close their gates and parking lots at night. Those *not* offering camping are open 7 a.m.-8 p.m. from May 1 to September 30, closing during the remainder of the year at 6:30 p.m.

Four state parks currently offer tent camping: **Sand Island State Recreation Area,** just a few minutes from downtown Honolulu; **Keaiwa Heiau State Recreation Area,** in the interior on the heights above Aiea; **Malaekahana Bay State Recreation Area,** a mile north of Laie on the windward coast; and **Kahana Valley State Park** between Punaluu and Ka'a'awa on the windward coast.

To camp at the four designated parks, you must acquire a permit (free) from the Dept. of Forestry, Division of State Parks, 1151 Punchbowl St., Honolulu, HI 96813, tel. 587-0300, open weekdays 8 a.m.-4:15 p.m. Oahu campsite **permit reservations** can be made no earlier than the fifth Wednesday before the first day of camping, but *must* be made at least one week in advance by writing a letter including your name, address, phone number, number of persons in your party, type of permit requested, and duration of your stay. The permits can be picked up on arrival with proof of identification.

On Oahu campsites are at a premium and people line up at 8 a.m. on the first-floor breezeway on the Beretania Street side of the issuing office, just outside the double glass doors, where you are given a number on a first-come first-served basis (usually no hassle except on three-day holiday weekends). After this, go to the third floor where the office is located.

Note: Camping is allowed *only* from 8 a.m. Fri. to 8 a.m. Wed. (closed all day Wed. and Thurs. for camping—other activities okay) with the shutdown, supposedly, for regrowth. Camping is allowed for only five consecutive days in any one month, and don't forget a parking permit for your vehicle, which must remain within the locked park gates at night. *Alooohaaa!*

County Parks

The city and county of Honolulu has opened 13 (changes periodically) of its 65 beach parks around the island to tent camping, and most allow trailers and RVs. Unfortunately, these are the very parks at which you're more likely to encounter hassles. A free permit is required, and camping is allowed for five days from Friday at 8 a.m. until the following Wednesday at 8 a.m., at which time your campsite must be vacated (no camping Wednesday and Thursday evenings). These campsites are also at a premium, but you can write for reservations and pick up your permits on arrival with proper identification. For information and reservations write or visit City and County of Honolulu, Dept. of Parks and Recreation, 650 S. King St., Honolulu, HI 96813, tel. 523-4525. Permits are also available from the satellite city halls around the island.

Note: All of the beach parks are closed during designated months (they differ from park to park) throughout the year. This is supposedly for cleaning, but really it's to reduce the possibility of squatters moving in. Make sure, if you're reserving far in advance, that the park will be open when you arrive! Don't count on the Parks and Recreation Department to inform you!

Private Campground

A private campground at **Malaekahana Beach** is located virtually next door to Malaekahana Bay State Recreation Area just north of Laie. Contact Network Enterprises, 56-335 Kamehameha Hwy., Laie, tel. 293-1736, Mon., Wed., Fri. 10 a.m.-6 p.m., other days 3-5 p.m. only.

Camping Gear And Rentals

If you've come without camping gear and wish to rent or purchase some try: **The Bike Shop,** 1149 S. King St., tel. 531-7071, renting tents at $30 for a weekend, $60 for the week, and backpacks at $20 for the weekend, $40 for the week;

or, **Omar the Tentman,** 1336 Dillingham Blvd., tel. 836-8785, who rents only one size tent that sleeps six to eight people (no backpacking tents) at $52 a weekend, $59 a week, and backpacks at $17 per weekend, $22 per week.

Note: Also see "What to Take."

HIKING

The best way to leave the crowds of tourists behind and become intimate with the beauty of Oahu is to hike it. Although the Neighbor Islands receive fewer visitors, a higher percentage of people hike them than Oahu. Don't get the impression that you'll have the island to yourself, but you will be amazed at how open and lovely this crowded island can be. Some cultural and social hikes can be taken without leaving the city, like a stroll through Waikiki and a historical walking tour of downtown Honolulu and Chinatown. But others—some mere jaunts, others quite strenuous—are well worth the time and effort.

Remember that much of Oahu is privately owned, and you must have permission to cross this land, or you may be open to prosecution. Usually private property is marked by signs. Another source that might stomp your hiking plans with their jungle boots is the military. A full 25% of Oahu belongs to Uncle Sam, and he isn't always thrilled when you decide to play in his back yard. Some of the finest walks (like to the summit of Mt. Kaala) require crossing military lands, much of which has been altered by very unfriendly looking installations. Always check and obey any posted signs to avert trouble. The following listings are by no means all-inclusive, but should help you to choose a trail that seems interesting and is within your ability level.

Diamond Head

The most recognized symbol of Hawaii, this is the first place you should head for a strikingly beautiful panorama of Waikiki and greater Honolulu. Called Leahi ("Casting Point") by the Hawaiians, it was named Diamond Head after a group of wild-eyed English sailors espied what they thought to be diamonds glistening in the rocks. Hawaii had fulfilled so many other dreams, why not a mountain of diamonds?! Unfortunately, the glimmer was caused by worthless calcite crystals. No fortune was made, but the name stuck.

To get there, follow Kalakaua Avenue south from Waikiki until it leads into Diamond Head Road, then quickly a sign points you to Diamond Head Crater. Pass through a tunnel and into the heavily militarized section in the center of the crater; the trail starts here. Although the hike is moderate, you should bring along water, a flashlight (a must), and binoculars if you have them. Run by the Division of State Parks, the park is open daily from 6 a.m. to 6 p.m. A sign at the beginning describes the rigors you'll encounter and informs that the trail is seven-tenths of a mile long and was built to the 760-foot summit of Leahi Point in 1908 to serve as a U.S. Coast Artillery Observation Station. It was heavily fortified during WW II, and part of the fun is exploring the old gun emplacements and tunnels built to link and service them.

Though only 10 minutes from Waikiki, wildflowers and chirping birds create a peaceful setting. When you come to a series of cement and stone steps, walk to a flat area to the left to find an old winch that hauled the heavy building materials to the top. Here's a wide panorama of the sea and Koko Head, and notice too that atop every little hillock is an old gun emplacement. Next comes a short but dark (bring a flashlight!) tunnel and immediately a series of 99 steps. You can avoid the steps by taking the trail to the left, but the footing is slippery and there are no guard rails. Following the steps is a spiral staircase that leads down into a large gun emplacement, through which you walk and come to another tunnel. If you haven't brought a flashlight, give your eyes a few minutes to adjust; there's enough light to make it. Once on top, another stairway and ladder takes you to the very summit.

Judd Trail

This is an excellent trail to take to experience Oahu's "jungle" while visiting the historic and picturesque **Nuuanu Pali.** From Honolulu take H-1 and turn onto Rt. 61, the Pali Highway. Turn right onto the Old Pali Highway, then right again onto Nuuanu Pali Drive. Follow it for just under a mile to Reservoir No. 2 spillway. The trail begins on the ocean side of the spillway and leads through fragrant eucalyptus and a dense stand of picture-perfect Norfolk pines. It continues through the forest reserve and makes a loop back to the starting point. En route you pass **Jackass Ginger Pool.** In the immediate area are "mud slides," where you can take a ride on a makeshift toboggan of *pili* grass, ti leaves, or a piece of plastic, if you've brought one. This activity is rough on your clothes, and even rougher on your body. The wet conditions after a rain are perfect. Afterward, a dip in Jackass Pool cleans the mud and refreshes at the same time. Continue down the trail to observe wild ginger, guava, and *kukui*, but don't take any confusing side trails. If you get lost head back to the stream and follow it until it intersects the main trail.

Tantalus And Makiki Valley Trails

Great sightseeing and hiking can be combined when you climb the road atop Tantalus. A range of trails in this area offer magnificent views. A few roads lead up Tantalus, but a good one heads past Punchbowl along Puowaina Drive; just keep going until it turns into Tantalus Drive. The road switchbacks past some incredible homes and views until it reaches the 2,013-foot summit, where it changes its name to Round Top Drive, then heads down the other side.

The best place to start is at the top of Tantalus at the **Manoa Cliff Trailhead,** where a number of intersecting trails give you a selection of adventure. Once on Round Top Drive, pass a brick wall with the name Kalaiopua Road imbedded in the stonework, and continue until you pass Forest Ridge Way, right after which is a large turnout on both sides of the road near telephone pole no. 56. To the right is the beginning of half-mile-long **Moleka Trail,** which offers some excellent views and an opportunity to experience the trails in this area without an all-day commitment. The trails are excellently maintained, often by the local Sierra Club. Your greatest hazard here is mud, but in a moment you're in a handsome stand of bamboo, and in 10 minutes the foliage parts onto a lovely panorama of Makiki Valley and Honolulu in the background. These views are captivating, but remember to have "small eyes"—check out the varied-colored mosses and fungi, and don't forget the flowers and fruit growing around you.

A branch trail to the left leads to Round Top Drive, and if you continue the trail splits into three: the right is the **Makiki Valley Trail,** which cuts across the valley starting at a Boy Scout camp on Round Top Drive and ending atop Tantalus; **Ualakaa Trail** branches left and goes for another half mile, connecting the Makiki Valley Trail with Puu Ualakaa State Park; straight ahead is the **Makiki Branch A Trail,** which descends for one-half mile, ending at the Division of Forestry Baseyard at the bottom of the valley.

On the mountainside of the Manoa Cliffs Trailhead is the **Connector Trail.** This pragmatic-sounding trail does indeed connect the lower trails with **Manoa Cliffs Trail,** skirting around the backside of Tantalus and intersecting the **Puu Ohia Trail,** which leads to the highest point on Tantalus and the expected magnificent view.

Maunawili Falls Trail

Maunawili Falls is on the other side of Nuuanu Pali, near Maunawili town. This trail offers adventure into Oahu's jungle, with a rewarding pool and falls at the end. At the third red light as you head down the windward side of the Pali Highway, make a right onto Auloa Road. In a few hundred yards, take the left fork onto Maunawili Road and follow it toward the mountains through a residential area. Turn right onto Aloha Oe Drive, follow it to the end, and make a right on Maleko Road that ends in a cul-de-sac. **Warning:** Do not trespass on any private land. There is no public right-of-way! Just before you get to the end of the cul-de-sac look for an open space on the right with a short trail leading down to a culvert. Follow the culvert for about 100 yards, and turn left onto a heavily used jeep trail that soon becomes a walking path. In 400 yards, at three telephone poles, the trail splits into three branches; take the center branch and go straight ahead downhill until you intersect a trail that leads right along the creek. This trail is very muddy, but worth it. Follow it for about 15 minutes until you come to Maunawili Falls—deep enough to dive in. You can also see an upper falls. Above them is an open field perfect for an overnight camp. To the left a path leads past a small banana plantation, along an irrigation ditch cut into the moun-

After a hike into the interior, refresh yourself with a dip in the pool of Maunawili Falls.

tainside, paralleled by a wooden walkway. Very few people venture into this safe but fascinating area.

Maunawili Demonstration Trail

This is one of the most easily accessible, and one of Oahu's newest trails. Soon after passing the Pali Lookout, which is clearly marked along the Pali Highway, you will go through a tunnel. Almost immediately, a sign points to a scenic overlook. Pull off into the parking area and walk back up the highway for about 100 yards where you'll see a break in the guardrail and a sign for *"Na'ala Hele,"* the Hawaiian Trail and Access System. The beauty of this trail is that it is reasonably flat with little elevation gain or loss as it winds its way along the windward side of the Koolau Range. The whine of the Pali Highway abates almost immediately and you are suddenly in a brilliant highland tropical forest. You can continue to the end (about three hours one-way) for a full day's hike, or just find a secluded spot after a mile or so for a picnic. The views are spectacular and there are vantage points where you can see the coast all the way from Rabbit Island to Chinaman's Hat. Remember, however, that like all Hawaiian trails, recent rainfall makes for treacherous footing.

Haula Loop Trails

Built by the Workers Civilian Conservation Corps (WCCC) during the Depression, these manicured trails run up and down two ridges and deep into an interior valley, gaining and loosing height as they switchback through the extraordinary jungle canopy. The **Gulch and Papali trails,** branches of the Hauula Loop Trail, start from the same place. The Hauula Trail is wide with good footing. There're a few stream crossings, but it's not muddy even after a heavy rain, which can shut down the Sacred Falls Trail just a few miles north. The hard-packed trail, covered in a soft carpet of ironwood needles, offers magnificent coastal views once you reach the heights, or you can look inland into verdant gulches and gullies (valleys).

You'll be passing through miniature ecosystems very reminiscent of the fern forests on the Big Island, but on a much smaller scale. The area flora is made up of ironwoods, passion fruit, thimbleberries, ohia, wild orchids, and fiddlehead ferns. To get there, head for Hauula on coastal Rt. 83 (Kamehameha Hwy.) and just past the 7-Eleven store, between mile markers 21 and 22, look inland for Hauula Homestead Road. Take it for a minute until you see the well-marked sign leading to the trails.

Sacred Falls

On coastal Rt. 83, between Hauula and Punaluu (mile markers 22 and 23), an HVB Warrior points you to Sacred Falls. Note that you *cannot* drive to the falls. An old commercial venture put out this misinformation, which persists to this day. The walk is a hardy stroll, so you'll need jogging shoes, not thongs. The area becomes a narrow canyon, and the sun sets early; don't start out past 3 p.m., especially if you want a dip in the stream. The trail was roughed up by Hurricane Ewa, and a sign along it says "Danger. Do not go past this point." Many people ignore this sign; the path is a little more treacherous but is passable.

The area's Hawaiian name was Kaliuwaa ("Canoe Leak"), and although the original name isn't as romantic as the anglicized version, the entire area was indeed considered sacred. In route, you pass into a very narrow valley where the gods might show disfavor by dropping rocks onto your head. Notice many stones wrapped with a ti leaf. This is an appeasement to the gods, so they're not tempted to brain you. Go ahead, wrap a rock; no one will see you! You can hear the falls dropping to the valley floor. Above you the walls are 1,600 feet high, but the falls drop only 90 feet or so. The pool below is ample for a swim, but the water is chilly and often murky. A number of beautiful picnic spots are on the large flat rocks.

North Oahu Treks
Some of the hiking in and around northwest Oahu is quite difficult. However, you should take a hike out to **Kaena Point,** where there is huge surf, sometimes 30 feet high. You have two choices: you can park your car at the end of the road past Dillingham Airfield on the north coast and hike in, or you can park your car at the end of the road past Makua on the Waianae coast and hike in. Both are about the same distance, and both are hardy but not difficult. The trail is only two miles, from each end, and few people come here except some local fishermen.

Peacock Flat is a good family-style trail that offers primitive camping. Follow Rt. 93 toward Dillingham Airfield and just before getting there turn left onto a dirt road leading toward the Kawaihapi Reservoir. If you want to camp, you need permits from the Division of Forestry and a waiver from the Mokuleia Ranch, tel. 637-4241, which you can get at their office, located at the end of a dirt road just before the one leading to Kawaihapi Reservoir. They will also provide instructions and a key to get through two locked gates before reaching the trailhead, if you decide to go in from that end. Heading through the Mokuleia Forest Reserve, you can camp anywhere along the trail, or at an established but primitive campground in Peacock Flat. This area is heavily used by hunters, who are mostly after wild pig.

Dupont Trail takes you to the summit of Mt. Ka'ala, highest point and by far the most difficult hike on the island. The last mile is downright dangerous, and has you hanging on cliff edges, with the bottom 2,000 feet below! This is not for the average hiker. Follow Rt. 930 to Waialua, make a left at Waialua High School onto a cane road, and follow it to the second gate, about 1.5 miles. Park there. You need a hiking permit from the Division of Forestry and a waiver from the Waialua Sugar Company, tel. 637-3521. Atop Ka'ala, although the views are magnificent, you'll also find a mushroom field of FAA satellite stations.

INFORMATION, EQUIPMENT, AND SAFETY

Hiking Groups And Information
The following organizations can provide information on wildlife, conservation, and organized hiking trips. The **Department of Land and Natural Resources,** Division of Forestry and Wildlife, 1151 Punchbowl St., Room 325, Honolulu, HI 96813, tel. 548-2861, is helpful in providing trail maps, accessibility information, hunting and fishing regulations, and general forest rules. Ask for a copy of their free *Island of Oahu Recreation Map.* It (and similar maps for the other islands) gives good information on hiking, camping, and hunting with a description of most trails. **Hawaiian Trail and Mountain Club,** P.O. Box 2238, Honolulu, HI 96804, meets behind Iolani Palace on Saturdays at 10 a.m., and Sundays at 8 a.m. Their hikes are announced in the *Honolulu Star Bulletin's* "Pulse of Paradise" column. **Hawaii Audubon Society** can be reached at P.O. Box 22832, Honolulu, HI 96822. **Sierra Club,** 1212 University Ave., Honolulu, HI 96826, tel. 538-6616, can provide you with a packet describing Hawaii's trails, charted by island, along with their physical characteristics and information on obtaining maps and permits. The packet costs $3, postage paid.

Equipment

Like everything else you take to Hawaii, your camping and hiking equipment should be lightweight and durable. Camping equipment size and weight should not cause a problem with baggage requirements on airlines: if it does, it's a tip-off that you're hauling too much. One odd luggage consideration you might make is to bring along a small **styrofoam cooler** packed with equipment. Replace the equipment with food items when you get to Hawaii; if you intend to car camp successfully and keep food prices down, you'll definitely need a cooler. You can also buy one on arrival for only a few dollars. You'll need a lightweight **tent,** preferably with a rainfly and a sewn-in floor. This will save you from getting wet and miserable, and will keep out mosquitoes, cockroaches, ants, and the few stinging insects on Oahu.

Sleeping bags are a good idea, although you can get along at sea level with only a blanket. Down-filled bags are necessary for Haleakala, Mauna Kea, Mauna Loa, or any high-elevation-camping—you'll freeze without one. **Campstoves** are needed because there's very little wood in some volcanic areas, it's often wet in the deep forest, and open fires are often prohibited. If you'll be car camping, take along a multiburner stove, and for trekking, a backpacker's stove will be necessary. The grills found only at some campgrounds are popular with many families that go often to the beach parks for an open-air dinner. You can buy a very inexpensive charcoal grill at many variety stores throughout Hawaii.

It's a great idea to take along a **lantern.** This will give added safety for campers. Definitely take a **flashlight,** replacement batteries, and a few small **candles.** A complete **first-aid kit** can be the difference between life and death, and is worth the extra bulk. Hikers, especially those leaving the coastal areas, should take **rain gear,** a plastic ground cloth, utility knife, compass, safety whistle, mess kit, water purification tablets, canteen, nylon twine, and waterproof matches. You can find plenty of stores that sell, and a few stores that rent, camping equipment; see the Yellow Pages under "Camping Equipment" as well as "Shopping" in the following travel chapters.

Safety

There are two things in Hawaii that you must keep your eye on to remain safe: humans and nature. The general rule is, the farther you get away from towns, the safer you'll be from human-induced hassles. If possible, don't hike or camp alone, especially if you're a woman. Don't leave your valuables in your tent, and always carry your money, papers, and camera with you. (See "Health and Well-being—Theft and Hassles.") Don't tempt the locals by being overly friendly or unfriendly, and make yourself scarce if they're drinking. While hiking, remember that many trails are well maintained, but trailhead markers are often missing. The trails themselves can be muddy, which can make them treacherously slippery and oftentimes knee-deep. Always bring food because you cannot, in most cases, forage from the land. Water in most streams is biologically polluted and will give you bad stomach problems if you drink it without purifying it first, either through boiling or with tablets. For your part, please don't use the streams as a toilet.

Precautions

Always tell a ranger or official of your hiking intentions. Supply an itinerary and your expected route, then stick to it. Twilight is short in the islands, and night sets in rapidly. In June sunrise and sunset are around 6 a.m. and 7 p.m., in December these occur at 7 a.m. and 6 p.m. If you become lost at night, stay put, light a fire if possible, and stay as dry as you can. If lost, walk on ridges and avoid the gulches, which have more obstacles and make it harder for rescuers to spot you.

Hawaii is made of volcanic rock which is brittle and crumbly. Never attempt to climb steep *pali* (cliffs). Every year people are stranded and fatalities have occurred on the *pali*. Be careful of elevation sickness, especially on Haleakala, Mauna Loa, and Mauna Kea. The best cure is to head down as soon as possible.

Heat can cause you to lose water and salt. If you become woozy or weak, rest, take salt, and drink water as you need it. Remember, it takes much more water to restore a dehydrated person than to keep hydrated; take small frequent sips. Be mindful of flash floods. Small creeks can turn into raging torrents with upland rains.

Never camp in a dry creek bed. Fog is only encountered at the 1,500- to 5,000-foot level, but be careful of disorientation. Generally, stay within your limits, be careful, and enjoy yourself.

Topographical And Nautical Charts
For in-depth topographical maps, write **U.S. Geological Survey, Federal Center, Denver, CO 80225.** In Hawaii, a wide range of topographical maps can be purchased at **Trans-Pa-** **cific Instrument Co.,** 1406 Colburn St., Honolulu, HI 96817, tel. 841-7538. For nautical charts, write **National Ocean Service,** 6501 Lafayette Ave., Riverdale, MD 20737-1199, tel. (301) 436-6990.

For a well-written and detailed hiking guide complete with maps, check out *Oahu Trails* (a book for each island is available) by Kathy Morey, published by Wilderness Press, 2440 Bancroft Way, Berkeley, CA 94704.

DIANA LASICH HARPER

BOB RACE

SPORTS AND RECREATION

Oahu is a playground for young and old with sports, games, and activities galore. Everyone can find something to enjoy, and most activities are free, relatively cheap, or once-in-a-lifetime thrills that are worth the money. The sea is the ideal playground. You can swim, snorkel, scuba, surf, fish, sail, canoe, kayak, windsurf, bodysurf, parasail, cruise, or merely stroll along the shore picking up shells or exploring tidepools.

If it can be ridden, sailed, glided, flown, bounced, smashed with a racquet, struck with a club, bat, or foot, or hooked with the right bait, you'll find it on Oahu. And lots of it! The pursuit of fun is serious business here, and you can find anything, sportswise, that you ever dreamed of doing. The island offers tennis and golf, along with plenty of horseback riding, hiking, hunting, and freshwater fishing. Spectator sports like baseball, basketball, polo, and especially football are popular. Whatever your desire or physical abilities may be, there'll be some activity that strikes your fancy.

One of the best tonics for relaxation is to play hard at something you thoroughly enjoy, so you're deliciously tired and fulfilled at day's end. For you this might be hooking onto an 800-pound marlin that'll test you to the limit, or per-

haps just giving yourself to the sea and floating on gentle waves. Hawaii is guaranteed to thrill the young, invigorate the once-young, and put a twinkle in your eye and a bounce in your step.

Note: Also see "The North Shore—Sporting Goods and Rentals," and "Getting Around—Sightseeing Tours" in the Out and About chapter.

GOLF

With over 30 private, public, and military golf courses scattered around such a relatively small island, it's a wonder that it doesn't rain golf balls. At present 19 links are open to the public, ranging from modest nine-holers to world-class courses whose tournaments attract the biggest names in golf today. Prices range from $25 up to $140 or more. An added attraction of playing Oahu's courses is that you get to walk around on some of the most spectacular and manicured pieces of real estate on the island. Some afford sweeping views of the coast, like the **Ko Olina Golf Club**, while others, like the **Pali Golf Course**, have a lovely mountain backdrop, or, like Waikiki's **Ala Wai Golf Course**, are set virtually in the center of all the downtown action.

GOLF COURSES OF OAHU

COURSE	PAR	YARDS	WEEKDAY FEES
Ala Wai Golf Course 404 Kapahulu Ave. Honolulu, HI 96851 tel. 296-4653	70	6,065	$20
Bay View Golf Center 45-285 Kaneohe Bay Dr. Kaneohe, HI 96744 tel. 247-0451	54	2,231	$20
Hawaii Country Club Kunia Rd. Kunia, HI 96759 tel. 621-5654	71	5,664	$55/60
Hawaii Kai Championship Golf Course 8902 Kalanianaole Hwy. Honolulu, HI 96825 tel. 395-2358	72	6,350	$75
Hawaii Kai Executive Golf Course 8902 Kalanianaole Hwy. Honolulu, HI 96825 tel. 395-2358	55	2,433	$25
Hawaii Prince Golf Club 91-100 4th Weaver Rd. Ewa Beach, HI 96706 tel. 944-4567	72	3,076	$50/135
Honolulu Country Club 1690 Ala Puunalu St. Honolulu, HI 96818 tel. 833-4541	73	6,808	$75
Kahuku Golf Course * x P.O. Box 143 Kahuku, HI 96731 tel. 293-5842	35	2,699	$18
Ko Olina Golf Club 92-1220 Alii Nui Dr. Ewa Beach, HI 96707 tel. 676-5300	72	6,867	$135
Links at Kuilima 57-091 Kamehameha Hwy. Kahuku, HI 96731 tel. 293-8574	72	6,795	$115/$125
Makaha Valley Country Club 84-627 Makaha Valley Rd. Waianae, HI 96792 tel. 695-7111	71	6,369	$70

GOLF COURSES OF OAHU

COURSE	PAR	YARDS	WEEKDAY FEES
Mid Pacific Country Club 266 Kaelepulu Dr. Kailua, HI 96734 tel. 261-9765	72	6,812	$130
Mililani Golf Club 95-176 Kualelani Ave. Mililani, HI 96789 tel. 623-2254	72	6,815	$75/80
Moanalua Golf Club * 1250 Ala Aolani St. Honolulu, HI 96819 tel. 839-2411	36	2,972	$25
Oahu Country Club 150 Country Club Rd. Honolulu, Hi 96817 tel. 595-3256	71	6,000	$110
Olomana Golf Links 41-1801 Kalanianaole Hwy. Waimanalo, HI 96795 tel. 259-7926	72	6,081	$65
Pali Golf Course 45-050 Kamehameha Hwy. Kaneohe, HI 96744 tel. 261-9784	72	6,493	$25
Pearl Country Club 98-535 Kanonohi St. Aiea, HI 96701 tel. 487-3802	71	6,924	$70/75
Sheraton Makaha Resort and Country Club P.O. Box 896, Makaha Valley Rd. Waianae, HI 96792 tel. 695-9544	72	7,091	$135
Ted Makalena Golf Course 93059 Waipio Point Access Rd., Waipahu, HI 96796 tel. 296-7888	71	5,976	$25
Waialae Country Club x √ 4997 Kahala Ave. Honolulu, HI 96816 tel. 734-2151	72	6,529	$65

Note: * = 9-hole course   x = no club rentals   √ = guests only

The **Hawaiian Open Invitational Golf Tournament** held in late January or February at the Waialae Country Club brings the world's best golfers. Prize money is close to $1 million, and all three major TV networks cover the event. This is usually the only opportunity the average person gets to set foot on this course.

Military personnel, or those with military privileges, are welcome to golf at a number of courses operated by all four branches of the service. Calling the respective bases provides all necessary information.

TENNIS

Grease up the old elbow because Oahu boasts over 168 county-maintained tennis courts. Get a

TENNIS COURTS OF OAHU

COUNTY COURTS

Under the jurisdiction of the Department of Parks and Recreation, 3908 Paki Avenue, Honolulu, HI 96815; tel. 923-7927. Courts listed are in Waikiki and main towns only. There are approximately 30 additional courts around the island.

LOCATION	NAME OF COURT	NO. OF COURTS	LIGHTED
Aiea	Aiea Recreation Center	2	Yes
Ewa	Ewa Beach Community Park	4	Yes
Kahala	Kahala Recreation Center	2	No
Kailua	Kailua Recreation Center	8	Yes
Kaimuki	Kaimuki Recreation Center	2	Yes
Kalakaua	Kalakaua Recreation Center	4	Yes
Kaneohe	Kaneohe District Park	6	No
Keehi	Keehi Lagoon Courts	12	No
Koko Head	Koko Head District Park	6	Yes
Maunawili	Maunawili Park	2	Yes
Pearl City	Pearl City Recreation Center	2	Yes
Sunset Beach	Sunset Beach Neighborhood Park	2	Yes
Wahiawa	Wahiawa Recreation Center	4	Yes
Waialua	Waialua Recreation Center	4	Yes
Waianae	Waianae District Park	8	Yes
Waikiki	Ala Moana Park	10	Yes
Waikiki	Diamond Head Tennis Center	7	No
Waikiki	Kapiolani Tennis Courts	4	Yes
Waimanalo	Waimanalo District Park	4	No
Waipahu	Waipahu Recreation Center	4	Yes

HOTEL AND PRIVATE COURTS THAT ARE OPEN TO THE PUBLIC

Honolulu	Hawaiian Regent Hotel (fee)	1	No
Honolulu	Ilikai Hotel, The Westin (fee)	7	Yes
Honolulu	King Street Courts (fee)	4	Yes
Honolulu	Waikiki Malia Hotel (fee for nonguests)	1	No
Kailua	Windward Tennis Club (fee)	5	Yes
Waianae	Makaha Resort (fee)	4	Yes

complete list of them by writing a letter of inquiry and enclosing a SASE to the Dept. of Parks and Recreation, Tennis Division, 3908 Paki Ave., Honolulu, HI 96815, tel. 923-7927. Also, plenty of hotel and private courts are open to the public for a fee, though a few hotels limit play to guests only. The accompanying chart is a partial listing of what's available.

SCUBA AND SNORKELING

If you think that Oahu is beautiful above the sea, wait until you explore below. The warm tropical waters and coral growth make it a fascinating haven for reef fish and aquatic plant life. You'll soon discover that Hawaiian waters are remarkably clear, with excellent visibility. Fish in every fathomable color parade by. Clusters of lavender, coral, red, and gold coral trees and over 1,500 different types of shells carpet the ocean floor. In some spots (like Oahu's Hanauma Bay) the fish are so accustomed to humans that they'll eat bread from your hand. In other spots, lurking moray eels add the special zest of danger. Sharks and barracuda pose less danger than scraping your knee on the coral or being driven against the rocks by a heavy swell. There are enormous but harmless sea bass and a profusion of sea turtles. All this awaits below Hawaii's waters.

Oahu has particularly generous underwater vistas open to anyone donning a mask and fins. Snorkel and dive sites, varying in difficulty and challenge, are accessible from the island. Sites can be totally hospitable, where families and first-time snorkelers can have an exciting but safe frolic, or accessible only to the experienced diver. All over the island are dive shops from which you can rent or buy all equipment, and where dive boats and instruction on all levels can be arranged. Particular spots are listed under "Beaches and Parks" in the travel sections, but some well-known favorites are Hanauma Bay, Black Point off Diamond Head, the waters around Rabbit Island, Sharks Cove on the North Shore, Wanalua Bay between Koko and Diamond Heads (good for green sea turtles), Magic Island near Ala Moana Beach Park, and some sunken ships and planes just off the Waianae coast.

exploring the reefs of Oahu

Scuba

If you're a scuba diver you'll have to show your "C Card" before local shops will rent you gear, fill your tanks, or take you on a charter dive. Plenty of outstanding scuba instructors will give you lessons towards certification, and they're especially reasonable because of the stiff competition. Prices vary, but you can take a three- to five-day semiprivate certification course, including all equipment, for about $375 (instruction book, dive tables, logbook extra charge). Divers unaccustomed to Hawaiian waters should not dive alone regardless of their experience. Most opt for dive tours to special dive grounds guaranteed to please. These vary also, but an *accompanied* single-tank dive where no boat is involved goes for about $65. For a single-tank boat dive, expect to spend $75. There are special charter dives, night dives, and photography dives. Most companies pick you up at your hotel, take you to the site, and return you home. Basic equipment rental costs $20-30 for the day, and most times you'll only need the top of a wetsuit.

Snorkeling

Scuba diving takes expensive special equipment, skills, and athletic ability. Snorkeling in comparison is much simpler and enjoyable to anyone who can swim. In about 15 minutes you can be taught the fundamentals of snorkeling—you really don't need formal instructions. Other snorkelers or dive shop attendants can tell you enough to get you started. Because you can breathe without lifting your head, you get great propulsion from the fins and hardly ever need to use your arms. You can go for much greater distances and spend longer in the water than if you were swimming. Experienced snorkelers make an art of this sport and you too can see and do amazing things with a mask, snorkel, and flippers. Don't, however, get a false sense of invincibility and exceed your limitations.

Those interested can buy or rent equipment in the dive shops listed below and in department stores. Sometimes condos and hotels have snorkeling equipment free for their guests, but if you have to rent it, don't do it from a hotel or condo, but go to a dive shop where it's much cheaper (see "Dive Shops and Rentals"). Expect to spend $5-8 a day for mask, fins, and snorkel. Many boats will take you out snorkeling or diving. Prices range from $40 (half day, four hours) to $70 (full day, eight hours); check "Getting Around—Sightseeing Tours" for many of the boats that do it all, from deep-sea fishing to moonlight cruises. A hotel's "activities center" can arrange these excursions for no extra charge. Do yourself a favor and wash all the sand off rented equipment. Most shops irritatingly penalize you $1 if you don't. All want a deposit, usually $30, that they put on a credit card slip and tear up when you return. Underwater camera rentals are now normal at most shops, and go for around $10-12 including film (24 shots), but not developing. Happy diving!

Dive Shops And Rentals

The following are dive shops with a good reputation. **Waikiki Diving**, at 1734 Kalakaua, and at 420 Nahua, tel. 955-5151, closed Sunday, does PADI certification. No snorkeling tours, but they rent snorkeling equipment at $6 for 24 hours. Certification courses cost $370. Open-water dive for beginners from shore is $50 one dive, $75 two dives. Try **Steve's Diving Adventures**, 1860 Ala Moana Blvd., tel. 947-8900; **South Sea Aquatics**, 1050 Ala Moana Blvd, tel. 538-3854; or **Hawaiian Divers**, 2344 Kamehameha Hwy., tel. 845-6644. **American Dive Oahu**, 3648 Waialae Ave., tel. 732-2877, is a full-service dive shop offering certification, shore and boat dives, and snorkeling adventures. **Snorkel Bob's**, tel. 735-7944, at the corner of Kapahulu and Date avenues, has very inexpensive deals on snorkeling equipment (rent the "better equipment," still a deal). Prices start at only $15 per week for full snorkel gear, which you can take to Maui, Kauai, and Big Island locations and return there ($3 extra). Snorkel Bob's also has underwater cameras and boogie boards for reasonable prices.

Surf and Sea, tel. 637-9887, is a complete dive shop on the North Shore in Haleiwa. **Aaron's Dive Shop**, at 602 Kailua Rd., Kailua, tel. 262-2333, open Mon.-Fri 8-8, Sat. till 6, Sun. till 5, is a full-service dive shop. A snorkel outfit is $7 for 24 hours. They have a four-day scuba certification course for $350, PADI. Introductory boat dive is about $75, off the beach is $75, but you get two dives.

Leeward Dive Center, 87-066 Farrington Hwy., Maili, tel. 696-3414, (800) 255-1574, offers PADI courses for $325. Introductory dives are $75, boat dives are $75 for two tanks, and it's $75 for night dives. They also do snorkeling with lessons and equipment for $36. The Leeward Dive Center's specially equipped dive boat, the *Kahanuolo*, departs daily from Wainae Boat Harbor at 8:30 a.m. and returns around 12 noon. They'll pick you up and return you to any Waikiki hotel. The above prices include all equipment and lunch aboard the boat.

Aloha Dive Shop, at Koko Marina (on the way to Hanauma Bay), tel. 395-5922, does it all from snorkeling to boat dives. Excellent rates. **Adventure Dive Hawaii**, tel. 235-4217 or 226-9814, owned and operated by Mark and Midori Imhoof, features introductory shore dives at Hanauma Bay for $50, along with private PADI certification courses for $350. They limit their number of divers to only six people so that the impact on the bay is kept at a minimum while the divers get optimum attention.

Snuba Tours Of Oahu

No that's not a typo. **Snuba**, at 2233 Kalakaua Ave., B-205A, Suite 1271, Honolulu, HI 96815,

Achilles tang (pāku'iku'i)

Hawaiian lionfish

red-lipped parrotfish

Moorish idol

manta ray

mottled moray (pūhi)

Potter's angelfish

REEF FISH

lagoon humu

trumpetfish

uhu

convict tang (manini)

blue-spotted cowfish

*threadfin
butterflyfish*

saddleback wrasse (hīnālea lau-wili)

*bluestripe
butterflyfish*

HAWAIIAN SHELLS

helmet

miter

auger

cone

cowrie

opihi

spindle

by ship's artist Francis Olmsted, circa 1840

tel. 396-6163 or 922-7762, offers a hybrid sport that is half snorkeling and half scuba diving. You have a regulator, a weight belt, mask, and flippers, and you're tethered to scuba tanks that float 20 feet above you on a sea-sled. The unofficial motto of Snuba is "secure but free." The idea is that many people become anxious diving under the waves encumbered by tanks and all the scuba apparatus. Snuba frees you. You would think that being tethered to the sled would slow you down, but actually you're sleeker and can make better time than a normal scuba diver. The sled is made from industrial-strength polyethylene and is 2.5 feet wide by 7.5 feet long, consisting of a view window and a belly in the sled for location of the scuba tank. If you get tired, just surface and use it as a raft. Snuba was invented by Mike Stafford of Placerville, California, as an aid to disabled people who wished to scuba. He got the idea from modern gold miners in the Mother Lode area who set a scuba tank on the side of the riverbank and run an air line down to the water to look for gold nuggets wedged under boulders. The first raft came off the assembly line in 1988.

Mick Riegel, the owner and operator of Snuba of Oahu, is one of the first to open a commercial venture in this newest of underwater sports. Mick and his staff conduct various tours throughout the day, including Snuba at Waikiki, daily 8:30 a.m.-3:30 p.m. on the half hour, $45; and the Snuba Half-Day Adventure, $95 including lunch.

SURFING

Surfing is a sport indigenous to Hawaii. When the white man first arrived he was astonished to see natives paddling out to meet the ships on long carved boards, then gracefully riding them into shore on crests of waves. The Hawaiians called surfing *he'enalu* (to "slide on a wave"). The newcomers were fascinated by this sport, recording it on engravings and woodcuts marvelled at around the world. Meanwhile, the Polynesians left records of surfing as petroglyphs and in *mele* of surfing exploits of times past. A local Waikiki beachboy by the name of Duke Kahanamoku won a treasure box full of gold medals for swimming at the Olympic Games of 1912, and thereafter he became a celebrity who toured the Mainland and introduced surfing to the modern world. Surfing later became a lifestyle, spread far and wide by the songs of the Beach Boys in the '60s. Now surfing is a sport enjoyed around the world, complete with championships, movies, magazines, and advanced board technology.

It takes years of practice to become good, but with determination, good swimming ability, and a sense of balance you can learn the fundamentals in a short time. At surf shops all around the island you can rent a board for very reasonable prices. The boards of the ancient *ali'i* were up to 20 feet long and weighed over 150 pounds, but today's board is made from ultralight foam plastic covered in fiberglass. They're about six feet long and weigh 12 pounds or so. Innovations occur every day in surfing, but one is the changeable "skeg" or rudder allowing you to surf in variable conditions.

The sport of surfing is still male-dominated, but women champions have been around for years. The most famous surfing beaches in the world are Sunset Beach and the Banzai Pipeline on North Shore Oahu. Every year the nationally televised Pro-Tour Surfing Championship is held there, usually in late November and December. It's only a matter of time before surfing becomes an Olympic sport.

One of the most brilliant books ever written on surfing is *Surfing, The Ultimate Pleasure,* by Leonard Lueras and designed by Fred Bechlen. Published by Workman Publishing of New York, a copy can be found at almost every surf shop.

All the Hawaiian islands have incredibly good surfing conditions, but Oahu is best. Conditions here are perfect for rank beginners up to the best in the world. Waikiki's surf is predictable, and just right to start on, while the Banzai Pipeline and Waimea Bay on the North Shore have some of the most formidable surfing conditions on earth. Makaha Beach in Waianae is perhaps the best all-around surfing beach, frequented by "living legends" in this most graceful sport.

If there is such a thing as "the perfect wave," Oahu's waters are a good place to look for it. Summertime brings rather flat wave action all around the island, but the winter months are a totally different story, with monster waves on the North Shore, and heavy surf at times even in the relative calm of Waikiki. *Never* surf without asking about local conditions, and remember that "a fool and his surfboard, and maybe his life, are soon parted." (See "Festivals, Holidays, and Events" for local and international surfing competitions on Oahu.)

Note: For **surfing conditions,** call 836-1952. Heed all warnings!

Surfing Lessons
A number of enterprises in Waikiki offer beach services. Often these concessions are affiliated with hotels, and almost all hotel activities desks can arrange surfing lessons for you. An instructor and board go for about $25 per hour. A board alone is half the price, but as in skiing, a few good lessons to start you off are well worth the time and money. Some reputable surfing lessons along Waikiki are provided by: Outrigger Hotel, 2335 Kalakaua Ave., tel. 923-0711; Hilton Hawaiian Village, 2005 Kalia Rd., tel. 949-4321; Halekulani Hotel, 2199 Kalia Rd., tel. 923-2311; Big Al Surfing School, 2210 Kalia Rd., tel. 923-4375. Also check near the huge rack of surfboards along Kalakaua Ave., just near Kuhio Beach at the Waikiki Beach Center, where you'll find a number of beachboy enterprises at competitive rates. Good ones are Waikiki Beach Services, tel. 924-4941, Beach Boys Inc., tel. 923-0711. In Haleiwa on the North Shore, try Surf and Sea, tel. 637-9887.

WINDSURFING AND BOOGIE BOARDING

The fastest growing water sport, both in Hawaii and around the world, is windsurfing. Technically called sailboarding, most people call this relatively new sport windsurfing, after the name of one of the most famous manufacturers of sailboards. A combination of surfing and sailing, the equipment is a rather large and stable surfboard mounted with a highly maneuverable sail. If it sounds difficult, most people find it slightly easier than surfing because you're mobilized by the wind and not at the mercy of the waves. You don't have to "read" the waves as well as a surfer, and like riding a bicycle, as long as you keep moving, you can hold your balance. Unlike male-dominated surfing, many women also windsurf. Kailua Bay has perfect conditions for this sport, and you can go there any day to see windsurfers skimming the waves with their multihued sails displayed like proud peacocks.

Windsurfing Lessons And Rentals
Far and away the most famous windsurfing beach on Oahu is Kailua Beach Park on the windward coast (see "Kailua and Vicinity—

Hobie Cats at Kealia Beach

Beaches" in the Windward Oahu chapter). Daily, a flotilla of windsurfers glide over its smooth waters, propelled by the always blowing breezes. Along the shore and in town a number of enterprises build, rent, and sell sailboards. There is also windsurfing along the North Shore (see "The North Shore—Shopping and Services" for rentals there). Commercial ventures are allowed to operate along Kailua Beach only on weekdays and weekend mornings, but weekend afternoons and holidays are *kapu!* Here are some of the best.

Kailua Sailboard Company, 130 Kailua Rd., tel. 262-2555, open 8:30 a.m.-5 p.m. daily, is a full-service sailboard store. Rentals are $30 per day (24 hours), half day $25, longer term available. Beginning group lessons are $39 for a three-hour session. During the week they have equipment right at the beach so you don't have to have a car to transport it. Weekends they provide a push cart or a roof rack at no additional charge. They also have boogie boards for $7.50 per day and two-person kayaks at $37.

Naish Hawaii, 155 A Hamakua Dr., tel. 262-6068, open 9-5 daily, are very famous makers of custom boards, production boards, sails, hardware, accessories, and repairs. They also have T-shirts, bathing suits, beach accessories, hats, and slippers primarily for men, but plenty of their fashions would be attractive on women as well. Naish is the largest and oldest windsurfing company in Hawaii. The famous Naish Windsurfing School, located at Kailua Beach, gives half day lessons, which include 90 minutes of personal instruction for $55 including all equipment; $75 for two people.

On the North Shore in Haleiwa, try **Surf and Sea,** tel. 637-9887.

Boogie Boards

If surfing or windsurfing is a bit too much for you, try a boogie board—a foam board about three feet long that you lie on from the waist up. You can get tremendous rides on boogie boards with the help of flippers for maneuverability. You can learn to ride in minutes and it's much faster, easier, and more thrilling than bodysurfing. Boogie boards are for sale all over the island and are relatively cheap. You can rent one from a dive or surf shop for a couple bucks, or buy your own for

$35-70. The most highly acclaimed boogie-boarding beach on Oahu is Sandy Beach. It also has the dubious distinction of being the most dangerous beach in Hawaii, with more drownings, broken backs, and broken necks than anywhere in the state. Waikiki is tame and excellent for boogie boarding, while Waimanalo Beach (see "Southeast Oahu—Waimanalo") is more for the intermediate boarder.

KAYAKS, HOBIES, WATER SKIS, ETC.

The **Windward Boats and Froome Boating Company,** tel. 261-2961, at 789 Kailua Rd., on the corner of Kailua Road and the Pali Hwy. just as you're entering town, rents Hobie Cats, power boats, kayaks and wave skis. Rates are: kayaks and wave skis, half day $25, full day $30, 24 hours $35; Hobies rent from $60 half day to $350 for the week for a 14-footer; a 16-footer is $80 half day, $400 week. Hobie Cat lessons are available.

If you like water-skiing, **Suyderhoud's Water Ski Center,** tel. 395-3773, at the Koko Marina Shopping center, can provide all your equipment, rentals, and lessons. Rates are $49 for two people, skis included, for a half-hour session.

Go Bananas Hawaii, 730 Kapapulu, tel. 737-9514, and at 98-406 Kamehameha Hwy., Pearl City, tel. 484-0606, are into kayaks, wave skis, and water toys. You can go for a guided kayak day tour (by appointment only); kayaks $25 per day, plus $20 per hour for the guide, with a reduced scale for longer periods. The store also sells aqua socks for walking on the reef, books, soaps, sunglasses, and T-shirts.

Twogood Kayaks Hawaii, tel. 262-5656 offers kayaking.

Note: Also see "Windsurfing Lessons And Rentals" above since many of those companies also rent other water equipment.

Hang Gliding, Parasailing And Jet Skis

For a once-in-a-lifetime treat try **Aloha Parasail,** tel. 521-2446. Strapped into a harness complete with lifejacket, you're towed aloft to glide effortlessly over the water. Aloha Parasail has free hotel pickup. Others are: **Big Sky Parasail,** at the Koko Marina Shopping Center, tel.

395-2760; and **Hawaii Kai Parasail,** at the Hawaii Kai Shopping Center, tel. 396-9224.

Sport Aviation of Hawaii, tel. 235-6307, sells hang gliders, but doesn't offer lessons. They will, however, give you a lot of tips on where to fly.

Waikiki Beach Services, tel. 924-4941, rents Jet Skis along Waikiki. Their rates are $45 for one hour, or $70 for two people on one ski for one hour. They also have parasailing; early bird special at 9 a.m. is $36, thereafter it's $45.

OTHER SPORTS

Horseback Riding

A different and delightful way to see Oahu is from the back of a horse. The following are a few outfits operating trail rides on different parts of the island. **Kualoa Ranch,** tel. 237-8515, by reservation only, in Kualoa on north windward Oahu, offers picnic rides into Kaaawa Valley. Hotel pick-up available. At **Turtle Bay Hilton,** tel. 293-8811, on the North Shore, nonguests are welcome; beach rides are offered daily except Monday with sunset rides on the weekends. **Sheraton Makaha Resort,** tel. 695-9511, offers escorted trail rides through Makaha Valley on leeward Oahu, daily except Monday. Hotel pick-up available.

Spectator Sports

Oahu is home to a number of major sporting events throughout the year. Many are "invitationals" that bring the cream of the crop from both collegiate and professional levels (see "Festivals, Holidays, and Events"). Here are the major sports happenings on the island.

Football is big in Hawaii. The University of Hawaii's Rainbows play during the normal collegiate season at Aloha Stadium near Pearl Harbor. In early January, the **Hula Bowl** brings together two all-star teams from the nation's collegiate ranks. You can hear the pads crack in February, when the NFL sends its best players to the **Pro Bowl.**

Basketball is also big on Oahu. The University of Hawaii's Rainbow Warriors play at the **Neal S. Blaisdell Center** in Honolulu at 777 Ward Street. Mid-April sees some of the nation's best collegiate hoopballers make up four

teams to compete in the **Aloha Basketball Classic.**

You can watch the Islanders of the Pacific Coast League play **baseball** during the regular season at Aloha Stadium. Baseball goes back well over 100 years in Hawaii, and the Islanders receive extraordinary fan support.

Watersport festivals include surfing events, usually from November through February. The best-known are: the **Hawaiian Pro Surfing Championships;** the **Duke Kahanamoku Classic; Buffalo's Big Board Classic;** and the **Haleiwa Sea Spree,** featuring many ancient Hawaiian sports. You can watch some of the Pacific's most magnificent yachts sail into the **Ala Wai Yacht Basin** in mid-July, completing their run from Los Angeles in the annual **Trans Pacific Yacht Race.**

GONE FISHING

Hawaii has some of the most exciting and productive "blue waters" in all the world. You'll find a statewide sport-fishing fleet made up of skippers and crews who are experienced professional anglers. You can also fish from jetties, piers, rocks, and shore. If rod and reel don't strike your fancy, try the old-fashioned throw net, or take along a spear when you go snorkeling or scuba diving. There's nighttime torch fishing that requires special skills and equipment, and freshwater fishing in public areas. Streams and irrigation ditches yield introduced trout, bass, and catfish. While you're at it, you might want to try crabbing for Kona and Samoan crabs, or working low-tide areas after sundown, hunting octopus, a tantalizing island delicacy. See the "Hawaiian Game Fish" chart in the "Food and Drink" section.

Deep-sea Fishing

Most game-fishing boats work the blue waters on the calmer leeward sides of the islands. Some skippers, carrying anglers who are accustomed to the sea, will also work the much rougher windward coasts and island channels where the fish bite just as well. Trolling is the preferred method of deep-sea fishing; this is done usually in depths of 1,000-2,000 fathoms (a fathom is six feet). The skipper will either "area fish," which means running in a crisscrossing pattern over a known productive area, or "ledge fish," which involves trolling over submerged ledges where the game fish are known to feed. The most advanced marine technology, available on many boats, sends sonar bleeps searching for fish. On deck, the crew and anglers scan the horizon in the age-old Hawaiian tradition—searching for seabirds clustered in an area, feeding on the very baitfish pursued to the surface by the huge and aggressive game fish. "Still fishing," or "bottom fishing" with hand lines, yields some tremendous fish.

One of the most famous fishing spots in Hawaii is **Penguin Banks** off the west coast of Molokai and the south coast of Oahu. "Chicken Farm" at the southern tip of the Penguin Banks is great trolling waters for marlin and mahimahi. The calm waters off the Waianae coast of Oahu, from Barber's Point to Kaena Point, yield marlin and *ahi*.

Charter Boats

The charter boats of Hawaii come in all shapes and sizes, but they are all manned by professional, competent crews and captains intimately knowledgeable of Hawaiian waters. Approximate rates are: private, full day $400-600, half day $250-350; share, full day $125, half day $85. Full days are eight hours, half days four, with three-quarter days and overnighters available too. No licenses are required. All tackle from 30 to 130 pounds is carried on the boats and is part of the service. Oftentimes soft drinks are supplied, but usually you carry your own lunch.

It is customary for the crew to be given any fish that are caught, but naturally this doesn't apply to trophy fish; the crew is also glad to cut off some steaks and fillets for your personal use. Honolulu's Kewalo Basin, only a few minutes from Waikiki, has the largest fleet of charter boats. Pokai Bay also has a fleet, and many charter boats sail out of Kaneohe Bay.

The vast majority of Oahu's fleet moors in **Kewalo Basin,** in Honolulu Harbor along Ala Moana Boulevard next to Fishermen's Wharf. The boat harbor is a sight in itself, and if you're contemplating a fishing trip, it's best to head down there the day before and yarn with the captains and returning fishermen. This way you can get a feel for a charter to suit you best.

Charter organizations include: **Island Charters,** tel. 536-1555; and **Ocean Fishing Adventures,** tel. 487-9060. Many private boats operating out of Kewalo Basin include: *Alii Kai,* tel. 521-3969; *Fish Hawk,* tel. 531-8338; *Sea Verse,* tel. 521-8829; and **E.L.O. Sport Fishing,** tel. 947-5208.

A few boats operate out of **Pokai Bay,** in Waianae on the northern leeward coast, and there are even a few berthed in Haleiwa on the North Shore.

The Game Fish

The most thrilling game fish in Hawaiian waters is marlin, generically known as "billfish" or *a'u* to the locals. The king of them is the blue marlin, with record catches well over 1,000 pounds. There're also striped marlin and sailfish, which often go over 200 pounds. The best times for marlin are during spring, summer, and fall. The fishing tapers off in January and picks up again by late February. "Blues" can be caught year-round, but, oddly enough, when they stop biting it seems as though the striped marlin pick up. Second to the marlin are tuna. *Ahi* (yellowfin tuna) are caught in Hawaiian waters of depths of 100-1,000 fathoms. They can weigh 300 pounds, but between 25 and 100 pounds is common. There's also *aku* (skipjack tuna) and the delicious *ono,* which average between 20 and 40 pounds.

Mahimahi is another strong, fighting, deep-water game fish abundant in Hawaii. These delicious fish can weigh up to 70 pounds. Shore fishing and baitcasting yield *papio,* a jack tuna. *Akule,* a scad (locally called *halalu*), is a smallish schooling fish that comes close to shore and is great to catch on light tackle. *Ulua* are shore fish and can be found in tidepools. They're excellent eating, average two to three pounds, and are taken at night or with spears.

O'io are bonefish that come close to shore to spawn. They're caught by baitcasting and bottom fishing with cut bait. They're bony, but they're a favorite for fish cakes and *poki. Awa* is a schooling fish that loves brackish water. It can get up to three feet long, and is a good fighter. A favorite for throw netters, it's even raised commercially in fishponds. Besides these there are plenty of goatfish, mullet, mackerel, snapper, various sharks, and even salmon. See also the "Hawaiian Game Fish" chart in the "Food and Drink" section.

Freshwater Fishing

Due to Hawaii's unique geology, only a handful of natural lakes and rivers are good for fishing. The state maintains two public freshwater fishing areas on Oahu. The **Wahiawa Public Fishing Area** is 300 acres of fishable waters in and around the town of Wahiawa. It's basically an irrigation reservoir used to hold water for cane fields. Species regularly caught here are large and smallmouth bass, sunfish, channel catfish, *tucunare,* oscar, carp, snakehead, and Chinese catfish. The other area is the **Nuuanu Reservoir no. 4,** a 25-acre restricted watershed above Honolulu in the Koolau Mountains. It's open for fishing only three times per year in May, August, and November. Fish caught here are tilapia and Chinese catfish.

Hawaii has only one native freshwater game fish, the *o'opu.* This gobie is an oddball with fused ventral fins. They grow to be 12 inches and are found on all islands, especially Kauai. Introduced species include largemouth and smallmouth bass, bluegills, catfish, *tucunare,* oscar, carp, and tilapia. The only trout to survive is the rainbow, found only in the streams of Kauai. The *tucunare* is a tough, fighting, good-tasting game fish introduced from South America, similar to the oscar, from the same region. Both have been compared to bass, but are of a different family.

Tilapia are from Africa and have become common in Hawaii's irrigation ditches. They're "mouth breeders" and the young will take refuge in their parents' protective jaws even a few weeks after hatching. Snakehead are eel-like fish that inhabit the reservoirs and are great fighters. Channel catfish can grow to over 20 pounds and bite best after sundown. There're also carp, and with their broad tail and tremendous strength, they're the poor man's game-fish. All of these species are best caught with light spinning tackle, or with a bamboo pole and a trusty old worm.

Fishing Rules

Fishing licenses (freshwater needed only) are good July 1-June 30. Licenses cost $7.50 for nonresidents, $3.50 for tourists (good for 30 days), $3.75 for residents and military personnel, $1.50 for children ages 9-15; they are free to senior citizens. Licenses are obtained from the

FRESHWATER FISH

tilapia

tucunare

Chinese catfish

oscar

Division of Conservation and Resources Enforcement (Oahu, tel. 548-8766) or from most sporting goods stores. For free booklets and information write Division of Aquatic Resources, 1151 Punchbowl St., Honolulu, HI 96813. All game fish may be taken year-round, except trout. Trout may only be taken on Kauai, and only for 16 days commencing on the first Saturday of August. Thereafter, for the remainder of August and September, trout can be taken only on Saturday, Sunday, and state holidays.

HUNTING

Most people don't think of Hawaii as a place for hunting, but actually it's quite good. Seven species of introduced game animals are regularly hunted, as well as 16 species of game birds. Not all species of game animals are open on all islands, but every island offers hunting. Please refer to "Sports" in the travel chapters for full details on hunting in particular areas on the island of Oahu.

General Hunting Rules

Hunting licenses are mandatory to hunt on public, private, or military land anywhere in Hawaii. They're good for one year beginning July 1, and cost $7.50 residents, $15 nonresidents, senior citizens free. Licenses are available from sporting goods stores and from the various offices of the Division of Forestry and Wildlife (information follows). This government organization also sets and enforces the rules, so contact them with any questions. Generally hunting hours are from a half hour before sunrise to a half hour after sunset. At times, there are "checking stations," where the hunter must check in before and after hunting.

Rifles must have greater than a 1,200-foot-pound muzzle velocity. Shotguns larger than .20 gauge are allowed, and muzzleloaders must have a .45 caliber bore or larger. Bows must have a minimum draw of 45 pounds for straight bows and 30 pounds for compounds. Arrows must be broadheads. Dogs are permitted only with some birds and game, and smaller caliber rifles and shotguns are permitted with their use, along with spears and knives. Hunters must wear orange safety cloth on front and back no smaller than a 12-inch square. Certain big-game species are hunted only by lottery selection; contact the Division of Forestry and Wildlife two months in advance. Guide service is not mandatory, but is advised if you're unfamiliar with hunting in Hawaii. You can hunt on private land only with permission, and you must possess a valid hunting license. Guns and ammunition brought into Hawaii must be registered with the chief of police of the corresponding county within 48 hours of arrival.

Information

Hunting rules and regulations are always subject to change. Also, environmental considerations often change bag limits and seasons. Make sure to check with the Division of Forestry and Wildlife for the most current information. Request "Rules Regulating Game Bird Hunting, Field Trials and Commercial Shooting Preserves," "Rules Regulating Game Mammal Hunting," and "Hunting in Hawaii." Direct inquiries to: Dept. of Land and Natural Resources, Division of Forestry and Wildlife Office, 1151 Punchbowl St., Honolulu, HI 96813, tel. 548-2861; on Maui, 54 S. High St., P.O. Box 1015, Wailuku, 96793, tel. 244-4352; on Hawaii, P.O. Box 4849, Hilo 96720, tel. 961-7221; on Lanai, 338 8th St., Lanai City 96763, tel. 565-6688; on Kauai, 3060 Eiwa St., P.O. Box 1671, Lihue 96766, tel. 245-4444; on Molokai, Puu Kapeelua Ave., Hoolehua 96729, tel. 553-5415.

Game Animals

All game animals on Hawaii have been introduced. Some are adapting admirably and becoming well entrenched, while the existence of others is still precarious. **Axis deer** originated in India and were brought to Lanai and Molokai, where they're doing well. The small herd on Maui is holding its own. Their unique flavor makes them one of the best wild meats, and they're hunted on Molokai and Lanai in March and April, by public lottery. **Feral pigs** are escaped domestic pigs that have gone wild and are found on all islands except Lanai. The stock is a mixture of original Polynesian pigs and all that came later. Hunted with dogs and usually killed with a spear or long knife, pig hunting is not recommended for the timid or tenderhearted. These beasts' four-inch tusks and fighting spirit make them tough and dangerous. **Feral goats** come in a variety of colors. Found on all islands

feral pig

LOUISE FOOTE

Gambel's quail

except Lanai, they have been known to cause erosion and are considered a pest in some areas, especially on Haleakala. Openly hunted on all islands, their meat when prepared properly is considered delicious.

Black-tailed deer come from the Rocky Mountains. Forty were released on Kauai in 1961; the herd is now stabilized at around 400 and they're hunted in October by public lottery. **Mouflon sheep** are native to Corsica and Sardinia. They do well on Lanai and on the windswept slopes of Mauna Loa and Mauna Kea, where they're hunt-

ed at various times by public lottery. **Feral sheep** haunt the slopes of Mauna Kea and Mauna Loa from 7,000 to 12,000 feet. They travel in flocks and destroy vegetation. It takes determination and a good set of lungs to bag one, especially with a bow and arrow. **Pronghorn** on Lanai, **feral cattle** on the Big Island, and **rock wallaby**, from Australia, who now make their home on Oahu, are not hunted.

Game Birds

A number of game birds are found on most of the islands. Bag limits and hunting seasons vary, so check with the Division of Forestry and Wildlife for details. **Ring-necked pheasant** are one of the best game birds, and found on all the islands. The **kalij pheasant** from Nepal is found only on the Big Island, where the **green pheasant** is also prevalent; some are found on Oahu and Maui. **Francolins**, gray and black, from India and the Sudan, are similar to partridges. They are hunted on all islands with dogs and are great roasted. There are also **chukar** from Tibet, found on the slopes of all islands; a number of **quail**, including the **Japanese and California** varieties; **doves;** and the **wild Rio Grande turkey**, which is found on all islands except Kauai and Oahu, although a few of the "featherless variety" have been known to walk the streets of Waikiki.

Feral goats have overpopulated and become pests. They roam from coast to mountaintop, depleting vegetation and causing considerable erosion.

LOUISE FOOTE

LOUISE FOOTE

ARTS AND CRAFTS

Referring to Hawaii as "paradise" is about as hackneyed as you can get, but when you combine it into "artists' paradise" it's the absolute truth. Something about the place evokes art (or at least personal expression) from most people. The islands are like a magnet: they not only draw artists to them, but they draw art *from* the artists. The list of literary figures who have visited Hawaii and had something inspirational to say reads like a freshman survey in literature: William Henry Dana, Herman Melville, Mark Twain, Robert Louis Stevenson, Jack London, Somerset Maugham, Joaquin Miller, and of course, James Michener.

The inspiration comes from the astounding natural surroundings. The land is so beautiful yet so raw; the ocean's power and rhythm is primal and ever-present; the riotous colors of flowers and fruit leap from the deep-green jungle background. Crystal water beads and pale mists turn the mountains into mystic temples, while rainbows come riding on the crests of waves. The stunning variety of faces begging to be rendered appears as if all the world sent a local delegation to the islands. And in most cases it did! Inspiration is everywhere, as is art, good or bad.

Sometimes the artwork is overpowering in itself and in its sheer volume. Though geared to the tourist's market of cheap souvenirs, there is hardly a shop in Hawaii that doesn't sell some item that falls into the general category of "art." You can find everything from carved monkey-face coconut shells to true masterpieces. The Polynesian Hawaiians were master craftsmen, and their legacy still lives in a wide variety of woodcarvings, basketry, and weavings. The hula is art in swaying motion, and the true form is rigorously studied and taken very seriously. There is hardly a resort area that doesn't offer the "bump and grind" tourist's hula and even these revues are accompanied by proficient local musicians. Nightclubs offer "slack key" balladeers and island music made on ukuleles, and Hawaii's own steel guitars spill from many lounges.

Vibrant fabrics, which catch the spirit of the islands, are rendered into muumuu and aloha shirts at countless local factories. They're almost a mandatory purchase! Pottery, heavily influenced by the Japanese, is well developed at numerous kilns. Local artisans fashion delicate jewelry from coral and olivine, while some ply the whaler's legacy of etching on ivory, called scrimshaw. There is a fine tradition of quilt-making, flower art in lei, and street artists working in everything from airbrush to glass. The following is an overview; for local offerings please see "Shopping" in each of the travel chapters.

ARTS OF OLD HAWAII

Since everything in old Hawaii had to be fashioned by hand, almost every object was either a work of art or at least a highly refined craft. With the "civilizing" of the natives, most of the "old ways" disappeared, including the old arts and crafts. Most authentic Hawaiian art exists only in museums, but with the resurgence of Hawaiian *roots,* many old arts are being revitalized, and a few artists are becoming proficient.

Magnificent Canoes

The most respected artisans in old Hawaii were the canoe makers. With little more than a stone adze and a pump drill, they built canoes that could carry 200 people and last for generations—sleek, well proportioned, and infinitely seaworthy. The main hull was usually a gigantic koa log, and the gunwale planks were minutely drilled and sewn to the sides with sennit rope. Apprenticeships lasted for years, and a young man knew that he had graduated when one day he was nonchalantly asked to sit down and eat with the master builders. Small family-sized canoes with outriggers were used for fishing, and perhaps carried a spear rack; large oceangoing double-hulled canoes were used for migration and warfare. On these, the giant logs had been adzed to about two inches thick. A mainsail woven from pandanus was mounted on a central platform, and the boat was steered by two long paddles. The hull was dyed with plant juices and charcoal, and the entire village helped launch the canoe in a ceremony called "drinking the sea."

carvings and weavings of old Hawaii

HAWAII STATE ARCHIVES

Carving And Weaving

Wood was a primary material, and craftsmen turned out well-proportioned and distinctive calabashes. Made mostly from koa, the luster and intricate grain was brought out with hand rubbing. Temple idols were a major product of woodcarving, and a variety of stone artifacts, including poi pounders, mirrors, fish sinkers, and small idols were turned out.

Hawaiians became the *best* basket makers and mat weavers in all of Polynesia. *Ulana* (mats) were made from *lau hala* (pandanus) leaves. Once split, the spine was removed and the leaves stored in large rolls. When needed they were soaked, pounded, and then fashioned into various floor coverings and sleeping mats. Intricate geometrical patterns were woven in, and the edges were rolled and well fashioned. Coconut palms were not used to make mats in old Hawaii, but a wide variety of basketry was made from the aerial root, *ie'ie*. The shapes varied according to use. Some were tall and narrow, some were cones, others were flat like trays, while many were woven around gourds and calabashes.

A strong tradition of weaving and carving has survived in Hawaii, and the time-tested material of *lau hala* is still the best, although much is now made from coconut fronds. You can purchase anything from beach mats to a woven hat and all share the qualities of strength, lightness, and air flow.

Feather Work

This highly refined art was only found on the islands of Tahiti, New Zealand, and Hawaii, while the fashioning of feather helmets and idols was unique to Hawaii alone. Favorite colors were red and yellow, which came only in a very limited number on a few birds such as the *o'o, i'iwi, mamo,* and *apapane.* Professional bird hunters in old Hawaii paid their taxes to *ali'i* in prized feathers. The feathers were fastened to a woven net of *olona* cord and made into helmets, idols, and beautiful flowing capes and cloaks. These resplendent garments were made and worn only by men, especially during battle when a fine cloak became a great trophy of war. Featherwork was also employed in the making of *kahili* and lei, which were highly prized by the noble *ali'i* women.

Tapa Cloth

Tapa, cloth made from tree bark, was common throughout Polynesia and was a woman's art. A few trees such as the *wauke* and *mamaki* produced the best cloth, but a variety of other barks could be utilized. First the raw bark was pounded into a feltlike pulp and beaten together to form strips. The beaters had distinctive patterns that also helped to make the cloth supple. They were then decorated by stamping, using a form of block printing, and dyed with natural colors from plants and sea animals, in shades of gray, purple, pink, and red. They were even painted with natural brushes made from pandanus fruit, with an overall gray color made from charcoal. The tapa cloth was sewn together to make bed coverings, and fragrant flowers and herbs were either sewn or pounded in to produce a permanent fragrance. Tapa cloth is still available today, but the Hawaiian methods have been lost, and most comes from other areas of Polynesia.

First Western Artists

When Captain Cook made first contact in 1778, the ship's artists immediately began recording things Hawaiian. John Webber and James Clevely made etchings and pen-and-ink drawings of Hawaiian people, structures, *heiau* and everyday occurrences that struck them as noteworthy or peculiar. William Ellis, ship's surgeon, also a fair hand at etching, was attracted to portraying native architecture. These three left a priceless and faithful record of what Hawaii was like at the moment of contact. Louis Choris, ship's artist with Otto Von Kotzebue in 1816, painted early portraits of King Kamehameha and Queen Kaahumanu, the two grandest figures in Hawaii's history. Jacques Arago, aboard the *Uranie* with the French Captain de Freycinet in 1819, recorded some gruesome customs of punishment of *kapu* breakers, and made many drawings of island people. Robert Dampier, who sailed on the *Blonde,* the ship that returned King Liholiho's body from England, recorded one of the earliest landscapes of Honolulu, a site which has continued to be depicted on film by more tourists than almost any other city on earth. These early artists merely set a trend that continues unabated to this day; artists endeavour to "capture" Hawaii, and they do so with every artistic medium available.

Modern Masters

Countless artists working at all levels of accomplishment try to match their skills to the vigor and beauty of the islands. Some have set the standards, and their names have become synonymous with Hawaiian art. Heading this list of luminaries are Huc Luquiens, Madge Tennent, Tadashi Sato, Jean Charlot, and John Kelly. Madge Tennent (1889-1972) was an Englishwoman who came to Hawaii via Samoa after spending years in South Africa and New Zealand. She worked in oils that she applied liberally and in bold strokes. Enamored with the people of Hawaii, her portraits are of a race striking in appearance and noble in character. Her works, along with those of other island artists, are displayed at the Tennent Art Foundation, on the slopes of Punchbowl on Oahu.

Huc Luquiens, former chairman of the Art Department at the University of Hawaii, was a master at etching, and was especially accomplished in dry point. His works, mainly island landscapes, are displayed in the Hawaiiana Collection of the Honolulu Academy of Arts. Maui-born Tadashi Sato, a superbly accomplished muralist, has produced such famous mosaics as the 30-foot *Aquarius* at the State Capitol in Honolulu, and the 60-foot *Portals of Immortality* at the Maui Memorial Gymnasium in Lahaina.

Frenchman Jean Charlot perfected his mural art in Mexico before coming to Hawaii in 1949. He is renowned for his frescoes and became a well-known art critic and the grand old man of Hawaiian art. He died in 1979 at the ripe old age of 90. John M. Kelly was in love with Hawaiian women; his etchings of them are both inspired and technically flawless. Kelly was infinitely patient, rendering his subjects in the minutest detail.

These artists are the "Big Five of Hawaiian Art"; their accomplishments should be seen as an "artistic gauge" of what Hawaii can inspire in an artist. By observing their works you can get an instant "art course" and a comparative view of the state of the arts in Hawaii.

LOUISE FOOTE

short feather capes for men of rank

Contemporary Artists

The crop of new artists making their mark always seems to be bounteous, and their works, heavily influenced by the "feeling of Hawaii," continue to be superb. The following list of artists, with a short description of their work, is by no means exhaustive. It merely shows the wide range of artwork available.

Richard Fields, a former Californian, now lives on Maui. The fascinating beauty of the *aina* is his inspiration that he depicts in his supra-realistic paintings of birds, mountains, clouds, flowers, and waterfalls. Richard creates his rich renditions using a mixed media of airbrush, acrylic, india ink, and stencils. His works are as striking and as inspiring as the ever-changing beauty of the islands.

Robert Nelson is a Maui artist who superbly transmits the integrated mystical life of land and sea. His watercolors are often diffused with the strange filtered light found beneath the waves. A conservationist, he has often depicted the gentle frolicking life of the whales that visit Hawaiian waters.

Bill Christian is a master of scrimshaw, which he renders on slate. He also produces fine oil paintings of the sea and old salts. A world-class artist, his works are displayed at art galleries on Maui as well as in the Smithsonian and the New Bedford Massachusetts Whaling Museum.

Pegge Hopper is often compared with Madge Tennent. She works in bold colors and strokes. Her subject matter is islanders, especially the delicacy and inner strength of women. Her works are displayed at various galleries, especially on Maui and Oahu, and are often available in limited-edition serigraphs.

John Costello, an Oahu artist, specializes in pointillism to capture the waves, women, and flora of Hawaii in a sensitive and mystical way. He co-owns and operates Kaala Art and Rainbow Island T's with his brother, Jim, in Haleiwa on North Shore Oahu. John's work as well as local artists' are showcased in their small shop.

Alapai Hanapi is a traditionalist sculptor who tries to recreate the motifs of his Hawaiian ancestors. He works in wood and stone with tools that he fashions himself. His driving force is "cultural awareness" and through his art he tells of the old ways. He lives simply with his wife

Hawaiian maiden by John Costello

and three daughters near an old fishpond on eastern Molokai. His work is known for its simplicity and is available at art shows periodically held throughout the islands.

Al Furtado is a freelance artist working in Honolulu. He specializes in capturing the movement of Hawaiian dance. His depictions are often larger than life with a strong sense of vitality and motion.

The following is a potpourri of other distinguished artists displayed at various galleries around the islands. Any work bearing their name is authentic island art considered to be superior by fellow artists. William Waterfall, photographer (see "Honolulu—Shopping"); Satoru Abe, sculptor; Ruthadell Anderson, weaver; Betty Tseng Yu-ho Ecke, *dsui* painter; Claude Horan, sculptor, ceramics; Erica Karawina, stained glass; Ron Kowalke, painter; Ben Norris, painter; Louis Pohl, printmaker; Mamoru Sato, sculptor; Reuben Tam, painter; Jean Williams, weaver; John Wisnosky, painter; John Young, painter.

ART INFORMATION

This section includes the names and addresses of guilds, centers, and organizations that dispense information on Hawaiian arts and crafts.

Arts Council of Hawaii, P.O. Box 50225, Honolulu, HI 96850, tel. 524-7120; Karl Ichida, executive director. A citizens' advocacy group for the arts providing technical assistance and information to individuals and groups. Publishes the *Cultural Climate,* a newsletter covering what's happening in the arts of Hawaii. Includes a calendar of events, feature articles, and editorials. Membership fee, $15, includes newsletter; nonmembers, 50 cents per issue.

Bishop Museum, 1525 Bernice St., Honolulu, HI 96819, tel. 847-3511. The world's *best* museum covering Polynesia and Hawaii. Exhibits, galleries, archives, demonstrations of Hawaiian crafts, and a planetarium. On the premises, Shop Pacifica has a complete selection of books and publications on all aspects of Hawaiian art and culture. Shouldn't be missed.

Contemporary Arts Center, 605 Kapiolani Blvd., Honolulu, HI 96813, tel. 525-8047. Promotes public awareness of contemporary art by providing gallery space, publicity, and exposure for local artists. Also houses a permanent collection and monthly exhibitions.

East Hawaii Cultural Council, P.O. Box 1312, Hilo, HI 96721. Publishes the *The Center Newspaper,* a monthly newsletter of what's happening artistically and culturally primarily on the Big Island. Includes a good monthly calendar of events with listings from exhibit openings to movies.

East-West Center Culture Learning Institute, Burns Hall 4076, 1777 East-West Rd., Honolulu, HI 96848, tel. 944-7691. At University of Hawaii campus. Dedicated to the sharing, exhibiting, and appreciation of arts, culture and crafts from throughout Asia and the Western world. Their bimonthly *Centerviews* includes an events calendar and topical editorials on the Pacific. Free.

East-West Journal, 1633 Kapiolani Blvd., Honolulu, HI 96814. Yearly guide to exhibition galleries featuring the work of locally renowned artists.

Hawaii Craftsmen, P.O. Box 22145, Honolulu, HI 96823, tel. 523-1974. Increases awareness of Hawaiian crafts through programs, exhibitions, workshops, lectures, and demonstrations.

Honolulu Academy of Arts, 900 S. Beretania St., Honolulu, HI 96814, tel. 532-8700. Collects, preserves and exhibits works of art. Offers public art education programs related to their collections. Also offers tours, classes, lectures, films, and a variety of publications.

Honolulu Symphony Society, 1000 Bishop St., Honolulu, HI 96813, tel. 537-6171. Provides professional-level music, primarily symphonic concerts.

Pacific Handcrafters Guild, P.O. Box 15491, Honolulu, HI 96818, tel. 538-7227. Focuses on developing and preserving handicrafts in Hawaii and the Pacific. They sponsor three major crafts fairs annually.

State Foundation on Culture and the Arts, 335 Merchant St., Room 202, Honolulu, HI 96813, tel. 586-0300. Began by state legislature in 1965 to preserve Hawaii's diverse cultural and artistic heritage. Publishes *Hawaii Cultural Resource Directory,* which lists most of the art organizations, galleries, councils, co-ops, and guilds throughout Hawaii. Very complete.

University of Hawaii at Manoa Art Gallery, 2535 The Mall, Honolulu, HI 96822, tel. 948-6888. Showcases contemporary artwork. Theme changes periodically.

ARTS TO BUY

Wild Hawaiian shirts or bright muumuu, especially when worn on the Mainland, have the magical effect of making wearers "feel" like they're in Hawaii, while at the same time eliciting spontaneous smiles from passersby. Maybe it's the colors, or perhaps it's just the "vibe" that signifies "party time" or "hang loose," but nothing says Hawaii like alohawear does. There are more than a dozen fabric houses in Hawaii turning out distinctive patterns, and many dozens of factories creating their own personalized designs. Oftentimes these factories have attached retail outlets, but in any case you can find hundreds of shops selling alohawear. Aloha shirts were the brilliant idea of a Chinese merchant in Honolulu, who used to hand-tailor them and sell them to the tourists who arrived by ship in the glory days before WW II. They were an instant success. Muumuu or "Mother Hubbards" were the idea of missionaries, who were appalled by Hawaiian women running about au naturel and insisted on covering their new Christian converts from head to foot. Now the roles are reversed, and it's Mainlanders who come to Hawaii and immediately strip down to as little clothing as possible.

Alohawear

At one time exclusively made of cotton, or from manmade yet naturally based rayon, these materials were and still are the best for any tropical clothing. Beware, however: polyester has slowly crept into the market! No material could possibly be worse than polyester for the island climate, so when buying your alohawear make sure to check the label for material content. Muumuu now come in various styles and can be worn for the entire spectrum of social occasions in Hawaii. Aloha shirts are still basically cut the same as always, but the patterns have undergone changes, and apart from the original flowers and ferns, modern shirts might depict an island scene, giving the impression of a silkscreen painting. A basic good-quality muumuu or aloha shirt starts at about $25 and is guaranteed to be worth its price in good times and happy smiles. The connoisseur might want to purchase *The Hawaiian Shirt, Its Art and History,* by R. Thomas Steele. It's illustrated with more than 150 shirts that are now considered works of art by collectors the world over.

Scrimshaw

This art of etching and carving on bone and ivory has become an island tradition handed down from the times of the old whaling ships. Although scrimshaw can be found throughout Hawaii, the center remains in the old whaling capital of Lahaina. Here along Front Street are numerous shops specializing in scrimshaw. Today, pieces are carved on fossilized walrus

scrimshaw

BOB RACE

ivory that is gathered by Inuit and shipped to Hawaii. It comes in a variety of shades from pure white to mocha, depending upon the mineral content of the earth in which it was buried. Elephant ivory or whale bone is no longer used because of ecological considerations, but there is a "gray market" in Pacific walrus tusks. Inuit can legally hunt the walrus. They then make a few minimal scratches on the tusks, which technically qualifies them to be "Native American art," and free of most governmental restrictions. The tusks are then sent to Hawaii as art objects, but the superficial scratches are immediately removed and the ivory is reworked by artisans. Scrimshaw is made into everything from belt buckles to delicate earrings and even into coffee-table centerpieces. The prices can go from a few dollars up into the thousands.

Woodcarvings

One Hawaiian art that has not died out is woodcarving. This art was extremely well developed among the old Hawaiians and they almost exclusively used koa because of its density, strength, and natural luster. It was turned into canoes, woodware, and furniture for the ali'i. Koa is becoming increasingly scarce, but many items are still available, though costly. Milo and monkeypod are also excellent woods for carving and have largely replaced koa. You can buy tikis, bowls, and furniture at numerous shops. Countless inexpensive carved items are sold at variety stores, such as little hula girls or salad servers, but most of these are imported from Asia or the Philippines and can be bought at any variety store.

Weaving

The minute you arrive in Hawaii you should shell out $2 for a woven beach mat. This is a necessity, not a frivolous purchase, but it definitely won't have been made in Hawaii. What is made in Hawaii is *lau hala*. This is traditional Hawaiian weaving from the leaves (*lau*) of the pandanus (*hala*) tree. These leaves vary greatly in length, with the largest over six feet, and they have a thorny spine that must be removed before they can be worked. The color ranges from light tan to dark brown. The leaves are cut into strips from one-eighth to one inch wide and are then employed in weaving. Any variety of items can be made or at least covered in *lau hala*. It makes great purses, mats, baskets, and table mats.

Woven into a hat, it's absolutely superb but should not be confused with a palm-frond hat. A *lau hala* hat is amazingly supple and even when squashed will pop back into shape. A good one is expensive ($25) and with proper care will last for years. All *lau hala* should be given a light application of mineral oil on a monthly basis, especially if it's exposed to the sun. For flat items, iron over a damp cloth and keep purses and baskets stuffed with paper when not in use. Palm fronds also are widely used in weaving. They, too, are a great natural raw material, but not as good as *lau hala*. Almost any item, such as a beach bag, woven from palm makes a good authentic yet inexpensive gift or souvenir, and many varieties are available in countless shops.

Gift Items

Jewelry is always an appreciated gift, especially if it's distinctive, and Hawaii has some of the most original. The sea provides the basic raw materials of pink, gold, and black coral, and it's so beautiful that it holds the same fascination as gemstones. Harvesting the coral is very dangerous work. The Lahaina beds off Maui have one of the best black coral lodes in the islands, but unlike reef coral these trees grow at depths bordering the outer limits of a scuba diver's capabilities. Only the best can dive 180 feet after the black coral, and about one diver per year dies in pursuit of it. Conservationists have placed great pressure on the harvesters of these deep corals, and the state of Hawaii has placed strict limits and guidelines on the firms and divers involved.

Pink coral has long been treasured by man. The Greeks considered it a talisman for good health, and there's even evidence that it has been coveted since the Stone Age. Coral jewelry is on sale at many shops throughout Hawaii, and the value comes from the color of the coral and the workmanship.

Puka (shells with little naturally occurring holes) and *opihi* shells are also made into jewelry. Many times these items are very inexpensive, yet they are authentic and great purchases for the price. Hanging macrame planters festooned with seashells are usually quite affordable and sold at roadside stands along with shells.

Hawaii produces some unique food items that are appreciated by most people. Various-sized jars of macadamia nuts and butters are great gifts, as are tins of rich, gourmet-quality Kona coffee, the only coffee produced in the United States. Guava, pineapple, passion fruit, and mango are often gift-boxed into assort-ments of jams, jellies, and spicy chutneys. And for that special person in your life, you can bring home island fragrances in bottles of perfumes and colognes in the exotic odors of gardenia, plumeria, and even ginger. All of the above items are reasonably priced, lightweight, and easy to carry.

HULA AND LEI

Hawaiian hula was never performed in grass skirts; tapa or ti-leaf skirts were worn. Grass skirts came to Hawaii from the Gilbert Islands, so if you see grass or cellophane skirts in a "hula revue," you'll know that it's not traditional. Hula, like all artforms, has its own highly specialized techniques. A dancer has to learn how to control every part of his or her body, including the facial expressions, which become very important and help to set the mood. The hands are extremely important and provide instant background scenery. For example, if the hands are thrust outwardly in an aggressive manner, this can be a battle; if they sway gently overhead, they refer to the gods or the early time of creation. They can easily become rain or clouds or the sun, sea, or moon. You must watch the hands to get the gist of the story, but the best comeback to this advice was the classic wisecrack, "You watch the parts you like, and I'll watch the parts I like."

Swaying hips, depending upon their motion, can be a long walk, a canoe ride, or sexual in-tercourse. The foot motion can portray a bat-tle, a walk, or any kind of movement or con-veyance. The overall effect is multidirectional synchronized movement.

The correct chanting of the *mele* is an integral part of the performance. These story-chants, combined with the various musical instruments that accompany the dance, make the hula very

much like opera, and are especially similar in the way the tale is unfolded.

Language Of The Lei

Every major island of Hawaii is symbolized by its own lei, made from a distinctive flower, shell, or fern. Each island has its own official color as well, which doesn't necessarily correspond to the color of the island's lei. Oahu, "The Gather-ing Place," is symbolized by yellow, the color of the tropical sun. Its flower is the delicate *ilima*, which resembles hibiscus and ranges in color from pastel yellow to a burnt orange. The blooms are about as large as a silver dollar and lei made from *ilima* were at one time reserved only for the *ali'i*, designating them as a royal flower.

THAT GOOD OLD ISLAND MUSIC

The missionaries usually take a beating when it's recounted how much Hawaiian culture they de-stroyed while civilizing the natives. However, they seemed to have done one thing right. They

man from the Sandwich Islands dancing

HAWAIIAN LEI

plumeria

crown

fern

ilima

lau hala

DIANA LASICH HARPER

taught the Hawaiians the diatonic musical scale and immediately opened a door filled with latent and superbly harmonious talent. The Hawaiians' chants, though sonorous, were repetitive; the emphasis was placed on historical accuracy and not on "making music." The Hawaiians, in short, didn't *sing* in the manner that Europeans did. But within a few years of the missionaries' arrival, they were belting out good old Christian hymns and one of their favorite pastimes became group and individual singing.

Early in the 1800s, Spanish *vaqueros* from California were imported to teach the Hawaiians how to be cowboys. With them came guitars and moody ballads. The Hawaiian *paniolos* (cowboys) quickly learned how to both punch cows and to croon away the long lonely nights on the range. Immigrants that came along a little later in the 19th century, especially from Portugal, helped create a Hawaiian-style music. Their biggest influence was a small four-stringed instrument called a *braga* or *cavaquinho*. One owned by Augusto Dias was the prototype of a homegrown Hawaiian instrument that became known as the ukulele. "Jumping flea," the translation of ukulele, is an appropriate name devised by the Hawaiians when they saw how nimble the fingers were as they "jumped" over the strings.

The Merry Monarch, King Kalakaua, and Queen Liliuokalani were both patrons of the arts

who furthered the Hawaiian musical identity at the turn of the century. Kalakaua revived the hula and was also a gifted lyricist and balladeer. He wrote the words to "Hawaii Pono," which became the national anthem of Hawaii and later the state anthem. Liliuokalani wrote the hauntingly beautiful "Aloha O'e," which is often pointed to as the "spirit of Hawaii" in music. Detractors say that its melody is extremely close to the old Christian hymn, "Rock Beside the Sea," but the lyrics are so beautiful and perfectly fitted that this doesn't matter.

Just prior to Kalakaua's reign a Prussian bandmaster, Capt. Henri Berger, was invited to head the fledgling Royal Hawaiian Band, which he turned into very respectable orchestra lauded by many visitors to the islands. Berger was open-minded and learned to love Hawaiian music. He collaborated with Kalakaua and other island musicians to incorporate their music into a Western format. He headed the band for 43 years until 1915, and was instrumental in making music a serious pursuit of talented Hawaiians.

Popular Hawaiian Music
Hawaiian music has a unique twang, a special feeling that says the same thing to everyone that hears it: "Relax, sit back in the moonlight, watch the swaying palms as the surf sings a lullaby." This special sound is epitomized by the

bandmaster Henri
Berger and the Royal
Hawaiian Band

HAWAII STATE ARCHIVES

bouncy ukulele, the falsetto voice of Hawaiian crooners, and by the smooth ring of the "steel" or "Hawaiian" guitar. The steel guitar is a variation that was originated by Joseph Kekuku in the 1890s. Stories abound of how Joseph Kekuku devised this instrument; the most popular versions say that Joe dropped his comb or pocketknife on his guitar strings and liked what he heard. Driven by the faint rhythm of an inner sound, he went to the machine shop at the Kamehameha School and turned out a steel bar for sliding over the strings. To complete the sound he changed the cat-gut strings to steel and raised them so they wouldn't hit the frets. Voila!—Hawaiian music as the world knows it today.

The first melodious strains of **slack-key guitar** can be traced back to the time of Kamehameha III, when Spanish cowboys (the forerunners of Hawaiian *paniolos*) from California were brought to the kingdom to run the wild cattle that had grown steadily in numbers ever since killing them was made *kapu* by Kamehameha I. The white man's gift had become a menace, growing in numbers to the point where they were even attacking grass houses for fodder. The Spanish cowboys roped, branded, and corralled them, and living up to the cowboy image, would pass lonesome nights on the range singing and playing their guitars. The Hawaiians, who made excellent cowboys, and their ears, recently tuned by the missionaries, picked up the melodies accompanied by the strange new instrument, and quickly "Hawaiianized" them. The Spanish had their way of tuning the guitar, and played difficult and aggressive music that did not sit well with Hawaiians, who were much more gentle and casual in their manners.

Hawaiians soon became adept at making their own music. At first, one person played the melody, but it lacked fullness. There was no body to the sound. So, as one *paniolo* fooled with the melody, another soon learned to play bass, which added depth. But, a player was often alone, and by experimenting learned that he could get the right hand going with the melody, and at the same time could play the bass note with the thumb to improve the sound. Singers also learned that they could "open tune" the guitar to match their rich voices.

Due to *kahunamism,* Hawaiians believed that knowledge was sacred, and what is sacred should be treated with utmost respect, which meant keeping it secret, except from sincere apprentices. Guitar playing became a personal artform whose secrets were closely guarded, handed down only to family members, and only to those who showed ability and determination. When old-time slack-key guitar players were done strumming, they loosened all the strings so that no one could figure out how they had it tuned. If they were playing, and some folks came by that were interested and weren't part of the family, the Hawaiians stopped what they were doing, put the guitar down, and put their foot on it across the strings to wait for the person to go away. As time went on, more and more Hawaiians began to play slack key, and a common repertoire emerged.

An accomplished musician could easily figure out the simple songs, once they had figured out how the family had tuned the guitar. One of the most popular tunings was the "open G." Old Hawaiian folks called it the "taro patch tune." Different songs came out, and if you were in their family and were interested in the guitar, they took the time to sit down and teach you. The way they taught was straightforward, and a test of your sincerity at the same time. The old master would start to play. They just wanted you to listen, get a feel for the music, not any more than that. You brought your guitar and *listened.* When you felt it, you played it, and the knowledge was transferred. Today, only a handful of slack-key guitar players know how to classically play the traditional tunes. The best-known and perhaps greatest slack-key player was Gabby Pahinui, with The Sons of Hawaii. He passed away recently, but left many recordings behind. A slack-key master still singing and playing is Raymond Kane. Raymond now teaches a handful of students his wonderful and haunting music. Not one of his students are from his own family, and most are *haole* musicians trying to preserve the classical method of playing.

Hawaiian music received its biggest boost from a remarkable radio program known as "Hawaii Calls." This program sent out its music from the Banyan Court of the Moana Hotel from 1935 until 1975. At its peak in the mid-1950s, it was syndicated on over 700 radio stations throughout the world. Ironically, Japanese pilots heading for Pearl Harbor tuned in island music as a signal beam. Some internationally famous classic tunes came out of the '40s and '50s. Jack Pitman composed "Beyond the Reef" in 1948; over 300 artists have recorded it, and it has sold well over 12 million records. Other million-sellers include: "Sweet Leilani," "Lovely Hula Hands," "The Crosseyed Mayor of Kaunakakai," and "The Hawaiian Wedding Song."

By the 1960s, traditional Hawaiian music began to die. Just too corny and light for those turbulent years, it belonged to the older generation and the good times that followed WW II. One man was instrumental in keeping Hawaiian music alive during this period. Don Ho, with his Tiny Bubbles, became the token Hawaiian musician of the '60s and early '70s. He's persevered long enough to become a legend in his own time, and his Polynesian Extravaganza at the Hilton Hawaiian Village packed visitors in until the early 1990s (see "Waikiki—Entertainment"). Ho now plays at the Waikiki Beachcomber four nights a week. Al Harrington, "The South Pacific Man," until his recent retirement had another Honolulu "big revue" that drew large crowds. Of this type of entertainment, perhaps the most Hawaiian is Danny Kaleikini, still performing at the Kahala Hilton, who entertains his audience with dances, Hawaiian anecdotes, and tunes on the traditional Hawaiian nose flute.

The Beat Goes On

Beginning in the mid-'70s, islanders began to assert their cultural identity. One of the unifying factors was the coming of age of "Hawaiian" music. It graduated from the "little grass shack" novelty tune and began to include sophisticated jazz, rock, and contemporary rhythms. Accomplished musicians whose roots were in traditional island music began to highlight their tunes with this distinctive sound. The best embellish their arrangements with ukuleles, steel guitars, and traditional percussion and melodic instruments. Some excellent modern recording artists have become island institutions. The local people say that you know if the Hawaiian harmonies are good if they give you "chicken skin."

Each year special music awards, **Na Hoku Hanohano,** or Hoku for short, are given to distinguished island musicians. The following are recent Hoku winners considered by their contemporaries to be among the best in Hawaii. If they're playing while you're there, don't miss them. **Loyal Garner,** who was awarded Female Vocalist of the Year for "I Shall Sing," is a truly wonderful artist. **Del Beazley,** who walked away with top honors for Male Vocalist of the Year, Contemporary Hawaiian Album, and Song of the Year, all from his fantastic album "Night and Day," is a wonderful performer. **Makaha Sons Of Niihau** captured a number of Hoku for Best Traditional Hawaiian Album, Best Group, and Album of the Year for their fantastic work "Ho'oluana." Led by Israel Kamakawiwoole, they are the best and shouldn't be missed. Best Contemporary Album went to **Hawaiian Style Band** for "Vanishing Treasures," while Single of the Year was awarded to **Bryan Kessler & Me No Hoa Aloha** for "Heiau," a haunting melody. Instrumental Album of the Year was awarded to **Susan Gillespie and Susi Hussong** for "Wedding Music," and Most Promising Artist was taken by **Kealohi** for "Kealohi."

Past winners of Hoku who have become renowned performers include: **Brothers Cazimero,** who are blessed with beautiful harmonic voices; **Krush,** who are highly regarded for their contemporary sounds; **The Peter Moon Band,** fantastic performers with a strong traditional sound; **Karen Keawehawai'i,** who has a sparkling voice and can be very funny when the mood strikes her; and **Henry Kapono,** formerly of Cecelio and Kapono, who keeps a low profile but is an incredible performer and excellent songwriter. His shows are noncommercial and very special. **Cecilio** is now teamed up with **Maggie Herron;** they are hot together and have a strong following in Honolulu. **The Beamer Brothers** are excellent performers and can be seen at various nightspots.

Some top-notch performers with a strong following are: Ledward Kaapana; Mango; Oliver Kelly; Ka'eo; Na Leo Pilimehana, whose "Local Boys" recently won a Hoku for Best Single; Freitas Brothers; Brickwood Galuteria, who won a double Hoku for Best Male Vocalist and Most Promising Artist; and Third Road Delite.

Classical And Chamber Music

A wide assortment of classical and chamber music is offered in Hawaii. The following organizations sponsor concerts throughout the year: Chamber Music Hawaii, 905 Spencer St., No. 404, Honolulu, HI 96822, tel. 531-6617; Classical Guitar Society of Hawaii, 1229 D. Waimanu, Honolulu, HI 96814, tel. 537-6451; The Ensemble Players Guild, P.O. Box 50225, Honolulu, HI 96850, tel. 735-1173; Hawaii Concert Society, P.O. Box 663, Hilo, HI 96721, tel. 935-5831; Honolulu Symphony Society, 1000 Bishop St., Suite 901, Honolulu, HI 96813, tel. 537-6171; Kauai Concert Association, 5867 Haaheo Pl., Kapaa, HI 96746, tel. 822-7593; Maui Philharmonic Society, 2274 S. Kihei Rd., Kihei, HI 96753, tel. 879-2962.

RADIO STATIONS

STATION	DIAL NUMBER	REMARKS
OAHU		
KCCN	AM 1420	Hawaiian music 24 hours. Indiscriminate selections will either delight or exasperate.
KDEO	AM 940, FM 102	Country
KPOI	FM 98	Rock
MAUI		
KAIM	AM 870, FM 95.5	Contemporary
KAOI	FM 95	Stereo
KPOA	FM 93.5	Hawaiian music 19 hours a day. Tropical jazz five hours a day.
HAWAII		
KBIG	FM 98	
KHLO.	AM 850	Country
KIPA	AM 620	Contemporary and requests
KKON	AM 790	Contemporary
KPUA	AM 670	Contemporary
KOAS	FM 92.1	Contemporary
KAUAI		
KFMN	FM 97	Contemporary, oldies
KONG	AM 570, FM 93.5	Contemporary and requests
KUAI	AM 720	Contemporary, surf report

Note: Not all stations may be received on all islands.

SHOPPING

You can't come to Oahu and *not* shop. Even if the idea of it doesn't thrill you, the lure of almost endless shops offering every imaginable kind of merchandise will sooner or later tempt even the most "big-waste-of-time" mumbler through their doors. So why fight it? And if you're the other type, who feels as though a day without shopping is like being marooned on a deserted island, have no fear of rescue, because everywhere on the horizon is "a sale, a sale!"

You can use "much much more" as either an aspersion or a tribute when describing Oahu, and nowhere does this qualifier fit better than when describing its shopping. Over a dozen major and minor shopping centers and malls are in Honolulu and Waikiki alone! Population centers around the island, including those in the interior, the south shore, windward shore, and North Shore, all have shopping centers in varying degrees—at the very least, a parking lot rimmed with a half-dozen shops that can provide immediate necessities.

On the Neighbor Islands, a major shopping mall is usually found only in the island's main city, with mom 'n' pop stores and small superettes taking up the slack. On Oahu, you've got these too, but you're never very far from some serious shopping centers. The tourist trade fosters the sale of art and artifacts, jewelry and fashions, and numerous boutiques selling these are strung around the island like a shell necklace. Food costs, in supermarkets, tend to be reasonable because Oahu is the main distribution center, and with all the competition, prices in general seem to be lower than on the other islands. If your trip to Hawaii includes a stop on Oahu, do most of your shopping here, because of the cut-rate prices and much greater availability of goods. When most Hawaiians go on a shopping spree, they head for Oahu. Don't underestimate a simple trip to the grocery store. Often, but not always, you can find uniquely Hawaiian gifts like coffee, macadamia nut liqueur, coconut syrup, and even an assortment of juices much cheaper than in the gift shops.

Note: The following are merely general listings; refer to "Shopping" in the travel sections for listings of specific shops, stores, and markets.

Honolulu Shopping Centers

Since it serves as the main terminal for The-Bus, you could make a strong case that **Ala Moana** Shopping Center is the heart of shopping on Oahu. At one time billed as the largest shopping center in the country, today it settles for being the largest in the state, with its hundreds of stores covering 50 acres. It's on Ala Moana Blvd., just across from the Ala Moana Beach Park. **The Ward Warehouse** is just a few blocks west of the Ala Moana Center, at 1050 Ala Moana Boulevard. The **Ward Center** on Ala Moana across from Ward Warehouse, is a relatively new shopping center that's gaining a reputation for some exclusive shops. (For more information on all of the above, turn to "Honolulu—Shopping.")

Waikiki Shopping

Shopping in Waikiki is as easy as falling off a surfboard. In two or three blocks of Kuhio and Kalakaua avenues are no less than seven

shell macrame

shopping centers. If that's not enough, there are hundreds of independent shops, plus plenty of street vendors. Main shopping centers include **Royal Hawaiian Shopping Center,** the **Waikiki Shopping Plaza,** and the **International Market Place,** an open-air shopping bazaar across from the Moana Hotel at 2330 Kalakaua Ave., open daily from 9 a.m. until the vendors get tired at night.

The **Hyatt Regency Shopping Center** is located on the first three floors of the Hyatt Regency Hotel, at 2424 Kalakaua Ave., tel. 922-5522. The **King's Village** is at 131 Kaiulani Ave., the **Waikiki Trade Center** is on the corner of Seaside and Kuhio avenues, and the **Rainbow Bazaar** is a unique mall located at the Hilton Hawaiian Hotel, at 2005 Kalia Road.

Around The Island

Heading east from Waikiki on Rt. 72, the first shopping opportunity is the **Niu Shopping Center** on your left, about four miles before Hanauma Bay. The **Time Supermarket** is known for good prices. Also on the left is the Koko Marina Shopping Center, just before Hanauma Bay, with a Liberty House, a few art galleries, and **Foodland Supermarket. Kailua** and **Kaneohe** bedroom communities have shopping malls. **Kahalua Sportswear,** along the Kahekili Hwy., about five minutes north of Byodo-In Temple, is a garment factory outlet store with decent prices and the ugliest collection of mannequins in the Pacific. Numerous shops are found along the North Shore from Haleiwa to Waimea, including surf, art, boutiques, and plenty of fast food and restaurants. The **Pearlridge Shopping Center** in Pearl City at the corner of the Kamehameha Hwy. and Waimano Home Rd. is a full shopping complex with over 150 stores. The **Waianae Mall** at 86-120 Farrington Hwy. serves the Waianae coast with a supermarket, drugstore, fast foods, and sporting goods.

Sundries

ABC has over a dozen mini-marts in and around Waikiki. Their prices are generally high, but they do have some good bargains on suntan lotions, sunglasses, and beach mats. The cheapest place to buy **film** is at **Sears, Woolworth's,** and **Longs Drugs.** All have good selections, cheap prices, and stores all over the island. **Francis Camera Shop** in the Ala Moana Center, tel. 946-2879, is extremely well stocked with accessories. For a large selection of military surplus and camping goods try the **Big 88** at 330 Sand Island Access Rd., tel. 845-1688.

If gadgetry fascinates you, head for **Shirokiya Department Store** at the Ala Moana and Pearlridge centers and in Waikiki. Besides everything else, they have a wonderful selection of all the gimcracks and doohickeys that Nippon has to offer. The atmosphere is somewhat like a trade fair. Those who can't imagine a tour with anything on their feet but Birkenstock can have their tootsies accommodated, but they won't be entirely happy. If you get a sole blowout, **Birkenstock Footprints** at Ala Moana Center, tel. 531-6014, will resole them for $14, but they want a full week to do it. For one-day service, they'll refer you to a shoemaker, **Joe Pacific** at the Ala Moana Center, tel. 946-2998, but he wants a toe-twisting $25 for the service!

Bookstores

Oahu has plenty of excellent bookstores. In Honolulu, try the **Honolulu Book Shops,** with three locations at the Ala Moana Center, tel. 941-2274, in downtown Honolulu at 1001 Bishop St., tel. 537-6224, and at the Pearlridge Center, tel. 487-1548. **Waldenbooks** is at the Pearlridge Center, tel. 488-9488, Kahala Mall, tel. 737-9550, and Waikiki Shopping Plaza, tel. 922-4154. For a fine selection of Hawaiiana try the **Bishop Museum and Planetarium Bookshop** at the Bishop Museum, 1525 Bernice St., tel. 847-3511, and at the **Mission Houses Museum** in downtown Honolulu at 553 S. King St., tel. 531-0481.

Rachel McMahan, Janice Beam, and Kathryn Decker have shopped their fingers to the bone for you and have written a small but definitive book entitled *The Shopping Bag.* It lists and describes shops all over Oahu from art supplies to toys and sporting goods.

Arts And Crafts

The following are a few of Oahu's many art shops and boutiques, just to get you started. An excellent place to find original arts and crafts at reasonable prices is along **The Fence** surrounding the Honolulu Zoo fronting Kapiolani

Park. Island artists come here every weekend 10 a.m.-4 p.m. to display and sell their artwork. The **Honolulu Academy of Arts** at 900 S. Beretania, open Tues.-Sat. 10 a.m.-4:30 p.m., Sun. 1-5 p.m., is not only great to visit, but has a fine gift shop that specializes in Asian art.

The same high-quality and authentic handicrafts are available in both the **Hawaiian Mission Houses Museum** and **Bishop Museum** gift shops (see "Bookstores" above). For Oriental art try **Gallery Mikado** and **Garakuta-Do**, both in Waikiki's Eaton Square Complex. **Ka'ala Art**, tel. 637-7533, in Haleiwa is a great one-stop shop for fine arts, pop art, and handicrafts, all by aspiring island artists. The **Punaluu Gallery**, tel. 237-8325, is the oldest gallery on the windward coast. It's been there over 30 years and is now operated by candle maker extraordinaire Scott Bechtol.

Flea Markets And Swap Meets
Amidst the junk, these are the cheapest places to find treasures. Two operate successfully on Oahu and have a regular following. **Aloha Flea Market**, weekends tel. 486-1529, weekdays tel. 732-9611, is at Aloha Stadium every Wed., Sat., and Sun. and most holidays 6 a.m.-3 p.m. It's the biggest flea market on Oahu, selling everything from bric-a-brac to real heirlooms and treasures.

Kam Swap Meet, tel. 483-5933, Kam Drive-In Theater, 98-850 Moanalua Rd., Pearl City, is open Wed., Thurs., Sat., and Sun. mornings. Regular stall holders to housewives cleaning out the garage offer great fun and bargains.

SUE STRANGIO EVERETTE

FESTIVALS, HOLIDAYS, AND EVENTS

In addition to all the American national holidays, Hawaii celebrates its own festivals, pageants, ethnic fairs, and a multitude of specialized exhibits. They occur throughout the year, some particular to only one island or locality, while others such as Aloha Week and Lei Day are celebrated on all the islands. Some of the smaller local happenings are semi-spontaneous, so there's no *exact* date when they're held. These are some of the most rewarding, because they provide the best times to have fun with the local people. Check local newspapers and the free island magazines for exact dates of some events.

The following events and celebrations are either particular to Oahu, or they're celebrated here in a special or different way. This central island has more festivities and events than all the others, and these times provide great social opportunities for meeting people. Everyone is welcomed to join in the fun, and most times the events are either free, or nominally priced. There's no better way to enjoy yourself while vacationing than by joining in with a local party or happening.

JANUARY

January 1: **Hauoli Makahiki Hou.** Start the New Year off right by climbing to the top of Koko Crater on Oahu. A great way to focus on the limitless horizons of the coming year and a great hangover remedy. See the HVB for details. Or continue the party with the **Sunshine Music Festival** rock concert at Diamond Head Crater.

January 2: **Queen Emma Museum Open House.** This is Queen Emma's birthday, and the public is invited to visit her summer home and view a well-preserved collection of her personal belongings; tel. 595-6291.

First Saturday: Watch the old pigskin get booted around in the **Hula Bowl Game,** Aloha Stadium, Honolulu. Annual college all-star football classic. Call Aloha Stadium, tel. 488-7731.

Mid-January to early February: **The Narcissus Festival** in Honolulu's Chinatown starts with the parade and festivities of Chinese New Year, with lion dances in the street, fireworks, a beauty pageant, and a coronation ball. For details call Welton Won at 533-3181.

Late January: **Robert Burns Night** at the Ilikai Hotel, Honolulu. Scots from Canada and mainland U.S. celebrate the birthday of Scotland's poet Robert Burns. For info call Louis Macphee, tel. 488-3839.

The **Cherry Blossom Festival** in Honolulu can begin in late January and last through March. Events include a Japanese cultural and trade show, tea ceremony, flower arranging, queen pageant, and coronation ball. Check newspapers and free tourist magazines for dates and times of various Japanese cultural events.

FEBRUARY

Early February: **NFL Pro Bowl.** Aloha Stadium, Honolulu. Annual all-star football game offering the best from both conferences. Aloha Stadium, tel. 488-7731.

Punahou School Carnival, Honolulu. Arts, crafts, and a huge rummage sale at one of Hawaii's oldest and most prestigious high schools. Great ethnic foods. You'd be surprised at what Hawaii's oldest and most established families donate to the rummage sale. Call 944-5711 for details.

The Hawaiian Open International Golf Tournament, in Honolulu at Waialae Country Club. Huge prize money lures the best PGA golfers to this tournament, which is beginning its second decade.

Mid-February: **Haleiwa Sea Spree** on Oahu's North Shore. Surfing championships, outrigger canoe races, and ancient Hawaiian sports, topped off by an around-the-island bicycle race. Competitions last four days.

Late February-early March: **Buffalo's Annual Big Board Surfing Classic** at Makaha Beach, Oahu. Features the best of the classic board riders. A real cultural event complete with entertainment, crafts, and food. A two-day event held the last weekend in February and again on the first weekend in March.

MARCH

·Remember **Buffalo's Big Board Classic** and the **Carole Kai Bed Race** down Kalakaua Ave. in Waikiki and a free concert at the Waikiki Shell the night before. There's a race and appearances by Hawaii's name entertainers in this fun-filled charity fund-raiser.

Hawaiian Song Festival and Song Composing Contest. Kapiolani Park Bandstand in Waikiki. Determines the year's best Hawaiian song. Presented by top-name entertainers.

Emerald Ball. An elegant affair sponsored by the Society of the Friendly Sons of St. Patrick

that features dinner as well as dancing to a big-name band. Also, the Saint Patrick's Day Parade. Kalakaua Ave., Waikiki.

Kamehameha School Annual Song Contest. Blaisdell Center Arena, Honolulu. Competition among secondary-grade students of Hawaiian ancestry. Kamehameha Schools, tel. 842-8211.

Late March: **Hawaiian Highland Gathering,** Honolulu. A gathering of the clans for Scottish games, competition, Scottish foods, highland dancing, and pipe bands. Great Scotsmen with kilts and lei too. Richardson's Field, Pearl Harbor, tel. 523-5050.

APRIL

Early April: **Easter Sunday.** Sunrise Service at the National Memorial Cemetery of the Pacific, Punchbowl Crater, Honolulu.

Annual Hawaiian Festival of Music. Waikiki Shell, Honolulu. A grand and lively music competition of groups from all over the islands and the Mainland. A music lover's smorgasbord offering everything from symphony to swing and all in between.

April 8: **Wesak or Buddha Day** on the closest Sunday to April 8. Celebrates the birthday of Gautama Buddha. Ornate offerings of tropical flowers at temples throughout Hawaii. Great sunrise ceremonies at Kapiolani Park, Honolulu. Mainly Japanese in their best *kimono.* Flower festival pageant and dance programs in all island temples.

Mid-April: **Aloha Basketball Classic,** Blaisdell Center Arena, Honolulu. Top college seniors are invited to Hawaii to participate in charity games made up of four teams. Blaisdell Center, tel. 527-5400.

MAY

May 1: **Lei Day.** May Day to the rest of the world, but in Hawaii red is only one of the colors when everyone wears a lei. Festivities throughout Hawaii with special goings-on at Kapiolani Park, Waikiki.

Early May: **Pacific Handcrafters Guild Fair,** at Ala Moana Park, Honolulu. An opportunity to see the "state of the arts" in Hawaii. Some of the islands' finest craftsmen in one spot selling their creations; tel. 538-7227.

Late May: **Memorial Day.** Special military services held at Honolulu, National Memorial Cemetery of the Pacific, on the last Monday in May. Call 546-3190.

50th State Fair, at Aloha Stadium, Honolulu. Agricultural exhibts, downhome cooking, entertainment, and produce. Lasts four weekends; tel. 536-5492.

JUNE

Early June: **Mission Houses Museum Fancy Fair,** Honolulu. A top-notch collection of Hawaii's best artists and craftsmen. A great chance to browse and buy. Also, foods and entertainment; tel. 531-0481.

June 11: **King Kamehameha Day** is a Hawaiian state holiday honoring Kamehameha the Great, Hawaii's first and greatest universal king. Lei-draping ceremony at King Kamehameha statue and parades complete with floats and pageantry featuring a ho'olaule'a (street party) in Waikiki. Civic Center, downtown Honolulu.

Mid-June: **Annual King Kamehameha Traditional Hula And Chant Competition.** Brigham Young University, Laie.

Annual Hawaiian Festival of Music, Waikiki Shell, Honolulu. A repeat of the April festivities, but no less of a music lover's delight as local and Mainland bands compete in genres from symphony to swing.

Late June: **Annual Japan Festival.** Dances and festivities in Honolulu at Kapiolani Park and the Blaisdell Center. Also, bon odori, the Japanese festival of departed souls, which features dances and candle-lighting ceremonies at numerous Buddhist temples throughout the islands. A special bon odori festival is offered at Haleiwa Jodo Mission, Haleiwa. These festivities change yearly and can be held anytime from late June to early August.

JULY

Early: **Tin Man Triathlon,** Honolulu. Over 1,000 triathletes gather to swim 800 meters, bike 25 miles, and finish with a 10,000-meter (6.2 miles) run around Diamond Head and back to Kapiolani Park in Waikiki. Call 533-4262.

Pan Am Clipper Cup Series. Boats from ports around the world sail to Oahu to navigate a series of triangles off Waikiki, along with one nonstop race from Ala Wai Harbor to Molokai, and an around-the-state nonstop race.

Trans Pacific Yacht Race, from Los Angeles to Honolulu during odd-numbered years. Yachties arrive throughout the month and converge on the Ala Wai Yacht Basin, where "party" is the password. They head off for Hanalei Bay, Kauai, to begin the year's yachting season.

July 4: **Hawaiian Islands Tall Ships Parade.** Tall-masted ships from throughout the islands parade from Koko Head to Sand Island and back to Diamond Head. A rare treat and taste of days gone by.

Mid-July: **Prince Lot Hula Festival,** Honolulu. A great chance for visitors to see authentic hula from some of the finest hula halau in the islands. Moanalua Gardens, tel. 839-5334.

Annual Ukulele Festival, Kapiolani Park Bandstand, Waikiki. Hundreds of ukulele players from throughout the islands.

Pacific Handcrafters Guild Fair, Thomas Square, Honolulu. A chance to see the "state of the arts" all in one locality. Browse, buy, and eat ethnic foods at various stalls.

Late July: **International Sailboard Championship Invitational** held at Diamond Head. Watch the amazing "aquabatics" as windsurfers run before the wind on their amazing one-man crafts.

AUGUST

Early August: **Honolulu Zoo Day,** Waikiki. A day of family fun where kids of all ages get a close-up look at the animals and a day of entertainment.

Hula Festival, Kapiolani Park, Waikiki. Recent hula graduates from Honolulu's Summer Fun classes perform hula they have learned. Some amazing bodily gyrations.

Late August: **Hawaiian Open State Tennis Championships,** Honolulu. Held at various courts around town offering substantial prizes. For infor call Don Andrews, tel. 923-9727.

Queen Liliuokalani Keiki Hula Competition, Kamehameha Schools, Honolulu. Children ages 5-12 compete in a hula contest. Caution: "Terminal Cuteness."

SEPTEMBER

Early September: **Waikiki Rough Water Swim,** Honolulu. A two-mile open-ocean swim from Sans Souci Beach to Duke Kahanamoku Beach. Open to all ages and abilities. Contact Gen Linuma, tel. 547-6410.

Late September: **Aloha Week.** There are major festivities on all of the islands, as everyone celebrates Hawaii's own "intangible quality," *aloha.* There are parades, luau, historical pageants, balls, and various other entertainment. The spirit of *aloha* is infectious and all are welcomed to join in. Check local papers and tourist literature for happenings near you. Downtown parades attract thousands, and even parking lots do their bit by charging a $1 flat fee during these festival times. The savory smells of ethnic foods fill the air from a multitude of stands, and the Honolulu Symphony performs at the Blaisdell Center, while free concerts are given at the Waikiki Shell.

Molokai to Oahu Canoe Race. Women (men in October) in Hawaiian-style canoes race from a remote beach on Molokai to Fort DeRussy in Honolulu. In transit they must navigate the rough Kaiwi Channel.

OCTOBER

Early October: **Pacific Handcrafters Guild,** Ala Moana Center Gallery, Honolulu. A fall show of the best works of Handcrafters Guild members. Perfect for early-bird and unique Christmas shopping.

Makahiki Festival, Waimea Falls Park, Oahu. Features Hawaiian games, crafts, and dances, reminiscent of the great Makahiki celebrations of ancient Hawaii. On an 800-acre tropical preserve.

Molokai to Oahu Canoe Race. Men (women in Sept.) navigate Hawaiian-style canoes across the rough Kaiwi Channel from a remote beach on Molokai to Fort DeRussy, Honolulu.

Oktoberfest. Where else would you expect to find German oom-pah bands, succulent wienerschnitzels, *und* beer, than in Honolulu. At the Budweiser Warehouse, 99-877 Iwaena St., Halawa Park, from noon until 10 p.m.

Mid-October: **Pan Am International Rugby Club Tournament.** Odd-numbered years. Watch the boys from throughout Oceania smash, clash, and collide in this rough and tumble sport. Queen Kapiolani Park, Honolulu. Contact Dick Gooch, tel. 836-6741.

Annual Orchid Plant And Flower Show. Hawaii's copious and glorious flowers are displayed. Blaisdell Center Exhibition Hall, Honolulu. Blaisdell Center, tel. 527-5400.

Late October: **Bishop Museum Festival.** A superb time to visit the world's best museum on Polynesia and Hawaii. Arts, crafts, plants, and tours of the museum and planetarium. A full day for the family, with special "back room" exhibits open to the public which are usually not seen. Bishop Museum, Honolulu, tel. 847-3511.

Aloha Week

NOVEMBER

Early November: **Ho'olaule'a in Waianae.** The military lets down its hair and puts on a display accompanied by top entertainers, food, and music in this very ethnic area. All-day event. Army Community Relations, tel. 438-9761.

November 11: **Veterans Day Parade.** National holiday. A parade from Fort DeRussy to Queen Kapiolani Park, Waikiki. American Legion, tel. 949-1140.

Christmas in November: **Mission Houses Museum Annual Christmas Fair.** Quality items offered by Hawaii's top craftsmen in an open-air bazaar; tel. 531-0481.

Late November: **Hawaiian Pro-Surfing Championships.** The best surfers in the world come to the best surfing beaches on Oahu. Wave action determines sites except for Men's Masters, which is always held at Banzai Pipeline, North Shore, Oahu. Big money and national TV coverage; tel. 521-8555.

Artists of Hawaii Annual Exhibition. The best works of Hawaii's contemporary fine artists. The Honolulu Academy of Arts, tel. 538-3693.

DECEMBER

Early December: **Hawaii International Film Festival,** East-West Center, Honolulu. The best art films from the East, West, and Oceania; tel. 944-7203.

Christmas celebrations: **Kamehameha Schools Christmas Concert,** Blaisdell Center Concert Hall, Honolulu, tel. 842-8211.

Pacific Handcrafters Guild Christmas Fair, Thomas Square, Honolulu. The best by the best, just in time for Christmas. Open air. Pacific Handcrafters, tel. 538-7227.

Mid-December: **Annual Honolulu Marathon.** An institution in marathon races. One of the best-attended and very prestigious races in the country, where top athletes from around the world turn out to compete; tel. 734-7200.

Annual Rainbow Classic. Invitational tournament of collegiate basketball teams. Blaisdell Center Arena, Honolulu, tel. 948-7523.

Aloha Bowl Game. Collegiate football. Aloha Stadium, Honolulu, tel. 488-7731.

PERFORMING ARTS EVENTS

The following offer top-notch performances at various times throughout the year: **Honolulu Symphony,** tel. 537-6191; **Hawaii Opera Theatre,** tel. 521-6537; **Honolulu Community Theatre,** tel. 734-0274; **Hawaii Performing Arts Company Theatre,** tel. 988-6131.

Ticketing

The Connection, a computerized ticketing service, open 24 hours, tel. 945-2867 or (800) 333-3388, handles all kinds of event ticketing for concerts, sporting events, theater performances, visiting Broadway plays, and most family attractions. You can call before you arrive in Hawaii and the tickets will be waiting for you at the venue's "Will Call Window." The Connection also has outlets on Oahu and Maui at all JR Music and House of Music stores. Payment is by cash or major credit card.

MUSEUMS, LIBRARIES, GALLERIES, GARDENS, AND A ZOO

Aloha Tower and Maritime Museum, at Ala Moana Blvd. and Bishop St., Honolulu, HI 96813, tel. 536-6373 or 548-5713. A landmark that said "Hawaii" to all who arrived by sea before planes took over. Great harbor and city views from top of tower. See also "Hawaii Maritime Center," below.

Army Museum, Fort DeRussy, P.O. Box 8064, Honolulu, HI 96815, tel. 543-2639. Official records, private papers, and photos documenting activities of the U.S. Army in east Asia and the Pacific islands. Access to holdings is by appointment.

Bishop Museum and Planetarium, 1525 Bernice St., Honolulu, HI 96819, tel. 847-3511. Open daily 9 a.m.-5 p.m., $7.95 for adults, $6.95 6-17, five and under free. The best collection in the world on Polynesia in general and Hawaii specifically. A true cultural treat. Should not be missed.

Children's Museum of Natural History, 1201 Ala Moana Blvd., Honolulu, HI 96814, Mon.-Fri. 9 a.m.-4 p.m., Sat. 9 a.m.-noon. Natural history and science exhibits.

The Contemporary Museum, under the direction of Merrill Rueppel, at 2411 Makiki Heights Rd., tel. 526-1322, open Tues.-Sat. 10 a.m.-4 p.m., Sun. noon-4 p.m., closed Mon., admission $4. The focus is on exhibitions, not collections, although works by David Hockney are on permanent display. Changing exhibits reflect different themes in contemporary art.

East-West Center, Burns Hall 4076, 1777 East-West Rd., University of Hawaii, Honolulu, HI 96848, tel. 944-7691. Cultural institute bringing together the peoples, art, history, and ways of East and West.

Episcopal Church in Hawaii, Queen Emma Square, Honolulu, HI 96813, tel. 536-7776. Records and photos of church ministry in Hawaii from 1862.

Foster Botanical Garden, 180 N. Vineyard Blvd. Open daily 9 a.m.-4 p.m., tel. 522-7065. Fifteen-acre oasis of exotic trees and rare plants.

Friends of Waipahu Cultural Garden Park, P.O. Box 103, Waipahu, HI 96797, tel. 677-0110. Re-creation of plantation village in the style of a living museum.

Hawaiian Historical Society, 560 Kawaiahao St., Honolulu, HI 96813, tel. 537-6271. Open Mon.-Fri. 10 a.m.-4 p.m. Extensive collection of 19th-century materials on Hawaiian Islands, including 3,000 photos, 10,000 books, maps, microfilm. Adjacent to Hawaiian Mission Children's Society. Should be seen together. Should not be missed.

Hawaiian Mission Children's Society, 553 S. King St., Honolulu 96813, tel. 531-0481. Open Tues.-Sat. 9 a.m.-4 p.m., Sun. noon-4 p.m., closed Monday. Admission is $3.50 adults, 75 cents children. Records, personal journals, letters and photos of early 19th-century Congregational missionaries to the Hawaiian Islands; archive of the Congregational Church in the Pacific. Shouldn't be missed.

Hawaiian State Archives, Iolani Palace Grounds, Honolulu, HI 96813, tel. 547-2355. Open Mon.-Fri. 7:45 a.m.-4:30 p.m. Archives of the government of Hawaii. Private papers of Hawaiian royalty and government officials, photos, illustrations, etchings recording Hawaiian history. For anyone seriously interested in Hawaii. Shouldn't be missed.

Hawaii Chinese Historical Center, 111 N. King St. Room 410, Honolulu, HI 96813, tel. 536-9302. Open 12 hours per week. Rare books, oral histories, and photos concerning the history of Chinese in Hawaii.

(CONTINUED ON NEXT PAGE)

MUSEUMS, LIBRARIES, GALLERIES, GARDENS, AND A ZOO

Hawaii Maritime Center at Pier 7, Honolulu Harbor, HI 96813, tel. 523-6151. Open daily 9 a.m.-5 p.m., admission is $7. A museum chronicling the exploration and exploitation of Hawaii by the seafarers who have come to its shores. Visit the famous double-hulled canoe *Hokule'a* and the tall-masted *Falls of Clyde*.

Hawaii Medical Library, Inc., 1221 Punchbowl St., Honolulu, HI 96813, tel. 536-9302. History of medicine in Hawaii.

Hawaii Pacific College Library. For college information call 544-0200.

Honolulu Academy of Arts, 900 S. Beretania St., Honolulu, HI 96814, tel. 532-8700. Object is to collect, preserve, and exhibit works of art (to conduct a public art education program related to the collection). Permanent and special exhibitions. Tours, classes, lectures, and films.

Honolulu Zoo, 151 Kapahulu Ave., tel. 521-3487. Open daily 9 a.m.-5 p.m. Quiet respite from hustle of Waikiki. Includes a collection of tropical birds as well as pandas, zebras, and gibbon apes. Great for kids of all ages.

Iolani Palace, P.O. Box 2259, Honolulu, HI 96804, tel. 536-3552. Iolani Palace Grounds. Performs all aspects of historic research, restoration, and refurbishing of palace. The only royal palace in the United States. Vintage artwork, antiques.

Kamehameha Schools, Kapalma Heights Rd., Honolulu, HI 96813, tel. 842-8620. Open Mon.-Fri. 7:30 a.m.-4 p.m. Traditional school for children of Hawaiian descent. Rare books, periodicals, slides on Hawaiiana.

Libraries: Oahu has more than a dozen libraries all over the island. The Central Administration number is 988-2194. Library for the Blind and Physically Handicapped is at 402 Kapahulu Ave., tel. 732-7767.

Punahou School, 1601 Punahou St., Honolulu, HI 96822, tel. 944-5823. Collection available by special arrangement. Institutional archives of the oldest private school in Hawaii.

Queen Emma's Summer Palace, 2913 Pali Hwy., Honolulu, HI 96817, tel. 595-3167. Restored historic home, built about 1848. Furniture and mementos of Queen Emma and her family. Some items belong to other members of royal family.

Sea Life Park, Makapuu Point, Waimanalo, HI 96795, tel. 259-7933. Varieties of Pacific marine plant and animal life, including several species of dolphins and whales. Feeding pool, Kaupa Village, turtle lagoon, restaurant, gift shop.

USS *Arizona* Memorial and Pacific Submarine Museum, Arizona Memorial Dr., Pearl Harbor, HI 96818, tel. 422-2771. A free tour of the sleek 184-foot white concrete structure that spans the sunken USS *Arizona*. Free Navy launches take you on the tour of "Battleship Row." Open Tues.-Sun. 8 a.m.-3 p.m. No reservations, first-come, first-served. Launches every 15 minutes. Visitor center offers graphic materials and film, reflecting events of the Pearl Harbor attack.

USS *Bowfin,* 11 Arizona Memorial Drive. Open daily 9:30 a.m.-4:30 p.m., tel. 423-1341. Fully restored WW II submarine. Insight into the underwater war. Self-guided tours. Fascinating. Next door to *Arizona* Memorial.

ACCOMMODATIONS

The innkeepers of Oahu would be personally embarrassed if you couldn't find adequate lodging on their island. So long as Oahu has to suffer the "slings and arrows" of development gone wild, at least you can find all kinds, qualities, and prices of places in which to spend your vacation. Of the nearly 60,000 rooms available in Hawaii, 35,000 are on Oahu, with 30,000 of them in Waikiki alone! Some accommodations are living landmarks, historical mementos of the days when only millionaires came by ship to Oahu, dallying as if it were their own private hideaway. When the jumbo jets began arriving in the early '60s, Oahu, especially Waikiki, began to build frantically. The result was hotel skyscrapers that grew faster than bamboo in a rainforest. These monoliths, which offered the "average family" a place to stay, marked a tremendous change in social status of visitors to Oahu. The runaway building continued unabated for two decades, until the city politicians, supported by the hotel keepers themselves, cried "Enough!" and the activity finally slowed down.

Now a great deal of money is put into refurbishing and remodeling what's already built. Visitors can find breathtakingly beautiful hotels that are the best in the land next door to more humble inns that can satisfy most anyone's taste and pocketbook. On Oahu, you may not get your own private beach with swaying palms and hula girls, but it's easy and affordable to visit one of the world's most exotic and premier vacation resorts. The following is merely an overview of the accommodations available on Oahu.

Note: For details and listings of specific accommodations, refer to the "Accommodations" section in the travel chapters, and the Hotel Index in the back of the book.

What, Where, And How Much

At almost anytime of year, bargains, plenty of them, may be found including **fly/drive/stay deals,** or any combination thereof, designed to attract visitors while keeping the prices down. You won't even have to look hard to find roundtrip airfare, room, and rental car for under

$500 a week from the West Coast, based on double occupancy. Rooms on Oahu may be found in all sorts of hotels, condos, and private homes. Some venerable old inns along **Waikiki Beach** were the jewels of the city when only a few palms obscured the views of Diamond Head. However, most of Waikiki's hotels now are relatively new high-rises. In Waikiki's **five-star** hotels, prices for deluxe accommodations, with all the trimmings, run about $200 per night. But a huge inventory of rooms go for half that amount and less. If you don't mind being one block from the beach, you can easily find nice hotels for $50-60. You can even find these prices in hotels on the beach, though most tend to be a bit older and heavily booked by tour agencies. You, too, can get a room in these, but expect the staffs to be only perfunctorily friendly, and the hotels to be a bit worn around the edges. Waikiki's side streets also hold many apartment-hotels that are, in effect, condos. In these you get the benefit of a full kitchen for under $75. Stays of a week or more bring further discounts.

Central Honolulu has few acceptable places to stay except for some no-frills hotels in and around Chinatown. Bad sections of Hotel Street have dives frequented by winos and prostitutes, not worth the hassle for the few dollars saved. Some upscale hotels around Ala Moana put you near the beach, but away from the heavy activity of Waikiki. For those passing through, a few **overnight-style** hotels are near the airport.

The remainder of the island, outside Waikiki, was mostly ignored as far as resort development was concerned. In the interior towns, and along the south and most of the windward coasts, you'll be hard pressed to find a room because there simply aren't any. Even today, only a handful of hotels are found on the leeward coast, mostly around **Makaha**, with the exception of the new and luxurious **Ihilani Resort and Spa.** The area has experienced some recent development with a few condos and some full resorts going up, but it remains mostly undeveloped. **Windward Oahu** does have a few established resorts at Turtle Bay and Punaluu, but most of the lodging there is in rentable beach houses and tiny, basic inns.

To round things off, there is a network of **bed and breakfast** homes, YM/WCAs, youth hos-tels, elderhostels, and summer sessions complete with room and board at the University of Hawaii (see "Honolulu—Accommodations" for details). Oahu also offers plenty of spots to pitch a tent at both state and county campgrounds.

HOTELS

Types Of Hotel Rooms

Even with the wide variety of other accommodations available, most visitors, at least first-timers, tend to stay in hotels. At one time, hotels were the only places to stay, and characters like Mark Twain were berthed at Kilauea's rude Volcano House, while millionaires and nobility sailed for Waikiki where they stayed in luxury at the Moana Hotel or Royal Hawaiian, which both still stand as vintage reminders of days past.

Today, there are over 62,000 hotel rooms statewide, and every year more hotels are built and older ones renovated. They come in all

Hilton Hawaiian Village

shapes and sizes, from 10-room, family-run affairs to high-rise giants. Most readily available and least expensive is a bedroom with bath, the latter sometimes being shared in the more inexpensive hotels. Some hotels also offer a studio, a large sitting room that converts to a bedroom; suites, bedrooms with sitting rooms; and apartments that have full kitchens plus at least one bedroom. Kitchenettes are often available, and they contain refrigerators, sinks, and stoves usually in a small corner nook, or fitted together as one space-saving unit. Kitchenettes cost a bit more, but save a bundle by allowing you to prepare some of your own meals. To get that vacation feeling while keeping costs down, eat breakfast in, pack a lunch for the day, and go out to dinner. If you rent a kitchenette, make sure all the appliances work as soon as you arrive. If they don't, notify the front desk immediately, and if the hotel will not rectify the situation ask to be moved or for a reduced rate. Hawaii has cockroaches (see "Health and Well-being"), so put all food away.

Hotel Rates: Add Nine Percent Tax

Every year Hawaiian hotels welcome in the New Year by hiking their rates by about 10%. A room that was $90 this year will be $99 next year, and so on. Hawaii, because of its gigantic tourist flow and tough competition, offers hotel rooms at universally lower rates than most developed resort areas around the world. Package deals, especially to Waikiki, almost throw in a week's lodging for the price of an air ticket. The basic daily rate is geared toward double occupancy; singles are hit in the pocketbook. Single rates are cheaper than doubles, but never as low as half the double rate; the most you get off is 40%.

Weekly and monthly rates will save you approximately 10% off the daily rate. Make sure to ask because this information won't be volunteered. Many hotels will charge for a double and then add an additional charge ($10 to $35) for extra persons. Some hotels, not always the budget ones, let you cram in as many as can sleep on the floor with no additional charge, so again, ask. Others have a policy of **minimum stay,** usually three days, but their rates can be cheaper. Also a **business/corporate** rate is usually available to anyone who can produce

a legitimate business card. A tax of **nine percent** is levied on all rooms!

Hawaii's **peak season** runs from just before Christmas until after Easter, and then again in early summer. Rooms are at a premium, and peak-season rates are an extra 10% above the normal daily rate. Oftentimes they'll also suspend weekly and monthly rates during peak season. The **off-peak** season is in late summer and fall, when rooms are easy to come by and most hotels offer lower rates. Here, subtract about 10% from the normal rate.

In Hawaiian hotels you always pay more for a good view. Terms vary slightly, but usually "ocean front" means your room faces the ocean and mostly your view is unimpeded. "Ocean view" is slightly more vague. It could be a decent view, or it could require standing on the dresser and craning your neck to catch a tiny slice of the sea sandwiched between two skyscrapers. Rooms are also designated and priced upward as **standard, superior, and deluxe.** As you go up, this could mean larger rooms with more amenities, or can merely signify a better view.

Plenty of hotels offer the **family plan,** which allows children under a certain age to stay in their parents' room free, if they use the existing bedding. If another bed or crib is required, there is an additional charge. Only a limited number of hotels offer the **American plan,** in which breakfast and dinner are included with the night's lodging. In many hotels, a refrigerator and a heating unit to make coffee and tea are provided free.

Paying, Deposits, And Reservations

The vast majority of Hawaiian hotels accept foreign and domestic traveler's checks, personal checks preapproved by the management, foreign cash, and most major credit cards. Reservations are always the best policy, and they're easily made through travel agents or directly by contacting the hotel. In all cases, bring documentation of your confirmed reservations with you in case of a mix-up.

Deposits are not always required to make reservations, but they do secure them. Some hotels require the first night's payment in advance. Reservations without a deposit can be legally released if the room is not claimed by 6 p.m. Remember, too, that letters "requesting reservations" are not the same as "confirmed reservations." In letters, include your dates of stay, type of room you want, and price. Once the hotel answers your letter, "confirm" your reservations with a phone call or follow-up letter and make sure that the hotel sends you a copy of the confirmation. All hotels and resorts have **cancellation requirements** for refunding deposits. The time limit on these can be as little as 24 hours before arrival to a full 30 days. Some hotels require full **advance payment** for your length of stay, especially during peak season or during times of crowded special events. Be aware of the time required for a cancellation notice *before* making your reservation deposit, especially when dealing with advance payment.

If you have confirmed reservations, especially with a deposit, and there is no room for you, or one that doesn't meet prearranged requirements, you should be given the option of accepting alternate accommodations. You are owed the difference in room rates if there is any. If there is no room whatsoever, the hotel is required to find you one at another comparable hotel and refund your deposit in full.

Amenities

All hotels have some of them, and some hotels have all of them. Air-conditioning is available in most, but under normal circumstances you won't need it. Balmy trade winds provide plenty of breezes, which flow through louvered windows and doors in many hotels. Ceiling fans are better than the air-conditioning. Televisions are often included in the rate, but not always. In-room phones are provided, but a service charge is usually tacked on, even for local calls. Swimming pools are very common, even though the hotel may sit right on the beach. There is always a restaurant of some sort, a coffee shop or two, a bar, a cocktail lounge, and sometimes a sundries shop. Some hotels also offer tennis courts or golf courses either as part of the premises or affiliated with the hotel; usually an "activities desk" can book you into a variety of daily outings, and the better hotels offer **concierge service.** Plenty of hotels offer laundromats on the premises, and hotel towels can be used at the beach. Bellhops get about $1 per bag, and maid service is free, though maids are customarily tipped $1-2 per day and a bit more if kitchenettes are involved. Waikiki hotels have the very annoying custom of charging for parking above and beyond the room rate! Outside of Waikiki, parking is usually free unless you opt for valet service. Hotels can often arrange special services like babysitters, all kinds of lessons, and often special entertainment activities. A few even have bicycles and some snorkeling equipment to lend. They'll receive and send mail for you, cash your traveler's checks, and take messages.

CONDOMINIUMS

The main qualitative difference between a condo and a hotel is in amenities. At a condo, you're more on your own. You're temporarily renting an apartment, so there won't be any bellhops and rarely a bar, restaurant, or lounge on the premises, though many times you'll find a sundries store. The main lobby, instead of having that grand entrance feel of many hotels, is more like an apartment house entrance, although there might be a front desk. Condos can be efficiencies (one big room), but mostly they are one- or multiple-bedroom affairs with a complete kitchen. Reasonable housekeeping items should be provided: linens, all furniture, and a fully equipped kitchen. Most have TVs and phones, but remember that the furnishings provided are all up to the owner. You can find brand-new furnishings that are top of the line, right down to garage sale bargains. Inquire about the furnishings when you make your reservations. Maid service might be included on a limited basis (for example, once weekly), or you might have to pay extra for it.

The method of paying for and reserving a condo is just about the same as for a hotel. However, requirements for deposits, final payments, and cancellation charges are much stiffer than in hotels. Make absolutely sure you fully understand all of these requirements when you make your reservations. Condos usually require a minimum stay, although some will rent on a daily basis, like hotels. Minimum stays when applicable are often three days, but seven is also commonplace, and during peak season, two weeks isn't unheard of. Swimming pools are common, and depending on the "theme" of the condo, you

1. Wahiawa pond (J.D. Bisignani)   **2.** Kawainui Canal, Kailua (J.D. Bisignani)
3. water lilies (J.D. Bisignani)

1. Waikiki skyline (J.D. Bisignani)   **2.** Royal Hawaiian Hotel (J.D. Bisignani)

can find saunas, weight rooms, jacuzzis, and tennis courts. Rates are about 10-15% higher than comparable hotels, with hardly any difference between doubles and singles. There is a nominal extra charge for more than two people, and condos can normally accommodate four to six guests. You can find clean, decent condos for as little as $200 per week, all the way up to exclusive apartments for well over $3000. Their real advantage is for families, friends who want to share, and especially long-term stays where you will always get a special rate. The kitchen facilities save a great deal on dining costs, and it's common to find units with their own small washers and dryers. Parking space is ample for guests, and like hotels, plenty of stay/drive deals are offered. You'll find condos all over Hawaii, but they're particularly prevalent on Maui.

Hotel/Condominium Information

The best source of hotel/condo information is the **Hawaii Visitors Bureau.** While planning your trip, either visit one nearby or write to them in Hawaii. (Addresses are given in "Information and Services—Hawaii Visitors Bureau.") Request a copy of their free and current *Member Accommodation Guide.* This handy booklet lists all the hotel/condo members of the HVB, with addresses, phone numbers, facilities, and rates. General tips are also given.

BED AND BREAKFAST

Bed-and-breakfast (B&B) inns are hardly a new idea. The Bible talks of the hospitable hosts who opened the gates of their homes and invited the wayfarer in to spend the night. B&Bs have a long tradition in Europe and were commonplace in 18th-century America. Now, lodging in a private home called a bed and breakfast is becoming increasingly fashionable throughout America, and Hawaii is no exception. Not only can you visit the Big Island, you can "live" there for a time with a host family and share an intimate experience of daily life.

Points To Consider

The primary feature of B&B homes is that every one is privately owned, and therefore uniquely different from every other. The range of B&Bs is

as wide as the living standards in America. You'll find everything from a semimansion in the most fashionable residential area to a little grass shack offered by a downhome fisherman and his family. This means that it's particularly important for the guest to choose a host family with whom his or her lifestyle is compatible.

Unlike at a hotel or a condo, you'll be living *with* a host (usually a family), although your room will be private, with private baths and separate entrances being quite common. You don't just "check in" to a B&B. In Hawaii you go through agencies (listed below), which act as go-betweens, matching host and guest. Write to them and they'll send you a booklet with a complete description of the B&B, its general location, the fees charged, and a good idea of the lifestyle of your host family. With the reservations application they'll include a questionnaire that will basically determine your profile: Are you single? Do you have children? Smoker? etc., as well as arrival and departure dates and all pertinent particulars.

Since B&Bs are run by individual families, the times that they will accept guests can vary according to what's happening in their lives. This makes it imperative to write well in advance: three months is good; earlier is too long and too many things can change. Four weeks is about the minimum time required to make all necessary arrangements. Expect a minimum stay (three days is common) and a maximum stay. B&Bs are not long-term housing, although It's hoped that guest and host will develop a friendship and that future stays can be as long as both desire.

B&B Agencies

A top-notch B&B agency is **Bed and Breakfast Hawaii,** operated by Evelyn Warner and Al Davis. They've been running this service since 1978, and their reputation is excellent. B&B Hawaii has a membership fee of $10 yearly. For this they mail you their "Directory of Homes," a periodic "hot sheet" of new listings, and all pertinent guest applications; add $1 for handling. Write Bed and Breakfast Hawaii, P.O. Box 449, Kapaa, HI 96746, tel. 822-7771 or (800) 733-1632.

One of the most experienced agencies, **Bed And Breakfast Honolulu Statewide,** at 3242 Kaohinanai Dr., Honolulu, HI 96817, tel. 595-

7533 or (800) 288-4666, owned and operated by Marylee and Gene Bridges, began in 1982. Since then, they've become masters at finding visitors the perfect accommodations to match their desires, needs, and pocketbooks. Their repertoire of guest homes offers more than 400 rooms, with half on Oahu and the other half scattered around the state. Accommodations from Marylee and Gene are more personally tailored than a hotel room. When you phone, they'll match your needs to their computerized in-house guidelines.

Other well-known agencies include the following. **Go Native Hawaii** will send you a directory and all needed information if you write to them at 65 Halaulani Pl., P.O. Box 11418, Hilo, HI, 96721, tel. 935-4178 or (800) 662-8483.

Pacific Hawaii Bed And Breakfast at 19 Kai Nanai Pl., Kailua, HI 96734, tel. 486-8838 or (800) 999-6026, lists homes throughout the state, but especially around Kailua/Kaneohe on Oahu's upscale windward coast.

Hawaiian Islands Vacation Rentals, 1277 Mokulua Dr., Kailua, HI 96734, tel. 261-7895 or (800) 258-7895, is owned and operated by Rick Maxey, who can arrange stays on all islands and help with interisland flights and car rental.

Babson's Vacation Rentals and Reservation Service, 3371 Keha Dr., Kihei, Maui, HI 96753, tel. 874-1166 or (800) 824-6409, is owned and operated by Ann and Bob Babson, a delightful couple who will try hard to match your stay with your budget.

Affordable Paradise, 226 Pouli Rd., Kailua, HI 96734, tel. 261-1693 or (800) 925-9065, specializes in Oahu B&Bs, but can arrange stays on all islands.

Two agencies specializing in beachfront villas, luxury condominiums, and exclusive estates are **Villas of Hawaii,** 4218 Waialae Ave., Suite 203, Honolulu, HI 96816, tel. 735-9000; and **Vacation Locations Hawaii,** P.O. Box 1689, Kihei, HI 96753, tel. 874-0077. Information on B&Bs can also be obtained from the **American Board of Bed and Breakfast Associations,** P.O. Box 23294, Washington, D.C. 20026.

OTHER ACCOMMODATIONS

Home Exchanges

One other method of staying in Hawaii, open to homeowners, is to offer the use of your home in exchange for use of a home in Hawaii. This is done by listing your home with an agency that facilitates the exchange and publishes a descriptive directory. To list your home and to find out what is available, write Vacation Exchange Club, 12006 111 Ave., Youngtown, AZ 85363; or Interservice Home Exchange, P.O. Box 87, Glen Echo, MD 20812.

Note: For **camping** information, see "Camping And Hiking." For **YM/WCA, Youth Hostels, Elderhostel,** and summer courses at the **University of Hawaii,** see "Honolulu—Accommodations," and "Waikiki—Accommodations."

DIANA LASICH HARPER

FOOD AND DRINK

Hawaii is a gastronome's Shangri-La, a sumptuous smorgasbord in every sense of the word. The varied ethnic groups that have come to Hawaii in the last 200 years have brought their own special enthusiasm and culture, and lucky for all, they didn't forget the cook pots, hearty ap petites, and exotic tastes of their homelands.

The Polynesians who first arrived found a fertile but barren land. Immediately they set about growing taro, coconuts, and bananas, and raising chickens, pigs, fish, and even dogs, though these were reserved for the nobility. The harvests were bountiful and the islanders thanked the gods with the traditional feast called the luau. The underground oven, the *imu*, baked most of the dishes, and participants were encouraged to feast while relaxing on straw mats and enjoying the hula and various entertainments. The luau is as popular as ever, and a treat that's guaranteed to delight anyone with a sense of eating adventure.

The missionaries and sailors came next and their ships' holds carried barrels of ingredients for the puddings, pies, dumplings, gravies, and roasts—the sustaining "American foods" of New England farms. The mid-1800s saw the arrival of boatloads of Chinese and Japanese peasants, who wasted no time making rice instead of bread the staple of the islands. The Chinese added their exotic spices, creating complex Sichuan dishes as well as workingmen's basics like chop suey. The Japanese introduced *shoyu*, sashimi, boxed (*bento*) lunches, delicate tempura, and rich, filling noodle soups. The Portuguese brought their luscious Mediterranean dishes with tomatoes and peppers surrounding plump spicy sausages, nutritious bean soups, and mouthwatering sweet treats like *malasadas* and *pao dolce* (sweet bread). Koreans carried crocks of zesty *kimchi*, and quickly fired up barbecue pits for *pulgogi*, a traditional marinated beef cooked over an open fire. Filipinos served up their tart *adobo* stews of fish, meat, or chicken in a rich sauce of vinegar and garlic.

Recently, Thai and Vietnamese restaurants have begun offering their irresistible dishes side by side with the fiery burritos from Mexican restaurants and the elegant cream sauces of

French restaurants. The ocean breezes of Hawaii not only cool the skin, but on them waft some of the most delectable aromas to make the taste buds thrill and the spirit soar.

THE CUISINES OF HAWAII

Hawaiian foods, oldest of all island dishes, are wholesome, well prepared, and delicious. All you have to do on arrival is notice the size of some of the local boys (and women) to know immediately that food to them is indeed a happy and serious business. An oft-heard island joke is that "local men don't eat until they're full, they eat until they're tired." Many Hawaiian dishes have become standard fare at a variety of restaurants, eaten sooner or later by anyone who spends time in the islands. Hawaiian food in general is called *kaukau,* cooked food is *kapahaki,* and something broiled is called *kaola* Any of these prefixes on a menu will let you know that Hawaiian food is served. Usually inexpensive, they'll definitely fill you and keep you going.

Traditional Favorites
In old Hawaii, although the sea meant life, many more people were involved with cultivating beautifully tended garden plots of taro, sugarcane, breadfruit, and various sweet potatoes (*uala*) than fishing. They husbanded pigs and barkless dogs (*ilio*), and prized *moa* (chicken) for their feathers and meat, but found eating the eggs repulsive. Their only farming implement was the *o'o,* a sharpened hardwood digging stick. The Hawaiians were the best farmers of Polynesia, and the first thing they planted was taro, a tuberous root that was created by the gods at the same time as man. This main staple of the old Hawaiians was made into poi. Every luau will have poi, a glutinous purple paste made from pounded taro root. It comes in liquid consistencies referred to as "one-, two-, or three-finger poi." The fewer fingers you need to eat it, the thicker it is. Poi is one of the most nutritious carbohydrates known, but people unaccustomed to it find it bland and tasteless, although some of the best, fermented for a day or so, has an acidic bite. Poi is made to be eaten *with* something, but locals who love it will pop it plain in their mouths and smack their lips. However, those unaccus-

tomed to it will suffer constipation if they eat too much.

A favorite popular dessert is *haupia,* a custard made from coconut. *Limu* is a generic term for edible seaweed, which many people still gather from the shoreline and eat as a salad or mix with ground *kukui* nuts and salt as a relish. A favorite Hawaiian snack is *opihi,* small shellfish (limpets) that cling to rocks. People gather them, always leaving some on the rocks for the future. They are cut from the shell and eaten raw by all people of Hawaii; as testament to their popularity they sell for $150 per gallon in Honolulu.

A general term that has come to mean hors d'oeuvres in Hawaii is *pu pu.* Originally the name of a small shellfish, now everyone uses the term for any "munchy" that's considered a finger food. A traditional liquor made from ti root is *okolehao.* It literally means "iron bottom," reminiscent of the iron blubber pots used to ferment it.

LUAU

To have fun at a luau you have to get into the swing of things. Basically a huge banquet, you eat and drink until you have trouble moving, somewhat like Thanksgiving on the beach. Entertainment is provided by local performers in what is invariably called a "Polynesian Revue." This includes the tourist's hula, the fast version with swaying hips and dramatic lighting, a few wandering troubadours singing Hawaiian standards, and someone swinging swords or flaming torches. All the Hawaiian standards like poi, *haupia, lomi* salmon, *lau lau,* and *kalua* pig are usually served. If these don't suit your appetite, various Asian dishes, plus chicken, fish, and roast beef might do. If you leave a luau hungry, it's your own fault!

Luau range in price $40-55 per person. The price oftentimes includes admission to the theme parks at which many are now presented. The least expensive, most authentic, and best luau are often put on by local churches or community groups. They are not held on a regular basis, so make sure to peruse the free tourist literature where they advertise. The following luau are institutions and have been operating for years. If you ask a local person "Which is the best?" you won't get two to agree. It's literally a matter of taste.

The **Royal Hawaiian Luau** on the Ocean Lawn of the Royal Hawaiian Hotel, every Mon. 6-9 p.m., tel. 923-7311, *is* the classic Hawaiian feast, complete with authentic foods, entertainment, and richly spiced with *aloha*. Authenticity is added by lawn seating on traditional *lau hala* mats (table seating too) while the sun sets on Waikiki Beach and the stars dance over Diamond Head. Entertainment is an hour-long Polynesian extravaganza featuring Tahitian and traditional hula, a Samoan fire dance, bold rhythmic drumming, and singing by Sam Bernard. The buffet is a lavish feast of *kalua* pig, salmon, mahimahi, steak, and sides of poi, *haupia,* and a sinful but scrumptious table of desserts like coconut cake, *lilikoi* chiffon pie, banana bread, and guava chiffon pie. You are presented with a fresh-flower lei and welcomed at the open bar for mai tais and other tropical drinks. Cost is $49.50 adults, $39.50 children under 12.

Chuck Machado's is open every Tues., Fri., and Sun. at 7 p.m., tel. 836-0249, at the Waikiki Outrigger Hotel. You can enjoy this great show just by strolling on the nearby beach.

Germaine's Luau, often claimed by local people to.be *the* best, is held at Ewa Beach, tel. 946-3111.

Paradise Cove Luau boasts a private beach with a shuttle bus departing Waikiki at 4 p.m. and returning by 10 p.m., tel. 945-3571. The **Great Hawaiian Luau** is held at Makapuu Point, tel. 926-8843.

TROPICAL FRUITS AND VEGETABLES

Some of the most memorable taste treats from the islands require no cooking at all: the luscious tropical and exotic fruits and vegetables sold in markets and roadside stands or found just hanging on trees, waiting to be picked. Make sure to experience as many as possible. The general rule in Hawaii is that you are allowed to pick fruit on public lands, but it should be limited to personal consumption. The following is a sampling of some of Hawaii's best produce.

Bananas
No tropical island is complete without them. There are over 70 species in Hawaii, with hundreds of variations. Some are for peeling and eating while others are cooked. A "hand" of bananas is great for munching, backpacking, or just picnicking. Available everywhere—and cheap.

Avocados
Brought from South America, avocados were originally cultivated by the Aztecs. They have a buttery consistency and a nutty flavor. Hundreds of varieties in all shapes and colors are available fresh year-round. They have the highest fat content of any fruit next to the olive.

Coconuts
What tropical paradise would be complete without coconuts? Indeed, these were some of the first plants brought by the Polynesians. When children were born, coconut trees were planted for them so they'd have fruit throughout their lifetime. Truly tropical fruits, they know no season. Drinking nuts are large and green, and when shaken you can hear the milk inside. You get about a quart of fluid from each. It takes skill to open one, but a machete can handle anything. Cut the stem end flat so that it will stand, then bore a hole into the pointed end and put in a straw or hollow bamboo. Coconut water is slightly acidic and helps to balance alkaline foods. Spoon meat is a custardlike gel on the inside of drinking nuts. Sprouted coconut meat is also an excellent food. Split open a sprouted nut, and inside is the yellow fruit, like a moist sponge cake. "Millionaire's salad" is made from

common banana

DIANA LASICH HARPER

the heart of a coconut palm. At one time an entire tree was cut down to get to the heart, which is just inside the trunk below the fronds and is like an artichoke heart except that it's about the size of a watermelon. In a downed tree, the heart stays good for about two weeks.

Breadfruit
This is a staple of the islands that provides a great deal of carbohydrates, but many people find the baked, boiled, or fried fruit bland. It grows all over the islands and is really thousands of little fruits growing together to form a ball.

Mangoes
These are some of the most delicious fruits known to humans. They grow wild all over the islands; the ones on the leeward sides of the islands ripen from April to June, while the ones on the windward sides can last until October. They're found in the wild on trees up to 60 feet tall, and the problem is how to stop eating them once you start!

Papayas
This truly tropical fruit has no real season, but is mostly available in the summer. They grow on branchless trees and are ready to pick as soon as any yellow appears. Of the many varieties, the "solo papaya," meant to be eaten by one person, is the best. Split them in half, scrape out the seeds, and have at them with a spoon.

Passion Fruit
Known by their island name of *lilikoi,* they make excellent juice and pies. They're a small yellow fruit (similar to lemons but smooth-skinned) mostly available in summer and fall, and many wild ones grow on vines, just waiting to be picked. Slice off the stem end, scoop the seedy pulp out with your tongue, and you'll know why they're called "passion fruit."

Guavas
These small round yellow fruits are abundant in the wild where they are ripe from early summer to late fall. Considered a pest—so pick all you want. A good source of vitamin C, they're great for juice, jellies, and desserts.

breadfruit

DIANA LASICH HARPER

Macadamia Nuts
The king of nuts was brought from Australia in 1892. Now it's the state's fourth-largest agricultural product. Available roasted, candied, or buttered.

Litchis
Called nuts but really a small fruit with a thin red shell. They have a sweet and juicy white flesh when fresh, and appear like nuts when dried.

Potpourri
As well as the above, you'll find pineapples, oranges, limes, kumquats, thimbleberries, and blackberries, as well as carambolas, wild cherry tomatoes, and tamarinds.

FISH AND SEAFOOD

Anyone who loves fresh fish and seafood has come to the right place. Island restaurants specialize in seafood, and it's available everywhere. Pound for pound, seafood is one of the best dining bargains on Oahu. You'll find it served in every kind of restaurant, and often the fresh catch-of-the-day is proudly displayed on ice in a glass case. The following is a sampling of the best.

Mahimahi
This excellent eating fish is one of the most common and least expensive in Hawaii. It's referred to as a "dolphin," but is definitely a fish and not a mammal at all. Mahimahi can weigh 10-65 pounds; the flesh is light and moist. This fish is broadest at the head. When caught it's a dark olive color, but after a while the skin turns irides-

HAWAIIAN GAME FISH

ono

ahi

uku

a'u

mahimahi

ulua

cent—blue, green, and yellow. Can be served as a main course or as a patty in a fish sandwich.

A'u

This true island delicacy is a broadbill swordfish or marlin. It's expensive even in Hawaii because the damn thing's so hard to catch. The meat is moist and white and truly superb. If it's offered on the menu, order it. It'll cost a bit more, but you won't be disappointed.

Ono

Ono means "delicious" in Hawaiian so that should tip you off to the taste of this wahoo, or king mackerel. Ono is regarded as one of the finest eating fishes in the ocean, and its white flakey meat lives up to its name.

Manini

These five-inch fish are some of the most abundant in Hawaii and live in about 10 feet of water. They school and won't bite a hook but are easily taken with spear or net. Not often on a menu, but they're favorites with local people who know best.

Ulua

This member of the crevalle jack family ranges between 15 and 100 pounds. Its flesh is white and has a steaklike texture. Delicious and often found on the menu.

Uku

This is a gray snapper that's a favorite with local people. The meat is light, firm, and grills well.

Ahi

A yellowfin tuna with distinctive pinkish meat. A great favorite cooked, or uncooked in sushi bars.

Moi

This is the Hawaiian word for "king." This fish has large eyes and a sharklike head. Considered one of the finest eating fishes in Hawaii, it's best during the autumn months.

Seafood Potpourri

Some other island seafoods found on the menu include limu, edible seaweed; opihi, a small shellfish (limpet) that clings to rocks and is considered one of the best island delicacies, eaten raw; aloalo, like tiny lobsters; crawfish, plentiful in taro fields and irrigation ditches; ahipalaka, albacore tuna; various octopuses (squid or calamari); and shark of various types.

A'ama are the ubiquitous little black crabs that you'll spot on rocks and around pier areas. They're everywhere. For fun, local fishermen will try to catch them with poles, but the more efficient way is to throw a fish head into a plastic bucket and wait for the crabs to crawl in and trap themselves. The a'ama are about as big as two fingers and make delicious eating.

Limu is edible seaweed that has been gathered as a garnish since pre-contact times, and is frequently found on traditional island menus. There's no other seaweed except limu in Hawaii. Because of this, the heavy, fishy-ocean smell that people associate with the sea, but which is actually that of seaweed, is absent in Hawaii.

ISLAND DRINKS

To complement the fine dining in the islands, the bartenders have been busy creating their own tasty concoctions. The full range of beers, wines, and standard drinks is served in Hawaii, but for a real treat you should try some mixed drinks inspired by the islands.

Kona coffee is the only coffee grown in America. It comes from the Kona District of the Big Island and it is a rich, aromatic, truly fine coffee. If it's offered on the menu, have a cup.

Drinking Laws

There are no state-run liquor stores; all kinds of spirits, wines, and beers are available in markets and shops, generally open during normal business hours, seven days a week. The drinking age is 21, and no towns are "dry." Legal hours for serving drinks depend on the type of establishment. Hours generally are: hotels, 6 a.m.-4 a.m.; discos and nightclubs where there is dancing, 10 a.m.-4 a.m.; bars and lounges where there is no dancing, 6 a.m.-2 a.m. Most restaurants serve alcohol, and in many that don't, you can bring your own.

Exotic Drinks

To make your experience complete, you must order one of these colorful island drinks. Most look very innocent because they come in pineapples, coconut shells, or tall frosted glasses. They're often garnished with little umbrellas or sparklers, and most have enough fruit in them to give you your vitamins for the day. Rum is used as the basis of many of them. It's been an island favorite since it was introduced by the whalers of last century. Here are some of the most famous: Mai tai, a mixture of light and dark rum, orange curaçao, orange and almond flavoring, and lemon juice; Chi-Chi, a simple concoction of vodka, pineapple juice, and coconut syrup, a real sleeper because it tastes like a milk shake; Blue Hawaii, vodka and blue curaçao; planter's punch, light rum, grenadine, bitters, and lemon juice—great thirst quencher. Singapore Sling is a sparkling mixture of gin, cherry, brandy, and lemon juice.

Local Brews

A locally brewed beer, **Primo,** manufactured under the auspices of the Joseph Schlitz Brewing Co. of Milwaukee, is a serviceable American brew in the German style, but lacks that full, hearty flavor of the European imports. In the early '70s it enjoyed an estimated 65% of the local market share, the highest in the nation, but after a bad batch was inadvertently released, sales plummeted and the local share fell to five percent, where it has since remained.

In the early '90s two local breweries folded, the Pacific Brewing Company that produced **Maui Lager,** and the Honolulu Brewing Company that produced **Koolau Lager** among others. Both breweries were critically acclaimed, but both geared their beers to the full bodied European taste. Local beer drinkers enjoy a much lighter brew, so sales of the new beers never really took off.

Undaunted, Paula Thompson, a young and energetic ad executive turned *beer meister,* has been brewing small batches of beer in her Kula home for years. A visiting uncle, involved in an Oregon brewery, suggested after tasting and enjoying one of her beers that Maui was perfect for a microbrewery of its own. Paula agreed, but to keep start-up costs down, she is brewing her **Whale Ale** and **Aloha Lager** at

the Blitz Weinhard Brewery in Portland, Oregon. Once the beer has been established, she hopes to move operations to Maui. Another island entrepreneur, Marcus Bender, much better capitalized, will be opening the Hawaii Brewery Development Co. on a 22 acre site on the Big Island of Hawaii, where the Planning Commission has already approved the project. Eager to bypass the pitfalls that swallowed past local breweries, Bender, going for volume, is positioning his **Big Island Beer** to compete directly with Budweiser, Coors, and Miller, avoiding the upscale market dominated by the imports.

MUNCHIES AND ISLAND TREATS

Certain "finger foods," fast foods, and island treats are unique to Hawaii. Some are a meal in themselves, but others are just snacks. Here are some of the best and most popular.

Pu Pu

Pronounced as in "Winnie the Pooh Pooh," these are little finger foods and hors d'oeuvres. They're everything from crackers to cracked crab. Often, they're given free at lounges and bars and can even include chicken drumettes, fish kabobs, and tempura. With a good display of them you can have a free meal.

Crackseed

A sweet of Chinese origin, these are preserved and seasoned fruits and seeds. Some favorites include coconut, watermelon, pumpkin seeds, mango, and papaya. Different tasting, they take some getting used to, but make great "trail snacks." Available in all island markets. Also look for dried fish (cuttlefish) on racks, usually near the crackseed. These are nutritious and delicious and make a great snack.

Shave Ice

This real island institution makes the Mainland "snow cone" melt into insignificance. Special machines literally shave ice to a fluffy consistency. It's mounded into a paper cone and you choose from dozens of exotic island syrups that are generously poured over it. You're given a straw and a spoon, and just slurp away.

Malasadas And Pao Dolce

Two sweets from the Portuguese. *Malasadas* are holeless donuts and *pao dolce* is sweet bread. They're sold in island bakeries and they're great for breakfast or just as a treat.

Lomi Lomi Salmon

This is a salad of salmon, tomatoes, and onions with garnish and seasonings. It often accompanies "plate lunches" and is featured at buffets and luau.

MONEY-SAVERS

Only one thing is better than a great meal: a great meal at a reasonable price. The following are island institutions and favorites that will help you to eat well and to keep prices down.

Those really determined to save money can always try this!

Kaukau Wagons

These are lunch wagons, but instead of being slick stainless-steel jobs, most are old delivery trucks converted into portable kitchens. Some say they're a remnant of WW II, when workers had to be fed on the job; others say the meals they serve took their inspiration from the Japanese *bento*, a boxed lunch. You'll see them parked along beaches, in city parking lots, or on busy streets. Usually a line of local people will be placing their orders, especially at lunchtime, a tip-off that they serve a delicious, nutritious island dish for a reasonable price. They might have a few tables, but basically they serve food to go. Most of their filling meals are about $4.50, and they specialize in the "plate lunch."

Plate Lunch

This is one of the best island standards. These lunches give you a sampling of authentic island food and can include teriyaki chicken, mahimahi, *lau lau*, and *lomi lomi* salmon, among others. They're served on paper or styrofoam plates, are packed to go, and usually cost less than $5.50. Standard with a plate lunch is "two-scoop rice," a generous dollop of macaroni salad, or some other salad. A full meal, they're great for keeping down food costs and for making an instant picnic. Available everywhere from *kaukau* wagons to restaurants.

Saimin

Special "saimin shops," as well as restaurants, serve this hearty Japanese-inspired noodle soup on their menu. Saimin is a word unique to Hawaii. In Japan, these soups would either be called *ramin* or *soba*, and it's as if the two were combined into saimin. These are large bowls of noodle soup, in a light broth with meat, chicken, fish, or vegetables stirred in. They cost only a few dollars and are big enough for an evening meal. The best place to eat saimin is in a little local hole-in-the-wall shop, run by a family.

Good Deals

Even some of the island's best restaurants in the fanciest hotels offer "early bird specials"—the regular menu offered for less, to diners who come in before the usual dinner hour, which is approximately 6 p.m. You can pay as little as half the normal price, and can dine in luxury on some of the best foods. Often advertised in the "free" tourist books, coupons for reduced meals might also include two for one, or limited dinners at a much lower price. Just clip them out.

Food Shopping
Around the island plenty of mom 'n' pop grocery stores provide fertile ground for a cultural exchange, but they're expensive. Oahu's large supermarkets include **Times, Safeway, Foodland,** and **Star Markets.** Preference is highly individual, but Times has a good reputation for fresh vegetables and good prices. Japanese **Holiday Mart** has stores around the island. They've got some bargains in their general merchandise departments, but because they try to be everything, their food section suffers, especially the fruits and vegetables.

A **Floating Farmer's Market** appears at different times and places around Honolulu. For example, on Wednesday mornings from 9:45 to 10:45 a.m., it's behind the fire station just north of the Honolulu Zoo in the tennis court (however, the location changes periodically). The vendors, who are mostly Filipino, drive up in small battered trucks and sell wonderful, fresh vegetables from their home plots at very reasonable prices. Big shots who bring in fruits and vegies from California and the like have been trying to weed these little guys out. The Honolulu Dept. of Parks regulates the time and place for the market, and you can get information at 527-6060.

Chinatown offers the **People's Open Market** at the Cultural Plaza, located at the corner of Mauna Kea and Beretania streets. Besides produce, you'll find fresh fish, meats, and poultry; the **Oahu Fish Market** is in the heart of Chinatown along King Street. The shops are run-down but clean, and sell everything from octopus to *kimchi.*

Health Food Stores
Brown rice and tofu eaters can keep that special sparkle in their eyes with no problem on Oahu—there are some excellent health food stores. Most have a snack bar where you can get a delicious and nutritious meal for bargain prices (see "Food" in the travel sections). **Down to Earth,** 2525 S. King St., tel. 947-7678, is an old standby where you can't go wrong; great stuff at great prices. **Kokua Co-op Natural Foods And Grocery Store,** at the corner of S. Beretania and Isenberg, tel. 941-1921, is open to the public Mon.-Sat. 9 a.m-8 p.m., Sun. 10 a.m.-7 p.m. It's full service store with organic and fresh produce, cheese, milk, juices, bulk foods, and breads. **Celestial Natural Foods,** at the Haleiwa Shopping Plaza on the North Shore, tel. 637-6729, is also top-notch. **Vim and Vigor** is at the Ala Moana Center, tel. 955-3600.

GETTING THERE

With the number of visitors each year approaching six million, and double that number of travelers just passing through, Hawaii is one of the easiest places in the world to get to . . . by plane. About 10 large U.S. airlines (and other small ones) fly to and from the islands; about the same number of foreign carriers, mostly from Asia and Oceania, touch down on a daily basis. In 1978 airlines were "deregulated." In 1984, the reign of the Civil Aeronautics Board (CAB), which controlled exactly which airlines flew where and how much they could charge, ended. Routes, prices, and schedules were thrown open to free competition. Airlines that had previously monopolized preferred destinations found competitors prying loose their strangleholds. Thus, Hawaii is now one of the most hotly contested air markets in the world. The competition between carriers is fierce, and this makes for "sweet deals" and a wide choice of fares for the money-wise traveler. It also makes for pricing chaos. It's impossible to give airline prices that will hold true for more than a month, if that long. But it's comforting to know that flights to Hawaii are cheaper today than they have been in years, and mile for mile are one of the best travel bargains in the industry. What's really important is to be familiar with the alternatives at your disposal, so you can make an informed travel selection. Now more than ever you should work with a sharp travel agent who's on your side.

Note: Handicapped travelers, please see "Health and Well-being—Help for the Disabled."

Brief Airline History

On May 20-21, 1927, the people of the world were mesmerized by the heroic act of Charles Lindbergh, The Lone Eagle, as he safely piloted his sturdy craft, *The Spirit of St. Louis*, across the Atlantic. With the Atlantic barrier broken, it took only four days for Jim Dole, of pineapple fame, to announce an air race from the West Coast to Hawaii. He offered the same first prize of $25,000 that Lindbergh had claimed, and to sweeten the pot he offered $10,500 for second place. The **Dole Air Derby** applied only to civilian flights, though the military was already at work attempting the Pacific crossing.

In August 1925, a Navy flying boat took off from near San Francisco, piloted by Commander John Rodgers. The seaplane flew without difficulty across the wide Pacific's expanse, but ran out of gas just north of the Hawaiian Islands and had to put down in a stormy sea. Communication devices went dead and the mission was given up as lost. Heroically, Rodgers and his crew made crude sails from the wing's fabric and sailed the plane to within 12 miles of Kauai, where they were spotted by an incredulous submarine crew. On June 28, 1927, Army Lieutenants Maitland and Hegenberger successfully flew a Fokker tri-motor land plane, *The Bird of Paradise,* from Oakland to Oahu in just under 26 hours.

On July 14, 1927, independent of the air derby, two indomitable pilots, Smith and Bronte, flew their *City of Oakland* from its namesake in California to a forced landing on the shoreline of Molokai. On August 16, 1927, eight planes lined up in Oakland to start the derby. The first to take off was the *Woolaroc*, piloted by Art Goebel and Bill Davis. It went on to win the race and claim the prize in just over 26 hours. Second place went to the appropriately named *Aloha,*

PACIFIC CROSSROADS

SOUTH AMERICA

NORTH AMERICA

ASIA

AUSTRALIA

NEW ZEALAND

HAWAII

MIDWAY

WAKE

GUAM

NEW GUINEA

PHILIPPINES

MANILA

HONG KONG

OKINAWA

KOREA

JAPAN

TOKYO

ALEUTIAN IS.

ANCHORAGE

SEATTLE

SAN FRANCISCO

LOS ANGELES

FIJI IS.

AMERICAN SAMOA

AUCKLAND

SYDNEY

TROPIC OF CANCER

EQUATOR

TROPIC OF CAPRICORN

2853 mi
2557 mi
2778 mi
2780 mi
3832 mi
5543 mi
5296 mi
4406 mi
5078 mi

2500 mi
2500 km

© MOON PUBLICATIONS, INC.

crewed by Martin Jensen and Paul Schluter, coming in two hours behind the *Woolaroc*. Unfortunately, two planes were lost in the crossing and two more in the rescue attempt, which accounted for 12 dead. However, the race proved that flying to Hawaii was indeed feasible.

WINGS TO HAWAII

There are two categories of airlines that you can take to Hawaii: **domestic,** meaning American-owned, and **foreign.** An American law, penned at the turn of the century to protect American shipping, says "only" an American carrier can transport you to and from two American cities. In the airline industry, this law is still very much in effect. It means, for example, that if you want a roundtrip San Francisco/Honolulu, you *must* fly on a domestic carrier, such as United or Pan Am. If, however, you are flying San Francisco to Tokyo, you are at liberty to fly a "foreign" airline such as Japan Air Lines, and you may even have a stopover in Hawaii, but you must continue on to Tokyo or some other foreign city and cannot fly JAL back to San Francisco. Canadians have no problem flying Canadian Pacific roundtrip from Toronto to Honolulu because this route does not connect two American cities, and so it is with all foreign travel to and from Hawaii. Travel agents all know this, but if you're planning your own trip be aware of this fact and know that if you're flying roundtrip it must be on a domestic carrier.

Kinds Of Flights

The three kinds of flights are the "milk run," direct, and nonstop. Milk runs are the least convenient. On these, you board a carrier, say in your home town, fly it to a gateway city, change planes and carriers, fly on to the West Coast, change again, and then fly to Hawaii. They're a hassle—your bags have a much better chance of getting lost, you waste time in airports, and to top it off, they're not any cheaper. Avoid them if you can.

On direct flights you fly from point A to point B without changing planes; it doesn't mean that you don't land in between. Direct flights usually do land once to board and deplane passengers, but you sit cozily on the plane along with your luggage and off you go again. Nonstop is just that, but can cost a bit more. You board and when the doors open again you're in Hawaii. All flights from the West Coast gateway cities are nonstop, "God willing," because there is only the Pacific in between!

Travel Agents

At one time people went to a travel agent the same way they went to a barber or beautician . . . loyally sticking with one. Most agents are reputable professionals who know what they're doing. They should be members of the American Society of Travel Agents (ASTA) and licensed by the Air Traffic Conference (ATC). Most have the inside track on the best deals, and they'll save you countless hours calling 800 numbers and listening to elevator music while on hold. Unless you require them to make very special arrangements, their services are free— the airlines and hotels that they book you into pay their commission.

If you've done business with a travel agent in the past, and were satisfied with the services and prices, by all means stick with him or her. If no such positive rapport exists, then shop around. Ask friends or relatives for recommendations; if you can't get any endorsements go to the Yellow Pages. Call two or three travel agents to compare prices. Make sure to give them equal information and be as precise as possible. Tell them where and when you want to go, how long you want to stay, class you want to travel, and any special requirements. Write down their information. It's amazing how confusing travel plans can be when you have to keep track of flight numbers, times, prices, and all the preparation info. When you compare, don't look only for the cheapest price. Check for convenience in flights, amenities of hotels, and any other fringe benefits that might be included. Then make your choice of agent; if he or she is willing to give you individualized service, stick with them from this point on.

Agents become accustomed to offering the same deals to many clients because they're familiar with making the arrangements and they worked well in the past. Sometimes these are indeed the best, but if they don't suit you, don't be railroaded into accepting them. Any good agent will work with you. After all, it's your trip and your money.

Package Tours

For the independent traveler, practical package deals that include only flight, car, and lodging are okay. Agents put these together all the time and they just might be the best, but if they don't suit you, make arrangements separately. A package *tour* is totally different. On these you get your hand held by an escort, eat where they want you to eat, go where they want you to go, and watch Hawaii slide by your bus window. For some people, this might be the way, but everyone else should avoid the package tour. You'll see Hawaii best on your own, and if you want a tour you can arrange one there, often cheaper. Once arrangements have been made with your travel agent, make sure to take all receipts and letters of confirmation (hotel, car) with you to Hawaii. They probably won't be needed, but if they are, nothing will work better in getting results.

Mainland And International Fares

There are many categories of airline fares, but only three apply to the average traveler: first class, coach, and excursion (APEX). Traveling **first class** seats you in the front of the plane, gives you free drinks and movie headsets, a wider choice of meals, more leg room, and access to VIP lounges, if they exist. There are no restrictions, no penalties for advance-booking cancellations or rebooking of return flights, and no minimum-stay requirements.

Coach, the way that most people fly, is totally adequate. You sit in the plane's main compartment behind first class. Your seats are comfortable, but you don't have as much leg-room or as wide a choice of meals. Movie headsets and drinks cost you a few dollars, but that's about it. Coach offers many of the same benefits as first class and costs about 30% less. You can buy tickets up until takeoff; you have no restrictions on minimum or maximum stays; you receive liberal stopover privileges, and you can cash in your return ticket or change your return date with no penalties.

Excursion or advance payment excursion (APEX) fares are the cheapest. You are accommodated on the plane exactly the same as if you were flying coach. There are, however, some restrictions. You must book and pay for your ticket in advance (7-14 days). At the same time, you must book your return flight, and under most circumstances you can't change either without paying a penalty. Also, your stopovers are severely limited and you will have a minimum/maximum stay period. Only a limited number of seats on any one plane are set aside for APEX fares, so book as early as you can. Also, if you must change travel plans, you can go to the airport and get on as a standby passenger using a discounted ticket, even if the airline doesn't have an official standby policy. There's always the risk that you won't get on, but you do have a chance, as well as priority over an actual standby customer.

Standby is exactly what its name implies: you go to the airport and wait around to see if any flights going to Hawaii have an empty seat. You can save some money, but cannot have a firm itinerary or limited time. Since Hawaii is such a popular destination, standbys can wait days before catching a plane. A company called **Stand Bys Ltd.** offers an up-to-the-minute newsletter and an 800 number, which gives you information on charter flights that haven't sold out. The service costs $45 per year, but you can save 15-60% on most tickets. Write to Stand Bys Ltd., 26711 Northwestern Hwy., Southfield, MI 48034, tel. (313) 352-4876.

Active and retired **military personnel** and their dependents are offered special fares on airlines and in military hostels. An excellent resource book listing all of these special fares and more is *Space-A* ($11.75 for book and first-class postage), available from Military Travel News, P.O. Box 9, Oakton, VA 22124. Plenty of money-saving tips.

Charters

Charter flights were at one time only for groups or organizations that had memberships in travel clubs. Now they're open to the general public. A charter flight is an entire plane or a "block" of seats purchased at a quantity discount by a charter company and then sold to customers. Because they are bought at wholesale prices, charter fares can be the cheapest available. As in package deals, only take a charter flight if it is a "fly only," or perhaps includes a car. You don't need one that includes a guide and a bus. Most importantly, make sure that the charter company is reputable. They should belong to the same organizations (ASTA and ATC) as most travel agents. If not, check into them at the local chamber of commerce.

More restrictions apply to charters than to any other flights. You must pay in advance. If you cancel after a designated time, you can be penalized severely or lose your money entirely. You cannot change departure or return dates and times. However, up to 10 days before departure the charter company is legally able to cancel, raise the price by 10%, or change time and dates. They must return your money if cancellation occurs, or if changed arrangements are unacceptable to you. Mostly they are on the up-and-up and flights go smoothly, but there are horror stories. Be careful. Be wise. Investigate!

Tips

Flights from the West Coast take about five hours; you gain two hours over Pacific Standard Time when you land in Hawaii. From the East Coast it takes about 11 hours and you gain five hours over Eastern Standard Time. Try to fly Mon.-Thurs., when flights are cheaper and easier to book. Pay for your ticket as soon as your plans are firm. If prices go up there is no charge added, but merely booking doesn't guarantee the lowest price. Make sure that airlines, hotels, and car agencies get your phone number too, not only your travel agent's, in case any problems with availability arise (travel agents are often closed on weekends). It's not necessary, but it's a good idea to call and reconfirm flights 24-72 hours in advance.

First-row (bulkhead) seats are good for people who need more legroom, but bad for watching the movie. Airlines will give you special meals (vegetarian, kosher, low cal, low salt) often at no extra charge, but you must notify them in advance. If you're "bumped" from an overbooked flight, you're entitled to a comparable flight to your destination within one hour. If more than an hour elapses, you get "denied-boarding compensation," which goes up proportionally with the amount of time you're held up. Sometimes this is cash or a voucher for another flight to be used in the future. You don't have to accept what an airline offers on the spot, if you feel they aren't being fair.

Taking your pet cat, or dog (including seeing-eye dogs) can pose great problems. See "What to Take—Pets and Quarantine."

When To Go

The prime tourist season starts two weeks before Christmas and lasts until Easter. It picks up again with summer vacation in early June and ends once more in late August. If possible, avoid these times of year. Everything is usually booked solid and prices are inflated. Hotel, airline, and car reservations, which are a must, are often hard to coordinate. You can save 10-50% and a lot of hassling if you go in the artificially created "off season," September to early December, and mid-April (after Easter) until early June. You'll not only find the prices better, but the beaches, hikes, campgrounds and even restaurants will be less crowded. The people will be happier to see you, too.

Traveling With Children

Fares for children ages 2-12 are 50% of the adult fare; children under two, not occupying a seat, travel free. If you're traveling with an infant or active toddler, book your flight well in advance and request the bulkhead seat or first row in any section and a bassinet if available. Many carriers have fold-down cribs with restraints for baby's safety and comfort. Toddlers appreciate the extra space provided by the front-row seats. Be sure to reconfirm, and arrive early to ensure this special seating. On long flights you'll be glad that you took these extra pains.

Although most airlines have coloring books, puppets, etc., to keep your child busy, it's always a good idea to bring your own. These can make the difference between a pleasant flight and a harried ordeal. Also, remember to bring baby bottles, formula, diapers, and other necessities, as many airlines may not be equipped with exactly what you need. Make all inquiries ahead of time so you're not caught unprepared.

Baggage

You are allowed two free pieces of luggage and a carry-on bag. The two main pieces can weigh up to 70 pounds each; a charge is levied for extra weight. The larger bag can have an overall added dimension (height plus width plus length) of 62 inches; the smaller, 55 inches. Your carry-on must fit under your seat or in the overhead storage compartment. Purses and camera bags are not counted as carry-ons and may be taken aboard. Surfboards and bicycles are about $15 extra. Although they make great mementos, remove all previous baggage tags from your luggage; they can confuse handlers. Attach a sturdy holder with your name and address on the handle, or use a stick-on label on the bag itself. Put your name and address inside the bag, and the address where you'll be staying in Hawaii if possible. Carry your cosmetics, identification, money, prescriptions, tickets, reservations, change of underwear, camera equipment, and perhaps a change of shirt or blouse in your carry-on.

Visas

Entering Hawaii is like entering anywhere else in the U.S. Foreign nationals must have a current passport and proper visa, an ongoing or return air ticket, and sufficient funds for the proposed stay in Hawaii. Canadians do not need a visa or passport, but must have proper identification such as passport, driver's license, or birth certificate.

Leaving Hawaii

Remember that before you leave Hawaii for the Mainland, all of your bags are subject to an **agricultural inspection,** a usually painless procedure taking only a minute or two. To facilitate

your departure, leave all bags unlocked until after inspection. There are no restrictions on beach sand, coconuts, dried flower arrangements, fresh flower lei, pineapples, certified pest-free plants, seashells, seed lei, and wood roses. However, avocado, litchi, and papaya must be treated before departure. Some other restricted items are berries, fresh gardenias, roses, jade plants, live insects, snails, cotton, plants in soil, soil itself, and sugarcane.

OAHU FLIGHT ARRIVALS

The old adage of "all roads leading to Rome" applies almost perfectly to Oahu, though instead of being cobblestones, they're sea lanes and air routes. Except for a handful of passenger ships still docking at Honolulu Harbor, and some limited nonstop flights to Maui and the Big Island, all other passengers to and from Hawaii are routed through **Honolulu International Airport.** These flights include direct flights to the Neighbor Islands, which means stopping over at Honolulu International and continuing on the same plane, or more likely changing to an interisland carrier whose fare is included in the original price of the flight.

HONOLULU AIRPORT

Honolulu International Airport

The state's only international airport is one of the busiest in the entire country, with hundreds of flights to and from cities around the world arriving and departing daily. In a routine year, over 15 million passengers utilize this facility. The two terminals (directions given as you face the main entranceway) are: the main terminal, accommodating all international and Mainland flights, with a small wing at the far-left end of the ground floor for a few commuter airlines; and the **interisland terminal** in a separate building at the far right end of the main terminal.

The ground floor of the **main terminal** is mostly for arriving passengers, and contains the baggage claim area, lockers and long-term storage, car rental agencies, and international and domestic arrival doors, which are kept separate. The second floor is for departing passengers, with most activity centered here, including ticket counters, shops, lounges, baggage handlers, and the entrance to most of the gates. From both levels you can board taxis and TheBus to downtown Honolulu and Waikiki.

The **interisland terminal** services flights aboard Hawaii's own interisland carriers (see following). It has its own snack bars, car rental booths, transportation to and from the city, lounges, information windows, and restrooms. It is only a leisurely five minutes stroll between the two terminals, which is fine if you don't have much baggage; if you do, there are plenty of shuttles every few minutes . . . supposedly! (See "Airport Transportation" following).

Services, Information, Tips

The main **information booth** is located on the ground level just near the central escalators. Besides general information, they have good maps of the airport, Oahu, Honolulu, and Waikiki. Also, inquiry booths lined up along the ground level and at the interisland terminal are friendly and helpful, but not always stocked with as many maps as the main information booth.

The **lost and found** is located on the ground level of the main terminal, and at the interisland terminal. The **post office** is across the street from the main entranceway toward the interisland terminal.

Lockers are located on both levels of the main terminal and at the interisland terminal, with a **baggage storage room** only on the ground floor of the main terminal. Locker rental is for a 24-hour period, with a refundable key deposit. You can rent lockers for a month or longer, but you must prepay and leave a deposit. The baggage storage accepts no personal checks, no prepayments, and no pets or perishables. You *must* have your claim ticket to retrieve your belongings. The service is well run, efficient, and unfriendly.

Money can be a hassle at the airport, especially getting change, which is a downright rip-off, and very bad public relations for visitors. Unfortunately, no one will give you change, putting you at the mercy of $1 bill-change machines located throughout the airport. These machines happily dispense $.85 for every $1 you put in, so if you want to make a phone call, or the like, you're out of luck. The snack bars will only change money for you with a purchase. For a state that prides itself on the *aloha* spirit and depends on good relations with its visitors, this is a ridiculously poor way of greeting people, or giving them a last impression before they return home. The **foreign currency exchange** is on the second floor of the main terminal along the concourse behind the United ticket window. Here, and at a few smaller exchanges on the ground floor, the charge is one percent per transaction on foreign currency, and the same on traveler's checks, no matter where they're from, with a minimum charge of $1.50.

To refresh and relax, you might visit the **Airport Mini-Hotel**, tel. 836-3044, on the second level central area of the terminal. You can have a shower for $8.18, which includes soap, towel, shampoo, deodorant, and hairdryers; an eighthour sleep in a private little room and a shower for $32.20; or a two hour nap after 9 a.m. for $19.08. Also, **The Shower Tree**, 3085 N. Nimitz Hwy., tel. 833-1411, is only five minutes from the airport with transportation available and luggage storage. Prices are the same as the Airport Mini-Hotel. If these seem a bit pricy, just use the public bathrooms for a quick wash, then choose any one of three small gardens near the central concourse to take a little nap. If you're there just for a short snooze, airport security won't bother you.

Airport Transportation

The **Wiki Wiki Shuttle** is a free bus that takes you between the main terminal and the interisland terminal. Staffed by courteous drivers, it is efficient, most of the time. When it's not, a nickname could be the "Tricky Tricky Shuttle." Transfer time between the two terminals is only about 10 minutes, which does not include baggage transfer. If you'll be going on to a Neighbor Island make sure the carrier you are using has an interline agreement with the Hawaiian domestic carrier. If not, you must fetch your own bags, place them on the shuttle, and bring them with you to the interisland terminal. Also, if a flight is delayed, it is up to the carrier to notify the Wiki Wiki Shuttle so that adjustments can be made, and they are waiting for you. If your carrier does not contact them, the shuttle bus will follow the normal schedule and may not arrive in time to get you to the interisland terminal. Usually, this is a routine procedure with few problems, but if your connecting schedule is tight, and especially if your carrier has no interline agreement (the airline or your travel agent can tell you) be aware and leave extra time!

Car rental agencies are lined up at booths on the ground floor of both terminals. Many courtesy phones for car rental agencies not at the airport are located in and around the baggage claim area; call for a free van to pick you up and take you to their nearby facility. This procedure even saves the hassle of maneuvering through heavy airport traffic—you usually wait at the island in the middle of the road just outside the baggage claim area. Make sure to specify the number of the area where you'll wait.

If you're driving to the airport to pick up or drop off someone, you should know about **parking.** If you want to park on the second level of the parking garage for departures, you must either take the elevator up to the fourth floor, or down to ground level, and from there cross the pedestrian bridge. There's no way to get across on levels two and three.

Public transportation to downtown Honolulu, especially Waikiki, is abundant. Moreover, some hotels have courtesy phones near the baggage claim area; if you're staying there, they'll send a van to fetch you. Current charges for taxis, vans, TheBus, and limousine service are posted just outside the baggage claim area, so you won't have to worry about being overcharged.

Taxis to Waikiki cost about $20-25, not counting bags. **Taxi Corporation,** tel. 944-8294, charges $18 per car load with no baggage charge. Splitting the fare with other willing passengers can save money. **Grayline** runs a small bus or van to Waikiki for about $5 with no baggage charge. Also, a number of vans and motorcoaches leave from the central island in the roadway just outside the baggage claim. They charge $5, but a wait of up to 45 minutes for one is not out of the ordinary. Moreover, they drop passengers at hotels all over Waikiki, so if you're not one of the first stops by chance, it could be an hour or so after reaching Waikiki before you're finally deposited at your hotel.

Airport Motor Coach, tel. 839-0911, open daily 6:30 a.m.-10 p.m., hotel pick-up, charges $4 per person Waikiki to the airport, and $5 per person from the airport to Waikiki.

You can take **TheBus** (no. 19 or no. 20) to Waikiki via the Ala Moana Terminal, from which you can get buses all over the island. If you're heading north pick up bus no. 20, 51, or 52 just outside the airport. TheBus only costs 85 cents (exact change), but you are allowed only one carry-on bag, which must be small enough to be held on your lap. Drivers are sticklers on this point.

DOMESTIC CARRIERS

The following are the major domestic carriers to and from Hawaii. The planes used are primarily DC-10s and 747s, with a smaller 727 flown now and again. A list of the "gateway cities" from which they fly direct and nonstop flights is given, but "connecting cities" are not. All flights, by all carriers, land at Honolulu International Airport, except for the limited direct flights to Maui and Hawaii. Only the established companies are listed. Entrepreneurial small airlines such as the now-defunct Hawaii Express pop up now and again and specialize in dirt-cheap fares. There is a hectic frenzy to buy their tickets and business is great for a while, but then the established companies lower their fares and the gamblers fold.

Hawaiian Air
One of Hawaii's own domestic airlines has entered the Mainland market. They operate a daily

flight from Los Angeles and San Francisco to Honolulu, with periodic flights from Anchorage, Las Vegas, Portland, and Seattle. The "common fare" ticket price includes an ongoing flight to any of the Neighbor Islands, and if you're leaving Hawaii, a free flight from a Neighbor Island to the link-up in Honolulu. Senior-citizen discounts for people age 60 or older are offered on trans-Pacific and interisland flights. Hawaiian Air's trans-Pacific schedule features flights between Honolulu and points in the South Pacific nearly every day: flights depart for Pago Pago and American Samoa, half continuing on to Apia, Western Samoa, and the rest flying to Tonga, with additional flights to New Zealand, Guam, Tahiti, and Rarotonga. Hawaiian Air offers special discount deals with Dollar rental cars and select major-island hotels. Contact Hawaiian Air at (800) 367-5320 Mainland, (800) 882-8811 in Hawaii.

United Airlines

Since their first island flight in 1947, United has become top dog in flights to Hawaii. Their Mainland routes connect over 100 cities to Honolulu. The main gateways are direct flights from San Francisco, Los Angeles, San Diego, Seattle, Portland, Chicago, New York, Denver, and Toronto. They also offer direct flights to Maui from San Francisco, Los Angeles, and Chicago, and from Los Angeles to the Big Island. United offers a number of packages, including flight and hotel on Oahu, and flight, hotel, and car on the Neighbor Islands. They interline with Aloha Airlines and deal with Hertz rental cars. They're the "big guys" and they intend to stay that way—their packages are hard to beat. Call (800) 241-6522.

American Airlines

American offers direct flights to Honolulu from Los Angeles, San Francisco, Dallas, and Chicago. They also fly from Los Angeles and San Francisco to Maui, with a connection in Honolulu. Call (800) 433-7300.

Continental

Flights from all Mainland cities to Honolulu connect via Los Angeles and San Francisco. Also available are direct flights from Australia and New Zealand to Honolulu. Call (800) 525-0280 or (800) 231-0856 for international information.

Northwest

Northwest flies from Los Angeles, San Francisco, and Portland via Seattle. There are onward flights to Tokyo, Osaka, Okinawa, Manila, Hong Kong, Taipei, and Seoul. Call (800) 225-2525.

Delta Airlines

In 1985, Delta entered the Hawaiian market; when it bought out Western Airlines its share became even bigger. They have nonstop flights to Honolulu from Dallas/Ft. Worth, Los Angeles, San Francisco, and San Diego; and now flights to Kahului, Maui, via Los Angeles or Honolulu. Call (800) 221-1212.

INTERISLAND CARRIERS

The only effective way for most visitors to travel between the Hawaiian islands is by air. Luckily, Hawaii has excellent air transportation that boasts one of the industry's safest flight records. The following airlines have competitive prices, with interisland flights at about $75 each way. You can also save money (about $15) if you **take the first or last daily scheduled flight.** This offer usually applies only to flights to and from Honolulu, but do check because the policy often changes. Another alternative is to **purchase a booklet of six flight vouchers.** You save about $7 per ticket, and they are *transferable.* Just book a flight as normal and present the filled-in voucher to board the plane. Vouchers are perfect for families or groups of friends, and can be purchased at any ticket office or at Honolulu International Airport.

Hawaiian Air, tel. (800) 367-5320 nationwide, (800) 882-8811 statewide, offers the most flights. From Honolulu to Kauai, 26 nonstop flights go from 5:40 a.m. to 8 p.m.; flights to Maui begin at 5:40 a.m. with one every 20 minutes or so until 8:05 p.m., and there are also regularly scheduled flights to Kapalua, West Maui Airport; flights to Hilo leave every 40 minutes from 5:50 a.m. to 6:55 p.m., and flights to Kona leave from 5:55 a.m. to 6:45 p.m. Also, daily flights are offered to Lanai and Molokai.

Aloha Airlines, tel. (800) 367-5250, 935-5771, connects Oahu to Kauai, Maui, and both Kona and Hilo on Hawaii. Aloha's routes to

INTERISLAND
AIR ROUTES

MAJOR AIRPORT
WITH FULL FACILITIES
SECONDARY AIRPORT

© MOON PUBLICATIONS, INC.

Kauai are: from Honolulu, 22 nonstop flights from 5:40 a.m. until 6:10 p.m.; to Maui, about 30 flights daily, with one departing every 20 minutes or so from 5:40 a.m. to 8:15 p.m.; to Kona, about 20 flights daily from 5:40 a.m. to 7:00 p.m.; and to Hilo, 12 flights from 5:50 a.m. to 7:00 p.m.

Aloha Island Air, tel. (800) 323-3345 nationwide, (800) 652-6541 statewide, offers scheduled flights to and from Honolulu, Princeville on Kauai, Molokai, and Lanai; and from Kahului, Kapalua, and Hana airports on Maui. There are three flights from Honolulu, with the first at 6:10 a.m. and the last at 5 p.m. Flights to and from the other destinations are scheduled at one or two per day and often involve a stopover.

FOREIGN CARRIERS

The following carriers operate throughout Oceania but have no U.S. flying rights. This means that in order for you to vacation in Hawaii using one of these carriers, your flight must originate or terminate in a foreign city. You can have a

stopover in Honolulu with a connecting flight to a Neighbor Island. For example, if you've purchased a flight on Japan Air Lines from San Francisco to Tokyo, you can stop in Hawaii, but you must then carry on to Tokyo. Failure to do so will result in a stiff fine, and the balance of your ticket will not be refunded.

Canadian Airlines International
Nonstop flights from Canada to Honolulu originate in Vancouver, Toronto, and Calgary; nonstop Pacific flights go to Fiji, Auckland, and Sydney, with connecting flights to other Pacific cities. Call (800) 426-7007.

Air New Zealand
Flights link New Zealand, Australia, and Fiji with Los Angeles via Honolulu. Also offered are a remarkable APEX fare from Los Angeles to New Zealand, with stops in Honolulu and Fiji; and a Super Pass fare that lets you stop in eight cities between Los Angeles and Australia. Occasionally, other special fares are offered. Call (800) 262-1234 for current information.

Japan Air Lines

The Japanese are the second-largest group, next to Americans, to visit Hawaii. JAL flights to Honolulu originate in Tokyo, Nagoya, and Osaka. There are no JAL flights between the Mainland and Hawaii. Call (800) 525-3663.

Philippine Airlines

Philippine Airlines flies between Los Angeles or San Francisco and Manila via Honolulu. Connections in Manila are available to most Asian cities. Call (800) 435-9725.

Qantas

Daily flights depart from San Francisco and Los Angeles for Sydney via Honolulu. Stopovers are possible in Fiji and Tahiti. Call (800) 622-0850.

China Airlines

Routes from Los Angeles to Taipei with stopovers in Honolulu and Tokyo are possible, but flights are not available year-round. Connections from Taipei to most Asian capitals. Call (800) 227-5118.

Korean Air

Korean Air offers some of the least expensive flights to Asia. Flights leave only from Los Angeles, stop in Honolulu, then continue either directly to Seoul or stop over in Tokyo. Connections to many Asian cities. Call (800) 421-8200.

Air Tungaru

Limited flights from Kiribati to Honolulu via Christmas Island and Tarawa. In Hawaii, call 735-3994.

Air Nauru

The South Pacific's richest island offers flights throughout Polynesia, including most major islands, with connections to Japan, Taipei, Hong Kong, Manila, Singapore, and Australia. In Hawaii, call 531-9766.

TRAVEL BY SHIP

American Hawaii Cruises

This American cruise ship company operates two 800-passenger ships, the SS *Independence* and the SS *Constitution*. These ships offer similar seven-day itineraries that circumnavigate and call at the four main islands. Their fares range from an inside "thrifty cabin" at $1095 to a luxury owner's suite for $3950. Children under 16 are often given special rates and cruise free June-Sept. when they share a cabin with their parents. You board the ship in Honolulu after a plane flight to the islands arranged by American Hawaii Cruises. Each ship is a luxury seagoing hotel and gourmet restaurant; swimming pools, health clubs, movies, and nightclubs are all part of the amenities. For details contact: American Hawaii Cruises, 550 Kearny St., San Francisco, CA 94108, tel. (800) 765-7000; from Canada call collect (415) 392-9400.

American Hawaiian Cruises' SS Independence

Alternatives

Other companies offering varied cruises include **P&O Lines,** which operates the *Sea Princess* through the South Pacific, making port at Honolulu on its way from the West Coast once a year.

Royal Cruise Line out of Los Angeles, or Auckland alternatively, sails the *Royal Odyssey*, which docks in Honolulu on its South Pacific and Orient cruise, $2200-4000.

The **Holland America Line** sails the *Rotterdam* on its 108-day Grand Circle cruise, departing Fort Lauderdale, passing around South America, and calling at Honolulu as it heads for Asia. Prices are $20,000-70,000. Call (800) 426-0327.

Society Expeditions offers a 42-day cruise throughout the South Pacific departing from Honolulu. Fares range $3000-9000. Call (800) 426-7794.

Information

Most travel agents can provide information on the above cruise lines. If you're especially interested in traveling by freighter, contact: **Freighter Travel Club of America,** P.O. Box 12693, Salem, OR 97309; or **Ford's Freighter Travel Guide,** P.O. Box 505, 22151 Clarendon St., Woodland Hills, CA 91367.

TOUR COMPANIES

Many tour companies advertise packages to Hawaii in large city newspapers every week. They offer very reasonable airfares, car rentals, and accommodations. Without trying, you can get roundtrip airfare from the West Coast and a week in Hawaii for $400-500 using one of these companies. The following companies offer great deals and have excellent reputations. This list is by no means exhaustive.

Note: For a list of **ecotours** and excursions available *in* Hawaii see "Getting Around." For ecotours *to* Hawaii see the following section.

SunTrips

This California-based tour and charter company sells vacations all over the world. They're primarily a wholesale company, but will work with the general public. SunTrips often works with American Trans-Air, tel. (800) 225-9920, when flying to Hawaii. American Trans-Air answers their phones Mon.-Fri. during normal business hours only. When you receive your SunTrip tickets, you are given discount vouchers for places to stay that are convenient to the airport of departure. Many of these hotels have complimentary airport pickup service, and will allow you to park your car, free of charge, for up to 14 days, which saves a considerable amount on airport parking fees. SunTrips does not offer assigned seating until you get to the airport. They recommend that you get there two hours in advance, and they ain't kidding! This is the price you pay for getting such inexpensive air travel. SunTrips usually has a deal with a car-rental company. Remember that everyone on your incoming flight is offered the same deal, and all make a beeline for the rental car's shuttle van after landing and securing their baggage. If you have a traveling companion, work together to beat the rush by leaving your companion to fetch the baggage and heading directly for the van as soon as you arrive. Pick your car up, then return for your partner and the bags. Even if you're alone, you could zip over to the car-rental center and then return for your bags without having them sit very long on the carousel. Contact SunTrips, 100 Park Center, P.O. Box 18505, San Jose, CA 95158, tel. (800) 662-9292, (800) 786-8747 in California, 941-2697 in Honolulu.

Council Travel Services

These full-service, budget-travel specialists are a subsidiary of the nonprofit Council on International Educational Exchange, and the official U.S. representative to the International Student Travel Conference. They'll custom-design trips and programs for everyone from senior citizens to college students. Bona fide students have extra advantages, however, including eligibility for the International Student Identification Card (ISIC), which often gets you discount fares and waived entrance fees. Groups and business travelers are also welcome. For full information, write to the main offices at Council Travel Services, 919 Irving St., Suite 102, San Francisco, CA 94122, tel. (415) 566-6222. Other offices are in Austin, Berkeley, Boston, Davis, Long Beach, Los Angeles, Miami, New York, Portland, San Diego, and Seattle.

Student Travel Network

You don't have to be a student to avail yourself of their services. Their main office is at 2500 Wilshire Blvd., Suite 920, Los Angeles, CA 90057, tel. (213) 380-2184. In Honolulu they're at 1831 S. King St., Honolulu, HI 96826, tel. 942-7755. STN also maintains offices in San Diego, San Francisco, Northridge (California), Toronto, and Vancouver, as well as throughout Australia and Europe.

Nature Expeditions International

These quality tours have nature as the theme. Trips are 15-day, four-island, natural-history expeditions, with emphasis on plants, birds, and geology. Their guides are experts in their fields and give personable and attentive service. Contact Nature Expeditions International at 474 Willamette, P.O. Box 11496, Eugene, OR 97440, tel. (503) 484-6529 or (800) 869-0639.

Ocean Voyages

This unique company offers seven- and 10-day itineraries aboard a variety of yachts in the Hawaiian Islands. The yachts, equipped to carry 2-10 passengers, ensure individualized sail training. The vessels sail throughout the islands, exploring hidden bays and coves, and berth at different ports as they go. This opportunity is for anyone who wishes to see the islands in a timeless fashion, thrilling to sights experienced by the first Polynesian settlers and Western explorers. For rates and information contact Ocean Voyages, 1709 Bridgeway, Sausalito, CA 94965, tel. (415) 332-4681.

Island Holiday Tours

This established, Hawaii-based company offers flights with American and United, and rental cars through Budget. Arrangements can also be made for tours, luau, helicopter rides, etc., on all islands. Contact Island Holiday Tours, 2255 Kuhio Ave., Honolulu, HI 96815, tel. (800) 448-6877.

Pleasant Hawaiian Holidays

A California-based company specializing in Hawaii, Pleasant Hawaiian Holidays makes arrangements for flights, accommodations, and transportation only. At 2404 Townsgate Rd., Westlake Village, CA 91361, tel. (800) 242-9244.

Ecotours To Hawaii

Sierra Club Trips offers Hawaii trips for nature lovers who are interested in an outdoor experience. Various trips include hikes over Maui's Haleakala, a kayak trip along the Na Pali Coast of Kauai, and a family camping spree in Kauai's Kokee region. All trips are led by experienced guides and are open to Sierra Club members only ($33 per year to join). For information contact the Sierra Club Outing Department, 730 Polk St., San Francisco, CA 94109, tel. (415) 776-2211.

Earthwatch allows you to become part of an expeditionary team dedicated to conservation and the study of the natural environment. An expedition might include studying dolphins in Kewalo Basin Marine Mammal Laboratory, or observing the ubiquitous mongoose from a hut high atop Mauna Kea. Basically, you become an assistant field researcher—your lodgings might be a dorm room at the University of Hawaii, and your meals might come from a remote camp kitchen. Fees vary and are tax deductible. If you are interested in this learning experience, contact Earthwatch, 680 Mt. Auburn St., P.O. Box 403-P, Watertown, MA 02272, tel. (617) 926-8200.

Backroads, 1516 Fifth St., Suite PR, Berkeley, CA 94710, tel. (510) 527-1555 or (800) 462-2848, arranges easy-on-the-environment bicycle and hiking trips to the Big Island. Basic tours include: six-day hiking/camping tour $698; six-day hiking/inn tour $1295; eight-day bicycle/inn tour $1495; and five-day bicycle/camping tour $649. Prices include hotel/inn accommodations or tent when applicable, most meals, and professional guide service. Airfare is not included, and bicycles and sleeping bags can be rented (b.y.o. okay!) for reasonable rates.

Far Horizons, P.O. Box 1529, 16 Fern Ln., San Anselmo, CA 94960, tel. (800) 552-4575, specializes in cultural discovery trips. A 12-day trip visits the islands of Hawaii, Lanai, and Oahu. Led by archaeologist Dr. Georgia Lee, an expert in Polynesian rock art, the expedition features stops at Hawaii's most famous *heiau,* petroglyph fields, museums, and historical homes. The cost is $3695 per person and includes trans-Pacific and international flights, accommodations, ground transportation, most meals, and entry fees.

Crane Tours, 15101 Magnolia Blvd., Sherman Oaks, CA 91403, tel. (800) 653-2545, owned and operated by Bill Crane, has been taking people kayaking and backpacking to the Big Island, Maui, and Kauai since 1976. Basic prices for these eco-adventures start at $650, with the most expensive tour around $800 (airfare not included).

Note: For **ecotours** *in* Hawaii see "Getting Around."

GETTING AROUND

Touring Oahu is especially easy, since almost every normal (and not so normal) mode of conveyance is readily available. You can rent anything from a moped to a pedicab, and the competition is very stiff, which helps keep prices down. A few differences separate Oahu from the other islands. To begin with, Oahu has a model public transportation system called TheBus—not only efficient, but very inexpensive. Also, Oahu is the only island that has a true expressway system, though along with it comes rush hour and traffic jams. A large part of Oahu's business is processing people, even if it's only to send them on to another island! The agencies operating these businesses on the island are masters at moving people down the road. With the huge volume of tourists that visit every year, it's amazing how smoothly it works. The following is a cross section of what's available and should help you to decide how you want to get around. Have fun! Also see "Waikiki—Sights" for more information about getting around in Waikiki.

CAR RENTALS

Does Hawaii really have more rental cars than pineapples? Oahu's Yellow Pages have eight pages of listings for car rental agencies. You can rent anything from a 60-passenger Scenic-cruiser to a 60-cc moped. Even so, if you visit the islands during a peak tourist frenzy without reserving your wheels in advance, you'll be marooned at the airport.

There's a tremendous field of cars and agencies from which to choose and they're cheaper than anywhere else in America. Special deals come and go like tropical rain showers; swashbuckling price-slashings and come-ons are common all over the rental car market. A little knowledge combined with some shrewd shopping around can save you a bundle. And renting a car is the best way to see the islands if you're going to be there for a limited time. Outside of Oahu, it simply isn't worth hassling with the poor public transportation system, or relying on your thumb.

Requirements

A variety of requirements are imposed on the renter by car agencies, but the most important clauses are common. Some of the worst practices being challenged are: no rentals to people under 25 and over 70, and no rentals to military personnel or Hawaiian residents! Before renting, check that you fulfill the requirements. Generally, you must be 21, although some agencies rent to 18-year-olds, while others still require you to be 25. You must possess a valid driver's license, with licenses from most countries accepted, but if you are not American, get an International Driver's License to be safe. You should have a major credit card in your name. This is the easiest way to rent a car. Some companies will take a deposit, but it will be very stiff. It could easily be $50 per day on top of your rental fees and sometimes much more. In addition, they may require a credit check on the spot, complete with phone calls to your employer and bank. If you damage the car, charges will be deducted from your deposit, and the car company itself determines the extent of the damages. Some companies *will not* rent you a car without a major credit card in your name, no matter how much of a deposit you are willing to leave.

When To Rent

On this one, you'll have to make up your own mind, because it's a "bet" that you can either win or lose big. But it's always good to know the odds before you plop down your money. You can reserve your car in advance when you book your air ticket, or play the field when you get there. If you book in advance, you'll obviously have a car waiting for you, but the deal that you made is the deal that you'll get—it may or may not be the best around. On the other hand, if you wait, you can often take advantage of excellent on-the-spot deals. However, you're betting that cars are available. You might be totally disappointed and not be able to rent a car at all, or you might make a honey of a deal.

If you're arriving during the peak seasons of Christmas, Easter, and late summer vacation, *absolutely book your car in advance.* They are all accounted for during this period, and even if you can find a junker from a fly-by-night, they'll price-gouge you mercilessly. If you're going off-peak, you stand a good chance of getting the car you want at the price you want. It's generally best to book ahead, but the majority of car companies have toll-free 800 numbers (listed below). At least call them for an opinion of your chances of getting a car upon your intended arrival.

Rates

If you pick up a car-rental brochure at a travel agency, notice that the prices for Hawaii rentals are about the lowest in the United States. The two rate options for renting are **mileage** and **flat rate.** A third type, **mileage/minimum,** is generally a bad idea unless you plan to do some heavy-duty driving. Mileage rate costs less per day, but you are charged for every mile driven. Mileage rates are best if you drive less than 30 miles per day—but even on an island that isn't much! The flat rate is best, providing a fixed daily rate and unlimited mileage. With either rate, you buy the gas; don't buy the cheapest because the poor performance from low octane eats up your savings.

Discounts of about 10-15% for weekend, weekly, and monthly rates are available. It's sometimes cheaper to rent a car for the week even if you're only going to use it for five days. Both weekly and monthly rates can be split between Neighbor Islands.

Warning: If you keep your car beyond your contract, you'll be charged the highest daily rate unless you notify the rental agency beforehand. Don't keep your car longer than the contract without notifying the company. They are *quick* to send out their repossession specialists. You might find your car gone, a warrant for your arrest, and an extra charge. A simple courtesy call notifying them of your intentions saves a lot of headaches and hassle.

What Wheels To Rent

The super-cheap rates on the eye-catcher brochures refer to subcompact standard shifts. The price goes up with the size of the car and with an automatic transmission. As with options on a new car, the more luxury, the more you pay. If you can drive a standard shift, get one! They're cheaper to rent and operate. Because many Hawaiian roads are twisty affairs, you'll appreciate the downshifting ability and extra control of a standard shift. AM/FM radios are good to have for entertainment and for weather and surf conditions. If you have the choice, take a car with cloth seats instead of sticky vinyl.

The average price of a subcompact standard shift, without a/c, is $30 per day, $120 per week (add about $8 per day—$50 per week—for an automatic), but rates vary widely. Luxury cars are about $10 per day more, with a comparable weekly rate. Most of the car companies, local and national, offer special rates and deals. These deals fluctuate too rapidly to give any hard-and-fast information. They are common, however, so make sure to inquire. Also, peak periods have "black outs" where normally good deals no longer apply.

Insurance

Before signing your car-rental agreement, you'll be offered "insurance" for around $10 per day. Since insurance is already built into the contract (don't expect the rental agency to point this out), what you're really buying is a waiver on the deductible ($500-1000), in case you crack up the car. If you have insurance at home, you will almost always have coverage on a rental car, including your normal deductible, but not all policies are the same, so check with your agent. Also, if you haven't bought their waiver, and you have a mishap, the rental agencies will put a claim against your major credit card on the spot for the amount of deductible, even if you can prove that your insurance will cover. They'll tell you to collect from your insurance company because they don't want to be left holding the bag on an across-the-waters claim. If you have a good policy with a small deductible, it's hardly worth paying the extra money for the waiver, but if your own policy is inadequate, buy the insurance. Also, most **major credit cards** offer complimentary car-rental insurance as an incentive for using their cards to rent the car. Simply call the toll-free number of your credit card company to see if this service is included.

Driving Tips

Protect your children as you would at home with car seats. Their rental prices vary considerably: Alamo offers them free of charge; National charges $3 per day; Hertz needs 48 hours notice; Dollar gives them free but they're not always available at all locations. Almost all the agencies can make arrangements if you give them enough notice. Check before you go and if all else fails, bring one from home.

There are few differences between driving in Hawaii and on the Mainland. Just remember that many people on the roads are tourists and can be confused about where they're going. Since many drivers are from somewhere else, there's hardly a "regular style" of driving in the islands. A farmer from Iowa accustomed to poking along on back roads can be sandwiched between a frenetic New Yorker who's trying to drive over his roof and a super-polite but horribly confused Japanese tourist who normally drives on the left.

In Hawaii, drivers don't honk their horns except to say hello, or in an emergency. It's considered rude, and honking to hurry someone might earn you a knuckle sandwich. Hawaiian drivers reflect the climate: they're relaxed and polite. Oftentimes, they'll brake to let you turn left when they're coming at you. They may assume you'll do the same, so be ready, after a perfunctory turn signal from another driver, for him or her to turn across your lane. The more rural the area, the more apt this is to happen.

It may seem like common sense, but remember to slow down when you enter the little towns strung along the circle-island route. It's easy to bomb along on the highway and flash through these towns, missing some of Hawaii's best scenery. Also, rural children expect *you* to be watchful, and will assume that you are going to stop for them when they dart out into the crosswalks.

The **H-1 and H-2 freeways** throw many Mainlanders a Polynesian "screwball." Accustomed to driving on super highways, Mainlanders assume that these are the same. They're not. Oahu's super highways are much more twisted, turned, and convoluted than most Mainland counterparts. Subliminally they look like a normal freeway, except that they've been tied into a Hawaiian knot. There are split-offs, crossroads, and exits in the middle of the exits. Stay alert and don't be lulled into familiar complacency.

B.Y.O. Car

If you want to bring your own car, write for information to: Director of Finance, Division of Licenses, 1455 S. Beretania St., Honolulu, HI 96814. However, unless you'll be in Hawaii for a bare minimum of six months and will spend all your time on one island, don't even think about it. It's an expensive proposition and takes time and plenty of arrangements. From California, the cost is at least $600 to Honolulu, and an additional $100 to any other island. To save on rental costs, it would be better to buy and sell a car there, or to lease for an extended period.

Car Rental Agencies

When you arrive at any of Hawaii's airports, you'll walk the gauntlet of car rental booths and courtesy phones shoulder to shoulder along the main hallways. Of the two categories of car rental agencies in Hawaii, each has its own advantage. The first category is the big international firms like Dollar, National, Hertz, Avis, and Budget. These big guys are familiar, easy to work with, sometimes offer special fly/drive deals with airlines, and live up to their promises. If you want your rental experience to be hassle-free, they're the ones. Also, don't be prejudiced against them just because they're so well known; sometimes they offer the best deal.

Hawaii has spawned a good crop of local entrepreneurial rental agencies. Their deals and cars can range, like rummage-sale treasures, from great finds to pure junk. These companies have the advantage of being able to cut deals on the spot. If nothing is moving from their lot on the day you arrive, you might get a real bargain. Unfortunately, mixed in this category is a hodgepodge of fly-by-nights. Some of these are small, but adequate, while others are a rip-off. Their cars are bad, their service is worse, and they have more hidden costs than a Monopoly board.

National Agencies

All of the following national companies have locations in Waikiki. The local phone numbers given are for the main location at Honolulu International Airport. Call for more details.

One of the best national firms with an excellent reputation for service and prices is **Dollar Rent A Car**, tel. 944-1544, (800) 367-7006, (800) 342-7398 in Hawaii. Their deals and service can't be beat.

Others include: **National Car Rental**, tel. 831-3800, (800) 227-7368; **Hertz**, tel. 831-3500, (800) 654-3131; **Avis**, tel. 834-5536, (800) 331-1212, (800) 831-8000 in Hawaii; **Budget**, tel. 922-3600, (800) 527-0700; **Alamo**, tel. 845-7511, (800) 327-9633; **Sears**, accepting Sears credit cards, tel. 599-2205, (800) 451-3600;

Thrifty, airport tel. 836-2388, Waikiki tel. 923-7383, toll-free (800) 367-2277.

Local Agencies

These firms offer bargain rates and older cars. Many of these rent without a major credit card, but they require a stiff deposit. Sometimes they even rent to those under 21, but you'll have to show reservations at a major hotel. Some where you usually make out all right are: **Aloha Funway Rentals,** airport tel. 831-2277, Waikiki tel. 942-9696, also exotics, jeeps, and mopeds; **Island,** tel. 839-2222 airport, 946-6666 Waikiki; **Sunshine,** tel. 836-0319 airport, 924-2866 Waikiki; and **VIP** (Very Inexpensive Prices), tel. 946-1671.

Fantasy And Vanity Rentals

The most distinctive and fun-filled cars on Oahu are the hotrods available from Waikiki's **Cruisin' Classics,** 2080 Kalakaua Ave., tel. 951-8331. They have a fleet of American and European classic cars that have been completely restored. Owner Don Pierce operates the company and has done the majority of the work himself on the 1928 Model-A Fords. He has completely reinforced the frame and incorporated a Mustang front suspension, engine, transmission, and rear end. They've all been updated with automatic transmissions and power steering (easy to drive). All are equipped with AM/FM cassette players and "oouugah" horns. Pick a roadster that'll seat four with the rumble seat, or a four-door convertible touring car, which seats five. Recent additions to the fleet are a 1959 pink Cadillac convertible, a 1960 Corvette, and a 1973 Corvette Stingray convertible. Prices start at $89 up to $250 for a stretch limo. They offer a collision damage waiver for an additional $14.95, or you can accept full responsibility. Insurance for these particular cars is not automatically covered by your credit card company, which is often *great views with only half the flats to worry about*

the case with normal rental cars. If your hotel is in the Waikiki area they'll fetch you in their stretch limo, and when you return their car, they'll take you back to your hotel.

Ferrari Rentals, also in Waikiki at 2080 Kalakaua Ave., tel. 942-8725, rents a magnificent Lamborghine Diablo for the equally magnificent price of $1100 per day, while their Ferrari Mondail is $400 a day, and a 1990 Jaguar XJSV-12 convertible goes for the mere pittance of only $250 per day.

Four-wheel Drives

If you're into 4WDs try: **United Car Rental,** tel. 922-4605; or **Aloha Funway Rentals,** tel. 834-1016.

PUBLIC TRANSPORTATION

TheBus

If Dorothy and her mates had TheBus to get them down the Yellow Brick Road, she might have chosen to stay in Oz and forget about Kansas. TheBus, TheBus, ThewonderfulBus is the always-coming, slow-moving, go-everywhere friend of the budget traveler. Operated by Oahu Transit Services, Inc. (OTS), it could

serve as a model of efficiency and economy in any city of the world. What makes it more amazing is that it all came together by chance, beginning as an emergency service in 1971. These brown, yellow, and orange coaches go up and down both the windward and leeward coasts, through the interior, while passing through all of the major and most of the minor towns in between, and most often stopping near the best sights.

The **direction** in which TheBus travels is posted after the number and the name of the town. They are designated as EB (eastbound toward Diamond Head) and WB (westbound toward the airport). The **fare** is only 85 cents adult, 25 cents for students between ages 6-18, while kids under five who can sit on their parent's lap aren't charged at all. The fare is paid in exact change upon entering. Even putting a $1 bill into the box and not expecting change is unacceptable. Adult **monthly bus passes,** good at any time and on all routes, are $20, but be aware that they are good only from the first to the last day of every month. If you buy a pass in midmonth, or even later, it is still $20! **Senior Citizens Bus Passes** are $15 and good for four years, or $6 for a discount fare ID also good for four years. Seniors must furnish proof of age, and will be given the pass within a few minutes of having an ID photo taken. Passes are available at **TheBus Pass Office,** open Mon.-Fri. 7:30 a.m.-3:30 p.m., at 811 Middle St., tel. 848-4500. Route 1, Kalihi Bus stops within a few feet of TheBus Pass Office.

Transfers are free and are issued upon request when entering TheBus, but you can only use them for ongoing travel in the same direction, and on a different line (numbered bus). They are also timed and dated, good for approximately one half-hour to one hour.

Get full **route and schedule information** by calling TheBus at 848-5555, 5:30 a.m.-10 p.m., or by visiting the information booth at the Ala Moana Terminal, where you can pick up fliers and maps. An excellent, inexpensive little guide is *Hawaii Bus and Travel Guide* by Milly Singletary, available in most bookstores. Recorded information on routes and attractions is available 24 hours a day at 296-1818.

The following are some popular destinations and their bus numbers, all originating from the Ala Moana Terminal: **Airport,** no. 19 or no. 20; *Arizona* **Memorial, Pearl Harbor,** no. 20, 50, 51, or 52 Wahiawa (not no. 52 Kaneohe); **Bishop Museum,** no. 2 School; **Chinatown,** no. 1, 2, 3, 4, 6, 8, 9, 11, 12, 50, or 52 Wahiawa; **Fisherman's Wharf,** no. 20 or 52 Kaneohe; Hanauma Bay, no. 1 or 57, beach bus weekends; **Honolulu (downtown),** no. 1, 2, 3, 4, 9, 11, or 12; **Pali Lookout,** not serviced; **Polynesian Culture Center,** both no. 52 buses, then a shuttle; **Queen Emma's Summer Palace,** no. 4; **Sea Life Park,** no. 57; **Waikiki Beach,** no. 2, 4, 8, 14, or 20.

The **Beach Bus,** no. 22, starts on Kuhio Ave. near Kalakaua Ave. and services all of the beach areas, including Hanauma Bay and Sandy Point; Sea Life Park is its terminus. Once a seasonal service, the **Beach Bus** now operates year-round.

Circling the island by bus is a terrific way to see the sights and meet people along the way. The circle route takes about four hours if you ride the entire loop, but you can use the transfer system to give yourself a reasonable tour of only the sights that strike your fancy. The **circle-island** bus is no. 52, but remember that there are two no. 52 buses, going in different directions. The buses are labeled: **no. 52 Wahiawa Kaneohe** goes inland to Wahiawa, north to Haleiwa, along the north shore, down the windward coast to Kaneohe and back over the *pali* to Honolulu; **no. 52 Kaneohe Wahiawa** follows the same route but in the opposite direction. If you'll be taking this bus to Pearl Harbor, be absolutely sure to take no. 52 Wahiawa Kaneohe, because if you took the other, you'd have to circle the entire island before arriving at Pearl!

Other Public Buses, Etc.
The **Waikiki Trolley,** tel. 526-0112, an open-air bus, will take you on a tour of Waikiki and Honolulu for $15 (all day pass, board, exit and re-board whenever you like).

Taxis
The law says that taxis are not allowed to cruise around looking for fares, so you can't hail them. But they do and you can, and most policemen have more important things to do than monitor cabs. Best is to summon one from your hotel or a restaurant. All are radio-dispatched, and they're usually there in a flash. The fares, posted on the taxi doors, are set by law and are fair, but still expensive for the budget traveler. The rates do change, but expect about $2.50 for the flag fall, and then 50 cents for each additional one-sixth mile. The airport to Waikiki is about $25, though luggage costs extra.

Of the many taxi companies, some with good reputations are: **SIDA,** a cooperative of owner-drivers, at 836-0011; **Aloha State Taxi,** tel. 847-3566; **Charley's,** tel. 531-1331; **TheCab,** tel. 533-4999. **City Taxi,** tel. 524-2121, offers competitive rates and a senior citizen discount. If you need some special attention like a Rolls-Royce limo, try: **Cloud 9 Limousines,** tel. 524-7999; for the **handicapped** and people in wheelchairs, **Handicabs,** tel. 524-3866.

ALTERNATIVE TRAVEL

Bicycles, Motorcycles, And Mopeds
Peddling around Oahu can be both fascinating and frustrating. The roads are well paved, but the shoulders are often torn up. Traffic in and around Honolulu is horrifying, and the only way to avoid it is by leaving very early in the morning. TheBus has no facilities for transporting your bike out of town, so an early departure is your only alternative. Once you leave the city, traffic, especially on the secondary interior roads, isn't too bad. Unfortunately, all of the coastal roads are heavily trafficked. Instead of a delicate road bike, you're better off renting a **cruiser** or **mountain bike,** which will allow for the sometimes poor road conditions and open up the possibilities of off-road biking. Even experienced mountain bikers should be careful on Oahu trails, which are often extremely muddy and rutted. Peddling around Waikiki, although congested, is usually safe, and a fun way of seeing the sights. Always lock your bike, and take your bike bag.

For info on biking on Oahu, contact **Hawaii Bicycling League,** P.O. Box 4403, Honolulu, HI 96813. This nonprofit corporation sponsors rides all over Oahu almost every weekend. Non-members are always welcome. The rides are multiple-level ability and are listed in the Hawaii Bicycling League's monthly newsletter, *Spoke-n-Words*. If you're into cycling and want a unique look at Oahu, don't miss these rides. Also see "Sightseeing Tours" following.

For bicycle rentals try: good old **Aloha Funway Rentals,** 2025 Kalakaua Ave., tel. 946-2766; **The Bike Way,** at 250 Ward Way, tel. 538-7433. For sales and repairs try: **The Bike Shop,** featuring Fuji, Mongoose, and Schwinn, at 1149 S. King St., tel. 531-7071; **McCully Bicycle,** featuring Specialized, Miyata, and Takara, at 2124 S. King, tel. 955-6329; and **The Bike Way,** featuring Bianchi and Univega, as above.

Motorcycles and mopeds are available from: **Aloha Funway Rentals,** tel. 942-9696; **Two Wheel Ventures,** tel. 943-0223; **Discount Moped Rentals,** tel. 941-3623.

Hitchhiking

Hitchhiking varies from island to island, both in legality and method. On Oahu, hitchhiking is legal, and you use the tried-and-true style of facing traffic and waving your thumb. But you can only hitchhike from bus stops! Not many people hitchhike and the pickings are reasonably easy, but TheBus is only 85 cents for anywhere you want to go and the paltry sum that you save in money is lost in "seeing time."

Two things against you: many of the people are tourists and don't want to bother with hitch-hikers, and many locals don't want to bother with nonlocal hitchhikers. When you do get a ride, most of the time it will be from a *haole* who is either a tourist on his own or a recent island resident. If you are just hitchhiking along a well-known beach area, perhaps in your bathing suit and obviously not going far, you can get a ride more easily. Women should exercise caution like everywhere else in the U.S., and avoid hitchhiking alone.

SIGHTSEEING TOURS

Guided land tours are much more of a luxury than a necessity on Oahu. Because of the excellent bus system and relatively cheap rental cars, you spend a lot of money for a narration and to be spared the hassle of driving. If you've come in a group and don't intend on renting a car, they may then be worth it. Sea cruises and air tours are equally luxurious, but provide glimpses of this beautiful island you'd normally miss. The following partial list of tour companies should get you started.

Note: For all activities, including snorkeling, scuba, all water sports, horseback riding, parasailing, golf, tennis, etc., please refer to "Sports and Recreation."

Land Tours

If you're going to take a land tour, you must have the right attitude, or it'll be a disaster. Your tour leader, usually driving the van or bus, is part instructor, comedian, and cheerleader. There's enough "corn" in his jokes to impress an Iowa hog. On the tour, you're expected to become part of one big happy family, and most importantly, to be a good sport. Most guides are quite knowledgeable about Oahu and its history, and they honestly try to do a good job. But they've done it a million times before, and their performance can be as stale as week-old bread. The larger the tour vehicle and the shorter the miles covered, the worse it is likely to be. If you still want a tour, take a full-day jaunt in a small van: you get to know the other people and the guide, who'll tend to give you a more in-depth presentation. Tips are cheerfully accepted. Also, be aware that some tours get kickbacks from stores and restaurants they take you to, where you don't always get the best bargains. Most companies offer free hotel pickup and delivery. Lunch or dinner is not included unless specified, but if the tour includes a major tourist spot like Waimea Falls Park or the Polynesian Culture Center, admission is usually included.

About eight different tours offered by most companies are variations on the same theme; since the prices are regulated, the cost is fairly uniform. The more popular are the **circle-island tour,** including stops at Diamond Head, Hanauma Bay, the windward and north shores, Waimea Falls, and perhaps the Mormon Temple and Dole Pineapple Pavilion, for about $50, and half for children. A **night tour** to the Polynesian Culture Center, including admission and dinner show, cost is $50. **Picnic tours,** and tours to **Byodo-In Temple,** go for around $40. Tours to **Punchbowl** and the *Arizona* **Memorial** are around $25.

1. Byodo-In Temple (J.D. Bisignani); 2. the moody *pali* from Kailau/Kaneohe (J.D. Bisignani);

1. windsurfing Oahu (J.D. Bisignani)   **2.** roadside fruitstand, Waiahole (J.D. Bisignani)

Some reputable companies include: **Akamai Tours,** tel. 971-3131; **Polynesian Adventure Tours,** tel. 922-0888; **Robert's Hawaii Tours,** tel. 523-5187; **Trans Hawaiian Tours,** tel. 735-6467; **E. Noa Tours,** tel. 599-2561; **Dole Pineapple Cannery Tour,** tel. 523-3653 (see "Honolulu—Sights"); and **Paradise Action Tours,** 307 Lewers St., tel. 926-9193, can arrange everything from Pearl Harbor Cruises to dinner shows. They also arrange condo/hotel reservations, car rental, and interisland tours at competitive prices.

Special Tours

The following are special tours that you should seriously consider. "Walking Tour of Chinatown," tel. 533-3181, by the Chinese Chamber of Commerce, leaves every Tuesday at 9:30 a.m. from in front of their offices at 42 N. King Street. You get a narrated three-hour tour of Chinatown for about $4, and an optional Chinese lunch for around $5. "Walking Tour of Honolulu, the 1800s," tel. 531-0481, is a two-hour tour led by a very knowledgeable volunteer from the Mission Houses Museum (see "Honolulu—Sights"), who is probably a member of the Cousin's Society and a descendant of one of the original Congregationalist missionaries to Hawaii. You're led on a wonderfully anecdoted walk through the historical buildings of central Honolulu for only $4 for the tour alone, and $7 if you combine it with a museum tour, every Wednesday and Thursday at 9:30 a.m., beginning from the Mission Houses Museum.

Honolulu Time Walks, 2634 S. King St., Suite 3, Honolulu, HI 96826, tel. 943-0731, offers fascinating interpretive walking tours focusing on the city's colorful past. The tours, ranging in price $2-40, sometimes including dinner, are thematic and change regularly. Expect topics like "The Revolution of 1893," "The lighter side of Old Honolulu," "Scandalous Days of Old Honolulu," and the very popular "Ghosts of Honolulu." Master storyteller Glen Grant, in costume, hosts many of the tours. Extremely authentic and painstakingly researched, these tours are immensely educational and entertaining. You can't find better. Reserve!

The **Hawaii Nature Center,** 2131 Makiki Heights Dr., Honolulu, HI, tel. 955-0100, is a nonprofit organization dedicated to environmental education through a "hands on" approach. Primarily geared toward school-age children, but welcoming the young at heart, the Hawaii Nature Center offers weekend community programs for families and the public to share in the wealth of Hawaii's magnificent natural environment through interpretive hikes, earth care projects, and nature crafts. This is a wonderful opportunity for visitors to explore Hawaii through direct interaction with the environment.

Oahu By Air

When you soar above Oahu, you realize just how beautiful this island actually is, and considering that the better part of a million people live in this relatively small space, it's amazing just how much undeveloped land still exists in the interior and even along the coast. The following are some air tours worth considering. Remember that small one- or two-plane operations come and go as quickly as cloudbursts. They're all licensed and regulated for safety, but if business is bad, the propellers stop spinning.

Novel air tours are offered from Dillingham Airfield, located in the northwest section of Oahu, a few miles down the Farrington Hwy. from Waialua. Once in the air, you can soar silently above the coast with **Glider Rides,** tel. 677-3404, an outfit offering one- or two-passenger piloted rides infinitely more exciting than the company's name. A plane tows you aloft and you circle in a five-mile radius with a view that can encompass 80 miles on a clear day. The rides are available daily, first-come, first-served, from 10 a.m. to 5 p.m. Cost is around $50 single, $70 double, and flights, depending upon air currents, last about 20 minutes (see "The North Shore—Beaches and Sights").

Islands in the Sky is a one-day flying extravaganza, offered by the most reputable island-based airline, **Hawaiian Air,** tel. 537-5100, that goes from Honolulu to Kona on the Big Island, on to Maui, and then back to Oahu for about $290.

Panorama Air Tours, tel. 836-2122 or (800) 367-2671, has tailor-made tours of Oahu and an all-encompassing "flightsee Hawaii tour" similar to Hawaiian Air's for about the same price. They fly smaller two-engined aircraft, and include the Big Island, Maui, and Kauai with a ground stop on each.

Helicopter companies rev up their choppers to flightsee you around the island, starting at $50 for a short trip over Waikiki. Prices rise from there as you head for the North Shore. Chopper companies include: **Hawaii Pacific Helicopters,** tel. 836-1561; **Kenai Air Hawaii,** one of the oldest and most reputable companies in the islands, tel. 836-2071; **Papillion Helicopters,** tel. 836-1566, another very well known and respected company; and **Royal Helicopters,** tel. 941-4683.

Sails And Dinner Cruises

If you're taking a tour at all, your best bet is a sail or dinner cruise. They're touristy, but a lot of fun, and actually good value. Many times money-saving coupons for them are found in the free tourist magazines, and plenty of street buskers in Waikiki give special deals. The latter are mostly on the up and up, but make sure that you know exactly what you're getting. Most of these cruises depart from the Kewalo Basin Marina, near Fisherman's Wharf, at 5:30 p.m. and cruise Waikiki toward Diamond Head before returning about two hours later. On board is a buffet, an open bar, live entertainment, and dancing. Costs vary but expect to spend about $50-60 per person. For cruises around Pearl Harbor and the *Arizona* Memorial see "Central Oahu—Aiea, Pearl City, and Vicinity."

Some of the better dinner sails and cruises follow. **Jada Yacht Charters,** tel. 955-0722, sails sister ships *Jada I* and *Jada II,* usually in tandem. Double-masted and with classic lines, they are the sharpest boats off Waikiki. Jada Charters takes you on a real sail, not a booze cruise where you stuff yourself on fried-to-death teriyaki chicken. They disembark at Ke'ehi Harbor, and will send a van to shuttle you back to Waikiki.

Aikane Catamarans, tel. 522-1533, is an established company with a number of boats sporting thatched roofs and Polynesian Revues. They offer sunset and morning cruises.

Windjammer Cruises, tel. 922-1200, sails out of Kewalo Basin on a sunset booze cruise.

Ali Kai Catamaran, tel. 522-1533, sails from Pier 5 every evening and presents a Polynesian dinner show complete with cocktails and dancing.

Royal Hawaiian Cruises, tel. 573-7001, sails from Pier 6 or Kewalo Basin on a nightly dinner cruise. They also offer Pearl Harbor cruises, and whalewatching in season.

For something different the **International Society for Krishna Consciousness** offers free rides on its *Jaludata,* along with free feasts (dogma sandwiches and karma entrees) on Sunday at 4:30 p.m. For information, *Hare Krishna, hare rama,* call 595-3947.

If you think that Oahu is beautiful topside, just wait until you see it below the waves. **Atlantis Submarines,** tel. 973-9800, (800) 548-6262, costs $80 adult, $39 children 12 and under, departs daily every hour on the hour from 7 a.m.-5 p.m., from the Hilton Hawaiian Village, where you board the Hilton Rainbow Catamaran that ferries you to the waiting sub. Once aboard, you're given a few instructions and then it's "run silent, run deep, run excited" for about one hour. The sub is amazingly comfortable. Seats are arranged so that everyone gets a prime view through the large windows, and the air is amazingly fresh. In early 1994 a brand new futuristic

dinner sail, Waikiki

sub was launched that measures 96 feet and carries 64 passengers. Outfitted with videocams, it allows the passengers to view the undersea world in every direction, while listening to explanations of the varied sea life through a multilanguage audio system. A thrill of a lifetime.

High-tech hits the high seas on the *Navatek I,* tel. 848-6360, a unique bi-hulled ship that guarantees the "most stable ride in the islands." Sailing from Pier 6, you have a choice of an early morning Pearl Harbor cruise, midday luncheon cruise, or the ultimate dinner cruise featuring gourmet food and some of the best island entertainers.

Captain Bob's Picnic Sail, tel. 926-5077 or (800) 262-8798, tours Kaneohe Bay daily and features lunch, and all you can drink, on its three- to four-hour sail for $65 adults, $45 children. You can work off lunch snorkeling or playing volleyball on the beach. The food is passable, but the setting offshore with the *pali* in the background is world-class.

Ecotourism In Hawaii
The following is a partial list of organizations, both public and private, that offer environmentally sound tours and outings throughout the Hawaiian Islands. (For ecotourism *to* Hawaii, see "Getting There.")

American Friends Service Committee, 2426 O'ahu Ave., Honolulu, HI 96822, tel. 988-6266 (Hawaii "Land Seminars").

EcoTours of Hawaii/Hawaiian Walkways, P.O. Box 2193, Kamuela, HI 96743, tel. 885-7759 (sea kayaking and mountain biking).

Eye of the Whale/Earthwalk Tours, P.O. Box 652, Davisville, RI 02854, tel. (401) 539-2401 (sailing and hiking).

Hawaii Audubon Society, 212 Merchant St., Suite 320, Honolulu, HI 96813, tel. 528-1432.

Hawaii Volcanoes National Park/Interpretation, P.O. Box 52, Hawaii Volcanoes National Park, HI 96718, tel. 967-7311 (hikes and talks).

The Nature Conservancy, 1116 Smith St., Suite 201, Honolulu, HI 96817, tel. 537-4508 (hikes).

Sierra Club, Moku Loa Group, P.O. Box 1137, Hilo, HI 96721, tel. 961-6978 (hikes and service trips).

Note: Also see "Camping and Hiking" and "Flora and Fauna" for more information.

DIANA LASICH HARPER

HEALTH AND WELL-BEING

In a recent survey published by *Science Digest,* Hawaii was cited as the healthiest state in the country to live in. Indeed, Hawaiian citizens live longer than anywhere else in America: men to 74 years on average and women to 78. Lifestyle, heredity, and diet help with these figures, but Hawaii is still an oasis in the middle of the ocean, and germs just have a tougher time getting there. There are no cases of malaria, cholera, or yellow fever. Because of a strict quarantine law, rabies is also nonexistent. On the other hand, tooth decay, perhaps because of the wide use of sugar and the enzymes present in certain tropical fruits, is 30% above the national average.

With the perfect weather, a multitude of fresh-air activities, soothing negative ionization from the sea, and a generally relaxed and carefree lifestyle, everyone feels better there. Hawaii is just what the doctor ordered: a beautiful natural health spa. That's one of the main drawing cards. The food and water are perfectly safe, and the air quality is the best in the country.

Handling The Sun
Don't become a victim of your own exuberance. People can't wait to strip down and lie on the sand like a beached whale, but the tropical sun will burn you to a cinder if you're silly. The burning rays come through easier in Hawaii because of the sun's angle, and you don't feel them as much because there's always a cool breeze. The worst part of the day is from 11 a.m. until 3 p.m. You'll just have to force yourself to go slowly. Don't worry; you'll be able to flaunt your best souvenir, your golden Hawaiian tan, to your green-with-envy friends when you get home. It's better than showing them a boiled lobster body with peeling skin! If your skin is snowflake white, 15 minutes per side on the first day is plenty. Increase by 15-minute intervals every day, which will allow you a full hour per side by the fourth day. Have faith; this is enough to give you a deep golden, uniform tan.

Haole Rot
A peculiar condition caused by the sun is referred to locally as *haole* rot. It's called this because it supposedly affects only white people, but you'll notice some dark-skinned people with the same condition. Basically, the skin becomes mottled with white spots that

refuse to tan. You get a blotchy effect, mostly on the shoulders and back. Dermatologists have a fancy name for it, and they'll give you a fancy prescription with a fancy price tag to cure it. It's common knowledge throughout the islands that Selsun Blue Shampoo has some ingredient that stops the white mottling effect. Just wash your hair with it and then rub the lather over the affected areas, and it should clear up.

Bugs

Everyone, in varying degrees, has an aversion to vermin and creepy crawlers. Hawaii isn't infested with a wide variety, but it does have its share. Mosquitos were unknown in the islands until their larvae stowed away in the water barrels of the *Wellington* in 1826 and were introduced at Lahaina. They bred in the tropical climate and rapidly spread to all the islands. They are a particular nuisance in the rainforests. Be prepared, and bring a natural repellent like citronella oil, available in most health stores on the islands, or a commercial product available in all groceries or drug stores. Campers will be happy to have mosquito coils to burn at night as well.

Cockroaches are very democratic insects. They hassle all strata of society equally. They breed well in Hawaii and most hotels are at war with them, trying desperately to keep them from being spotted by guests. One comforting thought is that in Hawaii they aren't a sign of filth or dirty housekeeping. They love the climate like everyone else, and it's a real problem keeping them under control. Many hotels post a little card in each room instructing you to call the desk if you spot a roach; they'll be happy to charge up to your room and annihilate it. Of a number of different roaches in Hawaii, the ones that give most people the jitters are big bombers over two inches long. Roaches are after food crumbs and the like, and very infrequently bother with a human. Be aware of this if you rent a room with a kitchenette or condo. If you are in a modest hotel and see a roach, it might make you feel better to know that the millionaire in the $600-a-night suite probably has them too. Bring your own spray if you wish, call the desk if you see them, or just let them be.

WATER SAFETY

Hawaii has one very sad claim to fame: more people drown here than anywhere else in the world. Moreover, there are dozens of yearly victims of broken necks, backs, and scuba and snorkeling accidents. These statistics shouldn't keep you out of the sea, because it is indeed beautiful, benevolent in most cases, and a main reason to go to Hawaii. But if you're foolish, the sea will bounce you like a basketball and suck you away for good. The best remedy is to avoid situations you can't handle. Don't let anyone dare you into a situation that makes you uncomfortable. "Macho men" who know nothing about the power of the sea will be tumbled into a Cabbage Patch Kid doll in short order. Ask lifeguards or beach attendants about conditions, and follow their advice. If local people refuse to go in, there's a good reason. Even experts get in trouble in Hawaiian waters. Some beaches, such as Waikiki, are as gentle as a lamb and you would have to tie an anchor around your neck to drown there. Others, especially on the north coasts during the winter months, are frothing giants.

While beachcombing, or especially when walking out on rocks, never turn your back to the sea. Be aware of undertows (the waves drawing back into the sea). They can knock you off your feet. Before entering the water, study it for rocks, breakers, reefs, and riptides. Riptides are powerful currents, like rivers in the sea, that can drag you out. Mostly they peter out not too far from shore, and you can often see their choppy waters on the surface. If caught in a "rip," don't fight to swim directly against it; you'll lose and only exhaust yourself. Swim diagonally across it, while going along with it, and try to stay parallel to the shore. Don't waste all your lung power yelling, and do rest by floating.

When bodysurfing, never ride straight in; come to shore at a 45-degree angle. Remember, waves come in sets. Little ones can be followed by giants, so watch the action awhile instead of plunging right in. Standard procedure is to duck under a breaking wave. You can even survive thunderous oceans using this technique. Don't try to swim through a heavy froth and never turn your back and let it smash you. Don't swim alone if possible, and obey all warning signs. Hawaiians want to entertain you and they don't put up signs just to waste money. The first rule is, "If in doubt, stay out."

Yikes!

Sharks live in all the oceans of the world. Most mind their own business and stay away from shore. Hawaiian sharks are well fed—on fish—and don't usually bother with unsavory humans. If you encounter a shark, don't panic! Never thrash around because this will trigger their attack instinct. If they come close, scream loudly. Portuguese men-of-war put out long floating tentacles that sting if they touch you. Don't wash it off with fresh water, as this will only aggravate it. Hot salt water will take away the sting, as will alcohol (the drinking or rubbing kind), aftershave lotion, and meat tenderizer (MSG), which can be found in any supermarket or Chinese restaurant. Coral can give you a nasty cut, and it's known for causing infections because it's a living organism. Wash the cut immediately and apply an antiseptic. Keep it clean and covered, and watch for infection.

Poisonous sea urchins, such as the lacquer-black *wana,* can be beautiful creatures. They are found in shallow tidepools and can only hurt you if you step on them. Their spines will break off, enter your foot, and burn like blazes. There are cures. Vinegar or wine poured on the wound will stop the burning. If not available, the Hawaiian method is urine. It might be ignominious to have

someone pee on your foot, but it'll put the fire out. The spines will disintegrate in a few days, and there are generally no long-term effects.

Hawaiian reefs also have their share of moray eels. These creatures are ferocious in appearance but will never initiate an attack. You'll have to poke around in their holes while snorkeling or scuba diving to get them to attack. Sometimes this is inadvertent on the diver's part, so be careful where you stick your hand while underwater.

HAWAIIAN FOLK MEDICINE AND CURES

Hawaiian folk medicine is well developed, and its cures for common ailments have been used effectively for centuries. Hawaiian *kahuna* were highly regarded for their medicinal skills, and Hawaiians were by far some of the healthiest people in the world until the coming of the Europeans. Many folk remedies and cures are used to this day and, what's more, they work. Some of the most common plants and fruits that you'll encounter provide some of the best remedies. When roots and seeds and special exotic plants are used, the preparation of the medicine is as painstaking as in a modern pharmacy. These prescriptions are exact and take an expert to prepare. They should never be prepared or administered by an amateur. For hospitals, doctors, and conventional medical help see "Information and Services."

This "denizen of the deep" is much more afraid of you than you are of him.

HOWARD LINDEMAN

KAREN McKINLEY

KUKUI (CANDLENUT)

Reaching heights of 80 feet, the *kukui* (candlenut) was a veritable department store to the Hawaiians, who made use of almost every part of this utilitarian giant. Used as a cure-all, its nuts, bark, or flowers were ground into potions and salves and taken as a general tonic, applied to ulcers and cuts as an effective antibiotic, or administered internally as a cure for constipation or asthma attacks. The bark was mixed with water and the resulting juice was used as a dye in tattooing, tapa-cloth making, and canoe painting, and as a preservative for fishnets. The oily nuts were burned as a light source in stone holders, and ground and eaten as a condiment called *inamona*. Polished nuts took on a beautiful sheen and were strung as lei. Lastly, the wood itself was hollowed into canoes and used as fishnet floats.

Common Curative Plants

Arrowroot, for diarrhea, is a powerful narcotic used in rituals and medicines. The pepper plant (*Piper methisticum*) is chewed and the juice is spat into a container for fermenting. Used as a medicine in urinary tract infections, rheumatism, and asthma, it also induces sleep and cures headaches. A poultice for wounds is made from the skins of ripe bananas. The peelings have a powerful antibiotic quality and contain vitamins A, B, and C, phosphorous, calcium, and iron. The nectar from the plant was fed to babies as a vitamin juice. Breadfruit sap is used for healing cuts and as a moisturizing lotion. Coconut is used to make moisturizing oil, and the juice was chewed, spat into the hand, and used as a shampoo. Guava is a source of vitamins A, B, and C. Hibiscus has been used as a laxative.

Kukui nut oil is a gargle for sore throats, a laxative, and the flowers are used to cure diarrhea. *Noni* reduces tumors, diabetes, and high blood pressure, and the juice is good for diarrhea. Sugarcane sweetens many concoctions, and the juice of toasted cane was a tonic for sick babies. Sweet potato is used as a tonic during pregnancy, and juiced as a gargle for phlegm. Tamarind is a natural laxative, and contains the most acid and sugar of any fruit on earth. Taro has been used for lung infections, thrush, and as suppositories. Yams are good for coughs, vomiting, constipation, and appendicitis.

HELP FOR THE DISABLED

A physically disabled person can have a wonderful time in Hawaii; all that's needed is a little pre-planning. The following is general advice that should help your planning.

Commission On Persons With Disabilities

This commission was designed with the express purpose of aiding handicapped people. They are a source of invaluable information and distribute self-help booklets free of charge. Any handicapped person heading to Hawaii should write first or visit their offices on arrival. For the *Aloha Guide To Accessibility* ($3), write or visit the head office at: Commission on Persons With Disabilities, 500 Ala Moana Blvd., Honolulu, HI 96813, tel. 586-8121; on Maui, 54 High St., Wailuku, Maui, HI 96793, tel. 243-5441; on Kauai, 3060 Eiwa St. #207, Lihue, Kauai, HI 96766, tel. 241-3308; on Hawaii, P.O. Box 1641, Hilo, HI 96820, tel. 933-7747.

General Information

The key for a smooth trip is to make as many arrangements ahead of time as possible. In advance, tell the transportation companies and hotels you'll be dealing with the nature of your handicap so that they can make arrangements to accommodate you. Bring your medical records and notify medical establishments of your arrival if you'll be needing their services. Travel with a friend or make arrangements for an aide on arrival (see the following section). Bring your own wheelchair if possible, and let airlines know if it is battery-powered; boarding interisland carriers requires steps. No problem: they'll board you early on special lifts, but they must know that you're coming. Many hotels and restaurants accommodate disabled persons, but always call ahead just to make sure.

Note: Guide dogs for the blind or visually impaired are subject to quarantine (see "What to Take—Pets and Quarantine").

Oahu Services
At Honolulu International, parking spaces are on the fourth floor of the parking garage near the elevator closest to the interisland terminal. Be aware, the **Wiki Wiki Bus** to town has steps.

Medical Services are available 24 hours a day at: Honolulu County Medical Society, tel. 536-6988; airport medical services, tel. 836-3341; visitor information, tel. 836-6417. For getting around, the City of Honolulu has a free curb-to-curb service for disabled persons, called **Handi-Van.** You must make arrangements for a pass 24 hours in advance. For a free handicapped bus pass for disabled but ambulatory people, write Handi-Van Pass, or Handicapped Bus Pass, 650 S. King St., Honolulu, HI 96813, tel. 524-4626. A private special taxi company is **Handi-Cabs of the Pacific** in Honolulu at 524-3866. **Avis** will rent cars with hand controls, tel. 836-5511.

For **medical equipment** the following Honolulu establishments rent all kinds of apparatus: **AAA Medical,** tel. 538-7021; **Abbey Rents,** tel. 537-2922; **Medical Supplies,** tel. 845-9522; **Honolulu Orthopedic,** tel. 536-6661. For **medical support and help** the following provide nurses, companions, and health aides—all require advance notice. **Hawaii Center for Independent Living,** tel. 537-1941; **Travel-Well International,** tel. 689-5420; **Voluntary Action Center,** tel. 536-7234.

PROSTITUTION

Though the small towns and villages are as safe as you can find anywhere in America, Hawaii isn't all good clean fun. Wherever there's a constant tourist flow, a huge military presence, and high cost of living, there will be those people that mama warned you about. Most of the heavy night action occurs in Waikiki around Kuhio and Kalakaua avenues, and on Chinatown's Hotel Street. Something about the *vibe* exudes sexuality. The land is raw and wild, and the settings are intoxicating. All those glistening bodies under the tropical sun and the carefree lifestyle are super-conducive to you know what! It's long been known as a great place for boy meets girl, or whomever, but there also exists "play for pay."

You can go two ways on the "sleaze" scene in Hawaii: ignore it and remain aloof and never see any; or, look for and find it with no trouble. The following is neither a condemnation nor an endorsement of how you should act and what you should do. It's merely the facts and the choice is up to you.

Prostitution—The Way It Was
Ever since the first ship arrived in 1778, Hawaii has known prostitution. At that time, a sailor paid for a woman one night for one iron nail. Funny, today they'll take a plastic card. Prostitution, rampant until the missionaries arrived in 1819, was indeed a major cause of the tragic population decline of the Hawaiian race. The tradition has carried on into this century. Iwilei was a notorious red-light district in Honolulu at the turn of the century. The authorities, many of whom were clientele, not only turned a blind eye to this scene, but semilegalized it. A policeman was stationed inside the "stockade" and police rules were listed on the five entrances. The women were required to have a weekly VD checkup from the Board of Health, and without a current disease-free certificate they couldn't work. Iwilei was even considered by some to be an attraction: when Somerset Maugham passed through the islands in 1916 on his way to Russia as a spy for England, he was taken here as if on a sightseeing tour. The long-established military presence in Hawaii

has also helped to keep prostitution a flourishing business. During WW II, troops were entertained by streetwalkers, houses of prostitution, and at dance halls. The consensus of the military commanders is that prostitution is a necessary evil, needed to keep up the morale of the troops.

The Scene Today

The two areas notorious for prostitution today are Kuhio and Kalakaua avenues in Waikiki, which are geared toward the tourist, and Hotel Street in downtown Honolulu, for servicemen and a much rougher trade. All sorts of women solicit on Kuhio and Kalakaua avenues— whites, blacks, and Asians—but the majority are young white women from the Mainland. They cruise along in the old-fashioned style, meeting your eyes and giving you the nod. As long as they keep walking the police won't roust them.

The prostitutes on Waikiki number about 300, and are very easy to spot, mostly hanging out across the street from the police station on Kalakaua or in front of the Hyatt. There was a great influx when Los Angeles cracked down for the 1984 Olympics, and Honolulu inherited many of the city's displaced streetwalkers.

Most hookers prefer Japanese clientele, followed by the general tourist, and lastly, the always-broke serviceman. In the terse words of one streetwalker queried about the preference for Japanese, she said, "They're small, clean, fast, and they pay a lot." Sounds like a streetwalker's dream! If anyone in Waikiki can speak Japanese, a hooker can.

Most are not "equal opportunity employees." Western guys, whether white or black, don't stand much of a chance. The prostitues are after the Japanese in a sort of crazy payback. The Japanese fish American waters, and the "pros" of Waikiki hook big Japanese fish.

A Honolulu policeman on his Kuhio Avenue beat said, "I can't do anything if they keep walking. It's a free country. Besides, I'm not here to teach anyone morals. . . . Last week a john "fell" out of an eight-story window and a prostitute was found with her throat slit. . .

I'm just on the front lines fighting herpes and AIDS. Just fighting herpes and AIDS, man." Unlike the days of Iwilei there is absolutely no official control or testing for VD.

Then there is Chinatown's Hotel Street (see "Chinatown—Nights" in the Honolulu chapter); it is as rough as guts. The girls are shabby, the bars and strip joints are shabbier, and the vibe is heavy.

Women can find male prostitutes on most of the beaches of Honolulu and Waikiki. Mostly these transactions take place during the day. Although many men make a legitimate living as "beach boys" instructing in surfing and the like, many are really prostitutes. It's always up to the woman to decide how far her "lessons" proceed.

Massage Parlors, Etc.

Besides streetwalkers, Honolulu and some of the Neighbor Islands have their share of massage parlors, escort services, and exotic dance joints. Most are in Honolulu, and some will even fly their practitioners to the Neighbor Islands if necessary. For massage parlors and "escort services" you can let your fingers do the walking—through 14 pages in the Honolulu Yellow Pages alone. Oddly enough, the "massage" listing is preceded by one for "marketing" and followed by one for "meat." Many legitimate massage practitioners in Hawaii can offer the best therapeutic massages in a variety of disciplines, including *shiatsu, lomi lomi,* and Swedish. Unfortunately, they share the same listings with the other kind of massage parlors. If the Yellow Pages listing reads something like "Fifi's Playthings—We'll rub it day or night, wherever it is," this should tip you off. Usually they offer escort services too, for both men and women.

Honolulu also has a number of exotic dance clubs, many along Kapiolani Boulevard (see "Honolulu—Entertainment"). Basically, they're strip joints with an extra twist. The dancers themselves are very attractive women who have been brought over from the Mainland. They can easily make $150 per night dancing, and the majority are not prostitutes. Their act lasts for three songs, and gets raunchier as it goes. If you invite a dancer to have a drink, it'll cost you $10, but it will be a real drink. This gets you nothing but conversation. The patron's drinks aren't as inflated as the scene would suggest, and some think it a bargain for the price of one drink to have a naked woman bumping and grinding just five feet away. Working the sexually agitated male crowd are women who can best be described as "lap sitters." They're almost always older Korean women who look as though they've been through the mill. They'll charge you $20 for a fake drink called *niko hana* (nothing), and then try to entice you over to a dark corner table, where they'll chisel $20 more, for all you can manage, or are brave enough to do, in a dark corner of a nightclub. Their chief allies are dim lights and booze.

ILLEGAL DRUGS

The use and availability of illegal, controlled, and recreational drugs are about the same in Hawaii as throughout the rest of America. Cocaine constitutes the fastest-growing recreational drug, and it's available on the streets of the main cities, especially Honolulu. Although most dealers are small-time, the drug is brought in by organized crime. The underworld here is mostly populated by men of Asian descent, and the Japanese *yakuza* is said recently to be displaying a heightened involvement in Hawaiian organized crime. Cocaine trafficking fans out from Honolulu.

A new drug menace hitting the Honolulu streets is known as "ice." Ice is smokable methamphetamine that will wire a user for up to 24 hours. The high lasts longer, and is cheaper than cocaine or its derivative, "crack." Users become quickly dependent, despondent, and violent because ice robs them of their sleep, along with their dignity. Its use is particularly prevalent among late-night workers. Many of the violent deaths in Honolulu have been linked to the growing use of ice.

However, the main drug available and commonly used in Hawaii is marijuana, which is locally called *pakalolo*. There are also three varieties of psychoactive mushrooms that contain the hallucinogen psilocybin. They grow wild but are considered illegal controlled substances.

Pakalolo Growing

About 25 years ago, mostly *haole* hippies from the Mainland began growing pot in the more remote sections of the islands, such as Puna on Hawaii and around Hana on Maui. They discovered what legitimate planters had known for

200 years: plant a broomstick in Hawaii, treat it right, and it'll grow. *Pakalolo,* after all, is only a weed, and it grows in Hawaii like wildfire. The locals quickly got into the act when they realized that they, too, could grow a "money tree." Hawaii's sugar and pineapple industries started to flag in the last decade and people had to do something to make ends meet. More than a few began to grow *pakalolo* (marijuana), now counted as one of the biggest, though illegal, cash crops in Hawaii.

As a matter of fact, the locals began resenting the *haole* usurpers, and a quiet and sometimes dangerous feud has been going on ever since. Much is made of the viciousness of the backcountry "growers" of Hawaii. There are tales of booby traps and armed patrols guarding their plants in the hills, but mostly it's a cat and mouse game between the authorities and the growers. If you, as a tourist, are tramping about in the forest and happen upon someone's "patch," don't touch anything. Just back off and you'll be okay. Pot has the largest monetary turnover of any crop in the islands, and as such, is now considered a major source of agricultural revenue. There are all kinds of local names and varieties of pot in Hawaii, the most potent being "Kona Gold," "Puna Butter," and "Maui Wowie." Though, actually, these names are all becoming passé.

THEFT AND HASSLES

Theft and minor assaults can be a problem, but they're usually not violent or vicious as in some Mainland cities. Mostly, it's locals with a chips on their shoulders and few prospects, who will ransack your car or make off with your camera. A big Hawaiian or local guy will be obliged to flatten your nose if you look for trouble, but mostly it will be sneak thieves out to make a fast buck.

From the minute you sit behind the wheel of your rental car you'll be warned about not leaving valuables unattended and locking your car up tighter than a drum. Signs warning about theft at most major tourist attractions help to fuel your paranoia. Many hotel rooms offer coin-operated safes, so you can lock your valuables away and be able to relax while getting sunburned. Stories abound about purse snatchings and surly locals who are just itching to give you a hard time. Well, they're all true to a degree, but Hawaii's reputation is much worse than the reality. In Hawaii you'll have to observe two golden laws: if you look for trouble, you'll find it; and, a fool and his camera are soon parted.

Theft

The majority of theft in Hawaii is of the "sneak thief" variety. If you leave your hotel door unlocked, a camera sitting on the seat of your rental car, or valuables on your beach towel, you'll be inviting a very obliging thief to pad away with your stuff. You have to learn to take precautions, but they won't be anything like those employed in rougher areas like South America or Southeast Asia; just normal American precautions.

If you must walk alone at night, stay on the main streets in well-lit areas. Always lock your hotel door and windows and place all valuable jewelry in the hotel safe. When you leave your hotel for the beach, there is absolutely no reason to carry all your traveler's checks, credit cards, or a big wad of money. Just take what you'll need for drinks and lunch. If you're uptight about leaving any money in your beach bag, just stick it in your bathing suit or bikini. American money is just as negotiable if it is damp. Don't leave your camera or portable stereo on the beach unattended. Ask a person nearby to watch them for you while you go for a dip. Most people won't mind at all, and you can repay the favor.

While sightseeing in your shiny new rental car, which immediately brands you as a tourist, again, don't take more than what you'll need for the day. Why people leave a camera sitting on the seat of their car is a mystery! Many people lock valuables away in the trunk, but remember that most good car thieves can "jimmy" it as quickly as you can open it with your key. If you must, for some reason, leave your camera or valuables in your car, lock them in the trunk or consider putting them under the hood. Thieves usually don't look there, and on most modern cars you can only pop the hood with a lever on the inside of the car. It's not fail-safe, but it's worth a try.

Campers face special problems because their entire camp is open to thievery. Most campgrounds don't have any real security, but who,

after all, wants to fence an old tent or a used sleeping bag? Many tents have zippers that can be secured with a small padlock. If you want to go trekking and are afraid to leave your gear in the campgrounds, take a large green garbage bag with you. Transport your gear down the trail and then walk off through some thick brush. Put your gear in the garbage bag and bury it under leaves and other light camouflage. That's about as safe as you can be. You can also use this same technique instead of leaving your valuables in your rental car. However, as nothing can be guaranteed, carrying the least amount possible is always better.

Hassles

Another self-perpetuating myth about Hawaii is that "the natives are restless." An undeniable animosity exists between locals, especially those with some Hawaiian blood, and *haole*. Fortunately, this prejudice is directed mostly at the "group" and not at the "individual." The locals are resentful against those *haoles* who came, took their land, and relegated them to second-class citizenship. They realize that this is not the average tourist and they can tell what you are at a glance. Tourists usually are treated with understanding and are given a type of immunity. Besides, Hawaiians are still among the most friendly, giving, and understanding people on earth.

Haole who live in Hawaii might tell you stories of their children having trouble at school. They could even mention an unhappy situation at some schools called "beat-up-a-*haole*" day, and you might hear that if you're a *haole* it's not a matter of *if* you'll be beaten up, but *when*. Truthfully, most of this depends upon your attitude and your sensitivity. The locals feel infringed upon, so don't fuel these feelings. If you're at a beach park and there is a group of local people in one area, don't crowd them. If you go into a local bar and you're the only one of your ethnic group in sight, you shouldn't have to be told to leave. Much of the hassle involves drinking. Booze brings out the worst prejudice on all sides. If you're invited to a beach party, and the local guys start getting drunk, make this your exit call. Don't wait until it's too late.

Most trouble seems to be directed toward white men. White women are mostly immune from being beaten up, but they have to beware of the violence of sexual abuse and rape. Although plenty of local women marry white men, it's not a good idea to try to pick up a local girl. If you're known in the area and have been properly introduced, that's another story. Also, girls out for the night in bars or discos can be approached if they're not in the company of local guys. If you are with your bikini-clad girlfriend, and a bunch of local guys are, say, drinking beer at a beach park, don't go over and try to be friendly and ask, "What's up?" You, and especially your girlfriend, just might find out. Maintain your own dignity and self-respect by treating others with dignity and respect. Most times you'll reap what you sow.

LOUISE FOOTE

WHAT TO TAKE

It's a snap to pack for a visit to Oahu. Everything is on your side. The weather is moderate and uniform on the whole, and the style of dress is delightfully casual. The rule of thumb is to pack lightly: few items, and light clothing both in color and weight. What you'll need will depend largely on your itinerary and your desires. Are you drawn to the nightlife, the outdoors, or both? If you forget something at home, it won't be a disaster. You can buy everything you'll need in Hawaii. As a matter of fact, Hawaiian clothing, such as muumuu and aloha shirts, is one of the best purchases you can make, both in comfort and style. It's quite feasible to bring only one or two changes of clothing with the express purpose of outfitting yourself while there. Prices on bathing suits, bikinis, and summer wear in general are quite reasonable.

Matters Of Taste

A grand conspiracy in Hawaii adhered to by everyone—tourist, traveler, and resident—is to "hang loose" and dress casual. Best of all, alohawear is just about all you'll need for comfort and virtually every occasion. The classic muumuu is large and billowy, and aloha shirts are made to be worn outside the pants. The best of both are made of cool cotton. Rayon is a natural fiber that isn't too bad, but polyester is hot, sticky, and not authentic. Not all muumuu are of the "tent persuasion." Some are very fashionable and form-fitted with peek-a-boo slits up the side, down the front, or around the back. *Holomuu* are muumuu fitted at the waist with a flowing skirt to the ankles. They are not only elegant, but perfect for "stepping out."

In The Cold And Rain

Two occasions for which you'll have to consider dressing warmly are visits to mountaintops and boat rides where wind and ocean sprays are a factor. You can conquer both with a jogging suit (sweat suit) and a featherweight, water-resistant windbreaker. If you're going to camp or trek, you should add another layer, a woolen sweater being one of the best. Wool is the only natural fiber that retains most of its warmth-giving properties even if it gets wet. Several varieties of "fleece" synthetics currently on the market also have this ability. If your hands get cold, put a pair of socks over them. Tropical rain showers can happen at any time so you might consider a fold-up umbrella, but the sun quickly breaks through and the warming winds blow.

Shoes
Dressing your feet is hardly a problem. You'll most often wear zoris (rubber thongs) for going to and from the beach, leather sandals for strolling and dining, and jogging shoes for trekking and sightseeing. A few discos require leather shoes, but it's hardly worth bringing them just for that. If you plan on heavy-duty trekking, you'll definitely want your hiking boots. Lava, especially a'a, is murderous on shoes. Most backcountry trails are rugged and muddy, and you'll need those good old lug soles for traction. If you plan moderate hikes, you might want to consider bringing rubberized ankle supports to complement your jogging shoes. Most drugstores sell them, and the best are a rubberized sock with toe and heel cut out.

Specialty Items
The following is a list of specialty items that you might consider bringing along. They're not necessities but most will definitely come in handy. A pair of binoculars really enhances sightseeing—great for viewing birds and sweeping panoramas, and almost a necessity if you're going whalewatching. A folding, Teflon-bottomed travel iron makes up for cotton's one major shortcoming, wrinkles; you can't always count on hotels to have irons. Nylon twine and miniature clothespins are handy for drying garments, especially bathing suits. Commercial and hotel laundromats abound, but many times you'll get by with hand-washing a few items in the sink. A transistor radio/tape recorder provides news, weather, and entertainment, and can be used to record impressions, island music, and a running commentary for your slide show. Hair dryer: although the wind can be relied upon to dry wet hair, it leaves a bit to be desired in the styling department. An inflatable raft for riding waves, along with flippers, mask and snorkel, can easily be bought in Hawaii but don't weigh much or take up much space in your luggage. If you'll be camping, trekking, or boating with only seawater available for bathing, take along "Sea Saver Soap," available from good sporting goods

stores. This special soap will lather in seawater and rinse away the sticky salt residue with it.

For The Camper
If you don't want to take it with you, all necessary camping gear can be purchased or rented while in Hawaii. Besides the above, you should consider taking the following: framed backpack or the convertible packs that turn into suitcases, daypack, matches in a waterproof container, all-purpose knife, mess kit, eating utensils, flashlight (remove batteries), candle, nylon cord, and sewing kit (dental floss works as thread). Take a first-aid kit containing Band-Aids, all-purpose antiseptic cream, alcohol swabs, tourniquet string, cotton balls, elastic bandage, razor blade, Telfa pads, and a small mirror for viewing private nooks and crannies. A light sleeping bag is good, although your fleecy jogging suit with a ground pad and light blanket or even your rain poncho will be sufficient. Definitely bring a down bag for mountainous areas. In a film container pack a few nails, safety pins, fishhooks, line, and bendable wire. Nothing else does what these do and they're all handy for a million and one uses. (See also "Hiking and Camping.")

Basic Necessities
As previously mentioned, you really have to consider only two "modes" of dressing in Hawaii: beachwear and casual clothing. The following is designed for the midrange traveler carrying one suitcase or a backpack. Remember that there are laundromats and that you'll be spending a considerable amount of time in your bathing suit. Consider the following: one or two pairs of light cotton slacks for going out and about, and one pair of jeans for trekking, or better yet, corduroys that can serve both purposes; two or three casual sundresses—muumuu are great; three or four pairs of shorts for beachwear and for sightseeing; four to five short-sleeved shirts or blouses and one long-sleeved; three or four colored and printed T-shirts that can be worn anytime from trekking to strolling; a beach coverup—the short terrycloth type is the best; a brimmed hat for rain and sun—the crushable floppy type is great for purse or daypack; two or three pairs of socks are sufficient, nylons you won't need; two bathing suits (nylon ones dry quickest); plastic bags to hold wet bathing suits

and laundry; five to six pairs of underwear; towels (optional, because hotels provide them, even for the beach); a first-aid kit, pocket-size is sufficient; suntan lotion and insect repellent; a daypack or large beach purse. And don't forget your windbreaker, perhaps a shawl for the evening, and an all-purpose jogging suit.

Pets And Quarantine
Hawaii has a very rigid pet quarantine policy designed to keep rabies and other mainland disease from reaching the state. All domestic pets are subject to **90 days' quarantine,** regardless of the fact that they may have current veterinary shot certificates. Unless you are contemplating a move to Hawaii, it is not feasible to take pets. For complete information, contact the Department of Agriculture, Animal Quarantine Division, 99-770 Moanalua Rd., Honolulu, HI 96701, tel. 488-8461.

ohia lehua flower

DIANA LASICH HARPER

INFORMATION AND SERVICES

Emergency

Police, fire, and ambulance can be summoned from anywhere on Oahu by calling **911**. Reach the **Coast Guard** for search and rescue at 536-4336 and the **Life Guard Service** at 922-3888.

Health Care

Full-service hospitals include: **Queen's Hospital,** 1301 Punchbowl St., Honolulu, tel. 538-9011; **Kaiser Foundation,** 1697 Ala Moana Blvd., Honolulu, tel. 949-5811.

Medical services and clinics include: **Doctors On Call,** tel. 971-6000 (for Japanese speaking doctors call 923-9966), for emergencies and "house calls" to your hotel, 24 hours a day; **Medi-Mart,** Waikiki, Royal Hawaiian Shopping Center, Bldg. A, Room 401, tel. 922-2335, open 9 a.m.-6 p.m.; **Waikiki Health Center,** 277 Ohua Ave., tel. 922-4787, for low-cost care including pregnancy and confidential VD testing, open 9 a.m-8 p.m. Mon.-Thurs., until 4:30 p.m. Fri., until 2 p.m. Saturday. You can get a free **blood pressure** check at the fire station in Waikiki, corner of Paki and Kapahulu streets, daily 9 a.m.-5 p.m.

For dental referral call **Dentist Information Bureau** at tel. 536-2135, 24-hour service.

Pharmacies around the island include: **Outrigger Pharmacy,** in Waikiki Outrigger Hotel, 2335 Kalakaua Ave., tel. 923-2529; **Kuhio Pharmacy,** at the corner of Kuhio and Nahua, tel. 923-4466, is full-service; **Longs Drugs,** in Honolulu at the Ala Moana Shopping Center, tel. 941-4433, and at the Kaneohe Shopping Center, tel. 235-4511; **Pay 'n' Save** at 86-120 Farrington Hwy., Waianae, tel. 696-6387.

For **alternative health care** try: **Acupuncture Clinic,** Waikiki Medical Bldg., 305 Royal Hawaiian Ave. Room 208, tel. 923-6939, open Mon.-Fri. 9 a.m.-4 p.m. (also see "Honolulu—Chinatown"); **Honolulu School of Massage,** 1750 Kalakaua Ave., tel. 942-8552, open 10 a.m.-6 p.m., with some later hours; **Ed Hoopai** is an excellent masseur whose motto is "You're in good hands," tel. 926-9045, at 250 Lewers St., second floor of the Outrigger Village Hotel, the suite above the pool. He deals basically in headaches, neck and shoulders, and lower backs. **Chiropractic Referral Service,** 700 Bishop St., tel. 521-5784, offers free information and referral to qualified chiropractors. Chiropractic Dial-a-Tape has taped messages for what ails, tel. 737-1111; on the leeward side is **Dr. Tom Smith,** 1222 Oneawa St., Kailua, tel. 261-4511, limited hours.

HAWAII VISITORS BUREAU OFFICES

Statewide HVB offices include: HVB Administrative Office, Waikiki Business Plaza, 2270 Kalakaua Ave., Suite 801, Honolulu, HI 96815, tel. 923-1811; Big Island HVB Hilo, 250 Keawe St., Hilo, HI 96720, tel. 961-5797; HVB, Big Island Kona Branch, 75-5719 W. Ali'i Dr., Kailua-Kona, HI 96740, tel. 329-7787; Kauai HVB, 3016 Umi St., Suite 207, Lihue, HI 96766, tel. 245-3971; Maui HVB, 250 Alamaha St., Suite N-16, Kahului, HI 96732, tel. 871-8691.

North America

Hawaii Visitors Bureaus are: **HVB Canada,** 205-1624 56th St., Delta, B.C., Canada V4L 2B1, tel. (604) 943-8555; **HVB Chicago,** 180 N. Michigan Ave., Suite 2210, Chicago, IL 60601, tel. (312) 236-0632; **HVB Los Angeles,** Central Plaza, 3440 Wilshire Blvd., Room 610, Los Angeles, CA 90010, tel. (213) 385-5301; **HVB New York,** Empire State Bldg., Suite 808, New York, NY 10018, tel. (212) 947-0717; **HVB San Francisco,** Suite 450, 50 California St., San Francisco, CA 94111, tel. (415) 392-8173; **HVB Washington D.C.,** 1511 K St. NW, Suite 415, Washington, D.C. 20005, tel. (202) 393-6752.

European Offices

HVB Belgium, Rue Couperin, #87 Bis, Boncelles 4100, tel. 32-41-38-1517.

HVB Germany, c/o Hans Regh Assoc., Postfach 930 247, Ginnheimer Landstrasse 1, D-6000, Frankfurt, tel. 49-69-70-4013.

HVB United Kingdom, 14 The Green, Richmond, TW9 1PX, England, tel. 44-81-332-6969.

Asia/Pacific Offices
HVB Australia, c/o Walshes World, 92 Pitt St., Sydney, N.S.W. 2000, tel. 61-2-235-0194.

HVB Hong Kong, Suite 3702-A, EIE Tower, Bond Centre, Queensway, Central, Hong Kong, tel. 852-526-0387.

HVB Japan, Hibiya Kokusai Bldg., 11th Fl., 2-2-3 Uchisaiwaicho, Chiyoda-ku, Tokyo 100, tel. 011-81-3-3580-2481.

HVB Korea, c/o Travel Press, 2nd Fl., West-in Chosun Hotel, C.P.O. Box 6445, Seoul 100-070, tel. 82-2-757-6781.

HVB Malaysia, c/o Pacific World Travel, 2.5 & 2.6 Angkasa Raya Bldg., Jalan Ampag, Kuala Lumpur 50450, tel. 60-3-244-8449.

HVB New Zealand, c/o Walshes World, 87 Queen St., 2nd Fl., Dingwall Bldg., Auckland, tel. 64-9-379-3708.

HVB Singapore, c/o Pacific Leisure, 3 Seah St., #01-04, Singapore 0718, tel. 65-338-1612.

HVB Taiwan, c/o Federal Transportation Co., 8th Fl., Nanking E. Road, Section 3, Taipei, tel. 886-2-507-8133.

HVB Thailand, c/o ADAT Sales, 8th Fl., Maneeya Center Bldg., 518/5 Ploenchit Rd., Bangkok 10330, tel. 66-2-255-6838.

OTHER INFORMATION SOURCES

The **Japanese Chamber of Commerce** has special information on things Japanese, tel. 949-5531; the **Chinese Chamber of Commerce** offers information and tours on Chinatown, tel. 533-3181. **State Foundation on Culture and Arts,** 335 Merchant St. Room 202, tel. 586-0300, dispenses information on what's happening culturally on Oahu. For general information, or if you have a hassle, try the **Office of Information and Complaints,** tel. 523-4385 or 523-4381. Write to any HVB office and request a copy of *Hawaii On A Budget,* a tabloid-style brochure that lists some of Hawaii''s least expensive accommodations and attractions.

Reading Material
Besides a number of special-interest Chinese, Japanese, Korean, Filipino, and military news-

The "HVB Warrior" is posted alongside the roadway, marking sites of cultural and historic importance.

papers, two major dailies are published on Oahu. The *Honolulu Advertiser,* tel. 525-8000, is the morning paper, and the *Honolulu Star Bulletin,* tel. 525-8000, is the evening paper. They combine to make a Sunday paper. A money-saving paper is the *Pennysaver,* tel. 521-9886, featuring classified ads on just about anything. Call for distribution points.

Don't miss out on the **free tourist literature** available at all major hotels, shopping malls, the airport, and stands along Waikiki's streets. They all contain up-to-the-minute information on what's happening, and a treasure trove of free or reduced-price coupons for various attractions and services. Always featured are events, shopping tips, dining and entertainment, and sightseeing. The main ones are: *This Week Oahu,* the best and most complete; *Spotlight Hawaii,* with good sections on dining and sightseeing. Two free tabloids, *Waikiki Beach Press* and *Island News,* offer entertainment calendars and feature stories of general interest to visitors. *Oahu Drive Guide,* handed out by all the major car rental agencies, has some excellent tips and orientation maps. Especially useful to get you started from the airport.

Note: For **bookstores,** see "Shopping," above, and "Shopping" or "Practicalities" in the travel chapters.

Post Offices And Libraries

Many small post offices are found in various towns around the island. The main post office in downtown Honolulu is at 3600 Aolele St., tel. 422-0770; in Waikiki at 330 Saratoga Rd., tel. 941-1062; in Kailua at 335 Hahani, tel. 262-7205; in Waianae at 86-015 Farrington Hwy., tel. 696-4032; in Haleiwa at 66-437 Kamehameha Hwy., tel. 637-5755; in Wahiawa at 115 Lehua, tel. 621-8496.

Oahu's libraries include: Hawaii State Library, in Honolulu at 478 S. King St., tel. 548-4775; Kailua Library, 239 Kuulei Rd., tel. 261-4611; Library for the Blind and Physically Handicapped, 402 Kapahulu Ave., tel. 732-7767; Waikiki branch next door, at 400 Kapahulu, tel. 732-2777.

Weather And Surf Conditions

For a weather report call 836-0234; for surfing conditions, call 836-1952; for Hawaiian waters report, tel. 836-3921.

Helpful Numbers

Arizona **Memorial,** tel. 922-1626; **Babysitting services,** tel. 923-8337, in Waikiki at 922-5575; **Bishop Museum,** tel. 922-1626; **Council of Churches,** tel. 521-2666; **Dept. of Agriculture,** plants, produce, regulations, etc., tel. 836-1415; **directory assistance,** tel. 1-411; Honolulu Harbor, daily ship arrival recording, tel. 537-9260; **Honolulu International Airport,** tel. 836-1411/6431; **time,** tel. 983-3211; **whale watch,** tel. 922-1626.

MONEY AND FINANCES

Currency

U.S. currency is among the drabbest in the world. It's all the same size and color; those unfamiliar with it should spend some time getting acquainted so that they don't make costly mistakes. U.S. coinage in use is: one cent, five cents, 10 cents, 25 cents, 50 cents, and one dollar (uncommon); paper currency is $1, $2 (uncommon), $5, $10, $20, $50, $100. Bills larger than $100 are not in common usage.

Banks

Full-service banks tend to open slightly earlier than Mainland banks, at 8:30 a.m. Mon.-Friday. Closing is at 3 p.m., except for late hours on Friday when most banks remain open until 6 p.m. Of most value to travelers, banks sell and cash traveler's checks, give cash advances on credit cards, and exchange and sell foreign currency.

Traveler's Checks

Traveler's checks are accepted throughout Hawaii at hotels, restaurants, car rental agencies, and in most stores and shops. However, to be readily acceptable they should be in American currency. Some larger hotels that often deal with Japanese and Canadians will accept their currency. Banks accept foreign-currency traveler's checks, but it'll mean an extra trip and inconvenience.

Credit Cards

More and more business is transacted in Hawaii using credit cards. Almost every form of accommodations, shop, restaurant, and amusement accepts them. For renting a car they're almost a must. With "credit card insurance" readily available, they're as safe as traveler's checks and sometimes even more convenient. Don't rely on them completely because there are some establishments that won't accept them, or perhaps won't accept the kind that you carry.

OTHER PRACTICALITIES

Telephone

Like everywhere else in the U.S., long-distance rates go down at 5 p.m. and drop even further from 11 p.m. until 8 a.m. the

> **The area code for all Hawaii is 808.**

next morning. From Friday at 5 p.m. until Monday morning at 8 a.m. rates are cheapest. Local calls from public telephones (anywhere on the same island is a local call) cost 25 cents. Calling between islands is a toll call, and the price depends on when and from where you call and for how long you speak. Emergency calls are always free. The area code for the entire state of Hawaii is 808. For directory assistance: local, 1-411; interisland, 1-555-1212; Mainland, 1-area code-555-1212; toll-free (800) 555-1212.

Time Zones

There is no "daylight saving time" observed in Hawaii. When daylight saving time is not observed on the Mainland, Hawaii is two hours behind the West Coast, four hours behind the Midwest, and five hours behind the East Coast. Hawaii, being just east of the international date line, is almost a full day behind most Asian and Oceanic cities. The number of hours Hawaii is behind these countries and cities are: Japan, 19 hours; Singapore, 18 hours; Sydney, 20 hours; New Zealand, 22 hours; Fiji, 22 hours.

Electricity

The same electrical current is in use in Hawaii as on the U.S. Mainland and is uniform throughout the islands. The system functions on 110 volts, 60 cycles of alternating current (AC). Appliances from Japan will work, but there is some danger of burnout, while those requiring the normal European current of 220 will not work.

Distance, Weights, And Measures

Hawaii, like all of the U.S., employs the "English method" of measuring weights and distances. Basically, dry weights are in ounces and pounds; liquid measures are in ounces, quarts, and gallons; and distances are measured in inches, feet, yards, and miles. The metric system, based on units of 10, is known but is not in general use. The Metric System chart at the back of the book should be helpful.

DIANA LASICH HARPER

BOB RACE

HONOLULU

Honolulu is *the* most exotic city in America. It's not any one attribute that makes this so; it's a combination of things. Honolulu's like an ancient Hawaiian goddess who can change her form at will. At one moment you see a black-eyed beauty, swaying provocatively to a deep and basic rhythm, and in the next a high-tech scion of the computer age sitting straight-backed behind a polished desk. The city is the terminus of "manifest destiny," the end of America's relentless westward drive, until no more horizons were left. Other Mainland cities are undoubtedly more historic, cultural, and perhaps, to some, more beautiful than Honolulu, but none come close to having all of these features in the same overwhelming combination. The city's face, though blemished by high-rises and pocked by heavy industry, is eternally lovely. The Koolau Mountains form the background tapestry from which the city emerges; the surf gently foams along Waikiki; the sun hisses fire-red as it drops into the sea, and Diamond Head beckons with a promise of tropical romance.

In the center of the city, skyscrapers rise as silent, unshakable witnesses to Honolulu's economic strength. In glass and steel offices, businesspeople wearing conservative three-piece uniforms are clones of any found on Wall Street. Below, a fantasia of people live and work. In nooks and crannies are an amazing array of arts, shops, and cuisines. In a flash of festival the streets become China, Japan, Portugal, New England, old Hawaii, or the Philippines.

New England churches, royal palaces, bandstands, tall-masted ships, and coronation platforms illustrate Honolulu's history. And what a history! You can visit places where in a mere twinkle of time past, red-plumed warriors were driven to their death over an impossibly steep *pali*, or where the skies were alive with screaming Zeros strafing and bombing the only American city threatened by a foreign power since the War of 1812. In hallowed grounds throughout the city lie the bodies of fallen warriors. Some are entombed in a mangled steel sepulchre below the waves, others from three wars rest in a natural bowl of bereavement and silence. And a nearby royal mausoleum holds the remains of those who were "old Hawaii."

Honolulu is the pumping heart of Hawaii. The state government and university are here. So are botanical parks, a fine aquarium and zoo, a floating maritime museum, and the world's foremost museum on Polynesia. Art flourishes like flowers, as do professional and amateur entertainment, extravaganzas, and local and world-class sporting events. But the city isn't all good clean fun. The seedier side includes "girlie" shows, raucous GI bars, street drugs, and street people. But somehow this blending and collision of East and West, this hodgepodge of emotionally charged history, this American city superimposed on a unique Pacific setting works well as Honolulu, the "Sheltered Harbor" of man and his dreams.

SIGHTS

The best way to see Honolulu is to start from the middle and fan out on foot to visit the inner city. You can *do* downtown in one day, but the sights of greater Honolulu require a few days to see them all. It's a matter of opinion where the center of downtown Honolulu actually is, but the King Kamehameha statue in front of Aliiolani Hale is about as central as you can get, and a perfect landmark from which to start. If you're staying in Waikiki, leave your rental car in the hotel garage and take TheBus (no. 2) for downtown sightseeing.

Note: For terrific **Living History Walking Tours** see "Getting Around—Sightseeing Tours—Special Tours" in the Out and About chapter.

Parking And Transportation, Downtown Honolulu

If you can't bear to leave your car behind, head for Aloha Tower. When you get to where you can see the Aloha Tower off the S. Nimitz Hwy., look for a sign pointing you left to "Piers 4 and 11, Aloha Tower." Enter to find plenty of parking. The traffic is not as congested here and the large lot is open 24 hours, at $1.00 per hour, with a four-hour maximum on the meter. Bring change, as none is available. You might have to come back and feed the meter again if you want to go as far as Chinatown, but this will be plenty of time for the local attractions that are well within walking distance.

For various sights outside the downtown area, your rental car is fine. Some shuttles running out to the *Arizona* Memorial are more expensive than TheBus (85 cents), but so convenient that they're worth the extra few coins. The **Waikiki Trolley,** tel. 526-0112, conducts tours throughout the downtown area. For $15 adults, $7.50 children, you can ride it all day long. It looks like a trolley but it's a bus that's been ingeniously converted.

DOWNTOWN HONOLULU

The **Statue of King Kamehameha** is at the junction of King and Mililani streets. Running off at an angle is **Merchant Street,** the oldest thoroughfare in Honolulu, and you might say its "the beginning of the road to modernity." The statue is much more symbolic of Kamehameha's strength as a ruler and unifier of the Hawaiian Is-

King Kamehameha I

lands than as a replica of the man himself. Of the few drawings of Kamehameha that have been preserved, none is necessarily a good likeness. Kamehameha was a magnificent leader and statesman, but by all accounts not very good-looking. This statue is one of three. The original, lost at sea near the Falkland Islands en route from Paris where it was bronzed, was later re-

covered, but not before insurance money was used to cast this second one. The original is in the town of Kapaau, in the Kohala District of the Big Island, not far from where Kamehameha was born, but although they supposedly came from the same mold, they somehow seem quite different. The third stands in Washington, D.C., dedicated when Hawaii became a state. The

Iolani Palace, the only royal residence in America

Honolulu statue was dedicated in 1883, as part of King David Kalakaua's coronation ceremony. Its black and gold colors are striking, but it is most magnificent on June 11, King Kamehameha Day, when 18-foot lei are draped around the neck and the outstretched arms.

Behind Kamehameha stands **Aliiolani Hale,** now the State Judiciary Building. This handsome structure, designed by an Australian architect and begun in 1872, was originally commissioned by Kamehameha V as a palace, but was redesigned as a general court building. It looks much more grand than Iolani Palace across the way. Kamehameha V died before it was finished, and it was officially dedicated by King Kalakaua in 1874. Less than 20 years later, on January 17, 1893, at this "hall of justice," the first proclamation by the Members of the Committee of Safety was read, stating that the sovereign nation of Hawaii was no more, and that the islands would be ruled by a provisional government.

Iolani Palace

As you enter the parklike palace grounds, notice the emblem of Hawaii in the center of the large iron gates. They're often draped with simple lei of fragrant *maile.* The quiet grounds are a favorite strolling and relaxing place for many government workers, especially in the shade of a huge banyan, purportedly planted by Kalakaua's wife, Kapiolani. The building, with its glass and ironwork imported from San Francisco, and its Corinthian columns, is the only royal palace in America. Iolani ("Royal Hawk") Palace, begun in 1879 under orders of King Kalakaua, was completed in December 1882 at a cost of $350,000. It was the first electrified building in Honolulu, and had a direct phone line to the Royal Boat House.

Non-Hawaiian island residents of the day thought it a frivolous waste of money, but here poignant scenes and profound changes rocked the Hawaiian islands. After nine years as king, Kalakaua built a **Coronation Stand** that temporarily sat in front of the palace (now off to the left). In a belated ceremony, Kalakaua raised a crown to his head and placed one on his queen, Kapiolani. During the ceremony, 8,000 Hawaiians cheered, while Honolulu's foreign, tax-paying businessmen boycotted. On August 12, 1898, after only two Hawaiian monarchs, Kalakaua and Liliuokalani (his sister), had resided in the palace, the American flag was raised up the flagpole following a successful coup that marked Hawaii's official recognition by the U.S. as a territory. During this ceremony, loyal Hawaiian subjects wept bitter tears, while the businessmen of Honolulu cheered wildly.

Kalakaua, later in his rule, was forced to sign a new constitution that greatly reduced his own power to little more than figurehead status. He traveled to San Francisco in 1891, where he died. His body was returned to Honolulu and lay in state in the palace. His sister, Liliuokalani, succeeded him; she attempted to change this constitution and gain the old power of Hawaii's sovereigns, but the businessmen revolted and the monarchy fell. Iolani Palace then became the main executive building for the provisional government, with the House of Representatives meeting in the throne room

*Washington Place,
Honolulu*

and the Senate in the dining room. It served in this capacity until 1968.

Iolani Palace is open to one-hour **guided tours only,** Wed.-Sat. 9 a.m.-2:15 p.m.; $5 adults, $2 children, with no children under five admitted. They're popular so make reservations at least a day in advance. Tickets are sold at a window at the Barracks, open Tues.-Sat. 8:30 a.m.-2:15 p.m. The Palace shop is open Tues.-Sat. 8:30 a.m.-3:30 p.m. For information and reservations call 522-0832.

Palace Grounds

Kalakaua, known as the "Merry Monarch," was credited with saving the hula. He also hired Henri Burger, first Royal Hawaiian Bandmaster, and together they wrote "Hawaii Pono," the state anthem. Many concerts were given from the Coronation Stand, which became known as the **Royal Bandstand.** Behind it is **Iolani Barracks** (Hale Koa), built in 1870 to house the Royal Household Guards. When the monarchy of Hawaii fell to provisional government forces in 1893, only *one* of these soldiers was wounded in a pathetic show of strength. The barracks were moved to the present site from nearby land on which the State Capitol was erected.

To the right behind the palace are the **State Archives.** This modern building, dating from 1953, holds records, documents, and vintage photos. A treasure trove to scholars and those tracing their genealogy, it is worth a visit by the general public to view the old photos on dis-

play. Free, open Mon.-Fri. 7:45 a.m.-4:30 p.m. Next door is the **Hawaii State Library,** housing the main branch of this statewide system. As in all Hawaii state libraries, you are entitled to a card on your first visit, and are then eligible to take out books. The central courtyard is a favorite lunch spot for many of the government workers. Some of the original money to build the library was put up by Andrew Carnegie. For information call 548-4775.

Government Buildings

Liliuokalani was deposed and placed under house arrest in the palace for nine months. Later, after much intrigue that included a visit to Washington, D.C., to plead her case and an aborted counterrevolution, she sadly accepted her fate and moved to nearby **Washington Place.** This solid-looking structure fronts Beretania Street and was originally the home of sea captain John Dominis. It was inherited by his son John Owen Dominis, who married a lovely young Hawaiian aristocrat, Lydia Kapaakea, who became Queen Liliuokalani. She lived in her husband's home, proud but powerless, until her death in 1917. Washington Place is now the official residence of the governor of Hawaii.

To the left of Washington Place is **St. Andrew's Cathedral.** Built in 1867 as an Anglican church, many of its stones and ornaments were shipped from England; Hawaii's monarchs worshiped here, and the church is still very much in use. To the right is the **War Memorial.**

Erected in 1974, it replaced an older memorial to the people who perished in WW II. A courtyard and benches are provided for quiet meditation.

Directly in front of you is the magnificent **Hawaii State Capitol,** built in 1969 for $25 million. The building itself is a metaphor for Hawaii: the pillars surrounding it are palms, the reflecting pool is the sea, and the cone-shaped rooms of the Legislature represent the volcanoes of Hawaii. It's lined with rich koa wood from the Big Island, and is further graced with woven hangings and murals, with two gigantic, four-ton replicas of the State Seal hanging at both entrances. The inner courtyard has a 600,000-tile mosaic, *Aquarius,* rendered by island artist Tadashi Sato, and on one side is a poignant sculpture of *Father Damien of the Lepers.* The State Legislature is in session January to March, and opens with dancing, music, and festivities at 10 a.m. on the third Wednesday in January, public invited. Peek inside, then take the elevator to the fifth floor for outstanding views of the city.

MISSION HOUSES MUSEUM

The days when tall ships with tattered sails crewed by rough seamen bore God-fearing missionary families dedicated to Christianizing the savage islands are alive in the halls and buildings of The Mission Houses Museum, 553 S. King St., Honolulu, HI 96813, tel. 531-0481. Across from Kawaiahao Church (oldest in Honolulu), the complex includes two main houses, a printing house annex, a library and a fine, inexpensive gift shop, and is operated by the **Hawaiian Mission Children's Society** (or Cousins' Society), whose members serve as guides and hosts. Many are direct descendants, or spouses of descendants, of the Congregationalist missionaries who built these structures. Tours are conducted Tues.-Sat. 9 a.m.-4 p.m., Sun. 12-4 p.m., closed Mondays. Guided tours of the Frame House, oldest wooden structure in Hawaii, 9:30 a.m.-3 p.m.; $3.50 admission, tel. 531-0481 (see "Special Programs" below).

Construction
If you think that precut modular housing is a new concept, think again. The first structure that you enter is the **Frame House,** the oldest wooden structure in Hawaii. Precut in Boston, it came along with the first missionary packet in 1819. Since the interior frame was left behind and didn't arrive until Christmas Day, 1820, the missionary families lived in thatched huts until it was erected. Finally the Chamberlain family occupied it in 1821. Many missionary families used it over the years, with as many as four households occupying this small structure at the same time. This is where the Christianizing of Hawaii truly began.

The missionaries, being New Englanders, first dug a cellar. The Hawaiians were very suspicious of the strange hole, convinced that the missionaries planned to store guns and arms in this "fort." Though assured to the contrary, King Liholiho, anxious to save face and prove his omnipotence, had a cellar dug near his home twice as deep and large. This satisfied everyone.

Notice the different styles, sizes, and colors of bricks used in the structures. Most of the ships of the day carried bricks as ballast. After unloading cargo, the captains either donated or sold the bricks to the missionaries, who incorporated them into the structures. A common local material was coral stone: pulverized coral was burned with lime to make a rudimentary cement, which was then used to bind cut-coral blocks. The pit that was used for this purpose is still discernible on the grounds.

Kitchen
The natives were intrigued with the missionaries, whom they called "long necks" because of their high collars. The missionaries, on the other hand, were a little more wary of their "charges." The low fence around the complex was symbolic as well as utilitarian. The missionaries were obsessed with keeping their children away from Hawaiian children, who at first ran around naked and played many games with overt sexual overtones. Almost every evening a small cadre of Hawaiians would assemble to peer into the kitchen to watch the women cook, which they found exceedingly strange because their *kapu* said that *men* did the cooking. In the kitchen, actually an attached cookhouse, the woodburning stove kept breaking down. More often than not, the women used the fireplace with its built-in oven. About once a week, they fired up the oven to make traditional New Eng-

land staples like bread, pies, cakes, and puddings. The missionaries were dependent on the Hawaiians to bring them fresh water. Notice a large porous stone through which they would filter the water to remove dirt, mud, and sometimes brackishness.

The Hawaiians were even more amazed when the entire family sat down to dinner, a tremendous deviation from their beliefs that separated men and women when eating. When the missionaries assembled to dine or meet at the "long table," the Hawaiians silently stood at the open door to watch the evening soap opera. The unnerved missionaries eventually closed the door and cut two windows into the wall, which they could leave opened but draped. The long table took on further significance. The one you see is a replica. When different missionaries left the islands, they, like people today, wanted a souvenir. For some odd reason, they elected to saw a bit off the long table. As years went by, the table got shorter and shorter until it was useless.

Residents

The house was actually a duplex. Although many families lived in it, two of the best known were the Binghams and the Judds. Much of the furniture here was theirs. Judd, a member of the third missionary company, assumed the duties of physician to all the missionaries and is-

landers. He often prescribed alcohol of different sorts to the missionary families for a wide variety of ailments; many records remain of these prescriptions, but not one record of complaints from his patients. The Binghams and Judds got along very well, and entertained each other and visitors, most often in the Judds' parlor because they were a little better off. The women would often congregate here to do their sewing, which was in great demand, especially by members of the royal household. Until the missionary women taught island girls to sew, providing clothing for Hawaii's royalty was a tiresome and time-consuming obligation.

The missionaries were self-sufficient, and had the unbounded energy of youth, as the average age was only 25. The husbands often built furniture for their families. Reverend Bingham, a good craftsman, was pressed by Queen Kaahumanu to build her a rocking chair after she became enamored of one made for Mrs. Bingham. The queen weighed almost 400 pounds, so building her a suitable chair was no slim feat! Still, the queen could only use it in her later years when she'd lost a considerable amount of weight. After she died, the Binghams asked for it to be returned, and it sits in their section of the house. Compare Bingham's chair to another in the Judds' bedroom, jury-rigged by a young missionary husband from a captain's chair. An understatement, found

left to right: Frame House, Printing House, Chamberlain House later in his diary, confirmed that he was not a carpenter.

When you enter the Judds' bedroom, note how small it is, and consider that two adults and five children slept here. As soon as the children were old enough, they were sent back to the Mainland for schooling, no doubt to relieve some of the congestion. Also notice that the windows were fixed, in the New England style, and imagine how close it must have been in these rooms. The Binghams' bedroom is also small, and not as well furnished. Bingham's shaving kit remains, and is inscribed with "The Sandwich Isles." In the bedroom of Mary Ward, a missionary woman who never married, the roof was raised to accommodate her canopy bed.

Another famous family that lived in the complex were the Cookes. When the missionary board withdrew its support, the Cookes petitioned them to buy the duplex, which was granted. Shortly thereafter, Mr. Cooke, who had been a teacher, formed a partnership with one Mr. Castle, and from that time forward Castle and Cooke grew to become one of Hawaii's oldest and most powerful corporations. The largest building in the compound is the **Chamberlain House.** This barnlike structure was completed in 1831 and used as a warehouse and living quarters for Levi Chamberlain's family. Goods were stored in most of the structure, while the family occupied three modest rooms.

Printing House

The missionaries decided almost immediately that the best way to convert the natives was to speak to them in their own language, and to create a written Hawaiian language which they would teach in school. To this end, they created the **Hawaiian alphabet,** consisting of 12 letters, including the five vowels and seven consonants. In addition, to disseminate the doctrines of Christianity, they needed books, and therefore a printing press. On the grounds still stands the Printing House, built in 1841 but first used as annex bedrooms by the Hall family. The original printing house, built in 1823, no longer exists. In the Printing House is a replica of the Ramage press brought from New England, first operated by Elijah Lewis. He returned to the Mainland when he was 24, and soon died of tuberculosis, but not before he had earned the distinction of being

the first printer west of the Rockies. Here were printed biblical tracts, textbooks, or anything that the king or passing captains were willing to pay to have printed. Although it took eight hours of hard work to set up one page to be printed, it is estimated that in the 20 years the press operated under the missionaries, over seven million pages were produced.

Gift Shop

While on the grounds make sure to visit the bookstore and gift shop. It's small but has an excellent collection of Hawaiiana, and some very inexpensive but quality items, such as tapa bookmarks for only 25 cents, and an outstanding collection of Niihau shellwork, considered the finest in Hawaii. The shelves hold tasteful items like woodcarvings, bread boards, hats, weavings, chimes, flags of old Hawaii, and stuffed pillows with classic Hawaiian quilt motifs. Also a good collection of Hawaiian dolls, for kids and adults. Between the bookstore and the research library are restrooms.

Special Programs

Along with other programs, the museum hosts Hawaii's only **living history program,** with actors who dress in fashions of the period and assume the roles of missionaries in 1830 Honolulu. Feel free to interact and ask questions, but remember that they stay in character, so the answers may surprise you. The living history program is usually offered on the last Saturday of the month, 10 a.m.-3 p.m., admission for adults $3.50. Other special programs are also offered like "Candlelight Tour of Honolulu, 1831," and a program that includes tea with the 19th century Reverend Hiram and Mrs. Sybil Bingham in their parlor, tel. 924-1911 for details. Also, consider a "Walking Tour of Honolulu," offered by the museum, that guides you through downtown Honolulu for two hours, hitting all the historic sights with an extremely knowledgeable narration by one of the museum's guides (see "Getting Around—Sightseeing Tours" in the Out and About chapter.

KAWAIAHAO CHURCH

This church, so instrumental in Hawaii's history, is the most enduring symbol of the original mis-

Kawaiahao Church

sionary work in the islands. A sign welcomes you and bids the blessing, "Grace and peace to you from God our Father." The church was constructed from 1836 until 1842 according to plans drawn up by Hiram Bingham, its minister. Before this, at least four grass shacks of increasing size stood here. One was destroyed by a sailor who was reprimanded by Reverend Bingham for attending services while drunk; the old sea dog returned the next day and burned the church to the ground. Kawaiahao ("Water of Hao") Church is constructed from over 14,000 coral blocks quarried from offshore reefs. In 1843, following Restoration Day, when the British returned the Hawaiian Islands to sovereignty after a brief period of imperialism by a renegade captain, King Kamehameha III uttered here the profound words in a thanksgiving ceremony that were destined to become Hawaii's motto, *"Ua mau ke ea o ka aina i ka pono,"* ("The life of the land is preserved in righteousness").

Other noteworthy ceremonies held at the church were the marriage of King Liholiho and his wife Queen Emma, who bore the last child born to a Hawaiian monarch. Unfortunately, little Prince Albert died at the age of four. On June

19, 1856, Lunalilo, the first king elected to the throne, took his oath of office in the church. A bachelor who died childless, he always felt scorned by living members of the Kamehameha clan, and refused to be buried with them at the Royal Mausoleum in Nuuanu Valley; he is buried in a tomb in the church's cemetery. Buried along with him is his father, Charles Kanaina, and nearby lies the grave of his mother, Miriam Kekauluohi. In the graveyard lies Henri Burger, and many members of the Parker, Green, Brown and Cooke families, early missionaries to the islands. Liliuokalani's body lay in state in the church before it was taken to the Royal Mausoleum. A jubilation service was held in the church when Hawaii became a state in 1959. Kawaiahao holds beautiful Christmas services with a strong Polynesian and Hawaiian flavor. Hidden away in a corner of the grounds is an unobtrusive adobe building, remains of a schoolhouse built in 1835 to educate Hawaiian children.

HAWAII MARITIME CENTER

The development of this center is a wonderful concept whose time has finally come. It's amazing that a state and former nation, whose discovery and very birth are so intimately tied to the exploration, navigation, and exploitation of the sea, has never had a center dedicated exclusively to these profoundly important aspects of its heritage. Now the Hawaii Maritime Center, at Pier 7, Honolulu Harbor, Honolulu, HI 96813, tel. 523-6151, is exactly that . . . and it needs your support as a visitor. The center, along with its museum in the **Kalakaua Boathouse,** now consists of three attractions: Aloha Tower, the beacon of hospitality welcoming people to Hawaii for six decades (not technically part of the center); the classic, and last remaining, fully rigged, four-masted *Falls of Clyde* floating museum; and the reproduction of a Hawaiian sailing canoe, *The Hokule'a,* which recently sailed back in time using ancient navigational methods to retrace the steps of Hawaii's Polynesian explorers. Take bus no. 8 or 20 from Waikiki and you're deposited right in front. Admission $7, all attractions. Open 9 a.m.-5 p.m. every day.

The Kalakaua Boathouse

The main building of the center is the two-storied Kalakaua Boathouse. Behind is Coasters, an American standard restaurant (see "Food—Inexpensive Dining Around Town"), and an area called Kalakaua Park, a garden and observation area perfect for lunch. Eighty-one steps lead to the "crow's nest," and "widow's walk," with great views of the harbor and city.

Upon entering you find a glass case filled with trophies and memorabilia from the days of King Kalakaua. His words have a sadly prophetic ring. "Remember who you are. Be gracious, but never forget from whence you came for this is where your heart is. This is the cradle of your life." Notice the phones installed throughout the capital in 1887, a few years before California had electricity. Kalakaua had previously installed telephones between his boathouse and the palace in 1878, just two years after Bell's invention. The bottom floor of the center recalls ancient fishing methods, and the traditional division of land and sea resources among the people.

Another fascinating display traces the development of surfing through the ages, from original boards, more like seagoing canoes at 18 feet long, until the modern debut of the fiberglass board. You can spot a vintage album of *Surfin Safari* by The Beach Boys. Here, too, is a land-surfing sled used for games during the Makahiki Festival. It measures six inches wide and 10-14 feet long. Trails to accommodate it were up to a mile long. Built on steep hills, they were paved in stone, layered with earth and topped with slippery grass. Once launched there was no stopping until the bottom. Yippee!

One corner of the museum is dedicated to tattooing, Polynesian and Western. It shows traditional tattoos worn by both men and women, and then how the Western style became more popular, as Hawaii was a main berth for sailors, who sported these living souvenirs from around the world. **Mail buoys** sounds uninteresting, but these tidbits of old Hawaiiana, still alive today, are fascinating. Fashioned from gaily painted metal cans, passing ships, mainly from Peru and Equador, still radio Honolulu Harbor that they are dropping one. Someone, anyone, who heard the message, would fetch then. Inside are little gifts for the finder, who takes the enclosed mail and sends it on its way.

King David Kalakaua

HAWAII STATE ARCHIVES

The second floor is dedicated to the discovery of Hawaii, both by the Polynesians and Westerners. Through ledgers, histories, and artifacts, it traces original discovery, Western discovery, the death of Captain Cook, and the role of the sea otter pelt, which brought the first whalers and traders after sandalwood. The whaling section is dripping with blood and human drama. Look at the old harpoons and vintage film footage. Yes, film footage, and photos. A remarkable display is of scrimshaw from the whaling days. Sailors would be at sea for five to seven years, and would have untold hours to create beauty in what were dismal conditions. Suspended from the ceiling are replicas of double-hulled sailing canoes, and one of only two fully restored skeletons of the humpback whale (this one is in diving position). One corner is a replica of H. Hatfield and Co., a whaling supply store of the era. The rear of the second floor shows steamships that cruised between Hawaii, Japan, and the East Coast, a nature exhibit of weather, marinelife, and volcanoes, and an auditorium with a video on the *Hokule'a* (see following).

Aloha Tower

When this endearing and enduring tourist cliche was built in 1926 for $160,000, the 184-foot, 10-story tower was the tallest structure on Oahu. As such, this landmark, with clocks embedded in all four walls, and emblazoned with the greeting and departing word, *Aloha,* became the symbol of Hawaii. Before the days of air transport, ocean liners would pull up to the pier to disembark passengers and on these "Steamer Days," festive well-wishers from throughout the city would gather to greet and lei the arriving passengers. The Royal Hawaiian Band would even turn out to welcome the guests ashore.

When you take the escalator up from the parking area, notice the huge U.S. Customs rooms that at one time processed droves of passengers. Today, the crowds are gone and the tower is quiet. Only a few harbormasters on the top floor oversee the comings and goings of cargo ships. When you enter the tower a sign claims that you can only get to the observation area on the top floor by elevator. You can walk up to the ninth floor if you want, but to get to the very top does necessitate taking the elevator, which has the dubious distinction of being one of the first elevators in Hawaii. Once atop the tower, you get the most remarkable view of the harbor and the city. A high-rise planned for just next door will surely ruin the view, but many people with good sense, and luckily with some clout, are fighting this project. A remarkable feature of the vista is the reflections of the city and the harbor in many of the steel and reflective glass high-rises. It's as if a huge mural were painted on them. The tower is open free of charge, daily 8 a.m.-9 p.m., though currently it is temporarily closed due to extensive contruction immediately surrounding the building. Check!

Falls Of Clyde

This is the last fully rigged, four-masted ship afloat on any of the world's oceans and has recently been designated as a National Historic Landmark. She was saved from being scrapped in 1963 by a Seattle bank that was attempting to recoup some money on a bad debt. The people of Hawaii learned of her fate and spontaneous-ly raised money to have the ship towed back to Honolulu Harbor. The *Falls of Clyde* was always a worker, never a pleasure craft. It served the Matson Navigation Company as a cargo and passenger liner from 1898 until 1920. Built in Glasgow, Scotland, in 1878, she was converted in 1906 to a sail-driven tanker; a motor aboard was used mainly to move the rigging around. After 1920, she was dismantled, towed to Alaska and became little more than a floating oil depot for fishing boats. Since 1968, the *Falls of Clyde* has been a floating museum, sailing the imaginations of children and grownups to times past, and in this capacity has perhaps performed her greatest duty.

Hokule'a

The newest and perhaps most dynamic feature of the center is the *Hokule'a.* This authentic re-creation of a traditional double-hulled sailing canoe captured the attention of the world when in 1976 it made a 6,000-mile roundtrip voyage to Tahiti. Piloted by Mau Piailug, a Caroline Islander, only ancient navigational techniques guided it successfully on its voyage. This attempt to relive these ancient voyages as closely as possible included eating traditional provisions only—poi, coconuts, dried fish, and bananas. Toward the end of the voyage some canned food had to be broken out!

Modern materials such as plywood and fiberglass were used, but by consulting many petroglyphs and old drawings of these original craft, the design and lines were kept as authentic as possible. The sails, made from a heavy cotton, were the distinctive crab-claw type. In trial runs to work out the kinks and choose the crew, she almost sank in the treacherous channel between Oahu and Kauai and had to be towed in by the Coast Guard. But the *Hokule'a* performed admirably during the actual voyage. The experiment was a resounding technical success, but it was marred by bad feelings between members of the crew who argued and drew racial boundary lines. Both Hawaiian and white crew members found it impossible to work as a team on the first voyage, thereby mocking the canoe's name, "Star of Gladness". The tension was compounded by the close quarters of more than a dozen men living on an open deck only nine feet wide by 40 feet long. The remarkable navigator Piailug refused to return to Hawaii with the craft and instead sailed back to his native island. Since then, the *Hokule'a* has made five more voyages, logging over 50,000 miles, with many racially mixed crews who have gotten along admirably.

The *Hokule'a,* sponsored by the Polynesian Voyaging Society, will make Pier 7 its home berth when not at sea. This double-hulled canoe, a replica of the ones that Captain Cook found so remarkable, will fascinate you too.

PALI HIGHWAY

Cutting across Oahu from Honolulu to Kailua on the windward coast is Rt. 61, better known as the Pali Highway. Before getting to the famous Nuuanu Pali Lookout at the very crest of the Koolau Mountains, you can spend a full and enjoyable day sightseeing. Stop en route at Punchbowl's National Memorial Cemetery, followed by an optional side trip to the summit of Tantalus for a breathtaking view of the city (see "Camping and Hiking—Hiking" in the Out and About chapter). You can also visit the **Royal Mausoleum** in the vicinity. Take the H-1 Freeway to Vineyard Boulevard (exit 22), cross the Pali Hwy. to Nuuanu Avenue and follow it to the mausoleum. In a minute or two, if you continue up Nuuanu Avenue, it intersects the Pali Hwy., but you'll have passed the Punchbowl turnoff (see following). This small chapel, built in 1865 by Kamehameha IV, holds the bodies of most of the royal family who died after 1825. Their bodies were originally interred elsewhere but were later moved here. The mausoleum at one time held 18 royal bodies but became overcrowded, so they were moved again to little crypts scattered around the grounds. Few tourists visit this serene place open weekdays 8 a.m.-4 p.m., tel. 536-7602.

About two miles past the Punchbowl turnoff, heading up the Pali Hwy. (exit 21-B off H-1), an HVB Warrior points you to the **Walker Home** across from Nuuanu Congregational Church. It's famous for its gardens, and at one time visitors were welcome to come and tour them for a fee. It's hard to tell if this is still happening. The gates are open and no signs tell you to keep out, but an unsmiling housekeeper backed by a steely-eyed German shepherd make you want to

wave from your car and keep rolling. Next comes Queen Emma's Summer Palace (see following) and the Daijingu Temple, a Baptist college, and a Catholic church. It almost seems as though these sects were vying to get farther up the hill to be just a little closer to heaven.

A sign, past Queen Emma's Palace, points you off to **Nuuanu Pali Drive.** Take it! This few-minutes' jog off the Pali Hwy. (which it rejoins) takes you through some wonderful scenery. Make sure to bear right as soon as you pull off and not up the Old Pali Hwy., which has no outlet. Immediately the road is canopied with trees, and in less than half a mile there's a bubbling little waterfall and a pool. The homes in here are grand, and the entire area has a parklike effect. One of the nicest little roads that you can take while looking around, this side trip wastes no time at all.

Queen Emma's Summer Palace

This summer home is more the simple hideaway of a well-to-do family than a grand palace. The 3,000-square-foot interior has only two bedrooms and no facilities for guests. The first person to put a house on the property was John George Lewis. He purchased the land for $800 from a previous owner by the name of Henry Pierce, and then resold it to John Young II. The exterior has a strong New England flavor, and indeed the house was prefabricated in Boston. The simple square home, surrounded by a lanai, was built from 1843 to 1847 by John Young II, Queen Emma's uncle. When he died, she inherited the property and spent many relaxing days here, away from the heat of Honolulu, with her husband King Kamehameha IV. Emma used the home little after 1872, and following her death in 1885 it fell into disrepair.

Rescued from demolition by the Daughters of Hawaii in 1913, it was refurbished and has operated as a museum since 1915. The palace, at 2913 Pali Hwy., tel. 595-3167, is open daily 9 a.m.-4 p.m., admission $6, children under 12 50 cents. Although it's just off the Pali Highway, the one and only sign comes up quickly, and many visitors pass it by. If you pass the entranceway to the Oahu Country Club just across the road, you've gone too far.

As you enter, notice the tall *kahili,* symbols of noble rank in the entranceway, along with *lau*

GREATER HONOLULU

TO WAIMANALO

KALANIANAOLE HWY 72

KAHALA HILTON

KEALAOLU

KAHALA AVE

KILAUEA

KAHALA RD

18th

DIAMOND HEAD RD

DIAMOND HEAD

H1

MAUNALANI HEIGHTS

ST. LOUIS HEIGHTS

MOILIILI KAIMUKI

WAIALAE AVE.

LUNALILO

DATE ST.

MONSARRAT

PAKI

KAPAHULU

MANOA

UNIVERSITY OF HAWAII

UNIVERSITY

ALA WAI CANAL

ALA WAI BLVD.

KALAKAUA

KAPIOLANI BLVD.

OHAU AVE

METCALF

KING

MCCULLY

KEEAUMOKU

KAPIOLANI BLVD.

LEWERS

KALIA

ALA MOANA SHOPPING

SEE "WAIKIKI" MAP

ALA WAI YACHT HARBOR

PUNAHOU ST.

ROUND TOP DR.

MAKIKI HEIGHTS

TANTALUS DR.

MAKIKI HTS. DR.

NEHOA

WILDER

PENSACOLA

PIIKOI

WARD

KEEAUMOKU

ALA MOANA BLVD.

KEWALO BASIN

ALA MOANA PARK

TO KAILUA AND QUEEN EMMA'S SUMMER PALACE

PACIFIC HEIGHTS

SEE "DOWNTOWN HONOLULU" MAP

PALI HWY.

61

NUUANU

PAUOA

PUNCHBOWL

SEE "PUNCHBOWL" MAP

H1

STATE CAPITOL

BISHOP

QUEEN ST.

ALA MOANA BLVD.

MAMALA BAY

TO KANEOHE

LIKELIKE HWY.

63

KAPALAMA

LILIHA

SCHOOL ST.

BISHOP MUSEUM

KING ST.

VINEYARD

BETHEL

CHINATOWN

DILLINGHAM BLVD

NIMITZ HWY.

ALOHA TOWER

HONOLULU HARBOR

SAND ISLAND ACCESS RD.

SAND ISLAND STATE RECREATION AREA

SAND ISLAND

KALIHI

90

KALIHI ST.

MOANALUA RD

MIDDLE RD.

78

TO PEAR CITY

PUULOA RD

92

90

KEEHI LAGOON

LAGOON DR.

TO PEARL HARBOR

HONOLULU AIRPORT

1 mi

1 km

N.B. ONLY MAIN ROADS SHOWN

© MOON PUBLICATIONS, INC.

1. and 2. hula dancers, Waimea Falls Park (J.D. Bisignani)

1. Hawaiian gallinule (R.J. Shallenberger)   **2.** orchid (J.D. Bisignani)

Prince Albert

hala mats on the floor, which at one time were an unsurpassed specialty of Hawaii. Today they must be imported from Fiji or Samoa. The walls are hung with paintings of many of Hawaii's kings and queens, and in every room are distinctive Hawaiian artifacts, such as magnificent feather capes, fans, and tapa hangings.

The furnishings have a very strong British influence. The Hawaiian nobility of the time were enamored with the British. King Kamehameha IV traveled to England when he was 15 years old; he met Queen Victoria, and the two become good friends. Emma and Kamehameha IV had the last child born to a Hawaiian king and queen on May 20, 1858. Named Prince Albert after Queen Victoria's consort, he was much loved but died when he was only four years old on August 27, 1862. His father followed him to the grave in little more than a year. The king's brother, Lot Kamehameha, a bachelor, took the throne but died very shortly thereafter, marking the end of the Kamehameha line; after that, Hawaii elected her kings. Prince Albert's canoe-shaped cradle is here, made in Germany by Wilhelm Fisher from four different kinds of Hawaiian wood. His tiny shirts, pants, and boots are still laid out, and there's a lock of his hair, and one from Queen Emma. In every room there are royal memorabilia. The royal bedroom displays a queen-size bed covered with an exquisite pink and purple tapa bedspread. There's

vintage Victorian furniture, and even a piano built in London by Collard and Collard. A royal cabinet made in Berlin holds porcelains, plates, and cups. After Queen Emma died, it stood in Charles R. Bishop's drawing room but was later returned. The grounds are beautifully manicured, and the house is surrounded by shrubbery and trees, many of which date from when the royal couple lived here. Restrooms are around back.

Walk around back past the basketball court and keep to the right. Soon you'll see a modest little white building. Look for a rather thick and distinctive rope hanging across the entranceway. This is the Shinto temple **Dai Jingu**. It's not nearly as spectacular as the giant trees in this area, but it is authentic and worth a quick look.

The Daughters of Hawaii have added a gift shop around back, which is open the same hours as the palace. It's small but packed with excellent items like greeting cards, lei, travel guidebooks, beverage trays (reproductions of the early Matson Line menus), little Hawaiian quilt pillows, needlepoint, wraparounds from Tahiti, T-shirts with Queen Emma's Summer Palace logo, and Niihau shellwork, the finest in Hawaii.

Nuuanu Pali Lookout

This is one of those extra-benefit places where you get a magnificent view without any effort at all. Merely drive up the Pali Hwy. to the well-marked turnout and park. Rip-offs happen, so take all valuables. Before you, if the weather is accommodating, an unimpeded view of windward Oahu lies at your feet. Nuuanu Pali ("Cool Heights") lives up to its name; the winds here are chilly, extremely strong, and funnel right through the lookout. You definitely need a jacket or windbreaker. On a particularly windy day just after a good rainfall, various waterfalls tumbling off the *pali* will actually be blown uphill! A number of roads, punched over and through the *pali* over the years, are engineering marvels. The famous "carriage road" built in 1898 by John Wilson, a Honolulu boy, for only $37,500, using 200 laborers and plenty of dynamite, was truly amazing. Droves of people come here, many in huge buses, and they all go to the railing to have a peek. Even so, by walking down the old road built in 1932 that goes off to the right, you actually get private and better views. You'll find the tallest point in the area, a huge needlelike rock. The wind is quieter here.

Nuuanu Pali figures prominently in Hawaii's legend history. It's said, not without academic skepticism, that Kamehameha the Great pursued the last remaining defenders of Oahu to these cliffs in one of the final battles fought to consolidate his power over all of the islands in 1795. If you use your imagination, you can easily feel the utter despair and courage of these vanquished warriors as they were driven ever closer to the edge. Mercy was not shown nor expected. Some jumped to their deaths rather than surrender, while others fought until they were pushed over. The estimated number of casualties varies considerably, from a few hundred to a few thousand, while some believe that the battle never happened at all. Compounding the controversy are stories of the warriors' families, who searched the cliffs below for years, and supposedly found bones of their kinsmen, which they buried. The Pali Lookout is romantic at night, with the lights of Kailua and Kaneohe in the distance, but the best nighttime view is from Tantalus Drive, where all of Honolulu lies at your feet.

HAWAII STATE ARCHIVES

engraving of Hawaii's unique pali by Barthelme Lauvergue, circa 1836

PUNCHBOWL, NATIONAL CEMETERY OF THE PACIFIC

One sure sign that you have entered a place of honor is the hushed and quiet nature that everyone adopts without having to be told. This is the way it is the moment that you enter this shrine. The Hawaiian name, Puowaina ("Hill of Sacrifice"), couldn't have been more prophetic. Punchbowl is the almost perfectly round crater of an extinct volcano that holds the bodies of nearly 25,000 men and women who fell fighting for the United States, from the Spanish-American War to Vietnam. At one time, Punchbowl was a bastion of heavy cannon and artillery trained on Honolulu Harbor to defend it from hostile naval forces. In 1943 Hawaii bequeathed it to the federal government as a memorial; it was dedicated in 1949, when the remains of an unknown serviceman killed during the attack on Pearl Harbor were the first interred.

As you enter the main gate, a flagpole with the Stars and Stripes unfurled is framed in the center of a long sweeping lawn. A roadway lined with monkeypod trees adds three-dimensional depth to the impressionistic scene, as it leads to the steps of a marble, altarlike monument in the distance. The eye has a continuous sweep of the field, as there are no elevated tombstones, just simple marble slabs lying flat on the ground. The field is dotted with trees, including eight banyans, a special tree and symbolic number for the many Buddhists buried here. Brightening the scene are plumeria and rainbow shower trees, often planted in Hawaiian graveyards because they produce flowers year-round as perennial offerings from the living to the dead when they can't personally attend the grave. All are equal here; the famous, like Ernie Pyle, the stalwart who earned the Congressional Medal of Honor, and the unknown who died alone and unheralded on muddy battlefields in godforsaken jungles. To the right just after you enter is the office, open Mon.-Fri. 9 a.m.-5 p.m. with brochures and restrooms. Tour buses, taxis, and limousines are lined up here. Don't leave valuables in your car.

To get to Punchbowl take the H-1 Freeway to Rt. 61, the Pali Highway, and exit at 21B. Im-

Punchbowl Cemetery

mediately get to the right, where a sign points you to Punchbowl. You'll make some fancy zigzags through a residential area, but it's well marked and you'll come to Puowaina Street, which leads you to the main gate. Make sure to notice landmarks going in, because as odd as it sounds, no signs lead you back out and it's easy to get lost.

The Monument

Like a pilgrim, you climb the steps to the monument, where on both sides marble slabs seem to whisper the names of the 20,000-plus servicemen, all MIAs whose bodies were never found but whose spirits are honored here. The first slabs on the right are for the victims of Vietnam, on the left are those from WW II, and you can see that time is already weathering the marble. They lie together, as they fought and died . . . men, boys, lieutenants, captains, private soldiers, infantrymen, sailors . . . from everywhere in America. "In proud memory . . . this memorial has been erected by the United States of America."

At the monument itself, built in 1966, is a chapel and in the middle is a statue of a woman, a woman of peace, a heroic woman of liberty. Around her on the walls are etched maps and battles of the Pacific War whose names still evoke passion: Pearl Harbor, Wake, Coral Sea, Midway, Iwo Jima, the Gilbert Islands, Okinawa. Many of the visitors are Japanese. Many of Hawaii's war dead are also Japanese. Four decades ago we battled each other with hatred and malice. Today, on bright afternoons we come together with saddened hearts to pay reverence to the dead.

UNIVERSITY OF HAWAII

You don't have to be a student to head for the University of Hawaii, Manoa Campus. For one, it houses the **East-West Center,** which was incorporated in 1975 and officially separated from the university; here nations from Asia and the Pacific present fascinating displays of their homelands. Also, Manoa Valley itself is one of the loveliest residential areas on Oahu (see following). To get to the main campus follow the H-1 Freeway to exit 24B (University Avenue). Don't make the mistake of exiting at the University's Makai Campus. Follow University Avenue to the second red light, Dole Avenue, and make a right onto campus. Stop immediately at one of the parking lots and get a parking map! Parking restrictions are strictly enforced, and this map not only helps to get you around, but saves you from fines or having your car towed away. Parking is 50 cents an hour, even for visitors, so think about taking TheBus, which services this area quite well.

Student Center

Make this your first stop. As you mount the steps, notice the idealized mural of old Hawaii: smiling faces of contented natives all doing interesting things. Inside is the **Information Center,** which dispenses info not only about the campus, but also about what's happening socially and culturally around town. They even have lists of cheap restaurants, discos, and student hangouts. Next door are typewriters available to nonstudents at $2 per day. The food in the cafeteria is institutional but cheap, and has a Hawaiian twist. The best place to eat is **Manoa Gardens** in the Hemingway Center, where you can get a tasty stir-fry or good vegetarian dishes for $3.50 and up.

The **University Bookstore** is excellent, open Mon.-Fri. 8:15 a.m.-4:15 p.m., Sat. 8:15-11:45 a.m. The bookstore is worth coming to for its excellent range of specialty items, like language tapes, and its extensive assortment of travel guidebooks. The **University Art Gallery** is on the third floor, and is worth a look. Free! The exhibits change regularly. Next to the gallery is a lounge filled with overstuffed chairs and big pillows, where you can kick back and even take a quick snooze. This is not a very social campus. By 4:30 or 5 p.m. the place is shut up and no one is around. Don't expect students gathered in a common reading room, or the activity of social and cultural events. When school lets out at the end of the day, people simply go home.

East-West Center

Follow Dole Avenue to East-West Road and make a left. Free tours, Wednesdays only at 1:30 p.m., originate from Imin Center-Jefferson Hall opposite Kennedy Theater. For more info contact the Friends of the East-West Center, 1777 East-West Rd., Honolulu, HI 96848, tel. 944-7691. The center's 21 acres were dedicated in 1960 by the U.S. Congress to promote better relations between the countries of Asia and the Pacific with the United States. Many nations, as well as private companies and individuals, fund this institution of cooperative study and research. John Burns Hall's main lobby dispenses information on what's happening, along with self-guiding maps. Imin Center-Jefferson Hall, fronted by Chinese lions, has a serene and relaxing Japanese garden behind, complete with a little rivulet and a teahouse named Jakuan, "Cottage of Tranquility." The murals inside are excellent, and it also contains a large reading room with relaxing couches.

The impressive Thai Pavilion was a gift from the king of Thailand, where it was built and sent to Hawaii to be reconstructed. This 23-ton, solid teak sala is a common sight in Thailand. The Center for Korean Studies (not part of the East-West Center) is also outstanding. A joint venture of Korean and Hawaiian architects, its inspiration was taken from the classic lines of Kyongbok Palace in Seoul. Most of the buildings are adorned with fine artworks: tapa hangings, murals, calligraphy, paintings, and sculpture. The entire center is tranquil, and along with the John F. Kennedy Theater of Performing Arts just across the road, is indeed fulfilling its dedication as a place of sharing and learning, culture and art.

MANOA VALLEY

Manoa Valley, a tropical palate of green ablaze with daubs of iridescent color, has a unique designation most aptly described as "urban rain forest." Although not technically true, the valley receiving more than 100 inches of rainfall per year is exceptionally verdant even by Hawaiian standards. However, it wasn't always so. In the late 1800s, the overpopulated valley was almost denuded of trees, only to be reforested by Dr. Lyons, the founder of Lyons Arboretum, who planted trees gathered from around the world. A literal backwater, the runoff from Manoa would flood the relatively dry Waikiki until the Ala Wai Canal was built in the 1920s as a catchment for its torrential flash floods. Only a short drive from arid Waikiki, Manoa was the first place in Hawaii where coffee was grown and where pineapple was cultivated. The great Queen Kaahumanu, who died here in 1832, favored the cool hills of the valley as a vacation spot to escape the summer heat. Manoa, favored by royalty ever since, has maintained itself as one of the most fashionable residential areas in Hawaii, even boasting its own country club at the turn of the century which is yet memorialized by the "Manoa Cup" held yearly at the Oahu Country Club. In 1893, just before annexation, a bewildered and beaten group of royalists came to Manoa to hide out. They were subsequently captured by a contingency of pursuing U.S. Marines and im-

THE LEGENDS OF MANOA VALLEY

Kahala-o-puna, known for her exceptional beauty, was betrothed to Kauhi, a young chief who was driven mad by unfounded jealousy. He falsely accused his lovely wife of faithlessness and killed her five times, only to have her resurrected each time by her sympathetic guardian *amakua*. Finally, left for dead, Kahala-o-puna was found by a young prince who fell in love with her. Beseeching his animal spirits, he brought her to life one last time, and through them turned the jealous Kauhi into a shark. Kahala-o-puna, warned never to go into the ocean, disobeyed, and was seized in the massive jaws of Kauhi, who fatally crushed the life from her never to be rekindled. The warm misty rains of Manoa are the tears of the mother of Kahala-o-puna, and the gentle winds are the soft sobs of her bereaved father, who together forever lament the loss of their beloved daughter.

Another legend sings of the spring, Wai-a-ke-akua, created spontaneously by the great gods Kane and Kaneloa, who came to visit this valley. While overindulging in *awa* they became intoxicated, and decided that they would dawdle in the lovely valley. Lying down, the gods could hear water running underground, so Kane took his great staff and struck the earth, causing Wai-a-ke-akua to appear. Because of the spring's divine origin, it became known as "water of the gods," making it *kapu* to all but the highest *ali'i*. When Kamehameha conquered Oahu, only he could drink from the spring, which flows with cool sweet water to this day.

prisoned in an area called "The Pen," located on the ground of the now defunct Paradise Park.

Taking Manoa Road past the University of Hawaii (see preceeding) you pass **Punahou School,** one of the oldest and most prestigious high schools in Hawaii. Built in 1841 from lava rock, children of the missionary families of wealthy San Franciscans attended, getting the best possible education west of the Rockies.

Manoa Road eventually crosses Oahu Avenue. Follow it to **Waioli Tea Room,** 3016 Oahu Ave., owned and operated by the Salvation Army, a small park with a snack bar that features fresh-baked pastries and serves lunch daily. Also featured here is the **Little Grass Shack** supposedly lived in by Robert Louis Stevenson when he was a resident of Waikiki. Visit the chapel with its distinctive stained-glass windows. Waioli Tea Room is open daily except Monday, 8 a.m.-3:30 p.m., luncheon served 11 a.m.-2 p.m. Reservations, tel. 988-2131.

Paradise Park, 3737 Manoa Rd. (at the very end), closed in late 1993, is 13 acres of lush tropical plants founded by James Wong about 25 years ago. Magnificent blooms compete with the wild plumage of 50 species of exotic birds. However, the Treetop (literally) Restaurant, located here and offering very good food and superlative views, is still operating.

BISHOP MUSEUM (STATE MUSEUM OF NATURAL AND CULTURAL HISTORY)

This group of stalwart stone buildings holds the greatest collection of historical relics and scholarly works on Hawaii and the Pacific in the world. Referring to itself as a "museum to instruct and delight," in one afternoon walking through its halls you can educate yourself about Hawaii's history and people and enrich your trip to the islands tenfold.

Officially named Bernice Pauahi Bishop Museum, its founding was directly connected to the last three royal women of the Kamehameha dynasty. Princess Bernice married Charles Reed Bishop, a New Englander who became a citizen of the then-independent monarchy in the 1840s. The princess was a wealthy woman in her own right, with lands and an extensive collection of "things Hawaiian." Her cousin, Princess Ruta Keeikolani, died in 1883 and bequeathed Princess Bernice all of her lands and Hawaiian artifacts. Together, this meant that Princess Bernice owned about 12% of all Hawaii! Princess Bernice died less than two years later, and left all of her land holdings to the **Bernice Pauahi Bishop Estate,** which founded and supported the Kamehameha School, dedicated to the education of Hawaiian children. (Though

Bishop Museum

this organization is often confused with the Bishop Museum, they are totally separate. The school shared the same grounds with the museum, but none of the funds from this organization were, or are, used for the museum.) Bernice left her personal property, with all of its priceless Hawaiian artifacts, to her husband, Charles. Then, when Queen Emma, her other cousin, died the following year, she too desired Charles Bishop to combine her Hawaiian artifacts with the already formidable collection and establish a Hawaiian museum.

True to the wishes of these women, he began construction of the museum's main building on December 18, 1889, and within a few years the museum was opened. In 1894, after 50 years in Hawaii, Bishop moved to San Francisco, where he died in 1915. He is still regarded as one of Hawaii's most generous philanthropists. In 1961, a science wing and planetarium were added, and two dormitory buildings are still used from when the Kamehameha School for Boys occupied the same site.

Getting There

To get there, take exit 20A off the H-1 Freeway, which puts you on Rt. 63, the Likelike Highway. Immediately get into the far right lane. In only a few hundred yards, turn onto Bernice Street, where you'll find the entrance. Or, exit H-1 onto Hofftailing Street, Rt. 61, exit 20B. Keep your eyes peeled for a clearly marked but small sign directing you to the museum. TheBus no. 2

(School-Middle Street) runs from Waikiki to Kapalama Street, from which you walk two blocks.

Admission And Information

The museum is located at 1525 Bernice St., Honolulu, HI 96817, tel. 847-3511, and is open seven days a week 9 a.m.-5 p.m. Admission is $7.95 adults, $6.95 6-17, five and younger free, but some exhibits and the planetarium are closed to children under six. It's sometimes best to visit on weekends because many weekdays bring teachers and young students who have more enthusiasm for running around than checking out the exhibits. Food, beverages, smoking, and flash photography are all strictly prohibited in the museum. The natural light in the museum is dim, so if you're into photography you'll need super-fast film (400 ASA performs only marginally). Before leaving the grounds make sure to visit **Hawaiian Halau,** where a hula is performed Mon.-Fri. at 1 p.m. Throughout the week, the hall offers demonstrations in various Hawaiian crafts like lei-making, featherwork, and quilting. The **planetarium** opens up its skies daily at 11 a.m. and 2 p.m.

There are special nighttime shows and family discount days offered; call 847-3511 for details. The snack shop has reasonable prices, and **Shop Pacifica,** the museum bookstore and boutique, has a fine selection of materials on Hawaii and the Pacific, and some authentic and inexpensive souvenirs. The **museum cafe** has a limited menu with dishes like Hawaiian fruit salad for $3.50; hamburger, $2.85; teriyaki burger, $2.65; and snacks like chili dogs, muffins, chips, and drinks.

Exhibits

It's easy to become overwhelmed at the museum, so just take it slowly. The number of exhibits is staggering: over 100,000 artifacts; almost 20 million(!) specimens of insects, shells, fish, birds, and mammals; an extensive research library; a photograph collection; and a fine series of maps. The main gallery is highlighted by the rich tones of koa, the showpiece being a magnificent staircase. Get a map at the front desk that lists all of the halls, along with a description of what theme is found in each, and a suggested route to follow. The following are just a small potpourri of the highlights that you'll discover.

To the right of the main entranceway is a fascinating exhibit of the old Hawaiian gods. Most are just called "wooden image" and date from the early 19th century. Among them are: Kamehameha's war-god, Ku; the tallest Hawaiian sculpture ever found, from Kauai; an image of a god from a temple of human sacrifice; and lesser gods, personal *amakua* that controlled the lives of Hawaiians from birth until death. You wouldn't want to meet any of them in a dark alley! Outside, in what's called the **Hawaiian Courtyard,** are implements used by the Hawaiians in everyday life, as well as a collection of

plants that are all identified. The first floor of the main hall is perhaps the most interesting because it deals with old Hawaii. Here are magnificent examples of *kahili*, feathered capes, plumed helmets . . . all the insignia and regalia of the *ali'i*. A commoner sits in a grass shack, a replica of what Captain Cook might have seen.

Don't look up! Over your head is a 55-foot sperm whale hanging from the ceiling. It weighed over 44,000 pounds alive. You'll learn about the ukulele, and how vaudevillians spread its music around the world. Hula-skirted damsels from the 1870s peer provocatively from old photos, bare-breasted and with plenty of "cheesecake." Tourists bought these photos even then, although the grass skirts they're wearing were never a part of old Hawaii but were brought by Gilbert Islanders. See authentic hula instruments like a "lover's whistle," a flute played through the nose, and a musical bow, the only stringed pre-European Hawaiian instrument.

Don't miss the koa wood collection. This accomplished artform produced medicine bowls, handsome calabashes, some simple home bowls, and others reputed to be the earthly home of the wind goddess, which had to be refitted for display in Christianized Iolani Palace. A model *heiau* tells of the old religion, and the many strange *kapu* that governed every aspect of life. Clubs used to bash in the brains of *kapu*-breakers are next to benevolent little stone gods, the size and shape of footballs, that protected humble fishermen from the sea. As you ascend to the upper floors, the time period represented becomes increasingly closer to the present. The missionaries, whalers, merchants, laborers, and Westernized monarchs have arrived. Yankee whalers from New Bedford, New London, Nantucket, and Sag Harbor appear determined and grim-faced as they scour the seas, harpoons at the ready. Great blubber pots, harpoons, and figureheads are preserved from this perilous and unglamorous life. Bibles, thrones, the regalia of power and of the new god are all here.

ART MUSEUMS AND GALLERIES

Honolulu Academy Of Arts

Enjoy the magnificent grounds of this perfectly designed building, a combination of East and

HAWAII STATE ARCHIVES

Princess Bernice

West with a Hawaiian roof and thick white stucco walls reminiscent of the American Southwest, created by architect Bertrum Goodhugh and benefactor Mrs. Charles Montague expressly as a museum. The museum, at 900 S. Beretania St. (TheBus no. 2) opposite Thomas Square, tel. 532-8700, is open Tues.-Sat. 10 a.m.-4:30 p.m., Sun. 1-5 p.m., closed Monday, suggested donation $4, free the first Wednesday of the month. Guided tours are conducted Tues.-Sat. at 11 a.m., Sunday at 1 p.m. The academy houses a brilliant collection of classic and modern art, strongly emphasizing Asian artwork.

James Michener's outstanding collection of Japanese ukiyo-e is here. The story goes that an unfriendly New York cop hassled him on his way to donate it to a New York City museum, while a Honolulu officer was the epitome of aloha when Michener was passing through, so he decided that his collection should reside here. This collection is currently displayed about six months per year, but a decision has been made to display it year-round. Magnificent Korean ceramics, Chinese furniture, and Japanese prints, along with Western masterworks from the Greeks to Picasso make the academy one of the most well-rounded art museums in America. Some collections are permanent while others change, so the museum remains dynamic no matter how many times you visit.

Enter through the foyer and pass to the courtyard that gets you away from the hustle and bustle of downtown. Great for a little respite from noise. Pass through double French doors to the thick white-walled galleries that create a perfect atmosphere for displaying fine works of art. Discover delights like Paul Gauguin's *Two Nudes on a Tahitian Beach,* James Whistler's *Arrangement in Black No. 5,* John Singer Sargent's *Portrait of Mrs. Thomas Lincoln Hansen Jr.* An entire wing is dedicated to religious art, while another holds furniture from medieval Europe. The courtyards are resplendent with statuary from the 6th century A.D. and a standing figure from Egypt, circa 2500 B.C. The Hawaiian climate is perfect for preserving artwork.

Stop at the **Academy Shop,** specializing in art books, museum repros, Hawaii out-of-prints, jewelry, notebooks, and postcards, open Tues.-Sat. 10 a.m.-4:30 p.m., Sunday 1-5 p.m., tel. 532-8704. The **Garden Cafe,** open Tues.-Sat.

11:30 a.m.-1 p.m., Thursday supper at 6:15 p.m., is in a garden under a canopy. They have a light but terrific menu, and besides, a trip to the academy demands a luncheon in the cafe. For menu and details see "Food—Art and the Sandwich."

The Contemporary Museum

Under the direction of Merrill Rueppel, at 2411 Makiki Heights Dr., tel. 526-1322, the museum welcomes you with two copper-green gates that are sculptures themselves. This open and elegant structure, the former Spalding House, has yielded six galleries, a shop, and an excellent gourmet restaurant, the Contemporary Cafe. Acquired through the generosity of the *Honolulu Advertiser's* stockholders, the building was donated to the museum as a permanent home in 1988. Surrounding it are three magnificent acres sculpted into Asian gardens perfect for strolling and gazing at the sprawl of Honolulu far below. The focus is on exhibitions, not collections, although works by David Hockney are on permanent display. Always changing exhibits reflect different themes in contemporary art. Open Tues.-Sat. 10 a.m.-4 p.m., Sun. noon-4 p.m., closed Mon., admission $4.

Tennent Art Foundation

At 201-203 Prospect St., on the *ewa* slope of Punchbowl, the foundation is open Tues.-Sat. 10 a.m.-noon, and Sun. 2-4 p.m., tel. 531-1987. Free. There is a library and the walls hold the paintings of Madge Tennent, one of Hawaii's foremost artists, as well as many other contemporary works. It's beautiful, quiet and worth a visit.

GARDENS, GUIDED TOURS, ETC.

Foster Botanical Garden

Many of these 15 acres of exotic trees have been growing in this manicured garden for over 100 years. At one time the private estate of Dr. Hillebrand, physician to the royal court, he brought many of the seedlings from Asia. Two dozen of these trees enjoy lifetime protection by the state. Located at 180 N. Vineyard Blvd., tel. 522-7065, open daily 9 a.m.-4 p.m., $1, self-guiding brochures. Guided tours Mon., Tues., and Wed. at 1:30 p.m. Many nature hikes on Oahu and the Neighbor Islands are sponsored by the gardens.

Moanalua Gardens

The private gardens of the Damon Estate, at 1352 Pineapple Pl., tel. 839-5334, were given to the original owner by Princess Bernice Bishop in 1884. Just off the Moanalua Freeway, and open to the public, these gardens are not heavily touristed, a welcome respite from the hustle and bustle of the city. Some magnificent old trees include a Buddha tree from Ceylon and a monkeypod called "the most beautifully shaped tree" in the world by *Ripley's Believe It or Not*. The Moanalua Foundation also sponsors walks deep into Moanalua Valley for viewing the foliage of "natural Hawaii." The free guided walks begin at 9 a.m. usually on weekends; make arrangements by calling 839-5334.

Dole Cannery Square

Look for the giant pineapple rising 200 feet into the air. A landmark of Honolulu, it was built in Chicago and erected here in 1928. It is still used as a reservoir and holds 100,000 gallons of water that's piped throughout the Dole Cannery, whose outer buildings were transformed in 1988 to a mini-mall that complements the ongoing Dole Cannery Tour. Located at 650 Iwilei Rd., tel. 548-4837, 45-minute tours are conducted daily 9 a.m.-5 p.m., with the last departing at 3 p.m. Admission $5, children under 12 free. Free parking included if you take your car, but ride the **Pineapple Transit,** tel. 523-DOLE, a van that runs 8:30 a.m.-3:30 p.m., stopping at many Waikiki hotels, 50 cents one-way. Upon entering the atrium area, look high on the walls to see reproductions of Dole Pineapple can labels. They're pop art, and convey a feeling of simpler times past. Here also is the **Food Court,** providing snacks, salads, sandwiches, and soups for a quick lunch.

The tour itself begins with a stereophonic slide show that details the development of pineapple as an industry in Hawaii. Plenty of memorabilia and vintage photos help create a sense of the past. You're then conducted right into the factory where workers are busy packing the fruit, and where you learn the process of how it makes it to the kitchen table. Observe

the newest generation of the marvelous Ginaca machine, first built in 1913 by Henry Ginaca, a draftsman hired by James Dole to modernize the industry. This whirring wonder can peel, core, cut, slice, and dice 100 fruits per minute. Within 20 minutes of reaching the machine, the canned fruit's ready for the grocer's shelf. After the tour, you're taken to a tasting room where you're offered complimentary . . . guess what?

On the second floor you'll find a cluster of shops laid out as traditional storefronts and featuring items made in Hawaii. Stop at the **Dole Logo Shop** for a T-shirt with a replica of a vintage pineapple can label, along with hats, gift items, and glassware all bearing the Dole logo. The **Island Moo Moo Works,** popular with local people, has racks of affordable muumuu and alohawear. The **Jungle Jerky Shop** has jerky of all sorts and sells stuffed animals, all life-size, as well as cotton cloth flowers. New shops like **Mamo Howell** and **Island Princess** have an added elegance with their fashions, or you can take care of your sweet tooth at **Sharyn's Hawaiian Island Cookies.** One of the nicest shops is the **Village Beach Shop.** They're a complete resortwear store with plenty of muumuu, sandals, and even boogie boards to choose from. They have a fine selection of T-shirts with gold designs by Ericka Paeis, a very creative and distinctive designer in the crowded field of Hawaiian T-shirts.

HONOLULU BEACHES AND PARKS

The beaches and parks listed here are found in and around Honolulu's city limits. World-famous Waikiki has its own entire section (see "Waikiki—Waikiki Beaches and Parks"). The good thing about having Waikiki so close is that it lures most bathers away from other city beaches, which makes them less congested. The following list contains most of Honolulu's beaches, ending at Fort DeRussy Beach Park, just a few hundred yards from where the string of Waikiki's beaches begin. Also see "Central Oahu—Aiea, Pearl City, and Vicinity."

Sand Island State Recreation Area

As you enter this 140-acre park by way of the Sand Island Access Rd., clearly marked off the

Nimitz Hwy., you pass through some ugly real estate—scrap yards, petrochemical tanks, and other such beauties. Don't get discouraged, keep going! Once you cross the metal bridge, a favorite fishing spot for local people, and then pass the entrance to the U.S. Coast Guard base, you enter the actual park, 14 acres landscaped with picnic and playground facilities. Follow the road into the park; you pass two observation towers that have been built in the middle of a grassy field, from where you can get an impressive view of Honolulu, with Diamond Head making a remarkable counterpoint. The park is excellently maintained, with pavilions, cold-water showers, walkways, and restrooms, all for day use only; the park closes at 6:30 p.m. However, the camping area is usually empty (state permit required). The sites are out in the open, but a few trees provide some shade.

Unfortunately, you're under one of the main glide paths for Honolulu International Airport. Many local people come to fish, and the surfing is good, but the beaches for snorkeling and swimming are fair at best. Some of the beach area is horrible, piled with broken stone, rubble, and pieces of coral. However, if you follow the road past the tower and park in the next lot, turn right and follow the shore up to a sandy beach. The currents and wave action aren't dangerous, but remember that this part of the harbor receives more than its share of pollutants. For delicious and inexpensive plate lunches, make sure to stop at Penny's just next door to Dirty Dan's Topless Go-Go Bar on your way down the access road.

La Mariana Yacht Sailing Club

This small marina at 50 Sand Island Access Road is a love song in the middle of an industrialized area. The marina is Annette La Mariana Nahinua's labor of love that has remained true since 1955. You can read her fantastic story on the menu of the marina's **Hideaway Restaurant**, which is the only real restaurant on Sand Island. In 1955 this area was forgotten, forsaken, and unkempt. Ms. Nahinua, against the forces of nature, and the even more unpredictable and devastating forces of bureaucracy, took this land and turned it into a yacht harbor. The main tools were indefatigable determination, God listening to her prayers, and a shovel and rake. It's one of the last enclaves of old Hawaii, a place to come for dinner, a drink, or just to look at the boats. The nighttime bartender, Mr. Lee, is friendly but stoic after decades of seeing and hearing it all. Annette, the founder, is now a little gray-haired woman, a motherly type in Birkenstocks, who lives right here above the Hideaway. In the daytime she wanders around spreading her magic while talking to old salts or new arrivals.

The marina is adjacent to an open waterway, which means that you don't have to pay for anchorage. It comes under the old "rights of sailors" to find a free port in which to berth. This unique setup has created an atmosphere in which a subculture of people have built subsistence shacks on the little islands that dot the bay. Some also live on old scows, shipshape yachts, or on very imaginative homemade crafts, afloat and semi-afloat on this tranquil bay. Many are disillusioned and disenfranchised Vietnam vets who have become misanthropes. You'll see the Stars and Stripes flying from their island hooches. Others are yachties who disdain being landlubbers, while others are poor souls who have fallen through the social net. La Mariana is a unique statement of personal freedom in a city where unique statements are generally not tolerated.

Kakaako (Point Panic) Beach Park

This small facility was carved out of a piece of land donated by the University of Hawaii's Biomedical Research Center. Next to Kewalo Basin Harbor, follow Ahuii Street, off Ala Moana Boulevard. You'll come to some landscaped grounds with a cold-water shower and a path leading to the bathing area. Kewalo Basin, developed in the '20s to hold Honolulu's tuna fleet, is home to many charter boats. If you're lucky, you may even spot a manta ray, which are known to frequent these waters. This area is poor for swimming, known for sharks, but great for bodysurfing. Unfortunately, novices will quickly find out why it's called Point Panic. A long seawall with a sharp dropoff runs the entire length of the area. The wave action is perfect for riding, but all wash against the wall. Beginners stay out! The best reason to come here is for the magnificent and unobstructed view of the Waikiki skyline and Diamond Head.

Ala Moana Park

Ala Moana ("Path to the Sea") Beach County Park is by far Honolulu's best. Most visitors congregate just around the bend at Waikiki, but residents head for Ala Moana, the place to soak up the local color. During the week, this beautifully curving white-sand beach has plenty of elbow room. Weekends bring families that come for every water sport Oahu offers. The swimming is great, with manageable wave action, plenty of lifeguards, and even good snorkeling along the reef. Board riders have their favorite spots, and bodysurfing is excellent. The huge area has a number of restrooms, food concessions, tennis courts, softball fields, a bowling green, and parking for 500 cars. Many Oahu outrigger canoe clubs practice in this area, especially in the evening; it's great to come and watch them glide along. A huge banyan grove provides shade and strolling if you don't fancy the beach, or you can bring a kite to fly aloft with the trade winds. Ala Moana Park stretches along Ala Moana Blvd., between the Ala Wai and Kewalo Basin boat harbors. It's across from the Ala Moana Shopping Center, so you can rush right over if your credit cards start melting from the sun.

Aina Moana ("Land from the Sea") State Recreation Area used to be called Magic Island because it was reclaimed land. It is actually the point of land stretching out from the eastern edge of Ala Moana, and although it has a different name, appears to be part of Ala Moana. All the beach activities are great here, too.

Kahanamoku Beach

This stretch of sand in front of the Hilton Hawaiian Village is named after Hawaii's most famous waterman, Duke Kahanamoku. The manmade beach and lagoon were completed in 1956. A system of pumps pushes water into the lagoon to keep it fresh. The swimming is great, and plenty of concessions offer surfboards, beach equipment, and catamaran cruises.

Fort DeRussy Beach

This is the last beach before reaching the Waikiki beaches proper. You pass through the right-of-way of Fort DeRussy military area, where you'll find restrooms, picnic facilities, volleyball courts, and food and beverage concessions. Lifeguard service is provided by military personnel—no duty is too rough for our fighting men and women! A controversy has raged for years between the military and developers who covet this valuable piece of land. The government has owned it since the turn of the century, and has developed what once was wasteland into the last stretch of non-cement, non-high-rise piece of real estate left along Waikiki. Since the public has access to the beach, and since Congress voted a few years back that the lands cannot be sold, it'll remain under the jurisdiction of the military.

If you are fascinated by the military and its history, visit **Battery Randolph** at Fort DeRussy, at the corner of Kalia and Saratoga roads. Plenty of displays and historical artifacts, free guided tour, open Tues.-Sun. 10 a.m.-4:30 p.m., tel. 543-2687. (For complete descriptions see "Sights—Free Sights and Curiosities" in the Waikiki chapter.)

ACCOMMODATIONS

The vast majority of Oahu's hotels are strung along the boulevards of Waikiki. Most are neatly clustered, bound by the Ala Wai Canal, and run eastward to Diamond Head. These hotels will be discussed in the Waikiki section. The remainder of greater Honolulu has few hotels, but those that do exist are some of Oahu's cheapest. Most are clean, no-frills establishments, with a few others at the airport, or just off the beaten track.

Oahu's YM/WCAs And YH

Oahu has a number of YM/WCAs from which to choose, and the only official youth hostel in the state. They vary as far as private room and bath are concerned, facilities offered, and prices. Expect to pay about $30 s with a shared bath, and about $32.50 d with a private bath.

The **YMCA Central Branch** (men only) at 401 Atkinson Dr., Honolulu, HI 96814, tel. 941-3344, is the most centrally located and closest to Waikiki. You can call ahead, but there are no reservations, no curfew, no visitors after 10 p.m.; it has an outside pool, singles, doubles, and private baths. This Y is located just across from the eastern end of Ala Moana Park, only a 10-minute walk to Waikiki.

YMCA Nuuanu (men only), 1441 Pali Hwy., Honolulu, HI 96813, tel. 536-3556, just near the intersection of S. Vineyard Blvd., is a few minutes' walk from downtown Honolulu. You'll find a modern, sterile facility with a pool, shared and single rooms, and private or communal showers; reservations accepted.

Armed Services YMCA, open to military personnel and civilians, both men and women, at 250 S. Hotel St., Honolulu, tel. 524-5600. No reservations, but a pool, single and double rooms, plenty of sporting facilities, and child care!

YMCA Atherton Branch, 1810 University Ave., Honolulu, tel. 946-0253. Near University of Hawaii, men and women students are given preferential treatment. Dormitory style, no recreational facilities. Cheapest in town, but there's a three-night minimum and a one-time membership fee.

YWCA Fernhurst, 1566 Wilder Ave., Honolulu, HI 96822, tel. 941-2231, just off Manoa Rd., across from the historical Punahou School. Singles and doubles with shared bath, women only. Weekly rates. Breakfast and dinner included (except Sunday) for low price. Doors closed at 11 p.m., but the night guard will admit later arrivals. Limited reservations depending on availability with deposit. Women can stay for up to one year, and many women from around the world add an international flavor.

The only official American Youth Hostel in Hawaii (more listed under Waikiki) is the **Honolulu International Youth Hostel,** 2323 A Seaview Ave., Honolulu, HI 96822, tel. 946-0591, located near the University of Hawaii. This YH is always busy, but will take reservations. AYH members with identity cards are given priority, but nonmembers are accepted on a space-available day-by-day basis. For information and reservations write to the manager, and include an SASE. For information and membership cards write American Youth Hostels, 1332 I St. NW, Suite 895, Washington, D.C. 20005.

Elderhostel, 100 Bolyston St., Suite 200, Boston, MA 02116, offers noncredit courses at Hawaii Loa College, Oahu. For people 60 years and older. Fees begin at $175 and include course, room, and board.

University Of Hawaii

Two six-week summer sessions beginning late May and in early July are offered to bona fide students of accredited universities at the University of Hawaii at Manoa, Oahu. Reasonable rates are available in residence halls (mandatory meals) and in apartments on campus; special courses have an emphasis on Polynesian and Asian culture and languages, including China and Japan. Unbeatably priced tours and outings to points throughout the islands for students and the general public can be arranged at the Summer Session Activities Office. For information, catalog, and enrollment, write Summer Session Office, University of Hawaii, 2500 Dole St., Krauss Hall 101, Honolulu, HI 96822, tel. 944-1014 or 949-0771.

Moderate/Expensive Hotels

The **Kobayashi Hotel** at 250 N. Beretania St., Honolulu, HI 96817, tel. 536-2377, is in Chinatown, and it's an old standby as an inexpensive but clean hotel. It's away from all the Waikiki action, and the spartan, linoleumed rooms rent for under $37. Plenty of travelers pass through here, and the hotel's restaurant serves authentic Japanese food at moderate prices.

The **Nakamura Hotel** is a little bit more "uptown" both price- and location-wise. It's at 1140 S. King St., Honolulu, HI 96814, tel. 537-1951. The rooms are well-appointed, carpeted, and have large bathrooms. Some a/c rooms face busy King Street; the *mauka* side rooms are quieter, with plenty of breezes to keep you cool. Often you can find a room at this meticulously clean hotel when others are booked up, only because it's out of the mainstream.

The **Pagoda Hotel,** 1525 Rycroft St., Honolulu, HI 96814, tel. (800) 367-6060, on Oahu 941-6611, behind Ala Moana Park between Kapiolani Blvd. and S. King Street. Because this hotel is away from the "action," you get very good value for your money. Rooms with kitchenettes start at about $55, with two-bedroom suites at around $90. All rooms have TV, a/c, and parking, and there's a swimming pool as well as access to the well-known Pagoda Restaurant.

Manoa Valley Inn

Another in the same category is the **Hawaii Dynasty Hotel,** at 1830 Ala Moana Blvd., tel. 955-1111. Rooms here are clean, decent, away from the action, and reasonably priced.

The **Ala Moana Americana,** 410 Atkinson Dr., Honolulu, HI 96814, tel. (800) 228-3278, on Oahu 955-4811, is another hotel where you're just off the Waikiki strip. It's located just behind Ala Moana Park between Ala Moana and Kapiolani boulevards, with a walking ramp connecting it directly with the Ala Moana Shopping Center. Rooms start at $90 and go up to around $250 for a two-bedroom suite (six people). There's a/c, TV, swimming pools, an all-night coffee shop, and the Summit Supper Club on the top of this 36-story hotel.

Manoa Valley Inn

The Manoa Valley Inn, at 2001 Vancouver Dr., Honolulu, HI 96822, tel. 947-6019 or (800) 634-5115, offers a magnificent opportunity to lodge in turn-of-the-century elegance. Formerly the John Guild Inn, this bed and breakfast was completely restored in 1982 and is listed on the National Register of Historic Places. Innkeeper Lisa Hookan-Holly offers a double bed with a shared bath, including continental breakfast, at a very reasonable $95, or a private suite for $120-175.

The exemplary continental breakfasts are prepared on the premises. In the morning, the aroma of fresh-brewed coffee wafts up the stairs. The breakfast selections are bran muffins, croissants, little sticky buns, fresh fruit of the sea-

son, and hand-squeezed juices. The daily and Sunday newspapers are available. Pick one and sink into the billowy cushions of a wicker chair on the lava-rock-colonnaded back porch. Both inside and out, you'll find coffee tables surrounded by overstuffed chairs and, nearby, decanters of port and sherry and dishes filled with chocolates. Every evening, wine and gourmet cheese, along with crackers and fresh fruits, are presented. All complimentary to guests.

The original structure was a very modest, two-story, boxlike home. It was situated on seven acres, but the demand for land by growing Honolulu has whittled it down to the present half acre or so. The grounds are well-kept, but small, so don't expect sweeping grand lawns. The original owner was Milton Moore, an Iowa lumberman. He sold it to John Guild in 1919, a secretary to Alexander and Baldwin, who basically created the structure that you see today. The home went through several owners and even did a stint as a fraternity house. It ended up as low-priced apartment units until it was rescued and refurbished by Rick Ralston, the owner of Crazy Shirts and one of Hawaii's successful self-made men, a patron of arts and antiques. He outfitted the house from his warehouse of antiques with furnishings not original to the house, but true to the period. The original structure was built in 1915. In 1919 the third floor was added, along with the back porch. A cottage with a white on white theme is available, and offers seclusion and privacy away from the main house.

FOOD

The restaurants mentioned below are outside of the Waikiki area, although many are close, even within walking distance. Others are located near Ala Moana, Chinatown, downtown, and the less touristed areas of greater Honolulu. Some are first-class restaurants; others, among the best, are just roadside stands where you can get a satisfying plate lunch. The restaurants are listed according to price range and location, with differing cuisines mixed in each range. Besides the sun and surf, it's the amazing array of food found on Oahu that makes the island extraordinary.

SHOPPING CENTER DINING

Ala Moana Shopping Center

The following are all located at the Ala Moana Shopping Center along Ala Moana Blvd, which has recently undergone a full face-lift. Most are located in the **Makai Food Court,** a huge central area where you can inexpensively dine on dishes from San Francisco to Tokyo. Counter-style restaurants serve island favorites, reflecting the multiethnic culinary traditions from around the Pacific. You take your dish to a nearby communal dining area, which is great for people-watching. The **China House** is open daily for lunch and dinner, tel. 949-6622. This enormous dining hall offers the usual selection of Chinese dishes, but is famous for its dim sum (served 11 a.m.-2 p.m.); you pick and choose bite-sized morsels from carts.

La Cocina, open daily for lunch and dinner, tel. 949-9233, serves Mexican food for under $5 with complimentary chips and salsa. Dining facilities and takeout service. Less spicy offerings to suit American tastes.

Michel's Baguette, first floor ocean side, is open weekdays 7 a.m.-9 p.m., Sat. till 5:30 p.m., Sun. 8 a.m.-5 p.m., tel. 946-6888. They specialize in French bread, pastries, and croissants baked on the premises. A good selection of tasty soups, salads, and sandwiches. A change from the ordinary burger.

Patti's Chinese Kitchen, first floor facing the sea, tel. 946-5002, has all the ambience

you'd expect from a cafeteria-style Chinese fast-food joint, plus lines about a block long. But don't let either discourage you. The lines move incredibly quickly, and you won't get gourmet food, but it's tasty, plentiful, and cheap. The Princess-Queen Special is steamed rice, fried rice or noodles, a chow mein, plus two entrees like sweet and sour pork or a chicken dish—for around $3. The Queen is the same, but add an entree—under $4. You can even have four entrees, which fills two large paper plates. The princesses who eat this much food aren't tiny-waisted damsels waiting for a rescuing prince—they can flatten anyone who hassles them on their own.

Ward Warehouse

This shopping center, located at 1050 Ala Moana Blvd., has a range of restaurants, from practical to semi-chic, all reasonably priced. **Beni Kai** is a Japanese restaurant that's beautifully appointed with a rock garden at the entranceway that continues to the inside. It's bright and airy, neo-Japanese traditional. Prices are reasonable, with set menu dishes like *unagi kabayaki* for $12.95, or miso-fried fish at $9.25. They have a wide selection of *don buri,* yakitori, and tempura for around $6. Open Mon.-Sat. 11 a.m.-2 p.m. for lunch, and for dinner from 5 p.m.

Nearby is the opposite side of the coin. A small lunch stand sells saimin and yakitori for under $4. Mostly you stand and eat, but there are a few tables in the common mall area. Also, for fast foods you'll find **Cookie Kitchen** and **The Old Spaghetti Factory,** serving a wide variety of pasta not quite like Mama makes, but passable, and at a reasonable price.

For those into health foods **Aloha Health Food,** primarily a vitamin and mineral store, has some prepared food and drinks in a cooler. Right across is **Coffee Works,** specializing in gourmet coffee and tea. They have a bakery and sandwiches for under $5, croissants $1.50. So take your vitamins on one side and get jazzed on the other. The **Farmer's Market** is not in the Ward Warehouse but just across the street, at 1020 Auahi, where you can pick up fresh produce and flowers.

Orson's Restaurant is a seafood house on the second floor. It's actually quite elegant considering the location, with a prize-winning sunset view of the small boat harbor at Kewalo Basin across the way. The inside, too, is richly appointed in wood and glass. Prices are $12-15 for fresh catch of the day complemented by an extensive wine list.

The **Chowder House** on the ground floor has fresh-grilled *ahi* ($8.25), snow crab salad ($5.95), Manhattan clam chowder ($2.25), clams and oysters on the half shell ($6), bay shrimp cocktail ($2.95), deep-fried shrimp ($5.85), and daily specials $5-8.

Ward Center

This upscale shopping center is directly across the street from Ala Moana Park and next door to the Ward Warehouse. The following are some of its restaurants and eateries, where you can enjoy not only class, but quality as well.

R. Fields Wine Co. is not really a restaurant, but a purveyor of exquisite food, fine wines, crackers, cookies, cheeses, imported pastas, and caviar. Most of the wines are top shelf Californian like Kiestler, Dominus, Opus I, Sutter Home (a fluke, left over from their catering business), and Robert Mondavi, with a nice vertical of their reserve wines going back to 1968. Older French wines, as well as German wines, are also available, and while you're there peruse the humidor for a fine cigar.

Chocoholics would rather visit the **Honolulu Chocolate Company** than go to heaven. Mousse truffles, Grand Marnier truffles, chocolate eggs with pistachio or English walnut all will send you into eye-rolling rapture. If you enter, forget any resolve about watching your weight. You're a goner!

For a quick lunch try **Mocha Java** or **Crepe Fever.** Both are yuppie, upscale, counter-service-type places with a few tables. Both have a selection of sandwiches with an emphasis on vegetarian. Crepe Fever has stuffed croissants and whole grain sandwiches. If you want a designer lunch, that's the place to go. For a double-fisted American sandwich with all the trimmings try **Big Ed's,** a deli serving of no-nonsense corned beef ($5.35), ham ($4.50), tuna salad

($4.25), or polish sausage. Takeout as well as sit down, with an actually good seating area away from the bustle at the south end of the shopping center.

Al Fresco's on the corner in the Ward Center is an upscale semi-deli and restaurant whose tables spill out into a little courtyard. Stay simple with a small pizza ($8.95) or Caesar salad ($6.95), or move onto smoked chicken with mustard-herb-butter pasta for $13.95, pesto with smoked salmon ($13.95), or boneless chicken breast ($14.95). Specials are available every day, like grilled eggplant for $8.95 up to blackened *onaga* ($19.95). This Mediterranean-style cafe is gourmet; while perhaps not designed for an elegant evening, it will give you gourmet food at reasonable prices.

The premier, or at least best-known, restaurant in the complex is **Keo's Thai Restaurant,** known for its mouthwatering Thai dishes and for its beautiful decor. The menu is extensive, with plenty of dishes for nonmeateaters. Prices can be quite reasonable for Thai noodles, chicken, shrimp, or vegetarian ($6.95-8.95), house salad ($4.95), green papaya salad ($4.95), spring rolls (four for $4.95), and tofu, shrimp, or chicken satay for under $9. Try the delicious soups like spicy lemon grass or Thai ginger for $3.75 per serving. Entrees like the Evil Jungle Prince have quite a spicy reputation, or tame down with Asian watercress stir-fried with garlic, yellow bean sauce, and beef, shrimp, or vegies ($6.95-8.95). Keo's has another location, and operates the Mekong I and II, simpler and less expensive restaurants. Keo's is known for its beautiful flower displays of torch ginger, orchids, or plumeria on every table, and you may eat inside or outside.

The **Yum Yum Tree** is an affordable American standard restaurant that features pies and cakes from its bakery, along with homestyle fresh pasta. They have an extensive dining area, quite cheerful with dark wood floors, ferns, hanging greenery, and an open-beam ceiling. Breakfast is 7 a.m.-noon, lunch 11 a.m.-5 p.m., dinner 5 p.m. to midnight, cocktails 7 a.m.-closing.

Compadres Mexican Restaurant, tel. 523-1307, open daily 11 a.m.-10:30 p.m., and until midnight on weekends, although part of a small chain with restaurants in Maui, San Francisco, Sacramento, and Palo Alto, offers made-to-order health conscious Mexican cuisine that was voted as the "Best on Oahu" by the small but discerning local Mexican population. The open-beamed dining room overlooking Ala Moana park is a mixture of "South Seas" and "south of the border" with plenty of ferns and foliage, round-topped wooden tables, bent-backed chairs upholstered in primary reds and greens, with Mexican masks, bronze parrots and ceramic macaws hanging from the walls and ceilings. The huge menu, featuring hand-made tortillas made either from white flour, whole wheat, blue corn, or regular old yellow corn, along with homemade chips and salsa uses no lard in any of the dishes except in carnitas, which are pork anyway. The most unique offerings are the **Quesadillas Internacionales,** priced $6.95-$8.95; flavors vary and can be Greek, filled with feta cheese and lamb; Baja with shrimp, spinach, and Monterey Jack cheese; Texas with chicken or steak and fiery sauce; or German with sausage, Monterey Jack cheese, honey mustard, and "Oh Chihuahua" sauerkraut. Beside quesadillas, there are standard burritos, tacos, and plenty of vegetarian selections like the Santa Fe Tamale or Compadres Tostada filled with beans, avocado, fresh salsa, and chopped olives. No dish is over $9. The bar complements the meal with a full selection of domestic and imported beer, 10 different kinds of tequila, margaritas by the glass or pitcher, and island exotic drinks for under $5. Compadres is an excellent choice for a "budget gourmet" meal in a hospitable atmosphere where the prices are right and the service excellent. There's even live music offered now and again. You can't go wrong!

Don't let the name **Andrew's Restaurant,** tel. 523-8677, fool you. It's actually an excellent continental restaurant on the second floor that makes its own pasta. Starters include *calamari fritto* ($6.25), wilted spinach salad ($3.50), and minestrone soup ($3); entrees are cannelloni ($13.95), frog legs ($16.75), a variety of veal dishes for under $20, and complete dinners with all the trimmings for $17-25.

Ryan's Grill, open Mon.-Sat. 11:15 a.m.-1:45 a.m., Sun. 5 p.m.-1:45 a.m., is an ultra-modern yet comfortable establishment appointed with black leather chairs, chrome railings, marble-topped tables, and a hardwood floor, which are all dominated by a huge bar and open kitchen. The menu offers standards along with nouveau cuisine and includes French onion soup ($6.59), sesame chicken salad ($8.50), or linguine with fresh basil and pine nuts ($7.95). Sandwiches are everything from hot Dungeness crab to a grilled chicken club, all for under $8. More substantial meals from the grill include Korean chicken ($7.95) or fresh blue marlin. The bar prepares all of the usual exotic drinks and has plenty of draught beer selections from which to choose. Most menu items along with plenty of munchies and *pu pu* are served until 1:00 a.m., so Ryan's Grill makes a perfect late night stop!

The Monterey Bay Canners Seafood Restaurant, open for lunch Mon.-Sat. 11 a.m.-4 p.m., for dinner Sun.-Thurs. 4 p.m.-11 p.m., Fri.-Sat. to midnight, Sun. brunch 10 a.m.-4 p.m., is a small California chain with a reputation for decent seafood at reasonable prices. Lunch from the sandwich board offers bay shrimp, bacon, and avocado ($7.25), a Kona burger ($6.25), or teriyaki chicken ($7.95). "Early bird specials," served daily 4-6 p.m., are priced at $9.95, and include baked mahimahi, blackened salmon, and shrimp or chicken curry. All come with soup or salad. For dinner, entrees might be deep fried shrimp for $15.95, or the very substantial grilled Seafest Special laden with lobster, crab legs, and shrimp for $18.95 (with chowder and salad add $2, children's menu available). The restaurant has live entertainment nightly 9 p.m.-1:30 a.m., usually provided by a local band like Fresh Catch that plays everything from Hawaiian favorites to contemporary music; happy hour, Wed.-Fri. 4:30-7:30 p.m., also brings live entertainment.

Restaurant Row

This new-age complex at 500 Ala Moana Blvd. (across from the Federal Building) points the way to "people-friendly" development in Honolulu's future. It houses shops and businesses, but mostly restaurants, all grouped together around a central courtyard and strolling area. Some restaurants are elegant and excellent, while others are passable and plain. But they are all in a congenial setting, and you can pick your palate and style preference as easily as you'd pick offerings at a buffet. Start at the central fountain area with its multicolored modernistic Lego-inspired tower. Every Saturday at 8 p.m. jazz is offered here overlooking the waterfront.

The **Sunset Grill,** tel. 521-4409, is on the corner. With wraparound windows, a long and open bar, and comfortable maple chairs, it lives up to its name. This is the place to come for a quiet evening drink in the downtown area. The food is prepared in full view on a kiawe-fired grill, wood-roasting oven, and Italian rotisserie. Choices include a variety of pasta, gourmet salads, calamari, fresh fish, oysters, chicken, veal, and lamb. Lunch is a wide variety of plump juicy sandwiches of turkey, sausage, beef, fish, or chicken. The chefs at the Sunset aren't afraid to blend East with West in a wide variety of creations. Open daily 11 a.m.-2 a.m., weekends from 9 a.m., with a late-night menu available on weekends.

The **Rose City Diner,** open Mon.-Thurs. 11 a.m.-11 p.m., Fri.-Sat., 11 a.m.-midnight, Sun., 11 a.m.-11 p.m., will take you back to a more innocent time in America when bobby-soxers sat on the hoods of their boyfriends' Chevys and listened to Buddy Holly on the AM radio. Fabian, Dion, Annette, or Ricky would feel right at home ordering burgers and BLTs from this classic menu, except that they would be better than ever. The waitresses wear pink uniforms with white aprons and jaunty hats. The booths, like a cool Elvis outfit, are pink and black. The walls are covered with pictures of five decades of actors and musicians: Satchmo, Jimmy Stewart, Ronald Reagan, Bogart, Elvis, Marlon, Sophia, Rock, Marilyn, Jane, Hitchcock, Lucy, Dezi, Fred, and Ethel—they're all here. Booths have table-top jukeboxes. Try a slider burger with grilled onions, or a miniburger served in a basket on top of French fries. Wash it all down with a root beer float, Cherry Coke, or a frothy malt.

Fast-food pawns will be happy to hear that **Burger King** is here too. **R. Fields Wine Co.,** for a do-it-yourself meal, is here with its gourmet wines, crackers, cheeses, escargot, caviar, and pâté. **Cheers** is a small bar open 11 a.m.-2 a.m. Stuck in the corner, it tries to live up to its TV namesake by welcoming the local execs and secretaries in for an after-work drink and chat. It's comfortable, friendly, sports-oriented, and smoky.

In the middle of the complex is **The Row,** an outdoor bar with finger food. The **Honolulu Chocolate Co.** is next. Like a smug little devil, it tempts with chocolate truffles, mocha clusters, and fancy nut rolls. So sin! You're on vacation. The **Paradise Bakery Cafe** is a simple counter restaurant with pie, coffee, and donuts.

Trattoria Manzo, tel. 522-1711, owned by Tony Manzo, offers very special Italian dishes from the Abruzzi, a coastal and mountainous region along the Adriatic known for its hearty cooking. Choose an antipasto from Italian cold cuts to clams in red wine sauce for $7 and under. Assorted soups and salads range from $3 to $6 for insalata calamari. Select your favorite pasta, and then cover it with one of 201 delectable sauces, most under $10. Chicken, veal, and steak are grilled, simmered in wine sauce, or made into parmigiana, or choose a traditional lasagna, gnocchi, or a good old pizza. The interior is sharp with neon strips, and black marble tables and chairs.

A few others in the Row include **CJ's Seafood,** open for lunch Mon.-Sat. 10:30 a.m.-2:30 p.m., dinner 5-10 p.m., with lunch specials for $5.25, and karaoke Thurs.-Sat. 10 p.m.-1:30 a.m.; and **Cafe Athena,** an indoor-outdoor restaurant with happy hour Mon.-Fri., when domestic beer and wine are $1.50.

INEXPENSIVE DINING AROUND TOWN

The following restaurants are located in and around the greater Honolulu area.

The **University of Hawaii,** Manoa Campus, hosts a number of restaurants, ranging from an inexpensive cafeteria to international cuisine at the East-West Center. Inexpensive to moderate restaurants include: **Manoa Gardens,** salad and snacks; **Campus Center Dining Room,** for full meals; and the **International Garden,** at Jefferson Hall in the East-West Center. For a great little lunch in a quiet setting in this area see the Waioli Tea Room.

At the Hawaii Maritime Center you'll find **Coasters Restaurant** tucked away in the rear overlooking Honolulu Harbor. American standards with a full complement from the sandwich board. Not great food, but a great setting and away from the bustle of Honolulu. More interesting and definitely more local is **Pier Eight Restaurant** sandwiched under the huge elevated pier area just nearby the Maritime Center. Basic, Chinese, fast food to go, open daily 10 a.m.-5 p.m.

King's Bakery and Coffee Shop is a favorite of local people, at 1936 S. King St. and Pumehana, tel. 941-5211 (one of three locations). They're open 24 hours, and get very busy around 6 p.m. when they allow only groups of two or more to sit in the few booths; the rest eat at the counter. The menu is American/Hawaiian/Asian. Full meals are around $5. Not great, but good and wholesome. The bakery has seven-grain or whole wheat bread, but mostly sells white fluffy stuff with tons of powdered sugar. However, they do offer "tofuti," a soft ice cream-like dessert made from healthful tofu. Their other locations are at the Kaimuki Shopping Center and Eaton Square. Across the street from King's Bakery are two inexpensive eateries, **McCully Chop Suey** and **Yoshi's Sushi Yakiniku Restaurant.**

Down to Earth Natural Foods, open Mon.-Sat. 10 a.m.-8:30 p.m., Sun. 10 a.m.-6 p.m., at 2525 S. King St., tel. 947-7678, is a kind of "museum of health food stores" serving filling, nutritious health food dishes for very reasonable prices. Sandwiches, like a whopping avocado, tofu, and cheese, are under $5. Daily full-meal specials, like vegie stroganoff, eggplant parmigiana, and lasagna are around $4, including salad. There are plenty of items on the menu that will fill you up for under $3. Healthwise, you can't go wrong! Just up the street at 2471 S. King, across from the Star Garden Market, is the tiny **Saimin Bowl Restaurant.** Their name says it all, and you can have a huge steaming bowl of soup for a few dollars.

Kokua Co-op Natural Foods And Grocery Store, at the corner of S. Beretania and Isenberg, tel. 941-1921, is open to the public Mon.-Sat. 9 a.m-8 p.m., Sun. 10 a.m.-7 p.m. It's a full-service store with organic and fresh produce, cheese, milk, juices, bulk foods, and breads.

Sekiya's Restaurant and Deli at 2746 Kaimuki Ave., tel. 732-1656, looks like a set from a 1940s tough-guy movie. The food is well prepared and the strictly local clientele will be amazed that you even know about the place.

Hale Vietnam, 1140 12th Ave. in Kaimuki, tel. 735-7581, is building an excellent reputation for authentic and savory dishes at very moderate prices. It gets the highest praise from local people, who choose it again and again for an inexpensive evening of delicious dining.

For a quick *bento* or sushi to go, try **Matsuri Sushi,** tel. 949-1111, at the corner of Kapiolani Blvd. and McCully. This quick-stop is perfect to pick up lunch on your way out of the Waikiki area.

Suehiro's at 1824 S. King, open daily for lunch and dinner, with takeout service, tel. 949-4584, gets the nod from local Japanese people. The menu here is authentic, the decor strictly Americana, and the food well prepared and moderately priced.

People's Cafe, 1300 Pali Hwy., is open Mon.-Sat. 10 a.m.-7:30 p.m., tel. 536-5789. Two going on three generations of the same Japanese family have been serving the full range of excellent and inexpensive Hawaiian food at this down-home restaurant. It's not fancy, but the food is good and the surroundings clean.

Coco's Coffee House at the corner of Kalakaua Ave. and Kapiolani Blvd. is an American standard that's open all night. It's like a million others in the U.S. where you can order a hot roast beef sandwich for a few bucks, or just sip a coffee into the wee hours, staying out of the weather.

Another of the same is the **Hungry Lion,** tel. 536-0148, at 1613 Nuuanu Avenue. Open 24 hours, it serves everything from Asian food to steaks. Many local people come here after a night out. Nothing special, but decent wholesome food on formica tables.

M's Coffee Tavern is a favorite with downtown office workers for great lunches, excellent coffee, and cocktails, at 124 Queen St., tel. 531-5739.

Walli Wok, tel. 943-1WOK, is a Chinese restaurant that delivers, but you must spend a minimum of $8. They'll come to anywhere in the downtown and Waikiki area, and are perfect for condo dinners or late-night snacks. The food is passable, and the servings are ample.

Two inexpensive yet authentic restaurants sit next door to each other at 1679 Kapiolani Blvd.; the **Kintoki Japanese Restaurant,** tel. 949-8835, and the **Sukyung Korean Restaurant.** This semi-seedy area has plenty of "girlie bars," but the food is good and authentic, with most items priced below $5.

Penny's Plate Lunches, on the Sand Island Access Rd. next to Dirty Dan's Topless Go-Go Joint, is one of the least expensive and most authentic Hawaiian plate-lunch stands you can find. The most expensive lunch is *lau lau,* pork and butterfish wrapped in a ti leaf, at around $3.50. You can also try baseball-sized *manapua* for around 60 cents. Penny's is out of the way, but definitely worth a stop.

You can't get much cheaper than free, and that's what the **International Society for Krishna Consciousness** offers every Sunday at 5:30 p.m. for its vegetarian smorgasbord. Their two-acre compound is just off the Pali Hwy. at 51 Coelho Way, tel. 595-4913. Of course there're a few chants for dessert. *Hare Krishna!*

Downtown Honolulu

In central Honolulu, mostly along Bishop Street's financial district, you'll find excellent and inexpensive restaurants that cater to the district's lunch crowd. One of the best is the **Croissanterie,** tel. 533-3443, at 222 Merchant St., open Mon.-Fri. 6 a.m.-9 p.m., Sat. to 4 p.m., closed Sunday. They serve up gourmet coffee and baskets of croissants stuffed with everything from tuna to strawberries and cream. Also offered are salads, soups, Japanese food, and a pasta table with lasagna and linguini with salad and garlic bread for under $5. The vintage building, which recently housed a bookstore, has brick walls, hardwood floors, and straight-backed cane chairs, all part of the decor in this sidewalk-style European cafe.

Another good place is **Al's Cafe** in the 1100 block of Bishop, open Mon.-Fri. 6 a.m.-4 p.m., Sat. 7 a.m.-1 p.m. Daily lunch specials like tuna or ham and cheese sandwiches and a medium soft drink or coffee for $3. Fast food in the area is **Jack in the Box, Taco Bell,** and **Pizza Hut** across the street from Woolworth's on Hotel Street. Heading down Hotel St. toward Chinatown you'll pass **Kathy's Kitchen,** at Bethel and Pauahi, where for around $4 you can get a plate lunch.

Art And The Sandwich

In Honolulu there are a few opportunities to feed your mind and soul along with satiating your appetite.

The **Garden Cafe,** tel. 531-8865, at the Honolulu Academy of Arts, 900 S. Beretania, is a classy place for lunch, Tues.-Sat. 11:30 a.m.-1 p.m., Thurs. supper at 6:15 p.m., set up in a garden of this excellent museum under a canopy. The cafe serves different soups like iced pumpkin soup with parsley, salads such as crunchy pea or orange, and sandwiches of ham with pepper jelly. Desserts run $1.50, with full luncheon at $7.50. The food is delicious, but be aware that the portions are not for the hungry, being designed primarily for patrons of the arts who seem to be wealthy matrons from the fashionable sections of Honolulu who are all watching their waistlines.

Don't let the Porsches, Mercedeses, and BMWs parked vanity plate to vanity plate in the parking lot discourage you from enjoying the **Contemporary Cafe,** tel. 523-3362 (reservations recommended), at the Contemporary Museum, 2411 Makiki Heights Drive. The small but superb menu is as inspired as the art in the museum, and the prices are astonishingly inexpensive. Dine inside or out, or perch on the porch. Appetizers are pâté, mussels, escargot, or smoked salmon for under $10. Soups and salads are home-smoked mahimahi and lingonberry salad, Malaysian shrimp salad, Greek salad, or chicken salad for under $11. Sandwiches are a fine selection including smoked breast of turkey or *ahi* Caesar for under $10. Desserts run from cheesecake to pecan pie, and beverages include homemade lemonade and cappuccino. For a wonderful cultural outing combined with a memorable lunch, come to the Contemporary Cafe. It's just so . . . contemporary!

Fast Foods And Treats

Fast-food fanciers and fanatics have nothing to fear on Oahu. There're enough quick stop eateries to feed an army, mainly because there is an Army, plus a Navy and a Marine Corps of young men and women on the island, not to mention the army of tourists. If you're after pizza, burgers, shakes, and fries, choose from 36 **McDonald's,** 13 or so **Jack-In-The-Boxes,** 24 **Pizza Huts,** 10 or so **Zippy's,** six **Wendy's,** a few **Farrell's** and good old **Dairy Queens.**

For **shave ice** try the **Waiola Store,** open Mon.-Sat. 7 a.m.-9 p.m., Sun. 8 a.m.-7:30 p.m., on the corner of Paani and Waiola. You can get it in Waikiki, but for the real stuff in all its syrupy glory come here.

MODERATE DINING AROUND TOWN

The following listings are for restaurants where two can dine for around $35. This does not include drinks.

The Hideaway Restaurant, at La Mariana Yacht Sailing Club, 50 Sand Island Access Rd. is the only real restaurant on Sand Island. Henry, for many years a ship's cook, can cook everything well—maybe not great, but well. If a Chinese person came here and wanted chop suey Henry could do it. If a guy wanted steak and potatoes, you got it! Pasta? Here it is! The Hideaway is an out-of-the-way place, local, and real Hawaiiana. This is where all the yachties come. The Hideaway serves appetizers, even escargot, for $6.75, chicken wings ($5.25), sautéed mushroom buttons ($5.25). From the broiler, rib-eye steak is $11.50. The most expensive is an eight-ounce filet mignon ($14.95). From the sea, deep-fried scallops ($10.50), shrimp scampi served over linguini ($10.95), ahi fresh fillet or steak cut for $10.95. That's the cheapest fresh ahi around.

Henry is also known for his onion rings. They're not on the menu; you have to know about them. Now you know. The Sunday brunch is excellent, but basic—eggs, potatoes, a slab of ham, rice, and toast for $3.50. Hard to beat. Inside hang Japanese glass floats that at night are diffused with different colors, providing mood lighting for the cozy black booths and wooden tables with high-backed wicker chairs.

Shiruhachi, at 1901 Kapiolani Blvd., tel. 947-4680, is a completely authentic Japanese sushi bar operated by Hiroshi Suzuki. As a matter of fact, until recently 90% of the clientele was Japanese, either visiting businessmen or locals in the know, and the menu was only in Japanese. However, everyone is more than welcome. With a beer, you get free otsumami (nibbles), with a wide selection of sushi and other finger foods like yakitori at about $2 for two skewers. A separate section of the restaurant turns into a cocktail lounge, somewhat like an akachochin, a neighborhood Japanese bar where people go to relax.

There's taped music and a dance floor. If you're into authentic Japanese, this is a great one.

Auntie Pasto's, at 1099 S. Beretania and the corner of Pensacola, tel. 523-8855, is open daily for lunch, dinner, and late nights. The vibe is upbeat pizza parlor, where you can even bring your own wine. Most of the Italian menu is around $6; the specialty is a fish stew loaded with morsels for about $12. Their large salad with garlic bread is cheap, and enough for two. No reservations necessary, quiet, comfortable.

TGI Fridays is a raucous singles' bar known for some delectable morsels such as stuffed potatoes, quiches, and the like. It's across the street from the Blaisdell Center at 950 Ward Ave., open daily 11 a.m.-2 p.m., tel. 523-5841. Plenty of swingers and college students keep the joint jumpin'.

Wo Fat's, at 115 N. Hotel St., tel. 533-6393, has had a little experience satisfying customers—the oldest eatery in Chinatown, it's been at the same location for over 80 years, and open for business for 100! Besides serving delicious food from a menu with hundreds of Cantonese dishes, the building itself is monumentally ornate. You're entertained just checking out the decor of lanterns, dragons, gilt work, and screens. Most dishes are reasonably priced and start at around $5. This restaurant is highly respected by the people of Chinatown and is part of the Chinatown tour offered by the Chamber of Commerce.

EXPENSIVE DINING AROUND TOWN

Sometimes only the best will do, and Honolulu can match any city for its fine restaurants. For more fine dining see "Waikiki."

Won Kee Seafood Restaurant, 100 N. Beretania, is a splurge joint where you get delicious seafood. Free parking on Maunakea Street. This is the place for Honolulu's in-the-know crowd. Tasteful and elegant surroundings.

The Chart House, at 1765 Ala Moana Blvd. near Ala Wai Yacht Harbor, is open daily 4 p.m. (Sun. 5 p.m.) till 2 a.m., tel. 941-6660. They offer a happy hour until 7 p.m., pu pu until midnight, and nightly entertainment. Shellfish specialties start at $15, with chicken and beef dishes a few dollars cheaper.

India House, 2632 S. King St., is open daily for lunch and dinner, tel. 955-7552. Extraordinary Indian dishes prepared by chef Ram Arora. A wide selection of curries, vegetarian dishes, special *naan* bread, kabobs, and fish *tikka*. Specialty desserts of homemade ice cream and toppings.

Windows of Hawaii sits atop the Ala Moana Building at 1441 Kapiolana Blvd., serving American and continental. Great views from this revolving restaurant. Lunch (sandwiches) for under $8, and complete dinners from $15. Extremely popular for its sunset view. Reservations, tel. 941-9138. Champagne brunch Sat. and Sun. 10 a.m.-2 p.m.

Keo's Thai Restaurant, 625 Kapahulu, open nightly 5:30-11 p.m., tel. 737-8240, has become an institution. It serves great Thai food at expensive prices. They pride themselves on the freshest ingredients, spices tuned up or down to suit the customer, and Keo's recipes taught to each chef personally. There's always a line, with a few benches in the parking lot for waiting customers, but no reservations are taken. The eight-page menu offers most of Thailand's delectables, and vegetarians are also catered to. You can save money and still have the same quality food at **Mekong II**, 1726 S. King, lunch and dinner, tel. 941-6184. Owned by Keo's, it's not as fancy.

Nuuanu Onsen, 87 Laimi Rd. (right off the Pali Hwy., just before Queen Emma's Summer Palace), tel. 538-9184, is one of Honolulu's best-kept secrets. This authentic Japanese teahouse serves a gourmet fixed menu. You leave your cares along with your shoes at the entrance, and are escorted by a kimono-clad waitress to your lacquered table, where you sit on tatami mats and enjoy the serenity of the garden framed by the shoji screens. The hostess plays geishalike teahouse games if you like. Here, you enjoy the experience as much as the meal.

ENTERTAINMENT

Dancing, Disco, And Lounge Acts
Anna Bannana's, at 2440 S. Beretania, tel. 946-5190, is the "top banana" for letting your hair down and boogying the night away. It's out by the university just across from Star Market. This dance joint has a laid-back atmosphere, reasonable beer prices, a small cover which goes to the band, no dress code, and a friendly student crowd. Dancing is upstairs, light dining downstairs, and a backyard to cool off between sets. Great place, great fun!

The **Club Jubilee**, at 1007 Dillingham Blvd., tel. 845-1568, sways with Hawaiian music every night but Monday. Listen to hula tunes on traditional and quickly fading slack key guitar. People from the audience, when moved by the music, will take to the dance floor or the stage for an impromptu performance. What they lack in.polish they make up for in sincerity. Everybody's welcome. Beer around $3, with plenty of *pu pu*, like watercress with mayonnaise and soy sauce, along with regular island munchies.

University of Hawaii students trumpet the mating call at **Moose McGillycuddy's**, at 1035 University Ave., tel. 944-5525, especially every Thursday, which is "Ladies Night." Standard but good food priced for the student pocketbook, and plenty of dancing.

Studebaker's, at Restaurant Row, 500 Ala Moana, tel. 526-9888, is a neon-lit, chrome deco bar with two red Studebakers in the window. Daytime it's a restaurant, but in the evening it's a disco and bar. From 4 to 7 p.m. enjoy the best deal with a one-drink minimum and inexpensive buffet, which can easily be a light dinner. The bartenders and cocktail waitresses climb on stage every hour and jitterbug for the audience, demonstrating classic "American Bandstand" routines and steps. One wall of glass bricks diffuses the light, and from the outside makes all the dancers look as if they're in a fishbowl. *Uptown* dress code, male and female peacocks welcome.

Rumours, in the Ala Moana American Hotel, 410 Atkinson St., tel. 955-4811, is an established disco that cranks up around 9 p.m. and features the newest in dance and rock videos. Also, the restaurant atop the building, Windows of Hawaii, supplements your dinner with an evening lounge act.

Tony Roma's, 98-150 Kaonohi St. in the Westridge Mall, Aiea, tel. 487-9911, offers a lounge act Sun. to Fri., and daily happy hour 4:30-8:30 p.m. with a special *pu pu* menu.

TGI Fridays, 950 Ward Ave., tel. 523-5841, is a lively night spot. Good food, large portions, reasonable prices, and music.

Pecos River Cafe, at 99-016 Kamehameha Hwy., tel. 487-7980, has country music by local country bands.

Note: Also see "Waikiki—Entertainment."

Freebies

At **Centerstage,** Ala Moana Center, various shows are presented—mostly music (rock, gospel, jazz, Hawaiian) and hula. Performances usually start at noon. The **Young People's Hula Show,** every Sun. at 9:30 a.m., is fast becoming an institution. Here, hula is being kept alive, with many first-time performers interpreting the ancient movements that they study in their *halau.*

The **Royal Hawaiian Band,** founded over 100 years ago, performs Fri. at noon on the Iolani Palace Bandstand.

Hilo Hattie, 700 Nimitz Highway, the largest manufacturer of alohawear in the state, conducts free tours of the factory, complete with complimentary shuttle ride from your hotel. Up to 80,000 garments are on display in the showroom. It's hard to resist spending: prices and craftsmanship are good, and designs are the most contemporary. Open daily 8:30 a.m.-5 p.m., tel. 537-2926.

The giant pineapple water tower off Iwilei Road guides you to the **Dole Pineapple Factory,** which has been completely refurbished into a mini-mall called the Dole Cannery Square, with distinctive Hawaiian shops and a cafeteria. Here, millions of Hawaii's fruit are canned, juiced, and sliced for shipment around the world. Free samples are available. The factory is busiest least during the winter months, but something fascinating is always going on. In the summertime, at the height of the harvest, this factory can process over three million cans of fruit per day! No reservations needed for small groups. Contact the Dole Company at 650 Iwilei Rd., tel. 523-3653, open 9 a.m.-3 p.m.

Girlie Bars And Strip Joints

You'll have no excuse if your maiden Aunt Matilda or local chapter of Fed Up Feminists Inc. ever catches you going into one of these joints, sonny boy! There's not even a hint of a redeeming social value here, and the only reason they're listed is to let you know where *not to go.* Many of these "lounges," as they're called, are strung along the 1600 and 1700 blocks of Kapiolani Blvd., and in the little alleys running off it. Mostly, tough-looking Asian men own or operate them, and they open and shut quicker than a streetwalker's heart. Inside are two types of women: the dancers and the "lap sitters," and there's definitely a pecking order in these henhouses. (For a full description, see "Health and Well-being—Prostitution"). Most patrons are local men or GI types, with only a smattering of tourists. Personal safety is usually not a problem, but a fool and his money are soon parted in these bars.

Here are some *without* the bad reputations that frequently go along with this type of clip joint. **Misty II Lounge,** operated by a Vietnamese guy, has been there five years, an eternity in this business; he immediately fires any girl with bad vibes. This club is at 1661 Kapiolani Blvd., tel. 944-1745. Just behind it in the little alleyway are the **Orchid, Musume,** and **Winners Club**—all about the same. Two clubs considered to be good ones by their patrons are **Butterfly Lounge,** 903 Keamoku, tel. 947-3012, and the **Stop Lite Lounge,** at 1718 Kapiolani, tel. 941-5838.

Chinatown's **Hotel Street** (see "Chinatown Nights") has hookers, both male and female, walking the heels off their shoes. They cruise during the day, but the area really comes alive at night. Mostly, these people are down-and-outers who can't make it against the stiff competition along the main areas of Waikiki. The clientele is usually servicemen and hard-core locals. A few clubs in this area offer strippers. Always be prepared for fights and bad vibes in any of these joints. A few that tourists have entered and survived include the **Zig Zag, My Way,** and **Hubba Hubba Club.**

SHOPPING

If you don't watch the time, you'll spend half your vacation moving from one fascinating store to the next. Luckily, in greater Honolulu the majority of shopping is clustered in malls, with specialty shops scattered around the city, especially in the nooks and crannies of Chinatown. For a general overview of what the island has for sale, along with listings for bookstores, flea markets, sundries, and art shops, see "Out and About—Shopping." For food shopping see "Out and About—Food and Drink."

Ala Moana Shopping Center

This is the largest shopping center in the state, and if you want to get all of your souvenir hunting and special shopping done in one shot, this is the place. It's on Ala Moana Blvd. just across from the Ala Moana Beach Park, open weekdays 9:30 a.m.-9 p.m., Sat. 9:30 a.m.-5:30 p.m., Sun. 10 a.m.-5 p.m., tel. 946-2811. Recently, the Ala Moana Shopping Center has taken off its comfortable Hawaiian shirt and shorts and donned designer fashions by Christian Dior and Charles Jordan. Local people are irritated, and they have a point, to a point. The center has plenty of downhome shopping left, but it now caters as much to the penthouse as it does to the one-room efficiency. It used to be where the *people* shopped, but now portions are being aimed at the affluent tourist, especially the affluent Japanese tourists who flaunt designer labels like politicians flaunt pretty secretaries. If anything, the shopping has gotten better, but you'll have to look around a bit more for bargains.

Plenty of competition keeps prices down, with more than enough of an array to suit any taste and budget. There are about 100 stores including all of Hawaii's major department stores like **Sears, Penney's,** and **Liberty House.** Utilitarian shops like shoe makers, eateries, banks, and boutiques feature everything from flowers to swim fins. It's also a great place to see a cross-section of Hawaiian society. Another pleasantry is a free hula show every Sunday at 9:30 a.m. on the **Centerstage** (see "Entertainment—Freebies" above). The **Hawaii Visitors Bureau** maintains an information kiosk just near Centerstage. The following is a mere sampling of what you'll find.

The restaurants in the **Makai Food Court** are exceptional, if not for taste, at least for price, and are unbelievable for the variety of cuisines represented. In a huge open area you'll find dishes from Bangkok to Acapulco, from Tokyo to San Francisco. Most of these restaurants have only counters for ordering, with tables in a common dining area. Great for people-watching, too!

A good one-stop store with plenty of souvenir-quality items at affordable prices is good old **Woolworth's.** They have all of the same sundries as Mainland stores, but plenty of Hawaiian and Oriental baubles fill the shelves, too. The film prices are some of the best.

House of Music sells records and tapes. This is a good store to shop for those island sounds that'll immediately conjure up images of Hawaii whenever they're played. Ground floor, tel. 949-1051.

The Honolulu Book Shop, tel. 941-2274, has the largest selection of books in the state, especially their Hawaiiana section. Books make inexpensive, easy-to-transport, and long-lasting mementos of your trip to Hawaii. Ground level near Centerstage.

Francis Camera Shop, tel. 946-2879, is a well-stocked camera store with a fine selection of merchandise sure to please the most avid camera buff. If you need something out of the ordinary for your camera bag, this is a good place to come. The staff is friendly and will spend time giving you advice. However, the best place to buy film is at **Sears** (no credit cards). **Woolworth's** and **Longs Drugs** also have good prices, but for cheap and fast developing try **Fromex Photo,** tel. 955-4797, street level, ocean side.

The Crackseed Center, tel. 949-7200, offers the best array of crackseed (spiced nuts, seeds, and fruits) that have been treats for island children for years. There're also dried and spiced scallops at $68 per pound and cuttlefish at $2.50 per pound—such a deal! Prices are inflated here, but their selection can't be beat, and you can educate yourself about these same products in smaller stores around the island. Crackseed is not to everyone's liking, but it does make a unique souvenir. Spirolina hunters can get their organic fix at **Vim and Vigor,** featuring vitamins, supplements, and minerals.

Shirikaya is a Japanese-owned department store between Penney's and Liberty House on the mountain side of the complex. They have a fascinating assortment of gadgetry, knickknacks, handy items, and nifty stuff that Nippon is so famous for. It's fun just to look around, and the prices are reasonable. Japanese products are also available at **Iida's,** a local store dating back to the turn of the century, featuring garden ornaments and flower-arrangement sets, tel. 946-0888.

Specialty shops in the center include: **The Ritz Department Store,** with high fashions for men and women; **Hawaiian Island Creations, Products of Hawaii,** and **Irene's,** all selling a wide assortment of island-made goods and souvenirs, from cheap to exquisite; **India Imports,** many unique items from the subcontinent, and eelskin products; **Tahiti Imports,** with bikinis, muumuu, and a wide selection of handicrafts from throughout Polynesia; **Jeans Warehouse** for you aloha buckaroos; and **San Francisco Rag Co.** for nice rags sewn together well.

Ward Warehouse

Located just a few blocks west of Ala Moana Center, at 1050 Ala Moana Blvd., open weekdays 10 a.m.-9 p.m., Sat. 10 a.m.-5 p.m., Sun. 11 a.m.-4 p.m., tel. 531-6411, this modern two-story complex lives up to its name as a warehouse, with a motif from bygone days when stout wooden beams were used instead of steel. The wide array of shops here includes a number of inexpensive restaurants (see "Food"), but the emphasis is on arts and crafts, with no less than 10 shops specializing in this field.

Give the tots their first lesson in impulse buying at **Hello Kiddie's,** a toy store, or at **Junior Co.,** or show them how a pro does it by wandering into **Be Be Sports** or **Blue Ginger** for men's and women's fashionable alohawear.

Kids of all ages will love **Neon Leon,** where you can buy masks, flying bats, puppets, a lot of neon, fake buns (yes those kind!), and a pineapple head if you've left yours at home.

Waldenbooks, tel. 533-2711, open daily 10 a.m.-9 p.m., Sunday to 6 p.m., has a tremendous selection of printed material. In this first-rate bookstore, you'll find the latest novels, a good section on Hawaiiana, and even travel guidebooks!

Repent past gluttonies at **Aloha Health Food,** primarily a vitamin and mineral store. Or dress your feet at **Thongs and Things,** with everything in thongs from spiked golfing thongs to Teva sandals, the best all-around footwear for the island. Upstairs is **Birkenstock Footprints,** with their wonderfully comfortable ugly ducklings. More shops are: **Island Sun Spots** featuring bikinis and sundresses; **Traditions,** a great junk shop; **Cotton Cargo** for comfortable and tasteful dresses; and **JR's Music Shop** for standard and contemporary music with plenty of tunes by local Hawaiian musicians.

Perhaps the premier shop in the Warehouse is **Nohea Gallery** (*nohea* means beautiful or handsome in Hawaiian), tel. 599-7927, owned and operated by Gail and Lorie Baron, who personally choose for display works by over 500 local artists and craftspeople. Some of the finest works are created by over 100 island woodworkers who make everything from rocking chairs and rolltop desks to traditional canoe paddles using rich grained woods like koa, mango, and rosewood. One of the most acclaimed woodworkers on display is **Kelly Dunn,** who, from his shop in Hawi on the Big Island, turns out bowls from Norfolk Island Pine that are so thin you can actually see through them. Other artists displaying their talents include: **Kurt McVay,** who creates masterpieces in glass primarily in cobalt blues and emerald greens highlighted with daubs of oranges and yellows; **Diana Lehr,** who uses oils and pastels to capture the dramatic skyscapes and colors of Hawaii's sunsets and sunrises; **Fabienne Blanc,** who works in ultravibrant watercolors creating surrealistic close-up images of plants and foliage; **Russell Lowrey,** Fabienne's husband, who watercolors and pastels, creating soft, feminine images of the islands; a very talented local couple, under the name of **Ulana O Kukui,** make beautiful jewelry such as rings of gold and silver that they fashion like traditional *lau hala* weaving along with fused and blown glass, and woven baskets of all natural materials; and

Rick Mills, a University of Hawaii professor, another glass artist who favors cobalt blue. Distinctive and affordable treasures include backgammon games, jewelry boxes, bowls, all kinds of jewelry, prints, and even distinctive post cards. Nohea Gallery is where you can see the "heart of Hawaii" through the eyes of its artists. Have a look!

Ward Center

Across the street from the Ward Warehouse, this relatively new shopping center is gaining a reputation for some exclusive shops. The Ward Center, open weekdays 10 a.m.-9 p.m., Sat. 10 a.m.-5 p.m., Sun. 11 a.m.-4 p.m., tel. 531-6411, is appointed in light wood and accentuated by brick floors that give the feeling of an intimate inside mall, although much is outside.

The Colonnade is a cluster of shops inside the Ward Center. It includes Regency Shoes, Lady Judith, a fine apparel shop, and Willowdale Galleries, twinkling with elegant antiques, crystal place settings, chandeliers, and even candelabra for those closet Liberace wannabes. It's like looking into a giant china closet filled with the best place settings and crystal.

Art A La Carte is a 12-member co-op featuring the works of well known island artists including Bunky Bakutis, Gail Bakutis, Connie Hustace, Mary Sylva, and Jackie Tanaguchi. Hanging on the walls are landscapes, seascapes, and a variety of portraits done in oils, paper, and watercolors, while glass cases hold the distinctive pit-fired ceramics of Bunky Bakutis.

Ladies will find exotic to erotic garments at The Blush Collection, while gentlemen can find that just right gift at Gems of the Pacific, which mainly deals in coral and black onyx jewelry. Villa Roma is a ladies' high fashion boutique, while Size Me Petite is for the smaller women and young girls, and Allure offers designer bikinis and bathing suits.

For a distinctive shop, check out Hawaiian Heritage, which is brimming with lustrous koa furniture—rocking chairs, four-poster beds, planter tables, and dining room tables and chairs, all beautifully executed.

Vibrating from a remote corner of the mall, where mystics feel more at home, is Sedona, tel. 531-8010, a metaphysical new-age store. Inside their shelves and cases are stocked with aroma therapy and massage oils, natural crystals, agates, books, jewelry, and consciousness-lifting tapes. Recharge your spiritual batteries with a personal psychic reading done by various practitioners in a private upstairs area.

Downtown Shopping

If you're touring the historical sights of downtown Honolulu, take a short stroll over to the corner of Bishop and King streets, as good a place as any to call the center of the financial district. The names atop the buildings, both vintage and new, trace "big business" in Hawaii. There's good food to be enjoyed in the restaurants in this area (see "Food") along with some shops stuck away in the corners of the big buildings. See also "Chinatown—Shopping." An enjoyable time can be had at the Dole Cannery Square, with shopping in its new mini-mall. Longs Drugs, tel. 534-4551, is at 1088 Bishop, and almost next door is Woolworth's, tel. 524-8980, for any sundries and necessities.

The full-service Honolulu Bookshop is on the corner of Bishop and Hotel, tel. 534-6224. The selections are excellent. Nautilus of the Pacific is at 1141 Bishop, specializing in estate jewelry and Hawaiian heirlooms, with plenty of sculptures and ceramics from Japan and China. Hawaiian Islands Stamp and Coin, tel. 531-6251, at 1111 Bishop St., street level in the International Savings Building, displays rare coins, stamps, and paper money of Hawaii, the U.S., and worldwide. Discount Store, at 65 S. Hotel St., sells TVs, VCRs, radios, and electronic gear. Amar's Sporting Goods, tel. 536-0404, at the corner of Bethel and Pauahi, is one of the bigger sporting goods stores on Oahu. The Lion Coffee Co., at 894 Queen St., tel. 521-3479, offers a great little tour of their roasting facilities and will mail out a colorful little newsletter on request. For classic Hawaiian shirts head for Bailey's Antique and Thrift Shop, 758 Kapahulu, tel. 734-7628, where you will find thousands of the vintage "collectible garments" on display. The best are made from rayon that was manufactured before 1950. Prices can range from $100 to $2,000.

Bargains And Discounts

For discounts and bargains, try the following. Crazy Shirts Factory Outlet, at 99-969 Iwaena St., Aiea, tel. 487-9919, sells seconds and discontinued styles, with a minimum savings of 50%. **Swimsuit Warehouse,** 870 Kapahulu Ave., Honolulu, tel. 735-0040, has women's swimsuits under $20, plus shorts and tops. **The Muumuu Factory,** 1526 Makaloa St., offers great sales—get there early and bring your helmet and shoulder pads to fight off the crowds. The **Hawaii Fashion Factory** at 1031 Auahi St., second floor, is just between the Ward Center and the Ward Warehouse. Fashions at factory prices, with the public welcome to visit the showrooms. **Goodwill Thrift Shop,** at 83 N. King, tel. 521-3105, displays the same bargains as on the Mainland, but with a wide assortment of alohawear. **Nearly New Thrift Shop,** 1144 Koko Head Ave., tel. 732-3272, has consignment sales of quality merchandise. **Symphony Thrift Shop,** 1923 Pensacola, tel. 524-7157, is a consignment shop for used clothing in excellent condition, and usually name brands. **The Discount Store,** 188 S. Hotel St., tel. 537-4469, boasts excellent prices on tape recorders, tapes, batteries, and electrical equipment. **Paradise Found Factory Outlet,** at 1108 Fort St. Mall, tel. 533-3658, is known for their quality shirts that sell for under $20. Tom Selleck, star of "Magnum P.I.," often wore shirts from Paradise Found.

Miscellaneous

Everyone, sooner or later, needs a good hardware store. You can't beat the selection at **Kilgo's,** 180 Sand Island Rd., tel. 845-3266. They have it all.

For camera and photo supplies **Central Camera** is a fine store in the downtown area where the salespeople are very helpful. Across from Hawaiian Telephone at 1164 Bishop St., tel. 536-6692. Open Mon.-Fri. 8:30 a.m.-4 p.m., Sat. 8:30-11 a.m. (Also see Ala Moana Shopping Center.) For **sporting goods** try: **Big 88,** 330 Sand Island Rd., tel. 845-1688, many military items; **Amar Sporting Goods,** 1139 Bethel St., tel. 536-0404, sporting goods, sportswear, and a full range of accessories and equipment.

anthurium

DIANA LASICH HARPER

CHINATOWN

Chinatown has seen ups and downs in the last 130 years, ever since Chinese laborers were lured from Guangdong Province to work as contract laborers on the pineapple and sugar plantations. They didn't need a fortune cookie to tell them that there was no future in plantation work, so within a decade of their arrival they had established themselves as merchants, mostly in small retail businesses and restaurants. Chinatown is roughly a triangle of downtown Honolulu bordered by Nuuanu Street on the southeast, N. Beretania Street on the northeast, and S. King St. forming the hypotenuse. Twice this area has been flattened by fire, once in 1886 and again in 1900. The 1900 fire was deliberately set to burn out rats that had brought bubonic plague to the city. The fire got out of control and burned down virtually the whole district. Some contended that the fire was allowed to engulf the district in order to decimate the growing economic strength of the Chinese. Chinatown reached its heyday in the 1930s when it thrived with tourists coming and going from the main port at the foot of Nuuanu Street.

Today, Chinatown is a mixed bag of upbeat modernization and run-down sleazy storefronts.

Although still strongly Chinese, there are Japanese, Laotians, Vietnamese, and even an Irish pub, O'Toole's, on Nuuanu Avenue. This is Asia come to life: meat markets with hanging ducks, and Chinese, Korean, Japanese, and Vietnamese food with their strange aromatic spices all in a few blocks. The entire district takes only 10 minutes to walk and is a world apart from "tourist" Oahu. Crates, live chickens, incredible shops, down-and-outers, tattoo parlors, and temples all can be found in this quarter. When Hotel Street meets River Street, with the harbor in the background, it all abruptly ends. This is a different Honolulu, a Pacific port, crusty and exciting.

AROUND CHINATOWN

Look for the pagoda roof of **Wo Fat's** on the corner of Hotel and Maunakea streets. This is the oldest chop suey house in Honolulu, started in 1886 by Mr. Wo Fat, a baker. It's a good landmark for starting your tour. If you want to clear your head from the hustle and bustle, visit the **Kuan Yin Temple,** where Buddha is always praised with some sweet-smelling incense. For peace and quiet, or to check out some old-timers playing checkers or dominoes, cross the river and enter **Aala Triangle Park.**

Treat yourself by walking a few minutes to **Foster Botanical Garden** at 180 N. Vineyard for a glimpse of rare and exotic flora from around the world. (See "Sights—Musuems, Galleries,

Gardens, and Tours.") While walking River Street, bordering Nuuanu Stream, behind the Cultural Plaza, notice what most people think is a temple but is really **Izumo Taisha Jinja,** a Japanese Shinto shrine. All the accoutrements of a shrine are here—roof, bell, prayer box. This one houses a male deity. You can tell by the

CHINATOWN

AALA ST.

NIMITZ HWY.

VINEYARD BLVD.

98

TO FOSTER BOTANIC GARDEN

AALA TRIANGLE PARK

NUUANU STREAM

AWA ST.

POST OFFICE

OPEN PEOPLE'S MARKET

RIVER ST.

CULTURAL PLAZA

KUKUI ST.

92

KEKAULIKE

WO FATS

HOTEL ST.

PAUAHI ST.

BERETANIA ST.

MAUNAKEA ST.

SMITH ST.

NUUANU AVE.

CHAPLIN LN.

FORT ST.

MARIN ST.

POLICE STATION

BETHEL ST.

ALA MOANA BLVD.

FORT ST.

S. KING ST.

BISHOP ST.

—N—

NOT TO SCALE

© MOON PUBLICATIONS, INC.

cross on the top. There's a ferroconcrete example of a *torii* gate.

Lum Sai Ho Tong, across the street from the Shinto shrine, is a basic Chinese Buddhist temple, very small. Below it is Edwin's Upholstery Shop, part of the temple.

You can easily do Chinatown on your own, but for another view and some extremely knowledgeable guides try the **Chinese Chamber of Commerce** tour, tel. 533-3181, which has been operating as a community service for almost 30 years. They'll guide you around Chinatown for only $4, with an optional $5 lunch at Wo Fat's. Or try the **Hawaiian Heritage Center Tour** from 1026 Nuuanu Ave., tel. 521-2749, every Mon., Wed., and Fri. at 9:30 a.m., for $4, and a lunch at Wo Fat's for $5. An excellent source of general information is the **Hawaii Chinese History Center,** 111 N. King St., Honolulu, HI 96817.

SHOPPING

For shopping head to the **Cultural Plaza,** on the corner of Maunakea and Beretania streets, but note that it has been struggling lately and shops come and go with regularity. It's more fun to look at than to shop. You'll find **Vin Ching Jade Center, Dragongate Bookstore, Excellent Jewelry Factory,** and **Peninsula Jewelry.** The Cultural Plaza **Moongate Stage** is the centerpiece. Here they perform Chinese dances and plays, and herald in the Chinese New Year. If there is a presentation (free), attend.

Nearby you'll find the **People's Open Market,** a co-operative of open-air stalls selling just about everything that Chinatown has to offer at competitive prices. Follow your nose to the pungent odors of fresh fish at **Oahu Fish Market** on King Street, where ocean delectables can be had for reasonable prices.

Pauahi Nuuanu Gallery, open weekdays 10:30-4, Sat. 9-1, at the corner of Pauahi and Nuuanu streets, is owned and operated by Lorna Dunn. It's small, but so are diamonds, and inside it's loaded with Hawaiian arts and crafts. The most impressive are the wooden bowls—light as a feather and thin as glass, made by Michael Ilipuakea Dunn, Lorna's son. Besides bowls there are little wooden jewelry boxes by Michael. Mythical carvings by Richard Morgan Howell

depict Hawaiian legends in wood and stone. Bruce Clark and Rick Mills, an instructor at the University of Hawaii, are glasswork artists. The painters represented are Laka Morton, a Kauai artist, Jianjie Jie, and Douglas Tolantino, a Filipino-Hawaiian, with heavy oils by Ellen Joseph Gilmore. Expensive prices, but quality work.

Waterfall Galleries, owned by award-winning photographer William Waterfall, are at 1160A Nuuanu St., tel. 521-6863. William runs the gallery, takes the photos, and collects the artwork that's here. The photography is all original. Plenty of the artwork comes from Asia, especially Balinese carvings and celadon pottery from Thailand, which is done in woodburning kilns and signed by the potter. William, while doing travel assignments, buys the artwork and schlepps them back. His gallery is full of sculptures, bas-reliefs, and masks from previous trips. So you don't know what you'll get when you come in here, but you can count on it being tasteful and original.

Pegge Hopper Gallery is next door to Waterfall Galleries. Ms. Hopper is one of the three most famous working artists in all of Hawaii. Her original works grace the walls of the most elegant hotels and homes in the islands. If you would like to purchase one of her bold and amazing serigraphs, this shop has the best and widest selection.

Cindy's Flower Shop is just next to Wo Fat's, and they have fresh lei at cheap prices. Located right where S. Beretania turns into N. Beretania, at Smith St. across from the Honolulu Towers, are a garland of flower shops like Lita's Lei and Mauna Kea Lei, famous for good products and prices. Also, at the corner of Pauahi and Maunakea look for **Aloha Lei and Flowers,** tel. 599-7725, who are locally famous for their lei, which they can ship to the Mainland.

At River and S. Beretania Streets is the **People's Open Market** every Monday 10 a.m.-11:15 a.m., selling fresh produce from local gardens.

The **Wingon Co.,** at 131 Hotel, has porcelain ware, but the feature is the big crocks of crackseed. If you want it the way it *was* made, this is it.

On the corner of Maunakea and Hotel you'll find **New World Fashions,** men's and women's wear, quality, value, and low prices.

Chinatown herbalist

Chinese Acupuncturists And Herbalists, Etc.
Ted J. Kaptchuk, O.M.D., in his excellent book *The Web That Has No Weaver* says, "Actually, Chinese medicine is a coherent and independent system of thought that has been developed over two millenia." Chinese practitioners, unlike their western counterparts, look at the entire individual, not just the acute symptom, and try to pinpoint what they refer to as "internal disharmony." Their diagnosis might be "dampness in the liver" or "fire in the kidney" for which they may prescribe a combination of acupuncture, herbs, dietary supplements and even exercise. The practitioners listed below are all licensed to practice Chinese medicine. A visit, where they will check your overall appearance and a number of "pulses," costs about $5. The herbs that they prescribe, usually dispensed from a wall of drawers labled with Chinese characters, will probably cost under $10 depending upon the malady.

Yuan Chai Tong Ltd. Oriental Herbs and **Dr. W.S. Lam,** licensed acupuncturist, occupy a storefront on the corner of River and N. King.

Nearby on Maunakea is **Fook Sau Tong's,** another Chinese herb specialist. Look in the window to see coiled snake skin, a few dried-out snakes, some flat-looking lizards, and who-knows-what. If you need the bounce put back in your step, maybe some tonics or a few needles in the ear are just what the doctor will order.

Kam Sang Chun, 1121 Nuuanu Ave., open daily 9 a.m.-noon and again 2-5:30 p.m., Sun., 9 a.m.-noon, is another long established acupuncturist and herbalist.

Down Smith St. is **Kam Mau Co.,** whose shelves are stacked with every conceivable (and inconceivable) Asian food. This is a great place to sample authentic crackseed. If your tummy revolts or if you need a quick tonic head next door to **Lai An Tong's** herb shop where some mashed antelope antler or powdered monkey brain will set you straight again.

CHINATOWN NIGHTS

Chinatown is relatively safe, especially during the daytime, but at night, particularly along infamous Hotel Street, you have to be careful. When the sun sinks, the neon lights and the area fires up. Transvestites and hookers slide down the street, shaking their wares and letting you know that they're open for business. Purchasing might leave you with a few souvenirs that you'd never care to *share* with the folks back home.

Not many tourists come this way. But walking down Hotel Street is really an adventure in and of itself. If you stay on the main drag, right down the middle, you'll be okay.

There are a lot of nondescript places like **China Bar** that open to the street like a wound oozing the odor of stale beer and urine. At Hotel and Nuuanu streets you'll find the Honolulu Police Department downtown substation.

The **Hubba Hubba Club,** with its live nude shows, no cover, and not too inflated drinks, is the best of Hotel Street. This is not a place for candy-asses, wimps, or missionaries. Simply put, there are naked women in here doing exotic and bizarre acts. The Hubba Hubba is basically a clip joint on the up and up. Inside are flashing lights, a runway, and $3 beers, with only mild pressure as you sit and watch the act.

As you walk down Hotel Street toward the river it gets sleazier. The **Zig Zag Club** is basically a gin joint. Interspersed is an assortment of peep shows, followed by the **Swing Club,** with disco dancing 10:30 a.m.-2:30 a.m., and then **Two Jacks Bar** (bar and cabaret). **Elsie's Bar,** at 145 N. Hotel St., open 6 a.m.-2 a.m., looks meaner than a tattooed snake, but it's a safe place. So if you want to have a night of fun and relaxation come in here. They offer Hawaiian music by the Puamana Serenaders along with fairly decent Hawaiian food. A few doors down are steps leading upstairs to the **Original Bath Palace.** The *original* place where drunken fools were taken to the cleaners.

FOOD

You can eat delicious ethnic food throughout Chinatown. If not Honolulu's best, the entire district, food-wise, is definitely Honolulu's cheapest. On almost every corner you've got places like **Mini Garden Noodle and Rice Shop** and **Cafe Paradise** for breakfast, lunch, and dinner. They're basic and cheap eateries whose ambience is a mixture of formica-topped tables and linoleum floors. In almost all, the food is authentic, with most featuring Asian food. You can easily get meals here for $3-5. Some eateries appear greasier than the Alaska Pipeline, so you'll have to feel them out. The local people eat in them regularly, and most are clean enough.

An example is **Neon's Filipino Restaurant** on S. Hotel near the Hubba Hubba Club. The sign says "Come in and have a halo halo, consists of many delicious fruits and flavor of canned juices. And by the way order a piece of custard." They serve Filipino dishes like *mongo am-palaya,* shrimp *pinakabet,* and *pancit* Canton for around $5.

Right at the corner of N. Hotel and Maunakea, you'll see **Wo Fat's Chinese Chop Suey,** tel. 533-6393, the oldest chop suey house in Hawaii, where you're guaranteed an authentic meal at reasonable prices. A visit to Chinatown is incomplete without lunch at Wo Fat's, or at least a tour of this extremely ornate restaurant. The three floors are covered with paintings of dragons, birds, flowers and a variety of land- and seascapes. Murals, carvings, and hanging lanterns create the mood of "rococo Chinese." The menu is like a small phone book, with literally hundreds of choices of fish, fowl, beef, and vegetarian dishes. It's hard to spend more than $10 per person, with many dishes considerably less.

Rosarina Pizza, New York Style, at N. Pauahi and Maunakea St., tel. 533-6634, is an alternative to the Asian cuisine. They will sell you a slice of pizza for only $1.40, or a whole pie ranging from a small cheese for $8 to a large combo at $15.25. You can also order a 12-inche sublike pastrami and provolone for $4.75, or an a la carte dinner like spaghetti with meat sauce or sausage, cannelloni, or manicotti, all for under $7.

Doong Kong Lau offers Hakka cuisine and sizzlers. It's on the river side of the Cultural Plaza, open Mon. 9 a.m.-9:30 p.m., Tues.-Sun. 8 a.m.-9:30 p.m., tel. 531-8833. Inside it's utilitarian with leatherette seats and formica tables. You come here for the food. Savories include stir-fried squid with broccoli for $5.95, stir-fried scallops with garlic sauce for $7.95, stir-fried oysters with black beans for $6.95, sizzle plates like seafood combo at $7.95, or shark fin with shredded chicken, $16.50. The menu reads, "The chief recommends deep fried shrimp with toast." Who's to argue with the chief! **Wan Kee Seafood Restaurant** is another restaurant in the Cultural Plaza. Locals swear by it, especially the lunch specials for $4.95.

The **Royal Kitchen,** tel. 524-4461, in the Cultural Plaza, is very popular with local families and business people. They're especially known for their takeout baked *manapua,* soft dough with pork and spices, and for their Chinese sausage, *lupcheung.* Open very early in the morning.

One place that you shouldn't miss is **Shung Chong Yuein,** a Chinese cake shop at 1027 Maunakea. Look in to see yellow sugar cakes, black sugar cakes, shredded coconut with eggs, salted mincemeat, Chinese ham with egg, lotus seeds, and steamed buns.

Chinatown Joe's, at the corner of Hotel and Nuuanu streets, tel. 534-3677, is a classic tavern complete with dart board and mugs of draft beer. Laid-back, local, and friendly, it's a good place to stop in for a breather, or to have a classic tuna, ham and Swiss, or pastrami sandwich.

Chinatown's Vietnamese Restaurants

A recent phenomenon is a number of excellent Vietnamese restaurants that have sprung up like bamboo sprouts along Chinatown's streets. The majority are meticulously clean, and the moderately priced food is "family-pride-gourmet." The decor ranges from oilcloth tablecloths topped by a "bouquet" of plastic flowers and a lazy Susan filled with exotic spices and condiments, to "down-to-earth chic" with some mood lighting, candles, and even linen place settings. As a group, they represent the best culinary deals on Oahu today. Many selections, like the grilled seasoned meatballs or marinated pork (under $8), come with noodles, fresh lettuce, mint, cucumber, bean sprouts, and ground peanut sauce that you wrap in layers of rice paper to make your own version of what can best be described as an "oriental taco." Simply moisten a few sheets of the rice paper in the bowl of water provided and wrap away. Great fun, and they'll show you how! There are plenty of savory vegetarian menu choices as well.

Maxime's Vietnamese Restaurant, 1134 Maunakea St., tel. 545-4188, open Tues.-Fri. 9 a.m.-9 p.m., Sat.-Sun. until 10 p.m., Mon. 5 p.m., is as authentic as its name is contrived. To get an idea, ask to use the bathroom. You'll pass through the cramped but meticulously cleaned kitchen filled with boiling pots that are tended by about three generations of the family. In the dining room, it's just formica tables and red Naugahyde chairs, but the people couldn't be more friendly. Try Maxime's special noodles with pork, shrimp, crab, bean sprouts, lettuce, and pork soup on the side for only $6.50, or an order of shrimp rolls—light aromatic rolls with

shrimp, pork, and garden vegetables and rice noodles rolled up in rice paper served with sauce for $4, or only $1.50 as an appetizer. The selections of *pho* soup, which can be beef or chicken (*pho ga*) come with rice noodles, onions, Chinese parsley, basil, bean sprouts, and wine. You can either have the meat in the soup or on the side, for only $4.50 or $5 for the jumbo size. Beverages are lemonade, iced coffee with condensed milk, jasmine tea, fresh coconut juice, sweet and sour lemon juice, and soybean milk. Top off your meal with desserts like caramel custard or sweet beans with coconut milk for under $2.00.

Royal Vietnam Restaurant, 1127 Maunakea St., tel. 524-1486, across from Maxime's, open daily 9 a.m.-10 p.m., is just as friendly, makes an attempt at decor, and is slightly higher priced. Specialties include barbecued quail with butter ($9.95) and braised prawns and black pepper gravy ($9.95). The hot-and-sour soups ("poolenty" for two) are wonderful. Try the Royal Seafood combination at $10.95, or catfish or shrimp hot and sour soup at $9.95. Less expensive, but great selections, are *bun,* shredded pork and vermicelli, with cucumbers and bean sprouts, mint, shredded lettuce, and roasted peanuts for $6.50, or spicy chicken and lemon grass for $6.95. Top off your meal with *che,* a sweet pudding for $1.95.

A Little Bit of Saigon, 1160 Maunakea, tel. 528-3663, open daily 10 a.m.-10 p.m., is the fanciest of the lot, although it is still quite basic. Specialties are "roll ups" that include savory beef, pork or chicken, served with lettuce, fresh herbs, vegetables, sweet and sour fish sauce, and peanut or pineapple and anchovy sauce along with thin rice paper that you use to roll-your-own for $5.95-$8.95. Good yet inexpensive selections are stir-fried vegetables that you can have either by themselves or with fresh fish, prawns, chicken, beef, tofu, or scallops, all for under $7.95. For the hearty appetite try the seven-course dinner for two at $29.95 that gives a good sample of the menu. Finish with agar served with tapioca and coconut milk for $1.75.

Pho May Vietnamese Restaurant, at 1029 Maunakea St., tel. 533-3522, open daily 9-9, is a fine family-operated restaurant. "Ambience free," the food more than makes up for it. Nothing is

1. anthurium (J.D. Bisignani)   **2.** You should have seen the frog! (J.D. Bisignani)

1. north coast, windward Oahu (J.D. Bisignani) **2.** the rainbow connection (J.D. Bisignani)

over $8. Specialties include Vietnamese soups of steak, well-done brisket and flank, tendon and tripe ($5.95), French bread and beef juicy cube ($5.95), and hot-and-sour soup for two bucks. With the soup they give you a stalk of fresh basil that you break up yourself, a spice that resembles cilantro, and sprouts that you add to the soup. Try shrimp and pork salad, crabmeat fried wonton, or spicy chicken curry. For under $10 you'll waddle away totally satiated.

To Chau Vietnamese Restaurant, at 1007 River, tel. 533-4549, and **Ha Bien,** next door to "Tattoo Parlor," serve basic Vietnamese fare for under $7 for most dishes. They're around the corner from the action of Hotel Street, and are family-oriented. Ha Bien is open strange hours, Mon. 8 a.m.-4 p.m., open the remainder of the week until 6 p.m.

Another Vietnamese restaurant is **My Canh,** tel. 599-1866, at 164 N. King St., open Mon.-Sat. 9-5, Sun. 9-3. Their menu reads, "You can select one specialty of the heart warming combination of the followings: rare steak well cooked, brisket and tendon, regular is $4.75, special is $5. BBQ meat spring for roll rice vermicelli is $5.25."

There's a really decent-looking Vietnamese restaurant called **Sau Duong** at 58 N. Hotel, tel. 538-7658, with home-cooked dishes like sour soup with fish ($8), lemon grass-spiced pork chop ($5.50), house specialties like fine sliced papaya salad with shrimp and pork ($3.75). Open for breakfast, lunch, and dinner.

GORDY OHLIGER

WAIKIKI

Waikiki ("Spouting Water") is like a fresh young starlet from the sticks who went to Hollywood to make it big, and did, though maybe too fast for her own good. Everyone always knew that she had a double-dip of talent and heart, but the fast lane has its heartaches, and she's been banged around a little by life. Even though her figure's fuller, her makeup's a little askew, and her high heels are worn down, she has plenty of chutzpah left, and when the curtain parts and the lights come up, she'll play her heart out for her audience.

Waikiki is a classic study of contradictions. Above all, it is an example of basic American entrepreneurialism taken to the nth degree. Along the main strip, high-powered businesspeople cut multimillion-dollar deals, but on the sidewalks it's a carnival midway with hucksters, handbillers, and street people selling everything decent and indecent under the tropical sun. To get a true feeling for Waikiki, you must put this amazing strip of land into perspective. The area covers only seven-tenths of a square mile, which at a good pace, you can walk in 15 minutes. On any given day, about 110,000 people crowd

its beaches and boulevards, making it one of the most densely populated areas on earth. Sixty thousand of these people are tourists; 30,000 are workers who commute from various towns of Oahu and cater to the tourists, and the remaining 20,000 actually call Waikiki home. The turnover is about 80,000 new tourists per week, and the pace never slackens. To the head shakers, these facts condemn Waikiki as a mega-growth area gone wild. To others, these same figures make Waikiki an energized, fun-filled place to be, where "if you don't have a good time, it's your own fault."

For the naive or the out-of-touch looking for "grass-shack paradise," the closest they'll come to it in Waikiki is painted on a souvenir ashtray. Those drawn to a smorgasbord of activities, who are adept at choosing the best and ignoring the rest, can't go wrong! People and the action are as constant in Waikiki as the ever-rolling surf.

History
The written record of this swampy area began in the late 1790s. The white man, along with his

historians, cartographers, artists, and gunpowder, were already an undeniable presence in the islands. Kalanikupule, ranking chief of Oahu, hijacked the *Jackall,* a small ship commanded by Captain Brown, with which he intended to spearhead an attack against Kamehameha I. The chief held the *Jackall* for a while, but the sailors regained control just off Diamond Head and sent the Hawaiians swimming for land. The ship then hastened to Kamehameha to report the treachery, and returned with his armada of double-hulled canoes, which beached along Waikiki. The great king then defeated Kalanikupule at the famous battle of Nuuanu Pali and secured control of the island. Therafter Waikiki, pinpointed by Diamond Head, became a well-known landmark.

Waikiki's interior was low-lying swampland, long known to be good for fishponds, taro, rice, and bananas, but hardly for living. The beach, however, was always blessed with sunshine and perfect waves, especially for surfing, a sport heartily loved by the Hawaiians. The royalty of Hawaii, following Kamehameha, made Honolulu their capital and kept beach houses at Waikiki. They invited many visiting luminaries to visit them at their private beach. All were impressed. In the 1880s, King Kalakaua was famous for his beach house hospitality. One of his favorite guests was Robert Louis Stevenson, who spent many months here writing one of his novels. By the turn of the 20th century Waikiki had become a highly exclusive vacation spot.

In 1901 the Moana Hotel was built, but immediately a protest was heard because it interfered with the view of Diamond Head. In 1906, Lucius Pinkham, then director of Hawaii's Board of Health, called the mosquito-infested area "dangerous and unsanitary," and proposed to drain the swamp with a canal so that "the whole place can be transformed into a place of unique beauty." By the early 1920s, the Ala Wai Canal was built, its dredgings used to reclaim land, and Waikiki was demarcated. By the end of the 1920s, the Royal Hawaiian Hotel, built on the site previously occupied by the royal beach house, was receiving very wealthy guests who arrived by ocean liner, loaded down with steamer trunks. They ensconced themselves at Waikiki, often staying for the duration of the season.

For about 40 years, Waikiki remained the enchanted domain of Hollywood stars, dignitaries, and millionaires. But for the brief and extraordinary days of WW II, which saw Waikiki barricaded and barb-wired, GIs—regular guys from the Mainland—were given a taste of this "reserved paradise" while on R&R. They brought home tantalizing tales of wonderful Waikiki, whetting the appetite of middle America.

Beginning just before statehood and continuing through the '60s to the mid-'70s, hotels and condos popped up like fertilized weeds, and tourism exploded with the advent of the jumbo jet. Discounted package tours began to haul in droves of economy-class tourists. Businesses catering to the tastes of penny-pinchers and first-timers elbowed their way into every nook and cranny. For the first time Waikiki began to be described as tacky and vulgar. For the old-timers, Waikiki was in decline. The upscale and repeat visitors started to snub Waikiki, heading for hidden resorts on the Neighbor Islands. But Waikiki had spirit and soul, and never gave in. In the last few years, its declining hotels started a campaign to regain their illustrious images. Millions upon millions of dollars have been poured into renovations and remodeling. Luxury hotels renting exclusive and expensive rooms have reappeared and are doing a booming business.

Waikiki Today

The Neighbor Islands are pulling more and more tourists away, and depending on your point of view, this is either a boon or a bust for Waikiki. Direct flights to Maui and the Big Island allow more tourists than ever to bypass Oahu, but still a whopping 80% of the people visiting the islands spend at least one night in a Waikiki hotel, which offer the lowest room rates in Hawaii. The sublime and the gaudy are neighbors in Waikiki. Exclusive shops are often flanked by buskers selling plastic hula dolls. Burgers and beer mingle their pedestrian odors with those of Parisian cuisine. Though Waikiki in many ways is unique, it can also come off as "Anytown, U.S.A." But most importantly it somehow works, and works well. You may not find "paradise" on Waikiki's streets, but you will find a willing "dancing partner," and if you pay the fiddler, she'll keep the beat.

Non-Americans, especially Japanese, still flock for dream vacations, mostly staying at

Waikiki hotels, 25% of which are owned by Japanese firms. Mainlanders and locals alike are disgruntled when they see the extent to which Waikiki has become a Japanese town. It's one of the only cities in America where you can have trouble ordering a meal or making a purchase if you don't speak Japanese! The visiting Japanese have been soundly warned by the tour operators before they arrive to never talk to strangers, especially someone on the street. Unfortunately for them, this means a vacation in which they never really leave Japan. They're herded into Japanese-owned shops and restaurants where prices are grossly inflated, and from which the tour operators get kickbacks. Local shopkeepers, not on the list, are aggravated. They say that the once-timid Japanese visitor will now show irritation if the shopkeeper doesn't speak Japanese, and will indignantly head for the door if there is no one provided to deal with them in their native tongue. Also, these visitors have been taught to bargain with American shopkeepers, who they are told inflate prices. This makes for some rugged interaction when the price is already fair, but the Japanese visitor won't believe it. Although a survey was done that says the Japanese tourist spends an average of $500 per day, as opposed to a Mainlander who spends $100 per day, the Japanese really don't spread their money around as much as you would think. The money spent in Japanese shops primarily goes back to Japan. It's an incestuous system that operates in Waikiki.

SIGHTS

To see Waikiki's attractions, you have to do little more than perch on a bench or loll on a beach towel. Its boulevards and beaches are world-class for people-watching. Some of its strollers and sunbathers are *visions,* while others are real *sights.* And if you keep your ears open, it's not hard to hear every American accent and a dozen foreign languages. Some actual sights are intermingled with the hotels, boutiques, bars, and restaurants. Sometimes, too, these very buildings are the sights. Unbelievably, you can even find plenty of quiet spots—in the gardens of Kapiolani Park, and at churches, temples, tearooms, and ancient Hawaiian special places sitting unnoticed amidst the grandiose structures of the 20th century. Also, both the Honolulu Zoo and Waikiki Aquarium are well worth a visit.

Getting Around
By far and away the best way to get around Waikiki is on foot. For one, it's easily walked from one end to the other in less than 20 minutes, and walking will save you hassling with parking and traffic jams. Also, TheBus and taxis are abundant, and along with rental cars, have been covered in the Out and About chapter under "Getting Around." Those who have opted for a rental car should note that many of the agencies operate Waikiki terminals, which for some can be more convenient than dropping your car at the airport on the day of departure. Check to see if it suits you. The following information is specific to Waikiki, and offers some limited alternatives.

In mid-1987, **pedicabs,** for all intents and purposes, were outlawed in Waikiki. There used to be 150-160 pedicabs that offered short taxi rides. They took people shopping, sightseeing, and between hotels, but basically they were a joy ride. Mainstream businesspeople considered them a nuisance, and there were rumors that some drivers dealt drugs, so they were finally outlawed. Now only 10-12 legal pedicabs operate in and around Waikiki. They're not allowed to go along Kalakaua Avenue, pick-up or drop-off at hotels, or use any of the main drags. They stay on the back streets or in the park, where they are constantly watched by the police. Charges are a hefty $3 per minute. The main customers are Japanese tourists who marvel at being peddled around town by a muscular *gaijin* in a rickshaw-type conveyance never seen in their own homeland any longer.

The **Waikiki Trolley,** tel. 526-0112, offers tours throughout Waikiki and downtown Honolulu. A day pass costs $15 adults, $7.50 children, and

WAIKIKI

© MOON PUBLICATIONS, INC.

MAMALA BAY

NOT ALL HOTELS ARE SHOWN

0.25 mi
0.25 km

TO DIAMOND HEAD
TO ALA MOANA SHOPPING CENTER

KAPIOLANI PARK

HONOLULU ZOO
WAIKIKI SHELL
KAPIOLANI PARK BANDSTAND
WAIKIKI AQUARIUM
THE FENCE (ART)

PAKI AVE.
MONSARRAT AVE.
KALAKAUA AVE.
KAPAHULU AVE.
ALA WAI BLVD.
KUHIO AVE.
PAOAKALANI
OHUA AVE.
KEALOHILANI
LILIUOKALANI
LEMON RD.

WAIKIKI BEACHSIDE
QUEEN KAPIOLANI
HOLIDAY INN
REGENT
HYATT REGENCY
KUHIO VILLAGE
WAIKIKI HANA
NIUMALU
PACIFIC MONARCH
KINGS
KOA
HAWAIIAN REGENT
KUHIO BEACH
SHERATON MOANA SURFRIDER
KUHIO MALL
KAIULANI AVE.
WAIKIKI BEACHCOMBER
MIRAMAR AT WAIKIKI
WAIKIKI TRADE CENTER
CORAL REEF
NAHUA
SEASIDE
LUNA
LEXINGTON HONOLULU
ISLAND COLONY
HONOLULU PRINCE
NOHONANI
ALOHA DR.
MANUKAI
ALOHA TOWERS
LEWERS
WAIKIKI SHOPPING PLAZA
BUSINESS PLAZA
INTERNATIONAL MARKET PLACE
ROYAL HAWAIIAN SHOPPING
HELUMOA
ROYAL HAWAIIAN
SHERATON WAIKIKI
OUTRIGGER REEF
WAIKIKI BEACH
HALEKULANI
BEACH WALK
SARATOGA
EDGEWATER
OUTRIGGER CORAL SEAS
BREAKERS
HOLIDAY ISLE
POST OFFICE
LAUULA ST.
SEASIDE
KUHIO AVE.
ALA WAI BLVD.
ALA WAI CANAL
ALA WAI ST.
KEONIANA ST.
MALUHIA RD.
KALIA RD.
PAOA PL.
FORT DERUSSY BEACH
HILTON LAGOON
BATTERY RANDOLPH MILITARY MUSEUM
HILTON HAWAIIAN VILLAGE
RAINBOW BAZAAR
WESTIN ILIKAI
PARK PLAZA WAIKIKI
HAWAIIAN MONARCH
McCULLY ST.
ENA RD.
HOBRON LN.
ALA MOANA BLVD.
KALAKAUA AVE.
92
ALA WAI YACHT HARBOR

Waikiki Trolley

you can get on and off as much as you like. The trolley is really an open-air bus, but it's well done and plenty of fun.

Waikiki does an excellent job of conveying traffic, both auto and pedestrian, along Kalakaua Avenue, the main drag fronting Waikiki. They've installed very clear yet unattractive combinations of stoplights and street names. These are metal L-shaped beams, painted a dull brown, that straddle the roadways, clearly pinpointing your location. Unfortunately, they match the area about as well as work boots match a hula dancer. To give the feeling of an outdoor strolling mall, sidewalks along Kalakaua have been widened and surfaced with red brick.

The **Kapiolani Park Kiosk** is on the corner of Kapahulu and Kalakaua avenues. The kiosk uses vintage photos to give a concise history of Kapiolani Park. An overview map shows all the features of the park. Information is available here concerning events at the Aquarium, Zoo, Waikiki Shell, the Kodak Hula Show, the Art Mart—a collection of island artists selling their creations along the Zoo fence (see "Shopping— The Fence"), and the Kapiolani Bandstand, where you're treated to free concerts by top-name bands and orchestras (see "Entertainment—Free or Small Fee Entertainment").

Public parking in Waikiki can be a hassle, although there are plenty of parking garages. A good place to park not far from the beach is the strip running parallel to Kapiolani Park at one end and along Saratoga Street at the other.

There are plenty of two-hour parking meters available, especially if you arrive before 9 a.m. Also, inexpensive (for Waikiki) parking is available at the ramp adjacent to the Waikiki 3 Theaters along Seaside Road, but only after 5:30 p.m.

Note: For terrific "Living History Walking Tours" see "Getting Around—Sightseeing Tours" in the Out and About chapter.

DIAMOND HEAD

If you're not sandwiched in a manmade canyon of skyscrapers, you can look eastward from anywhere in Waikiki and see Diamond Head. Diamond Head *says* Waikiki. Western sailors have used it as a landmark since the earliest days of contact, and the Hawaiians undoubtedly before that. Ships' artists etched and sketched its motif long before the names of the new-found lands of Hawaii, Waikiki, and Oahu

Diamond Head

Kapiolani Park

were standardized and appeared on charts as Owyhee, Whytete, and Woohoo. The Hawaiian name was Leahi ("Brow of the Ahi"); legend says it was named by Hi'iaka, Madame Pele's younger sister, because she saw a resemblance in its silhouette to the yellowfin tuna. The name "Diamond Head" comes from a band of sailors who found calcite crystals on its slopes and thought they'd discovered diamonds. Kamehameha I immediately made the mountain *kapu* until his adviser John Young informed him that what the seamen had found, later known as "Pele's tears," were, except as souvenirs, worthless. Diamond Head was considered a power spot by the Hawaiians. Previously, Kamehameha had worshipped at a *heiau* located on the western slopes, offering human sacrifice to his bloodthirsty war-god, Ku.

Geologically, the 760-foot monolith is about 350,000 years old, formed in one enormous explosion when seawater came into contact with lava bubbling out of a fissure. No new volcanic activity has been suspected in the last 200,000 years. The huge rock is now Hawaii's state monument and a national natural landmark. Its crater serves as a Hawaii National Guard depot; various hiking trails to the summit bypass installations left over from WW II (see "Out and About—Camping and Hiking"). Getting there takes only 15 minutes from Waikiki, either by TheBus no. 57 or by car along Diamond Head Road. The southeast (*makai*) face has some of the most exclusive and expensive real estate in the islands. The Kahala Hilton Hotel here is regarded by many to be one of the premier hotels in the world, and nearby is the super-snobbish Waialae Country Club. Many private estates—homes of multimillionaires, Hollywood stars, and high-powered multinational executives—cling to the cliffside, fronting ribbons of beach open to the public by narrow rights-of-way that oftentimes are hemmed in by the walls of the estates.

KAPIOLANI PARK

In the shadow of Diamond Head is Kapiolani Park, a quiet 140-acre oasis of greenery, just a coconut's roll away from the gray cement and flashing lights of Waikiki. It has proved to be one of the best gifts ever received by the people of Honolulu, ever since King Kalakaua donated this section of crown lands to them in 1877, requesting that it be named after his wife, Queen Kapiolani. In times past, it was the site of horse and car races, polo matches, and Hawaii's unique *pa'u* riders, fashionable ladies in long flowing skirts riding horses decked out with lei. The park was even the sight of Camp McKinley, the U.S. Army headquarters in the islands from 1898 to 1907.

It remains a wonderful place for people to relax and exercise away from the hustle of Waikiki. The park is a mecca for jogging and aerobics, with many groups and classes meeting here throughout the day. It also serves as the starting point for the yearly **Honolulu Marathon,** one of the most prestigious races in the world.

The beach part of the park, called Sans Souci, is very popular with local people and those wishing to escape the crowds, just a few beach-blanket lengths away.

Its **Waikiki Shell,** an open-air amphitheater, hosts many visiting musical groups, especially during Aloha Week. The Honolulu Symphony is a regular here, providing free concerts, especially on summer evenings. Nearby, the **Kapiolani Bandstand** hosts the Royal Hawaiian Band on Sunday afternoons. Also, under the shade of the trees toward Waikiki Beach, plenty of street entertainers, including clowns, acrobats, and jugglers, congregate daily to work out their routines to the beat of conga drums and other improvised music supplied by wandering musicians. Families and large groups come here to picnic, barbecue, and play softball. The park grounds are also home to the free **Kodak Hula Show** (see "Entertainment—Dinner Shows and Polynesian Extravaganzas"), Elks Club, prestigious Outrigger Canoe Club founded at the turn of the century, Waikiki Aquarium, and 45-acre Honolulu Zoo.

Just in front of the zoo, by the big banyan, are hundreds and hundreds of pigeons, the "white phantoms of Waikiki." In the morning they are especially beautiful darting through the sunshine like white spirits. Go to the Stop N Go or the ABC Store at the corner of Kapahulu and Kapiolani and buy birdseed. Take a few handfuls and stand among the pigeons. They will perch on your arms, shoulders, and head and peck away. If you're not wearing toe covering shoes be advised that if you drop seed between your toes, you'll get an instant and free pedicure by the hungry birds. This is great fun and free!

WAIKIKI AQUARIUM

The first Waikiki Aquarium was built in 1904, its entranceway framed by a *torii* gate. Rebuilt and restocked in 1954, it has just undergone another face-lift with a new entranceway, "touch tanks," and an opening directly to the sea. The aquarium, located at 2777 Kalakaua Ave. (TheBus no. 2), tel. 923-9741, is open daily 9 a.m.-5 p.m., admission $6 adults, $4 seniors, $2.50 youths 13-17, and free to children under 12. A self-guiding book describing the marinelife is available for $5, and an audio tour ("magic wand" device) in English and Japanese is 50 cents.

Although over 300 species of Hawaiian and South Pacific fish, flora, and mammals live in its sparkling waters, the aquarium is much more than just a big fish tank. The floor plan contains four galleries of differing themes, and a seal tank. The **South Seas Marine Life** exhibit shows fish found in waters from Polynesia to Australia. The tanks hold sharks, turtles, eels, rays, clams, a seahorse, and colorful coral displays. Another exhibit, **Micronesia Reef Builders,** is perhaps the most amazing of all. It contains live coral that seem more like extraterrestrial flowers than specimens from our own seas. Some are long strands of spaghetti with bulbous ends like lima beans, others are mutated roses, or tortured camellias, all moving, floating, and waving their iridescent purples, golds, and greens in a watery bouquet.

Watch the antics of the monk seals, shameless hams, from the side of their newly renovated 85,000 gallon tank, which now has a "variegated coastline" of natural nooks and crannies patterned after sections of Oahu's Pupukea and Kahe Point. Hawaiian monk seals are one of only two species of tropical seals on earth. Endangered, there are only about 1,500 individuals still surviving, and the "performances" are more of a detailed description of the seals day-to-day life in their dwindling environment. The three seals inhabiting the tank are all males, since placing a breeding couple would almost certainly result in the birth of a pup. Marine biologists anguished over the decision. It was felt that seals raised in captivity and then released back into the natural environment might introduce a devastating disease to the native population. This was considered too great a danger to risk.

The aquarium contains a bookshop with a tremendous assortment of titles on the flora and fauna of Hawaii. Restrooms are behind the bookshop area as you face the main gate. The University of Hawaii offers seminars and field trips through the aquarium, everything from guided reef walks to mini-courses in marine biology; information is available at the aquarium.

The Waikiki Aquarium is a very special opportunity for fun and education that will be enjoyed by the entire family. Don't miss it! (See The Northwestern Islands chapter).

Just near the aquarium is the **Waikiki Natatorium,** a saltwater swimming pool built in 1927 as a WW I memorial, which was allowed to decay over the years until it was closed in 1980. Plans are constantly afoot in the House of Representatives calling for a restoration, which may actually start soon.

HONOLULU ZOO

The trumpeting of elephants and chatter of monkeys emanates from the jungle across the street at the Honolulu Zoo, 151 Kapahulu Ave., tel. 923-7723, open daily 8:30 a.m.-4:30 p.m., with special shows in the summer at 6 p.m., admission $3, yearly pass $5. As you walk along or ride the tram, you find the expected animals from around the world: monkeys, giraffes, lions, big cats, a hippo, even a grizzly bear. The Honolulu Zoo has the *only* reptiles in Hawaii—three snakes in the Reptile House. Many islanders love this exhibit, because snakes in Hawaii are so exotic! But the zoo is much more than just a collection of animals. It is an up-close escapade through the jungle of Hawaii, with plants, trees, flowers, and vines all named and described. Moreover, the zoo houses Hawaii's indigenous birdlife, which is fast disappearing from the wild: Hawaiian gallinules, coots, hawks, owls, and the *nene,* the state bird, which is doing well in captivity, with breeding pairs being sent to other zoos around the world. The zoo is also famous for its Manchurian cranes, extremely rare birds from Japan, and for successfully mating the Galapagos turtle. A **petting zoo** of barnyard animals is great for kids. A concession stand serves typical junk food and soft drinks.

FREE SIGHTS AND CURIOSITIES

On the beach near the Surfrider Hotel are the **kahuna stones,** a lasting remnant of old Hawaii. The Hawaiians believed these stones were imbued with mana by four hermaphroditic priests from Tahiti: Kinohimahu, Kahaloamahu, Kapunimahu, and Kapaemahu (*mahu* in Hawaiian signifies homosexuality). They came to visit this Polynesian outpost in ancient times and left these stones for the people, who have held them in reverence for over 600 years. About 40 years ago, a group of local historians went looking for the stones but couldn't find them. Around that time, there was a bowling alley along the beach, and when it was finally torn down, it was discovered that the stones had been incorporated into the foundation. Today, the vast majority of visitors and islanders alike no longer revere the stones, often using them as a handy spot to scrape sand off their feet. *Kapuna* versed in the old ways say that the mana, once put in and strengthened by reverence, is now dissipating.

The **Urusenke Teahouse** is an authentic teahouse donated to Hawaii by the Urusenke Foundation of Kyoto. It is located at 245 Saratoga Rd., which lies along the Waikiki side of Fort DeRussy. Every Wed. and Fri. 10 a.m.-noon, tea master Yoshibuma Ogawa performs the ancient and aesthetic art of *chanoyu* (tea ceremony). The public is invited (free) to partake of the frothy *matcha,* a grass-green tea made from the delicate tips of 400-year-old bushes. To find delight and sanctuary in this centuries-old ritual among the clatter and noise of Waikiki offers a tiny glimpse into the often puzzling duality of the Japanese soul.

As you walk along Kalakaua Avenue, directly across from Waikiki Beach proper is **St. Augustine Catholic Church.** This modernistic building squashed between high-rises is worth a quick look. The interior, serene with the diffused light of stained glass, looks like a series of A-frames.

Believe it or not, you should pass through the McDonald's at the Royal Hawaiian Shopping Center to see a permanent collection of Hawaiian art on display. Among the exhibits are carvings, paintings, macrame, and featherwork. Many of the works are by Rocky Kaiouliokahihikoloehu Jensen, a famous island artist.

Even if you're not a guest at the following hotels, you should at least drop by their lobbies for a quick look. Dramatically different, they serve almost as a visual record of Waikiki's changing history. The **Moana Hotel,** the oldest, dating from 1901, is a permanent reminder of simpler times when its illustrious clientele would dance the night away at an open-air nightclub suspended over the sea. The Moana houses the Banyan Court, named for the enormous banyan tree just outside. From here, "Hawaii Calls" beamed Hawaiian music to the Mainland by shortwave for 40 years beginning in 1935. In its heyday, the show was carried by over 700 stations. The hotel's architecture is a classic example of the now quaint "colonial style."

Across the street are the giant, modernistic, twin towers of the **Hyatt Regency.** The lobby, like most Hyatts, is wonderful, with a huge waterfall and a jungle of plants, all stepped down the series of floors, making an effect like the "Hanging Gardens of Babylon." The **Pacific Beach Hotel,** at 2490 Kalakaua Ave., is a first-rate hotel and a great place to stay in its own right. But if you don't, definitely visit the lobby, where the Oceanarium Restaurant has an immense three-floor-high aquarium dedicated to holding 280,000 gallons of sea water. The old mafia dons used to send their rivals to "sleep with the fishes"; here, you have an opportunity to dine with the fishes. Usually you go snorkeling to watch the fish eat, but in this particular instance the fish watch you eat.

The **Royal Hawaiian Hotel,** built in 1927 on the site of the old royal beach house, once had fresh pineapple juice running in its fountains. Now surrounded by towering hotels, it's like a guppy in a sea of whales. However, it does stand out with its Spanish-Moorish style, painted in distinctive pink. In the old days, only celebrities and luminaries came to stay—who else could afford $3 per day? Although it's younger than the Moana, many consider it the grande dame of Hawaiian hotels. The entranceway is elegantly old-fashioned, with rounded archways, overstuffed couches, and lowboys. You pass through the lobby on a shocking cerise and green rug. All the rooms are appointed in the trademark pink, with matching towels, sheets, and pillowcases. When you visit the Royal Hawaiian, the most elegant lobby is not where you check in. Rather, turn right from there and follow the long hallway toward the sea. This becomes an open breezeway, with arches and columns in grand style. You'll come to a small circular area in the hotel. Here is the heart, with Diamond Head framed in the distance.

Battery Randolph Military Museum

The museum at Battery Randolph, with the hulks of tanks standing guard, is one long corridor where you feel the strength of the super-thick reinforced walls of this once-active gun emplacement. Located at Fort DeRussy, on the corner of Kalia and Saratoga roads, free guided tour, open Tues.-Sun. 10 a.m.-4:30 p.m., tel. 543-2687. The U.S. Battery Randolph once housed two 14-inch coast artillery rifles meant to defend Honolulu and Pearl harbors. The architecture is typical of the Taft Period forts constructed between 1907 and 1920. The battery is listed in the National Register of Historic Places. As you enter there is a shop dedicated to "things military," flying jackets to wall posters. Walk the halls to learn the military history of Hawaii traced as far back as Kamehameha I. Here are rifles, swords, and vintage photos of Camp McKinley, a turn-of-the-century military station in the shadow of Diamond Head.

A side room holds models of artillery used to defend Waikiki from times when Battery Ran-

Fort DeRussy tank

Moana Hotel

dolph was an active installation. One room shows how the guns worked in a method called "disappearing guns." The gun would raise up and fire and then disappear. The recoil of the gun would lock it back in position, and after it was reloaded a 50-ton counterweight would pop it up ready to fire. The explosive sound would rattle the entire neighborhood so they were seldom test-fired.

Exhibits show the fledgling days of Army aviation in Hawaii when on July 13, 1913, 14 officers began a military flying school. There are beautiful models of military equipment, especially one of an old truck unit. Then comes the ominous exhibit of "Rising Japan" with its headlong thrust into WW II. Hawaii, grossly overconfident, felt immune to attack because of the strong military presence. Photos from the '30s and '40s depict the carefree lifestyle of visiting celebrities like Babe Ruth and Shirley Temple, which ended abruptly on December 7, 1941 in the bombing of Pearl Harbor.

An entire room is dedicated to the Pearl Harbor attack and is filled with models of Japanese planes, aircraft carriers, and real helmets and goggles worn by the Zero pilots. Most interesting are the slice-of-life photos of Hawaii mobilized for war: defense workers, both men and women, sailors, soldiers, entertainers, and street scenes. Pamphlets from the time read, "Know Your Enemies," and there's a macabre photo of people gathered at a stadium to see a demonstration of the devasting effect of flame throwers that would

be employed upon the Japanese enemy. Bob Hope is here entertaining the troops, while a 442nd Regimental Battle Flag bears testament to the most decorated unit in American history, comprised mostly of *nisei* Japanese from Hawaii. Then come photos and exhibits from the soul-wrenching conflicts in Korea and Vietnam. Finally a room, like a whispering tomb, tells of the heroics of Hawaiian soldiers who have been awarded the Congressional Medal of Honor, almost all posthumously.

Make sure to go outside to the upper level exhibit where you'll see one of the old guns still pointing out to sea, which seems incongruous with sunbathers just below on the quiet and beautiful stretch of beach. On the upper deck are depth charges, torpedoes, and shells, along with a multimedia slide show. Your eyes will take a few minutes to refocus to the glorious sunshine of Waikiki after the cold gloom of the bunker. Perhaps our hearts and souls could refocus as well.

WAIKIKI BEACHES AND PARKS

In the six miles of shoreline from Gray's Beach fronting the Halekulani Hotel in central Waikiki to Wailupe Beach Park in Maunalua Bay just east of the Kahala Hilton, there are at least 17 choice spots for enjoying surf activities. Most of the central Waikiki beaches are so close to each other you can hardly tell where one ends and another begins. All of these are generally gentle, but as you head east the beaches get farther apart and have their own personalities. Sometimes they're rough customers. As always, never take *moana* for granted, especially during periods of high surf. To get information on the presence of lifeguards, call Honolulu Water Safety, tel. 922-3888; handicapped people can get information on specialized beach facilities and parks by calling 586-8121. Now that you've finally arrived at a Waikiki beach, the one thing left to do is kick back and R-E-L-A-X.

Waikiki Beach stretches for two miles, broken into separate areas. A multitude of concession stands offer everything from shave ice to canoe rides. It's not news that this beach is crowded. Sometimes when looking at the rows of glistening bodies, it appears that if one person wants to tan his other side, everybody else has to roll over with him. Anyone looking for seclusion here is just being silly. Take heart—a big part of the fun is the other people.

Umbrella stands set up along Waikiki Beach fronting Kalakaua rent boogie boards, surfboards, paddle boats, and snorkel gear. They're convenient, but their prices are much more ($5 for two hours) than many shops offering the same equipment (see "Out and About—Sports and Recreation"). The guys by the big banyan tree are slightly cheaper than those set up by the breakwater just before Kapiolani Park. However, all offer decent prices for surfing lessons ($15 per hour including board and lesson, stand-

ing guaranteed), and a $5 ride on an outrigger canoe, which gets you three waves and about 20 minutes of fun. Bargaining is acceptable.

Gray's Beach

This westernmost section's name comes from Gray's-by-the-Sea, a small inn once located here. The narrow white-sand beach lies in front of the Halekulani Hotel, which replaced Gray's. Take Lewers Street off Kalakaua Avenue and park along Kalia Road; a right-of-way is between the Reef and Halekulani hotels. The sea is generally mild here and the swimming is always good, with shallow waters and a sandy bottom. Offshore is a good break called **No. 3's,** a favorite with surfers.

Next door is **Royal Moana Beach,** lying between Waikiki's oldest manmade landmarks, the Moana and Royal Hawaiian hotels. Access is unlimited off Kalakaua Avenue. The inshore waters here are gentle and the bottom is sandy and generally free from coral. Offshore are three popular surfing areas, **Popular's, Queen's,** and **Canoes.** Many novices have learned to surf here because of the predictability of the waves, but with so many rookies in the water, and beach activities going on all around, you have to remain alert for runaway boards and speeding canoes.

Waikiki Beach Center
And Prince Kuhio Beach Center

When people say "Waikiki Beach," this is the section to which they're referring. Both beaches

Waikiki

front Kalakaua Avenue, and a long sand retaining wall called Slippery Wall fronts both beaches, creating a semienclosed saltwater pool. Here, you'll find surfing, canoeing, snorkeling, and safe year-round swimming along the gently sloping, sandy-bottomed shoreline. There are comfort stations, concession stands, and lifeguards. Be careful of the rough coral bottom at the Diamond Head end of Kuhio Beach. Covered with a coating of slick seaweed, Slippery Wall definitely lives up to its name. Though local youngsters play on the wall, the footing is poor and many knees have been scraped and heads cracked after spills from this ill-advised play. The surf on the seaward side of the wall churns up the bottom and creates deep holes that come up unexpectedly, along with an occasional rip current.

Kapiolani Beach Park

This is the only park along Waikiki with facilities for barbecueing and picnicking. Although it's only a short stroll down the beach from Waikiki, it gets much less use. This is where local families and those in the know come to get away from the crowds. In the park and along the beach are restrooms, volleyball courts, picnic tables, lifeguard towers, a bath house, and a concession stand. Activities include surfing, fishing, snorkeling, and year-round safe swimming. Just be careful of the rocky bottom that pops up unexpectedly here and there. Kapiolani Park incorporates **Sans Souci Beach** at the eastern end. This beach, in front of the Colony Surf and Kamaaina hotels, has unlimited access. Changing facilities are found at the deteriorating Honolulu Natatorium, a saltwater pool built in the '20s. Many families with small children come to Sans Souci because it is so gentle.

The **Natatorium** is in a sad state. Battles rage on whether it should be refurbished or torn down. Unless something has been done by the time you arrive, it's better to avoid its murky waters. Be careful of the rocky areas and dangerous dropoffs along the channel, especially in front of the Natatorium. **Kapiolani Park Center** is the beach closest to Waikiki. The swimming is good here, with the best part at the Waikiki end. The beach is at its widest, and the bottom is gently sloping sand. The area called **The Wall** has been designated as a special

bodysurfing area. Supposedly, board riders are restricted from this area, but if the surf is good they're guaranteed to break the rules. Experts can handle it, but novices, especially with runaway boards, are a hazard.

Around Diamond Head

Kaluahole Beach is located at the Waikiki side of Diamond Head. The water conditions are safe all year-round, but the beach is small and lies along a seawall. Once a large beach, it was paved over for building purposes. It has one public right-of-way, poorly marked and sandwiched between private homes. It's almost at the end at 3837 Kalakaua Avenue. The surfing in this area is generally good, and the breaks are known as "Tongg's," named after a local family that lived along this shore.

Diamond Head Beach Park is an unlimited access area along Beach Road (marked). It covers almost two acres of undeveloped shoreline. Unfortunately, the beach is very narrow and surrounded by unfriendly rock and coral. The waters, however, are quite protected and generally safe, except in periods of high surf. This area is good for fishing and finding quiet moments.

Kuilei Cliffs Beach Park lies below Diamond Head Road, with access available from three lookout areas along the road. You must walk down the cliff trails to the beaches below. Here are plenty of secluded pockets of sand for sunbathing, but poor swimming. The surf is generally rough, and the area is always frequented by surfers. Offshore is hazardous with submerged rocks, but this makes it excellent for diving and snorkeling—for experts only! Currents can be fierce, and you can be dashed against the rocks. Whales can sometimes be spotted passing this point, and to add to the mystique, the area is considered a breeding ground for sharks. Most visitors just peer down at the surfers from Diamond Head Road, or choose a spot of beach for peace and quiet.

Farther east is **Kaalawai Beach.** The swimming is good here and generally safe because of a protecting reef. Many locals come to this area to fish, and it is good for bodysurfing and snorkeling. The waters outside the reef are excellent for surfing, and produce some of the biggest waves on this side of the island. Access is by public right-of-way, marked off Ku-lumanu Place, or a small side road running off Kahala Avenue, or by walking along the shore-line from Kuilei Beach.

Kahala Beach, lying along Kahala Avenue, can be reached by a number of marked rights-of-way located between the high fences of es-tates in the area. The swimming is not particu-larly good, but there are plenty of pockets of sand and protected areas where you can swim and snorkel. Local people come to fish, and the surfing is good beyond the reef. The Ka-hala Hilton is located along this beach at the eastern end. The public can use "their" beach by walking from Kahala Beach. The swimming here is always safe and good because the hotel has dredged the area to make it deeper. Con-cession stands and lifeguards are provided by the hotel.

Wailupe Beach Park lies on the Waikiki side of Wailupe Peninsula in Maunalua Bay, and is the last beach covered by this chapter. This beach park, clearly marked off the Kalaniana'ole Highway, provides restrooms and picnic facili-ties. The swimming is safe, but the bottom can have either oozy mud or sharp coral in spots. Be careful of the boat channel surrounding the area because the deep dropoff is very abrupt.

ACCOMMODATIONS

Waikiki is loaded with places to stay: 170 prop-erties holding 30,000 rooms jammed into one square mile. And they come in all categories of hotels and condos, from deluxe to dingy. Your problem won't be finding a place to stay, but choosing from the enormous selection. Dur-ing "peak season" (Christmas to Easter and again in summer) you'd better have reserva-tions, or you could easily be left out in the *warm*. The good news is that, room for room, Waikiki is the cheapest place to stay in the state. Hotels along the beach tend to be slightly more ex-pensive than their counterparts on a side street or back lane. The beachfront hotels have the surf at the doorstep, but those a block away have a little more peace and quiet. The follow-ing listings are not exhaustive. They couldn't be! Here is just the best from all categories which you can use as a barometer to measure what's available.

INEXPENSIVE

Youth Hostels
Hale Aloha Youth Hostel is located in Waikiki at 2417 Prince Edward St., Honolulu, HI 96815, tel. 926-8313. Walk down Kalakaua until you see the Hyatt Regency. Two streets directly be-hind is Prince Edward. Directions are also avail-able at the Airport Information Counter. A dorm room bunk is $12. Couples only can rent a stu-dio for $25, which has to be reserved at least two weeks in advance with first night's deposit. No credit cards. The business office is open 8-10 a.m. and 5-9 p.m. The hostel closes at 11 p.m. and all must leave daily 10 a.m.-5 p.m. The maximum three-day stay, especially during peak seasons, can sometimes be extended at the discretion of the house parent. Requests must be made before 7:30 p.m. the previous day. Baggage may be left for the day for $1. Key de-posits will not be returned if keys are not re-turned by 10 a.m. Visitors are not allowed at any time. No alcohol or smoking. Chores are required. Lockers available.

Inter Club Hostel Waikiki, at 2413 Kuhio Ave., Honolulu, HI 96815, tel. 924-2636, has kitchen and laundry facilities and a relaxed is-land-style lounge. You must be an international traveler or an American with an onward-going ticket to bunk here. Rooms are dorm style (five beds in each), $15 per night plus $10 return-able "care deposit"; $45 double rooms, $10 key deposit. They accept reservations.

Hawaiian Seaside Hostel, 419 Seaside and Kuhio, Honolulu, HI 96815, tel. 924-3306, is a private hostel for international travelers, who must show a passport and an onward-going ticket. United States citizens are welcomed if they are travelers bound for a foreign destina-tion (onward-going ticket necessary). Rates are $9.75 for the first night, plus a $5.25 deposit which is returnable upon checkout. After the first night, the rates go up to $13 per night. Accommodations are in nine mixed dorms, each with five bunks. Each dorm has a complete kitchen and a bathroom, and other helpful amenities include free safe deposits, free long-term storage, laundry facilities, a lounge with a wide-screen TV, and free videos. The hostel, located on a cul-de-sac, is quiet for being so close to the action, and there is a lanai where you can socialize. Most of the international travelers that you will find there are Australians, British, Germans, and Swedes.

When the YHs are full try the **Waikiki Prince** just next door to Hale Aloha YH, at 2431 Prince Edward St., tel. 922-1544. Listed as a hotel, it is about the cheapest in Waikiki at about $25-35 per night during low season.

The **Waikiki Hostel** for now, but their name changes regularly, at 1946 Ala Moana Blvd. no. 212, Honolulu, HI 96815, tel. 949-3382, offers dormitory rooms at $10 the first two nights, $14 thereafter, $90 weekly. All dorm rooms have a/c, cable TV, a fridge, and a bath. The hostel provides laundry facilities and limited cooking facilities along with free tea and coffee, boogie boards, and masks. They'll also shuttle you to and from the airport (free) if their van is running.

Honolulu's YM/WCAs and official American Youth Hostel are near, but not technically in Waikiki. Find a complete list under "Honolulu—Accommodations."

Inexpensive Hotels And Condos

The **Waikiki Hana Hotel** at 2424 Koa Ave., Honolulu HI 96815, tel. 926-8841 or (800) 367-5004, sits just behind the massive Hyatt Regency on a quiet side street. The hotel has just 73 rooms, so you won't get lost in the shuffle, and the friendly staff go out of their way to make you feel welcome. The Waikiki Hana is surrounded by high-rise hotels, so there's no view, but the peace and quiet just one block from the heavy action more than makes up for it. Rooms start at a very reasonable $80 and go to $115 for a superior with kitchenette. All rooms have telephones, a/c, color TV, in-room safes, and are gaily appointed with bright bedspreads and drapes. The **Super Chef Restaurant**, on the ground floor of the hotel, is one of the best in Waikiki for atmosphere, food, and very reasonable prices. On-site parking is another good feature in crowded Waikiki. For a quiet, decent, but basic hotel in the heart of Waikiki, the Waikiki Hana can't be beat!

The **Waikiki Beachside Apartment Hotel,** at 2556 Lemon Rd., Honolulu, HI 96815, tel. 923-9566, is owned and operated by Mr. and Mrs. Wong, who keep a close eye on who they admit, as they run a very "decent" clean hotel. They rent weekly and monthly, charging from $285 to $1000, off-season cheaper. Per diem rooms are sometimes available, but you have to speak to Mrs. Wong first. Furnished units have full kitchens and baths with twin beds and a convertible sofa and accommodate up to three people at no extra charge. There are laundry facilities, but no maid service is available. Reservations are reluctantly accepted (they like to see you first), and parking is extra. Mrs. Wong says that they are going to renovate the hotel because it has become run-down. There are no firm plans for completion, but when and if they are carried out, the rates will go up. Be advised!

The **Outrigger Coral Seas Hotel,** at 250 Lewers St., Honolulu, HI 96815, tel. 923-3881 or (800) 367-5170, is an old standby for budget travelers. This is the epitome of the economy tourist hotel and houses **Perry's Smorgasbord.** It's one of the Outrigger Hotels, and seems to get all the hand-me-downs from the others in the chain. There's a restaurant, cocktail lounge, TV, pool, and parking. Rates are an economical $65-75, extra person $15, and just a few dollars more for a kitchenette. Not to everyone's taste, but with plenty of action and the beach is only a few steps away.

The **Edgewater Hotel,** at 2168 Kalia Rd., Honolulu, HI 96815, tel. 922-6424, is another budget standby in the palpitating heart of Waikiki. Rates begin at a reasonable $45 s, to $110 for a suite, $15 extra person. Facilities include a swimming pool, a good Italian restaurant, parking, TV, and maid service. Kitchenettes cost slightly extra.

The **Royal Grove Hotel,** at 151 Uluniu Ave., Honolulu, HI 96815, tel. 923-7691, run by the Fong family, gives you a lot for your money. You can't miss its "paint-sale pink" exterior, but inside it's much more tasteful. The older and cheaper wing is about $40 per room, the newer upgraded wing with a/c is around $45-75. Most are studios and one-bedroom apartments with full facilities. A tiny pool in the central courtyard offers some peace and quiet away from the street. The Royal Grove passes the basic tests of friendliness and cleanliness. It's used but not abused. During low season they offer reduced weekly and monthly rates.

Hale Pua Nui, at 228 Beachwalk, Honolulu, HI 96815, tel. 923-9693 or 921-4398, offers very reasonable accommodations only a few minutes walk from Waikiki Beach. A studio apartment with a kitchenette is only $40 off season, and $55 during peak season, additional person $5. Hale Pua Nui, clean and adequate, is a touch above spartan, with ceiling fans but no a/c, cable TV, phone, and fully equipped kitchen. Unfortunately, the "House of the Big Flower" is a bit wilted. The hotel is geared to repeat clientele, mostly from Canada, who book a year in advance, and not really open to new clientele, especially those who just drop in. If you want a room, call well in advance, and they will send you a form with the house rules (plenty). Remember, too, that there is no elevator, so you must carry your bags to the upper floors.

A two-minute walk puts you on Waikiki Beach when you stay at the **Waikiki Malihini Hotel,** 217 Saratoga Road, Honolulu, HI 96815, tel. 923-9644 or 923-3095, which bills itself as a "small, plain hotel with no extra frills. Just a place to stay in an excellent location." And, that's just what it is! In a semi-quiet area just across from Fort De Russy, the hotel's 30 units have kitchenettes, daily maid service, fans (no a/c in most units), rental TV, and convenient but not complimentary parking next door. The management, not unfriendly but not overly congenial either, "strongly requests" that you contact them and fill out a card that will inform them of your dates-of-stay, number-in-party, etc., *before* they will make reservations. A well laid lava rock wall in front provides some privacy for a small picnic area complete with tables and charcoal grills. Rates are studios $45-48, lanai studios $50-55, and one-bedroom apartments $65-75 (some have a/c). There's a three-day minimum stay during peak season, and payment is by cash only!

MODERATE HOTELS AND CONDOS

The **Queen Kapiolani Hotel** is at 150 Kapahulu Ave., Honolulu, HI 96815, tel. 922-1941 or (800) 367-5004. With its off-the-strip location and magnificent views of Diamond Head, this is perhaps the best, and definitely the quietest, hotel for the money in Waikiki. You're only seconds from the beach, and the hotel provides a spacious lobby, parking, a restaurant, TV, a/c, shops, and a swimming pool. Rates begin at $110 standard to $120 for a superior; a few rooms have kitchenettes. The main lobby has been rejuvenated with a $2 million face-lift. The stately marble columns have been redone, new wallpaper has been applied, and the shopping area has been upgraded. The overall effect is open and airy with the living mural of Diamond Head in the background. Select rooms have been made first-class with new carpeting, draperies, furnishing, and amenities. Most boast a spectacular view of Diamond Head. An excellent choice for the money; for reservations write directly to Hawaiian Pacific Resorts, 1150 S. King St., Honolulu, HI 96814, tel. 531-5235. Also featured, in the Peacock Dining Room, is one of the best buffets in Waikiki (see "Food—Moderate").

You can't beat the value at the **Pacific Monarch Hotel/Condo** located directly behind the Hyatt Regency at 142 Uluniu Ave., Honolulu, HI 96815, tel. 923-9805 or (800) 777-1700. It offers some great features for a moderately priced hotel. Fully furnished studios begin at $95, one-bedroom apartments from $130, all a/c, with on-site parking; standard rooms are available, too. The rooms are bright and cheery with full baths, living/dining areas, and cable TV. End units of each floor are larger, so request one for a large or shared party. The swimming pool, with a relaxing jacuzzi, perches high over Waikiki on the 34th floor of the hotel, offering one of the best cityscapes in Honolulu. The lobby is sufficient but small. It's accented with a lava fountain and two giant brass doors. A security key allows guests through the main door to the elevators. Save money and have a great family experience by setting up temporary housekeeping at the Pacific Monarch.

The **Outrigger Hotels** chain has 23 locations in and around Waikiki offering thousands of rooms. Many of the hotels are on quiet side streets, others are on the main drags, while still more perch on Waikiki Beach. Although most are not luxurious, they do offer good accommodations and all have pools, restaurants, a/c, TV, and parking. Rates vary slightly from hotel to hotel: some have kitchen facilities and cost $75 d to $300 for a suite, $10-15 extra person. Special discounts of 20% are offered to travelers over 50 years old. For information contact Outrigger Hotels Central Reservations, 3443 S. Galena Dr., Denver, CO 80231, tel. (800) 462-6262. Three of their best hotels in Waikiki are the **Outrigger Reef, Outrigger Waikiki** (both on the beach), and the **Outrigger Prince Kuhio.**

You can capitalize on the off-beach location of the **Aston Honolulu Prince,** at 415 Nahua St., Honolulu, HI 96815, tel. 922-1616 or (800) 922-7866, where you'll find a hotel/condo offering remarkably good value for your money. The hotel/condo, under the auspices of general manager Charles St. Sure, invites you into its fully furnished one- and two-bedroom suites. All offer a/c, color cable TV, fully equipped kitchens, and daily maid service. Prices begin at $80 for a standard room, $125 one bedroom, and $145 two bedroom, with substantial discounts during low season. The apartments are oversized, with a huge sitting area that includes a sofa bed for extra guests. The Honolulu Prince is not fancy, but it is clean, decent, and family-oriented. A fine choice for a memorable vacation at affordable prices.

The **Breakers Hotel,** 250 Beach Walk, Honolulu, HI 96815, tel. 923-3181 or (800) 426-0494, is a very friendly family-style hotel, where if you're a repeat visitor, the staff remembers your name. Only minutes from the beach, this little gem of a hotel somehow keeps the hustle and bustle far away. Every room has a kitchenette and overlooks the shaded courtyard of coconut and banana trees. The rates for studios are $88-95 s, $91-97 d, additional person $8. The garden suites, which are equipped for up to four people, are $120-146. All units have a full kitchenette, a/c, color TV, a safe, and limited parking. There is also a swimming pool, and the Hotel Cafe Terrace where you can have a snack or light meal. Studios begin at $75, one bedroom at $110, all fully furnished.

The **Waikikian Hotel,** 1811 Ala Moana Blvd., Honolulu, HI 96815, tel. 949-5331 or (800) 367-5124, is at the north end of Waikiki near the Ala Moana Boat Harbor and is surrounded by ultramodern high-rise hotels. This character-laden hotel is only two stories, and is an enclave of peace amidst hustle and bustle. There is a feeling of days gone by as you move down the charming walkway through painstakingly cared-for grounds. Ferns, palms, and flowers line the walk, and at night it is accentuated with lighted torches. If you know what to expect you'll be happy with this hotel; not luxury, but a double dip of character. The grounds front the very safe beach of the Hilton Hawaiian Village Lagoon with a short walk to the waves of Waikiki. Prices are reasonable beginning at $77, with family suites for $140.

Sometimes you just hit it lucky, and find yourself in a situation where you get more for your money than you expected, and delightfully so. The **Waikiki Beachcomber Hotel,** 2300 Kalakaua Ave., Honolulu, HI 96815, tel. 922-4646, (800) 622-4646 Mainland, or (800) 338-6233 Canada, is definitely one of those *sometimes* things. The Beachcomber, living up to its name, is just a minute from the beach, and with a professional and amiable staff, knows exactly what you want and how to deliver it. The guest rooms, outfitted in rattan furniture and painted in soothing tropical tones, all feature a private lanai, a/c, TV, phone, and convenient refrigerator. On the property is a pool, the Beachcomber Restaurant, long famous for its live KCCN Aloha Friday Luncheon Buffet, boutique shops, and a lounge for evening relaxation. The rates for guest rooms range from $120 to $280 for a suite with $15 for an additional person, children under 17 free in their parents' room. A fantastic special at only $99 puts you in a city view room with a rental car included or a breakfast buffet for two. To stay within budget, while having a quality experience, the Beachcomber is a sure bet!

The **Ilima Hotel,** 445 Nohonai St., Honolulu, HI 96815, tel. 923-1877 or (800) 367-5172, is two streets back from the Ala Wai Canal and overlooks the Ala Wai Golf Course. This condostyle hotel is a few blocks from the beach—quiet atmosphere and budget rates. They have just completed a $1.5 million renovation, featuring waveless waterbeds in their deluxe suites.

Studio units begin at a reasonable $86, $10 extra pp, one bedroom $109, two bedroom $176. All units have full kitchens, a/c, and TV, along with a pool, parking, and maid service. Good value.

Miramar at Waikiki, 2345 Kuhio Ave., Honolulu, HI 96815, tel. 922-2077 or (800) 367-2303, is in the heart of Waikiki. The hotel, refurbished and renamed in the last few years, offers generous-size rooms, with lanai, a pool, a restaurant, a/c, TV, and parking. Rates range from $90-105, $20 extra per person.

All you have to do is literally roll out of bed, walk out your door, and pick a spot on Waikiki Beach when you stay at the **Aston Waikiki Shores Condominium,** at 2161 Kalia Rd., Honolulu, HI 96815, tel. 926-4733 or (800) 367-2353. Individually owned, the decor in each unit differs, but most are tasteful with island-style furnishings, and all are immense. Typical is a one-bedroom laid out with a sitting area, living room, dining area, two baths with dressing rooms, and a kitchen complete with microwave, dishwasher, coffee maker, and garbage disposal. To make your stay more pleasant, there's daily maid service, private lanai, cable TV, in-room washers and dryers, beach towels, limited parking, and children stay free with their parents. Rates, especially for what you get, are very reasonable, and start at $150 for a studio with deluxe ocean view, and go up to $385 for a two bedroom deluxe ocean front (10% off-season discount, ask!).

A reasonably priced accommodation is the **Coconut Plaza Hotel,** at 450 Lewers St., tel. 923-8828 or (800) 882-9696. Rates are about $100 for a double during peak season. Off-season is cheaper, with a special day rate of $50 for bona fide business travelers. A complimentary continental breakfast is offered daily in the lobby. All rooms are fully air-conditioned, and there is a hotel pool.

Twinkling lights descending the residential valleys of the Koolaus with Diamond Head framed in perfect symmetry are an integral part of the natural room decor of the **Aston Waikiki Sunset Hotel,** 229 Paoakalani St., Honolulu, HI 96815, tel. 922-0511, (800) 922-7866 Mainland, or (800) 321-2558 Hawaii, one of Waikiki's newest suite-hotels. Charmingly refurbished from head to toe in 1991, the Waikiki Sunset, al-

though *feeling* like a condominium, offers all of the comfort and convenience of a hotel including 24-hour front desk service, daily maid service, and amenities like a swimming pool, sauna, tennis court, travel desk, mini-mart, and even a restaurant. The entrance, cooled by Casablanca fans whirring over marble floors, sets the mood for this charming hotel tucked away only one block from the Waikiki strip. Suites range from comfortable studios at $119, to deluxe two-bedroom units for $315 (penthouse available). All feature full kitchens outfitted with a large refrigerator, coffee maker, electric stove and oven, disposal, and complete utensils for in-room cooking and dining. All suites feature a private lanai and entertainment center with remote-control color TV, and a tiled bath with a Japanese-style *ofuro,* a soaking tub perfect for the start of a cozy evening. The larger suites have a sitting room, modern and chic with rattan furniture, a bar/breakfast nook, and separate master bedroom. The **Manbow Inn,** on the sixth floor, open 7:30 a.m.-9 p.m., serves breakfast, lunch, and dinner at reasonable prices. The mini-mart, open 7 a.m.-11 p.m., provides everything from suntan lotion to takeout pizza. Here, too, you can rent sporting equipment like snorkel sets and boogie boards, with a 10% discount offered to hotel guests.

Varying shades of Italian Trabertine marble covered with pink floral carpets, filigreed mirrors, tables of black lacquer bearing Chinese porcelains, and ornate Louis XV chests under cut crystal chandeliers are the signature touches of the chinoiserie decor (combination of Chinese and European) at the **Aston Waikiki Beachside Hotel,** 2452 Kalakaua Avenue, Honolulu, HI 96815, tel. 931-2100, (800) 922-7866 Mainland, (800) 445-6633 Canada, or (800) 321-2558 Hawaii, another of Aston's boutique hotels. A Chinese lord and his concubine sit under an umbrella in a hand-painted silk portrait, while two bronze lions guard the marble staircase leading to a formal parlor on the second floor. Here, white silk couches with puffy pillows, a magnificent Chinese folding screen depicting courtly life, and an 18th-century Chinese secretary in red and black lacquer especially made for the "British market" are the decor. Outside, a tiny courtyard serenaded by a bubbling Italian fountain is set with wooden tables protected by canvas umbrellas. Mornings are perfect here with complimentary coffee and croissants. In the 12 floors above, only 77 luxurious rooms await, ranging in price from $160 for a superior to $290 for a VIP ocean front (ask for discounted specials). Small, but space-consciously designed, the rooms are vibrant with melba peach carpet and wallpaper with a counterpoint of black. Amenities include air-conditioning, or functional windows to catch the Waikiki breeze, an entertainment center with remote-control color TV and VCR, a mini-fridge stocked with a selection of complimentary soft drinks, and a voice mail message system. Your stay is made even more relaxing with twice daily maid service and turndown service with a special treat left on your pillow, a free morning newspaper, and concierge service for all activities and travel plans. Tastefully decorated, the rooms are appointed with Chinese vases, folding screens painted with birds and flowers, jewelry boxes, and goosedown pillows imported from London. The bathrooms are done in Italian marble and feature glass shower stalls (no baths), floor-to-ceiling mirrors, pedestal sinks with black fixtures from Germany, his-and-her *yukata* (robes), a makeup mirror, a hair dryer, and bath products including shampoo, moisturizer, and French-milled soaps. Ocean view rooms have their own lanai, but be aware that some inside rooms are windowless.

A tunnel of white thumbergia tumbling from a welcoming arbor leads to the entrance of the **Aston Waikiki Beach Tower Hotel,** 2470 Kalakaua Ave. Honolulu, HI 96815, tel. 926-6400, (800) 922-7866 Mainland, or (800) 321-2558 Hawaii, one of Waikiki's newest mini-luxury suite hotels. A lustrous patina shines from brown on tan marble floors while glass-topped tables of black and gold lacquer hold magnificent displays of exotic blooms, and fancy French mirrors and cut glass chandeliers brighten the small but intimate reception area. Enter your suite through a vestibule of brown marble and glass onto a white carpet leading to a combination dining/living room. This common area, accented with contemporary paintings and highlighted by koa trim, offers a full wet bar, drum and glass tables, high-backed chairs, a pastel rainbow couch, and an entertainment center with remote-control TV. The ultramodern kitchen is complete with standard-sized refrigerator with ice maker, a rice cooker, a blender, a coffee maker, a microwave, a four-burner stove and oven, a dishwasher, a double sink, and koa cabinets. The master bedroom has its own entertainment center and private lanai from which you can overlook Waikiki. The bathroom has a double sink, commode, and shower, and a huge walk-in closet holding a complimentary safe, steam iron and board, and a washer and dryer. Rates range from $305 for a one-bedroom superior to $475 for a two-bedroom deluxe with the two-bedroom penthouse at $575, and the two-bedroom Presidential at $800. Special amenities include twice daily maid service, turndown service, concierge desk, valet parking, a paddle tennis court, a swimming pool, spa and sauna, and also meeting rooms and a family plan.

Upon arrival, step onto a path of white tile leading through a tiny but robust garden to a translucent dome sheltering the outdoor reception area of the **Aston Waikiki Joy Hotel,** a lotus flower that blooms in the heart of Waikiki, at 320 Lewers St., Honolulu, HI 96815, tel. 923-2300, (800) 922-7866 Mainland, or (800) 321-2558 Hawaii. Blocks of glass, veined marbles in pinks, whites, and grays, and polished chrome are part of its petals. Immediately, marble steps rise to a veranda, where every morning a complimentary continental breakfast is served accompanied by the soft background chanting of a tiny fountain. The hotel, with only 94 rooms is divided into two towers, the Hibiscus and the Gardenia (housing only suites). It's intimate enough to make everyone feel like an honored guest. Typical rooms in the Hibiscus Tower, $99-125, are amazingly spacious. You enter through a vestibule to find an ultramodern room of slate blue and pastel pink contrasted with the embossed effect of a tan Berber carpet. Two accommodating wicker chairs wait to hug you with their overstuffed pillow arms. At the foot of each bed is an ottoman, great for perching on while dressing, and a dresser built in as part of the wall. The hotel rooms each feature a refrigerator and writing desk, which has a believable rendition of Miss Muffet's tuffet as its chair. A king-sized bed with a slanted headboard perfectly designed for propping pillows is the "nerve center" of the room. Here, in easy reach, is a dimmer switch for all lighting, a temperature control, and a phone featuring a personalized voice message system. In front of the bed is an entertainment center with remote-control color TV and a stereo system with tape deck. The bathroom, done in pastel barber stripes, is a sanctuary of relaxation where you can slide every evening into a large and bubbling jacuzzi tub. The suites, in the Gardenia Tower, $120-220, feature a bedroom and attendant sitting area complete with couch, and a large private lanai. Suite kitchens have a standard-sized refrigerator, two-burner stove, double sink, microwave, toaster, and coffee maker. Here too, the bathrooms feature the wonderful jacuzzi tub. The Waikiki Joy is also very special with a 15-room karaoke studio, the largest and most modern in Waikiki (reservations recommended). The karaoke studio also features a lounge at the entrance, open weekdays 5 p.m.-2 a.m., weekends until 4 a.m., where you can order exotic drinks, standard cocktails, assorted iced teas, and island inspired *pu pu* from tofu to breaded calamari sticks. The hotel restaurant is **Cappucino's** (see "Food") a European-style bistro featuring live entertainment on the weekends. The Waikiki Joy, aptly named, is the epitome of the adage that "wonderful things come in small packages," but in this case, the wonderful thing *is* the package!

DELUXE

Hilton Hawaiian Village

This glorious first-rate hotel, an oasis of tranquility, sits in its own quiet corner of Waikiki. The Hilton, at 2005 Kalia Rd., Honolulu, HI 96815, tel. 949-4321 or (800) 445-8667, is at the far western end of Waikiki, just below Fort DeRussy. Enter along 200 yards of the private hotel driveway, passing the village, a small mall with exclusive shopping and dining. Facing you are the Hilton's "towers," the Tapa, the Diamond Head, the Rainbow, and the prestigious Alii Tower. Rainbow Tower, so called because of the huge multistoried rainbow on the entire side of this building, is, according to the *Guinness Book of World Records,* the tallest ceramic-tile mosaic in the world. All the rooms are deluxe with magnificent views. Amenities include color TV,

a/c, self-service bar, refrigerator, 24-hour room service, voice mail, and a safe for personal belongings. Children will also be delighted with the **Rainbow Express,** a year-round program that entertains and educates with everything from hula lessons to a trip to the Honolulu Zoo ($10 half-day, $20 full lunch included).

The Alii Tower pampers you even more with a private pool with nightly gourmet *pu pu,* turndown service, fresh flowers, fruit baskets, concierge service, flowers, a fitness center, a sauna, and bath accessories. Rates are $195-350 throughout the Village, and from $240-375 in the Alii Tower.

The towers form a semicircle fronting the beach, not a private beach because none can be private, but about as private a public beach as you can get. Few come here unless they're staying at the Hilton. It's dotted with palms—tall royal palms for elegance, shorter palms for shade. The property has three pools. The main pool, surrounded by luxuriant tropical growth, is the largest in Waikiki. The lagoon area creates the music of water in bubbling rivulets, tiny waterfalls, and reflecting pools. Torches of fire, and ginger, banana trees, palms, ferns, and rock gardens are the grounds. The concierge can arrange a guided tour of the grounds (free) by a groundskeeper, who will explain the habitat, life cycle, and characteristics of each plant.

The *action* of Waikiki is out there, of course, just down the driveway, but you don't feel it unless you want to. Relax and enjoy the sunset accompanied by music at any one of 10 lounges like the **Shell Bar,** or in the main foyer where another small casual bar swings to the tunes of a piano stylist. Exotic and gourmet dining from throughout the Pacific rim is available at the Village's 10 restaurants, especially the hotel's signature **Bali by the Sea** and **Golden Dragon** restaurants (see "Food").

As you pull into the driveway there's a geodesic dome, like a giant stereo speaker, where headliner John Hirokawa stars in the **Magic of Polynesia,** a magic show and Polynesian extravaganza performed twice nightly. Also, Charro, a superb flamenco guitarist and comedienne, along with her fabulous international "koochie koochie" show, performs in the Tropic Showroom nightly Tues.-Sat. (see "Entertainment" for both). The hotel has everything to keep its "villagers" contented and happy. As a complete destination resort where you can play, relax, shop, dine, dance, and retreat, the Hilton Hawaiian Village knows what it's about and has found its center.

Halekulani Hotel

The Halekulani Hotel, in mid-Waikiki at 2199 Kalia Rd., Honolulu, HI 96815, tel. 923-2311 or (800) 367-2343, was an experiment of impeccable taste that paid off. A few years ago the hotel was completely rebuilt and refurnished with the belief that Waikiki could still attract the luxury-class visitor, and that belief has proven accurate. Since opening, the hotel has gained international recognition, and has been named as a member of the prestigious Leading Hotels of the World, and Preferred Hotels and Resorts Worldwide. The soothing serenade of the Halekulani begins from the moment you enter the porte cochere where an impressive floral display of protea, anthuriums, orchids, and ferns arranged in the *sogetsu* style of *ikebana* by Kanemoto-san awaits to welcome you. The property was first developed in 1907 by Robert Lewers as a residential grouping of bungalows, none of which survive. However, still preserved is the **Main Building,** dating from the 1930s when the hotel became a fashionable resort owned by Juliet and Clifford Kimball. The Main Building, a plantation-style mansion, houses the hotel's award winning **La Mer Restaurant,**

along with the **Orchids Dining Room,** serving breakfast, lunch, and dinner; **Lewer's Lounge** for an intimate cocktail and nightly entertainment; and the very genteel **Living Room,** where you can enjoy afternoon tea and watercress sandwiches (see "Food—Classy Dining," or "Entertainment"). Notice the Main Building's distinctive "Dickey Roof," patterned after a Polynesian longhouse, perfectly sloped in such as way as to catch island breezes while repelling a sudden rain squall. Wander the grounds to be pleasantly surprised that a full 50% is given to open space accented with trimmed lawn, reflecting pools, and bubbling fountains. The **Orchid Pool,** with its signature mosaic orchid, is always inviting and within earshot of the foaming surf. Close by is **House Without a Key,** an indoor/outdoor buffet restaurant also serving light snacks and perhaps the best locale in all of Waikiki for a sunset cocktail. Upon arrival, you are escorted directly to the privacy of your own guest room where you register. Awaiting is a platter of fine china bearing a display of fresh fruit and complimentary "Bakeshop" chocolates. Each evening, with turndown service, a dainty orchid and delicate shell are left upon your pillow, along with a once-per-week recipe card from one of the fine hotel restaurants. Enter the guestroom through a solid teak door into an antechamber that opens into a room, done in seven shades of white. The floors are covered in rich Berber carpet while the king-sized beds are dressed with a distinctive Hawaiian quilt.

the Dragon Room at the Hilton Hawaiian Village

For ultimate relaxation and added convenience, all of the rooms feature a writing desk, small couch, reclining chair, and marble-topped accessory tables softly lit by Oriental-style lamps. A remote controlled entertainment center, minifridge, three telephones, an in-room safe, and a collection of wooden and satin covered hangers complete the amenities. Sliding louvered doors lead to a tiled lanai, private and perfect for in-room dining. The bathroom, with floor to ceiling tile, features a deep soaking tub, a shower stall, two sinks, a separate commode, and a hairdryer. The louvered and glass doors can be opened so that you have a view from your tub directly past the lanai to Diamond Head in the distance. Prices are $245-425 guest room, $580-3500 suite, and $45 extra per person. Additional amenities include swimming pool, beach service, daily newspapers, free local telephone calls, and a full service fitness center where you can sign up to go on a fun run with world-class marathon runner Max Telford. The Halekulani awaits to show you its version of classic island charm. You won't be disappointed.

Sheraton Moana Surfrider

The Moana, at 2365 Kalakaua Ave., Honolulu, HI 96815, tel. 922-3111 or (800) 325-3535, is the oldest and most venerable hotel in Waikiki. Now operated by Sheraton Hotels, it has recently completed a $50 million upgrade, which has restored the class and beauty for which the Moana has long been famous. More than just recapturing turn-of-the-century grandeur, the Moana has surpassed itself by integrating all of the modern conveniences. The original Italian Renaissance style is the main architectural theme, but like a fine opera, it joins a variety of architectural themes that blend into a soul-satisfying finale. The restoration has connected the three main buildings, the Moana, Ocean Lanai, and Surfrider, to form an elegant complex of luxury accommodations, gourmet dining, and distinctive shopping. The renovated Moana, filled with memories of times past, is magical. It's as if you stood spellbound before the portrait of a beautiful princess of long ago, when suddenly her radiant granddaughter, an exact image, dazzling in jewels and grace, walked into the room.

You arrive under the grand columns of a porte cochere, where you are greeted by doormen in crisp white uniforms and hostesses bearing lei and chilled pineapple juice. The lobby is a series of genteel parlor arrangements conducive to very civilized relaxation. Art, urns, chandeliers, sofas, koa tables, flowers, vases, and pedestaled glass-topped tables wait in attendance. An elevator takes you to the second floor, where a room filled with 80 years of memorabilia whispers names and dates of the Moana's grand past. After a fresh chilled glass of pineapple juice, you are escorted to check-in.

Upstairs, the rooms are simple elegance. Queen-sized beds in the Banyan Wing, rattan chairs, and fat fluffy pillows and bedspreads extend their waiting arms. All rooms have a/c, and the Banyan Wing features a remote-control master keyboard for TV, lights, and music. But this is the Moana! Sachet-scented closets hold *yukata* (robes), terry slippers, and satin hangers. Bathrooms are tile and marble appointed with huge towels and stocked with fine soaps, shampoos, creams, makeup mirrors, and a bathroom scale, which you can hide under the bed.

Being the first hotel built in Waikiki, it sits right on the beach with one of the best views of Diamond Head along the strip. A swimming pool with sundeck is staffed with attentive personnel, and the activities center can book you on a host of activities, including a classic outrigger canoe ride or a sunset sail on a catamaran. Three restaurants, a grand ballroom, a snack bar, and two lounges take care of all your dining needs. Rooms in the Moana wing overlook Banyan Court, scene of a nightly entertainment that can be chamber music provided by a pianist or harpist. Open the windows, allowing the breezes to billow the curtains while the waves of Waikiki join with the music below in a heavenly serenade. Rooms are $195-315, with suites priced $260-340; $25 each additional person. The Sheraton Moana Surfrider is a superb hotel offering exemplary old-fashioned service.

Royal Hawaiian Hotel

The Royal Hawaiian, second oldest hotel built along Waikiki, at 2255 Kalakaua Ave., Honolulu, HI 96815, tel. 923-7311 or (800) 325-3535, provides an ongoing contemporary experience in turn-of-the-century charm. The Royal Hawaiian has also recently completed a $25 million restoration, which has recaptured the grand elegance of days past. Doors first opened in 1927, at a cost of $4 million, an unprecedented amount of money in those days for a hotel. The Depression brought a crushing reduction to Hawaiian tourism, bringing the yearly total down from a whopping 22,000 to under 10,000 (today more visitors arrive in one day), and the Royal became a financial loss. During WW II, with Waikiki barb-wired, the Royal was leased to the Navy as an R&R hotel for sailors from the Pacific Fleet. After the war, the hotel reverted to Matson Lines, the original owner, and reopened in 1947 after a $2 million renovation. Sheraton Hotels purchased the Royal in 1959, built the Royal Tower Wing in 1969, sold the hotel in 1975, but continued to remain as operating managers.

Original double doors featured one solid door backed by a louvered door so you could catch the ocean breezes and still have privacy. Today, the hotel is fully air-conditioned, so the old doors

the Royal Hawaiian Hotel

have been removed and new solid rosewood doors carved in the Philippines have replaced them. Rooms might have four-poster beds, canopies, twins, or kings, depending upon your preference. All rooms have remote-control TV, refrigerators, electronic safes, and computer hookups on telephones for lap-top computers. Furniture is French provincial, with bathrooms fully tiled. Completely renovated rooms in the original section have kept the famous pink motif, but are slightly more pastel. They have a marble tile bathroom, a brass butler, louvered drawers, and a huge bed. The tall ceilings are even more elegant with molded plaster cornices. Guests are treated to banana bread on arrival, a daily newspaper, and turndown service with a complimentary late-night sweet treat. Preferential tee-off times at the Makaha Resort are also offered. Each floor of the original Royal has a pool elevator, so guests in beachwear don't clash with the early evening black-tie set. A Hospitality Suite is provided for early morning check-ins or late check-outs and offers complimentary shower facilities, maid service six times during the day, coffee-making facilities, and a sitting and lounging area.

Some of the prestige suites are truly luxurious and feature huge balconies with tiled floors, where a party of 25 could easily be entertained. The tastefully carpeted bedrooms boast a quilt-covered bed heaped with a half-dozen pillows. The huge bathrooms overlook the beach and have a small built-in jacuzzi. In the massive Governor's Suite is a formal dining room, two huge bedrooms, two magnificent sitting areas; one a formal parlor, the other an "informal" rec-room. The Royal Towers, an addition dating from 1969, are preferred by many guests because every room has an ocean view. From the balcony of most, you look down onto the swimming pool, the beach, palm trees, and Diamond Head in the distance. A basic guestroom is $235-425, with suites ranging from $350 to over $1600.

If you stay at the Royal Hawaiian, you can dine and sign at the Moana Surfrider, Sheraton Waikiki, or Princess Kaiulani, all operated by Sheraton Hotels. One of the best features of the Royal, open to guest and nonguest, is the remarkable luau every Monday night (see "Food and Drink—Luau" in the Out and About chapter), and the extraordinary food and entertainment provided Tues.-Sat., by the Brothers Cazimero in the hotel's famous and elegant Monarch Dining Room (see "Entertainment"). The Royal Hawaiian, a Waikiki classic, is worth a visit even if you don't stay there. (See "Sights").

Hawaiian Regent Hotel

The Hawaiian Regent, at 2552 Kalakaua Ave., Honolulu, HI 96815, tel. 922-6611 or (800) 367-5370, has a long history of treating guests like royalty. The hotel now stands on what was the original site of Queen Liliuokalani's summer cottage. The Regent was the first major Hawaiian project of master designer Chris Hemmeter, famed for his magnificent Westin Kauai and Hyatt Regency Waikaloa hotels. The grand tradition of the hotel is reflected in the open sweeping style that marks a Hemmeter project. After almost two decades, the Regent appears extremely modern becasue its design was so visionary when it was built. With almost 1,400 units, the hotel ranks as the third-largest hotel in Hawaii after the Hilton Hawaiian Village and the Sheraton Waikiki. Rates are from $135 for a standard room to $695 for a deluxe suite. Children are especially taken care of with the "Keiki K.A.I. Club," a summer program, and honeymooners can choose a junior suite with special amenities for a reduced price. All rooms are oversized and include cable TV, a/c, nightly turndown service, and in-room safes. You can step across the street to mingle with the funseekers on Waikiki Beach, or relàx at one of the hotel's two pools. A championship Laykold tennis court is open from sunrise to sunset, with lessons and rackets available. The hotel offers a variety of exclusive shops in an off-lobby mall area like Shirokiya and Sandcastles for alohawear and evening wear. An on-site beauty shop and Japanese acupressure/massage service are there to revitalize you after a hard day of having fun in the sun. The Regent is renowned for its fine dining, entertainment, and late-night disco. The **Lobby Bar** is a perfect spot to perch while listening to relaxing Hawaiian music. The **Cafe Regent**, an open-air restaurant just off the main lobby, is open for breakfast, buffet, and lunch selections 6 a.m.-2:30 p.m. The **Tiffany Restaurant**, dinner only, has casual dining in an elegant atmosphere, with a stained-glass ceiling

and shuttered windows (see "Food"). The **Ocean Terrace,** designed for kicking back and watching life go by, is a poolside bar serving sandwiches and hamburgers at very good prices. The premier restaurant of the hotel, and one of Waikiki's consistently best, is the awardwinning **The Secret,** previously known as the Third Floor (see "Food"), where you can not only dine in Polynesian splendor, but be treated to a magnificent selection of wines collected by Richard Dean, one of only two sommeliers in all of Hawaii.

Enjoy a daily international buffet or spectacular Sunday brunch at **The Summery,** or a traditional Japanese meal at the **Regent Marushin.** You won't be told to hush while you dance or relax to the sounds of live music in **The Library.** And, if you have "dancing feet" take them to **The Point After,** one of Waikiki's swingingest high-tech discos, which will rock you until the wee hours. If you're after peace and quiet, head for the **Garden Courtyard,** a multipurpose area in the center of the hotel. Sit among flowers and full-grown coconut and bamboo trees. Every Mon., Wed., and Fri. 10 a.m.-noon learn lei-making, hula, or even Hawaiian checkers from *kapuna* who come just to share their *aloha.* The Hawaiian Regent is a first-class hotel that really knows how to make you feel like a visiting monarch. Rule with joy!

Park Plaza Waikiki

While the valets park your car, climb the marble staircase or take the chrome and glass-etched escalator one floor to the reception area where Jun Keneko's mural, *The Hawaii Wall,* fashioned from colorful tiles, black and white painted stripes, and precisely placed painted dots, will mirror your excitement of being in Hawaii. The Park Plaza Waikiki, 1956 Ala Moana Blvd., Honolulu, HI 96815, tel. 941-7275, (800) 367-6070, or (800) 437-7275, one of Waikiki's newest hotels, has only been open since 1992. The main lobby, mostly in tile, is bright and colorful with strong straight lines. Listen for the tinkling notes of a player piano that will lead you to the **Heliconia Bar,** where comfortable leather stools equipped with arm- and backrests are perfect for an afternoon's lounging. Along the bar's walls are original Picasso porcelains: magnificent, provocative, and stunningly simple. Among the works are practical serving plates named *Three Sardines* and a water pitcher shaped like a human face. On the second floor is a reading room with papers from around the world, a pool where room service will deliver snacks and sandwiches, and a complete fitness room where you can exercise or schedule a massage after winding down in the sauna. An entire wing called **The Gallery** is designated as an official extension of the Contemporary Museum, and displays the best of Hawaiian artists, with exhibits changing every eight weeks. The hotel has 313 rooms, including 45 suites that all feature air-conditioning, private lanai, twice-daily maid service, in-room refreshment centers, which include wet bars and complimentary coffee service, an in-room safe, hair dryers, bathrobes, a daily newspaper, three telephones, voice mail, and remote-control TV and VCR. The Park Plaza also welcomes business travelers with its executive business center, which provides mail service, cellular phones, fax service, and computer hook-ups. There is a splendid meeting facility and a concierge service that will take care of anything from renting snorkel gear to getting you a helicopter ride. Rates are: $120 standard, city or ocean view; $140 superior, city view; $160 deluxe; the Plaza suites are $200-240 with luxury suites going for $400-500; and the grand luxury Royal Amethyst Suite goes for $2000; additional person $25. Corporate rates are available, and children 18 years of age and under stay free when sharing. Rollaway beds and cribs are also complimentary. In a standard to deluxe room, you enter the wall to wall carpeted guest room through a vestibule of textured wallpaper and white-on-tan marble to find a king-sized bed with upholstered headboard flanked by two pine end tables, and an armoire that functions as the entertainment center. The small and efficient bathrooms feature a tub or choice of standard shower or hand-held shower, a pedestal sink, and a fine collection of toiletries. The top floor, reserved for the hotel suites and featuring butler service, are named after gemstones. A typical suite, huge by any standard, has a magnificent master bedroom where you can't help feeling like an honored guest in a king-sized bed with recessed headboard specially designed to accommodate pillows so that the entire bed becomes a grand chaise lounge

from which you can enjoy the view or the private entertainment center. The living area is a combination dining room complete with oak table and parlor with beautifully upholstered chairs, a writing desk, a sectional sofa that doubles as a lounge, another entertainment center, and a full wet bar for entertaining in your room. The bathroom is wonderful with a jacuzzi tub. The Park Plaza, because of its "off the strip" location, is one of the most reasonably priced luxury class hotels in Waikiki.

Hawaii Prince Hotel

The dynamic seascape of the tall masted ships anchored in the Ala Wai Yacht Harbor, reflect in the shimmering pink-tinted glass towers of the Hawaii Prince Hotel, at 100 Holomoana St., Honolulu, HI 96815, tel. 956-1111 or (800) 321-6248, the city's newest luxury hotel. Opposite the harbor, and through the main reception area, ultramodern with burnished chrome and lustrous marble, is framed in a sweep of curved glass the busy streets of the city. The twin towers, Diamond Head and Ala Moana, are scaled by a glass elevator affording wide-angled vistas of the Honolulu skyline. Decorated in green and tan with light pine paneling, the rooms, all ocean view, feature a marble-topped desk with full mirror, a/c, functional windows, and a full entertainment center with remote-control color TV and VCR. Each room has its own refrigerator, walk-in closet with complimentary safe and terry cloth robes, and a king-sized bed with fluffy down pillows. The marble bathrooms have separate shower stalls, tubs, and commodes with a full set of toiletries, lighted makeup mirrors, and hair dryers. Room rates are from $200 for an Oceanfront Marina to $330 for an Oceanfront Top (floors 30-33), while suites range $450-2500, $35 extra person. Special business rates are offered (ask when booking) along with the Prince Three-night Special at $550 double occupancy with a daily full American breakfast for two, airport limousine transfer, and unlimited golf package. Great deal! Ride the elevator to the fifth floor, where you will find a keyhole-shaped pool and canvas shade umbrellas overlooking the harbor below. Other amenities include three excellent restaurants, the Takanawa, Prince Court, and Hakone (see "Food"), a small but adequate fitness room, turndown service, valet parking, and a Waikiki/Ala Moana Shuttle. The Hawaii Prince boasts its own golf course, the **Hawaii Prince Golf Club,** the only one of its kind belonging to a Waikiki hotel. Located at Ewa Beach, 35 minutes away by complimentary shuttle, the Arnold Palmer-designed 27-hole championship course (see the "Golf Courses of Oahu" chart in the Out and About chapter) includes a fully equipped golf shop, practice range, putting greens, chipping greens, locker, and shower facilities, clubhouse dining, and tennis courts (special Golf Packages available). The Hawaii Prince, located at the "gateway to Waikiki" is away from the action of the frenetic Waikiki strip, but close enough to make it easily accessible.

Kahala Hilton

Cast-up treasures of sand-tumbled glass is the theme captured in the distinctive multihued chandeliers that hang from the 30-foot vaulted ceilings of the grand hallway, the entrance to the Kahala Hilton. Long considered a standard-setter for Hawaiian deluxe hotels, the Kahala Hilton, 5000 Kahala Ave., Honolulu, HI 96816, tel. 734-2211 or (800) 367-2525, is not technically in Waikiki, but in Kahala, an exclusive residential area just east of Diamond Head. The hotel, built 30 years ago, is proud that most of its key employees have been there from the first days and that they have formed lasting friendships with guests who happily return year after year. Surrounded by the exclusive Waialae Country Club (not even hotel guests are welcome unless they are members), the hotel gives a true sense of peace and seclusion and rightly boasts a "Neighbor Island Experience" only minutes from bustling Waikiki. A grand staircase fashioned from lava rock wears a living lei of green ferns and purple orchids, as it descends to the **The Maile Lounge,** a formal restaurant, and the last of its kind that still offers dinner dancing. The menu features appetizers like fresh sashimi, Russian caviar, tender breast of duck, and seared fresh foie gras. Soups can be lobster bisque or gazpacho followed by a Maile salad or Caesar salad. Entrees are sumptuous with Maine lobster, swordfish, fresh catch prepared various ways, and specialties like roast duckling, chicken Wellington, and roast rack of lamb Provençale. The hotel's informal **Plumeria Cafe** is famous for its impossible-to-resist pastries, while the seaside **Hala Terrace,** open for breakfast, lunch, and dinner, hosts the legendary **Danny Kaleikini Show** (see "Entertainment"). A beach shack offers all kinds of pool-side snacks and boasts the best hamburgers on Oahu.

The hotel, fronting the sheltered Mauna Lua Bay, features a perfect crescent beach, swimming pool, and beach cabana with all watersports gear available including kayaks, paddleboats, and scuba gear (free lesson daily). Behind, a waterfall cascading from a free-form stone wall forms a rivulet that leads to a dolphin lagoon (feeding daily at 11 a.m., 2 p.m., and 4 p.m.) and a series of saltwater ponds teeming with reef fish.

Average rooms are extra-large and feature tropic-perfect parquet floors, done in light pastels in a nouveau-European style, and all feature either an ocean view or sweeping mountain view that overlooks the manicured golf courses. The marble-tiled bathrooms are also extra-large and await you with lounging *yukata,* feature a "lady's side" with a *rightfully* larger dressing area, makeup mirror, hair dryer, personal sink, and soaking tub, while the "man's side" holds a mini-fridge and shower stall. Rates are $180-495 d, $495-1800 for a suite. The Kahala Hilton isn't for everyone, but there's no doubt that you get all that you pay for. Recently, because of a lease snafu, the hotel was put up for sale. With the new owners will come extensive renovations that will preserve the spirit and taste so well earned by the classic hotel, but at the same time will make it glamorous once again.

FOOD

The streets of Waikiki are an international banquet, with over a dozen cuisines spreading their tables for your enjoyment. Because of the culinary competition, you can choose restaurants in the same way that you peruse a smorgasbord, for both quantity and quality. Within a few hundred yards are all-you-can-gorge buffets, luau, dinner shows, fast foods, ice cream, and jacket-and-tie restaurants. The free tourist literature runs coupons, and placards advertise specials for breakfast, lunch, and dinner. Bars and lounges often give free *pu pu* and finger foods that can easily make a light supper. As with everything in Waikiki, its restaurants are a close-quartered combination of the best and the worst, but with only a little effort it's easy to find great food, great atmosphere, and mouthwatering satisfaction.

Note: At many of the moderately priced restaurants listed below and at all of the expensive restaurants *reservations are highly recommended*. It's much easier to make a two-minute phone call than it is to have your evening spoiled, so please call ahead. Also, many of the restaurants along the congested Waikiki strip provide valet parking (usually at no charge), or will offer validated parking at a nearby lot. So check when you call to reserve. Attire at most Hawaiian restaurants is casual, but at the better restaurants it is dressy casual, which means close-toed shoes, trousers, and a collared shirt for men, and a simple but stylish dress for women. At some of the very best restaurants you won't feel out of place with a jacket, but ties are not usually worn. For a list of **luau** in greater Honolulu, including Waikiki, see "Food and Drink—Luau" in the Out and About chapter.

INEXPENSIVE

Eggs And Things, at 1911 Kalakaua Ave., just where it meets McCully, tel. 949-0820, is a late-night institution open from 11 p.m. until 2 p.m. the following afternoon. A number of discos are just around the corner, so the clientele in the wee hours is a mix of revelers, hotel workers, boat captains, and even a hooker or two. The decor is wooden floors and formica tables, but the waitresses are top-notch and friendly. The food is absolutely excellent and it's hard to spend over $10. Daily specials are offered 1-2 a.m., while the morning special 5-8 a.m. gets you three pancakes and two fresh eggs cooked as you like for just a few dollars. Waffles and pancakes are scrumptious with fresh fruit or home-made coconut syrup. Besides the eggs and omelettes the most popular item is fresh fish, which is usually caught by the owner himself, Mr. Jerry Fukunaga, who goes out almost every day on his own boat. It's prepared Cajun-style, or sautéed in garlic and butter, with two fresh eggs and a choice of pancakes, rice, or home-fried potatoes. Prices vary according to market price. Casual attire is acceptable, and BYO wine or beer is okay.

Around the corner is **The Dynasty Restaurant,** tel. 947-3771, at 1778 Ala Moana Blvd., in Discovery Bay across from the Ilikai Hotel. They have an enormous menu of various Chinese cuisines that is acceptable but not memorable. They are friendly and courteous, and open daily 10 a.m.-6 a.m. For a very late night repast after "doing the town," their food definitely hits the spot!

Almost across the street and tucked into a nook close to the Hilton Hawaiian Village is the **Saigon Cafe,** at 1831 Ala Moana Blvd., tel. 955-4009, open daily 6:30 a.m.-10 p.m. Along with the delightful Vietnamese restaurants that have sprung up in Chinatown. The Saigon Cafe is a friendly, meticulously clean, unpretentious, family-run affair that definitely offers "budget gourmet" food. Order tureens of soup for two, spiced with lemon grass, hot garlic sauce, and floating with dollops of seafood, chicken, beef, tofu, or pork for under $7. Roll your own spring rolls, which come with slices of meat, fresh vegetables, mint, dipping sauces, and transparently thin rice paper that you dip in water to soften before rolling away. Noodle dishes are large and hearty, while breakfast brings an assortment of eggs, pancakes, and waffles. It's hard to spend more than $10 on a meal that is not only delicious, but fresh, made to order, and healthy as well. Great choice!

Da Smokehouse, 470 Ena Rd., tel. 946-0233, open daily 11:30 a.m.-midnight, is one of those places where the food is excellent, but you wouldn't want to eat there. Why? Because it is primarily a takeout restaurant with only a few booths stuck in the back where *da* smoke and *da* grease from *da* wood-fired smoker is *da* decor. Actually, owner Shirley Jones has recently moved *da* wood-fired smoker out back and added a few new tables. *Da* decor is now compromised. Next will come color coordinated table ware. God forbid! Your choices are smoked beef, pork, chicken, and ham all served picnic style, with two choices of sides including homemade potato salad, baked beans, rice, or cole slaw. Price ranges are chicken, smoked ham, or smoked beef brisket sandwiches for $6, one-quarter barbecue chicken for $5.05, grilled ham, pork spareribs or beef back ribs for $10.45, or a side of pork for $24. The combo plate of all of the above, which can easily feed four, is only $20. No liquor, so BYO. Free delivery makes Da Smokehouse a perfect alternative to inflated room service prices at surrounding hotels, or for a home-cooked dinner in your condo. You'll love it!

Hippo's, 468 Ena Rd., tel. 944-8466, open daily 11 a.m.-midnight, is a *loco* Mexican restaurant painted yellow with a bunch of artistic junk hung like a giant mobile from the ceiling. Happy hour 3-6:30 p.m. brings pitchers of margaritas for $7.95, and pitchers of beer for $5.95. Appetizers are everything from Texas Fondue (what can it be?) for $5.75 to taco salads for $6.25, with a bowl of homemade chili only $4. Traditional favorites like chimichangas, kahlua pork enchiladas, corn tortillas with beans and beef, and burrito ranchero are priced from $6.95 to $10. They even have Sicilian-style pizza ranging in price from $7.45 for a small to $19.50 for a large with the works. If you don't fancy a meal, try one of the specialty coffee drinks like Cafe Mexico or Cafe Frangelico, for under $5. Hippo's is a fun, relaxed restaurant where you can have a good south-of-the-border meal. *Bienvenidos!*

Ena Restaurant, 432 Ena Rd., tel. 951-0818, open daily 10 a.m.-11:30 p.m., is a small Chinese restaurant with little atmosphere, but with good food at good prices. Appetizers and soups include crispy won ton $2.95, chicken salad $5.95, and scallop soup for $2.95. Lunch specials like lemon chicken or beef with vegetables are $4.75, while entrees like mixed seafood and vegetables, fillet of fish in hot red sauce, roast duck, twice-cooked Sichuan-style pork, or Hunan-style tofu are from $5.95 to $8.95. The Ena Restaurant, away from the hustle and bustle, is a good choice for a basic meal with no frills.

Ruffage Natural Foods, at 2442 Kuhio, tel. 922-2042, is one of a very few natural food restaurants in Waikiki. They serve regular as well as nonfish sushi, a wide assortment of tofu sandwiches, natural salads, tofu burgers, fresh island fruits, and smoothies. Everything is homemade, and they try to avoid, as much as possible, processed foods. Just about everything on the menu is less than $5. It's a small hole-in-the-wall type eatery that's easy to miss. A few tables outside under a portico is the ambience.

Ezogiku is a chain of Japanese restaurants. Open till the wee hours, these no-atmosphere restaurants serve inexpensive hearty bowls of Sapporo *ramen* (renowned as the best), curry rice, and *gyoza*. They have multiple locations in and around Waikiki at 2083 Kuhio Ave., 2420 Koa Ave., 2546 Lemon Rd., and 2141 Kalakaua Avenue. Ezogiku is a no-frills kind of place. Small, smoky, counter seating, and totally authentic. They're so authentic that on their dishes they spell *ramen* as *larmen*. You not only eat inexpensively, but you get a very authentic example of what it's like to eat in Japan . . . cheaply. Eat heartily for around $6.

The Jolly Roger is an American standard restaurant with a Hawaiian flair. If you're after good old-fashioned tuna salad sandwiches, hot roast beef, a tostada even, or just plain soup and salad, this would be your best bet in Waikiki. The Jolly Roger has two locations, at 2244 Kalakaua (always too crowded so the service suffers), and 150 Kaiulani, where it's slightly quieter. Actually the Kaiulani restaurant borders on tasteful with a dark green decor accented with bronze, pleasant booth seating, and a profusion of ferns and hanging plants. Both are open 6:30 a.m.-1 a.m. Breakfasts are waffles, pancakes, omelettes, and meats, but try their orange bread as standard or French toast. A lunch special is hamburger steak, $4.95, with dinners well under $10. Happy hour is 6 a.m.-6 p.m., when exotics are poured for $1.75, draft beer $1.50, free *pu pu* from 4-6 p.m. Nightly entertainment in the bar section, especially The Blue Kangaroo at the Kalakaua Ave. Jolly Roger (see "Entertainment").

Man Lee's Chinese Restaurant, 124 Kapahulu, tel. 922-6005, is a basic Chinese restaurant that offers daily lunch and dinner specials. The atmosphere is quiet since it's around the corner from most of the action, and the food is acceptable but not memorable. A belly-filler only.

Wong and Wong, at 1023 Maunakea, tel. 521-4492, is a simple and basic Chinese restaurant where you can have a good and filling meal at a reasonable price. Many people who live and work in and around Waikiki choose to go here for Chinese food.

Perry's Smorgy, at 2380 Kuhio Ave., tel. 926-9872, and at the Coral Seas Hotel, 250 Lewers St., tel. 923-3881, is the epitome of the budget travelers' "line 'em up, fill 'em up, and head 'em out" kind of restaurant. There is no question that you'll waddle away stuffed, but forget about any kind of memorable dining experience. When you arrive, don't be put off by the long lines. They move! First, you run a gauntlet of salads, breads, and potatoes, in the hopes that you'll fill your plate. Try to restrain yourself. Next comes the meat, fish, and chicken. The guys serving up the roast beef are masters of a whole lot of movement and very little action. The carving knife whips around in the air, but does very little damage to the joint of beef. A paper-thin slice is finally cut off and put on your plate with aplomb. The carver then looks at you as if you were Oliver Twist asking for more. Added pressure comes from the long line of tourists behind, who act as if they have just escaped from a Nazi labor camp. The breakfast buffet is actually very good, with all the standard eggs, meats, juices, and rolls, and the food in general, considering the price, is more than acceptable. You can't complain.

Pizzeria Uno, at 2256 Kuhio (and Seaside), tel. 926-0646, is part of a small chain that allows each of its locations to be individual, although the deep-dish "Chicago-style" pizza re-mains the same. Open daily 11 a.m.-midnight, live entertainment Wed.-Sat.; express lunch Mon.-Fri. 11-3, with specials including soup or salad. Appetizers like pizza skins, potato-flavored pizza wedges with onions and zesty cheese for $4.75, and individual-size pizzas for $5.95 keep prices down. Large pizzas like Spinoccoli are different flavored with spinach, fresh broccoli, a blend of cheeses, and a little garlic for $10.95. Also, burgers and sandwiches, with names like The Big Frankie, not a teenie-weanie, mark Pizzeria Uno as a casual, fun-filled restaurant. Happy hour, 11 a.m.-6 p.m., is good value with draft beer at 95 cents, and all tropical drinks for $1.95. Breakfast is a "sunrise special," two golden-brown pancakes, two strips of bacon, and an egg for $1.99 6 a.m.-noon. Modern and upbeat with black and white decor. On the beaten track, but worth a stop.

The **Waikiki Seafood and Pasta Co.** is at the Outrigger Surf Hotel, 2280 Kuhio Avenue. Dinners are good but not memorable, and range from inexpensive to reasonable. Fresh pasta starts from golden- herb pasta for $5.95 and pasta of the day for $6.95. Other dishes are calimari marinara ($9.95), veal piccata ($12.95), and calimari steak Italiana ($10.95). Specials like vegie lasagna are $6.95 with the most expensive at $14 for veal parmigiana. Good value, and acceptable food. A change from deep-fried mahimahi.

Peking Garden, 307 Royal Hawaiian Ave., tel. 922-3401, is a hole-in-the-wall eatery just behind the Waikiki Medical Center heading *mauka.* They serve Chinese-American food basically in the form of filling plate lunches for around $3.50. A good choice is the Peking fried chicken.

Shorebird Beach Broiler, open for breakfast, lunch, and dinner (from 5 p.m.), is on the beach behind the Outrigger Reef Hotel at 2169 Kalia Rd., tel. 922-2887, giving this budget restaurant the best gourmet location in all of Waikiki. Here you'll find a limited but adequate menu of cook-your-own selections for under $15 (discount tickets save you more). Walk through the lobby to the beach for a remarkable sunset while dining. Included is a good, fresh salad bar of vegetables and fruits. Beverages are included, the setting is wonderful, and the value excellent, but you do pay extra for bread. Karaoke is offered nightly for all those Don Ho "wannabes."

Ferdinand's, in the Coral Reef Hotel, 2299 Kuhio Ave., tel. 923-5581, is a no-nonsense place running specials and discount tickets. Basically it's an American standard restaurant with a Hawaiian flavor. An attempt is made at entertainment, a Don Ho clone singing in the background. The food is decent but not memorable; with discounts two can eat for around $15. Besides inexpensive food, they have inexpensive drinks at happy hour, beers $1 or $1.25. They also have free *pu pu* 4-6 p.m. Breakfast special is a choice of two pancakes or toast and jelly with bacon or sausage, or an egg any style for $2.99.

The **Holiday Inn,** at 2570 Kalakaua Ave., has very reasonable basic American food in the street-level dining room. Breakfast specials for $1.99 bring you pancakes, eggs, and bacon. Dinner features specials for $10 and under, like roast beef for $8.95.

Hamburger Mary's, at 2109 Kuhio, tel. 922-6722, has two claims to fame. It serves homestyle food at reasonable prices, and has long been famous as a gay and lesbian hangout. The decor, given the open structure of the building facing Kuhio, is actually quite nice. The front is a terrace with a brick floor, round tables, and wrought-iron chairs. The *inside* area has a little grass shack motif, with curios hanging from the ceiling—old glass bottles, chandeliers, a flying angel, even an old surfboard. The back room holds a pool table and a dance floor. Rock and roll is always happening. Breakfast is served all day long. At lunch they feature salads such as a fresh garden salad for $5.25, or "stuff your own" (your choice of papaya, avocado, or tomato stuffed with chicken, tuna, cream cheese, or cheddar cheese) for $7.25. Big hearty Hamburger Mary sandwiches are the Mary burger ($4.25), avocado burger ($6.25), and meatless sandwiches like avocado or cheddar cheese for under $6. Soups and sides are plentiful, but try a bowl of homemade beef chili for $3.50. A great people-watching spot with good food at moderate prices.

Waikiki Waialana Restaurant, 2211 Kuhio Ave., in the Outrigger Waikiki Malia Hotel, tel. 923-7621, open 24 hours, offers daily dinner specials for around $7.95. Included is a crisp salad bar and a huge well-done baked potato. The beverages are not included, but for the price, the food is a good value.

The Islander Coffee House, on Lewers St., tel. 923-3233, in the Reef Towers Hotel, open daily 6 a.m.-midnight, has inexpensive breakfasts of two pancakes, eggs, and bacon for $2.69. They also offer steak and eggs Benedict for $4.29, chef salad ($6), hamburgers under $5, and specials every day for inexpensive prices. No dining experience whatsoever, but down-home prices in the heart of Waikiki.

The **Mongolian Barbecue,** at the Kuhio Mall, 2301 Kuhio Ave., tel. 923-2445, open daily 11 a.m.-10 p.m., would make Genghis Khan smile. He could feed his army for peanuts. There is no decor, but this is a very good and inexpensive place to eat. For $13.95 you get the Full Mongolian, for which you make a selection of beef, chicken, pork, lamb, vegies, sauces, and spices from chilled serving trays. Then you watch them cook your order in the fire pit. Included is rice and a famous, homemade sesame bun. If you've got the room, you can go back for a second round. Children under 12 get the same treatment for $8.95. If it sounds like too much, try the Quick Mongolian for $6.95, which is the same but the items are selected for you by the servers, and no seconds. The Mini-Mongolian for $5.95 is your choice of beef, lamb, chicken, or pork with vegies, served with rice or homemade bun. Limited fish selections as well. Good and "budget gourmet."

The **Beach Street Cafe,** in the Outrigger Reef Hotel, 2169 Kalia Rd., open daily 7 a.m.-9 p.m., is literally on the beach. Breakfast, 7-11 a.m., starts at $2.99 for a scrambled-egg platter, and just $1.95 for cereal and yogurt. Other munchies like burgers and plate lunches are under $4. Cafeteria-style, the cafe has no decor except for a huge open window that frames the living sculpture of Waikiki.

Kapahulu Avenue

Once Kapahulu Avenue crosses Ala Wai Boulevard, it passes excellent inexpensive to moderately priced restaurants, strung one after the other. Kapahulu was the area in which the displaced Chinese community resettled after the great Chinatown fire at the turn of the century. Kapahulu basically means "poor soil," and unlike most areas of Hawaii could barely support vegetables and plants. Undaunted, the Chinese brought in soil with wagons and wheelbarrows, turning the area productive and verdant.

The first is **Rainbow Drive-In,** at the corner of Kanaaina Avenue. It's strictly local, with a kids' hangout feel, but the plate lunches are hearty and well-done for under $4. Another of the same, **K C Drive-In,** just up the road a few blocks at 1029 Kapahulu, specializes in waffle dogs, shakes, and even has carhops. Both are excellent stops to pick up plate lunches on your way out of Waikiki heading for the H-1 Freeway.

The first sit-down restaurant on the strip is **Irifune Japanese Restaurant,** at 563 Kapahulu, tel. 737-1141, open daily for lunch 11:30 a.m.-1 p.m. and for dinner 5-9:30 p.m., directly across from **Zippy's,** a fast-food joint. Irifune serves authentic, well-prepared Japanese standards in its small dining room. Most meals begin at $6, with a nightly special for around $8. You're also given a card that is punched every time you eat there; after 20 meals, you get one free. Irifune is a great deal for Japanese food, and is much cheaper and easily as good as most other Japanese restaurants on the Waikiki strip. A winner!

The next restaurant in line is **Ono Hawaiian Foods,** 726 Kapahulu, tel. 737-2275, open Mon.-Sat. 10:30 a.m.-7:30 p.m., an institution in downhome Hawaiian cooking. This is the kind of place that a taxi driver takes you when you ask for "the real thing." It's clean and basic, with the decor being photos of local performers—all satisfied customers—hung on the wall. If you want to try *lomi lomi* salmon, poi, or *kalua* pig, this is *da kine place, brah!* Prices are cheap. And, if you have a sweet tooth, try **Leonard's Bakery,** which specializes in *malasadas* and *pao dolce.*

The **Rama Thai Restaurant,** on the corner of Kapahulu and Winam streets, across from New World Chinese Restaurant, open daily for dinner 5-10 p.m., tel. 735-2789, is *uptown* with some track lighting and linen tablecloths, but the prices and food are still *downtown* Bangkok. A wonderful choice is *satay* beef appetizer for $6.95, or chicken and ginger soup in a coconut-milk spicy broth ($6.95), and red Thai curried beef, chicken, or scallops for $6.95. Almost half of the menu is vegetarian. All items are a la carte, so

it's not that cheap; a complete meal costs around $15. The fish-ball soup is out of this world, with plenty for two. The tofu in coconut milk is also a great choice.

To round out the multicultural cuisines of Kapahulu Avenue, try **Jo-Ni's Restaurant and Bakery,** at 1017 Kapahulu, tel. 735-8575, serving traditional Filipino dishes with many American and Hawaiian standards.

Fast Foods And Snacks

There are enough formica-tabled, orange-colored, golden-arched, belly-up-to-the-window places selling perfected, injected, and inspected ground cow, chicken, and fish to feed an army . . . and a navy, and marine corps too. Those needing a pre-fab meal can choose from the royal **Burger King** and **Dairy Queen,** Jack-in-his-Box, Ronnie McDonald, Pizza Hut-2-3-4, **Wendy's,** and dippy **Zippy's Drive-In.** Fast food addicts easily find your pushers throughout Waikiki!

Farrell's Restaurant, at the International Market Place and the Royal Hawaiian Center serves ice cream and a good selection of sandwiches and soups for decent prices. Along Kalakaua Avenue are **Baskin Robbins** and **Häagen Dazs.** For cheap Italian try the **Noodle Shop** In the Waikiki Sand Villa Hotel, tel. 922-4744.

Minute Chef, across from the Sheraton Moana Surfrider Hotel, on Kalakaua Ave., has hamburgers for 99 cents, cheeseburgers $1.19, sandwiches $2.50, and roast beef for about $3.99. A change of pace from the styrofoam box-type fast foods. Not bad, for cheap fast food.

Zorro's, at 2310 Kuhio Ave., tel. 926-5555, is your basic pizza parlor that includes a limited menu of pasta, sandwiches, and salad. The standard 16-inch pizza ranges from $10.99 to $19.89 depending upon toppings. Pastas are all under $6, and sandwiches under $5. Open 10 a.m.-4 a.m. with free delivery.

You can't miss the pink, white, and magenta of **J.R.'s Fast Food Plate Lunch Restaurant,** at the corner of Lewers and Helumoa, where $6 or less will get you a hefty plate of rice, macaroni salad, and a slice of teriyaki beef, roast pork, or mahimahi. The food is fair, the portions hefty, and with a touch of local color is far superior to the nondescript national fast food chain restaurants in the area. Upstairs is a dining veranda where you can perch above the endless crowd.

The **Patisserie,** at 2330 Kuhio, tel. 922-9752, offers fresh French pastries, coffee, and sandwiches. They're not bad for this neck of the woods. Fairly decent food at acceptable prices. Good for early mornings if you want just a light breakfast. The **Patisserie** adjacent to the Edgewater Hotel, at 2168 Beach Walk, open 6:30 a.m.-9 p.m., offers sundaes, ice cream, fresh baked pastries, and hefty deli sandwiches like the Black Forest Ham for $4.50, or have lasagna for $3.50. A breakfast special, served 6:30-9 a.m., includes scrambled eggs, toast, and your choice of ham, bacon or Portuguese sausage for only $2.25. If the Waikiki sun is, God forbid, shaded by clouds, you can prepare yourself for its return by focusing on the blazing yellow walls of this sandwich shop! Two more Patisseries can be found around town, one at 33 S. King St., the other in the Amfac Building in downtown Honolulu.

Fatty's Chinese Fast Food, 2345 Kuhio, tel. 922-9600, is very inexpensive. For about $3.50 you get a giant plate of Chinese fast food. A belly-filler only, but not bad.

MODERATE

Roberto and Laura Magni, a couple from Milano, one day discussed moving to Hawaii. With Italian spontaneity and gusto, they looked at each other and simultaneously said "perche no!" **Caffelatte,** at 339 Saratoga Rd. (across from the P.O.), tel. 924-1414, open daily 5:30 p.m.-1 a.m., on the second floor of a clapboard "New England-Hawaiian style" house encircled by a veranda, is the result of their impetuousness. The cosmopolitan interior, simple and basic, is white on green with wrought iron tables set with starched white linens. Hardwood floors, framed paintings both traditional and modern, a horse-shoe bar, and subdued globed lighting complete the casual but stylish effect. The Mediterranean-inspired service is slow, but very friendly, and very professional. Each waitperson is intimately familiar with the menu, and will be happy to recommend and describe each

dish. The menu features homemade pasta ranging in price $11.50-20 with offerings like Spaghetti Paradiso with tomato sauce, or *daglia talle,* a flat thin pasta with Italian sausage for $12.50. Traditional favorites are sure to please with lasagna Leonardo da Vinci at $15, various polenta smothered in everything from a simple calamari to brosola, a rolled and herb-stuffed steak, gnocchi for $14.50, and ricotta and spinach ravioli at $17. Top off dinner with Italian desserts like peaches and strawberries in wine, or oranges and bananas in Russian vodka. The bar serves Italian wine by the bottle or glass, along with bubbling spumante and various champagnes. Italy in Hawaii? . . . *Perche no?*

The **Super Chef Restaurant,** tel. 926-7199, at the Waikiki Hana Hotel, 2424 Koa Ave., is a sleeper. It is definitely one of *the* best moderately inexpensive restaurants in Waikiki, where you can get an *almost* gourmet meal for a terrific price. Being in a small hotel on a side street keeps the crowds away, so the quality of the food and service never suffers. The restaurant decor is not spectacular, but it is classy with small linen-covered tables and drum-seat chairs in a open and cheery room. The staff is very friendly, and the chefs prepare each meal individually behind a tile counter. Breakfast is served 6:30-10:30 a.m., when they feature buttermilk pancakes, bacon and ham, or Portuguese sausage with a large juice for just $2.25; or choose a *wiki wiki* breakfast of pastry, juice, and Kona coffee for only $1.75. No lunch menu, but dinner is served 5-10 p.m. One special is a complete dinner of steak with two lobster tails for only $11.95, or rack of lamb for $8.95. The portions are moderate but definitely not miniscule, and on top of it the cooking is just a half step below excellent. Definitely worth a try.

The **Waikiki Broiler,** in the Edgewater Hotel, 2168 Kalia Rd., open daily 6 a.m.-9 p.m., displays multiple personalities depending on where you choose to sit. All are pleasant! Dine al fresco at the Patio Bar and start your day with a "breakfast special" of pancakes, two strips of bacon, and one egg for $2.49. In the afternoon, the Patio Bar, accented with brass rail, comfortable stools, and tables shaded by umbrellas, becomes more of a bistro/beer garden where you can enjoy hand-mixed exotic drinks while listening to a guitarist daily 4-6 p.m. The

1. Punchbowl Crater (J.D. Bisignani) **2.** Hanauma Bay Park (J.D. Bisignani)
3. Kaneohe Bay (J.D. Bisignani)

1. the Pali Highway (Dr. Janos Balogh) **2.** Diamond Head (J.D. Bisignani)

main dining room, brightened with paintings of flowers and birds, and light fixtures that look like melted ice cream cones, is as homey as a kindly old *tutu's* kitchen. Here, for lunch, you can order teriyaki chicken breast with rice or fries for $3.49, and for dinner a complete teriyaki steak dinner for two for only $15.95. Evening specials like freshly caught *ahi,* mahimahi, or marlin are a reasonable $13.25. The main lounge area, comfortable with tall wooden stools surrounding drum-topped tables, serves handmade mai tais daily 6-9 p.m., for $1.75. Evenings the inside bar rocks with a live band 9 p.m.-1:30 a.m., with karaoke on Sunday and Monday. The Waikiki Broiler is a terrific, moderately priced restaurant, where the food, if not quite outstanding, is definitely worth the price.

The **Peacock Dining Room,** at the Queen Kapiolani Hotel, 150 Kapahulu, tel. 922-1941, open 5:30-9 p.m., offers one of the most outstanding buffets in Waikiki for both price and quality. Different nights feature different cuisines. All are special but the Japanese buffet on Wednesday and Thursday and the seafood buffet on Friday are extraordinary. All range from $12.95 to $15.95. The room itself is tasteful with white tablecloths and full service. Every time you return to the buffet just leave your empty plate and it will be taken away for you. Help yourself from an amazing array of entrees that are expertly prepared. The salad bar is extremely varied, and the desserts will make you wish that you saved room. Excellent value.

Tiffany's Steakhouse, at the Hawaiian Regent, 2552 Kalakaua, tel. 922-6611, dinner 6-9:30 p.m., is a casual restaurant featuring thick juicy steaks, a varied and ample salad bar, and a good selection of fresh seafood. Evenings are magical because of a stained-glass ceiling illuminated by backlighting. The furnishings are European contemporary that counterpoint louvered windows all around. Tables are set with pink tablecloths and heavy crystal ware with the subdued lighting and ceiling fans adding comfort and romance to your meal. The menu begins with escargot ($6.95), soups and chowder (under $4), and a seafood bar for $6.95. The house specialties are generous portions of prime rib ($19.95), filet mignon ($21), short rib ($18.50), tempura ($18.50), and seafood Newburg ($17.95). A la carte salad bar is $7.95. Tiffany's

is that special blend of elegant and casual where you can dine in style and still be presented with a moderate check.

Carlos Castaneda wouldn't even notice as he walked past two psychedelic green cactuses into **Pepper's,** at 150 Kaiulani Ave., tel. 926-4374, open daily for lunch 11:30 a.m.-4 p.m., dinner 4 p.m.-1:30 a.m. The interior is Yuppie-Mex with a wraparound rectangular bar with a fat wooden rail, and low ceilings done in a Mexican-style stucco. The specialties of the house are prepared in a wood-fired oven for that hearty outdoor flavor in the heart of "Rancho Waikiki." Light meals are chicken taco salad for $9.95, the Pepper club ($6.95), and tuna melt ($5.95), with a good selection of salads. But you can get these anywhere so go "south of the border" for burrito madness ($8.50), complete flautas dinner ($9.95), or selections from the lava-rock grill like marinated chicken breast ($12.95), or baby-back ribs (full slab, $15.95). You can also pick Mexican favorites like tacos, enchiladas, and fajitas, all served with rice, beans, and Mexican salad. Nothing on the Mexican side is more than $12.95, with most around $9. Eat *hombre!*

Eating at **Caffe Guccinni,** at 2139 Kuhio Ave., tel. 922-5287, open daily 4-10:30 p.m., is like following a Venetian gondolier to his favorite restaurant. It's not fancy but the food is good and plentiful, and the pasta is made fresh daily. The staff is usually a cook and a waiter who seats you at one of a dozen tables, most outdoors. They're easy to miss because they're stuck back off the street, which means a nice, quiet area. For a light meal choose garlic bread ($2.50) and Caesar salad ($6.98), or for a full meal try one of the house specialties (with soup or salad), like eggplant parmigiana, pasta contesto, spaghetti and meatballs, or manicotti, all under $11. The cappuccino and espresso are freshly brewed and extraordinarily good. For dessert have *cannoli,* a flaky pastry stuffed with ricotta and smothered with slivers of almond and chocolate—excellent!

Hernando's Hideaway, at 2139 Kuhio, tel. 922-7758, open daily 10:30 a.m.-2 a.m., sits well off the street and is a very casual Mexican restaurant where the emphasis is on plenty of good food and having a good time. Tables are mostly outside under an awning, and every day a special drink is featured, with $2 margaritas during happy hour. Some of the best offerings are chicken enchilada dinner for $6.75, or an overstuffed calzone for $5.75. Every night, 6-7 p.m. is "power hour," when all well drinks are $1, followed by "pizza hour" 7-8 p.m., when pizza is only $1 per slice. All this activity attracts a younger crowd of both resort workers and vacationers. You can eat until you're as stuffed as a burrito for under $10.

The **New Orleans Bistro,** at 2139 Kuhio, tel. 926-4444, open 5 p.m.-midnight, along with its zesty Cajun and creole dining, offers jazz nightly. The chef, from New Orleans, has put together a small but superb sampler menu of the finest in Cajun cooking. The prices are a touch expensive, but if you're bored with the average offerings of mahimahi and teri chicken, you'll be glad that you found the Bistro. They've done the most with this limited location. The tables, covered in pink tablecloths, are arranged so that there is an intimate and romantic feeling, and somehow the hustle and bustle of Kuhio has been minimized. Appetizers begin at $4.95 and sharpen your palate with deep-fried calimari, oysters Bienville, or Gulf Coast oysters baked on the half shell topped with New Orleans classic cream sauce laced with shrimp for $10.95. Salads are basically $5 and include beefsteak tomato (Maui Feast) and house salad of hearts of palms ($4.95). Entrees are mesquite-grilled lemon herb chicken ($12.95), Louisiana fresh fried catfish ($14.95), blackened fish du jour (seasonal price), or smoked *kalua* shrimp and angel hair pasta ($15.95). If amphibians and reptiles pique your fancy there're frog legs and alligator tenderloins barbecued, blackened, or deep-fried with cocktail sauce, served with Cajun rice and vegies for $19.95. A good choice for a different dining experience.

Bobby McGee's Conglomeration, at the Colony East Hotel, 2885 Kalakaua, tel. 922-1282, open Mon.-Thurs. 5:30-10 p.m., Fri., Sat., and Sun. 5-11 p.m. This is a riproaring fun-filled place for the entire family. One of those rare combinations that caters to all ages and all pocketbooks, and foodwise it won't let you down. The waiters and waitresses are all in costume, so you might be served your meal by Batman or Annie Oakley. The interior has numerous rooms, so you can sit close to the disco dance floor in case you have the overwhelming urge to twist off

a few calories, or you can sit in a quiet room well away from the music. Create your own combos by mixing and matching selections like fried clam strips, top sirloin, deviled crab, and island chicken. Pick any two for $14.95, any three for $16.95, each additional $3.95. Also, traditional dishes are top sirloin for $13.75, mahimahi macadamia for $8.95, or lasagna for $8.25. Children's menu for under $5. Plus an assortment of sandwiches for $5. All entrees come with the salad bar, which is set up in an old bathtub. If you can't make up your mind where to dine, Bobby McGee's is a sure bet.

Pieces of Eight is in the Coral Seas Hotel, tel. 923-6646, open daily 5-11 p.m., happy hour 4-6 p.m., piano bar nightly. This steak and seafood house has managed to create a comfortable and relaxed atmosphere where they serve up excellent steaks and very good fish dishes at a moderate price. The decor is dark wood and burnished brass in a romantically lit main room. A piano stylist tinkles in the background. It's the perfect combination of restaurant that will match itself to your mood. Come for that special night out or just a casual evening meal. "Early birders" 5-7 p.m. can pick selections like garlic chicken or fish 'n' chips with salad bar for $6.95. Entrees are 10-ounce top sirloin ($13.95), ground beef sirloin ($8.95), filet mignon ($15.95), and mahimahi amandine ($11.95). All dinners include choice of potato, rice, or bread and salad bar is $3.50 extra. A great choice for good food and a pleasant setting at affordable prices. The **Cellar Bar** open from noon to the wee hours serves exotic drinks and light meals like a simple pizza, hamburger, or fish bake combination. If you are out on the town, it is a good choice to munch while enjoying a video game or a game of pool.

The House of Hong, 260 Lewers St., tel. 923-0202, open daily 11 a.m.-10:30 p.m., Sun. from 4 p.m., is a standard, no surprises Chinese restaurant with a flair. The decor borders on tasteful with some tables outfitted in starchy white tablecloths accented by inlaid wall murals and painted ceilings of China scenes. The Cantonese lunch special is weekdays 11 a.m.-3 p.m. for $5.95, with "early bird specials" 4-6 p.m.—dishes like egg flower soup, chicken chow mein, sweet and sour pork, crispy wonton, fried rice, fortune cookie, and Chinese tea for $9.95. Not great, but no complaints either.

The **Oceanarium** at the Pacific Beach Hotel, 2490 Kalakaua Ave., tel. 922-1233, offers a full breakfast, lunch, and dinner menu. For lunch, try the tropical fruit plate at $7.50, or an entree such as Cajun five-spice chicken for $7.50. Dinner appetizers like Cajun calimari begin at $4.95, while entrees like New York peppercorn steak are $19.95, and specials like live Maine lobster

MAke Sure you eat here ASK About early Buffet Dinner

A Good place for lunch

...ch-... in ...er. ...ip-...um

...alia ...om ...eal ...ne. ...airs

and white linen table cloth set with crystal. Antipasti selections include escargot ($8.25) and spinach salad ($7.75). Combine these with pasta dishes like spaghetti puttanesca, a savory dish of fillet of anchovy and melted butter cooked in a hot sauce with tomatoes and black olives ($10.75). Complete dinners, ranging in price $17.95-24.95, include choice of minestrone soup or dinner salad, and lasagna, eggplant or tortellini. Trattoria is a good choice for a moderate restaurant with a pleasant atmosphere and better than average cooking.

Benihana of Tokyo, at the Hilton Rainbow Bazaar, 2005 Kalia Rd., open daily for lunch 11:30 a.m.-2 p.m., and for dinner 5:30-10:30 p.m., tel. 955-5955, is a medium-priced Japanese restaurant for those who are jittery about the food and prices. Meals are designed to fit *gaijin* taste, and cooks flash their knives and spatulas at your table—as much a floor show as a dining experience. Good, basic Japanese food, *teppan*-style.

Rascals on Kuhio, at the Kuhio Mall, 2301 Kuhio Ave., tel. 922-5566, is open for dinner only, and doubles as a nightclub with late-night suppers served until 3 a.m. and dancing until 4 a.m. Varied menu of seafood, featuring Cajun-style shrimp soup.

Mandarin Palace, at the Miramar Hotel, 2345 Kuhio Ave., tel. 926-1110, is open for lunch and dinner. Highly rated for its Asian cuisine in a full-blown Chinese atmosphere.

The **Seafood Emporium,** Royal Hawaiian Shopping Center, 2201 Kalakaua Ave., tel. 922-5477, is moderately priced for seafood, with one of the island's largest selections of domestic and imported fish. A good choice for a reasonable lunch or dinner.

The Great Wok of China, Royal Hawaiian

C... ...s de... ...s pr... ...t, w... ...d ve... ...e st...

g... ...1, w... ...ur m... ...r, w... ...re h... ...se

you get the exact same buffet for $7.50. Every day is slightly different, but you can count on a huge assortment of food that is sure to please.

White and pink canvas umbrellas shade the outdoor tables of the **Cafe Princess Garden,** just next to its sister restaurant the **Cafe Princess** (indoor restaurant with full table service), both set in a carved garden grotto surrounded by the Royal Hawaiian and Sheraton hotels. Here, in the heart of Waikiki, but buffered from the crowds, you can enjoy a reasonably priced breakfast special of two scrambled eggs, link sausage, and a croissant for $3.50, or lunch specials, served 11:30 a.m.-5 p.m., like soup and a sandwich for $6.50 or a plate lunch for $5.75. Dinner specials served 5-10 p.m. in the Princess Garden feature steak and lobster for $18.95, while those opting for the inside Cafe Princess can choose jumbo prawns or charbroiled steak for $16.95, or roast prime rib for $11.95. The outdoor Cafe Princess Garden is an excellent people-watching perch from which to enjoy happy hour drinks, 11:30 a.m.-6 p.m., and 10 p.m. until closing, when mai tais are $2.25, pitchers of Bud are $5.50, and frothy chi-chis are only $3.

CASUAL GOURMET

The following restaurants are unique in that they serve inspired gourmet food in lovely settings for very reasonable prices. Though technically not in Waikiki, but located almost next door to each other in Hawaii Kai about 20 minutes away, both are definitely worth the trip.

OnJin Kim creates with food in the same way that a great maestro conducts a symphony orchestra . . . each instrument, distinctive in its own voice, is embraced into the whole. This executive chef draws upon innate talents honed to perfection at the world's finest culinary schools, and then, like a true virtuoso, adds her own intangible ingredients of imagination and heart. The result is the finest dishes of contemporary French, Italian, and Japanese cuisine offered side by side in a glorious melody of flavor and presentation. OnJin is a "nouveau purist," respecting each culinary style with the blending of taste left to the menu selection. Her creations are offered at the **Hanatei Bistro,** 6650 Kalanianaole Hwy., Honolulu HI, 96825, tel. 396-0777, located in the Hawaii Kai Executive Plaza II, open for dinner daily 5:30-10 p.m. Sunday is extra special with brunch served 10 a.m.-1:30 p.m., presenting a fantastic display including sushi bar, snow crab and shrimp cocktails, made-to-order omelettes of all descriptions, carved slabs of prime rib done to perfection, and a "thank the lord it's Sunday and my sins are forgiven" dessert table, all for only $19.95. The dining room, with floor to ceiling windows, is very simple with a minimal amount of decorating creating a Japanese inspired theme. The lattice-covered ceiling, hung with both tasteful chandelier and huge origami crane, is curved like the roof of a Buddhist temple. The curved roof picks up again over an elevated section reminiscent of a classic tea pavilion. Black and red lacquered partitions separate the two areas while the soothing waters of two miniature ponds purl in the background. Appetizers are everything from charred *ahi* at $8.50 to curried- chicken spring rolls at $5.95. The sashimi menu features individual classic offerings like *hamachi* at $5, or special orders for two like Nihon Sensu, three sashimi selections presented on a Japanese fan at $12, or the superb Nihonbashi, five sashimi selections presented on a miniature Japanese cedar bridge at $24. Pasta, half orders as appetizers or full orders as entrees, include capellini with black sturgeon and red salmon caviar at $9/$18, and prawn ravioli also at $9/$18. Soups, all $5, are a seafood suimono, a

blend of French and Japanese traditions with seafood, mushrooms, tofu, and green onions, to a hearty four-onion soup with glazed croutons. The entrees, reflecting OnJin's philosophy of "neo-purist" cuisine, include filet mignon in a merlot sauce, tempura battered seafood and vegetables with dipping sauces, veal scallopini in a savory Madeira sauce, *opakapaka,* luscious Hawaiian pink snapper in a delicate Chinese sesame chile sauce, and *sanshuno sakana,* butter fish in miso, salmon in a salt crust, and teriyaki *unagi* (eel). The most expensive entree is $22, with most priced under $20. The specialty of the house is Bouillabaisse de Chef OnJin, a medley of various seafood simmered in saffron, lemon grass, and plum tomatoes at $26, with regional specials offered with the changing of the seasons. Completely satiate your taste buds with a scrumptious dessert like creme brulee, spiced apple puff, tiramisu cheesecake, or throw all caution to the wind and indulge in the very wicked chocolate macadamia nut torte. At Hanatei, the service is impeccable, and a complete wine list complements all dishes. This is adventurous gourmet dining at its best.

The word "genius" is oftentimes overused and misapplied, causing it to loose its oomph, but when it comes to creativity with food, Roy Yamaguchi is a genius, par excellence! **Roy's Restaurant,** 6600 Kalanianaole Hwy. and Keahole Dr., tel. 396-7697, in Hawaii Kai Corporate Plaza, open Sun.-Thurs. 5:30-9:30 p.m., until 10:30 p.m. Fri.-Sat., presents Euro-Asian cuisine (Pacific Rim) at its very best. The young master chef, through experimentation and an unfailing sense of taste, has created dishes using the diverse and distinctive flavors of French, Italian, Chinese, Japanese, Thai, and Hawaiian cuisine and blended them into a heady array of culinary delights that destroy the adage that "east is east and west is west." The twain have definitely met, and with a resounding success. Roy's dining room is "elegant casual" much like the food, featuring an open kitchen, and although pleasant enough with a superb view, it is not designed for a lengthy romantic evening. Roy's dining philosophy seems to be the serving of truly superb dishes posthaste with the focus on the "food as the dining experience," not the surroundings. The presentation of every dish, under the direction of executive chef Gordon Hopkins, who has been with Roy's since its inception, is flawless, and as pleasing to the eye as it is titillating to the palate. The mastery is in "the blend," which can take you to heights of satiation rarely experienced before. Start with the wild mushrooms with polenta and macadamia nut oil, or potstickers with lobster miso sauce, or even an individual *imu*-oven pizza smothered with grilled chicken, feta cheese, olives, and pesto, all for under $8. Salads feature island-grown greens and vegetables and include such wonderful concoctions as crispy calamari with lemon grass and vinaigrette at $6.95, and Chinese chicken with candied pecans and soy ginger dressing at $6.95. Entrees are wonders like grilled loin of lamb with rosemary, crabmeat, and risotto sauce at $17.95, or a nightly special such as lemon grass encrusted mahimahi with crispy duck cakes in *lilikoi* mustard sauce for $22.95. Desserts by pastry chef Rick Chang are also superb, and include individually prepared (order at beginning of dinner) fresh fruit cobbler in sauce anglaise, or a richer than rich chocolate souffle. Although Roy's has only been open since 1988, it is *the* trend setter in new and inspired cuisine, receiving the praise and adulation of other fine chefs throughout the Islands who try to mimic and match Roy's flair and style.

CLASSY DINING

Halekulani Hotel Dining

Softly the soprano sea sings, while the baritone breeze whispers in melodious melancholy, as you float ephemerally above the waves at **La Mer,** the signature dinner restaurant at the Halekulani Hotel. Splendid in its appointment, the walls, filigreed panels of teak covered in Chinese silk screen, are predominantly browns and whites, the traditional colors of Hawaiian tapa. The ceiling, too, is a work of art, with carved panels trimmed in bronze. Seating is in high-backed upholstered chairs with armrests, and every table is either illuminated by flickering candles or by recessed ceiling lamps that seem to drip the soft gold light of the melting sun upon the table. The hotel's executive chef and chef de cuisine of La Mer, George Mavrothalassitis (Chef

Mavro), was gifted at birth with all of the ingredients to make a great chef . . . a passionate Greek heart inherited from his father, an artistic soul from his Austrian mother, and a Frenchman's devoted love affair with food. Chef Mavro creates culinary masterpieces of Hawaiian regional cuisine using only the finest and best ingredients that are impeccably presented by a highly professional wait staff. Each dish, prepared by La Mer's twelve cooks at their own stations, must pass final inspection by the chef, and if they are found to be at all flawed or simply unartistic, they never reach the dining room. The menu is magnificent and begins with zucchini torte of sautéed *kahuku* prawns at $19, or kiawe-wood smoked Norwegian salmon with shallot and chive sauce at $17. Next comes onaga baked in thyme and rosemary rock salt crust with a fresh herb sauce at $38, sautéed fish coated with cumin and rosemary in a light curry at $26, or filet mignon with oysters in a pinot noir and chervil sauce at $34. All are wonderful; the best however are three selections of full course table d'hôte priced from $65 to $95. Courses are sumptuous and can be poached *papio* with scallop mousse served with lobster sauce, or poached *onaga* with wilted greens and three-caviar sauce. All come with a marvelous selection of fine French cheeses served with walnut bread and a wonderful dessert. Some desserts prepared by pastry chef Franz Schier are chilled white nougat with candied fruit and guava coulis, and a warm brownie with cognac sabayon, at $12. La Mer sets the standard of haute Hawaiian regional cuisine, and if you were to choose one restaurant for a night of culinary bliss, this is a perfect choice.

The House Without a Key, open for breakfast 7-10 a.m. buffet, lunch 11 a.m.-5 p.m., and dinner 5-9 p.m., is a casual outdoor-indoor restaurant in a magnificent oceanside setting. Named after the first novel written about Charlie Chan, Honolulu's famous fictional detective, the restaurant offers unsurpassed views in every direction, and is perhaps the best spot on the island to enjoy a sunset cocktail. Although casual, the seating is very comfortable with padded chairs at simple wood-trimmed tables. The breakfast buffet, including fresh omelettes, is $18.50. Lunch offers main course salads like Oriental chicken salad, grilled beef fajita salad, or a pasta dish like seafood penne or spaghetti bolognese all for under $15. Sandwiches range from a classic triple-decker club sandwich at $12, to grilled mahimahi on nori bread for $15, while entrees are New York steak at $21 or grilled salmon at $19. Dinner starts with cocktail *pu pu,* including chilled jumbo shrimp at $13.50 or scallops wrapped in bacon for $10.50, with the sandwiches, salads and entrees about the same as the lunch menu. Desserts, designed to soothe your palate as the setting sun soothes your soul, include chocolate macadamia-nut creme pie, Toblerone chocolate mousse, or *lilikoi* cheesecake all priced at $6. Entertainment, nightly 5-8 p.m., performed by **The Islanders,** or the **Hiram Olsen Trio** is great for "dancing under the stars." Remember, the door is never locked at House Without a Key.

White, purple, and yellow orchids tumble from trellises, cascade from clay planters, and always grace your table at **Orchids Dining Room,** also at the Halekulani, open daily 7:30-11 a.m. breakfast, 11:30 a.m.-2 p.m. lunch, and 6-10 p.m. dinner, and is another seaside, indoor-outdoor restaurant. Specializing in contemporary American cuisine, Orchids is also famous for its fabulous Sunday brunch at $29.50 adults, $18.50 children. Executive chef Shawn Smith makes freshness a priority, buying ingredients as locally as possible . . . vegetables, beef, prawns, and especially fish. Beautifully appointed with teak wood and Hawaiian eucalyptus flooring, the setting is casual-elegant with white starched linen tablecloths, captain-style chairs with blue and white pillows, and of course heavy silver and crystal. Arranged with a bilevel central dining area that spreads out to a covered veranda, all tables enjoy a panoramic view of the sea with Diamond Head in the distance. Start the day with a continental breakfast including fresh fruit juice, pastry basket, and beverage at $12.50, or an American breakfast with all of the above plus eggs and a breakfast meat at $16.50, or try Japanese style with grilled fish, steamed rice, pickles, miso soup, seaweed, and green tea, at $19.50. There's also a frittata for $13, whole wheat pancakes with macadamia nuts and coconut syrup at $9, or just a basket of pastries and coffee for $6.75. The daily brunch is served 8:30-10 a.m., at $20.75. Start your engine with a mimosa, Bloody Mary, screw-driver, or tropical fruit, along with eggs Benedict, frittata, smoked salmon and cream cheese, and various pastries. Lunch begins with an assortment of delicious appetizers like seared *ahi* with mustard shoyu for $15, or a simple salad of mixed greens with various dressings for $6. Soups, all priced at $5, include Portuguese bean and chilled tropical fruit soup. Special dishes are an assortment of pasta under $15, curry including lamb, Thai chicken for around $18, and broiled Hawaiian fish with herbs at $18. A full course table d'hôte is $25, and all desserts are $6.50. Dinner entrees are luscious seafood platters of charbroiled *a'u* with kula tomato and herbed pasta at $27, pepper crusted opakapaka at $29.50 or rack of lamb Provençale at $33. A taster's menu at $54 is a full five course meal including a symphony of desserts.

Hilton Hawaiian Village Dining

The Hilton Hawaiian Village, at 2005 Kalia Rd., is one of the finest destination resorts in Hawaii. Its two signature restaurants, both *Travel Holiday* award winners, complement the resort perfectly. **Bali by the Sea,** tel. 941-2254, open daily for dinner 6-10 p.m., may sound like Indonesian cuisine, but it's more continental than anything else. The setting couldn't be more brilliant. Sit by the open windows so that the sea breezes fan you as you overlook the gorgeous Hilton beach with Diamond Head off to your left. The room is outfitted in a blue paisley carpet, high-backed, armrest-type chairs, white tablecloths, and classical place settings with silver service. Upon ordering, you are presented with a complimentary platter of hors d'oeuvres. Choose appetizers like gratin of oysters with julienne of duck, or fettuccini with wild mushrooms with prosciutto and sun-dried tomatoes. Soups are bisque of shrimp and lobster or a classic French onion. Entrees are a magnificent selection of fish from Hawaiian waters baked, sautéed, or broiled and then covered in a variety of sauces from fresh basil to mint and tomato vinaigrette. Meat entrees are breast of chicken and lobster, or medallions of venison simmered in pears, cranberry, and *poivrade* sauce. The meal ends with a fine presentation of desserts, or a complimentary "steaming chocolate Diamond Head." Bali by the Sea is a superb choice for an elegant evening of fine dining.

The **Golden Dragon,** tel. 946-5336, open nightly for dinner 6-10 p.m., would tempt any knight errant to drop his sword and pick up chopsticks. This too is a fine restaurant where the walls are decorated with portraits of emperors, and the plates carry the Golden Dragon motif. The interior color scheme is a striking vermilion and black, with the chairs and tables shining with a lacquerware type of patina. The floor is dark koa. Outside, the terrace has pagoda-style canopies under which you may dine. Obviously the Golden Dragon isn't your average chop suey house, but the menu has all of the standard Chinese fare from lemon chicken to . . . well, chop suey, but it doesn't end there. The food is expertly prepared, and two fine choices are the exotic Imperial Beggar's Chicken (for two), which takes 24 hours notice to prepare, and Chef Dai's Selection (for two), which includes lobster in black bean sauce, shrimp, almond duck, beef in rice wine, duck fried rice, and a special dessert all for only $40. For a first-class restaurant with impeccable food and service, the prices at the Golden Dragon are very, very reasonable.

Around Waikiki

One of the most laudable achievements in the restaurant business is to create an excellent reputation and then to keep it. **Nick's Fishmarket** at the Waikiki Gateway Hotel, 2070 Kalakaua, tel. 955-6333, open nightly for dinner 6-11:30 p.m., has done just that . . . and keeps doing it. Many gourmets consider Nick's *the* best dining in Waikiki, and it's great fun to find out if they know what they're talking about. Owner Randy Schoch pays personal attention to every detail at Nick's, while executive chef Mariano Lalica creates the culinary magic. Lalica placed first in the "Seafood Olympics" recently held in Hawaii, and is a marvel at preparing fresh fish, which he accents with Thai peanut sauce and balsamic vinegar, rock shrimp sauce with stone ground mustard and macadamia nuts, or roasted garlic and sundried tomato vinaigrette. Adventurous and highly skilled, Chef Lalica, like the master of an old sailing ship, will take you to culinary ports of call rarely, if ever, visited. Highly professional waiters, knowledgeable about every dish, are friendly and efficient, and always at hand to suggest just the right wine from the extensive list to perfectly complement your choice of dish. Start with fresh-baked clams casino ($9.95), smoked salmon ($10.50), or, if you're in the mood, how about beluga caviar (don't ask). For soup order the Fish Market Chowder, while the Caesar salad prepared at your table has long won honors as the best available west of California! Although Nick's is primarily renowned for its fish, don't overlook the veal, steaks, and chicken with sides of pasta. An excellent choice is one of Nick's complete dinners featuring entree, soup or salad, vegetables, and hot drink. Other great choices are veal picatta, succulent rack of lamb with a Hawaiian mango chutney, and perfectly prepared abalone imported from the cold waters of the California coast. The sinless along with those expecting salvation "tomorrow" will enjoy the dessert menu, which features Nick's van-banna pie, a tempting concoction of banana mousse and almond vanilla ice cream dripping with a caramel sauce, New York inspired cheesecake, or a lighter tropical sorbet. A "Cafe Menu" has recently been added from which you can order until the wee hours while listening to live entertainment in the lounge area. Lobster fried rice, crispy calamari, pasta a la Hawaii, or plump tacos can all be enjoyed, and are all very reasonably priced under $10. Dancing to live music is featured nightly along with special events such as wine tasting evenings scheduled throughout the year. The bar prepares a host of exotic island drinks along with a fine cup of cappuccino, and is known for its extensive microbrewery beer selections. If you had only one evening in Waikiki and you wanted to make it memorable, you'd have a hard time doing better than Nick's Fishmarket.

Sergio's, at the Ilima Hotel, 445 Nohonani, open daily for dinner 5:30-11:30 p.m., tel. 926-3388, is one of the finest Italian restaurants in Honolulu. The interior is romantic, subtle, and simple with a combination of booths and tables. Sergio prepares foods from all regions of Italy, blending and matching hearty peasant soups, fresh salads, and antipasti garnished with aromatic cheeses and spicy prepared meats, pasta dishes, entrees, and desserts. The more than a dozen choices of pasta come with sauces of savory meat, or delicate vegetables, and seafood. Entrees of chicken, beef, and fresh fish make your taste buds rise and shout "Bravo! Sergio! Bravo!"

Michel's, at the Colony Surf Hotel, 2895 Kalakaua Ave., tel. 923-6552, open daily 7 a.m.-10 p.m., is literally on the beach, so your appetite is piqued not only by sumptuous morsels, but by magnificent views of the Waikiki skyline boldly facing the Pacific. The interior is "neo-French elegant," with the dining rooms appointed in soft pastels, velour chairs with armrests, white tablecloths, crystal chandeliers, heavy silver service, and tasteful paintings. The bar is serpentine and of polished koa. Michel's Sunday brunch is legendary. Choose an entree and the remainder of the brunch comes with it. Suggestions are baked avocado with crab meat for $26, or the renowned eggs Benedict for $22. You get a choice of broiled fresh grapefruit with sherry, sliced oranges and melon, fresh Hawaiian pineapple slices, or Puna papaya with limes, along with a sparkling champagne cocktail, and baskets of banana or blueberry muffins and Kona coffee. Daily breakfasts are a wild mushroom omelette ($8.50), or breakfast steak and eggs ($14.50), Belgian waffles ($9.50), and buttermilk pancakes ($7.50). Lunch is appetizers like baked oysters Michel ($10), or Michel's Reuben sandwich ($10). Fruits of the sea are steamed king crab leg for $27, and from the grill come spring lamb chops ($17). Dinner is *magnifique* with fresh Maine lobster on ice ($27), delicate baby coho salmon garnished with shrimp served in its own sauce ($37), or tournedos rossini, a center cut of tenderloin with goose liver and truffles. The dining experience at Michel's is completely satisfying with outstanding food and outstanding service, all in an outstanding setting.

The Secret is the signature restaurant at the Hawaiian Regent, 2552 Kalakaua, tel. 922-6611, open nightly 6-9:30 p.m. As you enter, you pass an arrangement of cornucopias, some holding fresh fruits and fish, while others brim over with gourds, Indian corn, bread turtles, and alligators. A wheelbarrow is loaded with nuts. The decor in the main room is high-back, peacock, wicker chairs, where you're wrapped in the arms of bamboo in a boothlike atmosphere. The room is open-beam construction overlooking Waikiki Beach. In the center is a koi pond with gas torches lit for that extra touch. Hanging from the ceiling are banners that give you the feeling of being at a medieval feast, Polynesian style. Strolling minstrels, The Anacan's, play a seemingly infinite melody of moody contemporary tunes, while a harpist gives an impression of heavenly strains on Monday evenings. Waiters are extremely professional, providing insightful tips to the menu that they have memorized. The Secret is renowned for its fine wines, with over 340 selections expertly managed by Richard Dean, one of only two master sommeliers in all of Hawaii. Within the restaurant is a wine room that can hold a private party of 12 that may choose from a special menu. As you peruse the menu you are presented with a plate of freshly baked Indian *naan* bread. Select the hors d'oeuvres bar, which has smoked salmon, caviar, and duck pâté, enough for a meal for a reasonable $14. Specialties are a Casserole des Fruits de Mer (lobster, scallops, shrimp, and *opacapaca* in fennel sauce), and medallions of venison all priced around $35. The Secret has a long and well-deserved reputation as one of the finest eating establishments in Waikiki. A romantic dinner here will long be remembered.

Matteo's, in the Marine Surf Hotel, 364 Seaside, tel. 922-5551, open 6 p.m.-2 a.m., is a wonderfully romantic Italian restaurant that sets the mood even outside by welcoming you with a red canopy and brass rail that leads to a carved door of koa and crystal. Inside is dark and stylish, with high-backed booths, white tablecloths, and marble-top tables. On each is a rose, Matteo's signature. Dinners begin with hot antipasti priced $7-14, such as stuffed mushrooms a la Matteo, seafood combo or cold antipasto for two. Light fare of *ensalada e zuppa* (salad and soup), hearts of romaine lettuce, or clam soup matched with garlic bread or pizza bread make an inexpensive but tasty meal. Entree suggestions are chicken *rollatini*, veal *rollatini* (rolled veal stuffed with bell peppers, mushrooms, onions, spinach, and mozzarella), or *bragiola* (rolled beef with mozzarella cheese, garlic, fresh basil, and baked with marinara sauce), all under $20. Complete dinners come with Matteo's special salad, pasta, vegetables, and coffee or tea and include mahimahi Veronica (sautéed fish in lemon sauce and seedless grapes) or veal parmigiana and are priced under $28. Pastas are very reasonable and besides the usual linguine dishes include gnocchi and manicotti a la Matteo. An extensive wine list complements the food. If you are out for a special evening of fine dining and romance, Matteo's will set the mood, and the rest is up to you.

The **Surf Room** is in the Royal Hawaiian Hotel, 2259 Kalakaua Ave., tel. 923-7311. The menu is solid but uninspired. However, the setting couldn't be lovelier, and the buffet is staggeringly huge.

Hy's Steak House, 2440 Kuhio Ave., tel. 922-5555, is one of those rare restaurants that is not only absolutely beautiful, but serves great food as well. Decorated like a Victorian sitting room, its menu offers things other than steaks and chops, but these are the specialties and worth the stiff-upper-lipped price.

Restaurant Suntory, Royal Hawaiian Shopping Center, tel. 922-5511, is a very handsome restaurant with different rooms specializing in particular styles like *shabu shabu, teppanyaki,* and sushi. The prices used to be worse, but they're still expensive. However, the food preparation and presentation are excellent, and the staff is very attentive.

Furusato Sushi, right next to the Hyatt Regency at 2424 Kalakaua Ave., tel. 922-4991, and **Furusato Tokyo Steak,** downstairs, are both expensive but top-notch Japanese restaurants. The food and service are authentic, but they are geared toward the Japanese tourist who expects, and almost demands, to pay high

prices. In the steakhouse, expect steak since very little else is on the menu. Upstairs is sushi. Free valet parking is great for this congested part of Waikiki.

The **Hawaii Prince Hotel**, 100 Holomoana St., tel. 956-1111, features three distinctive restaurants. **Takanawa,** with posts of *sugi* pine, floor-to-ceiling windows, and a koi pond in the center of a Japanese garden, is the hotel's sushi bar. **The Prince Court,** the main dining room, offers breakfast, lunch, and dinner. Breakfast, served 5:30-11 a.m., starts with juices and fruits ($4-7), seasonal berries and cream ($6), continental breakfast ($10.50), and a buffet breakfast ($15). Lunches start with appetizers like grilled fresh mozzarella ($6.50), barbecued Pacific oysters and fried onions ($9.50), and Cobb salad with Dungeness crab ($9.50). Sandwiches like sliced avocado, tomato, sprouts, and cucumber in pocket bread start at $6.50, while pasta selections are $9-13.50. Dinner offers entrees like the fresh fish of the day, cooked five possible ways including being baked in a cornbread crust or sautéed with angel hair pasta for a reasonable $17.50, or a mixed grill of local slipper lobster, *kahuku* shrimp, and sea scallops for $24. **Hakone,** the hotel's fine Japanese restaurant, is appointed with shoji screens and wooden tables with high-backed chairs in front of a glass wall that frames the still life of the Ala Wai Yacht Harbor. Dishes are typical, with set menus (*teishoku*) of chicken teriyaki ($23), katsura steak ($29.50), and the Kaiseki Hakone, a full seven course meal for $60.

ENTERTAINMENT

Waikiki swings, beats, bumps, grinds, sways, laughs, and gets down. If Waikiki has to bear being called a carnival town, it might as well strut its stuff. Dancing (disco and ballroom), happy hours, cocktail shows, cruises, lounge acts, Polynesian extravaganzas, and the street scene provide an endless choice of entertainment. Small-name Hawaiian trios, soloists, pianists, and sultry singers featured in innumerable bars and restaurants woo you in and keep you coming back. Big-name island entertainers and visiting international stars play the big rooms. Free entertainment includes hula shows,

ukulele music, street musicians, jugglers, artists, and streetwalkers. For a good time, nowhere in Hawaii matches Waikiki. Also see "Honolulu—Entertainment" for other listings in and around greater Honolulu.

Bars, Happy Hours, And Lounge Acts
Brother Noland is a local talent who appears here and there around town. He's the cutting edge for ethnic Hawaiian groups playing hot reggae, originals, and plenty of Stevie Wonder, solo or with a group, and shouldn't be missed.

Steve and Theresa are excellent Hawaiian musicians. Their sound is a melodious mixture of traditional and contemporary. Accomplished musicians with beautiful voices, they often appear at various venues around town.

In the Park Shore Hotel, 2586 Kalakaua Ave., **The Bar** is a quiet, relaxing place to have a drink. Sometimes, a guest pianist plays.

The **Irish Rose Saloon,** at 227 Lewers, presents live entertainment nightly with dancing till 4 a.m., and features sporting events on their big-screen TV. Happy hour is 3-8 p.m. It's right across the street from the Outrigger Coral Seas Hotel, just at the entrance of the Al Herrington Show.

A great little bar, the **Brass Rail** serves up cold draft beer and deli sandwiches. They're into sports and especially Monday Night Football, which usually begins in Hawaii at 7:30 p.m. Located on the ground floor of the Outrigger Waikiki Hotel, at 2335 Kalakaua.

The **Rose and Crown Pub** in King's Village has a pianist playing sing-along favorites in what is a very close rendition of an English-style pub. They have daily specials; for example, on Saturday if you wear your Rose and Crown hat you have happy hour prices all night long. So drink hearty, and hold on to your hat! The crowd is intent on swilling beer and partying. Noisy, raucous, and fun.

Key Largo is a *bar,* and bars are not so easy to find in Waikiki. Stuck away at 142 Uluniu St., it attracts a mostly local crowd, especially Wed.-Sat. when they feature live rock and roll bands. Key Largo doesn't have the vibe of a rough joint, but it is the sort of place where a fool and his teeth can easily be parted.

Jolly Roger Restaurant, at 2244 Kalakaua and 150 Kaiulani (see "Food") presents a changing mixture of live music nightly in their lounge, open until 2 a.m. A good spot for listening to music and enjoying conversation around the bar. The **Crow's Nest,** above the Jolly Roger restaurant at 2244 Kalakaua, features local and visiting entertainers. If **Blue Kangaroo,** a hilarious comedy act, is playing, don't miss them. The entertainers, Mike Drager and Jay Cook, have been singing and playing their guitars and various other stringed instruments together for over 25 years. They first played at the Crow's Nest in 1972, and in their own words "can't believe the sumbitch lasted this long." Their ribald songs are extremely egalitarian . . . they insult all races, creeds, and sexes equally. As the night gets later their humor gets raunchier. Be forewarned, and have a ball.

The Grapevine, corner of Prince Edward and Uluniu streets, presents low-key live music. Artists change, but expect a guitarist playing soulful Hawaiian music.

In the International Market Place, the **Cock's Roost Steak House** offers free entertainment, with no minimum or cover.

The Brothers Cazimero have an excellent and well-deserved reputation as one of Hawaii's finest duos, singing a lovely blend of Hawaiian and contemporary music. You can usually catch them at the Royal Hawaiian Hotel's Monarch Room. Dinner and cocktail shows are Tues.-Sat. at 7 p.m. Alohawear is fine, tel. 923-7311.

Baron's Studio, Waikiki Plaza Hotel, tel. 946-0277, is home to jazz vocalist Azure McCall. Open nightly, quiet drinks, fine background tunes.

The **Polynesian Pub,** 2490 Kalakaua, tel. 923-3683, offers happy hour nightly and contemporary Hawaiian music. Right-priced drinks, no cover.

The Garden Bar, Hilton Hawaiian Village, tel. 949-4321, features John Norris and the New Orleans Jazz Band on Sun. 2-6 p.m. Also, at the hotel's Paradise Lounge, **Olomana,** a contemporary Hawaiian trio, performs weekend evenings 8 p.m.-midnight, no cover.

The five-star Halekulani Hotel offers superb nightly entertainment. There is no lovelier location for a sunset cocktail than **House Without a key,** where The Islanders or The Hiram Olsen Trio perform contemporary tunes nightly 5-8:30 p.m. Gracing the stage are two former Miss Hawaii's, Kanoe Miller and Debbie Nakanelua, who perform their inspired hula on alternate evenings. Sunday brunch at the hotel's **Orchids Dining Room** is made even more genteel with the musical strains of harpist, Susanne Hussong, accompanied by flutist Susan Gillespie, who perform the hit songs of Broadway musicals. Nightly 9 p.m.-12:30 a.m, from the wood-paneled **Lewers Lounge** flows the liquid sweetness of jazz vocalist Loretta Ables, accompanied by Jim Howard on keyboard and Bruce Hamada

*the distinctive mural
at The Wave*

on bass. On Sunday and Monday, Billy Kurch, a pianist/vocalist takes over and performs contemporary tunes.

Flashback, two shows nightly except Sunday, at the Waikiki Terrace Hotel, recreates the legends of the '50s. Elvis lives!

The Honolulu Comedy Club, nightly except Monday, at the Ilikai Hotel, tel. 922-5998, presents most of Hawaii's and many of the Mainland's hottest comedians.

Discos, Dancing, And Nightclubs

Ballroom dancers will enjoy **Tea Dancing at the Royal** in the Monarch Room of the Royal Hawaiian Hotel, featuring the 14-piece Del Courtney Orchestra, Mon. 5:30-8:30 p.m. The **Maile Lounge** at the Kahala Hilton, tel. 734-2211, offers live music for ballroom dancing nightly.

Nick's Fishmarket at the Gateway Hotel, 2070 Kalakaua (see "Waikiki—Food"), swings with contemporary dance music until 1:30 a.m. A mixed crowd, but mostly a mature crowd who have stayed on to dance after a magnificent meal that Nick's is known for. Music is provided by No Excuse, headliners who make Nick's their home when not on tour.

The **Paradise Lounge** in the Rainbow Tower of the Hilton Hawaiian Village is a jazz nightclub, perfect for a night of relaxing entertainment. They have a pianist nightly and a polished wooden dance floor. Weekends bring a variety of jazz ensembles for your listening and dancing pleasure. Perfect for a romantic evening.

The Wave is a rock 'n' roll and new wave hotspot with live music nightly, 1877 Kalakaua Ave., tel. 941-0424. It has become an institution of late-night fun and dancing. The crowd is mixed, and you can either choose to dance, perch upstairs in the balcony behind glass where you can check out the dancers below, or have a few drinks and some conversation. The Wave is a sure bet for a night of fun.

Pink Cadillac, at 478 Ena, is just around the corner from the Wave. Open till 2 a.m., its large dance floors rock with merrymakers ages 18 and up. It's a happening place for younger rockers. Alcohol is served, but if you are under 21 you'll be braceleted, which means you can't drink. The cover charge is $10 for ages 18-21, $5 over 21.

The following are disco nightclubs in and around Waikiki. Most have videos, a theme, a dress code of alohawear and shoes, no sandals, and start hopping around 9 p.m. with the energy cutoff around 4 a.m.

The **Jazz Cellar,** 205 Lewers St., features mostly live rock and roll and some jazz. The place jumps till 4 a.m. and has plenty of special nights like "Thirsty Tuesdays" and "Ladies' Night." Put on your dancin' shoes and casual attire, tel. 923-9952.

Lewers Street Annex, at 270 Lewers, is a basic disco dance spot featuring Top 40 tunes. The clientele is mostly young visitors and some local workers who stop in for a late-night drink. A special feature is their "12 o'clock high," basically happy hour prices noon-midnight. Standard drinks $1.50, domestic beers $1.50, margaritas and mai tais $1.50. Good for casual drinking, dancing, and meeting people.

The Infinity, at the Sheraton Waikiki, presents golden oldies and contemporary live music nightly from 8 p.m. Good dance floor.

The **Blue Water Cafe,** 2350 Kuhio Ave., once the home of live music, now has disco and videos. It's distinguished by its copper and brass appointment, including full copper doors to the restrooms, and pillars covered in copper.

The **3-D Ballroom,** 2260 Kuhio, is a crummy little joint two floors up with super-loud music for teeny-boppers and punkers.

The Point After, 2552 Kalakaua Ave., tel. 922-6611, is a local favorite with a dress code. Fatso sofas can be found in this football-theme nightspot.

Red Lion Dance Palace, 240 Lewers St., tel. 922-1027, offers high-tech video, disco, and a pool bar. Beachwear is OK. Open 2 p.m.-4 a.m.

Masquerade and **Phaze,** next door to each other at the corner of McCully and Kalakaua avenues, feature a heavy sound system and wild light shows. Cutting-edge videos, great dance floors, and wild tunes till 4 a.m.

Cilly's, 1909 Ala Wai Blvd., tel. 942-2942; **Annabelle's** at the Westin Ilikai, 1777 Ala Moana Blvd., tel. 949-3811; and **Steel Wings,** also at the Westin Ilikai, are well-known discos where you can't help having a good time. All have reputations as swinging nightspots.

Exotic live dancers, like exotic live plants, need a unique atmosphere in which to bloom. Both seem to crave light, one sunlight, the other a spotlight. Most of the flashy fleshy nightspots of Waikiki used to be a few blocks away along Kapiolani Blvd. (see "Health and Well-being—Prostitution" in the Out and About chapter), but they have been moving ever closer to the heart of Waikiki. Now they are strung along Kuhio Avenue, where they're easily recognizable by their garish neon lights advertising their wares. The Kuhio Avenue exotic dance spots are supposedly a step up in class from their Kapiolani Boulevard counterparts, but when their dancers strip to the buff, the difference is hardly noticeable . . . or very noticeable, depending upon point of view. The names of the strip joints really don't matter, just look for the signs of "exotic dancers." Usually a $10 cover and $5 for a drink.

Dinner Shows And Polynesian Extravaganzas

The **Don Ho Show,** an institution that played at the Hilton Hawaiian Village for years, is no longer. Mr. Ho has moved to the Waikiki Beachcomber at 2300 Kalakaua Ave., tel. 922-4646, where he plays two shows nightly, Thurs.-Sun. The 7 p.m. dinner show costs $46, and the 9 p.m. cocktail show is $28. Either show is recommended. Gone is the glitz and glamour, just Ho and his organ much in the same way as he performed at Duke Kahanamoku's Club in the 1960s. Don Ho is still a great performer, and "the godfather of modern Hawaiian music." Professional funster **Frank De Lima** hosts "Tropical Madness" in the Polynesian Palace nightly except Mon., at 9 p.m. De Lima, supported by a cast of various loonies, is guaranteed to tickle your funny bone, "island style."

The Kahala Hilton, tel. 734-2211, presents **An Evening With Danny Kaleikini.** This extraordinary island entertainer has been captivating audiences here for almost 30 years. This show has class; it doesn't draw the large budget-oriented crowds. Two shows nightly except Sun., dinner show at 7 p.m., cocktail show at 9 p.m.

The Hilton Dome at the Hilton Hawaiian Village fills with magical vibrations when headliner **John Hirokawa** suddenly appears out of nowhere. The **Magic of Polynesia** is a journey into the realm of enchantment and beauty that the entire family can enjoy. Slight of hand, disappearing maidens, swaying hula dancers, fantastic costumes and audience participation are all part of the magical extravaganza. Two shows nightly: dinner seating at 6:30 p.m., adults $45, children $31; cocktail show at 9 p.m., adults $25, children $17.

Society of Seven, a well established local ensemble, appears nightly except Sunday at the Outrigger Main Showroom.

If you missed them the first time, here's your chance to see the world's greatest entertainers when unbelievably realistic impersonators perform **Legends in Concert,** a Las Vegas-style spectacular presented nightly at the Aloha Showroom of the Royal Hawaiian Shopping Center.

The Ainahau Showroom at the Sheraton Princess Kaiulani Hotel presents the **Sheraton Spectacular Polynesian Revue,** nightly for dinner and cocktail shows at 5:30 and 8 p.m.

Free Or Small Fee Entertainment

Check the newspapers and free tourist literature for times to the following events.

The **Royal Hawaiian Band** plays free concerts on Sunday afternoons at the bandstand in Kapiolani Park, oftentimes with singers and hula dancers. Also in the park, free concerts are periodically given by a variety of local and visiting musicians at the Waikiki Shell.

The **Kodak Hula Show** (small admission) is very popular. The show is held on Tues., Thurs., and Fri. at 10 a.m. in Kapiolani Park, but people start lining up at 8 a.m.; be there by 9 if you want a seat. You sit on bleachers with 3,000 people, while Hawaiian *tutu* bedecked in muumuu, lei, and smiles play ukuleles and sing for the ti-leaf-skirted dancers. You can buy film and even rent a camera, as befits the show's sponsor, the Eastman Kodak Company—snap away with abandon. The performance dates back to 1937, and some of the original dancers, now in their eighties, still participate. At the finale, the dancers line up on stage with rod-lettered placards that spell out H-A-W-A-I-I, so you can take your own photo of the most famous Hawaiian postcard. Then the audience is invited down for a free hula lesson. People who are too hip hate it, *kamaaina* shy away from it, but if you're a good sport, you'll walk away like everyone else with a big smile on your face.

A potpourri of contemporary entertainment is also found in Kapiolani Park on weekends. Just across from the zoo, musicians, jugglers, clowns, unicyclists, and acrobats put on a free, impromptu circus. Some of the best are B.J. Patches, Twinkles, and Jingles from a local troupe called Clown Alley.

The **Ukulele Tree Hawaiian Music Show** is held in the Outrigger East Hotel Sat., Sun., and Mon. 5-7 p.m., free, where local musicians and sometimes well-known guests come to play and be heard. For information call 922-5353.

The **Royal Hawaiian Shopping Center** provides free entertainment throughout the week: quilting, *lau hala* weaving, pineapple cutting, and free hula lessons every Friday at 10 a.m. with Aunti Maiki Aiu Lake.

Molehu I Waikiki, a nightly torch lighting ceremony complete with authentic hula performed by various *halau,* is offered to the public free of charge at Kuhio Beach Park. For information contact 923-1094.

Na Mea Hula, under the direction of *kuma hula* Karla Akiona, takes place every Friday 5:30-7 p.m., at the Sheraton Waikiki Hotel, tel. 922-4422. Preceeding the hula, the prèsentation includes lei-making, conch shell blowing, a *kahiko* procession, and a torch lighting ceremony.

Aunty Bella's Leis, 2200 Kalakaua Ave., gives free lei-making classes Mon., Wed., and Fri. at 10:30 a.m. The flowers are free and you keep the lei that you string.

At the Shore Bird Restaurant, 2160 Kalia, a **female bikini beauty** contest is held on Sun. at 4 p.m. You can win $400 for first prize, second prize $150, third $50. All finalists receive dinner for two at the Shore Bird Beach Broiler and much more.

Sometimes, "free" tickets to some of Waikiki's most popular Polynesian Extravaganzas are handed out by condo time-share outfits stationed in booths along the main drags. For attending their sales presentations, usually 90 minutes, you can get tickets, but they might be the toughest freebies you've ever earned. The presentation is a pressure cooker where hardened sales pros try every imaginable technique to get you to sign . . . "right now, because this is the only time that this deal can be offered." If you're really interested in time-sharing, the deals aren't too bad, but if you're there only for the tickets, what a waste of time!

SHOPPING

The biggest problem concerning shopping in Waikiki is to keep yourself from burning out over the endless array of shops and boutiques. Everywhere you look someone has something for sale, and with the preponderance of street stalls lining the boulevards, much of the merchandise comes out to greet you. The same rule applies to shopping as it does to everything in Waikiki—class next door to junk. Those traveling to the Neighbor Islands should seriously consider a shopping spree in Waikiki, which has the largest selection and most competitive prices in the islands. A great feature about shopping in Waikiki is that most shops are only a minute or two from the beach. This enables your salehound companion to hunt while you relax. There's no telling how much money your partner can save you! "Ingrate! This bathing suit could have cost $50, but I got it for $25. See, you saved $25 while you were lying here like a beached whale." Everyone concerned should easily be mollified. Charge!

The Fence

The best place to find an authentic island-made souvenir at a reasonable price is at **The Fence,** located along the fence of the Honolulu Zoo fronting Kapiolani Park. The new offical name is **Artists of Oahu/Sunday Exhibit.** Some of the island's best artists congregate here to display and sell their works on Wednesday and weekends 10 a.m.-4 p.m. Individual artists are only allowed to display one day a week. The Fence was the good idea of Honolulu's current mayor, Frank Fasi, who decided that Oahu's rich resource of artists shouldn't go untapped. There are plenty of excellent artists whose works are sure to catch your fancy.

Gifts And Souvenirs

If you would really like to return from the islands with a unique gift try **Hawaiian Pillows and Kits,** tel. 734-5032. The pillowcases are excellent renditions of the distinctive style of quilting developed in Hawaii after being introduced by the missionaries of last century. Rose Tam-Hoy, the owner, shows her handiwork at the Sheraton Moana's Banyan Courtyard on Fridays and at various other hotels throughout the week. Rose is a wealth of knowledge on Hawaiian quilting, and is happy to offer demonstrations and lessons.

Another islander demonstrating and selling Polynesian crafts is Faitu Powell of **Powell's Souvenirs,** tel. 926-6797. Faitu also sets up a small display at the Moana on Friday, and across the way at the Princess Kaiulani on Saturdays. She specializes in handmade hula skirts,

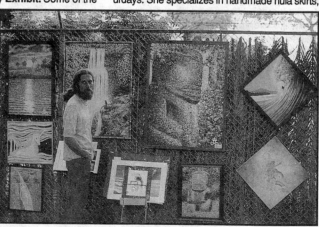

John Costello, artist

lei, head bands, *haku,* and a variety of handicrafts. All of her souvenirs are authentic.

Fine Japanese art can be seen and purchased at two outstanding shops in Waikiki's Eaton Square, **Gallery Mikado** and **Garakuta-Do.**

ABC Stores scattered throughout Waikiki were founded by a local man, Sid Kosasa, who learned the retail business from his father. This "everything store" sells groceries, sundries, and souvenirs. Prices are good, especially on specials like lotions and beach mats. Very convenient.

On Kalakaua between Kealohilani and Ohua streets above the ABC Store is **Lowest Factory Prices.** They've got very good prices on all-cotton shirts and muumuu, a rarity. Every price tag offers 10% off.

Those who just couldn't return home without a deep Hawaiian tan can be helped by visiting **Waikiki Aloe.** They specialize in skin-care products, lotions, and tanning supplies. In the Royal Hawaiian Shopping Center and the Kuhio Mall.

The **Waikiki Business Plaza,** 2270 Kalakaua Ave., houses a number of jewelry stores. In one stop you can get a pretty good idea of prices and availability. Look for jewelry boxes laden with jade, gold, turquoise, pearls, coral, and *puka* shells, and eel, snake, and leather goods.

Military Shop of Hawaii has an entire wall dedicated to military patches, along with clothes, memorabilia, and collectibles. At 1921 Kalakaua Ave., tel. 942-3414.

Those with good taste but a limited budget should check out **Hawaiian Wear Unlimited,** liquidators of alohawear from most of Hawaii's big manufacturers. Located at the Royal Hawaiian Shopping Center, open daily 9 a.m.-10 p.m. Also, **Robin Claire** "resale boutique" sells used designer clothing. At 1901 Kapiolani Plaza, tel. 941-8666.

Kite Fantasy, 2863 Kalakaua Ave., tel. 922-KITE, is sure to have an aerial toy to tickle your fancy. Kapiolani Park across the road is one of the best spots around to fly a kite, and they give free kite-flying lessons regardless of whether you purchase a kite or not; daily display at 11 a.m. and 2 p.m. Next door to the old Natatorium and the New Otani Hotel, you'll see their multicolored kites floating in the breeze. Inside they have the "finest collection of kites, windsocks,

and toys" in Hawaii. The phenomenal winds in Hawaii that generate good waves and good windsurfing conditions also generate excellent kite-flying conditions. Hardly a day goes by that there isn't wind enough to get a kite up. And, because the winds are so gusty and changeable, it makes for some fantastic kite-flying acrobatics. Nearby in the park is what they call the Kite Tree, where kite flyers congregate in the evening. So if you're interested, go fly a kite!

Waikiki Fashion Center, 2310 Kuhio, next door to Zorro's, sells alohawear like plenty of other stores, but the prices are pretty good, and they even feature an ad for $5 off with a purchase of $20 or more.

For a full range of **photo supplies** at bargain prices try: **Woolworth's,** 2224 Kalakaua Ave.; **Fox Photo** in the International Market Place and the Waikikian and Reef Towers hotels; and **Photo Stores** here and there along Kalakaua, Kuhio, Kalia, and Lewers streets. **Island Camera and Gift Shop,** on Kalakaua across from the Moana Hotel, is a small but full-service camera store. Handbillers often give money-saving coupons to a variety of photo stores.

Duty-free goods are always of interest to international visitors. You can find a duty-free store on Royal Hawaiian Ave., just behind Woolworth's. Also, if you want to see a swarm of Japanese jostling for position in a tiny little store trying to feed a buying frenzy, that's the spot.

Waikiki Shopping Centers

The largest credit card oasis is the **Royal Hawaiian Shopping Center.** This massive complex is three stories of nonstop shopping, running for three blocks in front of the Sheraton and Royal Hawaiian hotels. It's open daily 9 a.m.-10 p.m., till 9 p.m. on Sun., tel. 922-0588. This complex provides an excellent mixture of small intimate shops and larger department stores. There's a **post office** on the second-floor "B" building. The second and third floors of this shopping center are pretty quiet. It's off the street so not as many tourists find their way here. It's a good place to do some comparative browsing before making your purchases.

Where the Royal Hawaiian Shopping Plaza ends the **Waikiki Shopping Plaza** begins, but on the other side of the street. Here, you'll find

Waikiki Bazaar

multilevel shopping. The mall's centerpiece is a five-story waterfall, an impressive sculpture of water and plexiglass. Another feature of this mall is Waikiki Calls, a free hula show. The plaza is open daily 9 a.m.-11 p.m., tel. 923-1191.

The **International Market Place** is an open-air shopping bazaar that feels like Asia. Its natural canopy is a huge banyan, and the entire complex is across from the Moana Hotel at 2330 Kalakaua Ave., open daily from 9 a.m. until the vendors get tired at night, tel. 923-9871. Among some fine merchandise and a treasure or two is great junk! If you're after souvenirs like bamboo products, shellwork, hats, mats, lotions, alohawear, and carvings, you can't do better than the International Market Place. The worst thing is that everything starts to look the same; the best is that the vendors will bargain. Make offers and try hard to work your way through the gauntlet of shops without getting scalped. Check out the Elvis Store and Museum, which must be seen to be believed.

Directly behind the marketplace is the **Kuhio Mall,** at 2301 Kuhio Avenue. Basically the same theme with open-air shops: gifts, fashions, food, and handmade artifacts. Enjoy the free Polynesian Show nightly at 7 and 8 p.m. This is a little older, funkier mall, one grade up from what you would find in the International Market Place and Duke's Alley. If you want a low-key place to discover "treasure junk" this mall is good. It's even better than the International Market Place because it's more low-key. There aren't nearly

as many people here and the salespeople are not as pushy.

For those who can't stand to waste an opportunity to shop, they can do so while passing through **Duke's Alley,** a shortcut between Kuhio and Kalakaua avenues. Here you'll find a row of stalls selling basically the same merchandise as in the International Market Place.

The **Hyatt Regency Shopping Center,** also called the **Atrium Shops,** is located on the first three floors of the Hyatt Regency Hotel, 2424 Kalakaua Ave., tel. 922-5522, open daily 9 a.m.-11 p.m. The 70 or so shops are mighty classy: if you're after exclusive fashions or a quality memento, this is the place. There's a continental-style sidewalk cafe, backed by a cascading indoor waterfall. Often free entertainment and fashion shows are put on by the various shops.

Smaller Malls
King's Village, at 131 Kaiulani Ave., just next to the Hyatt Regency, takes its theme from last century, where boardwalks pass 19th-century look-a-like shops, complete with a changing-of-the-guard ceremony nightly at 6:15 p.m. This attractive complex offers free entertainment and attracts some of the best local street artists, who usually set up their stands at night. The **Waikiki Trade Center** is on the corner of Seaside and Kuhio avenues with some of Waikiki's most elegant shops, featuring sophisticated fashions, exquisite artwork, and fine dining. The **Rainbow Bazaar** is a unique

mall located at the Hilton Hawaiian Hotel, 2005 Kalia Road. Fun just to walk around, shops feature three main themes: Imperial Japan, Hong Kong Alley, and South Pacific Court.

The Waikiki Bazaar is on Kalakaua across from a brand-new building called A.N.A. Kalakaua Center, a multihued building in pastels. It's beautiful. Reminiscent of newer constructions seen in Japan. The Bazaar is bizarre. Upstairs, and in little booths, is an orgy of porno shops. A person who couldn't read Japanese *katakana* wouldn't know that they said "porno." The Bazaar is there expressly for the use of Japanese tourists.

Street Artists And Vendors

You don't have to try to find something to buy in Waikiki—in fact, if you're not careful, the merchandise will come after you! This takes place in the form of street vendors, who have been gaining a lot of attention lately. Some view them as a colorful addition to the beach scene, others as a nuisance. These carnival-type salespeople set up their mobile booths mainly along Kalakaua Avenue, with some on Kuhio Avenue and the side streets in between. In dealing with them you can have a positive experience if you remember two things: they have some pretty nifty junk, and you get what you pay for.

Also, street artists set up their palettes along busy thoroughfares, and especially at the entrances to small shopping malls. Most draw caricatures of patrons in a few minutes for a few dollars—fun souvenirs.

Right here under the Waikiki banyan is a gentleman named Coco who makes coconut-frond hats, basically a dying art. Just near the canoe rides, you'll see his hats and baskets. Depending on the hat, you can get one for $15 or so. The baskets, good for holding fruit, incidentals, or whatever, are a real souvenir of Hawaii. With Coco making them right before your very eyes, you can't get more authentic than that. Coco says you can still learn how to weave in the Hawaiian tradition. His dad, Uncle Harry Kuikai, weaves at the Royal Hawaiian Shopping Center every Tues. and Thurs. 9:30-11:30 a.m. He'll teach you the basics of weaving and you can make your own souvenir (free). For longer-term tourists, there's an eight-week weaving class sponsored by the Kamehameha School. Just call the high school and inquire as to time and fees.

As you walk around Waikiki you'll see plenty of street-side booths offering unbelievable prices like "rent a car for $5, a jeep for $15, Pearl Harbor Cruise $5, Don Ho Show $20." Why so cheap? It's basically an advertising firm that signs you up to listen to a 90-minute spiel on a time-share condo. What happens during and after the 90-minute hard pitch is up to you, but you do get the payoff at the end.

plumeria

BOB RACE

CENTRAL OAHU

For most uninformed visitors, central Oahu is a colorful blur as they speed past in their rental cars en route to the North Shore. Slow down, there are things to see! For island residents, the suburban towns of Aiea, Pearl City, Mililani, and Wahiawa are home. Both routes heading north from Honolulu meet in **Wahiawa,** the island's most central town. The roads cross just near the entrance to **Schofield Barracks,** a warm-up target for Japanese Zeros as they flew on their devastating bombing run over Pearl Harbor.

Wahiawa was of extreme cultural and spiritual importance to the early Hawaiians. In town are **healing stones,** whose mystic vibrations were said to cure the maladies of sufferers. In a field not far from town are the **Kukaniloko,** the royal

birthing stones, where the ruling *ali'i* labored to give birth to the future nobles of the islands. While in town you can familiarize yourself with Oahu's flora by visiting the **Wahiawa Botanic Garden,** or take a quick look at a serene Japanese temple.

As you gain the heights of the **Leilehua Plateau,** sandwiched between the Waianae and Koolau ranges, a wide expanse of green is planted in cane and pineapple. Just like on supermarket shelves, Del Monte's **Pineapple Variety Garden** competes with Dole's **Pineapple Pavilion,** a minute up the road. As a traveler's way station, central Oahu blends services, amenities, and just enough historical sites to warrant stretching your legs, but not enough to bog you down for the day.

WAHIAWA AND VICINITY

Wahiawa is like a military jeep: basic, ugly, but indispensable. This is a soldiers' town, with servicemen from Schofield Barracks or nearby Wheeler AFB shuffling along the streets. Most are young, short-haired, short-tempered, and dressed in fatigues. Everywhere you look are cheap bars, burger joints, run-down discos perfumed with sweat and

spilled beer, and used-furniture stores. Route 99 turns into Rt. 80 which goes through Wahiawa, crossing California Avenue, the main drag, then rejoins Rt. 99 near the Del Monte Pineapple Variety Garden. Wahiawa has seemingly little to recommend it, and maybe because of its ugliness, when you do find beauty it shines even brighter.

SIGHTS

Wahiawa Botanic Garden

In the midst of town is an oasis of beauty, 27 acres of developed woodlands featuring exotic trees, ferns, and flowers gathered from around the world. Located at 1396 California Ave., they're open daily except Christmas and New Year's, 9 a.m.-4 p.m., admission free. The parking lot is marked by an HVB warrior; walk through the main entranceway and take a pamphlet from the box for a self-guiding tour. When it rains, the cement walkways are treacherously slippery, especially if you're wearing thongs. The nicer paths have been left natural, but they can be muddy. Inside the grounds are trees from the Philippines, Australia, Africa, and a magnificent multihued Mindanao gum from New Guinea. Your senses will be bombarded with fragrant camphor trees from China and Japan, and the rich aroma of cinnamon. Everywhere are natural bouquets of flowering trees, entangled by vines and highlighted by rich green ferns. Most specimens have been growing for a minimum of 40 years, so they're well established.

The Healing Stones

Belief in the healing powers of these stones has been attracting visitors since ancient times. When traveling down Oahi Street (Rt. 80) take a left on California Avenue, and follow it to Kaalalo Place. To glimpse the religion of Hawaii in microcosm, in a few blocks you pass the Riusenji Soto Buddhist Mission, followed by the healing stones, next door to Olive United Methodist Church. If you've never experienced a Buddhist temple, make sure to visit the grounds of **Riusenji Soto Mission.** Usually no one is around, and even if the front doors are locked you can peer in at an extremely ornate altar graced by Buddha, highlighted in black lacquer and gold. On the grounds look for a stone *jizo*, patron of travelers and children. In Japan he often wears a red woven hat and bib, but here he has on a straw hat and muumuu.

An HVB Warrior marks the stones, just past the Kaalala Elementary School, across the street from a beautiful eucalyptus grove. A humble cinder-block building built in 1947 houses the stones. When you swing open the iron gate it strikes a deep mournful note, as if it were an instrument designed to announce your presence and departure. Inside the building, three stones sit atop rudimentary pedestals. Little scratches mark the stones, and an offertory box is filled with items like oranges, bread, a gin bottle, coins, and candy kisses. A few votive candles flicker before a statue of the Blessed Virgin.

Kukaniloko, The Birthing Stones

Follow Rt. 80 through town for about a mile. At the corner of Whitmore Avenue is a red light: right takes you to Whitmore Village and left puts you on a dirt track that leads to another eucalyptus grove marking the birthing stones. About 40 large boulders are in the middle of a field with a mountain backdrop. One stone looks like the next, but on closer inspection you see that each has a personality. The royal wives would come here, assisted by both men and women of the ruling *ali'i,* to give birth to their exalted offspring. The baby's umbilical cord, a sacred talisman, would be hidden in the cracks and crevices of the stones. Near the largest palm tree is a special stone that appears to be fluted all the way around, with a dip in the middle. It, along with other stones nearby, seem perfectly fitted to accept the torso of a woman in a reclining position. Notice that small fires have been lit in the hollows of these stones, and that they are discolored with soot and ashes.

Schofield Barracks

Stay on Rt. 99, skirt Wahiawa to the west, and go past the entrance to Schofield Barracks. Schofield Barracks dates from the turn of the century, named after Gen. John Schofield, an early proponent of the strategic importance of Pearl Harbor. A sign tells you that it is still the "Home of the Infantry, Tropic Lightning." If you enter here through the McComb Gate, you can visit the **Tropic Lightning Museum** with memorabilia going back to the War of 1812. There are planes from WW II, Chinese rifles from Korea, and deadly *pungi* traps from Vietnam.

The museum has lost many of its exhibits in recent years. They've been taken to the Army Museum in Waikiki. But the base is still interesting to visit and remains one of the prettiest military installations in the world. With permission, you can proceed to the Kolekole Pass, from where you get a sweeping view of inland and coastal Oahu. While heading north on 99 as you pass Schofield Barracks, notice a few run-down shops about 50 yards past the entrance. Stop here and look behind the shops at a wonderful still life created by the Wahiawa Reservoir (good fishing; see "Sports and Recreation—Freshwater Fishing" in the Out and About chapter).

Pineapples

A few minutes past the entrance to Schofield Barracks, Rt. 803 bears left to Waialua, while Rt. 99 goes straight ahead and begins passing rows of pineapple. At the intersection of Rt. 80 is the **Del Monte Variety Garden.** You're free to wander about and read the descriptions of the history of pineapple production in Hawaii, and of the genetic progress of the fruit made famous by the islands. This exhibit is much more educational and honest than the **Dole Pineapple Pavilion** just up the road, the one with all the tour buses lined up outside. You too can enter and pay $1.50 for a sad little paper plate half filled with pineapple chunks. Or how about 60 cents for a glass of canned pineapple juice from a dispenser that you'd find in any fast-food store. Unless the pineapple harvest has been abundant, you can't even buy a fresh fruit, and when you can, they're no cheaper or fresher than those in any grocery store. The Dole Pineapple Pavilion is firmly entrenched along the tourist route, but as a positive public relations scheme it is a blunder!

Kukaniloko, royal birthing stones

Schofield Barracks

PRACTICALITIES

Food And Shopping

Dot's Restaurant, off California Ave. at 130 Mango St., tel. 622-4115, is a homey restaurant specializing in American-Japanese food that gives a good square meal for your money. The interior is a mixture of Hawaiian/Asian in dark brown tones. Lunch specials include butterfish, teriyaki chicken, pork, or beef plates all for around $4.50. Miso soup is $2, and simple Japanese dishes go for about $3.50. The most expensive item on the menu is steak and lobster for $15. Dot's is

nothing to write home about, but you definitely won't go hungry.

If you're into fast foods, no problem. The streets are lined with **Jack in the Box** elbowing **Ronald McDonald,** who's trying to outflash the old **Burger King.**

The streets of Wahiawa are lined with stores that cater to residents, not tourists. This means that the prices are right, and if you need supplies or necessities, this would be a good place to stock up. On the corner of California and Oahi streets is a **Cornet Store,** an old-fashioned five and dime, where you can buy anything from suntan lotion to a crock pot. The **Big Way Supermarket** is at the corner of California and Kilani avenues.

AIEA, PEARL CITY, AND VICINITY

The twin cities of Aiea and Pearl City, except for the USS *Arizona* Memorial and perhaps a football game at Aloha Stadium, have little to attract the average tourist. Mainly they are residential areas for greater Honolulu, and for the large numbers of military families throughout this area.

PEARL HARBOR: USS *ARIZONA* MEMORIAL

Even as you approach the pier from which you board a launch to take you to the USS *Arizona,* you know that you're at a shrine. Very few spots in America carry such undeniable emotion so

easily passed from one generation to another: here, Valley Forge, Gettysburg, not many more. On that beautiful, cloudless morning of December 7, 1941, at one minute before 8 o'clock, the United States not only entered the war, but lost its innocence forevermore.

The first battle of WW II for the U.S. actually took place about 90 minutes before Pearl Harbor's bombing, when the USS *Ward* sank an unidentified submarine sliding into Honolulu. In Pearl Harbor, dredged about 40 years earlier to allow superships to enter, the heavyweight champions of America's Pacific Fleet were lined up flanking the near side of Ford's Island. The naive deployment of this "Battleship Row" prompted a Japanese admiral to remark that never, even in times of maximum world peace, could he dream that the military might of a nation would have its unprotected chin stuck so far out, just begging for a right cross to the jaw. When it came, it was a roundhouse right, whistling through the air, and what a doozy!

Well before the smoke could clear and the last explosion stopped rumbling through the mountains, 3,581 Americans were dead or wounded, six mighty ships had sunk into the ooze of Pearl, 12 others stumbled around battered and punch-drunk, and 347 warplanes were useless heaps of scrap. The Japanese fighters had hardly broken a sweat, and when their fleet, located 200 miles north of Oahu, steamed away, the "east wind" had indeed "rained." But it was only the first squall of the American hurricane that would follow.

Getting There

There are a few options on how to visit Pearl Harbor and the USS *Arizona* Memorial. If you're driving, the entrance is along Rt. 99, the Kamehameha Highway, about a mile south of Aloha Stadium; well-marked signs direct you to the parking area. If you're on H-1 west, take exit 15A, and follow the signs. You can also take TheBus, no. 50, 51, or 52 from Ala Moana Center, or no. 20 Airport from Waikiki, and be dropped off within a minute's walk of the entrance. Depending upon stops and traffic, this can take well over an hour.

Arizona Memorial Shuttle Bus, tel. 839-0911, a private operation from Waikiki, takes about 20 minutes and will pick you up at most Waikiki hotels. They charge $2 one-way; reservations are necessary. Returning, no reservations are necessary; just buy a ticket from the lady selling them under the green umbrella in the parking lot.

The **Arizona Memorial Visitor Center** is a joint venture of the U.S. Park Service and the Navy, and is free! The Park Service runs the theater and museum, and the Navy operates the shuttle boats that take you out to the memorial shrine. The complex is open daily 7:30 a.m.-5 p.m., with daily programs 8 a.m.-3 p.m. (closed Thanksgiving, Christmas, New Year's Day), when you can visit the museum and the theater, and take the shuttle boats out to the memorial. If the weather is stormy, or waves rough, they won't sail. For recorded information call 422-0561 or 422-2771. As many as 3,000 people visit per day, and your best time to avoid delays is before 9:30 a.m.

Also, a number of boats operate out of Kewalo Basin doing **Pearl Harbor Cruises.** Costing about $15 for an extensive tour of Pearl Harbor, they are not allowed to drop passengers off at the memorial itself.

Bookstore And Theater

As you enter, you're handed a numbered ticket. Until it's called, you can visit the bookstore/gift

Under attack: The Japanese attack on Pearl Harbor set off a chain of events that would make the U.S. the domineering power of the Pacific.

Arizona *Memorial*

shop and museum, or if the wait is long, the USS *Bowfin* moored within walking distance (see following). The bookstore specializes in volumes on WW II and Hawaiiana. The museum is primarily a pictorial history, with a strong emphasis on the involvement of Hawaii's Japanese citizens during the war. There are instructions of behavior to "all persons of Japanese ancestry," from when bigotry and fear prevailed early in the war, as well as documentation of the 442nd Battalion, made up of Japanese soldiers, and their heroic exploits in Europe, especially their rescue of Texas's "lost battalion." Preserved newspapers of the day proclaim the "Day of Infamy" in bold headlines.

When your number is called you proceed to the comfortable theater where a 20-minute film includes actual footage of the attack. The film is historically factual, devoid of an overabundance of flag waving and mom's apple pie. After the film you board the launch: no bare feet, no bikinis or bathing suits, but shorts and shirts are fine. Twenty years ago visitors wore suits and dresses as if going to church!

The Memorial

The launch, a large mostly open-air vessel handled and piloted with professional deft, usually by women Naval personnel, heads for the 184-foot-long alabaster memorial straddling the ship that still lies on the bottom. Some view the memorial as a tombstone; others see it as a symbolic ship, bent by struggle in the middle,

but raised at the ends pointing to glory. The USS *Arizona* became the focus of the memorial because her casualties were so severe. When she exploded, the blast was so violent that it lifted entire ships moored nearby clear out of the water. Less than nine minutes later, with infernos raging and huge hunks of steel whizzing through the air, the *Arizona* was gone. Her crew went with her; nearly 1,100 men were sucked down to the bottom, and only 289 somehow managed to struggle to the surface. To the left and right are a series of black and white moorings bearing the names of the ships that were tied to them on the day of the attack.

The deck of the memorial can hold about 200 people; a small museum holds the ship's bell, and a chapel-like area displays a marble tablet with the names of the dead. Into a hole in the center of the memorial, flowers and wreaths are dropped on special occasions. Part of the superstructure of the ship still rises above the waves, but it is slowly being corroded away by wind and sea water. The flag, waving overhead, is attached to a pole anchored to the deck of the sunken ship. Sometimes, on weekends, survivors from the attack are aboard to give firsthand descriptions of what happened that day. Many visitors are Japanese nationals, who often stop and offer their apologies to these Pearl Harbor survivors, distinguished by special military-style hats. The Navy ordered that any survivor wishing to be buried with his crew members had that right. In 1982 a diver took a stainless-steel container of the ashes of one of the survivors to be laid to rest with his buddies.

Nearby Attractions

The **USS** *Bowfin,* a WW II submarine moored within walking distance of the *Arizona* Memorial Center, has been turned into a self-guiding museum, open 9:30 a.m.-4:30 p.m., admission $6 adults, $1 children ages 6-12. In the little compound leading to the sub is a snack bar with some tables, a few artillery pieces, and a torpedo or two. As you enter, you're handed a telephonelike receiver; a recorded transmitted message explains about different areas on the sub. The deck is made from teak wood, and the deck guns could go fore or aft depending on the skipper's preference. You'll also notice two anchors; one, under a fresh coat of paint, was salvaged from the pink sub used in the film *Operation Petticoat.*

As you descend, you feel as if you are integrated with a machine, a part of its gears and workings. In these cramped quarters of brass and stainless steel lived 90 to 100 men, all volunteers. Fresh water was in short supply, and the only man allowed to shower was the cook. Officers were given a dipper of water to shave with, but all the other men grew beards. With absolutely no place to be alone, the men slept on tiny stacked shelves, and only the officers could control their light switches. The only man to have a miniscule private room was the captain.

Topside, twin 16-cylinder diesels created unbelievable noise and heat. A vent in the passageway to the engine room sucked air with such strength that if you passed under it, you'd be flattened to your knees. When the sub ran on batteries under water, the quiet became maddening. The main bunk room, not much bigger than an average bedroom, slept 36 men. Another 30 or so ran the ship, while another 30 lounged. There was no night and day, just shifts. Coffee was constantly available, as well as fresh fruit, and the best mess in all the services. Subs of the day had the best radar and electronics available. Aboard were 24 high-powered torpedoes, and ammo for the topside gun. Submariners, chosen for their intelligence and psychological ability to take it, knew that a hit from the enemy meant certain death. The USS *Bowfin* is fascinating and definitely worth a visit.

The Navy holds an **open house** on one of its ships berthed at Pearl Harbor on the first Saturday of each month. For information call 474-8139. You must enter through the main Nimitz Gate, and then follow the signs to the ship, which is usually at the Bravo or Mike piers. On your way to the docking area you stop at the Family Services area where you can pick up some snacks or ice cream at a Baskin-Robbins concession. The sailors conducting the tour are polite and knowledgeable, and the tour is free. Those never in the service can always spot the officers—the guys with the white shoes. Take TheBus to the Nimitz Gate, or if you've

USS Bowfin,
WW II submarine

visited the *Arizona* Memorial, a convenient shuttle connects for only 50 cents.

The **Pacific Submarine Museum** is also reached through the Nimitz Gate. It's free but you need a pass from the gate. It's open Wed.-Sun. 9:30 a.m.-5 p.m., tel. 471-0632.

BEACHES AND SIGHTS

As you travel up Aiea Heights Road, an exit off H-1, you get a world-class view of Pearl Harbor below. It's not glorious because it is industrialized, but you do ride through suburban sprawl Hawaiian style until you come to the end of the road at **Keaiwa Heiau State Recreation Area.** In the cool heights above Aiea, these ancient grounds have a soothing effect the minute you enter. Overnight tent camping is allowed here, with exceptionally large sites (permit needed, see main "Out and About—Camping and Hiking"); for the few other visitors, the gates open at 7 a.m. and close at 6:30 p.m. As you enter the well-maintained park (a caretaker lives on the premises), tall pines to the left give a feeling of alpine coolness. Below, Pearl Harbor lies open, like the shell of a great oyster.

Keaiwa Heiau was a healing temple, surrounded by gardens of medicinal herbs tended by Hawaii's excellent healers, the *kahuna lapa'au*. From the gardens, roots, twigs, leaves, and barks were ground into potions and mixed liberally with prayers and love. These potions were amazingly successful in healing Hawaiians before the white man brought his diseases. Walking onto the stone floor of the *heiau,* it's somehow warmer and the winds seem quieter. Toward the center are numerous offerings, simple stones wrapped with a ti leaf. Some are old, while others are quite fresh. Follow the park road to the **Aiea Loop Trail,** which heads back 4.5 miles roundtrip onto one of the ridges descending from the Koolaus. Pass through a forest of tall eucalyptus trees, viewing canyons to the left and right. Notice, too, the softness of the "spongy bark" trees growing where the path begins. Allow three hours for the loop.

Blaisdell County Park's waters, which can be considered part of Pearl Harbor, are too polluted for swimming. It's sad to think that at the turn of the century it was clear and clean enough

to support oysters. Pearl Harbor took its name from Waimomi, "Water of Pearls," which were indeed harvested from the oysters and a certain species of clam growing here. Today, sewage and uncountable oil spills have done their devastation. Recently, oysters from the Mainland's East Coast have been introduced, and are being harvested from the mud flats. Supposedly, they're fit to eat. Facilities include a pay phone, tables, and restrooms. Access is off Rt. 99 just past Aloha Stadium and before you enter Pearl City.

Keehi Lagoon Beach Park is also polluted, but some people do swim here. The park is at the northern tip of Keehi Lagoon, at 465 Lagoon Dr., just past the **Pacific War Memorial** on Rt. 92 (the Nimitz Highway). Here are restrooms, picnic facilities, and a pay phone. Local people use the area for pole fishing and crabbing.

The **Hawaii Plantation Village,** 94-695 Waipahu St., Waipahu, HI 96797, tel. 677-0110, offers a stroll down memory lane into a once working plantation village. The small group of homes is a testament to the hard work performed by Hawaii's plantation communities. Reservations are recommended, and admission is by donation.

PRACTICALITIES

Accommodations

Except for long-term, accommodations are virtually nonexistent in this area. Luckily a few **bed and breakfast** homes provide some alternatives (see "Accommodations—Bed and Breakfast" in the Out and About chapter. One of the most interesting is the home of Corry and Helga Trummel, who reside in Pacific Palisades above Pearl City. What started out as a tract house has become a living museum. Helga has been collecting and inheriting art since she was a little girl in prewar Germany. Every nook and cranny has a curio from Europe, Asia, or Hawaii, and Helga loves to share her artwork and the fascinating stories of her youth. The first floor is completely dedicated to the guests. There's a music room, a library with a fine collection of books on WW II and the western states, two bedrooms, and a separate cottage in the back. Out here too is a small pool, dry sauna, and an observation platform high on the hill. Inside, as you mount the steps to the second floor you're greeted by a wooden statue of a woman with a bowl on her head, original oil paintings, and a grandfather clock, all from the last century. Enter the breakfast nook and suddenly you're in a German hunting lodge. The green and white table and benches painted with flowers are over 100 years old. Gaze around to see a stuffed bear, antique sitar, a mountain goat, stag, stuffed ducks, a collection of beer steins, a white moose head, pronghorn, and a bar. All in what once was a tract house kitchen! The main house is furnished like a very rich German chocolate cake; maybe not to everyone's taste, but definitely more than filling!

The **Pepper Tree Apartment Hotel,** at 98-150 Lipoha Pl., Aiea, HI 96701, tel. 488-1993, offers furnished studios and apartments, all with complete kitchens and baths, TV, and phones. A laundromat and swimming pool are also available. Many military personnel use this facility as temporary housing.

Shopping, Dining, And Services

The main shopping center in Aiea is the **Pearl-ridge Shopping Center,** tel. 488-0981, open Mon.-Sat. 10 a.m.-9 p.m., Sun. to 5 p.m., with prices geared toward island residents, not tourists, so you have a good chance of coming away with a bargain. Some of the larger stores include Liberty House, J.C. Penney, Sears, Star Supermarket, Longs, Waldenbooks, and Woolworth's. There are also 16 theaters, two food courts with over 30 restaurants, plus 150 smaller boutiques and specialty shops. The entire complex is air-conditioned, and serviced by an in-house monorail for your shopping convenience.

Buzz's Steak House, 98-751 Kuahao Pl. (at the corner of Moana Loa and Kaahumanu), tel. 487-6465, sometimes open for lunch, nightly for dinner, is futuristic, like something a kid would build with an erector set. It'd be perfect if it were down by the sea, where you could see something, but from where it's located you can peer at Pearl Harbor in the distance, or have a world-class view of the freeway. The steakhouse is owned and operated by an old island family whose business grew into a small chain of restaurants from their original location in Kailua.

This is one of the remaining three. Buzz's is an institution where islanders go when they want a sure-fire good meal. There's a salad bar and you prepare your own charbroiled steaks and fish. The prices are reasonable.

The **Waimalu Shopping Plaza,** located along Kaahumanu St. between the Kamehameha Hwy. (Rt. 99) and the H-1 Freeway, has a small cluster of shops and restaurants. There's a **Times Supermarket,** open 24-hours with its pharmacy and deli, and the **Good Health Store,** open 9 a.m.-7 p.m., Sat. 11 a.m.-6 p.m., selling food supplements and minerals. In the same complex is **Stuart Anderson's Cattle Co.,** tel. 487-0054, open daily for lunch and dinner. The lounge is open until 2 a.m. weekends, serving huge steaks and all the trimmings.

Across the road is the **Elephant and Castle Restaurant,** at 98-1247 Kaahumanu, tel. 487-5591, open daily for lunch and dinner, breakfast only on weekends. This restaurant has done an excellent job of creating an English-style pub atmosphere. The interior is cool and rich with red velvet, heavy chairs, tapestries, open beams, with a pool table and dart boards in the pub area. Nightly, it's one of the best places in the area for a beer and a chat. The food is good too. For example, try English fish 'n' chips ($4.95), a burger platter ($5), hot sandwiches ($5), or soup and sandwich ($4.75). Specials on weekends are English prime rib dinner, (queen-sized $10.95, king-sized $14.95), New York steak ($14.95), and seafood scampi ($10.95). Enjoy merry old England Hawaiian style.

The **Pearl City Tavern,** at 905 Kamehameha Hwy. (corner of Waimano Home Dr.), tel. 455-1045, is the best restaurant in the Pearl City/Aiea area. The cuisine is a combination of seafood, steaks, and mainstream Japanese. They're famous for their "monkey bar," which houses rhesus monkeys behind the bar in a glass cage. After a couple of stiff belts some customers mistakenly think that they're looking into a mirror. There's a fish tank bubbling away and a separate tank for live Maine lobsters, a specialty of the house. Choose a table or romantic booth in the huge dining room appointed with Japanese scrolls, a huge lantern, and shoji screens. For lunch try escargot ($5.50), seafood *pu pu* ($2.15), chef salad ($8), shrimp Louie ($7.50), or a bowl of Boston clam chowder for only $1.50.

Dinner is delicious with a choice of chicken Oriental salad ($6), prime rib ($15.75), fillet of mahimahi ($15), or seafood Newburg ($15.75). Or choose three different entrees for $25 from: soft-shell crab, shrimp and scallops, king crab legs, and roast prime rib. Dinners include won ton soup or salad, potatoes, french bread and butter. Complete Japanese dinners are miso soup and trimmings, rice and tea, and a choice of any three of the following entrees: broiled fish, sashimi, beef teriyaki, butterfish *misoyaki,* or chicken teriyaki at $17.25 per person. If you're in the Pearl Ridge/Aiea area and want a special night out, this is the place!

BOB RACE

SOUTHEAST OAHU

KOKO HEAD TO WAIMANALO

It's amazing how quickly you can leave the frenzy of Waikiki behind. Once you round the bend past Diamond Head and continue traveling east toward Koko Head, the pace slackens measurably . . . almost by the yard. A minute ago you were in traffic, now you're cruising. It's not that this area is undeveloped; other parts of the island are much more laid-back, but none so close to the action of the city. In the 12 miles you travel from Honolulu to Waimanalo, you pass the natural phenomenon of Koko Crater, a reliable blowhole, the most aquatically active underwater park in the islands, and a string of beaches, each with a different personality.

Man has made his presence felt here, too. The area has some of the most exclusive homes on the island, as well as Hawaii Kai, a less exclusive project developed by the visionary businessman Henry Kaiser, who 20 years ago created this harbinger of things to come. There's Sea Life Park, offering a day's outing of fun for the family, plus shopping centers, the mostly Hawaiian town of Waimanalo, and Bellows Air

Force Base, unused by the military and now one of the finest camping beaches on the island. Besides camping, few accommodations are found out here, and few restaurants. This lack of development preserves the area as scenic and recreational, prized attributes that should be taken advantage of before this sunny sandbox gets paved over.

SIGHTS, BEACHES, AND PARKS

The drive out this way accounts for half of the 360 degrees of what is called **The Circle Route.** Start by heading over the Pali Highway down to Kailua, hitting the sights on the way, or come this way first along Diamond Head Road to Rt. 72 as you make the loop back to the city. The only consideration is what part of the day you'd rather stop at the southeast beaches for a dip. For the most part, the beaches of this area *are* the sights, so both are combined in this one section. The road abounds with scenic points and overlooks. This is the part of Oahu that's absolutely beautiful in its undevelopment. It's hard to find a road on any of the Hawaiian islands that's going to be more scenic than this. At first the countryside is dry because this is the leeward side. But as you approach Waimanalo it gets much more tropical. The road is a serpentine ribbon with one coastal vista after another, a great choice for a joy ride just to soak in the sights. The following listings assume that you follow Rt. 72 from Waikiki to Waimanalo. For beaches between Waikiki and the following, please see "Sights—Waikiki Beaches and Parks" in the Waikiki chapter.

Maunalua Bay

Maunalua ("Two Mountain") Bay is a four-mile stretch of sun and surf between Diamond Head and Koko Head, with a beach park about every half mile. The first is **Waialae Beach County Park** in Kahala. Go straight ahead on Kahala

Avenue for one minute instead of going left on Rt. 72 to join H-1 on to Haunauma Bay. This section is the Beverly Hills of Honolulu, as many celebrities like Tom Selleck and Carol Burnett have homes here. The least expensive home in this section easily pushes $1 million asking price. Waialae is a popular windsurfing spot, crowded on weekends. It's a small beach park with basic amenities in a beautiful location where Makapuu Head wraps around and gives the impression that there are two islands off in the distance, but it's just the way Oahu bends at this point.

Next comes **Kawaikui Beach Park.** No lifeguard, but the conditions are safe year-round, and the bottom is shallow, muddy, and overgrown with seaweed. In times past, islanders came to the confluence of a nearby spring to harvest special *limu* that grow only where fresh water meets the ocean. You'll find unlimited access, parking stalls, picnic facilities, and rest-

KOKO HEAD TO WAIMANALO

rugged southeast coast

rooms. Few people use the park, and it's ideal for sunning, but for frolicking in the water, give it a miss.

In quick succession come **Niu and Paiko beaches,** lying along residential areas. Although there is public access, few people take advantage of them because the swimming, with a coral and mud bottom, is less than ideal. Some residents have built a pier at Niu Beach past the mudflats, but it's restricted to their private use. Paiko Lagoon is a state bird sanctuary; binoculars will help with sightings of a variety of coastal birds.

The residential area in the hills behind **Maunalua Bay Beach Park** is Hawaii Kai, built by Henry Kaiser, the aluminum magnate. The controversial development was often denigrated as "suburban blight." Many felt it was the beginning of Oahu's ruination. The park fronts Kuapa Pond, at one time a huge fishpond, later dredged by Kaiser, who used the dredged material to build the park, which he donated to the city in 1960. Now, most of the land has been reclaimed except for Koko Marina, whose boat launch constitutes the primary attraction of the park. You'll find a large sandy parking area where **Paradise Jet Skis** (look for a tent) rents self-powered skis, pricey at $40 per hour, tel. 235-1612.

Except for the boat launch (the only one on this side of the island), the area is of little recreational use because of the mud or coral bottom. However, swimming is possible and safe, but be careful of the sudden drops created by the dredged boat channels. Two undeveloped parks are located at the end of Poipu Drive, **Kokee and Koko Kai parks.** The currents and beach conditions make both unsuitable for swimming, but they're popular with surfers. Few others come here, but the views of the bay are lovely with glimpses of Molokai floating on the horizon to the south.

Hanauma Bay State Underwater Park

One of the premier beach parks in Hawaii is located in the sea-eroded crater of an extinct volcano just below Koko Head. People flock here to snorkel, scuba, picnic, and swim. During the day, the parking lot at the top of the hill overlooking the crescent bay below looks like a used car lot, jammed with Japanese imports, vans, and tour buses. A shuttle bus (75 cents) runs up and down the hill, and you can rent snorkeling equipment at the concession stand for $6 per day. If you want to avoid the crowds come in the early morning or after 4 p.m. when the sun dips behind the crater, and most tourists leave on cue. There's still plenty of daylight, so plan your trip accordingly.

The reef protects the bay and sends a maze of coral fingers right up to the shoreline. A large sandy break in the reef, **Keyhole,** is a choice spot for entering the water and for swimming. The entire bay is alive with tropical fish. Many have become so accustomed to snorkelers that they've lost their fear entirely, and willingly accept food from your fingers—some so rudely you had better be careful of getting your fingers nibbled. The county provides lifeguards, restrooms, showers, picnic facilities, a pavilion, and food concession.

Before you enter the water, do yourself a favor and read the large bulletin board near the pavilion that describes conditions. It divides the bay into three areas ranging from beginner to expert, and warns of sections to avoid. Be especially careful of **Witches Brew,** a turbulent area on the right at the mouth of the bay that can wash you into the **Molokai Express,** a notoriously dangerous rip current. Follow a path along the left-hand seacliff to **Toilet Bowl,** a natural pool that rises and falls with the tides. If the conditions are right, you can sit in it to float up and down in a phenomenon very similar to a flushing toilet.

Note: Environmental Alert. Because severe overuse was threatening the fragile ecosystem of the bay, tour companies are now banned from dropping people in the park expressly for snorkeling. Tour buses can now only stop at the top of the hill for a 15 minute overview, and then must leave. People wishing to explore the bay may come by rental car, moped, bicycle, or city bus, which has a stop within the park. However, if you drive, once the parking lot is filled, it is closed! And, the park is closed to all visitors on Wednesday mornings until noon when sorely needed maintenance is performed. Also, please do not feed the fish anything but approved fish food. Peas and bread are only appetizing to largemouthed fish and severely cut down on the variety of fish that would normally live within the reef. Most importantly, the very reef is being destroyed by people walking upon it. Please do everything you can to avoid this. A few tour companies have tried to continue bringing people into the park and have found ways to violate the *spirit,* if not the *letter* of the restrictions. Please do not patronize them. With care, Hanauma Bay will remain beautiful for all future generations.

Koko Head Hike

For a sweeping view, hike to the summit of **Koko Head,** not to be confused with Koko Crater, another good hike but farther east on Rt. 72 (see following). To start your trek, look for a paved road closed off to vehicles by a white metal fence, on the right before the road to the

parking lot. A 15-minute hike takes you to the 646-foot summit of Koko ("Blood") Head. This was the last place that young, wandering Madame Pele attempted to dig herself a fiery nest on Oahu; as usual, she was flooded out by her jealous sister. From the summit you get an unobstructed view of Molokai 20 miles across the Kaiwi Channel, the bowl of Hanauma Bay at your feet, and a sweeping panorama of Diamond Head and the Koolau Mountains. Below are two small extinct craters, Nono'ula and Ihi'ihilauakea.

Koko Crater

Koko Crater's Hawaiian name is Kohelepelepe ("Fringed Vagina"). Legend says that Pele's sister, Kapo, had a magical "flying vagina" that could fly and that she could send anywhere. Kamapua'a, the pig-god, was intent on raping Pele when Kapo came to her aid. She dispatched her vagina to entice Kamapua'a, and he followed it to Koko Head, where it made the crater and then flew away. Kamapua'a was unsuccessful when taking a flying leap at this illusive vagina.

You can either hike or drive to the crater. To begin the hike, look for the road to the "Hawaii Job Corp Training Center" just across from Hanauma Bay. Follow the road down past a rifle range and park at the job training building. Behind is an overgrown tramway track. The remaining ties provide a rough but adequate stairway to the top. At the 1,208-foot summit is an abandoned powerhouse and tramway station. The wood is rotted and the floors are weak! The crater itself lies 1,000 feet below. An easier but less exciting route is to follow Rt. 72 for two miles to Wawamalu Beach near the Hawaii Kai Golf Course, and then take a left on Kealahou Street. Nearby is a walking path that leads into the crater. On the floor of Koko Crater is a botanical garden that, due to the unique conditions, specializes in succulents.

Halona Cove

As you round a bend on Rt. 72 you come to the natural lookout of Halona Cove, which means "The Peering Place," an excellent vantage point from which to see whales in season. Just before Halona, a sign will point you to the **Honolulu Japanese Casting Club,** with a stone wall and a monument. The monument at one time was of O Jisan, the Japanese god of protection, destroyed by overzealous patriots during WW II. The current monument was erected after the war, and O Jisan was carved into it. Below is a secluded little beach that's perfect for sunbathing. The only way to it is to scramble down the cliff. Swim only on calm days, or the waves can pull you out to sea and then suck you into the chamber of the famous **Halona Blowhole** just around the bend. There's a turnout at the blowhole for parking. The blowhole is a lava tube at the perfect height for the waves to be driven into it. The water compresses, and the pressure sends a spume into the air. Be extremely cautious around the blowhole. Those unfortunate enough to fall in face almost certain death.

Sandy Beach Park
Sandy Beach is one of the best bodysurfing beaches on Oahu, and the most rugged of them all. More necks and backs are broken on this beach than on all the other Oahu beaches combined. But because of the east-breaking waves, and bottom, the swells are absolutely perfect for bodysurfing. The lifeguards use a flag system to inform you about conditions. The **red flag** means "stay out." When checking out Sandy Beach, don't be fooled by bodysurfers who make it appear easy. These are experts, intimately familiar with the area, and even they are injured at times. Local people refer to the beach as "Scene Beach" because this is where young people come to strut their stuff. This is where the boys are because this is where the girls are. There are restrooms, a large parking area, and two lifeguard towers. Rip-offs have happened, so don't leave valuables in your car. *Kaukau* wagons park in the area, selling a variety of refreshments.

As the road skirts the coastline, it passes a string of beaches that look inviting but are extremely dangerous because there is no protecting reef. The best known is **Wawamalu**, where people come to sunbathe only. Across the road is **Hawaii Kai Golf Course**, tel. 395-2358. You have a choice of two courses: the Championship, offering a full round of golf with beautiful views, challenging holes, and excellent greens; or the Executive, a shorter par-three course for those with limited time. This is an excellent public course, but the greens fee is high.

The lifeguards do a great job at Sandy Beach

Makapuu Beach Park
This beach park is below Makapuu ("Bulging Eye") Point, a projection of land marking Oahu's easternmost point, and a favorite launching pad for hang gliding. Makapuu is *the* most famous bodysurfing beach in the entire state, but it can be extremely rugged; more people are rescued here than at any other beach on Oahu (except Sandy Beach). In winter the conditions are hazardous, with much of the beach eroded away, leaving exposed rocks. With no interfering reef, the surf can reach 12 feet—perfect for bodysurfing, if you're an expert. Board riding is prohibited. In summer, the sandy beach reappears, and the wave action is much gentler, allowing recreational swimming. There are restrooms, lifeguard towers with a flag warning system, and picnic facilities.

Offshore is **Manana ("Rabbit") Island.** Curiously, it does resemble a rabbit, but it's so named because rabbits actually live on it. They were released there in the 1880s by a local rancher who wanted to raise them but who was aware that if they ever got loose on Oahu they could ruin much of the crop lands. During the impotent counterrevolution of 1894, designed to reinstate the Hawaiian monarchy, Manana Island was a cache for arms and ammunition buried on its windward side. Nearby is tiny Kaohikaipu ("Turtle") Island, which, along with Manana, is reserved as a seabird sanctuary.

1. seaside vista, windward Oahu (J.D. Bisignani)   **2.** Waikiki sunset (J.D. Bisignani)

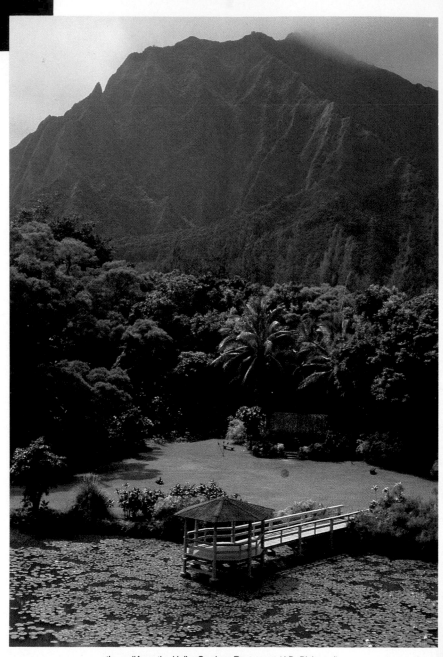

the *pali* from the Haiku Gardens Restaurant (J.D. Bisignani)

Sea Life Park Hawaii

Overlooking Makapuu Point and nestled below the lush Koolau Mountains is Sea Life Park Hawaii, a cluster of tanks holding an amazing display of marine animals that live freely in the ocean just a few hundred yards away. Admission for adults is $19.95, juniors $8.95, and children $3.95. Open daily 9:30 a.m.-5 p.m., Fri. until 10 p.m., tel. 259-7933 or (800) 767-8046. A free shuttle bus runs from major Waikiki hotels (call for details), or take TheBus no. 57 from Ala Moana Center, or no. 58, which comes straight up Kuhio Avenue. The park hosts a variety of shows by trained seals, whales, and dolphins, along with the informative Ocean Science Theater. The park's most impressive feature is the **Hawaiian Reef Tank,** a massive 300,000-gallon fish bowl where guests come face to face with over 2,000 specimens of the island's rich marinelife as they descend three fathoms down an exterior ramp. At **Whaler's Cove,** tall tales and legends of old Hawaii are retold while the park's dolphins cavort using the offshore Rabbit Island as a backdrop.

Outside the entrance turnstile is a shopping complex and the new **Sea Lion Cafe.** Here too is the **Pacific Whaling Museum,** free admission, housing one of the largest collections of whaling artifacts and memorabilia in the Pacific. The Whaler's Cove has a replica of a whaling ship called the *Essex Nantucket.* Sea lion food is available, and there's a public feeding daily at 11:30 a.m., 1:30 p.m., and 3:30 p.m., also 5 p.m. on Friday. Sea Life Park Hawaii is a great learning and entertaining experience for the entire family, or for anyone interested in exploring Hawaii's fascinating marinelife.

Kaupo Beach Park

This is the first park that you come to along the southeast coast that is safe for swimming. It is between Sea Life Park and Waimanalo. The park is undeveloped and has no lifeguards, so you are advised to exercise caution. The shore is lined with a protective reef or rocks, and the swimming is best beyond the reef. Close to shore, the jutting rocks discourage most swimmers. Surfers frequent Kaupo, especially beginners, lured by the ideal yet gentle waves.

Kaiona Beach Park

Just before you enter the ethnically Hawaiian town of Waimanalo, you pass Kaiona Beach Park, which you can spot because of the semipermanent tents pitched there. Local people are very fond of the area, and use it extensively. Look inland to view some remarkable cliffs and mountains that tumble to the sea. The area was at one time called Pahonu, "Turtle Fence," because a local chief who loved turtle meat erected a large enclosure in the sea into which any turtle that was caught by local fishermen had to be deposited. Parts of the pond fence can still be seen. Facilities include restrooms, showers, and a picnic area. Swimming is safe year-round, and tent and trailer camping are allowed with a county permit.

Rabbit Island

Bellows Beach

Waimanalo

This small rural town was at one time the center of a thriving sugar plantation owned by the *hapa* Hawaiian nobleman, John Cummins, who was responsible for introducing rabbits to Manana Island. It has fallen on hard times ever since the plantation closed in the late 1940s, and now produces much of Honolulu's bananas, papayas, and anthuriums from small plots and farms. The town sits in the center of Waimanalo Bay, which is the longest (3>% miles) stretch of sand beach on Oahu. To many people, especially those from Oahu, it is also the best. Few but adequate travelers' services are in town (see "Services" below).

The **Olomana Golf Links,** tel. 259-7926, is a 6,000-yard, relatively easy, par-72 course, inexpensive and close to town. It's also a good place to go for breakfast. You think you're in Waimanalo when you pass a 7-Eleven Store and McDonald's in a built-up area, but that isn't it. You keep going about a mile or two and and then you'll come to the older section of town which is Waimanalo proper.

Waimanalo County Beach Park, as you enter town by the 7-Eleven and McDonald's, provides camping with a county permit. The beach is well protected and the swimming is safe year-round. Snorkeling is good, and there are picnic tables, restrooms, and recreational facilities, including a ball park and basketball courts. This park is right in town, and not secluded from the road. Although the facilities are good, the setting could be better.

Just outside of town is **Waimanalo Bay State Recreation Area,** which remains largely undeveloped, and is much better situated. The access road is hard to spot, but just after McDonald's look for a tall wire fence with the poorly marked entrance in the center. It is good for picnicking and swimming, which can sometimes be rough. The area, surrounded by a dense ironwood grove, is called "Sherwood Forest," due to many rip-offs by thieves who fancy themselves as Robin Hood, plundering the rich and keeping the loot for themselves. Guess who the rich guys are? Fortunately, this problem of breaking into cars is diminishing, but take necessary precautions. This is the best beach on this section of the island.

Bellows Field Beach County Park, a one-time active Air Force base, is now one of Oahu's finest beach parks, and there's camping too! As you enter a sign warns that "This military installation is open to the public only on the following days: weekends—12:00 noon Friday to 6:00 a.m. Monday; federal and state holidays—6:00 a.m. to 6:00 a.m. the following day. Camping is authorized in this park by permit from the City and County of Honolulu, Parks and Recreation Board, only." They mean it! The water is safe for swimming year-round, but lifeguards are on duty only during the above-stated hours. Bodysurfing and board surfing are also excellent in the park, but snorkeling is mediocre. Surfboards are not allowed in the area between the two lifeguard towers. After entering the main gates, follow the road for about two miles to the beach area. You'll find picnic tables, restrooms, and cold-water showers. The combination of shade trees and adjacent beach make a perfect camping area. The park is marked by two freshwater streams, Waimanalo and Puha, at either end.

SERVICES

Except for the excellent camping, you're limited when it comes to accommodations in this area. **Hawaiian Family Inns,** a small cooperative of private homes in and around Hawaii Kai, provides European-style bed and breakfast. Each home differs slightly, but most have a private entrance, bath, yard and beach privileges, and some kitchen facilities. Daily rates are a reasonable $35, less during the off-season, with weekly and monthly discounts available. The three homes involved can be reached by calling 395-3710, 395-4130, or 395-8153.

The first place to pick up supplies as you head east on Rt. 72 is at the **Times Super Market** in the **Niu Valley Shopping Center,** located about halfway between Diamond Head and Koko Head. In the shopping center is **The Swiss Inn,** tel. 377-5447, an authentic Swiss restaurant where the owner/chef pours love and attention into every dish. The food is superb, well prepared, and reasonably priced for the quality. After your meal, have dessert at **Dave's Ice Cream,** also in the center.

Note: For Hawaii Kai's two outstanding gourmet restaurants, **Roy's** and **Hanatei,** see "Food—Casual Gourmet" in the Waikiki chapter.

Koko Marina Shopping Center
Located along the highway in Hawaii Kai, this center is the largest and easiest access shopping center that you'll find on the way to Hanauma Bay. For photo supplies and sundries, try **Thrifty Drugs, Ben Franklin's, Clic Photo, and Surfside Camera.** There are two banks, a **Waldenbooks,** and a satellite city hall for camping permits (tel. 395-4481). **Foodland** provides most supplies for picnics and camping, and you can dine at Chuck's Steak House, McDonald's, Magoo's Pizza, Baskin-Robbins Ice Cream, Sizzler, Kentucky Fried Chicken, and Kozo Sushi.

The **Aloha Dive Shop** at the Koko Marina is a full-service dive shop. You can rent or buy snorkeling and scuba gear. So, if you haven't picked up rentals from Waikiki and you're heading out to Hanauma Bay, come here. They have plenty of different dives. They start at $52 for beginners, $62 for certified divers, and $295 for certification courses (three days), featuring all-boat diving at Manalua Bay and Koko Head and Diamond Head.

The Japanese own the Koko Marina Center. In the center are thrill-ride (jet-skis, parasails, etc.) booking agencies that will take non-Japanese tourists, but are more for the Japanese tourists who come here by the bus load and immediately head out on one of these thrill rides. They've already booked from Japan, so it's all set up and off they go.

Upstairs, on the water side of the Koko Marina, is **American Sports Ltd.,** tel. 395-5319. They offer jet-skiing and snorkeling, and can book you into parasailing and scuba diving as well. Their special deal is jet-skiing, snorkeling, plus lunch for $49. Lunch is a sandwich and French fries, or, *bento* if you prefer.

Waimanalo And Vicinity Practicalities
For a tasty and inexpensive lunch try any of a number of *kaukau* wagons around Sandy Beach.

As you enter Waimanalo, look on the right for a sandwich-board sign painted with a bright red chili pepper that marks the **Bueno Nalo Cafe** at 41865 Kalanianaole Hwy. (next door to Bobby's Market), open daily 11:30 a.m.-9 p.m., tel. 259-7186, which offers a very tasty and inexpensive selection of Mexican food a la Hawaiiana. Hearty *menudo* soup covered in melted cheese is only $3.95 while a la carte tacos, tostadas, tamales, and burritos range $2.25-3.50, and combination dinners are priced at $8.95-9.95. The service is friendly, the atmosphere relaxed, and the food is much better than average.

A short "mile" past Bueno Nalo is **Mel's Market,** where you can pick up almost all camping supplies. Waimanalo town is growing up. As you enter you'll find a **7-Eleven** and **McDonald's.** The **Waimanalo BBQ,** just near the 7-Eleven and the P.O., open daily 10 a.m.-5 p.m., is an open air "cafe" that prepares huge plate lunches including kalua pig, shrimp, pork adobo, and grilled mahimahi for only $4! They also have a mixed plate of three items for $5, and shave ice for dessert. The food is delicious, the atmosphere as local as you can get, and the service friendly. It's a great stop to pick up a picnic lunch. The restrooms, unfortunately, leave a little to be desired.

Keep going along the Kalanianaole Hwy. for a mile or so to find **Waimanalo Shopping Center** in the middle of town. Here are **Jack-in-the-Box, Subway Sandwiches, Dave's Ice Cream,** two gas stations, and a bank. You can do all your business, pick up lunch and supplies, and head on down the road or go to the beach. In the shopping center is also a **visitor information booth, Woolworth's,** and **Waimanalo Market.**

Frankie's Drive-In, at the bottom of the hill a minute or so past Jack-in-the-Box, is a local favorite plate lunch drive-in, where you can fill up on teriyaki beef or chicken, fried mahimahi, or

hamburger steak along with two big scoops of rice and a whack of mac-salad for under $5. Frankie's is great for takeout that can be enjoyed at one of the nearby beaches. Their specialty is a *lilikoi* milkshake, a true island delight!

Pine Grove Village is an open-air bazaar where local people come to sell handmade products and produce. The majority of items are authentic and priced well below similar products found in Honolulu. Participants and times vary, but a group is usually selling daily until 6 p.m. Some excellent buys include local fruits and vegetables, lei, shellwork, hand-dipped candles, bikinis, jewelry, and leather goods. Price haggling is the norm; when the seller stops smiling, that's about the right price.

The **Olomana Golf Course,** at 41-1801 Kalanianaole Hwy., Waimanalo is a good place to go for breakfast. The menu is uninspired American-standard with an island twist, but the view is very good and the prices reasonable.

BRIAN BARDWELL

WINDWARD OAHU

Oahu's windward coast never has to turn a shoulder into a harsh and biting wind. The trades do blow, mightily at times, but always tropical warm, perfumed with flowers, balmy and bright. Honolulu is just 12 miles over the hump of the *pali,* but a world apart. When *kamaaina* families talk of going to "the cottage in the country," they're most likely referring to the windward coast. In the southern parts, the suburban towns of **Kailua** and **Kaneohe** are modern in every way, with the lion's share of the services on this side. Kailua has Oahu's best windsurfing beach and a nearby *heiau,* preserved and unvisited, while Kaneohe sits in a huge bay dotted with islands and reef. The coastal **Kamehameha Highway** (Rt. 83) turns inland to the base of the *pali,* passing the **Valley of the Temples,** resplendent with universal houses of worship. At **Kahaluu** starts a string of beaches running north, offering the full range of Oahu's coastal outdoor experience. You can meander side roads into the mountains near the Hawaiian villages of **Waiahole** and **Waikane,** where the normal way of life is ramshackle cottages on small subsistence farms.

The coast bulges at **Ka'a'awa,** where the **Crouching Lion,** a natural stone formation, seems ready to pounce on the ever-present tour buses that disturb its repose. North is **Punaluu,** famous for **Pat's,** the only resort in the immediate area, and for **Sacred Falls State Park,** a short hike to a peak at Oahu's beautiful and natural heart (if it isn't muddy). Suddenly, you're in manicured **Laie** where Hawaii's Mormon community has built a university, a temple perfect in its symmetry, and the **Polynesian Cultural Center, a sanitized replica of life in the South Seas, Disney style. The northern tip at** Kahuku, site of one of Oahu's oldest sugar mills, is where the **North Shore** begins. Kahuku Point houses two refuges, one for wildlife, and the other for Oahu's only nudist camp, both protecting endangered species from humanity's prying eyes.

It makes little difference in which direction you travel the windward coast, but the following will be listed from south to north from Kailua to Kahuku. The slight advantage in traveling this direction is that your car is in the right-hand lane, which is better for coastal views. But, as odd as it may seem, this dynamic stretch totally changes its vistas depending upon the direction that you travel. You can come one way and then retrace your steps, easily convincing yourself that you've never seen it before. The road is clearly marked with mile markers. They decrease as you head north from Kaneohe on Rt. 83, the Kamehameha Highway. Also see "Out and About—Camping and Hiking" for trails in the area.

Beaches And Parks

Over a dozen beaches line the 24 miles of the windward coast from Kailua to Kahuku. The majority offer a wide range of water sports and camping. A few offshore islands, refuges for Hawaiian waterbirds, can be visited and explored. You can walk to these islands during low tide, and even camp there. See "Out and About—Camping and Hiking" for other state and county parks not along the coast.

KAILUA AND VICINITY

The easiest way into Kailua ("Two Seas") is over the Koolaus on Rt. 61, the Pali Highway. As soon as you pass through a long tunnel just after the Nuuanu Pali Lookout (see "Honolulu—Sights") and your eyes adjust to the shocking brilliance of sunshine, look to your right to see Mt. Olomana. Its 1,643-foot peak is believed to be the volcanic origin of Oahu, the first land to emerge from the seas. Below lies Kailua and the Kawainui swamp, perhaps the oldest inhabited area on this side of the island. Kamehameha I, after conquering Oahu in 1795, gave all this land to his chiefs who had fought for him. The area became a favorite of the ruling *ali'i* until the fall of the monarchy at the turn of this century. The Kawainui Canal drains the marsh and runs through Kailua. A good vantage point from which to observe it is along Kalaheo Ave., the main road running along the coast in Kailua. Kailua has approximately 45,000 people, technically making it the state's largest windward city. It's developed with shopping centers, a hospital, and the *best* windsurfing beach in the state (see below). For a full description of windsurfing activities at Kailua Beach please refer to "Out and About—Sports and Recreation." Four golf courses surround the town, and a satellite city hall dispenses **camping permits.**

SIGHTS

A good touring loop is to continue straight on Rt. 61 until it comes to the coast. Turn right onto Kalaheo Road, which takes you along the coast to Kailua Beach Park. In the waters offshore will be a spectacle of windsurfers, with their sails puffed out like the proud chests of multicolored birds. To the left of the beach is **Mokapu ("Sacred Area") Peninsula,** home of the Kaneohe Marine Corps Base. Notice that the rock that separates the peninsula creates a large natural archway navigable by sizable boats. Most of the little islands in the bay are bird sanctuaries. The farthest, **Moku Manu,** is home to terns and man-o'-wars, birds famous for leading fishermen to schools of fish. Up on the coastal bluffs is a gray house with a flat roof, the residence of a local woman called the "Birdlady of Kailua." The woman has a reputation for taking care of any sick or injured birds that people bring to her. Her entire home is carved from rock, including the chairs and table. Every once in a while tours are offered to the house for a few dollars. They're irregular, so check the local papers, and you may be lucky enough to be there at just the right time.

A'alapapa Drive gains the heights from the beach and takes you through an area of beautiful homes until you come to **Lanikai Beach.** At one time trees came down to the shoreline, but it has steadily eroded away. The Navy attempted to start a retaining reef by dumping barge loads of white bath tile just offshore. Their efforts were not successful, but many homes in town now have sparkling, new, white-tiled bathrooms! As A'alapapa Drive loops back to town, it changes names to Mokulua; a pulloff here affords an expansive panorama of the bay below. By daytime it's enjoyable, but in the evening local kids come here to hang out and drink beer.

WINDWARD OAHU
KAILUA TO KAHUKU

JAMES CAMPBELL
WILDLIFE REFUGE
KII POND

TO
HALEIWA

KAHUKU

83

MALAEKAHANA BAY

LAIE BEACH PARK
LAIE BAY

LAIE

POLYNESIAN
CULTURAL
CENTER

POUNDERS BEACH
KOKOLOLIO BEACH

HAUULA BEACH PARK

HAUULA

MAKAO BEACH

PUNALUU

SACRED FALLS
STATE PARK

PUNALUU BEACH PARK

MAHIE PT.

KAHANA BAY
BEACH PARK

MAKAUA BEACH PARK
SWANZY BEACH PARK

KAUHIIMAKAOKALANI
(CROUCHING LION)

KAAAWA

KAAAWA BEACH PARK

KAHANA
VALLEY
STATE
PARK

MAKAHONU PT.

SUGAR MILL
RUINS (1864)

KUALOA CO. REGIONAL PARK

KOOLAU RANGE

MOKOLII I.
(CHINAMAN'S HAT)

WAIKANE

WAIAHOLE BEACH PARK

WAIAHOLE

KAPAPA I.

KAALAEA

PYRAMID
ROCK

KANEOHE BAY

MOKU MANU
SEABIRD SANCTUARY

MOKAPU PT.

KAHALUU

836

KANEOHE
MARINE CORPS
AIR STATION

MOKAPU

BYODO-IN
TEMPLE

HEEIA

83

MOKU O LOE
(COCONUT I.)

MOKAPU PENINSULA

KANEOHE

H3

KAILUA

KAILUA BAY

KAILUA BEACH PARK

KAWAINUI
SWAMP

MOKU LUA IS.

LANIKAI

LIKELIKE HWY

NUUANU PALI
STATE PARK

PALI HWY

63

61

MT. OLOMANA
(1643 ft)

KALANIANAOLE HWY

BELLOWS FIELD
BEACH PARK

WAIMANALO
BAY

72

TO
WAIMANALO

HONOLULU

H1

0   2 mi
0   3 km
-N-

© MOON PUBLICATIONS, INC.

Ulupoa Heiau

Ulupoa is dedicated to the Ulu line of *ali'i*, who were responsible for setting up *heiau* involving the sacred birth of chiefs. Oftentimes the umbilical cord was cut just as a drum was sounded, then the cord (*piko*) was placed in a shallow rock depression at a *heiau*. This temple, supposedly built by the legendary *menehune,* shows remarkable stone craftsmanship, and measures 140 feet wide and 30 feet high. Atop the temple is a pathway that you can follow. Notice small stones wrapped in ti leaves placed as offerings. To get there, as you approach Kailua on Rt. 61 look for a red light and a 7-Eleven store. Turn left onto Uluoa Street, following it to Manu Aloha Street, where you turn right. Follow it to the end and park in the YMCA lot.

BEACHES

Along the shoreline of an exclusive residential area, just south of Kailua, sits **Lanikai Beach.** Three clearly marked rights-of-way run off Mokulua Drive, the main thoroughfare. No facilities, but good snorkeling and swimming year-round, with generally mild surf and a long, gently sloping, sandy beach. The beach runs south for almost a mile, broken by a series of seawalls designed to hold back erosion. Many small craft use the sandy-bottomed shore to launch and land. Popular with local people, but not visited much by tourists.

Kailua Beach Park is the main beach in the area. In the last few years, it has become the windsurfing capital of Hawaii. Local people complain that at one time the beach was great for family outings, with safe conditions and fine facilities. Now the wind has attracted a daily flotilla of windsurfers, kayak racers, and jet-skiers. The congested and contested waters can be dangerous for the average swimmer. Many windsurfers are beginners, so if you're a swimmer, be careful of being run over. The conditions are similar to out-of-control skiers found on the slopes of many mountains. The windsurfing area is clearly marked with buoys, which recently were moved 100 yards northeastward, making the area larger.

The park boasts a pavilion, picnic facilities, restrooms, showers, lifeguards, a boat ramp, and a food concession. The surf is gentle year-round, and the swimming safe. Children should be careful of the sudden dropoffs in the channels formed by the Kaelepulu Canal as it enters the sea in the middle of the beach park. Good surfing and diving are found around Popoi'a Island just offshore. Follow Rt. 61 through Kailua until it meets the coast, and then turn right on S. Kalaheo St. following it to the beach park. For sailboard rentals and instruction see "Sports and Recreation—Windsurfing" in the Out and About chapter.

Kailua Beach, the windsurfing capital of Oahu

Kalama Beach is reached by making a right onto N. Kalaheo. This beach has no facilities and is inferior to Kailua Beach Park, but the swimming is good, and sections of the beach have been made off-limits to any surf-riding vehicles.

PRACTICALITIES

Accommodations

The **Kailua Beachfront Vacation Homes** offer two completely furnished and ready-to-move-into rental homes with a minimum stay of five days. The one-bedroom home rents for $95-110 for up to four persons, the three-bedroom home is $190-220 for up to six persons. Located along S. Kalaheo, they are just minutes from Kailua Beach Park. For peak seasons like Christmas and Easter, making reservations up to a year in advance is not unusual. Normally reservations are made three to six months in advance. Homes have telephones, color TVs, beach furniture, parking, maid service on request, and barbeques. The three-bedroom has a full kitchen with electric stove, a large refrigerator, dishwasher, washer and dryer, and all lanai furniture. The smaller house is complete except for dishwasher. For information and reservations write Kailua Beachfront Vacation Homes, 133 Kailuana Pl., Kailua, HI 96734, tel. 261-3484.

One of the finest guest homes in Kailua is **Sharon's Serenity**, tel. 263-3634. This beautiful property sits on a quiet side street fronting the picturesque Kawainui Canal. Sharon goes out of her way to make you feel comfortable and welcome. The fridge is always filled with cold beer and soft drinks, and the coffee is always fresh-perked. Sharon also takes the time to sit with you, giving advice on where to dine, what to see, and a candid description of activities that are worthwhile. She also goes weekly to the People's Market (she'll take you along early Thursday morning) for lovely island blooms including anthuriums, ginger, and heliconia, which she arranges and places throughout the home to add a touch of beauty. The meticulously clean, beautifully appointed home features guest rooms with color TV, Mexican tile throughout, a spacious family room, swimming pool, lanai, and

beautiful views of the *pali* and the bay. The main guest room has its own attached private bath done in tile and oak cabinetry. In here, the bed is queen-sized, and next to it is a comfortable leather recliner with green-shaded reading lamp close at hand. Another bedroom could easily accommodate a family, with a large double bed and a twin bed set up like a daybed. It features in-room sliding doors for privacy and its own bath just across the hall. Rates are $45-50 s, $60-65 d, with a self-contained but very tiny and inexpensive "Lemon Room" (named for its color, not because you'll be squeezed) that is available on request. The price includes a continental or bacon and egg breakfast (bacon and eggs available every day but Thursday), which Sharon will have waiting in the morning. Sharon's Serenity is an excellent choice for the windward coast, and perfect for getting away from it all.

Pacific Hawaii Bed and Breakfast lists private homes in and around Kailua. Rates and homes differ dramatically, but all are guaranteed to be comfortable and accommodating. For details see "Accommodations—Bed and Breakfast" in the Out and About chapter.

Food

The **Kailua Shopping Center**, 540 Kailua Rd., has one of the very best restaurants for value in Kailua, the **Barbecue East**, tel. 262-8457, open Mon.-Sat. 11 a.m.-9 p.m., Sun. 1-9 p.m., last Sun. of the month 5-9 p.m. The prices are terrific, the service friendly, and the food is delicious in this formica and linoleum decor restaurant. It's really the international potpourri that Hawaii is famous for because with every plate you get Korean kimchi, Japanese miso soup, Hawaiian fish, American macaroni salad, and a bit of coleslaw. If that's not all the peoples of Hawaii accounted for, then what is? Specials include *ahi jun* or teriyaki, butterfish, or scallops *jun* for $6.95. The sashimi special is *ahi* sashimi with fried scallops, fried oysters, kalbi beef, barbecued chicken, and sides for $10.75. You can even have a sashimi mixed plate of barbecued chicken and beef, sashimi, and the works for only $7.45. Korean specials are *kalbi* beef, *pulgogi*, or chicken *mando* and all the trimmings for $8.95. They also serve beer and wine. The best choice for the money in Kailua, but no decor whatsoever.

If you want to save even more, at the other end of the shopping plaza is **Okazu-ya**, just a takeout lunch window, Japanese and Korean style. In the same small complex is **Chef's Grill** Sandwich and Plate Lunch, and a **Baskin-Robbins** for your sweet tooth.

Hekili Street: Kailua's Restaurant Row

The 100 block of Hekili Street could be Kailua's version of Honolulu's Restaurant Row. Along this street is the **No Name Bar,** tel. 261-8725, just across from the bowling alley. The No Name Bar is for beer-drinking types who want a good meal as well. They have Sunday morning football at 7:30 a.m., and serious Monday night football at 6:30 p.m. Open Mon.-Fri. 3 p.m.-2 a.m., Sat. 11 a.m.-2 a.m., Sun. 3 p.m.-midnight, happy hour 4-7 p.m., with live entertainment nightly. Choices include salads like Cobb salad for $6.50, or No-name salad of ham, turkey, Swiss, provolone, eggs, and cukes for $6.95. Mixed plates can be empanadas—fresh-baked pastry filled with chick peas, olives, Cheddar, and spicy Mexican sauce ($6.95)—or sausage bread ($5.95 small, $7.50 large). Chili is $3.95, and sandwiches are under $7.

The **Princess Chop Suey** is your basic chop suey joint two doors down from the No Name. Open Mon.-Sat. 10:30 a.m.-9 p.m., Sun. noon-9 p.m., tel. 839-0575. Naugahyde booths and formica tables. Everything under $7.95.

Next door is **Sisco's Cantina,** tel. 262-7337, featuring complete Mexican cuisine, open Sun.-Thurs. 11 a.m.-10 p.m., Fri. and Sat. 11 a.m.-11 p.m. Tostadas, tacos, burritos, enchiladas, and chiles rellenos are all under $10. More expensive dishes are shrimp Veracruz ($14), fajitas ($16.25, for two $20.95). All come with Mexican corn, sautéed Tex-Mex mushrooms, and salad. Inside, the south-of-the-border atmosphere is created with hanging piñatas, stucco walls, and blue-tile tables. A minute down the street is **Detroit Italian Deli,** featuring subs and ice cream.

Onesto's Ristorante Italiano, at 117 Hekili St., tel. 261-8688, is open daily except Monday; lunch is 11 a.m.-2 p.m., dinner is 5:30 p.m.-9:30 p.m., Fri.-Sat. until 10 p.m. Onesto's has brought a touch of "la dolce vita" Italian-style to Kailua. The lunch menu starts with appetizers like antipasto for two at $3.80, sautéed mushrooms for $3.80, and Caesar salad for two or more at $3.80 per person. Pasta dishes, a staple of Onesto's, are linguine with chicken, anchovy linguine with mushrooms, or linguine arrabiata, with tomato sauce and sautéed bacon, all priced under $8. Seafood offerings are calamari marinara for $6.80, or the fresh catch (usually *ono*), which is prepared scampi style with picante or garlic sauce for under $10. Meat and poultry entrees are chicken marsala ($7.50), chicken Sorrentino, served with eggplant, mozzarella cheese, mushrooms, butter, and marsala wine ($8.50). Dinner entrees are "un poco molto expensivo" than lunch. A good choice is Sicilian chicken with roasted potatoes and onions served with linguine ($10.80), or shrimp linguine ($11.80). Seafoods like calamari marinara or shrimp saltimbocca with eggplant, mozzarella cheese, prosciutto, mushrooms, butter and white wine are $11.80. Pasta dishes, in small (about $2 less) and regular-size servings, are linguine with meat sauce, rigatoni with ricotta, and fettucini Alfredo all for under $10. There's even a small deli area selling bread and pasta by the pound. Desserts including amaretto or cappuccino gelato, and New York-style cheesecake are about $3, but opt for the *torta deicato Italiano,* also $3. Onesto's, although not quite haute cuisine, offers a pleasant setting, and very decent food, especially for the money.

Around Town

Let the pungent aroma of garlic frying in olive oil lead you to **Assaggio's Ristorante Italiano,** 354 Uluniu St., tel. 261-2772, open Mon.-Fri. for lunch, 11:30 a.m.-2:30 p.m., dinner nightly 5-10 p.m. You are welcomed into a bright and open room done in the striking colors of black, red, teal, and magenta. A wall running down the center of the restaurant separates the bar from the dining room, where tables covered in white linen and black upholstered chairs line the long window area. The typical Italian menu, served with crusty Italian bread, begins with antipasti priced $5.90-9.90, fresh clam scampi at $6.90, and the light and classic prosciutto and melon at $6.90. Soups are pasta fagioli (macaroni and beans, the favorite of Italian contadina), minestrone, tortellini imbrodo (tortellini with ricotta in broth), or vichysoisse served as a cup or bowl, for $1.90 or $2.90. Pasta ranging in price $8-12 includes linguine, fettuccini, and ziti. Dishes come in two sizes, small (about $2 less) and regular, and are covered in marinara, clam, carbonata, or pesto sauce. Entrees are chicken cacciatore or chicken rolatini, stuffed with ricotta cheese, both at $12.90; baked ziti with eggplant and mozzarella for $9.90; or lasagna for $11.90. Meat dishes are New York steaks, pork chops, or *osso bucco* (veal shanks with onions), all for around $14.90. From the sea comes fresh fish sautéed in garlic oil for $15.90, scallops and shrimp in wine, garlic butter, and snow peas for $17.90, or calamari alla parmigiana at $12.90. Desserts are homemade cheesecake, cannelloni, spumoni, and chocolate mousse all around $4. The full bar serves imported and domestic beers, liquors, coffees, espressos, and plenty of wine varietals.

El Charro Avitia, 14 Oneawa St., tel. 263-3943, open daily for lunch and dinner, is a better than average Mexican restaurant. Simple yet tasteful, the south-of-the-border inspired decor is achieved with adobelike arches, wooden tables, Mexican ceramics placed here and there, and plenty of cacti and hanging plants. The menu features combination dinners of burritos, chili verde, enchiladas, or tacos, all priced under $10. The specialty of the house is the fresh fish Veracruzana, as good as you'll find anywhere, carne asada, or *camarones al mojo de ajo* (jumbo shrimp sautéed in butter, garlic, and white wine), all for under $14, and all served with rice, black beans, fresh vegetables, and a fresh fruit garnish. Less expensive dishes are chimichangas, burritos, taco salad, and Mexican pizza, which is two deep fried tortillas topped with cheddar cheese, jack cheese, beans, tomatoes, olives, and lettuce, all around $9. Huevos Mexicana, rancheros, and revueltos, served throughout the day, are $7.50. The bar mixes a mean margarita, which come in normal sizes up to a fiesta 40-ounce that will definitely have you yelling *olé!* El Charro Avitia is definitely worth the money!

Just up Oneawa St., across from the **Taco Bell,** is **Ching Lee Chop Suey,** a down-home, inexpensive Chinese restaurant where you can have a complete meal for under $5.

You'll first notice **Someplace Else,** at the corner of Aulike and Kuule Rd., tel. 262-8833, because of the huge multicolored umbrellas in the outside patio area. This is Kailua's upscale yuppie restaurant. It's open 11 a.m.-2 a.m., food service till 10 p.m., no breakfast except Sun. brunch from 9 a.m. It's a jungle in there with hanging plants, ferns, and flowers in every nook and cranny. Lunch brings a broiled *ono* sandwich ($7.25), chicken almond salad ($6.25), or crab-stuffed tomato ($8.95). The extensive menu continues with omelettes, and appetizers like escargot ($6.95), stuffed mushrooms ($6.95), and clam chowder, French onion, gazpacho, and soup of the day for under $5. South-of-the-border selections are burritos, chimichangas, and the like for around $8. The broiler fires up with top New York steak ($16.95), barbecued ribs ($13.95), and chicken marsala ($12). If you are looking for a place to "do lunch," or an evening of civilized conversation, don't go anywhere until you've tried Someplace Else.

Buzz's Original Steakhouse, at 413 Kawailoa Rd., tel. 261-4661, is really *the* original steakhouse of this small island chain owned by the Schneider family. Buzz's is just across the road from Kailua Beach Park, situated along the canal. This restaurant is an institution with local families. It's the kind of place that "if you can't think of where to go, you head for Buzz's." The food is always good, if not extraordinary. They have top sirloin ($14.95), pork chops ($13.95), chicken teri ($11.75), fresh fish (usually about $18), and mahimahi ($12.95). Salad bar is included with all entrees, and separately for $7.95. Everything is charbroiled.

Saeng's Thai Cuisine, at 315 Hahani, tel. 263-9727, open Sat.-Sun. 5-9:30 p.m., Mon.-Fri. 11 a.m.-2:30 p.m. and again from 5-9:30 p.m., offers spicy Thai food with an emphasis on vegetarian meals. Appetizers and starters are Thai crisp noodles ($5.25), sautéed shrimp ($9.95), salads like green papaya salad ($5.25), *yum koong* (shrimp salad, $7.95), and chicken coconut soup ($6.95). Specialties include spicy stuffed calimari $9.95, Thai red curry ($7.95), and a la carte beef, pork, and chicken dishes, all under $8. Vegetarians can pick from mixed vegies with yellow bean paste ($5.95), mixed vegies with oyster sauce ($5.95), or zucchini tofu ($5.95). Saeng Thai is a good change of pace at a decent price.

Orson's Bourbon House, along the main drag at five Hoolai St., tel. 262-2306, is just behind the Burger King on a little side street. This Cajun-style restaurant prepares blackened *ahi* as a medium-rare fish (wonderful as appetizer, but can do as an entree for $9), fried calimari ($7.95), and *mufaletas* (a sub sandwich New Orleans style). Special of the day could be fresh silver salmon sautéed for $12.50. The decor is fine dining with white starched tablecloths and fresh flower bouquets, while the bar area is rich with koa wood trim. Nightly entertainment is lively with everything from Hawaiian to jazz.

Captain Bob's Picnic Sail, tel. 926-5077 or (800) 262-8798, tours Kaneohe Bay daily and features lunch and all-you-can-drink on its three-to four-hour sail, $65 adults, $45 children. You can work off lunch snorkeling or playing volleyball on the beach. The food is passable, but the setting offshore with the *pali* in the background is world class. Captain Bob also has a good reputation for community spirit, often taking local children's groups out on his boats. For most people desiring to see the waters along the windward coast while spending a pleasant afternoon, this is the best bet.

Uluniu Street: Inexpensive Dining

Uluniu Street has inexpensive places to eat, one after the other. After making a left from Kuulei Road (Rt. 61) onto Oneawa, a main thoroughfare, turn right onto Uluniu just at the large Kailua Furniture. First is an authentic hole-in-the-wall Japanese restaurant, **Kailua Okazuya.** They specialize in *donburi,* a bowl of rice smothered with various savories. Try their *o yakodon buri,* chicken and egg with vegetables over rice for under $4. They serve plate lunches and a sushi special that can't be beat, which includes fresh fish, shrimp, abalone, and octopus for only $5! Next door is **Insam Korean Restaurant,** with more of the same Korean style, and up the street is the **New Chinese Garden,** a basic Chinese restaurant with decent prices. None of these restaurants are remarkable, but will fill you up with good enough food for a very reasonable price.

Shopping And Services

The two towns of Kailua and Kaneohe have the lion's share of shopping on the windward coast. You can pick up basics in the small towns as you head up the coast, but for any unique or hard-to-find items, Kailua/Kaneohe is your only bet. The area offers a few shopping centers. The **Windward Mall,** at 46-056 Kamehameha Hwy., Kaneohe, tel. 235-1143, open weekdays 9:30 a.m.-9 p.m., Sat. to 5:30 p.m., Sun. 10 a.m.-5 p.m., is the premier, full-service mall on the windward coast. Besides department stores like Liberty House and Sears, there are shops selling everything from shoes to health foods.

The **Kaneohe Bay Mall** across from the Windward Mall is a little more down-home, and features a Longs Drugs, especially good for photo supplies. The **Aikahi Park Shopping Center** along Kaneohe Bay Dr., at the corner of Mokapu Blvd., is a limited shopping center whose main shops are a Safeway and a Sizzler Restaurant. The **Kailua Shopping Center,** at 540 Kailua Rd., also has limited shopping that includes a **Time's Supermarket,** open till 10 p.m., and a well-stocked **Honolulu Bookshop,** tel. 261-1996, open Mon.-Fri. 9:30-9, Sat. 9:30-5:30, Sun. till 5 p.m., for a full range of reading material. There's also a **Cornet Store** along Kailua Ave. for sundries, lotions, and notions, and a **Longs Drugs.**

Thursday mornings bring a **farmers' market** into town for only one hour, 8:50-9:50 a.m. Those in the know arrive early to get a number at their favorite stalls, which can sell out within minutes of opening. Great for fresh flowers and fruits.

You might pick up an heirloom at **Heritage Antiques,** at the corner of Kailua Rd. and Amakua St., tel. 261-8700, open daily 10-5:30, which is overflowing with Asian, Hawaiian, and Americana antiques. Here too are **jewelers,** H.W. Roberts and J.K. Phillips, who also specialize as gemologists. **Hunter Antiques,** across the street from Heritage Antiques, specializes in Depression glass.

You'll find just about anything at **Holiday Mart** on Hahani Road., or picnic supplies at the landmark **Kalapawai Store,** at the corner of Kailua and Kalaheo roads, which marks the best entrance to Kailua's windsurfing beaches.

Campers can reach the **satellite city hall** for information and permits by calling 261-8575. A **post office** is at the corner of Kailua and Hahani, just across from the Hawaiian National Bank. Medical aid is available from **Castle Medical Center,** tel. 261-0841. The **Family and Urgent Medical Care** is at 660 Kailua Rd., tel. 263-4433.

KANEOHE AND VICINITY

The bedroom community of Kaneohe ("Kane's Bamboo") lies along Kaneohe Bay, protected by a huge barrier reef. Within the town is **Hoomaluhia Regional Park,** so large that guided hikes are offered on a daily basis. Offshore is Moku o' Loe, commonly called **Coconut Island.** It became famous as the opening shot in the TV show "Gilligan's Island," although the series itself was shot in California. In ancient times, it was *kapu* and during WW II served as an R&R camp for B-29 crews. Many of the crews felt the island had bad vibes, and reported having a streak of bad luck. In recent times, Frank Fasi, Honolulu's current mayor, suggested that Hawaii's gate-crashing guests, Ferdinand and Imelda Marcos, should lease Coconut Island. It never happened.

SIGHTS

In the northern section of town is **He'eia Pier,** launching area for the *Coral Queen,* tel. 247-0375, a glass-bottomed boat that sails throughout the bay. It is a popular attraction, so make reservations. Fortunately, in recent years, the once crystal-clear bay, which was becoming murky with silt because of development, is clearing again due to conservation efforts.

A sandbar has been building in the center of Kaneohe Bay that has made a perfect anchorage for yachts and powerboats. These boat people drop anchor, jump off, and wade to the bar through waist-deep, clear waters. It has become an unofficial playground where you can fling a Frisbee, drink beer, fly a kite, or just float around. Part of the sand bar rises above the water and some barbecue chefs even bring their hibachis and have a bite to eat. Surrounding you is Kaneohe Bay with Chinaman's Hat floating off to your right, and a perfect view of the *pali* straight ahead. The epitome of la dolce vita, Hawaiian style.

Senator Fong's Plantation, at 47-285 Pulama Rd., Kaneohe, HI 96744 (near Kahaluu), tel. 239-6775, open daily 9 a.m.-4 p.m., with guided tram tours running 10:30 a.m.-3 p.m., admission $8.50 adults, $5 children. Hawaii's newest attraction is a labor of love created by Senator Hiram Fong, who served as the state senator from 1959 to 1976. Upon retirement he returned to his home, and ever since has been beautifying the gardens he started over 40 years ago. The result is 725 acres of natural beauty. When you first arrive, there is a large open-air pavilion housing a snack window serving sandwiches, plate lunches, and saimin. Inside is also a small but well-appointed souvenir shop where you can get everything from aloha shirts to postcards. Notice a table set with baskets of flowers where you can make your own keepsake lei for $5.

For a fun-filled day on Kaneohe Bay, far from the crowds of Waikiki, try **North Bay Boat Club's** "A Day on the Bay," located on the grounds of Schrader's Windward Marine Resort, 47-039 Lihikai Dr., Kaneohe, tel. 239-5711, ext. 112. "Your day" includes hotel pick-up, barbecue lunch, open bar, windsurfing, kayaking, snorkeling, and sailing. Scuba introductory dives and jet-ski rides are also available at extra cost from **Wave Riders of Kaneohe,** tel. 239-5711, who offer a self-propelled tour around the bay on a jet-ski for $40 per hour, or $60 for two people for an hour.

All Hawaii Cruises, tel. 926-5077, features a snorkel/sail with Captain Bob, who has an excellent reputation with local people. Your adventure includes hotel pick-up, barbecue lunch, open bar, a four-hour sail, glass-bottom viewing, and reef walking. This is an excellent opportunity to view the awesome beauty of the windward coast.

BEACHES

Kaneohe Bay offers **Kaneohe Beach Park, Heeia State Park,** and **Laenani Beach Park,** all accessible off Rt. 836 as it heads northward along the coast. All are better for the views of Kaneohe Bay than for beach activities. They have restrooms and a few picnic tables. The water is safe year-round, but it's murky and lined with mudflats and coral heads. The same conditions hold true for **Waiahole Beach Park** about four miles north, but this area is much less developed, quieter, and good for beachcombing.

© MOON PUBLICATIONS, INC.

Heeia State Park lies along Rt. 836 between Kaneohe and Kahaluu and is designated as an "interpretive park." It sits high on Kealohi Point overlooking Heeia Fishpond below. Kealohi translates as "The Shining," because it was a visible landmark to passing voyagers, but there is a much deeper interpretation. To the Hawaiians this area was a "jumping-off point into the spirit world." It was believed that the souls of the recently departed came to this point and leapt into eternity. The right side, Heeia-kei, was the side of light, while the left side, Heeia-uli, was the domain of darkness. The wise *kahuna* taught that you could actually see the face of God in the brilliant sun as it rises over the point.

On the grounds are a main hall, pavilion, restrooms, and various short walks around the entire area with magnificent views of Kaneohe Bay. The park contains numerous indigenous plants and mature trees, the perfect laboratory for the educational goals set by The Friends of Heeia State Park. As an interpretive park, programs are offered for the community and visitors alike. Bernadette Lono, the Director of Hawaiian Studies, gives personal tours of the area. Her family has been part of this *ahuapua* (ancient land division) for countless generations. Bernadette first acquaints you with the area by asking you to sit Hawaiian style on the grass. The earth or *aina* is fundamental to the Hawaiian belief system, and you should start connected to it. She goes on to explain the symbiotic relationship between inland farmers whose fields stretched to Eolaka, the top of the *pali*, and the fishermen who plied the waters of Mokapu on the other side of the peninsula.

Below, Heeia Fishpond is now privately owned by a Mr. Brooks, who has taken over the management of the pond from the Bishop Estates on a 20-year lease. He will raise mullet (*ama*), the traditional fish raised by the ancient Hawaiians and *kapu* to all except the *ali'i*.

PRACTICALITIES

Accommodations
The **Bayview Apartment Hotel** has fully furnished one- and two-bedroom units at $64 for one bedroom, $82 for two. Three-day minimum

stay, but you can stay for one or two if there's room. The hotel is a no-frills cinderblock building that is clean and friendly. There's parking, TV, swimming pool, no in-room phones, but an intercom calls you to the front desk. For reservations and information write Bayview Apartment Hotel, 44-707 Puamohala St., Kaneohe, HI 96744, tel. 247-3635.

The **Schrader's Windward Marine Resort** in Kaneohe has fully furnished apartments. It calls itself "a small rural resort," and although not far from city lights, it's definitely off the beaten track—literally on the edge of Kaneohe Bay, so close that it boasts fishing from the lanai of some apartments. Follow Rt. 836 from Kahaluu for a few minutes until you spot the Pineapple Hut (a tourist trap) and St. John's by the Sea Church. Turn here down Lihikai Drive to the resort.

There are 53 units here, but they differ greatly as they sprawl along the bay. The gray building, a housing project clone along the road front, is part of the place, and oddly enough are some of the most expensive units at $85-100 per night. All units have living rooms, color TV, phones, daily maid service, refrigerators and a/c, but only 19 have stoves and these rent for $65-200 per night. Least expensive with a full kitchen is $65. The rooms are spotless but old. Because of the age of the building, it's as if you've gone back 30 years to old Hawaii. The resort houses a fair number of TLA people (Temporary Lodging for Military). This is the only place for them to stay on the island.

The best deal for the money is a one-bedroom away from the road and facing the bay. If you call and specify any unit with a lanai you're going to get at least a partial view of the bay. The resort also offers motorboats, kayaks, sailboards, and small sailboats through its sister organization, North Bay Boat Club. Get a break at Wave Runners of Kaneohe (jet-skis) and Twilight Cruise, a narrated cruise of the bay every Tuesday evening on a pontoon boat. Discounts offered on long stays, and may include a package deal with Thrifty car rental.

For information write Schrader's Windward Marine Resort, 47-039 Lihikai Dr., Kaneohe, HI 96744, tel. (800) 367-8047, ext. 239, Canada (800) 423-8733, ext. 239, on Oahu 239-5711.

Dining And Nightlife
Fortunately, or unfortunately, Kaneohe is a bit of a wasteland as far as tourist services, nightlife, and eating out are concerned. Most people who live here head for the action in Honolulu. There are a few limited choices. **Fuji's Delicatessen,** at 45-270 Wm. Henry Rd., tel. 235-3690, is a local favorite known for its downhome Japanese, Korean, and Hawaiian cooking served family style on long communal tables.

If you're looking for a real cultural experience, head for **Bob's Saimin,** at 46-132-A Kahuhipa St., tel. 247-7878, especially late in the evening where you can get hearty bowls of soup and a selection of barbecued meats for inexpensive prices. The best deal in town is at **Kim Chee One,** at 46-010 Kamehameha Hwy., tel. 235-5560, which has a few sister restaurants scattered around Oahu. The setting is plain, but you'll have trouble finishing the excellent Korean mixed barbecued plate for $6.95, easily enough for two.

KAHEKILI HIGHWAY

Where Rt. 83 intersects the Likelike Highway on the southern outskirts of Kaneohe, it branches north and changes its name from the Kamehameha Highway to the Kahekili Highway until it hits the coast at Kahaluu. This four-mile traverse passes two exceptionally beautiful valleys: Haiku Valley and the Valley of the Temples. Neither should be missed.

SIGHTS

Haiku ("Abrupt Break") Gardens is a lovely section of a commercial area that includes a restaurant (see below) and some quiet condominiums. After you pass a community college, Haiku Road is past two red lights. Turn left here and proceed for about one-half mile until you see the entrance. The gardens date from the mid-1800s, when Hawaiian *ali'i* deeded 16 acres to an English engineer named Baskerville. He developed the area, creating a series of spring-fed lily ponds, a number of estate homes, and planting flowers, fruits, and ornamental trees. Later a restaurant was built, now owned by the Ing family, and the grounds became famous for their beauty, often used for outdoor weddings and special gatherings.

You're welcome to walk through the gardens. Proceed from the restaurant down a grassy area to a pond, where perhaps you'll attract an impromptu entourage of ducks, chickens, and guinea fowl that squawk along looking for handouts. Amidst the lush foliage is a grass shack used for weddings. A path leads around a larger pond whose benches and small pavilions are perfect for contemplation. The path leads under a huge banyan, while a nearby bamboo grove serenades with sonorous music if the wind is blowing.

Valley Of The Temples

The concept of this universal faith cemetery is as beautiful as the sculpted *pali* that serves as its backdrop. A rainy day makes it better. The *pali* explodes with rainbowed waterfalls, and the greens turn a richer emerald, sparkling with dewdrops. Don't miss the Valley of the Temples Memorial Park, 47-200 Kahekili Hwy., tel. 239-8811. Admission is $2 per person or *kamaaina* rates of $5 per carload, but you have to prove you're from Hawaii. High on a hill sits a Christian chapel, an A-frame topped by a cross. The views can be lovely from up here, but unfortunately the large windows of the chapel perfectly frame some nondescript tract housing and a Pay 'n' Save supermarket below. Great planning!

Byodo-In Temple

The crown jewel of the valley is **Byodo-In Temple** ("Temple of Equality"), a superbly appointed replica of the 900-year-old Byodo-In of Uji, Japan (depicted on the 10-yen coin). This temple dates from June 7, 1968, 100 years to the day when Japanese immigrants first arrived in Hawaii. It was erected through the combined efforts of an American engineering firm headed by Ronald Kawahara in accordance with a plan designed by Kiichi Sano, a famed Kyoto landscape artist. Remove your shoes before entering the temple. A three-ton brass bell, which you're invited to strike after making an offering, creates the right vibrations for meditation, and symbolically spreads the word of Amida Buddha.

The walls hold distinctive emblems of different Buddhist sects. Upstairs wings are roped off, with no entry permitted. Stand on the gravel path opposite the main temple. You'll see a grating with a circle cut in the middle. Stick your face in to see the perfectly framed contemplative visage of Buddha. Cross a half-moon bridge to the left of the temple and follow the path to a small gazebo. Here a rock, perfectly and artistically placed, separates a stream in two, sending the water to the left and right. The pagoda at the top of the path is called the Meditation House. Go to this superbly manicured area to get a sweeping view of the grounds. In front of the Meditation House is a curious tree; pick up one of the fallen leaves, and feel the natural velvet on the backside.

The grounds are alive with sparrows and peacocks, and from time to time you'll hear a curious-sounding "yip, yip, yip" and clapping hands. Follow it to discover Mr. Henry Oda, who will be surrounded by birds taking crumbs from his fingers, as well as a boiling cauldron of koi in the waters below with mouths agape demanding to be fed. He has taken over for the recently retired Mr. Hisayoshi Hirada, the original "Birdman of Byodo-In." Mr. Hirada translates his first name into "long live a good man," and he, well into his 80s, is living proof. Mr. Hirada began training the birds and carp of Byodo-In after his *first* retirement. He would come daily to feed the fish, clapping his hands while he did so. Soon the Pavlovian response took over. Simultaneously, a small and courageous bird, which Hirada-san calls Charlie, began taking crumbs from his fingers.

Charlie and the Birdman

Mr. Oda does a great job of showing visitors around, but old-timers say that there is no one like Mr. Hirada, and if he happens to be there while you're visiting, you have been blessed by the great Buddha of Byodo-In. A small gift shop selling souvenirs, cards, and some refreshments is to the right of the temple. If you wish to photograph the complex, it's best to come before noon, when the sun is at your back as you frame the red and white temple against the deep green of the *pali*.

Kahaluu

This town is at the convergence of the Kahekili Highway and the Kamehameha Highway (Rt. 83) heading north. Also, Rt. 836, an extension of the Kamehameha Highway, hugs the coastline heading down to Kailua/Kaneohe. It offers some of the most spectacular views of a decidedly spectacular coast, with very few tourists venturing down this side road. Kahaluu Town is a gas station and a little tourist trap selling junk just in case you didn't get enough in Waikiki. The Hygienic store sells liquor, groceries, soda, and ice, all you'll need for an afternoon lunch. The Waihee Stream, meandering from the *pali*, empties into the bay and deposits fresh water into the ancient **Kahaluu Fish Pond,** a picture-perfect tropical setting. So picture-perfect is the place that it has provided the background scenery to TV and Hollywood productions such as an episode from "Jake and the Fat Man," a setting for *Parent Trap II,* and the famous airport and village scene from *The Karate Kid II.* All of the movie sets have been torn down, but you can still overlook the fishpond by taking a short walk just behind the bank in town.

WAIAHOLE AND VICINITY

If you want to fall in love with rural, old-time Oahu, go to the northern reaches of Kaneohe Bay around Waihole and Waikane, a Hawaiian grassroots area that has so far eluded development. Alongside the road are many more fruit stands than in other parts of Oahu. For a glimpse of what's happening look for the Waiahole Elementary School, and turn left up Waiahole Valley Road. The road twists its way into the valley, becoming narrower until it turns into a dirt track. Left and right in homey, ramshackle houses lives down-home Hawaii, complete with taro patches in the back yards. Another road of the same type is about one-half mile up Rt. 83 just before you enter Waikane. If you're staying in Waikiki, compare this area with Kuhio Avenue only 45 minutes away!

Route 83 passes a string of beaches, most with camping. Offshore from Kualoa County Park is Mokolii ("Small Reptile") Island, commonly called **Chinaman's Hat** (between mile marker 30 and 31) due to its obvious resemblance to an Oriental chapeau. If the tides are right, you can walk out to it (sneakers advised because of the coral), where you and a few nesting birds have it to yourself. Kualoa Park has undergone extensive renovations. There is an expansive parking area, plenty of picnic tables, and a huge grassy area fronting the beach. The road passes through what was once sugarcane country. Most of the businesses failed last century, but you will see the ruins of the Judd Sugar Works a mile or so before reaching Ka'a'awa. The dilapidated mill stands although it was closed more than a century ago. Entering is not advised!

Kualoa County Regional Park

With the *pali* in the background, Chinaman's Hat Island offshore, and a glistening white strand shaded by swaying palms, Kualoa is one of the finest beach parks on windward Oahu. One of

Chinaman's Hat

the most sacred areas on Oahu, the *ali'i* brought their children here to be reared and educated, and the area is designated in the National Register of Historic Places. It has a full range of facilities and services, including lifeguards, restrooms, and picnic tables. The park is open daily 7 a.m.-7 p.m., with overnight camping allowed with a county permit (mandatory). The swimming is safe year-round along a shoreline dotted with pockets of sand and coral. The snorkeling and fishing are good, but the real treat is walking the 500 yards to Chinaman's Hat at low tide. You need appropriate footgear (old sneakers are fine) because of the sharp coral heads. The island is one of the few around offshore Oahu that is not an official bird sanctuary, although many shorebirds do use the island and should not be molested.

Because of its exposure to winds, Kualoa is sometimes chilly. Although the park is popular, it is not well marked. It lies along Rt. 83, and if you're heading north, look for a red sign to the Kualoa Ranch. Just past it is an HVB Warrior pointing to the park and Chinaman's Hat. Heading south the entrance is just past the HVB Warrior pointing to the Kualoa Sugar Mill ruins.

PRACTICALITIES

Food And Shopping
The **Haiku Gardens Restaurant,** true to its name, sits surrounded by a fragrant garden in a lovely, secluded valley (see "Kahekili Highway" above). The restaurant after massive renovations has opened as a **Chart House,** a small chain with an excellent reputation for good food at reasonable prices.

The **Hygienic Store** along Rt. 83 just past the Valley of the Temples sells groceries and supplies. It's flanked by stalls selling fruits and shellwork at competitive prices.

Kahaluu Sportswear, at 47-102-A1 Wailehua Rd., along the Kahekili Hwy. about five minutes past Byodo-In Temple, open daily until 10 p.m., is a garment factory outlet store that sells inexpensive alohawear. Some is made from unbearable and unwearable polyester, but a great deal are made from cotton or rayon. Prices are about 10-20% cheaper than what you'll find in the malls, or city area, though the mannequins, mostly armless and legless, are a sad lot.

Follow the Kahekili Hwy. to Rt. 83 past Waiahole and Waikane, where you'll find some of the best roadside fruit stands on Oahu. One is located just near the Waiahole Elementary School (mile marker 34.5), and another just a few minutes north along Rt. 83 has cold drinking coconuts. Do yourself a favor and have one. Sip the juice and when it's done, eat the custardlike contents. A real island treat, nutritious and delicious.

KA'A'AWA TOWN AND VICINITY

SIGHTS

When you first zip along the highway through town you get the impression that there isn't much, but there's more than you think. The town stretches back toward the *pali* for a couple of streets. On the ocean side is **Ka'a'awa Beach Park,** a primarily local hangout. Across the road is the post office, and the **Ka'a'awa Country Kitchen,** which serves breakfast and plate lunches, where you can easily eat for $5. They have a few tables, but the best bet is to get your plate lunch and take it across the street to the beach park. Next door is a **7-Eleven** with gas and incidentals. Behind the post office is **Pyramid Rock,** obviously named because of its shape.

Oahu's *pali* is unsurpassed anywhere in the islands, and it's particularly beautiful here. Take a walk around. Stroll the dirt roads through the residential areas and keep your eyes peeled for a small white cross on the *pali* just near Pyramid Rock. It marks the spot where a serviceman was killed during the Pearl Harbor invasion. His spirit is still honored by the perpetually maintained bright white cross. While walking you'll be treated to Ka'a'awa's natural choir— wild roosters crowing any time they feel like it, and the din of cheeky parrots high in the trees. A pair of parrots escaped from a nearby home about 10 years ago, and their progeny continue to relish life in the balmy tropics.

As you come around the bend of Mahie Point, staring down at you is a very popular stone formation, the **Crouching Lion.** Undoubtedly a tour bus or two will be sitting in the lot of the Crouching Lion Inn. As with all anatomical rock formations, it helps to have an imagination. Anyway, the inn is much more interesting than the lion. Built by George Larsen in 1928 from roughhewn lumber from the Pacific Northwest, the huge stones were excavated from the site itself. The inn went public in 1951 and has been serving tourists ever since (for menu and prices see "Practicalities" below).

Ka'a'awa And Kahana Bay Beaches

Three beach parks in as many miles lie between Ka'a'awa Point and Kahana Bay. The first heading north is **Ka'a'awa Beach County Park,** a popular camping beach (county permits) with restrooms, lifeguards, and picnic facilities. An offshore reef running the entire length of the park makes swimming safe year-round. There's a dangerous rip at the south end of the park at the break in the reef.

Swanzy County Park, two minutes north, also has camping with a county permit. The sand and rubble beach lies below a long retaining wall, often underwater during high tide. The swimming is safe year-round, but is not favorable because of the poor quality of the beach. Swanzy is one of the best squidding and snorkeling beaches on the windward coast. A break in the offshore reef creates a dangerous rip, and should be avoided.

Kahana Bay County Park is a full-service park with lifeguards, picnic facilities, restrooms,

near Ka'a'awa

the area's only boat launch, and camping (county permit). Swimming is good year-round, although the waters can be cloudy at times. A gentle shorebreak makes the area ideal for bodysurfing and beginner board riders. This entire beach area is traditionally excellent for *akule* fishing, with large schools visiting the offshore waters at certain times of year. It once supported a large Hawaiian fishing village; remnants of fishponds can still be seen. On the mountainside is **Kahana Valley State Park** amidst a mixture of ironwoods and coconut trees. There are restrooms, fresh water, and picnic tables. Few visit here, and it's perfectly situated for a quiet picnic.

Huilua Fish Pond lies between Ka'a'awa and Punaluu, not far from the Paniola Cafe (about mile marker 25.8). Look to the mountainside for Trout Farm Road and immediately to your right, on the ocean side, is the fishpond. Spot a small bridge and a great launching area for a canoe, kayak, or flotation device. Once in, go left under the traffic bridge. Follow Kahana Stream as it gets narrower and narrower (but passable) as it heads inland. You can even use the overhanging ferns to pull yourself along. It's deep so be aware. If you go to the right, you'll reach the bay. It's fairly safe until you come to open ocean. TheBus stop is directly across from the launching area so you can get off here, enjoy the sights, and then continue on.

PRACTICALITIES

Crouching Lion Inn

There was a time when *everyone* passing through Ka'a'awa stopped at the Crouching Lion Inn. Built in 1926, it was the only place *to* stop for many, many years. The inn has seen its ups and downs, and now, fortunately, it is under new management and on the upswing again. The inn, along Rt. 83 in Ka'a'awa, tel. 237-8511, open daily for lunch 11 a.m.-3:30 p.m., and for dinner 5-9 p.m., is beautiful enough to stop at just to have a look, but if you want a reasonably quiet meal, avoid lunchtime and come in the evening when all of the tour buses have long since departed. Sitting high on a verdant green hill, the inn's architectural style is a mixture of Southwestern and Hawaiian-country. Inside it is cozy with a few fireplaces as well as open-beamed ceilings, while the view from the veranda is especially grand. Lunch can be a simple order of Portuguese bean soup that comes with a delicious flavored bun at only $3.75 per bowl, or appetizers like royal shrimp cocktail, sashimi, honey garlic shrimp, or oysters on the halfshell ($6.25-8.95). Salad entrees are a Crunchy Lion Louie with your choice of shrimp or snowcrab at $8.95, or a papaya stuffed with tuna salad for $7.25. Regular entrees are chopped steak, chicken macadamia, or kahlua pork plate all priced under $10. Sandwiches like a grilled Reuben are under $8, while various burgers cost $6.50-8. Dinner entrees, with fresh-baked rolls, soup or salad, vegetables, and choice of rice, potatoes, or garlic pasta, include pepper steak, teriyaki steak, filet mignon, or prime rib for $18.50-22.95. Chicken macadamia, broiled chicken, and kahlua pork go for $14.95, while seafood selections and vegetarian pleas-ing stir-fry tempura complete the menu. The inn's famous mile-high coconut pie, macadamia nut cream pie, or double-crusted banana pie for under $4, are absolutely delicious. To com-plement your menu selection there is also a full bar serving cocktails, beer, wine, and liquors.

On the premises is the **Livingstone Gal-leries,** open daily 11 a.m.-7 p.m., tel. 237-7165, which display original prints, sculptures, and edition prints of both internationally acclaimed and local island artists. The artists displayed in-clude: **Jiang, He Neng,** and **Hede Guang,** all of the Yunnan School of Art that emerged in China after long years of repression under the Mao regime. Using various media including pastels, watercolors, and chalk the Yunnan artists have created works reminiscent of stained-glass win-dows that seemingly pre-existed inside their souls waiting for the light to illuminate their beau-ty. Other artists include father and son Edgardo and Walfrido Garcia. Dad, Edgardo, lives on the North Shore and does sunsets, waves, and wind-tortured palm trees, while Walfrido spe-cializes in fantastic seascapes that often include Pele, the goddess of fire. Also represented are the works of **Tony Bennett,** the famous croon-er, which burst with intense emotion; the fan-tastic underwater-earth-cosmic paintings of **John Pitre** or **Dana Queen,** his wife and col-league; the foggy coasts and misty *pali* cap-tured by **Somner;** bronze sculptures by Uni-versity of Hawaii economics professor **Bruce Stanford;** and the terminally cute children ren-dered by **Mary Koski.** Also displayed is **Bever-ly Fettig,** an Oahu artist long renowned for her land and seascapes; and finally, **Dawson,** who renders sculptures of faces and masks in a neo-classic Greek style.

PUNALUU AND HAUULA

PUNALUU

When islanders say Punaluu ("Coral Diving") they usually combine it into the phrase "Pat's at Punaluu" because of the famous resort that's been delighting local people and visitors for years (at mile marker 23.2). It's a favorite place to come for a drive in the "country." Punaluu is a long and narrow ribbon of land between the sea and the *pali*. Its built-up area is about a mile or so long, but only a hundred yards wide. It has gas, supplies, camping, and some of the cheapest accommodations anywhere on Oahu, along with the **Punaluu Art Gallery,** operated by Scott Bechtol, famous candle artist (for both see "Practicalities" following). On the northern outskirts of town, a sign points to **Sacred Falls,** an excellent hike, weather permitting (see "Out and About—Camping and Hiking").

A few hundred yards south of Pat's is **St. Joachim Church.** There's nothing outstanding about it, merely a one-room church meekly sit-ting on a plot of ground overlooking the sea. But it's real home-grown, where the people of this district come to worship. Just look and you might understand the simple and basic lifestyle that still persists in this area.

HAUULA

This speck of a town is just past Punaluu be-tween mile markers 21 and 22. The old town center is two soda machines, two gas pumps, and two limited supply stores, Masa's and Ching Jong Leong's. Another store, Segame's, sells cold beer and liquor. At the estuary of a stream is **Aukai Beach Park,** a flat little beach right in the middle of town. A **7-Eleven** and a little church up on the hill with the *pali* as a back-drop add the seemingly mandatory finishing touches. Just near the bus stop on the south end, look for a local man who is usually there selling lei. The flowers and vines are fresh-picked from the immediate area, and the prices and authenticity are hard to beat.

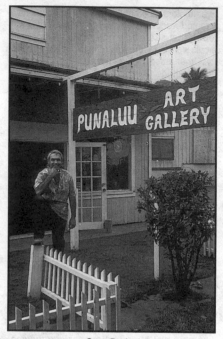

Scott Bechtol

Outdoor enthusiasts will love the little-used **Hauula Loop Trails.** These ridge trails head up the valleys gaining height along the way. They offer just about everything that you can expect for a Hawaiian trail, the mountains, the valleys, and vistas of the sea. Built by the Civilian Conservation Corps during the Depression, the trails are wide, and the footing is great even in rainy periods which can shut down the nearby **Sacred Falls Trail.** (See "Out and About—Camping and Hiking").

BEACHES

Right along the highway is **Punaluu Beach County Park.** Punaluu provides shopping, and the beach park has restrooms, cooking facilities, camping by permit (recently closed, so check) but no lifeguards. The swimming is safe year-round inside the protected reef. Local fishermen, usually older Filipino men who are surf-

casting, use this area frequently. They're friendly and a great source of information for anyone trying to land a fish or two. They know the best baits and spots to dunk a line.

Hauula Beach County Park is an improved beach park with lifeguards, picnic facilities, restrooms, pavilion, volleyball court, and camping (permit). Safe swimming year-round inside the coral reef, with good snorkeling; surfing is usually best in the winter months. Rip currents are present at both ends of the beach at breaks in the reef, and deep holes in the floor of a brackish pond are formed where Maakua Stream enters the sea. Across the road are the ruins of the historic **Lanakila Church** (1853), partially dismantled at the turn of the century to build a smaller church near Punaluu.

PRACTICALITIES

Accommodations
Pat's at Punaluu Condominium, at mile marker 23.2, P.O. Box 359, Hauula, HI 96717, tel. 293-8111 or (800) 845-8799, is definitely in the "budget category," so don't expect deluxe accommodations. The "used but not too abused" units are clean, and you will get what you pay for. Rates on a sliding scale depend upon the length of your stay: $68-76 for a guest room; $72-80 for a large deluxe; $76-84 one bedroom; $120-140 three bedroom. Pat's has a great beach, parking, TV, a restaurant, a swimming pool, and weekly maid service. They offer a "room 'n' wheels" package, and discounts on long stays. Pat's is off the beaten track, so definitely call ahead to check room availability. Turning up and expecting a room is a foolish gamble. This is a condo, not a hotel, so one-night stays are not the norm, and few services are provided. Next to the restaurant is a small convenience store that may or may not look open. But inside (separate business) is a small desk, open 8:30 a.m.-1 p.m., where you register. Another rental office on the property is open until 9 p.m., but check-in after that costs extra since someone has to stay around to let you in.

The **Countryside Cabins** are a wonderful, inexpensive, and definitely funky place to stay. They're owned and operated by Margaret Naai, still sparkling at 92 years old. The entrance is hard to spot, but it's located *mauka* about 5-10 minutes past Pat's at Punaluu. Look for the small white sign that says "Cabins." Completely furnished studios are $25 daily, $175 weekly, $475 monthly. Unfurnished rooms are $20 nightly, $140 weekly, $300 monthly. Margaret will reserve a room for you if you send a $10 deposit. She's a peach, but she's getting on in years, so it would be best to send a SASE envelope with your deposit and not count on her to remember. For information and reservations, write Countryside Cabins, 53-224 Kamehameha Hwy., Hauula HI 96717, tel. 237-8169.

Food And Shopping

An institution along the windward coast, **Pat's at Punaluu,** tel. 293-8111, open daily except Monday 11 a.m.-9 p.m., and breakfast on the weekends only, has an extraordinary view of the coast. The interior is quite tasteful with open beams, ceiling fans, high-backed wicker chairs, and a long polished koa bar. The feeling is warm, peaceful, and very tropical. There's a little bandstand, some fish tanks, and a large lava rock wall that counterpoints the white stucco. Breakfast (weekends only) features three-egg omelettes, bacon or sausage and eggs, or a local artery clogging "locomoco" for under $6. Lunch includes a variety of appetizers from beer-battered mahimahi for $6.95 to grilled sate with peanut sauce for $7, along with dragon wings or roasted chicken basted with a pepper sauce for $5.25. For the lighter appetite, salads are a simple house garden salad for $5.25, to the Pacific seafood salad at $10.75, while sandwiches range from a kahlua pork sandwich $7.50 to a crab and shrimp salad sandwich for $8.95. Full meals are served with salad, potato or rice, rolls, and vegetables, and include a captain's platter of seasonal fish and seafood in a crispy beer-batter tempura at market price, or a Hawaiian plate of kahlua pork, grilled fish, *lomi* salmon, and steamed rice, available as a plate lunch or dinner at $7.95 or $10.75. From the grill, order baby-back ribs, country lamb chops, or a grilled saloon steak for under $20. No trip to Pat's is complete without sampling the fresh tarts famous since 1945—your choice of banana, pineapple, or coconut ladled into an oven-fresh tart shell and mounded with whipped cream.

Pat's is also famous for mai tais, made fresh, and so laced with booze that if you intend on driving, it would be good to have a designated driver. Pat's, long renowned as a good, old-fashioned, Hawaiian-style restaurant, has been going through a transition in the last few years. Luckily, it is definitely back on the right track. The previous owners tried to make it a tourist trap complete with a mediocre cafeteria to cater to the tour-bus crowd. The new owners have reclaimed Pat's and saved it from a fate worse than deep-fried mahimahi. They're restoring Pat's to its old island-style tradition, and doing an admirable job. Pat's is back, and is definitely worth a stop.

The **Punaluu Art Gallery,** in Punaluu around mile marker 24, tel. 237-8325, open daily 10:30 a.m.-6:30 p.m., formerly owned by Dorothy Zoler, is the oldest art gallery on windward Oahu. The new owner, candle artist Scott Bechtol, remains dedicated to showcasing the works of an assortment of the finest artists that the North Shore has to offer. Scott is well known for his wonderful sculpted candles, all made from the finest beeswax. Some are lanterns shaped like a huge pita bread with the top third cut off. The remainder is sculpted with a scene that glows when the candle is lit. Others are huge tikis, dolphins, or flowers, all inspired by the islands. There's even a 10-foot whale! Some of the larger candles are $70, and the man-size tiki is about $800, but smaller candles are only $5, and Scott's unique "crying tiki" sells for only $20. Scott creates all of this beautiful glowing art with just one precision carving tool . . . a Buck knife! Another artists shown is Bill Cupit, who creates "bananascapes." Bill removes the outer bark from the banana tree, then he tears and cuts it to make a scene of boats or mountains. The result is a three-dimensional piece. Bill's wife is an artist who specializes in seascapes made with seaweed, while Christine Diana uses fossilized wood to render "Tiny Treasures," miniature paintings of Hawaiian scenes. Other beauty is added by Janet Holiday's silk screen prints, Peter Hayward's oil paintings, and the dramatic tropical beauty of the North Shore captured by long-time resident, Edgardo Garcia. The Punaluu Art Gallery is a jewel case of manmade beauty surrounded by natural beauty. They harmonize perfectly.

The **Sacred Falls Bazaar,** seaside on the north end of Punaluu, open daily 9:30 a.m.-6:30 p.m., sells an assortment of neat touristy junk including aloha shirts, shell lei, tie-dyed T-shirts, and a small shelf with fresh island fruit. A minute further north is the **Jhing Leong Store,** painted shocking pink, where you can pick up a smattering of supplies.

In Hauula look for the **Hauula Kai Center,** a small shopping center with a **post office** and a **Pay 'n' Save** for everything from film to swim fins, and the **Village Food Mart,** open 9-9 weekdays, 9-5 Sunday for all food needs. Also, look for **Lotus Inn Chop Suey,** tel. 293-5412, where you'll get a tasty and filling meal daily 10 a.m.-9

p.m. for under $6. A full menu of Cantonese-style food includes ginger chicken, shrimp, and beef. Happy hour runs 3-7 p.m., when well drinks cost $1.25 and are accompanied by free *pu pu*. The shopping center also features the **Bethlehem Baking Company,** open daily 6:30 a.m.-6 p.m., with an assortment of yummies including sweet homemade breads of pineapple and coconut.

Also in Hauula is the **Rainbow Shopping Plaza,** an unabashed tourist trap, classic in its obvious tastelessness. Here you'll find beads and baubles, the **Rainbow Barbecue** for something to eat and the **Rainbow Lounge** where you can have a drink.

LAIE TO KAHUKU

LAIE

The "Saints" came marching into Laie ("Leaf of the Ie Vine") and set about making a perfect Mormon village in paradise. What's more, they succeeded! The town itself is squeaky clean, with well-kept homes and manicured lawns that hint of suburban Midwest America. Dedicated to education, they built a branch of **Brigham Young University** (BYU) that attracts students from all over Polynesia, many of whom work in the nearby Polynesian Cultural Center. The students vow to live a clean life, free of drugs and alcohol, and not to grow beards. In the foyer of the main entrance look for a huge mural depicting Laie's flag-raising ceremony in 1921, which symbolically established the colony. The road leading to and from the university campus is mazelike but easily negotiable.

The first view of the **Mormon Temple,** built in 1919, is very impressive. Square, with simple architectural lines, this house of worship sits pure white against the *pali,* and is further dramatized by a reflecting pool and fountains spewing fine mists. This tranquil, shrine-like church is open daily 9 a.m.-9 p.m., when a slide show telling the history of the Laie colony is presented, along with a guided tour of the grounds. "Smoking is prohibited, and shirts (no halter tops) must be worn to enter." The temple attracts more visitors than any

other Mormon site outside of the main temple in Salt Lake City.

Polynesian Cultural Center
The real showcase is the Polynesian Cultural Center. PCC, as it's called by islanders, began as an experiment in 1963. Smart businessmen said it would never thrive way out in Laie, and tourists didn't come to Hawaii for *culture* anyway. The PCC now rates as one of Oahu's top tourist attractions, luring about one million visitors annually. Miracles do happen! PCC is a nonprofit organization, with proceeds going to the Laie BYU, and to maintaining the center itself.

Covering 42 acres, the primary attractions are seven model villages including examples from Hawaii, Samoa, the Marquesas, Fiji, New Zealand, Tonga, and Tahiti. Guides lead you through the villages either on a walking tour, or by canoe over artesian-fed waterways. A shuttle tram runs outside the center, and will take you on a guided tour to the BYU campus, the Temple, and a short tour of the community (it would be okay except for the missionary hard sell). The villages are primarily staffed with people from the representative island homelands. Remember that most are Mormons, whose dogma colors the attitudes and selected presentations of the staffers. Still, all are genuinely interested in dispensing cultural knowledge about their traditional island ways and beliefs, and almost all are characters who engage in lighthearted bantering with their willing audience. The undeniable family spirit and pride at PCC makes you feel welcome, while providing a clean and wholesome experience, with plenty of attention to detail.

The morning begins with the **Fiafia Festival,** a lei greeting that orients you to the center. Next comes **Music Polynesia,** a historical evolution of island music presented by singers, musicians, and dancers. A brass band plays from 5:30 p.m., touring the different villages, and the **Pageant of Canoes** sails at 2 and 3 p.m. The largest extravaganza occurs during an evening dinner show called **This is Polynesia.** Beginning at 7:30 p.m., the center's amphitheater hosts about 3,000 spectators for this show of music, dance, and historical drama. The costumes and lighting are dramatic and inspired; it's hard to believe that the performers are not professionals. Soon to open is an **Imax,** a wraparound movie screen that attempts to give you a real sense of what it's like to take a canoe around the shores of Fiji, or to tramp the mountains of New Zealand.

Food is available from a number of snack bars, or you can dine at the **Gateway,** which serves you a buffet dinner as part of a package including the Polynesian extravaganza. A luau, and a Mission Buffet are offered now and again, usually at 5:30 p.m., so there's plenty of time to eat and then catch the show if you desire.

PCC is open daily except Sunday 12:30 p.m.-9 p.m. General admission to the center is $25 adult, $12.50 children, under five free. There are also a variety of other packages available including an all-day pass, with dinner buffet and evening show for around $50, children $25. For more information contact PCC at 293-3333 or (800) 367-7060. TheBus no. 52 leaves from Ala Moana to the center and takes about two hours. Most island hotels can arrange a package tour to PCC.

PRACTICALITIES

Accommodations
The **Laniloa Lodge Hotel,** 55-109 Laniloa St., Laie, HI 96762, tel. 293-9282 or (800) 526-4562, is just outside the Polynesian Culture Center, and has been recently given a face-lift. Rooms are $70-85 standard, $90-105 deluxe, $100-130 two bedroom deluxe, $10 additional person. They also offer a special rate if you purchase two all-day tickets to the Polynesian Cultural Center. All rooms have a/c, TV, and there's parking, a pool, and a restaurant that closes early on Sundays, but McDonald's is next door.

Kekeala Hale is a condominium rental fronting Kekeala Beach, at 55-113 Kamehameha Hwy., Laie, HI 96762, tel. 293-9700. They call themselves "private Polynesia at its best," and being as secluded as they are, they have a point. Cottages are over a thousand square feet with a full kitchen and bath, with one king and four twin beds in each unit. A tennis court on the property is featured. Rates for cottages that sleep six to 12 (using foam pads) are $240 daily, $600 for a weekend, $1440 weekly. Rates for a cottage sleeping four to six are $120 daily, $720 weekly. All require a three-day minimum.

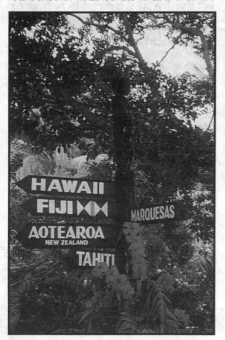

Polynesian Cultural Center

Lora Dunn's House is at 55-161 Kamehameha Hwy., Laie, HI 96762, tel. 293-1000 (between mile markers 19 and 20, ocean side). Lora admits people on a first-come, first-served basis, but will happily take phone reservations for which she requires a deposit. Chances of turning up and finding a vacancy are poor, so at least call from the airport to check availability. A separate studio for two people is $175, while the downstairs self-contained unit of her home, which is larger and can accommodate four people, runs about $350 per week. Good value in a quiet, if not spectacular, setting.

Note: Also see "Beaches" following, some of which have camping facilities.

Food And Shopping

When you enter Laie you will be greeted by the Stars and Stripes flying over the entrance of the Polynesian Cultural Center. Next door is a whopper of a **McDonald's,** and in keeping with the spirit of Polynesian culture, it looks like a Polynesian longhouse. Just next door is the **Laniloa Lodge,** whose restaurant features breakfast specials for under $4, and complete dinners with soup, salad, vegies, and Kona coffee for only $10.95. They're open every day for breakfast until 8 p.m., except Sunday when the restaurant closes at 2 p.m. The food is wholesome but ordinary at the Laniloa Lodge, tel. 293-5888.

On the ocean side of the road is **Masa's Market,** which couldn't be more local with counters stocked with everything from lotus root to lamb. At the north end of Laie, you'll pass **TT Surf Shop,** about the only shop in this neck of the woods offering snorkel equipment, surf boards, or boogie boards. A few minutes south, is the **Haaula Kai Shopping Center** (see "Hauula—Practicalities"), which provides a small variety of dining spots and shopping.

Between Kahuku and Laie is a new **Laie Shopping Center** where you'll find a large and modern **Foodland,** along with a **Bank of America,** and a small convenience store, **Lindy's Food.** The most interesting shop is the **Hawaiian-Polynesian Cultural Supply,** tel. 293-1560, open 9:30 a.m.-5 p.m. weekdays, half day Saturday, a rare and unique hula supply store. They feature fine Polynesian crafts used in the hula like *ip'u* (gourd drums), hula skirts, headdresses,

beads, and shell lei. There are other accoutrements and art items like koa bowls, carved turtles, and mother-of-pearl necklaces. All items are handmade in Tahiti, Samoa, Tonga, and Hawaii, basically from throughout Polynesia. T-shirts, sweatshirts, and suntan oil are also sold. All items offered are authentic, and the storekeepers are friendly and informative regarding the hula. A great store in which to browse and to pick up a unique and *real* souvenir. Also see "Kahuku—Practicalities" following.

BEACHES

At the southern end of Laie is **Pounder's Beach,** so named by students of BYU because of the pounding surf. The park area is privately owned, open to the public, with few facilities (a few portable outhouses and picnic tables). This beach experiences heavy surf and dangerous conditions in the winter months, but its excellent shoreline break is perfect for bodysurfing. The remains of an old pier at which interisland steamers once stopped is still in evidence.

Laie Beach County Park is an unimproved beach park with no facilities, but a one-mile stretch of beach. The shoreline waters are safe for swimming inside the reef, but wintertime produces heavy and potentially dangerous surf. Good snorkeling, fishing, and throw-netting by local fishermen; get there by following the stream from the bridge near the Laie Shopping Mall.

Camping Beaches

Kakela Beach was a privately owned facility where camping was allowed. Now under the Department of State Parks, it is being renovated and may open again for camping (See "Out and About—Camping and Hiking" for information.

Malaekahana Bay State Recreation Area is the premier camping beach along the north section of the windward coast. Separated from the highway by a large stand of shade trees, it offers showers, restrooms, picnic facilities, and camping (state permit). Offshore is Moku'auia, better known as **Goat Island.**

The island is only a stone's throw from shore. Reef walkers or tennis shoes are advised. You can reach this seabird sanctuary by wading across the reef during low tide. You'll find a

*Kahuku Mill
Shopping Center*

beautiful crescent white-sand beach and absolute peace and quiet. The swimming inside the reef is good, and it's amazing how little used this area is for such a beautiful spot. Be aware that there are two entrances to the park. The north entrance, closest to Kahuku, puts you in the day-use area of the park, where there are restrooms and showers. Further offshore, about 200-300 yards, is a small island. *You can not wade to this island. It is too far, and the currents are strong.* The entrance to the camping section is south a minute or two (around mile marker 17) and is marked by a steel gate painted brown and a sign welcoming you to Malaekahana Bay State Recreation Area. You must be aware that the gates open at 7 a.m. and close at 6:45 p.m.

KAHUKU

This village, and it is a village, is where the *workers* of the North Shore live. Kahuku is "fo' real," and a lingering slice of what *was* not so long ago. Do yourself a favor, and turn off the highway for a two-minute tour of the dirt roads lined by proudly maintained homes that somehow exude the feeling of Asia.

Practicalities
You can pick up supplies at the **Kahuku Superette** clearly marked along Rt. 83, or better yet look for a little white *kaukau* wagon that sits

across the roadway from the school. They sell great food that they bring from Honolulu's Chinatown fresh every day. Unfortunately, they're here only during school hours, when you can pick up a tasty and inexpensive lunch.

Keep a sharp eye out for a truck and a sign featuring fresh shrimp for $6.95 just along the road. Follow it to **Ahi's Kahuku Restaurant,** operated by Roland Ahi and son, open daily 10 a.m.-9 p.m. The shrimp couldn't be fresher as it comes from Pacific Sea Farms, an aquaculture farm just a few minutes away. The longest that these plump babies have been out of the water is 48 hours, so you are definitely getting *the* best. In this no-frills, but super-friendly restaurant, you can have your shrimp cooked to order as scampi, deep-fried, tempura, a cocktail, or sautéed. You get about eight shrimp, depending on the size. The shrimp is the pièce de résistance, but they have basic sandwiches like tuna and hamburger, both under $4, and entrees like spaghetti with meat sauce for $5.95, and steak and mahimahi combo for $10.95. Complete meals come with green salad, fresh vegetables, rice, and tea. They also serve beer and wine, and on Friday nights, Charlie Kualoha, a wonderfully talented local musician, performs everything from country to contemporary Hawaiian. Ahi's serves all of its great food with authentic *aloha*. Stop in! You'll be glad you did!

On the north end of town is the **Mill Shopping Center,** which is really the town's old sugar mill that has been recycled. The interior is dominated by huge gears and machinery, power panels, and crushers that are the backdrop for a string of shops, a restaurant, and the Kahuku Theater. The 10-foot gears and conveyor belts have all been painted with bright colors, and seem like a display of modern art pieces. Outside is a **Circle K** food store and gas station, **Lee's Gifts and Jewelry, Island Snow** for shave ice, **Tropical Memories Jeweler,** and a post office.

Chucho's Mexican Restaurant and **J-Gem's Plate Lunches** defy the adage that "two things can't occupy the same space at the same time." These "window service" restaurants, tel. 293-2110, open daily except Sunday 7 a.m.-8 p.m., are two separate establishments serving very different menus but operating out of the same window. They're located under the veranda behind the gas station at the Mill Shopping Center. J-Gem's offers breakfast selections like Portuguese sausage, eggs, and rice ($2.99), or a stack of pancakes ($1.99). The most expensive plate lunch is a teri beef combo ($4.99), or choose a fishburger ($2.25) or *lumpia,* an island favorite by way of the Philippines ($3.99). Chucho's offers tacos, tostadas, burritos, quesadillas, and taquitos all for under $2.95, and dinner combinations with rice and beans ($3.65-4.95). Both get the "thumbs up" from local people who say their food is great.

About one mile northwest of Kahuku heading toward Haleiwa, you'll pass the **Royal Hawaiian Prawn and Shrimp Farm.** Notice a patchwork quilt of ponds shored up with mud, very similar to rice paddies, where the succulent crustaceans are raised. The general public is invited to stop by and purchase the little beauties.

Just past is the **Tanaka Plantation Store,** at 56-901 Kamehameha Hwy., Kahuku, a refurbished turn-of-the-century company store that now houses a clutch of boutiques and shops. Make sure to visit **Paul Wroblewski's Antiques and Collectibles,** open daily 10 a.m.-

5:30 p.m., "unless they are closed." Blown to Oahu's North Shore from Kauai by Hurricane Iniki, Paul has reopened his shop and once again jammed it with Hawaiian artifacts, old bottles, costume jewelry, license plates, fishing floats, netsuke, scrimshaw, a collection of Marilyn Monroe memorabilia, and a full line of antique jewelry. Paul's an amiable fellow, and is open to any reasonable offer.

Next door is **Fairly Galleries,** featuring posters, prints, and a bit of jewelry, along with **Coconuts,** open daily 9 a.m.-6 p.m., tel. 293-7865, with bathing suits, T-shirts, straw hats, alohawear, towels, silver jewelry, and postcards. They also have a snack counter with sandwiches and espresso featured.

Perhaps the most interesting shop in the complex is the **Amazonian Forest Store,** open daily 11 a.m.-6 p.m., owned and operated by Brazilian world travelers Cesar Olivera and Katia Ferz. They specialize in authentic artifacts gathered from the Amazon and other rainforest regions around the world, including Hawaii and Indonesia. Some of the most amazing artifacts are headdresses and paintings by Brazil's Xindu Indians, along with basketry, parasols, coconut purses, string and cotton hammocks, and semi-precious gemstones gathered from throughout South America. If these aren't enough to make you "bug eyed" perhaps a Brazilian string bikini will.

Geographical Note
The following chapter, "The North Shore," begins at the west end in Waialua/Haleiwa and works eastward toward Kahuku. That's because most people visiting the North Shore proceed in this direction, while those heading for "Windward Oahu" start in Kailua/Kaneohe and proceed up the coast. So, the end of this chapter follows geographically with the end of "The North Shore" chapter. Don't let it throw you.

BOB RACE

THE NORTH SHORE

This shallow bowl of coastline stretches from Kaena Point in the west to Turtle Bay in the east. **Mount Ka'ala,** verdant backdrop to the area, rises 4,020 feet from the Waianae Range, making it the highest peak on Oahu. The entire stretch is a day-tripper's paradise with plenty of sights to keep you entertained. But the North Shore is synonymous with one word: surfing. Thunderous winter waves, often measuring 25 feet (from the rear!) rumble along the North Shore's world-famous surfing beaches lined up one after the other—**Waimea Bay, Ehukai, Sunset, Banzai Pipeline.** They attract highly accomplished athletes who come to compete in prestigious international surfing competitions. In summertime *moana* loses her ferocity and lies down, becoming gentle and safe for anyone.

Haleiwa, at the junction of the Farrington Highway (Rt. 930) heading west along the coast and the Kamehameha Highway (Rt. 83) heading east, is fast becoming the central town along the North Shore. The main street is lined with restaurants, boutiques, art galleries, small shopping malls, and sports equipment stores. **Waialua,** just west, is a "sugar town" with a few quiet condos for relaxation. Farther west is **Dillingham A.F.B.** (inactive), where you can arrange to fly above it all in a small plane or soar silently in a glider. The road ends for vehicles not far from here, and then your feet have to take you to Kaena Point, where *the* largest waves pound the coast. Heading east, you'll pass a famous *heiau* where human flesh mollified the gods. Then come the great surfing beaches and their incredible waves. Here and there are tidepools rich with discovery, a monument to a real local hero, and **Waimea Falls Park,** the premier tourist attraction of the North Shore.

BEACHES AND SIGHTS

The main attractions of the North Shore are its beaches. Interspersed among them are a few sights definitely worth your time and effort. The listings below run from west to east. The most-traveled route to the North Shore is from Honolulu along the H-2 freeway, and then directly to the coast along Rt. 99 or Rt. 803. At Weed Circle or Thompson Corner, where these routes reach the coast, turn left along the Farrington Highway, following it to road's end just before Kaena Point, or turn right along the Kamehameha Highway (Rt. 83), which heads around the coast all the way to Kailua.

Be aware that *all* North Shore beaches experience very heavy surf conditions with dangerous currents from October through April. The waters, at this time of year, are not for the average swimmer. Please heed all warnings. In summertime, leap in!

ALONG THE FARRINGTON HIGHWAY, RT. 930

Waialua
The first town is Waialua ("Two Waters"). Take Waialua Beach Road just off the Weed Traffic Circle coming north on Rt. 99, or follow the signs off the Farrington Highway. At the turn of the century, Waialua, lying at the terminus of a sugar-train railway, was a fashionable beach community complete with hotels and vacation homes. Today, it's hardly ever visited, and it's

not uncommon to see as many horses tied up along the main street as it is to see parked cars in this real one-horse town. Sundays can also attract a rumble of bikers who kick up the dust on their two-wheeled steeds.

The sugar mill, an outrageously ugly mechanical monster, is still operating and is central to the town. Quiet Waialua, with its main street divided by trees running down the middle, *is* rural Oahu. There's a general store for supplies, a post office, and snacks at the **Sugar Bar,** a restaurant in the old Bank of Hawaii building. If you're returning to Haleiwa take Haleiwa Road, a back way through residential areas. Look for Paalaa Road on the right and take it past a small Buddhist temple that holds an *o bon* festival honoring the dead, traditionally observed in July.

Mokuleia Beach County Park And Dillingham Airfield
Mokuleia is the main public access park along the highway. It provides picnic facilities, restrooms, lifeguards, a playground area, and camping (county permit). In summertime, swimming is possible along a few sandy stretches protected by a broken offshore reef. Mokuleia Army Beach, across from the airfield, is a wider

THE NORTH SHORE

© MOON PUBLICATIONS, INC.

bikers at Waialua

strand of sand. It's very private, and the only noise interrupting your afternoon slumber might be planes taking off from the airfield. A minute farther toward Kaena is an unofficial area with a wide sand beach. During the week you can expect no more than half dozen people on this 300-yard beach. Remember that this is the North Shore and the water can be treacherous. Careful! Five minutes past the airfield, the road ends. This is a good place to check out giant waves.

Across the road is **Dillingham Airfield,** small but modern, with restrooms near the hangars and a new parking area. A public phone is available in hangar G-1. Most days, especially weekends, a few local people sell refreshments from their cars or trucks. The main reason for stopping is to take a small plane or glider ride. **Glider Rides,** tel. 677-3404, takes you on a 20- to 30-minute flight for $40 single, $60 double. The owner is Bill Star, who has been flying from here since 1970. They fly seven days a week starting at about 10 a.m. on a first-come, first-served basis. They suggest you bring a camera and arrive before 5 p.m. to get the best winds. There's always a pilot with you to make sure that your glider ride is a *return* trip. Another glider operation is **Mile High Glider Rides.** They fly for 30 minutes, and they offer a sit-up-front-and-try-the-controls-type ride complete with acrobatics and instruction. They fly out of hangar no. 10, and charge about $80 per ride. **Surf Air Tours,** tel. 637-7003, flies Cessna 172s or 206s

for a half-hour along the North Shore for $30 per person, or a longer "circle-island tour" for $50 per person. It's worthwhile, but the glider ride is more exceptional.

In quick succession after Dillingham Airfield comes undeveloped **Kealia Beach,** safe during calm periods, and **Mokuleia Army Beach,** improved and open to the public. Local people have erected semipermanent tents in this area and guard it as if it were their own. **Camp Harold Erdman** is next, one of the best-known camps on Oahu. This YMCA facility is named after a famous Hawaiian polo player killed in the '30s. The facility is used as a summer camp for children, throughout the year for special functions, and as a general retreat area by various organizations. Access is limited to official use.

Kaena Point

Kaena Point lies about 2.5 miles down the dirt track after the pavement gives out. Count on three hours for a return hike and remember to bring water. The point can also be reached from road's end above Mahuka on the Waianae (leeward) side of the island. Kaena has *the* largest waves in Hawaii on any given day. In wintertime, these giants can reach above 40 feet, and their power, even when viewed safely from the high ground, is truly amazing. Surfers have actually plotted ways of riding these waves, which include being dropped by helicopter with scuba tanks. Reportedly, one surfer named Ace Cool has already done it. For the rest of us mortals . . .

"who wants to have that much fun anyway!" Kaena Point is the site of numerous *heiau*. Due to its exposed position, it, like similar sites around the islands, was a jumping-off point for the "souls of the dead." The spirits were believed to wander here after death, and once all worldly commitments were fulfilled, they made their "leap" from earth to heaven. Hopefully, the daredevil surfers will not revive this tradition!

HALEIWA AND VICINITY

Haleiwa ("Home of the Frigate Birds") has become the premier town of the region, mainly because it straddles the main road and has the majority of shopping, dining, and services along the North Shore. **Haleiwa Alii Beach Park** is on the western shores of Waialua Bay, which fronts the town. This beach park is improved with restrooms, lifeguard tower, and a small boat launch. Lifeguards staff the tower throughout the summer, on weekends in winter. The shoreline is rocks and coral with pockets of sand, and although portions can be good for swimming, the park is primarily noted for surfing, in a break simply called "Haleiwa."

When you come into Haleiwa, just past Pizza Hut and McDonald's, notice on the right-hand side of the road a sign that says "Weinberg Village." Look and you will see one-room, decent, modern . . . shacks! The idea was good— "to create low rent homes for the poor and homeless" with funds bequeathed for this purpose by Mr. Weinberg, a social-minded philanthropist. However, each of the tiny units costs $40,000 to build, and the people residing here have to pay $300 per month rent. Moreover, they are supposed to be torn down in five years!

Head eastward and cross the **Anahulu River Bridge.** Park for a moment and walk back over the bridge. Look upstream to see homes with tropical character perched on the bank with a bevy of boats tied below. The scene is reminiscent of times gone by.

A much better park is **Haleiwa Beach Park,** clearly marked off the highway on the eastern side of Waialua Bay. Here you'll find pavilions, picnic facilities, lifeguards, restrooms, showers, food concessions, and camping (county permit). The area is good for fishing, surfing, and most importantly, for swimming year-round! It's about the only safe place for the average person to swim along the entire North Shore during winter.

Kawailoa Beach is the general name given to the area stretching all the way from Haleiwa Beach County Park to Waimea Bay. A string of beaches, **Papailoa, Laniakea,** and **Chun's Reef,** is just off the road. Cars park where the access is good. None of these beaches is suitable for the recreational swimmer. All are surfing beaches, with the most popular being Chun's Reef.

typical rural Buddhist temple, outskirts of Haleiwa

WAIMEA BAY AND VICINITY

The two-lane highway along the North Shore is pounded by traffic; be especially careful around Waimea Bay. The highway sweeps around till you see the steeple of **St. Peter and Paul Mission** with the bay below. The steeple is actually the remnants of an old rock-crushing plant on the site. **Waimea Bay Beach County Park** has the largest rideable waves in the world. This is the heart of surfers' paradise. The park is improved with a lifeguard tower, restrooms, and a picnic area.

During a big winter swell, the bay is lined with spectators watching the surfers ride the monumental waves. In summertime, the bay is calm as a lake. People inexperienced with the sea should not even walk along the shorebreak in winter. Unexpected waves come up farther than expected, and a murderous rip lurks only a few feet from shore. The area is rife with tales of heroic rescue attempts, many ending in fatalities. A plaque commemorates Eddie Aikau, a local llfeguard credited with making thousands of rescues. In 1978, the *Hokule'a,* the Polynesian Sailing Society's double-hulled canoe, capsized in rough seas about 20 miles offshore. Eddie was aboard, and launched his surfboard to swim for help. He never made it, but his selfless courage lives on.

Waimea Falls Park
Look for the well-marked entrance to Waimea Falls Park, mountain side from the bay, and then drive for quite a way into the lush valley before coming to the actual park entrance. Along with the Bishop Museum, the park is the most culturally significant travel destination on Oahu. Although open to the public and more than happy to welcome visitors, Waimea Falls Park has not lost sight of its ancient *aloha* soul, which it honors while providing a wonderful day of excitement and education. Primarily a botanical garden, with a fascinating display of flowers and plants all labeled for your edification, the Waimea Arboretum collects, grows and preserves extremely rare specimens of Hawaii's endangered flora. If you choose not to walk, an open-air tour bus will take you through, narrating all the way. A

thrilling event is the professional diving from the 55-foot rock walls into the pool below Waimea Falls, along with the feeding of peacocks, geese, guinea fowl, and jungle fowl scheduled throughout the day. Culturally enlightening are displays of ancient hula (*kahiko*) performed by very accomplished dancers, a display of Hawaiian games, carving demonstrations, and walks along forest paths that end at fascinating historical sites. On the property is Hale o Lono, one of the island's largest and most ancient *heiau* dedicated to the god Lono. Admission is $19.95 adults, $8.95 juniors, and $3.95 children, open daily 10 a.m.-5:30 p.m., tel. 638-8511. The **Proud Peacock** (see "Practicalities—Food") serves dinner until 9 p.m. Monthly (check the free tourist literature), on the Friday night closest to the full moon, beginning at 8:30 p.m., the park offers a free, guided moon-viewing tour.

Pupukea Beach Park
A perfect place to experience marinelife is the large tidepool next to Pupukea Beach Park, the first one north of Waimea Bay, across the street from the Shell gas station. A long retaining wall out to sea forms a large and protected pool at low tide. Wear footgear and check out the pools with a mask. Don't be surprised to find large sea bass. A sign warns against spearing fish, but the local people do it

all the time. Be careful not to step on sea urchins, and stay away from the pool during rough winter swells, when it can be treacherous. The beach park has restrooms, picnic facilities, and fair swimming in sandy pockets between coral and rock, but only in summertime. County camping with a permit used to be allowed at this beach park, and may be available again.

The middle section of the park is called **Shark's Cove,** though no more sharks are here than anywhere else. The area is terrific for snorkeling and scuba in season. Look to the mountains to see **The Mansion** (see following), and next to it the white sculpture of the **World Unity Monument.** If you had to pick a spot from which to view the North Shore sunset, Pupukea Beach Park is hard to beat!

Farther down the road, as you pass mile marker 9 you can't help noticing a mammoth redwood log that has been carved into a giant statue representing an ancient Hawaiian. Peter Wolfe, the sculptor, has done a symbolic sculpture for every state in the union, this being his 50th. This statue is extremely controversial. Some feel that it looks much more like an American Indian than a Hawaiian, and that the log used should have been a native koa instead of an imported redwood from the Pacific Northwest. Others say that its *intention* was to honor the living and the ancient Hawaiians, and that is what's important. Just off to the left a small shop sells plants, towels, and shellwork from the Philippines.

Puu O Mahuka Heiau

Do yourself a favor and drive up the mountain road leading to the *heiau* even if you don't want to visit it. The vast and sweeping views of the coast below are incredible. About one mile past Waimea Bay the highway passes a Foodland on the right. Turn here up Pupukea Road and follow the signs. There is a warning at the beginning of the access road, but the road is well maintained and many people ignore the sign.

Puu O Mahuka Heiau is large, covering perhaps five acres. Designated as a state historical site, its floorplan is huge steps, with one area leading to another just below. The *heiau* was the site of human sacrifice. People still come to pray as is evidenced by many stones

wrapped in ti leaves placed on small stone piles lying about the grounds. In the upper section is a raised mound surrounded by stone in what appears to be a central altar area. The *heiau's* stonework shows a high degree of craftsmanship throughout, but especially in the pathways. The lower section of the *heiau* appears to be much older, and is not as well maintained.

Drive past the access road leading to the *heiau* and in a minute or so make a left onto Alapio Road. This takes you through an expensive residential area called **Sunset Hills** and past a home locally called **The Mansion**—look for the English-style boxwood hedge surrounding it. The home was purported to be Elvis Presley's island hideaway. Almost next door are the grounds of the **Nichiren Buddhist Temple,** resplendent with manicured lawns and gardens. This area is a tremendous vantage point from which to view Fourth of July fireworks lighting up Waimea Bay far below.

Waimea Falls Park

THE GREAT SURFING BEACHES

Sunset Beach runs for two miles, the longest white-sand beach on Oahu. Winter surf erodes the beach, with coral and lava fingers exposed at the shoreline, but in summertime you can expect an uninterrupted beach usually 200-300 feet wide. The entire stretch is technically Sunset Beach, but each world-famous surfing spot warrants its own name though they're not clearly marked and are tough to find . . . exactly. Mainly, look for cars with surfboard racks parked along the road. The beaches are not well maintained either. They're often trashed, and the restrooms, even at Waimea Bay, are atrocious. The reason is politics and money. Efforts all go into Waikiki, where the tourists are. Who cares about a bunch of crazy surfers on the North Shore? They're just a free curiosity for the tourists' enjoyment!

The **Banzai Pipeline** is probably the best-known surfing beach in the world. Its notoriety dates from *Surf Safari,* an early surfer film made in the 1950s, when it was dubbed "Banzai" by Bruce Brown, maker of the film. The famous tubelike effect of the breaking waves comes from a shallow reef just offshore, which forces the waves to rise dramatically and quickly. This forces the crest forward to create "the Pipeline." A lifeguard tower near the south end of the beach is all that you'll find in the way of improvements. Parking is along the roadway. Look for Sunset Beach Elementary School on the left, and the Pipeline is across the road. You can park in the school's lot on non-school days.

Ehukai Beach County Park is the next area north. It has a lifeguard tower and restroom, and provides one of the best vantage points from which to watch the surfing action on the Pipeline and Pupukea, the area to the right.

Don't expect much when you come to **Sunset Beach County Park** itself. Except for a lifeguard tower, there is nothing. This beach is the site of yearly international surfing competitions. Almost as famous as the surfing break is the **Sunset Rip,** a notorious current offshore that

NORTH SHORE SURF BEACHES

SUNSET BEACH

BANZAI PIPELINE

83

SHARKS COVE

FOODLAND

PUPUKEA RD.

RUBBER DUCKIES

BEACH PARK

"THREE TABLES"

CATHOLIC CHURCH

PINBALLS

MARIJUANA'S

WAIMEA BAY

TO HALEIWA

NOT TO SCALE

© MOON PUBLICATIONS, INC.

grabs people every year. Summertime is generally safe, but never take *moana* for granted.

Geographical Note

The previous chapter, "Windward Oahu," begins in Kailua/Kaneohe and works its way up the coast simply because most people visiting that coast approach it from the south. Those heading for the North Shore usually come from Haleiwa in the west and proceed northeast toward Kahuku. So, the end of this chapter follows geographically with the end of the "Windward Oahu" Chapter. Don't let it throw you.

PRACTICALITIES

ACCOMMODATIONS

Places to stay are quite limited along the North Shore. The best deals are beach homes or rooms rented directly from the owners, but this is a hit-and-miss proposition, with no agency handling the details. You have to check the local papers. The homes vary greatly in amenities. Some are palaces, others basic rooms or shacks, perfect for surfers or those who consider lodging secondary. Check the bulletin boards outside the Surf and Sea Dive Shop in Haleiwa and Foodland supermarket.

Deluxe
The **Turtle Bay Hilton Golf and Tennis Resort** is a first-class resort on Turtle Bay, the northern extremity of the North Shore, P.O. Box 187, 57-091 Kamehameha Hwy., Kahuku, HI 96731, tel. 293-8811 or (800) HILTONS. Once a Hyatt hotel, it was built as a self-contained destination resort and is surrounded by sea and surf on Kuilima Point, which offers protected swimming year-round. The entrance road to the hotel is lined by blooming hibiscus that outline a formal manicured lawn. In 1993, *Golf Magazine* rated the 27-hole, Arnold Palmer-inspired Links at Kuilima one of the "top 10 best new courses in the U.S., while *Tennis Magazine* rated the hotel's tennis facilities among the top fifty tennis resorts in the entire world! The resort also offers a pool, full water activities including windsurfing and scuba lessons, horseback riding, shopping, and the fanciest dining on the North Shore (see "Food" following). Since the hotel is an oasis unto itself, you should *always* call ahead to book any of these activities, even as a guest staying at the hotel, to avoid disappointment. There's very little shopping in this area, so if you're after film, or basic picnic supplies, stop at the hotel's mini- mall. The resort's newest feature is a seaside **Wedding Chapel,** splendid with open-beamed ceiling, stained glass, and eight-foot beveled windows that can be thrown open to allow the ocean breezes to waft through. All guest rooms are ocean view, but not all are oceanfront. Oceanfront is slightly more expensive, but is worth the price, especially from December to April when humpback whales cavort in the waters off the point. Rooms are furnished with full baths, a mini-fridge, a dressing room, a large vanity, ample closets, a/c, and remote control cable TV. Junior suites come complete with a library, a large bathroom and changing room, two couches, a sitting area, a queen-sized bed, and a large enclosed lanai. The Hilton has upgraded and refurbished with new carpets, drapes, bedspreads, and hibiscus patterned wallpaper. Rates are: ocean view $170; ocean lanai $190; oceanfront $210; cabanas $320; and suites $390-$1350; $25 extra person. The Hilton family plan allows children free when they stay in a room with their par-

Turtle Bay

ents. The Hilton is a first-class destination resort, but because of its fabulous, yet out-of-the-mainstream location, you get much more than what you pay for. The Turtle Bay Hilton is an excellent choice for a vacation with the feel of being on a Neighbor Island.

Ke Iki Hale is a small condo complex operated by Alice Tracy, 59-579 Ke Iki Rd., Waimea, HI 96712, tel. 638-8229. Pass the Foodland supermarket heading north, and look for a school sign. Turn left to the beach to find the condo. The property has 200 feet of private beach with a sandy bottom that goes out about 300 feet (half that in winter). The condo is quiet with a home-away-from-home atmosphere. Rates are: one-bedroom beachfront, $125 per day, $770 per week, $2400 per month; two-bedroom beachfront, $150 per day, $975 per week, $2500 per month. Units on the grounds with no beachfront are about 25% less.

Surfer Rentals
The North Shore of Oahu has long been famous for its world-class surfing. The area attracts enthusiasts from around the world who are much more concerned with the daily surfing report than they are with deluxe accommodations. The Kamehameha Highway is dotted with surfer rentals from Haleiwa to Turtle Bay. Just outside their doors are the famous surfing breaks of Marijuana's, Rubber Duckies, and Pinballs, all famous and known to world-class surfers. Some of these accommodations are terrific, while others are barely livable. Here's a sample of what's offered.

Backpacker's Vacation Inn and Hostel, 59-788 Kamehameha Hwy., Haleiwa, HI 96712, tel. 638-7838 (courtesy phone at airport, no charge), specializes in budget accommodations for surfers, backpackers, and families. Owned and operated by the Foo Family, the main building in this small cluster of buildings is at mile marker 6, the fourth driveway past the church tower coming from Waimea Bay. There are a number of facilities and room styles which could put you on the beach or mountainside, depending on availability and your preference. Basic rates are $14-16 for a bunk in the hostel-style rooms, which includes cooking and laundry facilities, and TV in the communal room. Each room has four bunks, microwaves, a shower, and a bath. The feeling is definitely not deluxe, but it is adequate. A complex on the beach, $70 daily, $420 weekly, sleeps four, has a complete kitchen, two double beds, a roll-out couch, a ceiling fan, and a world-class view of the beach from your lanai. The back house, on the mountainside, is farther away from traffic and is amongst the trees. It's on stilts, and has an open ceiling and rustic common area. Rates are $40 for the main rooms (two people), a private loft for $25 (it gets hot up there), or share a bunk for $14. The Vacation Inn has only one rule: use common sense, and clean up after yourself. They provide free boogie boards and snorkeling gear. Airport transportation (directly opposite the baggage claim) is free *to* the inn and $5 for the return trip. Everyone's friendly and laid-back. Book ahead. A good choice.

The **Plantation Village** at 59754 Kamehameha Hwy., tel. 638-7838, operated by Backpacker's (see preceeding) lies across from Three Tables Beach by Shark's Cove, between mile markers 6 and 7. It's on TheBus line and only a five-minute walk from a Foodland store for supplies. The Plantation Village, once a real Filipino working village, has cottages by the sea, secure behind a locked gate, and furnished with cable, stereo, linens, a full kitchen, dishes, washers and dryers, ice machines, and cleaning service. Many of the fruit trees on the grounds provide the guests with complimentary bananas, papayas, breadfruit, or whatever is ripe. Prices are $16 for a shared room and bath with two or three others. Ask for Unit 2, which is the same price, but a tiny private room. The small (300 square feet) private cottages, once the homes of real plantation workers, sleep two and are $40 per night, or $245 per week. A $100 per night deluxe cottage sleeps four, and you get a large front lanai, two couches, wicker furniture in a sitting room, cable TV, a/c, fan, full bath with vanity, and kitchen fully furnished with microwave, stove, and fridge. The Backpacker's van (see preceeding) also services the Plantation Village. During surfing season the place is booked out. Reserve one month in advance, full deposit during high season (Dec.-Feb.), one-half deposit other months. No refund policy in high season.

FOOD

Inexpensive

McDonald's golden arches rise above Haleiwa as you enter town. Historic Haleiwa Theater was torn down so that the world could have another Egg McMuffin. Here too is a **7-Eleven** convenience store. Almost next door is **Pizza Hut.** Besides pizza, their salad bar isn't bad.

Between the two, but a culinary world apart, **Celestial Natural Foods,** tel. 637-6729, open weekdays 9 a.m.-6:30 p.m., Sun. 10-6, sells natural and health foods, and serves vegetarian meals at the snack bar. Smoothies are $2.50; most sandwiches and a variety of salads are under $3.50. The food is healthful and nutritious, but portions are definitely not for the hungry.

Cafe Haleiwa, a hole-in-the-wall eatery on your left just as you enter town, serves one of the best breakfasts on Oahu. Their "dawn patrol" 6-7 a.m. includes eggs and whole-wheat pancakes for $2.50. Specials of the house are whole-wheat banana pancakes, French toast, spinach and mushroom quiche, and steaming-hot Kona coffee. One of the partners, Jim Sears, is called "the wizard of eggs" and has built up a local following. The cafe attracts many surfers, so it's a great place to find out about conditions.

If you're tired or just need a pick-me-up head for the North Shore Marketplace (after McDonald's, mountain side), where you'll find the **Coffee Gallery,** open daily 6 a.m.-9 p.m., tel. 637-5571, which has the largest selection of fresh roasted gourmet coffees in Hawaii, including Kona coffees and international selections of organically grown coffee from Sumatra, Indonesia, Guatemala, and South America. You can enjoy a steaming cup from their full service espresso bar along with fresh carrot juice, and vegan pastry made without dairy products or eggs. Other more bliss-inducing pastries are blackberry apple crumble pie, super chocolaty brownies, fresh fruit bars, and racks of various cookies and muffins. Every day there is a homemade soup, fresh salad, and a fine selection of deli sandwiches that range from a vegetarian garden burger on a whole wheat bun with lettuce and tomatoes, Maui onion, guacamole, and a side of tortilla chips to a turkey sandwich, or pita bread filled with eggplant, pesto, and vegies all priced around $4.95. Sit outside in the shaded and screened dining area and watch the character laden "characters" of the North Shore come and go.

The **China Inn** here serves a variety of inexpensive dishes like sweet and sour pork ($3.50), sweet and sour fish ($3.25), and hamburgers. Take it out to the shade of the lanai. A minute past is the **Haleiwa Chinese Restaurant,** tel. 637-3533, open daily 10 a.m.-9 p.m. The interior is basic but the food is very good. Their steamed sea bass and *kung pao* chicken are both excellent. A gigantic bowl of tofu soup is $4, while most main courses are under $6. One of the best inexpensive eateries on the North Shore.

You can tell by the tour buses parked outside that **Matsumoto's** is a very famous store on the North Shore. What are all those people after? Shave ice. This is one of the best places on Oahu to try this island treat. Not only do the tourists come here, but local families often take a "Sunday drive" just to get Matsumoto's shave ice. Try the Hawaiian Delight, a mound of ice smothered with banana, pineapple, and mango syrup.

The **Country Drive-In** is across from Haleiwa Shopping Center. They have plate lunches (20 varieties), smoothies, and country breakfasts like corned-beef hash and fried eggs with breakfast meat for $2.25. Quick and good.

The tiny town of Waialua (see "Beaches and Sights-Along The Farrington Highway, Rt. 930") is home to **The Sugar Bar,** located in the old Bank of Hawaii Building. They feature an international cuisine, hot dogs from America to bratwurst from Germany. *Magnifique!*

East from town, across from Shark's Cove, is **Shark's Shack,** a *usually* open lunch wagon that'll fix you a sandwich or rent you snorkeling gear. Next door is **Pupukea Shave Ice** for an island treat. Farther toward Sunset Beach (around mile marker 9) look for **Diamico's Pizza,** open for breakfast, lunch, and dinner, (slow but friendly service), and the Sunset Beach store, home of Ted's Bakery.

Moderate/Expensive

Steamer's in the Haleiwa Shopping Plaza, tel. 637-5071, is a clean and modern restaurant serving seafood, beef, and chicken. There's plenty of brass, paneled walls, and low lighting.

Lunches are especially good with a wide choice of omelettes from $5, including one made from crab, shrimp, and mushrooms; all come with blueberry or French muffins. Whet your appetite with sushi or steamed clams, or have a full fish dinner starting at $10. Dining daily 11 a.m.-11 p.m., bar until 2 a.m.

Rosie's Cantina, also in the plaza, open Sun.-Thurs. 7 a.m.-10 p.m, Fri.-Sat. 7 a.m.-11 p.m., prepares hearty Mexican dishes for a good price. The inside is "yuppie Mex" with brass rails, painted overhead steam pipes, and elevated booths. Expect to pay $4 for enchiladas and burritos, while meat dishes are $8-9. Order the enchilada stuffed with crab for $9; add a salad and two could easily make this a lunch. **Pizza Bob's** across the way has an excellent local reputation, and its little pub serves up delicious pizza, salad, lasagne, and sandwiches.

The **Proud Peacock,** Waimea Falls Park, tel. 638-8531, is open daily for lunch and dinner. It's fun to dine here even if you don't enter the park. From the dining room, you can look into some of the nicest gardens while feeding crumbs to the peacocks. The beautiful mahogany bar was made in Scotland almost 200 years ago. You can have a light soup and salad, but their seafood *pu pu* platter is hard to beat. Roast pork and roast beef are well-prepared favorites here. A Moonlight Buffet 5-9 p.m. is served to adults for $9.95, children 12 and under $5.95, on two full-moon nights a month. Included are prime rib, chicken, mahimahi, and Hawaiian-style pork. Guided tours begin at 8:30 p.m. sharp.

Jameson's by the Sea, 62-540 Kamehameha Hwy., tel. 637-4336, is open daily for lunch, dinner, and cocktails. Located at the north end of Haleiwa overlooking the sea, its outdoor deck is perfect for a romantic sunset dinner while inside the romantic mood is continued with track lighting, shoji screens, cane chairs with stuffed pillows, candles with shades, and tables resplendent with fine linen. Appetizers include a salmon plate ($8.95), stuffed mushrooms with escargot ($6.50), and fresh oysters ($8.95). Chowder and salad are under $7. Try the Yokohama soup, as well as salad with any of the homemade dressings. Main dishes like mahimahi, stuffed shrimp, shrimp curry with mango chutney, and sesame chicken range

$16-25. For dessert have the lemon macadamia nut chiffon pie for $3.50. The bar is quiet at night and serves a variety of imported beers; try South Pacific, imported from New Guinea; the dining room closes at 10 p.m. and the bar an hour later. Reservations highly recommended. Request a window seat for the sunset.

The **Chart House,** at 66-011 Kamehameha Hwy., Haleiwa, tel. 638-8005, open daily for dinner 5-10 p.m., for lunch Thurs.-Sun. 11 a.m.-3 p.m., is part of a small chain known for good food, located in a green cinder-block building on the left before you cross the Anahulu River bridge. Although purely utilitarian on the outside, the inside is modern and tasteful with plenty of tile work, track lighting, bent-back chairs, and ceiling fans. Most appetizers, ranging from artichokes to chowder are under $5, while the salad bar (included with an entree) is $11.95 a la carte. Steaks, the specialty of the house, are priced $17.95-22.95, while chicken breast teriyaki is a reasonable $15.95, and seafood from salmon to shrimp Sante Fe are all under $22. Specials are offered daily, and there's a "wine of the month" chosen to enhance your meal. For dessert try the mud pie or the key lime pie. Although the Chart House is not quite gourmet, the food is good and wholesome, with the price right for what you get.

Classy Dining

If you're looking for gourmet dining in an incredibly beautiful setting head for the Turtle Bay Hilton Golf and Tennis Resort (see "Accommodations" preceeding). The **Cove Restaurant,** open 6-9:30 p.m. (reservations advised), is the signature restaurant at the resort and welcomes you for an evening of fine dining. Slowly stroll a wooden walkway loading past tiny waterfalls and a profusion of plants to the main room that overlooks the manicured grounds and pool. Start with lobster bisque in a puff pastry shell or a variety of fresh island salads for $6. Move on to filet mignon, veal chops, fresh tiger prawns, and lobster that you choose fresh from the tank. The fresh catch, always an excellent choice, is a very reasonable $19.95. If you really want to treat yourself, order the North Shore potpourri, a silver bowl mounded with ice that cradles *opihi*, shrimp, sashimi, oysters, and fresh fish that come with savory dipping sauces from a basic shoyu and hot mustard to a papaya salsa. Enjoy dessert while gazing through floor-to-ceiling windows that frame the living mosaic of Turtle Bay turned brilliant by a legendary North Shore sunset.

The **Seatide Room** is synonymous with Sunday brunch. It enjoys a wonderful reputation, and if friends or family come visiting, islanders take them here to impress. Brunch is buffet style 9 a.m.-2 p.m. and features mounds of fresh fruits and pastries, fresh-squeezed fruit juices, imported cheeses, eggs Florentine and Benedict, fresh fish, seafood, sashimi, shrimp, crab claws, and flowing champagne. Reservations not taken, $25 adults. Expect a wait, which goes easily as you enjoy the magnificent scenery.

The **Palm Terrace** is the most "ordinary" of the hotel's restaurants, but ordinary par excellence!. Open 6:30 a.m.-10 p.m., the restaurant serves hearty American favorites from all 50 states, supplemented by dishes from around the world. You can dine on smoked Pacific fish, saimin with crispy bread, curried chicken papaya, or a seafood tostada. You will enjoy lunch sandwiches like Portuguese sausage on rye or a clubhouse special. There are hamburgers, of course—the basic burger, right down to a North Shore burger with grilled onions and peppers. For dessert order a cinnamon tulip; macadamia nut ice cream, split bananas, chocolate, and Kahuku watermelon all in a cinnamon tostada pastry shell. The views overlooking Turtle Bay combined with excellent value for the money make the Palm Terrace the best *ordinary* restaurant on the North Shore.

A wonderful culinary addition to the hotel is the **Asahi,** open Thurs.-Mon. 5:30-9:30 p.m., a Japanese restaurant with a full-service sushi bar. Dine on delectables made right before your eyes by master sushi chefs from Japan, or the more timid can choose a Japanese standard like teriyaki chicken, or the Asahi combination dinner of beef teriyaki and lobster tail, all served with salad, rice, and miso soup.

The **Bay View Lounge** is a casual restaurant/nightclub offering a deli-luncheon buffet. It's open 11:30 a.m.-1 a.m. and serves complimentary *pu pu* around sunset, which is a perfect time to drop in. On weekends the Bay View Lounge is the hotspot disco, ID required after 9 p.m.; dress code is collared shirts and close-toed shoes.

SHOPPING AND SERVICES

Art Galleries And Shops

Ka'ala Art, open 9 a.m.-6 p.m. daily, tel. 637-7065, as you enter Haleiwa (across from McDonald's), is a perfect place to stop, with some of the best shopping on the North Shore. The brothers Costello, John and Jim, who own and operate the shop, are knowledgeable, longtime residents of the North Shore who don't mind dispensing directions and information. The premier items are John's original artwork, wonderful paintings that are impressionistic and magical, with many of these unique designs silk-screened onto 100% cotton T-shirts or made into inspiring posters. John has also turned his hand to carvings of dolphins and other Hawaiian themes. Also featured are fine carvings from Tonga, Tahiti, and Bali that John has hand-selected on his travels, along with excellent examples of local Hawaiian wood carvings. Small but wonderful items are tapa cloth made by Sella, a Tongan woman who lives nearby, batiks from Thailand, and jewelry made locally and from Asia. The Costello brothers travel to buy, and they have a keen eye for what's happening and distinctive. Brother Kevin offers a fine selection of imported clothing from Thailand, which is available through the gallery by appointment. A rainbow has spilled in a corner of the shop, where 100% cotton pareu ($18-35) from Hawaii, Tahiti, and Indonesia vibrate in living color. More "art-clothing" includes a rack of beach coverups designed by John, and tie-dyed and silk-screened using ecologically minded nontoxic, colors. There's also a fine postcard selection just to remind the folks back home that you are in Hawaii.

Iwa Gallery, open daily except Tuesday 10:30 a.m.-6:30 p.m., is across the street from the Protestant church, founded in 1892, and next door to Aoki's Shave Ice. This co-op shows the efforts of local artists who have been juried in order to place their artwork on consignment. Featured are the fine candle sculptures of **Scott Bechtol** (see "Windward Oahu—Punaluu and Hauula"). Other artists displayed at the gallery include: Angela Kanas, a watercolor artist who does fanciful renditions of Hawaiian gods, goddesses, and traditional folk; Janet Stewart, who depicts island themes like Madame Pele lying with the blood of her hot lava flowing from her body, or a *keiki* hula dancer with a look of concentration on her face, or a kindly *tutu* in a red muumuu; Bill Cupit uses the bark of banana trees to create entire island scenes like ships departing a sheltered harbor; Peter Hayward, well into his eighties, works in oils creating translucent waves crashing on lonely shores. Serigraphs and cards by Janet Holaday are often depictions of flowers in bold primary colors; Peggy Pai, born and raised in China, creates silk batik with ephemeral, beautiful, cloudy landscapes; James Rack uses his palette and brush to catch scenes of idyllic Hawaii; and Norman Kelly catches children at play or surfers on towering waves in his fluid watercolors.

Wyland Gallery, across the street from the Haleiwa Shopping Center, is open daily 9 a.m.-6 p.m., tel. 637-7498. Wyland is a famous environmental artist known for his huge whale and marinelife murals, in addition to watercolors and fine oil paintings. The gallery is large, spacious, and well lit. Everything has a Hawaiian or sea theme, and there's even a huge fish tank filled with tropical fish. Delight at the magnificent bronze sculptures by Dale Evers, depicting whales and manta rays in sublime frozen movement. There're modern sepia-tone photos by Kim Taylor Reese, watercolors of Hawaiian maidens by Janet Stewart, lithographs by Roy Tabora of palms trees and cliffs with Michelangelo skies, bronze dolphins by Christopher Bell, wood sculptures by Kerry Sweet, Margaret Keene's lithographs of children with big eyes, and Sue Phillipson's oils of island flowers. You can walk away with a limited-edition lithograph by Wyland with original watercolor mark framed in koa for $940. If the original artwork is too expensive, there're posters, mini-prints, and postcards. Wyland's gold jewelry sculpture is also beautiful, distinctive, and affordable.

North Shore Marketplace

The North Shore Marketplace, along the Kamehameha Highway between McDonald's and the Haleiwa Shopping Center, is a small complex with some inexpensive and unique shops. The most interesting shop is **Jungle Gem's,** tel. 637-6609, open 10 a.m.-6 p.m., with a metaphysical assortment of crystals, crystal balls,

African trading beads, and gems. The shop specializes in locally made jewelry that is reasonably priced and of excellent quality. The owners, Brent Landberg and Kimberely Moore, are knowledgeable gemologists and fine jewelers who do much of the work on display. Next door the **Island Wear Factory Outlet** has inexpensive alohawear.

Another good shop is **More or Less Beach Wear,** tel. 638-6859, open 9 a.m.-6 p.m. daily, where they make custom bathing suits and sell hand-painted T-shirts by local artists. The owner and chief designer, Lucinda Vaughen, will take a personal hand in fitting and designing just the right suit for you.

Birds of Aloha, open daily except Monday 10:30 a.m.-5:30 p.m., tel. 638-5214, specializes in hand-fed baby parrots, macaws, cockatoos, and African grays. These living rainbows of color cost from $1500 to $5000, and can be brought back to the mainland without being quarantined. Rossi Baker, the owner, hatched

Ka'ala Art

the birds herself and is happy to talk about them, and will allow you to hold the birds and to take pictures.

Northshore Books, tel. 637-3202, open 10 a.m.-6:30 p.m., is a general purpose bookstore with racks of used books with an emphasis in Hawaiiana, metaphysics, New Age, and children's literature. The bookstore also has selections of posters, note cards, and bookmarks.

Along The Kamehameha Highway

As you move down the Kamehameha Highway from west to east you'll pass in rapid succession the **Haleiwa Flower Shop** on the left selling lei and fresh-cut flowers. Next comes **Oogenesis Boutique,** with original fashions for women, and almost next door is **Haleiwa Acupuncture Clinic,** tel. 637-4449, with Richard Himmelmann, in cooperation with Healing Touching Massage by Brenda McKinnon, and chiropractic care by Dr. Edward Bowles, who will make house calls.

On the right is **A Guy Selling Shells.** He specializes in hanging baskets made from bubble and cowrie shells. Prices range from $50 down to $5, with most coming from the Philipines.

The **Consignment Shop,** behind the Country Kitchen, sells well-chosen junk and previously owned ladies' apparel and accessories, artwork, clothing, and towels.

Haleiwa Shopping Center

This shopping center provides all the necessities in one-stop shopping: boutiques, pharmacy, photo store, and general food and merchandise. It's in the center of Haleiwa, tel. 622-5179. Some shops are: **Rix** with jewelry, women's fashions, and alohawear; **Exotic Gourmet Ice Cream Palace; Et Cetera's,** a tiny but jampacked souvenir store with woodcarvings, teas, alohawear, and shells; **Space And Lace** sells hats, slippers, shoes, towels, and sunglasses; **Liquor Galley,** open daily 9 a.m.-midnight, is a full-service liquor store; and **Haleiwa Family Health Center** is a walk-in clinic, tel. 524-2527, open 8 a.m.-5 p.m. daily, closed Sunday.

Food Shopping

For food and picnic supplies try the **Haleiwa IGA,** tel. 637-5004, in the Haleiwa Shopping

Haleiwa

Center, or **Foodland,** along the highway past Waimea Bay, tel. 638-8081.

Services

The best sources of general **information** for the North Shore are the bulletin boards outside of Surf and Sea and the Foodland supermarket.

As you enter Haleiwa from the west, you'll pass a **Shell** gas station and a full-service **post office.**

Sporting Goods And Rentals

The following shops are all located along the Kamehameha Highway, the main drag through Haleiwa, heading from west to east.

Across the road from the Shell gas station just as you enter the west end of town is **Excell Wet Suits and Water Sports,** a full-service surf shop that rents snorkeling gear. On the right is **Kayak Oahu,** tel. 637-6565, who rent kayaks and will provide tips on where to go.

Raging Isle Sports, in the North Shore Marketplace, tel. 637-7707, 10 a.m.-6 p.m. daily, is primarily a surf shop and manufacturer of Barnfield's Raging Isle Boards, but they rent and sell bikes, and you can pick up items from a pair of shorts to a tennis racket. The bikes are an assortment of beach cruisers and mountain bikes that rent $10-20 daily and $55-115 weekly. They also service and repair bikes.

Race Hawaii, 66-249 Kamehameha Hwy., tel. 637-SURF, open 9 a.m.-6 p.m. daily, 8 a.m.-7 p.m. during top season, is a famous surfboard design shop owned by Scott Bucknall, who has patented the x-fin skeg design. They rent boards during the surf season and sell bathing suits, biking pants, and T-shirts bearing their logo.

Hawaii Surf and Sail, 66-214 Kamehameha Hwy., open 8:30 a.m.-7:30 p.m., tel. 637-5373, has surfboards (rental $10 per day), sailboards, and accessories.

For a full range of surfing, snorkeling, and diving equipment try **Surf and Sea** near the Union 76 gas station in Haleiwa. They've got boogie boards, masks and fins, tanks, weights, surfboards, and sailboards. They can even arange flights from Dillingham Airfield.

Fantasy Cycles, 66-134 Kamehameha Hwy., tel. 637-3221, open 10 a.m.-7 p.m., Sun. 10 a.m.-3 p.m., is owned by Bob Frattin. He rents bikes for $15 a day or $63 per week. Bob will start off entry-level riders with a map and riding pointers, and will also take riders on trail tours that include lunch. You must be experienced, and the ride is not for the beginner or couch potato.

... but a diversion, the most common is upon the water ...
the men lay themselves flat upon an oval piece of plank ...
they wait the time for the greatest swell that sets on shore,
and altogether push forward with their arms to keep on its top,
it sends them in with a most astonishing velocity ...

JAMES KING, CIRCA 1779

BOB RACE

THE LEEWARD COAST

The Waianae ("Mullet Waters") coast, the lee-ward face of Oahu, is separated physically from the rest of the island by the Waianae Range. Spiritually, culturally, and economically, the separation is even more profound. This area is Oahu's last stand for ethnic Hawaiians, and for that phenomenal cultural blending of people called *locals*. The idea of "us against them" permeates the consciousness of the area. Guidebooks, government pamphlets, and word of mouth warn tourists against going to Waianae because "the natives are restless." If you follow this poor advice, you not only miss the last of undeveloped coastal Oahu, but the absolute pleasure of meeting people who will treat you with genuine *aloha*. Along the coast are magnificent beaches long known for their surf, new condos and developments nestled in secure valleys, and prime golfing. Inland, roads will take you to the roof of Oahu. Waianae is the home of small farms, run-down shacks, and families that hold luau on festive occasions, where the food and entertainment are the real article. Anyone lucky enough to be invited into this quickly disappearing world will be blessed with one of the last remaining authentic cultural experiences in Hawaii.

The possibility of hassles shouldn't be minimized because they do happen, but every aggressor needs a victim. The biggest problem is thievery, of the sneak-thief variety. You're marked as a tourist because of your new rental car. If you leave valuables in it, or lying unattended on the beach, they have a good chance of disappearing. But who does silly things like this *anywhere* in the U.S.? You won't be accosted, or held up at gunpoint, but if you bother a bunch of local guys drinking beer, you're asking for trouble. Moreover, the toughness of Waianae is self-perpetuating, and frankly the locals *like* the hard reputation. A few years back a feature writer reported that when he visited Waianae some toughs threw rocks at him. No one had ever reported this before, but after a big stink was made about it, more and more people had rocks thrown at them when they visited here. In recent years *pakalolo* has had a tremendous effect on the area. Local guys began growing and smoking it. This brought some money back into the depressed region, and it changed

THE LEEWARD COAST

(map)

KAENA PT.

KAENA PT. STATE PARK

PUU PUEO
(768 ft)

KAENA PT.
ST. PARK

FARRINGTON HWY.

KEAWAULA

TO
HALEIWA

YOKOHAMA
BAY BEACH
COUNTY PARK

MAKUA

POOHUNA PT.

OHIKILOLO
BEACH

MAKUA VALLEY

WAIANAE

KEAAU BEACH
COUNTY PARK

KEPUHI
BEACH

FARRINGTON HWY.

KEPUHI PT.

PUU KEAAU
(2650 ft)

MAKAHA STREAM

MAKAHA VALLEY

RANGE

MAKAHA
BEACH
COUNTY PARK

MAKAHA

93

MAUNA LAHILAHI
BEACH COUNTY PARK

WAIANAE
REGIONAL PARK

WAIANAE VALLEY RD.

POKAI BAY BEACH
COUNTY PARK

WAIANAE

LUALUALEI BEACH
COUNTY PARK

TO
SCHOFIELD
BARRACKS

MAILI

MAILI BEACH
COUNTY PARK

MAIPALAOA BEACH

LUALUALEI NAVAL RD.

ULEHAWA BEACH
COUNTY PARK

MAILI PT.

LUALUALEI

NANAKULI

NANAKULI BEACH
COUNTY PARK

KAHE PT. BEACH
COUNTY PARK

0   2 mi

0   3 km

93

MAKAKOLE RD.

KALAELOA BLVD.

H-1

90

TO
HONOLULU

WAIMANALO
RD.

BARBERS PT. BEACH
COUNTY PARK

© MOON PUBLICATIONS, INC.

the outlook of some of the residents. They felt a camaraderie with other counterculture people, many of whom happened to be *haole*. They could relax and not feel so threatened with pursuing an often elusive materialistic path. Many became more content with their laid-back lifestyle, and genuinely less interested with the materialistic trip all the way around.

In truth, *we* shouldn't be warned about *them*, but vice versa. The people of Waianae are the ones being infringed upon, and it is they who, in the final analysis, will be hassled, ripped off, and ultimately dispossessed. Recent articles by Oahu's Development Conference strongly state that future development will center on the island's northwestern shore . . . the Waianae coast! A few rocks are poor weapons against developmental progress, which is defined by the big boys with the big dreams and the big bucks to back them up.

BEACHES AND SIGHTS

The Waianae coast is very accessible. One road takes you there. Simply follow the H-1 freeway from Honolulu until it joins the Farrington Hwy. (Rt. 93). It runs north, opening up the entire coast. A handful of side roads lead into the interior, and that's about it! A strange recommendation, but sensible on this heavily trafficked road, is to drive north to the end of the line and then stop at the scenic sights on your way back south. This puts you on the ocean side of the highway where you won't have to worry about cutting across two lines of traffic, which can be a steady stream making it tough to navigate. The Bus no. 51 runs the entire Waianae coast and stops at all of the following beaches.

Note: Many of the beach parks along this coast offer **camping**, but their status periodically changes to **no camping** without notice. Many of the other campers are local people in semipermanent structures; the reason that the status changes quickly is to prevent these people from squatting. Also, remember that this is the leeward coast, which gets plenty of sunshine. Many of the beach parks do not have shade trees, so be prepared. June is the prettiest month because all the flowers are in bloom, but it's one of the worst times for sunburn. The entire coast is great for snorkeling, with plenty of reef fish. However, keep your eyes on the swells,

and always stay out during rough seas, when waves can batter you against the rocks. The parks listed below run from south to north.

HEADING NORTH

Barbers Point Beach County Park
The first beach is Barbers Point Beach County Park, at the end of Kalaeloa Boulevard. Turn down it where H-1 and the Farrington Hwy. join. The point was named after Capt. Henry Barber, who was shipwrecked here in 1795. Few people, even island residents, visit this beach park. It's in an industrial area and the shoreline is rocky. One pocket of white-sand beach is open to the public, though it fronts a private residence. The swimming is safe only in summer, and you'll find picnic facilities, restrooms, and camping (county permit).

Kahe And Hawaiian Electric Beach County Parks
Kahe and Hawaiian Electric beach county parks are just where the Farrington Hwy. curves north along the coast. They're the first two *real* Waianae beaches, and they're symbolic. You come around the bend to be treated to an absolutely pristine view of the coast with the rolling sea, a

Waianae coast

white-sand beach, a cove, and the most hideous power plant you've ever seen. Kahe Beach County Park offers restrooms, a pavilion, and picnic facilities. The beach is poor except for a section just east of the improved park. Swimming is dangerous except on calm summer days. The Hawaiian Electric Beach Park, across from the power plant, is known as "Tracks" to island surfers because of the railroad tracks that run along the shore here. Facilities include picnic tables, a pavilion, restrooms, showers, and parking along the highway. The white-sand beach is wide, and the swimming generally safe. The mild waves are perfect for learning how to surf. If you keep your eyes trained out to sea, the area is beautiful. Don't look inland!

Nanakuli Beach County Park

Nanakuli Beach County Park is on the southern outskirts of Nanakuli ("Pretend to be Deaf") town, which is the first real town of the Waianae coast. If you get to the red light you've gone a little too far. The beach park is community-oriented, with recreational buildings, basketball courts, a baseball diamond, and kiddies' play area. Camping has been permitted with a county permit. Lifeguards work on a daily basis, and the swimming is generally safe except during periods of high winter surf. The northern end of the beach, called Kalanianaole, is generally calmer than the southern end. They're divided by a housing project, but connected by a walkway. The southern section is fronted by a cliff with a small cove below. During periods of calm surf, the waters are crystal clear and perfect for snorkeling.

Ulehawa Beach County Park

Ulehawa Beach County Park, just north of Nanakuli, offers restrooms, picnic facilities, lifeguards, and sometimes camping. The best swimming is in a sandy pocket near the lifeguard tower. Surf conditions make for good bodysurfing. Most of the park, along a rocky cliff, is undeveloped. Here you'll find unlimited fishing spots. A shallow lagoon is generally safe for swimming year-round. As always, it's best to check with the local people on the beach.

Maili Beach County Park

Maili Beach County Park is at the southern end of Maili ("Many Small Stones") town. It lies between two streams coming down from the mountains. Amenities include restrooms, picnic facilities, a lifeguard tower, and camping . . . sometimes! The best swimming is in front of the lifeguard tower. The beach is broken into three parts by a housing development. In wintertime the beach disappears, but it returns wide and sandy for the summer. Most of the park is undeveloped. In town is a **7-Eleven** and gas stations. As you drive through town notice a giant outcropping, Maili Point, which meets the sea like a giant fist. It has the same dominant presence as Diamond Head. When you go through town you'll see what's been happening around here since development has come to Waianae. Pull off at Maili Beach County Park, and to your right are the modest homes of local people. Look up the coast to where the mountains come down to the sea. Out on that headland you can see a giant resort and on the bending backbone leading up to it modest homes of the local people. The beach is at least 300 yards long, and family-oriented. Plenty of coral pockets offer good snorkeling. Don't just jump in. Ask the locals or swing by the lifeguard tower to make sure that it's safe.

Lualualei Beach County Park

Lualualei Beach County Park has restrooms, camping sometimes, and picnic facilities. The entire park is largely undeveloped and lies along low cliffs and raised coral reef. Swimming is almost impossible. It's primarily good for fishing and looking.

Pokai Beach County Park

Pokai Beach County Park is one of the nicest along the Waianae coast, located just south of Waianae town. It provides restrooms, camping sometimes, lifeguards, and a boat ramp, which brings plenty of small craft into the area. Don't be surprised to see a replica of a double-hulled canoe, often used for publicity purposes. It last appeared in a beer commercial. The park is clean, well maintained, reasonably secure, and family-oriented. There's surfing, snorkeling, and safe swimming year-round. If you're heading for one beach along Waianae, this is a top choice.

To get a look at a small working harbor or to hire a fishing boat, visit **Waianae Boat Harbor** as you head north from town. Huge installed stones form an impressive manmade harbor, with everything from luxury yachts to aluminum fishing boats. To head inland take **Waianae Valley Road.** You quickly gain the heights of the Waianae Range, and eventually come to a sentry box with a soldier inside. From here Kolekole Road is closed to the public, but if you stop and identify yourself, you'll be given permission to go to **Kolekole Pass.** The awesome view is well worth the trip.

Makaha Beach County Park

Makaha Beach County Park is famous for surfing, and as you approach, you can't help spotting a dominant headland called **Lahi Lahi,** which was a one-time island. Called "Black Rock" by the local fishermen, and used as a landmark, it still marks Makaha. Surfing competitions have been held here since the Makaha International Surfing Competition began in 1952. In recent years, a local lifeguard named Richard "Buffalo" Keaulana, known to all who've come here, has begun the Annual Buffalo Big Board Riding Championship. Paul Strauch, Jr., inventor of the "hang five," comes to Makaha whenever he has a chance, along with Buffalo's sons and other pro surfers, many of whom live in the area. The swimming can be dangerous during high surf, but excellent on calm days. Winter brings some of the biggest surf in Hawaii. Always pay heed to the warnings of the lifeguards.

Although Makaha can translate as "water breaking out to sea" because of the area's propensity of damming runoff waters from the mountains behind the beach until enough pressure forces it to "break out," there is another meaning for Makaha that doesn't help its image. The second translation meaning "Fierce," aptly describes a gang of bandits who long ago lived in the surrounding hills and terrorized the region. They would wait for small bands of people walking the road, then swoop down and relieve them of their earthly goods. If you follow Makaha Valley Road inland, you pass condos and high-rises clinging to the arid walls of this leeward valley. Surrounded by an artificial oasis of green, this developed resort area provides golfing and all the amenities of a destination resort. Stop in at the Sheraton Makaha to ask permission to visit the **Kaneaki Heiau,** a 17th-century temple restored by the resort under the direction of the Bishop

Buffalo at Makaha Beach

Museum. This temple was dedicated to Lono, the benevolent god of harvest and fertility. The grass and thatched huts used as prayer and meditation chambers, along with a spirit tower, have all been replicated.

Once past Makaha, the road gets rugged, with plenty of private places to pull off. This crab claw of land, which ends at Kaena Point, forms a bay. The seascape demands attention but look into the interior. The mountains seem naturally terraced as they form dry, deep valleys. All are micro-habitats, each different from the other. On top of one notice a gigantic golf ball, really a radar tracking station, that lets you know you're coming to the end of the passable road.

Keaau Beach County Park

Keaau Beach County Park has restrooms, picnic facilities, and camping (county permit). The improved part of the park has a sandy beach, but mostly the park is fronted by coral and lava, and is frequented mostly by fishermen and campers. The unimproved section is not good for swimming, but it does attract a few surfers, and is good for snorkeling and scuba but only during calm periods. The improved section is a flat grassy area with picnic tables, shade trees, and pavilions.

Yokohama Bay

Yokohama Bay is the end of the line. The pavement ends here, and if you're headed for Kaena Point (see "The North Shore—Beaches and Sights") you'll have to walk. Yokohama Bay is a long stretch of sandy beach that is mostly unimproved. A lava-rock bathhouse is on the right, just after the entrance. The area was named because of the multitude of Japanese fishermen who came to this lonely site to fish. It's still great for fishing! The swimming can be hazardous because of the strong wave action and rough bottom, but the snorkeling is superb. Mostly the area is used by surfers and local people, including youngsters who dive off the large lava rocks. This is inadvisable for people unfamiliar with the area. Yokohama is a great place to come if you're after a secluded beach. Weekdays, you'll have it to yourself, with a slightly greater number of people on the weekends. Definitely bring cold drinks, and remember that there are no shade trees, so a hat or beach umbrella is a necessity. Many camp here unofficially.

Notice a rugged beach area, marked by dumped household appliances, just south of Yokohama Bay. Notice broken-down vans and makeshift tents of ripped tarps put up by local people who have staked out this area and who live here semipermanently. If you're looking for trouble, you've found the right spot.

Kaneana Cave is a few minutes south on your left as you head back down the coast. You probably didn't notice it on your way north because of the peculiar land formation that conceals the mouth in that direction. Unfortunately, people have come here with spray cans and trashed the cave. If you can overlook that, it's a phenomenon—a big one. You can spot it by looking for three cement blocks, like road dividers, right in front of the entrance. It's at the foot of a 200-foot outcropping of stone. When you see local people defacing the natural beauty like this, it's hard to believe that the Hawaiians had such a spirit bond with the *aina*.

PRACTICALITIES

ACCOMMODATIONS

Except for camping, there are no inexpensive places to stay along the Waianae coast. Some local people let rooms for a good rate, but there is no way to find this out in advance. Your best bet is to check out the **bulletin board** at the Food Giant Supermarket in Waianae. Accommodations range from moderate to expensive, with Makaha Valley being the most developed resort area of Oahu outside of Waikiki. Except for the Sheraton Makaha Resort, all are condos and require a minimum stay of seven days.

The **Maili Cove** rents one-bedroom apartments for $350-450 per week. They have a swimming pool, parking, TV, along with a few hotel units. Located at 87-561 Farrington Hwy., Waianae, HI 96792, tel. 696-4447.

The **Makaha Beach Cabanas** are in Makaha along the beach just past the high school. All units have a lanai overlooking the water. They're not fancy, but are spotlessly clean and serviceable. All units are fully furnished with complete kitchens; from $350 per week. Contact the Makaha Beach Cabanas, 84-965 Farrington Hwy., tel. 696-7227.

The **Makaha Shores** are privately owned units that overlook a beautiful white-sand beach and provide great viewing of the surfers challenging the waves below. All units are fully furnished with weekly rates of $290 studio, $400 one-bedroom, and $500 two-bedroom. Contact the condo at 84-265 Farrington Hwy., Makaha, HI 96792, tel. 696-7121.

The least expensive accommodations are at the **Makaha Surfside.** The beach is rocky near the condo, but it makes up for this with two pools and a sauna. All units are individually owned and fully furnished. Weekly rates begin at $290 studio to $400-475 for a one-bedroom. Daily rates range from $30 to $60. For information

typical camping beach, leeward coast

write Makaha Surfside, 85-175 Farrington Hwy., Makaha, HI 96792, tel. 696-2105.

Makaha Valley Towers rise dramatically from Makaha Valley, but they don't fit in. They're either a testament to man's achievement or ignorance, depending on your point of view. In keeping with the idea of security, you drive up to a gate manned by two guards. You're stopped, asked your business, and sent unsmilingly on your way. The condo provides fully furnished units, a/c, TV, and pool. Weekly rates are $365 studio, $400-500 one-bedroom. If you're staying in this ill-fitting high-rise, at least try to get a top floor where you can take advantage of the remarkable view. For rates and information: Makaha Valley Towers, 84-740 Kili Dr., Makaha, HI 96792, tel. 695-9055.

The **Sheraton Makaha Resort** is famous for its hideaway golf course, among the top five on Oahu. The Sheraton has done an exemplary job with the units, some of the nicest on the island. This is a true destination resort with a complete list of activities, including horseback riding, tennis, two swimming pools, and a full complement of hotel-sponsored beach and water activities (although the ocean is a few miles away). Rooms begin at $110 to $340 for a suite. For information and reservations, write Sheraton Makaha Resort, P.O. Box 896, Waianae, HI 96792, tel. 695-9511 or (800) 325-3535.

The courtiers anxiously waited for the grand night when the torches would be lighted and the drums beaten to announce the lovely princess as she was presented to the assembled *ali'i*. Those closest to the young beauty were confident that their years of training had refined the grace and nobility that matched her dignified heritage. She had proven to be an enthusiastic and willing student, endearing herself to all because of her gaiety, sweetness, and loving heart. But to assume her rightful place with the most powerful in the land, she would have to gain the self-possessed assurity that only comes from the wisdom of experience. It is much the same with the **Ihilani Resort and Spa,** at 92-1001 Olani St., Kopolei, HI 96707, tel. 679-0079, (800) 626-4446, Oahu's newest luxury resort that officially opened its doors in December 1993. The hotel, an alabaster specter floating amidst the 640 emerald-green acres of the Ko Olina Resort, rises above a white-sand beach 25 minutes southwest of the airport (simply follow the H-1 expressway to the clearly marked Ko Olina exit). You approach the resort by way of a cobblestone drive that winds its way up to a porte cochere where valets and lei-bearing hostesses wait to greet you. The open breezeway leads to a towering glass-domed atrium brightened by cascading trellised flowers, and ringed by living green ferns. Below, rivulets trickle through a series of free-form ponds, some like glass-reflecting sculptures, others alive and tinkling a natural refrain. The guest rooms, huge at almost 700 square feet, are pleasantly appointed in pastels and white and all feature a/c, ceiling fans, louvered doors, remote-control entertainment centers, in-room safes, mini bars, and luxurious cushioned teak furniture including a dining table and lounge awaiting you on your private lanai. A futuristic feature is a bedside master control telephone system from where you can regulate the room's lighting, a/c, and voice mail service at the touch of a finger. Bathrooms, an intricate play of marble and tile, feature double sinks, hair dryers, a basket of fine toiletries, separate commode and shower stalls, and deep over-sized tubs. Evening brings turndown service when little gifts of mineral bath gels or soothing facial compresses are left on your pillow, compliments of the spa. Other amenities are 24-hour room service, concierge service, tennis courts, and a beauty salon.

The green velvet of the **Ko Olina Championship Golf Course,** designed by Ted Robinson, and already named as one of the finest courses in America by the prestigious *Golf Digest,* fronts the hotel. Open since 1990, the course is fully matured and has already hosted a number of prestigious tournaments.

Dining at the Ihilani is in the masterful and infinitely creative hands of executive chef, Katsuo Sugiura (Chef Suki), who has created dishes in what he describes as "Tropical Pacific." This fantastic blending of east and west relies heavily on locally grown herbs, vegetables, meats, and most importantly, island seafood. It is a blissful marriage built on Mediterranean, Oriental, and Hawaiian cuisine that can easily be influenced by Scandinavian, Caribbean and Southwestern ingredients. Mostly, Chef Suki is an artist who is constantly experimenting and creating new presentations on a daily basis. Using smoking techniques that he has perfected over the years, Suki not only creates distinctive individual dishes, but he creates them especially for each guest, sealing the recipe and repeating it when you return, if you so desire. The Ihilani's signature restaurant is the dinner-only **Azul,** complemented by a magnificent wine cellar, with breakfast, lunch, and dinner served at the open-air **Naupaka Terrace.** Health-conscious cuisine is offered at the **Spa Cafe,** on the fourth level of the Ihilani Spa; traditional Japanese fare at the **Kyuan Restaurant;** while golfers or those into a more casual setting will enjoy club house dining at the Ko Olina Golf Course's **Niblick Restaurant.**

Located in a separate facility just a short walk across from the main entrance is the **Ihilani Spa,** a magnificently soothing, revitalizing, and uniquely Hawaiian spa experience. Under the direction of Lisa Dobloug, the facility is centered around Thalasso water therapy, a computer-controlled water-jet massage utilizing fresh sea water and seaweed. After being immersed in this state-of-the-art tub, you move on to the Vichy Shower, Grand Jet, or Needle Pavilion, where 12 shower heads poke stimulating sprays into every nook and cranny. Next, the superbly trained staff offers hands-on experiences in the form of therapeutic massage including Swedish, *lomi lomi,* or *shiatsu.* You can also opt for a manicure, pedicure, or skin rejuvenating facial. To keep trim and supple, head for the fitness facility on the third level where you will find a lap pool, jacuzzi, aerobics room, and strengthening equipment. With time and maturity, the Ihilani Resort and Spa, tucked away from the madding crowd, gives every indication of becoming one of Oahu's premier destinations.

FOOD

For anyone with an urge to eat a two-scoop plate lunch, no problem. Little drive-in lunch counters are found in almost every Waianae town. Each serves hearty island food such as teriyaki chicken, pork, or mahimahi for under $5. A good one is the **Makaha Drive-In.** Another popular spot is **Red Baron Pizza** in the Waianae Mall, tel. 696-2396.

You also see plenty of fruit sellers parked along the road. Their produce couldn't be fresher, and stopping provides you not only with the perfect complement to a picnic lunch but with a good chance to meet some local people.

For your shopping and dining needs in Nanakuli, try the **Pacific Shopping Mall,** where you'll find **Sac and Save Supermarket,** the largest in the area. In the complex is **Nanakuli Chop Suey Restaurant,** open 10 a.m.-8:30 p.m., tel. 668-8006, serving standard Chinese fare at local down-home prices (chicken dishes under $5, beef or pork to $4.75). Just behind McDonald's is the **Eden BBQ Lounge,** with sit-down and takeout Korean food at moderate prices, tel. 668-2722, open 10-9 daily.

The **Waianae Mall** is a complete shopping facility. Don't worry about bringing supplies or food if you're on a day excursion. You'll find all that you need at the mall, which includes Cathay Deli, Red Baron Pizza, Subway Sandwiches, Woolworth's, Big-Way Supermarket, and Pay 'n' Save Drugs. Have no fear if you're addicted to fast foods. Some major franchises have decided that your trip to leeward Oahu wouldn't be complete without something processed in a styrofoam box. **Burger King** is in the mall, and in town **McDonald's** golden arches rise alongside the highway just across from **Taco Bell.** If you're looking for ethnic flavor try the **Tamura Supermarket,** which stocks plenty of ingredients used in ethnic foods. You'll spot a number of gas stations in the middle of town, along with a **Domino's Pizza, Circle K,** and a **7-Eleven** convenience store.

Makaha has **Makaha Drive-In,** a plate lunch stand, **Woolworth's,** and a shopping basket of neighborhood markets.

Salvatore's, 87-064 Farrington Hwy., tel. 696-6121, open daily 8 a.m.-10 p.m., weekend entertainment sometimes featuring a live band, is located about halfway between Waianae and Maili, and is the "hot spot" in these parts serving the best food for the money in Makaha. Located on the second floor, you have a pretty good perch from which to view the coast. Painted sea-blue and cloud-white, the open beamed interior has a nautical theme with ship's ladders, glass lanterns, and heavy cargo nets placed here and there. Half of Salvatore's is a full bar, and the other a dining area. The breakfast menu offers French toast at $2.95, all you can eat hotcakes for $5.95, eggs Benedict for $6.95, and a variety of omelettes priced $4.95-5.95. The lunch buffet, offered daily except Sunday 11 a.m.-3 p.m., gives you a choice of fresh fruits, salads, vegetables, chili, rice, soup, pasta of the day, and chicken and fish prepared various ways.

The regular lunch menu includes burgers from $4.95, French-dipped, barbecue, teriyaki, and turkey club sandwiches at $5.95, or choose the salad bar for $5.95. The dinner menu features gourmet pasta priced $6.95-13.95, grilled garlic chicken or ground sirloin for $9, fish and chips for $7.95, and combination dinners like barbecued teriyaki beef, ribs, and chicken basket at $13.95. From the bar order beer, domestic or imported, cocktails of every description, or one of the house wines.

The **Sheraton Makaha** has a number of restaurants ranging from sandwich bars to elegant dining. The Kaala Room features an impressive menu of fresh fish, steaks, and continental cuisine. Get a table with a long sweeping view of the valley, wonderful at sunset. Open daily for dinner, tel. 695-9511. The hotel's Pikake Cafe serves breakfast, lunch, and dinner with an assortment of sandwiches and international dishes.

The **Food Giant** grocery store in Waianae has a good selection of Oriental and Hawaiian food. To know what's happening along the Waianae coast check out the bulletin board in front.

Note: For other restaurant choices see the Ihilani Resort and Spa under "Accommodations."

Arts And Crafts

The **Waianae Hawaiian Cultural and Art Center** offers workshops in lei-making, *lau hala* weaving, hula, and the Hawaiian language. They welcome people either to observe or participate in their programs. For times and schedules contact the **State Foundation of Culture and Arts,** tel. 586-0300.

Sports and Recreation

The **Leeward Dive Center,** tel. 696-3414 or 800-255-1574, is a full-service dive shop offering rentals, scuba and snorkel excursions and certification courses. See "Sports and Recreation—Dive Shops" in the Out and About chapter.

THE NORTHWESTERN ISLANDS

Like tiny gems of a broken necklace, the Northwestern Hawaiian Islands spill across the vast Pacific. Popularly called the **Leewards,** most were discovered last century, oftentimes by hapless ships that ground to a sickening halt on their treacherous, half-submerged reefs. Their captains left their names: Lisianski, Kure, French Frigate Shoals, Hermes, and Pearl. Even today, craft equipped with the most modern navigational devices must be wary in these waters. They remain among the loneliest outposts on the face of the earth.

Land And Climate
The Leewards are the oldest islands of the Hawaiian chain, believed to have emerged from the sea at least six million years ago; some experts say 25 million years! Slowly they floated northward past the suboceanic hotspot as the other islands were built. Measured from **Nihoa Island,** about 100 miles off the northern tip of

Kauai, they stretch for just under 1,100 miles to **Kure Atoll,** last of the **Midway Islands.** There are 13 islets, shoals, and half-submerged reefs in the chain. Most have been eroded flat by the sea and wind, but a few tough volcanic cores endure. Together they make up a land mass of approximately 3,400 acres, the largest being the Midways at 1,280 acres, and the smallest the **Gardner Pinnacles** at just over 2.5 acres. The climate is similar to that of the main islands with a slightly larger variance. Temperatures sometimes dip as low as 50 degrees and climb as high as 90 degrees.

Administration And History
Politically, the Leewards are administered by the city and county of Honolulu, except for the Midway Islands, which are under federal jurisdiction. None are permanently inhabited, except for some lonely military and wildlife field stations on Midway, Kure, and the French

Frigate Shoals. All are part of the **Hawaiian Islands National Wildlife Refuge,** established at the turn of the century by Theodore Roosevelt. In precontact times, some of the islands supported a Tahitian culture markedly different from the one that emerged on the main Hawaiian islands. Necker Island, for example, was the only island in the entire Hawaiian archipelago on which the inhabitants carved stone figures with a complete head and torso. On many of the others, remnants of *heiau* and agricultural terracing attribute to their colonization by precontact Hawaiians. Over the years, natives as well as Westerners have exploited the islands for feathers, fertilizer, seals, and fish.

The islands are closely monitored by the U.S. Fish and Wildlife Agency. Permission to land on them is granted only under special circumstances. Studies are underway to determine if the waters around the islands can support some commercial fishing, while leaving a plentiful supply of food for the unique wildlife of these lonely islands.

Wildlife

Millions of seabirds of various species have found permanent sanctuary on the Leewards, using them as giant floating nests and rookeries. Today the populations are stable and growing, but it hasn't always been so. On Laysan, at the turn of the century, egg hunters came to gather uncountable albatross eggs, selling the albumen to companies making photographic paper. They brought their families along, and their children's pets, which included rabbits. The rabbits escaped and multiplied wildly. In no time they invaded the territories of the **Laysan honeycreeper, rail,** and **millerbird,** rendering them extinct. Laysan has recovered and is refuge to over six million birds, including the rare and indigenous **Laysan teal** and **finch.**

An amazing bird using the rookeries is the **frigate bird.** The male can blow up its chest in a mating ritual like a giant red heart-shaped balloon. Also known as **man-of-war birds,** they oftentimes pirate the catches of other birds, devour chicks, and even cannibalize their own offspring.

Some of the most prolific birds of the Leewards are terns, both the delicate all-white **fairy tern** and its darker relative, the **sooty tern.** Other distinctive species include a variety of boobies, and the **Laysan albatross,** which has a wingspan of 10-12 feet, the world's largest.

Besides birds, the islands are home to the **Hawaiian monk seal,** one of only two species of indigenous Hawaiian mammals. These beautiful

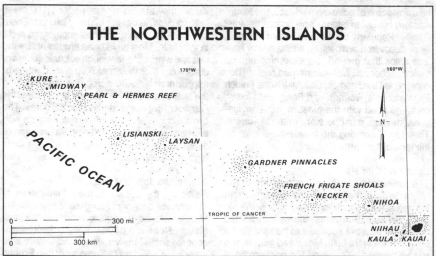

THE NORTHWESTERN ISLANDS

KURE
MIDWAY
PEARL & HERMES REEF
LISIANSKI
LAYSAN
PACIFIC OCEAN
170°W
160°W
N
GARDNER PINNACLES
FRENCH FRIGATE SHOALS
NECKER
NIHOA
TROPIC OF CANCER
0 — 300 mi
0 — 300 km
NIIHAU
KAULA KAUAI
© MOON PUBLICATIONS, INC.

monk seal

and sleek animals were hunted to near extinction for their skins. Man encroached on their territory more and more, but now they are protected as an endangered species. About 1,000 individuals still cling to existence on various islands.

The **green turtle** is another species that has found a haven here. They were hunted to near extinction for their meat and leather, and of the few colonies around the world, the largest in the U.S. is on the French Frigate Shoals.

*unique figurine of
Necker Island*

BOOKLIST

INTRODUCTORY

Aloha, The Magazine of Hawaii and the Pacific. Davick Publications, P.O. Box 49035, Escondido, CA 92046. This excellent bimonthly magazine is much more than just slick and glossy photography. Special features may focus on sports, the arts, history, flora and fauna, or just pure island adventure. *Aloha* is equally useful as a "dream book" for those who wish that they could visit Hawaii, and as a current resource for those actually going. One of the best for an overall view of Hawaii, and well worth the subscription price.

Barrow, Terrence. *Incredible Hawaii.* Rutland, VT: Tuttle, 1974. Illustrated by Ray Lanternman. A pocket-sized compilation of oddities, little-known facts, trivia, and superlatives regarding the Hawaiian Islands. Fun, easy reading, and informative.

Cohen, David, and Rick Smolan. *A Day in the Life of Hawaii.* New York: Workman, 1984. On December 2, 1983, 50 of the world's top photojournalists were invited to Hawaii to photograph a variety of normal life incidents occurring on that day. The photos are excellently reproduced, and are accompanied by a minimum of text.

Day, A.G., and C. Stroven. *A Hawaiian Reader.* New York: Appleton, Century, Crofts, 1959. A poignant compilation of essays, diary entries, and fictitious writings that takes you from the death of Captain Cook through the "statehood services."

Emphasis International. *On the Hana Coast.* Honolulu: Emphasis International Ltd., 1983. Text by Ron Youngblood. Sketches of the people, land, legends, and history of Maui's northeast coast. Beautifully illustrated with line drawings, vintage photos, and modern color work. Expresses true feeling and insight into people and things Hawaiian by letting them talk for themselves. An excellent book capturing what's different and what's universal about the people of the Hana District.

Friends of the Earth. *Maui, The Last Hawaiian Place.* New York: Friends of the Earth, 1970. A pictorial capturing the spirit of Maui in 61 contemporary color plates along with a handful of historical illustrations. A highly informative as well as beautiful book printed in Italy.

Hawaii Magazine. 1400 Kapiolani Blvd., Suite B, Honolulu, HI, 96814. This magazine covers the Hawaiian Islands like a tropical breeze. Feature articles on all aspects of life in the islands with special departments on travel, happenings, exhibits, and restaurant reviews. Up-to-the-minute information, and a fine read.

Hopkins, Jerry. *The Hula.* Edited by Rebecca Crockett-Hopkins. Hong Kong: APA Productions, 1982. Page after page of this beautifully illustrated book sways with the dynamic vibrancy of ancient Hawaii's surviving artform. Hopkins leads you from dances performed and remembered only through legends to those of past and present masters captured in vintage and classic photos. For anyone interested in the history and the spirit of Hawaii portrayed in its own unique style of expressive motion.

Island Heritage Limited. *The Hawaiians.* Norfolk Island, Australia: Island Heritage Ltd., 1970. Text by Gavan Daws and Ed Sheehan. Primarily a "coffee table" picture book that lets the camera do the talking with limited yet informative text.

Judd, Gerritt P., comp. *A Hawaiian Anthology.* New York: MacMillan, 1967. A potpourri of observations from literati such as Twain and Stevenson who have visited the islands over the years. Also, excerpts from ordinary people's journals and missionary letters from early times down to a gleeful report of the day that Hawaii became a state.

Krauss, Bob. *Here's Hawaii.* New York: Coward, McCann Inc., 1960. Social commentary in a series of humorous anecdotes excerpted from this newspaperman's column from the late

'60s. Dated, but in essence still useful because people and values obviously change very little.

Lueras, Leonard. *Surfing, The Ultimate Pleasure.* New York: Workman Publishing, 1984. An absolutely outstanding pictorial account of Hawaii's own sport—surfing. Vintage and contemporary photos are surrounded by well-researched and written text. Bound to become a classic.

McBride, L.R. *Practical Folk Medicine of Hawaii.* Hilo, HI: Petroglyph Press, 1975. An illustrated guide to Hawaii's medicinal plants as used by the *kahuna lapa'au* (medical healers). Includes a thorough section on ailments, diagnosis, and the proper folk remedy to employ. Illustrated by the author, a renowned botanical researcher and former ranger at Volcanoes National Park.

Michener, James A. *Hawaii.* New York: Random House, 1959. Michener's fictionalized historical novel has done more to inform *and* misinform readers about Hawaii than any other book ever written. A great tale with plenty of local color and information that should be read for pleasure and not considered fact.

Naturist Society Magazine. P.O. Box 132, Oshkosh, WI 54920. This excellent magazine not only *uncovers* bathing-suit-optional beaches throughout the islands, giving tips for naturalists visiting Hawaii, but also reports on local politics, environment, and conservation measures from the health-conscious nudist point of view. A fine publication.

Piercy, LaRue. *Hawaii, This and That.* Hilo, HI: Petroglyph Press, 1981. Illustrated by Scot Ebanez. A 60-page book filled with one-sentence facts and oddities about all manner of things Hawaiian. Informative, amazing, and fun to read.

Rose, Roger G. *Hawaii: The Royal Isles.* Honolulu: Bishop Museum Press, 1980. Photographs by Seth Joel. A pictorial mixture of artifacts and luminaries from Hawaii's past. Includes a mixture of Hawaiian and Western art depicting island ways. Beautifully photographed with highly descriptive accompanying text.

Wilkerson, James A., M.D., ed. *Medicine for Mountaineering.* 3rd ed. Seattle: The Mountaineers, 1985. Don't let the title fool you. Although the book focuses on specific health problems that may be encountered while mountaineering, it is the best first-aid and general health guide available today. Written by doctors for the layman to use until help arrives, it is jam-packed with easily understandable techniques and procedures. For those intending extended treks, it is a must.

HISTORY/POLITICAL SCIENCE

Albertini, Jim, et al. *The Dark Side of Paradise, Hawaii in a Nuclear War.* Honolulu: cAtholic Action of Hawaii. Well-documented research outlining Hawaii's role and vulnerability in a nuclear world. This book presents the antinuclear and antimilitary side of the political issue in Hawaii.

Apple, Russell A. *Trails: From Steppingstones to Kerbstones.* Honolulu: Bishop Museum Press, 1965. This "Special Publication #53" is a special-interest archaeological survey focusing on the trails, roadways, footpaths, and highways and how they were designed and maintained throughout the years. Many "royal highways" from pre-contact Hawaii are cited.

Ashdown, Inez MacPhee. *Old Lahaina.* Honolulu: Hawaiian Service Inc., 1976. A small pamphlet-type book listing most of the historical attractions of Lahaina Town, past and present. Ashdown is a life-long resident of Hawaii and gathered her information firsthand by listening to and recording stories of ethnic Hawaiians and old *kamaaina* families.

————. *Ke Alaloa o Maui.* Wailuku, Hi.: Kamaaina Historians Inc., 1971. A compilation of the history and legends of sites on the island of Maui. Ashdown was at one time a "lady in waiting" for Queen Liliuokalani and has since been proclaimed Maui's "Historian Emeritus."

Bell, Roger. *Last Among Equals: Hawaiian Statehood and American Politics.* Honolulu: University of Hawaii, 1984. Documents Hawaii's long and rocky road to statehood, tracing political partisanship, racism, and social change.

Cameron, Roderick. *The Golden Haze*. New York: World Publishing, 1964. An account of Captain James Cook's voyages of discovery throughout the South Seas. Uses original diaries and journals for an "on the spot" reconstruction of this great seafaring adventure.

Daws, Gavan. *Shoal of Time, A History of the Hawaiian Islands*. Honolulu: University of Hawaii Press, 1968. A highly readable history of Hawaii dating from its "discovery" by the Western world down to its acceptance as the 50th state. Good insight into the psychological makeup of the influential characters that formed Hawaii's past.

Department of Geography, University of Hawaii. *Atlas of Hawaii*. 2nd ed. Honolulu: University of Hawaii Press, 1983. Much more than an atlas filled with reference maps, it also contains commentary on the natural environment, culture, sociology, a gazetteer, and statistical tables. Actually a mini encyclopedia.

Feher, Joseph. *Hawaii: A Pictorial History*. Honolulu: Bishop Museum Press, 1969. Text by Edward Joesting and O.A. Bushnell. An oversized tome laden with annotated historical and contemporary photos, prints, and paintings. Seems like a big "schoolbook," but extremely well done. If you are going to read one survey about Hawaii's historical, social, and cultural past, this is the one.

Fuchs, Lawrence. *Hawaii Pono*. New York: Harcourt, Brace and World, 1961. A detailed, scholarly work presenting an overview of Hawaii's history, based upon psychological and sociological interpretations. Encompasses most socio-ethnological groups from native Hawaiians to modern entrepreneurs. A must for social historical background.

Handy, E.S., and Elizabeth Handy. *Native Planters in Old Hawaii*. Honolulu: Bishop Museum Press, 1972. A superbly written, easily understandable scholarly work on the intimate relationship of pre-contact Hawaiians and the *aina* (land). Much more than its title implies, this book should be read by anyone seriously interested in Polynesian Hawaii.

The Hawaii Book. Chicago: J.G. Ferguson, 1961. Insightful selections of short stories, essays, and historical and political commentaries by experts specializing in Hawaii. Good choice of photos and illustrations.

Hawaiian Children's Mission Society. *Missionary Album*. Honolulu: Mission Society, 1969. Firsthand accounts of the New England missionaries sent to Hawaii and instrumental in its conversion to Christianity. Down-home stories of daily life's ups and downs.

Heyerdahl, Thor. *American Indians in the Pacific*. London: Allen and Unwin Ltd., 1952. Theoretical and anthropological accounts of the influence on Polynesia of the Indians along the Pacific coast of North and South America. Fascinating reading, with unsubstantiated yet intriguing theories presented.

Ii, John Papa. *Fragments of Hawaiian History*. Honolulu: Bishop Museum, 1959. Hawaii's history under Kamehameha I as told by a Hawaiian who actually experienced it.

Joesting, Edward. *Hawaii: An Uncommon History*. New York: W.W. Norton Co., 1972. A truly uncommon history told in a series of vignettes relating to the lives and personalities of the first white men in Hawaii, Hawaiian nobility, sea captains, writers, and adventurers. Brings history to life. Absolutely excellent!

Lee, William S. *The Islands*. New York: Holt, Rinehart, 1966. A socio-historical set of stories concerning *malihini* (newcomers) and how they influenced and molded the Hawaii of today.

Liliuokalani. *Hawaii's Story By Hawaii's Queen*. Rutland, VT: Tuttle, 1964. A moving personal account of Hawaii's inevitable move from monarchy to U.S. Territory by its last queen, Liliuokalani. The facts can be found in other histories, but none provides the emotion or point of view as expressed by Hawaii's deposed monarch. A "must" read to get the whole picture.

Nickerson, Roy. *Lahaina, Royal Capital of Hawaii*. Honolulu: Hawaiian Service, 1978. The story of Lahaina from whaling days to present, spiced with ample photographs.

Smith, Richard A., et al., eds. *The Frontier States*. New York: Time-Life Books, 1968. Short and concise comparisons of the two newest states: Hawaii and Alaska. Dated information, but good social commentary and an excellent appendix suggesting tours, museums, and local festivals.

Takaki, Ronald. *Plantation Life and Labor in Hawaii, 1835-1920.* Honolulu: University of Hawaii Press, 1983. A perspective of plantation life in Hawaii from a multiethnic viewpoint. Written by a nationally known island scholar.

MYTHOLOGY AND LEGENDS

Beckwith, Martha. *Hawaiian Mythology.* Honolulu: University of Hawaii Press, 1970. Forty-five years after its original printing, this work remains the definitive text on Hawaiian mythology. Beckwith compiled this book from many sources, giving exhaustive cross-references to genealogies and legends expressed in the oral tradition. If you are going to read one book on Hawaii's folklore, this should be it.

Colum, Padraic. *Legends of Hawaii.* New Haven: Yale University Press, 1937. Selected legends of old Hawaii reinterpreted, but closely based upon the originals.

Elbert, S., comp. *Hawaiian Antiquities and Folklore.* Honolulu: Univerity of Hawaii Press, 1959. Illustrated by Jean Charlot. A selection of the main legends from Abraham Fornander's great work, *An Account of the Polynesian Race.*

Melville, Leinanai. *Children of the Rainbow.* Wheaton, Ill.: Theosophical Publishing, 1969. A book on higher spiritual consciousness attuned to nature, which was the basic belief of pre-Christian Hawaii. The appendix contains illustrations of mystical symbols used by the *kahuna.* An enlightening book in many ways.

Thrum, Thomas. *Hawaiian Folk Tales.* Chicago: McClurg and Co., 1907. A collection of Hawaiian tales from the oral tradition as told to the author from various sources.

Westervelt, W.D. *Hawaiian Legends of Volcanoes.* Boston: Ellis Press, 1916. A small book concerning the volcanic legends of Hawaii and how they related to the fledgling field of volcanism at the turn of the century. The vintage photos alone are worth a look.

NATURAL SCIENCES

Abbott, Agatin, Gordon MacDonald, and Frank Peterson. *Volcanoes in the Sea.* Honolulu: University of Hawaii Press, 1983. A simplified yet comprehensive text covering the geology and volcanism of the Hawaiian Islands. Focuses upon the forces of nature (wind, rain, and surf) that shape the islands.

Boom, Robert. *Hawaiian Seashells.* Honolulu: Waikiki Aquarium, 1972. Photos by Jerry Kringle. A collection of 137 seashells found in Hawaiian waters, featuring many found nowhere else on earth. Broken into categories with accompanying text including common and scientific names, physical descriptions, and likely habitats. A must for shell collectors.

Brock, Vernon, and W.A. Gosline. *Handbook of Hawaiian Fishes.* Honolulu: University of Hawaii Press, 1960. A detailed guide to most of the fishes occurring in Hawaiian waters.

Carlquist, Sherwin. *Hawaii: A Natural History.* New York: Doubleday, 1970. Definitive account of Hawaii's natural history.

Carpenter, Blyth, and Russell Carpenter. *Fish Watching in Hawaii.* San Mateo, CA: Natural World Press, 1981. A color guide to many of the reef fish found in Hawaii and often spotted by snorkelers. If you're interested in the fish that you'll be looking at, this guide will be very helpful.

Fielding, Ann, and Ed Robinson. *An Underwater Guide to Hawaii.* Honolulu: University of Hawaii Press, 1987. If you've ever had a desire to snorkel/scuba the living reef waters of Hawaii and to be familiar with what you're seeing, get this small but fact-packed book. The amazing array of marinelife found througout the archipelago is captured in glossy photos with accompanying informative text. Both the scientific and common names of specimens are given. This book will enrich your underwater experience and serve as an easily understood reference guide for many years.

Hamaishi, Amy, and Doug Wallin. *Flowers of Hawaii*. Honolulu: World Wide Distributors, 1975. Close-up color photos of many of the most common flowers spotted in Hawaii.

Hawaii Audubon Society. *Hawaii's Birds*. Honolulu: Hawaii Audubon Society, 1981. A field guide to Hawaii's birds, listing the endangered indigenous species, migrants, and introduced species that are now quite common. Color photos with text listing distribution, description, voice, and habits. Excellent field guide.

Hosaka, Edward. *Shore Fishing in Hawaii*. Hilo, HI: Petroglyph Press, 1984. Known as the best book on Hawaiian fishing since 1944, this book receives the highest praise because it has born and bred many Hawaiian fishermen.

Hubbard, Douglass, and Gordon MacDonald. *Volcanoes of the National Parks of Hawaii*. Volcanoes, HI: Hawaii Natural History Association, 1982. The volcanology of Hawaii, documenting the major lava flows and their geological effect on the state.

Island Heritage Limited. *Hawaii's Flowering Trees*. Honolulu: Island Heritage Press. A concise field guide to many of Hawaii's most common flowering trees. All color photos with accompanying descriptive text.

Kay, E. Alison, comp. *A Natural History of the Hawaiian Islands*. Honolulu: University of Hawaii Press, 1972. A selection of concise articles by experts in the fields of volcanism, oceanography, meteorology, and biology. An excellent reference source.

Kuck, Lorraine, and Richard Togg. *Hawaiian Flowers and Flowering Trees*. Rutland, VT: Tuttle, 1960. A classic field guide to tropical and subtropical flora illustrated in watercolor. A "to the point" description of Hawaiian plants and flowers with a brief history of their places of origin and their introduction to Hawaii.

Merlin, Mark D. *Hawaiian Forest Plants, A Hiker's Guide*. Honolulu: Oriental Publishing, 1980. A companion guide to trekkers into Hawaii's interior. Full-color plates identify and describe the most common forest plants encountered.

————. *Hawaiian Coastal Plants*. Honolulu: Oriental Publishing, 1980. Color photos and botanical descriptions of many of the plants and flowers found growing along Hawaii's varied shorelines.

Merrill, Elmer. *Plant Life of the Pacific World*. Rutland, VT: Tuttle, 1983. The definitive book for anyone planning a botanical tour to the entire Pacific Basin. Originally published in the 1930s, it remains a tremendous work.

Nickerson, Roy. *Brother Whale, A Pacific Whale-watcher's Log*. San Francisco: Chronicle Books, 1977. Introduces the average person to the life of earth's greatest mammals. Provides historical accounts, photos, and tips on whale-watching. Well written, descriptive, and the best "first time" book on whales.

Sohmer, S. H., and R. Gustafson. *Plants and Flowers of Hawaii*. Honolulu: University of Hawaii Press, 1987. Sohmer and Gustafson range the vegetation zones of Hawaii, from mountains to coast, introducing you to the wide and varied floral biology of the islands. They give a good introduction to the history, and the uniqueness of the evolution of Hawaiian plantlife. Beautiful color plates are accompanied by clear and concise plant descriptions, with the scientific and common Hawaiian names listed.

Stearns, Harold T. *Road Guide to Points of Geological Interest in the Hawaiian Islands*. Palo Alto, Ca.: Pacific Books, 1966. The title is almost as long as this handy little book that lets you know what forces of nature formed the scenery that you see in the islands.

van Riper, Charles, and Sandra van Riper. *A Field Guide to the Mammals of Hawaii*. Honolulu: Oriental Publishing. A guide to the surprising number of mammals introduced into Hawaii. Full-color pages document description, uses, tendencies, and habitat. Small and thin, makes a worthwhile addition to any serious trekker's backpack.

TRAVEL

Morey, Kathy. *Maui Trails*. Berkeley: Wilderness Press, 1993. Morey's books are specialized, detailed trekker's guides to Hawaii's outdoors. Complete with useful maps, historical references, official procedures, and plants and animals encountered along the way. If you're focused on hiking, these are the best to take along. *Maui Trails, Hawaii Trails,* and *Kauai Trails* are also available.

Riegert, Ray. *Hidden Hawaii*. Berkeley, CA: And/Or Press, 1992. Ray offers a "user friendly" guide to the islands.

Stanley, David. *South Pacific Handbook*. 5th ed. Chico, CA: Moon Publications, 1993. The model upon which all travel guides should be based. Simply the best book in the world for travel throughout the South Pacific.

Sutton, Horace. *Aloha Hawaii*. New York: Doubleday, 1967. A dated but still excellent guide to Hawaii providing sociological, historical, and cultural insight. Horace Sutton's literary style is the best in the travel guide field. Entertaining reading.

Thorne, Chuck. *The Diver's Guide to Maui*. Kahului, Hi.: Maui Dive Guide, 1984. A no-nonsense snorkeler's and diver's guide to Maui waters. Extensive maps, descriptions, and "straight from the shoulder" advice by one of Maui's best and most experienced divers. A must for all levels of divers and snorkelers.

Thorne, Chuck, and Lou Zitnik. *A Divers' Guide to Hawaii*. Kihei, HI: Hawaii's Diver's Guide, 1984. An expanded diver's and snorkeler's guide to the waters of the six main Hawaiian Islands. Complete list of maps with full descriptions, tips, and ability levels. A must for all levels of snorkelers and divers.

Warner, Evie, and Al Davies. *Bed and Breakfast Goes Hawaiian*. Kapaa, HI: Island Bed and Breakfast, 1990. A combination bed and breakfast directory and guide to sights, activities, events, and restaurants on the six major islands.

COOKING

Alexander, Agnes. *How to Use Hawaiian Fruit*. Hilo, HI: Petroglyph Press, 1984. A full range of recipes using delicious and different Hawaiian fruits.

Fitzgerald, Donald, et al., eds. *The Pacific House Hawaii Cookbook*. Pacific House, 1968. A full range of Hawaiian cuisine including recipes from traditional Chinese, Japanese, Portuguese, New England, and Filipino dishes.

Gibbons, Euell. *Beachcombers Handbook*. New York: McKay Co., 1967. An autobiographical account of this world-famous naturalist as a young man living "off the land" in Hawaii. Great tips on spotting and gathering naturally occurring foods, survival advice, and recipes. Unfortunately the lifestyle described is long outdated.

Margah, Irish, and Elvira Monroe. *Hawaii, Cooking with Aloha*. San Carlos, CA: Wide World, 1984. Island recipes including *kalua* pig, *lomi* salmon, and hints on decor.

LANGUAGE

Boom, Robert, and Chris Christensen. *Important Hawaiian Place Names*. Honolulu: Boom Enterprises, 1978. A handy pocket-sized book listing most of the major island place names and their translations.

Elbert, Samuel. *Spoken Hawaiian*. Honolulu: University of Hawaii Press, 1970. Progressive conversational lessons.

Elbert, Samuel, and Mary Pukui. *Hawaiian Dictionary*. Honolulu: University of Hawaii, 1971. The best dictionary available on the Hawaiian language. The *Pocket Hawaiian Dictionary* is a less expensive condensed version of this dictionary adequate for most travelers with a general interest in the language.

GLOSSARY

Words marked with an asterisk (*) are used commonly throughout the islands.

a'a*—rough clinker lava. *A'a* has become the correct geological term to describe this type of lava found anywhere in the world.

ahupua'a—pie-shaped land divisions running from mountain to sea that were governed by *konohiki*, local *ali'i* who owed their allegiance to a reigning chief

aikane—friend; pal; buddy

aina—land; the binding spirit to all Hawaiians. Love of the land is paramount in traditional Hawaiian beliefs.

akamai—smart; clever; wise

akua—a god, or simply "divine." You'll hear people speak of their family or personal *amakua* (ancestral spirit). Favorites are the shark or the *pueo* (Hawaiian owl).

ali'i*—a Hawaiian chief or noble

aloha*—the most common greeting in the islands; can mean both hello or goodbye, welcome or farewell. It can also mean romantic love, affection, or best wishes.

amakua—a personal or family spirit, usually an ancestral spirit

aole—no

auwe—alas; ouch! When a great chief or loved one died, it was a traditional wail of mourning.

ewa—crooked; place-name for west Honolulu, used as a directional term

halakahiki—pineapple

halau—originally a longhouse, now used mostly to describe hula halau, i.e., a hula school

hale*—house or building. Often combined with other words to name a specific place such as Haleakala ("House of the Sun") or Hale Pai ("Printing House").

hana*—work; combined with *pau* means end of work or quitting time

hanai—literally "to feed." Part of the true *aloha spirit*. A *hanai* is a permanent guest, or an adopted family member, usually an old person or a child. This is an enduring cultural phenomenon in Hawaii, in which a child from one family (perhaps that of a brother or sister, and quite often one's grandchild) is raised as one's own without formal adoption.

haole*—a word that at one time meant foreigner, but which now means a white person or Caucasian. Many etymological definitions have been put forth, but none satisfies everyone. Some feel that it signified a person without a background, because the first white men could not chant their genealogies as was common to Hawaiians.

hapa*—half, as in a mixed-blooded person being referred to as *hapa haole*

hapai*—pregnant; used by all ethnic groups when a *keiki* is on the way

haupia*—a coconut custard dessert often served at luau

heiau*—a traditional Hawaiian temple. A platform made of skillfully fitted rocks, upon which structures were built and offerings made to the gods.

holomuu*—an ankle-length dress that is much more fitted than a muumuu, and which is often worn on formal occasions

hono—bay, as in Honolulu ("Sheltered Bay")

ho'oilo—traditional Hawaiian winter that began in November *hoolaulea*—any happy event, but especially a family outing or picnic

hoomalimali—sweet talk; flattery

huhu—angry; irritated

hui—a group; meeting; society. Often used to refer to Chinese businesspeople or family members who pool their money to get businesses started.

hukilau—traditional shoreline fish-gathering in which everyone lends a hand to *huki* (pull) the huge net. Anyone taking part shares in the *lau* (food). It is much more like a party than hard work, and if you're lucky you'll be able to take part in one.

hula—a native Hawaiian dance in which the rhythm of the islands is captured by swaying hips and stories told by lyrically moving hands. A *halau* is a group or school of *hula*.

huli huli—barbecue, as in *huli huli* chicken

i'a—fish in general. *I'a maka* is raw fish.

imu—underground oven filled with hot rocks and used for baking. The main cooking feature at luau, used to steam-bake pork and other succulent dishes. The tending of the *imu* was traditionally for men only.

ipo—sweetheart; lover; girlfriend or boyfriend

kahili—a tall pole topped with feathers, resembling a huge feather duster. It was used by an *ali'i* to announce his or her presence.

kahuna—priest; sorcerer; doctor; skillful person. *Kahuna* had tremendous power in old Hawaii, which they used for both good and evil. The *kahuna ana'ana* was a feared individual because he practiced "black magic" and could pray a person to death, while the *kahuna lapa'au* was a medical practitioner bringing aid and comfort to the people.

kai—the sea. Many businesses and hotels employ *kai* as part of their name.

kalua—roasted underground in an *imu*. A favorite island food is *kalua* pork.

kamaaina—a child of the land; an old-timer; a longtime island resident of any ethnic background; a resident of Hawaii or native son or daughter. Hotels and airlines often offer discounts called "*kamaaina* rates" to anyone who can prove island residency.

kanaka—man or commoner; later used to distinguish a Hawaiian from other races. Tone of voice can make it a derisive expression.

kane—means man, but actually used to signify a relationship such as husband or boyfriend. Written on a door it means "Men's Room."

kaola—any food that has been broiled or barbecued

kapu—forbidden; taboo; keep out; do not touch

kapuna—a grandparent or old-timer; usually means someone who has gained wisdom. The statewide school system now invites *kapuna* to talk to the children about the old ways and methods.

kaukau—slang word meaning food or chow; grub. Some of the best food in Hawaii comes from the "*kaukau* wagons," trucks that sell plate lunches and other morsels.

kauwa—a landless, untouchable caste once confined to living on reservations. Members of this caste were often used as human sacrifices at *heiau*. Calling someone *kauwa* is still considered a grave insult.

kava—a mildly intoxicating traditional drink made from the juice of chewed awa root, spat into a bowl, and used in religious ceremonies

keiki—child or children; used by all ethnic groups. "Have you hugged your *keiki* today?"

kiawe—an algaroba tree from South America commonly found in Hawaii along the shore. It grows a nasty long thorn that can easily puncture a tire. Legend has it that the trees were introduced to the islands by a misguided missionary who hoped the thorns would coerce natives into wearing shoes. Actually, they are good for fuel, as fodder for hogs and cattle, and for reforestation, none of which you'll appreciate if you step on one of their thorns or flatten a tire on your rental car!

koa—a hard, fine-grained native Hawaiian wood preferred as a material to fashion furniture and bowls

kokua—help. As in "Your *kokua* is needed to keep Hawaii free from litter."

kona wind*—a muggy subtropical wind that blows from the south and hits the leeward side of the islands. It usually brings sticky hot weather and one of the few times when air-conditioning will be appreciated.

konane—a traditional Hawaiian game, similar to checkers, played with pebbles on a large flat stone used as a board

koolau—windward side of the island

kuhina nui—the highest regent in the days of the monarchy

kukui—a candlenut tree whose pods are polished and then strung together to make a beautiful lei. Traditionally the oil-rich nuts were strung on the rib of a coconut leaf and used as a candle.

kuleana—homesite; the old homestead; small farms. Especially used to describe the small spreads on Hawaiian Homes Lands on Molokai.

Kumulipo*—ancient Hawaiian genealogical chant that records the pantheon of gods, creation, and the beginning of humankind

la—the sun. Often combined with other words to be more descriptive, such as *La*haina ("Merciless Sun") or Haleaka*la* ("House of the Sun").

lanai*—veranda or porch. You'll pay more for a hotel room if it has a lanai with an ocean view.

lani—sky or the heavens

lau hala*—traditional Hawaiian weaving of mats, hats, etc., from the prepared fronds of the pandanus (screw pine)

lei*—a traditional garland of flowers or vines. One of Hawaii's most beautiful customs. Given at any auspicious occasion, but especially when arriving or leaving Hawaii.

lele—the stone altar at a *heiau*

limu—edible seaweed of various types. Gathered from the shoreline, it makes an excellent salad. It's used to garnish many island dishes and is a favorite at luau.

lomi lomi—traditional Hawaiian massage; also, raw salmon made into a vinegared salad with chopped onion and spices

lua*—the toilet; the head; the bathroom

luakini—a human-sacrifice temple. Introduced to Hawaii in the 13th century at Wahaula Heiau on the Big Island.

luau*—a Hawaiian feast featuring poi, *imu*-baked pork, and other traditional foods. Good ones provide some of the best gastronomical delights in the world.

luna—foreman or overseer in the plantation fields. They were often mounted on horseback and were renowned either for their fairness or cruelty. They represented the middle class, and served as a buffer between plantation workers and white plantation owners.

mahalo*—thank you. *Mahalo nui* means "big thanks" or "thank you very much."

mahele—division. The "Great Mahele" of 1848 changed Hawaii forever when the traditional common lands were broken up into privately owned plots.

mahimahi*—a favorite eating fish. Often called a dolphin, but a mahimahi is a true fish, not a cetacean.

mahu—a homosexual; often used derisively like "fag" or "queer"

maile—a fragrant vine used in traditional lei. It looks ordinary but smells delightful.

maka'ainana—a commoner; a person "belonging" to the *aina* (land), who supported the *ali'i* by fishing and farming and as a warrior

makai—toward the sea; used by most islanders when giving directions

make—dead; deceased

*malihini**—newcomer; tenderfoot; recent arrival

malo—the native Hawaiian loincloth. Never worn anymore except at festivals or pageants.

*mana**—power from the spirit world; innate energy of all things animate or inanimate; the grace of god. Mana could be passed on from one person to another, or even stolen. Great care was taken to protect the *ali'i* from having their mana defiled. Commoners were required to lie flat on the ground and cover their faces whenever a great *ali'i* approached. *Kahuna* were often employed in the regaining or transference of mana.

manauahi—free; gratis; extra

manini—stingy; tight. A Hawaiianized word taken from the name of Don Francisco *Marin*, who was instrumental in bringing many fruits and plants to Hawaii. He was known for never sharing any of the bounty from his substantial gardens on Vineyard Street in Honolulu.

*mauka**—toward the mountains; used by most islanders when giving directions

mauna—mountain. Often combined with other words to be more descriptive, such as Mauna Kea ("White Mountain").

mele—a song or chant in the Hawaiian oral tradition that records the history and genealogies of the *ali'i*

menehune—the legendary "little people" of Hawaii. Like leprechauns, they are said to have shunned humans and possess magical powers. Stone walls said to have been completed in one night are often attributed to them. Some historians argue that they actually existed and were the aboriginals of Hawaii, inhabiting the islands before the coming of the Polynesians.

moa—chicken; fowl

*moana**—the ocean; the sea. Many businesses and hotels as well as places have *moana* as part of their name.

moe—sleep

moolelo—ancient tales kept alive by the oral tradition and recited only by day

*muumuu**—a "Mother Hubbard," an ankle-length dress with a high neckline introduced by the missionaries to cover the nakedness of the Hawaiians. It has become fashionable attire for almost any occasion in Hawaii.

nani—beautiful

nui—big; great; large; as in *mahalo nui* (thank you very much)

ohana—a family; the fundamental social division; extended family. Now used to denote a social organization with grass-roots overtones, as in the "Protect Kahoolawe Ohana."

okolehau—literally "iron bottom"; a traditional booze made from ti root. *Okole* means "rear end" and *hau* means "iron," which was descriptive of the huge blubber pots in which *okolehau* was made. Also, if you drink too much it'll surely knock you on your *okole*.

*ono**—delicious; delightful; the best. *Ono ono* means "extra or absolutely delicious."

opihi—a shellfish or limpet that clings to rocks and is gathered as one of the islands' favorite *pu pu*. Custom dictates that you never remove all of the *opihi* from a rock; some are always left to grow for future generations.

opu—belly; stomach

pahoa—a dagger, as used by ancient Hawaiians

pa'hoehoe*—smooth, ropey lava that looks like burnt pancake batter. *Pa'hoehoe* is now the correct geological term used to describe this type of lava found anywhere in the world.

pakalolo—marijuana; the state's most productive cash crop

pake—a Chinese person. Can be derisive, depending on tone in which it is used. It is a bastardization of the Chinese word meaning "uncle."

pali*—a cliff; precipice. Hawaii's geology makes them quite common. The most famous are the *pali* of Oahu, where a major battle was fought.

paniolo*—a Hawaiian cowboy. Derived from the Spanish *espaniola*. The first cowboys brought to Hawaii during the early 19th century were Mexicans from California.

papale—hat. Except for the feathered helmets of the *ali'i* warriors of old Hawaii, hats were generally not worn. However, once the islanders saw their practical uses and how fashionable they were, they began weaving them from various materials and quickly became experts at manufacture and design.

pau*—finished; done; completed. Often combined into *pau hana,* which means end of work or quitting time.

pa'u—long split skirt often worn by women when horseback riding. Last century, an island treat was *pa'u* riders in their beautiful dresses at Kapiolani Park in Honolulu. The tradition is carried on today at many of Hawaii's rodeos.

pilau—stink; bad smell; stench

pilikia—trouble of any kind, big or small; bad times

poi*—a glutinous paste made from the pounded corm of taro which ferments slightly and has a light sour taste. Purplish in color, it's a staple at luau, where it is called "one-, two-, or three-finger" poi, depending upon its thickness.

pono—righteous or excellent

pua—flower

puka*—a hole of any size. *Puka* is used by all island residents, whether talking about a pinhole in a rubber boat or a tunnel through a mountain.

punalua—the tradition of sharing mates in practice before the missionaries came. Western seamen took advantage of it, and this led to the spreading of contagious diseases and eventually to the ultimate demise of the Hawaiian people.

punee*—bed; narrow couch. Used by all ethnic groups. To recline on a *punee* on a breezy lanai is a true island treat.

pu pu*—an appetizer; a snack; hors d'oeuvres; can be anything from cheese and crackers to sushi. Oftentimes, bars or nightclubs offer them free.

pupule—crazy; nuts; out of your mind

pu'u—hill, as in Pu'u Ulaula ("Red Hill")

tapa*—a traditional paper cloth made from beaten bark. Intricate designs were stamped in using beaters, and natural dyes added color. The tradition was lost for many years but is now making a comeback, and provides some of the most beautiful folk art in the islands.

taro*—the staple of old Hawaii. A plant with a distinctive broad leaf that produces a starchy root. It was brought by the first Polynesians and was grown on magnificently irrigated plantations. According to the oral tradition, the life-giving properties of taro hold mystical significance for Hawaiians, since it was created by the gods at about the same time as humans.

ti—a broad-leafed plant that was used for many purposes, from plates to hula skirts (never grass). Especially used to wrap religious offerings presented at the *heiau*.

tutu*—grandmother; granny; older woman. Used by all as a term of respect and endearment.

ukulele*—*uku* means "flea" and *lele* means "jumping," so literally "jumping flea"—the way the Hawaiians perceived the quick finger movements used on the banjolike Portuguese folk instrument called a *cavaquinho*. The ukulele quickly became synonymous with the islands.

wahine*—young woman; female; girl; wife. Used by all ethnic groups. When written on a door it means "Women's Room."

wai—fresh water; drinking water

wela—hot. *Wela kahao* is a "hot time" or "making whoopee."

wiki*—quickly; fast; in a hurry. Often seen as *wiki wiki* (very fast), as in "Wiki Wiki Messenger Service."

HOTEL INDEX

RESTAURANT INDEX

INDEX

Italicized page numbers indicate information in captions, charts, illustrations, maps, or special topics.

ABOUT THE AUTHOR

Joe Bisignani is a fortunate man because he makes his living doing the two things that he likes best: traveling and writing. Joe has been with Moon Publications since 1979 and is the author of *Japan Handbook, Big Island of Hawaii Handbook, Kauai Handbook, Hawaii Handbook,* and *Maui Handbook*. When not traveling, he makes his home in Northern California.

MOON HANDBOOKS—THE IDEAL TRAVELING COMPANIONS

Moon Handbooks provide travelers with all the background and practical information he or she will need on the road. Every Handbook begins with in-depth essays on the land, the people, their history, arts, politics, and social concerns—an entire bookshelf of introductory information squeezed into a one-volume encyclopedia. The Handbooks provide accurate, up-to-date coverage of all the practicalities: language, currency, transportation, accommodations, food and entertainment, and services, to name a few. Moon Handbooks are ideal traveling companions: informative, entertaining, and highly practical.

To locate the bookstore nearest you that carries Moon Travel Handbooks or to order directly from Moon Publications, call: (800) 345-5473, Monday-Friday, 9 a.m.-5 p.m. PST.

THE PACIFIC/ASIA SERIES

BALI HANDBOOK   by Bill Dalton
Detailed travel information on the most famous island in the world. 428 pages.   **$12.95**

BANGKOK HANDBOOK   by Michael Buckley
Your tour guide through this exotic and dynamic city reveals the affordable and accessible possibilities. Thai phrasebook. 214 pages.   **$10.95**

BLUEPRINT FOR PARADISE: How to Live on a Tropic Island   by Ross Norgrove
This one-of-a-kind guide has everything you need to know about moving to and living comfortably on a tropical island. 212 pages.   **$14.95**

FIJI ISLANDS HANDBOOK   by David Stanley
The first and still the best source of information on travel around this 322-island archipelago. Fijian glossary. 198 pages.   **$11.95**

INDONESIA HANDBOOK   by Bill Dalton
This one-volume encyclopedia explores island by island the many facets of this sprawling, kaleidoscopic island nation. Extensive Indonesian vocabulary. 1,000 pages.   **$19.95**

JAPAN HANDBOOK   by J.D. Bisignani
In this comprehensive new edition, award-winning travel writer J.D. Bisignani offers to inveterate travelers, newcomers, and businesspeople alike a thoroughgoing presentation of Japan's many facets. 950 pages.   **$22.50**

MICRONESIA HANDBOOK: Guide to the Caroline, Gilbert, Mariana, and Marshall Islands
by David Stanley
Micronesia Handbook guides you on a real Pacific adventure all your own. 345 pages.   **$11.95**

NEW ZEALAND HANDBOOK   by Jane King
Introduces you to the people, places, history, and culture of this extraordinary land. 571 pages. **$18.95**

OUTBACK AUSTRALIA HANDBOOK   by Marael Johnson
Australia is an endlessly fascinating, vast land, and *Outback Australia Handbook* explores the
cities and towns, sheep stations, and wilderness areas of the Northern Territory, Western
Australia, and South Australia. Full of travel tips and cultural information for adventuring,
relaxing, or just getting away from it all. 355 pages.   **$15.95**

PHILIPPINES HANDBOOK   by Peter Harper and Evelyn Peplow
Crammed with detailed information, *Philippines Handbook* equips the escapist, hedonist, or
business traveler with thorough coverage of the Philippines's colorful history, landscapes, and
culture. 600 pages.   **$17.95**

SOUTHEAST ASIA HANDBOOK   by Carl Parkes
Helps the enlightened traveler discover the real Southeast Asia. 873 pages.   **$21.95**

SOUTH KOREA HANDBOOK   by Robert Nilsen
Whether you're visiting on business or searching for adventure, *South Korea Handbook* is an
invaluable companion. Korean glossary with useful notes on speaking and reading the
language. 548 pages.   **$14.95**

SOUTH PACIFIC HANDBOOK   by David Stanley
The original comprehensive guide to the 16 territories in the South Pacific. 740 pages.   **$19.95**

TAHITI-POLYNESIA HANDBOOK   by David Stanley
All five French-Polynesian archipelagoes are covered in this comprehensive guide by
Oceania's best-known travel writer. 235 pages.   **$11.95**

THAILAND HANDBOOK   by Carl Parkes
Presents the richest source of information on travel in Thailand. 568 pages.   **$16.95**

THE HAWAIIAN SERIES

BIG ISLAND OF HAWAII HANDBOOK   by J.D. Bisignani
An entertaining yet informative text packed with insider tips on accommodations, dining, sports
and outdoor activities, natural attractions, and must-see sights. 350 pages.   **$13.95**

HAWAII HANDBOOK   by J.D. Bisignani
Winner of the 1989 Hawaii Visitors Bureau's Best Guide Award and the Grand Award for
Excellence in Travel Journalism, this guide takes you beyond the glitz and high-priced hype and
leads you to a genuine Hawaiian experience. Covers all 8 Hawaiian Islands. 879 pages.   **$15.95**

KAUAI HANDBOOK   by J.D. Bisignani
Kauai Handbook is the perfect antidote to the workaday world. Hawaiian and pidgin glossaries.
236 pages.   **$9.95**

MAUI HANDBOOK   by J.D. Bisignani
"No fool-'round" advice on accommodations, eateries, and recreation, plus a comprehensive
introduction to island ways, geography, and history. Hawaiian and pidgin glossaries. 393 pages.
$14.95

HONOLULU~WAIKIKI HANDBOOK: The Island of Oahu   by J.D. Bisignani
A handy guide to Honolulu, renowned surfing beaches, and Oahu's countless other diversions.
Hawaiian and pidgin glossaries. 354 pages.   **$14.95**

THE AMERICAS SERIES

ALASKA-YUKON HANDBOOK   by Deke Castleman and Don Pitcher
Get the inside story, with plenty of well-seasoned advice to help you cover more miles on less money. 460 pages.   **$14.95**

ARIZONA TRAVELER'S HANDBOOK   by Bill Weir
This meticulously researched guide contains everything necessary to make Arizona accessible and enjoyable. 445 pages.   **$16.95**

BAJA HANDBOOK: Mexico's Western Peninsula including Cabo San Lucas   by Joe Cummings
A comprehensive guide with all the travel information and background on the land, history, and culture of this untamed thousand-mile-long peninsula. 362 pages.   **$15.95**

BELIZE HANDBOOK   by Chicki Mallan
Complete with detailed maps, practical information, and an overview of the area's flamboyant history, culture, and geographical features, *Belize Handbook* is the only comprehensive guide of its kind to this spectacular region. 263 pages.   **$14.95**

BRITISH COLUMBIA HANDBOOK   by Jane King
With an emphasis on outdoor adventures, this guide covers mainland British Columbia, Vancouver Island, the Queen Charlotte Islands, and the Canadian Rockies. 381 pages.
$15.95

CANCUN HANDBOOK   by Chicki Mallan
Covers the city's luxury scene as well as more modest attractions, plus many side trips to unspoiled beaches and Mayan ruins. Spanish glossary. 257 pages.   **$13.95**

CENTRAL MEXICO HANDBOOK: Mexico City, Guadalajara, and Other Colonial Cities   by Chicki Mallan
Retrace the footsteps of Cortés from the coast of Veracruz to the heart of Mexico City to discover archaeological and cultural wonders. 391 pages.   **$15.95**

CATALINA ISLAND HANDBOOK: A Guide to California's Channel Islands
by Chicki Mallan
A complete guide to these remarkable islands, from the windy solitude of the Channel Islands National Marine Sanctuary to bustling Avalon. 245 pages.   **$10.95**

COLORADO HANDBOOK   by Stephen Metzger
Essential details to the all-season possibilities in Colorado fill this guide. Practical travel tips combine with recreation—skiing, nightlife, and wilderness exploration—plus entertaining essays. 416 pages.   **$17.95**

COSTA RICA HANDBOOK   by Christopher P. Baker
Experience the many wonders of the natural world as you explore this remarkable land. Spanish-English glossary. 574 pages.   **$17.95**

IDAHO HANDBOOK   by Bill Loftus
A year-round guide to everything in this outdoor wonderland, from whitewater adventures to rural hideaways. 282 pages.   **$14.95**

JAMAICA HANDBOOK by Karl Luntta
From the sun and surf of Montego Bay and Ocho Rios to the cool slopes of the Blue Mountains, author Karl Luntta offers island-seekers a perceptive, personal view of Jamaica. 230 pages. **$14.95**

MONTANA HANDBOOK by W.C. McRae and Judy Jewell
The wild West is yours with this extensive guide to the Treasure State, complete with travel practicalities, history, and lively essays on Montana life. 427 pages. **$15.95**

NEVADA HANDBOOK by Deke Castleman
Nevada Handbook puts the Silver State into perspective and makes it manageable and affordable. 400 pages. **$14.95**

NEW MEXICO HANDBOOK by Stephen Metzger
A close-up and complete look at every aspect of this wondrous state. 375 pages. **$14.95**

NORTHERN CALIFORNIA HANDBOOK by Kim Weir
An outstanding companion for imaginative travel in the territory north of the Tehachapis. 765 pages. **$19.95**

NORTHERN MEXICO HANDBOOK: The Sea of Cortez to the Gulf of Mexico
by Joe Cummings
Directs travelers from the barrier islands of Sonora to the majestic cloud forests of the Sierra Madre Oriental to traditional villages and hidden waterfalls in San Luis Potosí. 500 pages. **$16.95**

OREGON HANDBOOK by Stuart Warren and Ted Long Ishikawa
Brimming with travel practicalities and insiders' views on Oregon's history, culture, arts, and activities. 461 pages. **$15.95**

PACIFIC MEXICO HANDBOOK by Bruce Whipperman
Explore 2,000 miles of gorgeous beaches, quiet resort towns, and famous archaeological sites along Mexico's Pacific coast. Spanish-English glossary. 428 pages. **$15.95**

TEXAS HANDBOOK by Joe Cummings
Seasoned travel writer Joe Cummings brings an insider's perspective to his home state. 483 pages. **$13.95**

UTAH HANDBOOK by Bill Weir
Weir gives you all the carefully researched facts and background to make your visit a success. 445 pages. **$14.95**

WASHINGTON HANDBOOK by Archie Satterfield and Dianne J. Boulerice Lyons
Covers sights, shopping, services, transportation, and outdoor recreation, with complete listings for restaurants and accommodations. 419 pages. **$15.95**

WYOMING HANDBOOK by Don Pitcher
All you need to know to open the doors to this wide and wild state. 495 pages. **$14.95**

YUCATAN HANDBOOK by Chicki Mallan
All the information you'll need to guide you into every corner of this exotic land. Mayan and Spanish glossaries. 391 pages. **$15.95**

THE INTERNATIONAL SERIES

EGYPT HANDBOOK by Kathy Hansen
An invaluable resource for intelligent travel in Egypt. Arabic glossary. 522 pages. **$18.95**

MOSCOW-ST. PETERSBURG HANDBOOK by Masha Nordbye
Provides the visitor with an extensive introduction to the history, culture, and people of these two great cities, as well as practical information on where to stay, eat, and shop. 260 pages. **$13.95**

NEPAL HANDBOOK by Kerry Moran
Whether you're planning a week in Kathmandu or months out on the trail, *Nepal Handbook* will take you into the heart of this Himalayan jewel. 378 pages. **$12.95**

NEPALI AAMA by Broughton Coburn
A delightful photo-journey into the life of a Gurung tribeswoman of Central Nepal. Having lived with Aama (translated, "mother") for two years, first as an outsider and later as an adopted member of the family, Coburn presents an intimate glimpse into a culture alive with humor, folklore, religion, and ancient rituals. 165 pages. **$13.95**

PAKISTAN HANDBOOK by Isobel Shaw
For armchair travelers and trekkers alike, the most detailed and authoritative guide to Pakistan ever published. Urdu glossary. 478 pages. **$15.95**

STAYING HEALTHY IN ASIA, AFRICA, AND LATIN AMERICA
by Dirk G. Schroeder, Sc D, MPH
Don't leave home without it! Besides providing a complete overview of the health problems that exist in these areas, this book will help you determine which immunizations you'll need beforehand, what medications to take with you, and how to recognize and treat infections and diseases. Includes extensively illustrated first-aid information and precautions for heat, cold, and high altitude. 200 pages. **$10.95**

TIBET HANDBOOK: A PILGRIMAGE GUIDE
by Victor Chan
This remarkable book is both a comprehensive trekking guide to mountain paths and plateau trails, and a pilgrimage guide that draws on Tibetan literature and religious history. 1104 pages. **$30.00**

MOONBELTS

Made of heavy-duty Cordura nylon, the Moonbelt offers maximum protection for your money and important papers. This all-weather pouch slips under your shirt or waistband, rendering it virtually undetectable and inaccessible to pickpockets. One-inch-wide nylon webbing, heavy-duty zipper, one-inch quick-release buckle. Accommodates traveler's checks, passport, cash, photos. Size 5 x 9 inches. Black. **$8.95**

**New travel handbooks may be available that are not on this list.
To find out more about current or upcoming titles,
call us toll-free at (800) 345-5473.**

IMPORTANT ORDERING INFORMATION

FOR FASTER SERVICE: Call to locate the bookstore nearest you that carries Moon Travel Handbooks or order directly from Moon Publications:

(800) 345-5473 • **Monday-Friday** • **9 a.m.-5 p.m. PST** • fax (916) 345-6751

PRICES: All prices are subject to change. We always ship the most current edition. We will let you know if there is a price increase on the book you ordered.

SHIPPING & HANDLING OPTIONS: 1) Domestic UPS or USPS first class (allow 10 working days for delivery): $3.50 for the first item, 50 cents for each additional item.

Exceptions:
  • **Moonbelt** shipping is $1.50 for one, 50 cents for each additional belt.
  • Add $2.00 for same-day handling.
  • UPS 2nd Day Air or Printed Airmail requires a special quote.
  • International Surface Bookrate (8-12 weeks delivery):
    $3.00 for the first item, $1.00 for each additional item. Note: Moon Publications cannot guarantee international surface bookrate shipping.

FOREIGN ORDERS: All orders that originate outside the U.S.A. must be paid for with either an International Money Order or a check in U.S. currency drawn on a major U.S. bank based in the U.S.A.

TELEPHONE ORDERS: We accept Visa or MasterCard payments. Minimum order is US$15.00. Call in your order: (800) 345-5473, 9 a.m.-5 p.m. Pacific Standard Time.

ORDER FORM

Be sure to call (800) 345-5473 for current prices and editions or for the name of the bookstore
nearest you that carries Moon Travel Handbooks • 9 a.m.–5 p.m. PST
(See important ordering information on preceding page)

Name: _____ Date: _____

Street: _____

City: _____ Daytime Phone: _____

State or Country: _____ Zip Code: _____

QUANTITY	TITLE	PRICE

Taxable Total_____

Sales Tax (7.25%) for California Residents_____

Shipping & Handling_____

TOTAL_____

Ship: ☐ UPS (no PO Boxes)   ☐ 1st class   ☐ International surface mail

Ship to: ☐ address above   ☐ other _____

Make checks payable to: **MOON PUBLICATIONS, INC.** P.O. Box 3040, Chico, CA 95927-3040
U.S.A. We accept Visa and MasterCard. **To Order:** Call in your Visa or MasterCard number, or send
a written order with your Visa or MasterCard number and expiration date clearly written.

Card Number: ☐ **Visa**   ☐ **MasterCard**

☐ ☐ ☐ ☐   ☐ ☐ ☐ ☐   ☐ ☐ ☐ ☐   ☐ ☐ ☐ ☐

Exact Name on Card: _____

expiration date:_____

signature_____

W/94

WHERE TO BUY THIS BOOK

BOOKSTORES AND LIBRARIES:
Moon Publications Handbooks are sold worldwide. Please write
our sales manager for a list of wholesalers and distributors in
your area that stock our travel handbooks.

TRAVELERS:
We would like to have Moon Publications Handbooks available
throughout the world. Please ask your bookstore to write or
call us for ordering information. If your bookstore will not order
our guides for you, please write or call for a free catalog.

MOON PUBLICATIONS, INC.
P.O. BOX 3040
CHICO, CA 95927-3040 U.S.A.
TEL: (800) 345-5473
FAX: (916) 345-6751

TRAVEL MATTERS

Travel Matters is Moon Publications' quarterly newsletter. It provides today's traveler
with timely, informative travel news and articles.
You'll find resourceful coverage on:

- **Money**—What does it cost? Is it worth it?
- **Low impact travel**—tread lightly travel tips
- **Special interest travel**—cultural tours,
  environmental excursions, outdoor recreation,
  adventure treks, and more
- **Travel styles**—families, seniors, disabled travelers,
  package and theme tours
- **Consumer reviews**—books, language aids, travel
  gadgets, products, and services
- **Facts and opinions**—reader's letters and Moon
  Handbook author news
- **Moon Handbook booklist**—the latest titles and
  editions, and where and how to purchase them

To receive a free copy of *Travel Matters*, write Moon Publications Inc., P.O. Box 3040,
Chico, CA 95927-3040, or call toll-free (800) 345-5473, Monday–Friday,
9 a.m. – 5 p.m. Pacific Standard Time.

THE METRIC SYSTEM

To compute centigrade temperatures, subtract 32 from Fahrenheit and divide by 1.8. To go the other way, multiply centigrade by 1.8 and add 32.

1 inch = 2.54 centimeters (cm)
1 foot = .304 meters (m)
1 mile = 1.6093 kilometers (km)
1 km = .6124 miles
1 fathom = 1.8288 m
1 chain = 20.1168 m
1 furlong = 201.168 m
1 acre = .4047 hectares
1 sq km = 100 hectares
1 sq mile = 2.59 square km
1 ounce = 28.35 grams
1 pound = .4536 kilograms
1 short ton = .90718 metric ton
1 short ton = 2000 pounds
1 long ton = 1.016 metric tons
1 long ton = 2240 pounds
1 metric ton = 1000 kilograms
1 quart = .94635 liters
1 US gallon = 3.7854 liters
1 Imperial gallon = 4.5459 liters
1 nautical mile = 1.852 km